CELEBRATING
50 YEARS
Texas A&M University Press
publishing since 1974

Francisco Amangual, Trustee of the Presidio

ELMA DILL RUSSELL SPENCER SERIES
IN THE WEST AND SOUTHWEST

Francisco Amangual, Trustee of the Presidio

Administration, Dereliction,
and the Flying Squadrons in the
Comandancia General,
1680–1810

Roland Rodríguez

TEXAS A&M UNIVERSITY PRESS
COLLEGE STATION

Copyright © 2024 by Roland Rodríguez
All rights reserved
First edition

∞ This paper meets the requirements of ANSI/NISO Z39.48–1992
(Permanence of Paper).
Binding materials have been chosen for durability.
Manufactured in the United States of America

Library of Congress Cataloging-in-Publication Data

Names: Rodríguez, Roland, author.
Title: Francisco Amangual, trustee of the presidio : administration,
    dereliction, and the flying squadrons in the Comandancia General,
    1680–1810 / Roland Rodríguez.
Description: First edition. | College Station : Texas A&M University Press,
    [2024] | Series: Elma Dill Russell Spencer series in the West and
    Southwest | Includes bibliographical references and index.
Identifiers: LCCN 2024000486 | ISBN 9781648431463 (cloth) | ISBN
    9781648431470 (ebook)
Subjects: LCSH: Amangual, Francisco, Captain, 1739–1812—Military
    leadership. | Spain. Ejército. Segunda Compañía Volante de San Carlos
    de Parras—Biography. | Spaniards—Texas—Biography. | Military
    bases—Provincias Internas (New Spain)—Management. | Civil-military
    relations—Provincias Internas (New Spain) | Texas—History—To 1846. |
    San Antonio (Tex.)—History, Military—18th century. | BISAC: HISTORY /
    United States / State & Local / Southwest (AZ, NM, OK, TX) | HISTORY /
    Wars & Conflicts / General | LCGFT: Biographies.
Classification: LCC F389 .R63 2024 | DDC 976.4/02092 [B]—dc23/eng/20240109
LC record available at https://lccn.loc.gov/2024000486

For
Ray Hernández-Durán
and Kurt Simmons

Contents

Acknowledgments ix

Introduction.. 1

CHAPTER ONE. Presidial Units, *Volantes*, and Amangual
in the Frontier, 1700–1786 25

CHAPTER TWO. "Truly Elected" Paymaster, Civil and Military
Administration, and Service to the King, 1781–1793 51

CHAPTER THREE. "The Detachment Cannot Be Effective and
I Will Not Be Responsible" The *Reglamento* of 1772,
Situational Strategies, and Slander.................................... 77

CHAPTER FOUR. Managing Soldiers, Questionable Accounts,
and a Case of Contraband, 1792...................................... 123

CHAPTER FIVE. Further Accusations, Considerable Numbers
of Apache, and His Majesty's Assurance 164

CHAPTER SIX. Defending the Numbers, a New Century,
and Forty Years of Service... 204

CHAPTER SEVEN. Change of Command, the 1808 Expedition,
and the Road Home 241

Conclusion... 275

Epilogue 283

Appendix 1 285

Appendix 2 287

Appendix 3 289

Appendix 4 293

Notes 295

Bibliography. 399

Index 417

Acknowledgments

The writing of this book found inspiration in the cover art for Andrés Tijerina's *Tejanos and Texans Under the Mexican Flag* (1994). For several reasons, Theodore Gentilz's nineteenth-century painting *Sobre La Huella* captured my attention, and Tijerina's discussion of the borderlands mounted patrol, the so-called flying squadrons or *compañías volantes*, spurred on my imagination. My early research of Mexico's *chinacos*, the leather-and-silver adorned equestrian guerillas of the French Intervention period, led me first to Gentilz's depiction of these similarly attired men on horseback. Identified by Tijerina as *volantes*, they appear to be surveying a barren desertscape of Texas. Within the content of Tijerina's book I first learned about this specialized unit of the presidial cavalry and, further, about a *mallorquín* soldier named Francisco Amangual. For the textual introductions and pictorial representations derived from his important scholarship, I am deeply indebted to Andrés. Without his encouragement and fellowship, the story that follows would not exist.

I thank my professors in the Department of Art and Art History at the University of New Mexico for providing a stimulating and supportive environment for me to explore the history of art with an emphasis on the intersection of *text* and *image*. No mere study of iconography in coursework here. Rather, I was trained in a systematic process of engaging with objects of inquiry by foregrounding the social, political, economic, and intellectual context of their production, use, and circulation. Colonial *Ibero*-American specialist Raymond Hernández-Durán expected me to think broadly and inclusively, and he spent years training me to critically assess art objects, to (re)interpret textual and pictorial sources, and to systematize the historical enterprise writ large. From him I learned how to grapple with a wide array of theoretical frameworks as mechanisms to assess meaning and purpose in the trans-Atlantic "colonial" world. With persistence, Ray turned me into a colonial scholar. For that, I am grateful.

The late Mayanist scholar Flora Clancy expanded my intellectual horizons by supporting my interest in nineteenth-century México while animating my thinking about the wide array of achievements by pre-Conquest First Peoples. Since it seemed only natural for me to dovetail history coursework with my art history program of studies, I was fortunate to have the opportunity to study with UNM History professors Bárbara Reyes, in classes focused on the multi-ethnic borderlands, and Cynthia Radding, in seminars examining the eighteenth- and nineteenth-century Ibero-Indigenous *Américas*.

I am particularly indebted to Dr. Radding for encouraging my specialized coursework, for her unending support as I merged art historical inquiry with that of viceregal administration and periodization, and for introducing me to the late Professor Richard Greenleaf. As an Art History masters degree candidate, I received a Richard E. Greenleaf Graduate Fellowship from the Latin American and Iberian Institute (LAII). As such, I worked with Dr. Greenleaf, albeit in a limited capacity, but such brief interactions were rewarding because they challenged my preconceptions about the colonial historical experience. I will never forget Dr. Greenleaf's great generosity with his time and critique as I worked on a project, suggested by him, involving an intellectual skirmish between two influential Dominican clerics in seventeenth-century Guatemala.

This cohesive program of scholarly study at UNM was largely responsible for setting me on the path toward further development of the skills necessary for working with colonial documents. I applied this rigorous training to my doctoral program in borderlands history at UTEP.

At the University of Texas in El Paso, I thank faculty members Professors Charles Martin and Ignacio Martínez for agreeing to be on my dissertation committee. Sincere appreciation to Dr. Martin for his valuable critique and urging me on towards revising and publishing the manuscript. While at UNM, I met University of Arizona Department of Art History faculty member Stacie Widdifield, a foremost authority in nineteenth-century Mexican art history. Motivated by her insightful work in various publications in two languages, I was determined to have Dr. Widdifield serve on my committee, and I am grateful for her participation and continuous support.

My research benefitted from the unstinting knowledge of and assistance by several archivists who have contributed to this study in immeasurable ways. I remain grateful to Elena Pérez-Lizano, Archives Bureau Chief, and all the archivists at the State Archives of New Mexico and the former State Historian of New Mexico Estevan Rael-Gálvez; to José Montelongo, Librarian for Mexican Studies, at the Nettie Benson Latin American Collection at the University of Texas in Austin; to the late Ann Massmann and her staff at the Center for Southwest Research at the Zimmerman Library of the University of New Mexico; Jill Crane at St. Mary's University in San Antonio for the interlibrary loan of the Index of the Laredo Archives; Scott

Acknowledgments xi

Cossel at the University of Arizona Library for his electronic delivery of a remarkable 284-page document inclusive of material related to the First, Second, and Third *compañías volantes* of Nueva Vizcaya; to June Can at the Beinecke Rare Book and Manuscript Library at Yale University for five digitized images that clarified numerical data pertaining to the 1808 Amangual expedition, and to the staff of the Daughters of the Republic of Texas Library Collection, my deep appreciation. I give unbridled blessings to Aryn Glazier, Jessica Meyerson, and Justin Kovar at the Dolph Briscoe Center for American History at the University of Texas at Austin for their ongoing assistance in obtaining scans of not yet digitized documents in the Béxar Archives necessary to my research. I extend that same enthusiastic praise to archivists David Carlson and Liliana Villanueva of the Spanish Archives at the Béxar County Clerk's Office in San Antonio for generous access to documents dealing with Amangual's final years. Another round of applause to Aryn Glazier at the Béxar Archives for expediting images of documents cited in this book, and to Garrett Gibson of the Gilcrease Museum in Tulsa for permission to use Lino Sánchez y Tapia's captivating "Soldado Mexicano Presidial," a favorite image of mine from the nineteenth century. For assistance in obtaining permissions to publish images from their archives, I extend deep appreciation to Catie Carl of the Palace of the Governors Photo Archives at the New Mexico History Museum and to Brian Moeller and Stephanie Arias at The Huntington Library in California.

I am the beneficiary and proud recipient of regional-specific funding to support my research with fellowships from the Office of the State Historian of New Mexico, the Historical Society of New Mexico, the Jane Sánchez Legacy Fund, a Dodson Research Grant from the University of Texas at El Paso, the Tom Lea Institute at the University of Texas at El Paso, and the Latin American and Iberian Institute at the University of New Mexico. By receiving the very first CHIPOTLE (Chicano, Hispano, Latino Program) Fellowship from the University Libraries (UNM), I curated two art exhibitions for the University's Zimmerman Library and its Herzstein Latin American Reading Room Gallery.

I am especially grateful to John Wheat, Archives Translator at the Briscoe Center for American History at the University of Texas in Austin, for his kind assistance with the digitized colonial documents held at the Béxar Archives. Having John's good opinion of several of my attempts at difficult translations has been enormously satisfying, and I appreciate his willingness to share with me his extraordinary knowledge of the complex, and often frustrating, syntax of eighteenth-century Castilian. This project is that much more cohesive because of his good counsel, and I am much wiser from his help. Any remnant errors in translation are exclusively mine.

Texas A&M University Press Director Jay Dew's unflagging belief in the tale I had to tell has sustained me professionally over the past seven years. For his commitment to a new narrative about presidio life and administration, I am forever in his debt. For the peer reviewers' positive commentary, I am profoundly grateful.

Finally, words here cannot adequately express my deep appreciation to my dissertation chair and main advisor, Professor Jeffrey Shepherd, for his invaluable direction with the content of the dissertation, for his enduring patience, and his unfailing good humor throughout my often-dispirited trajectory as a doctoral candidate. Were it not for Jeff's presence in the UTEP Department of History, I would have left that program long ago and my research and this book would have likely never materialized. For his unwavering faith in me and perceptive critique of my work, I remain forever grateful. It is not for nothing that I thank Jeff, also, for always being a gentleman.

To Kurt Simmons, a very long time ago you gave me the gift of your friendship, and you have helped me turn the complicated into the straightforward, make sense of the nonsensical, and you never gave up on me. For that, I owe you my life. Thank you for believing in my soldiers and in Captain Amangual as much as I do. I am not deserving of your kindness, boundless patience, and grown man goofiness. BFF, this book would not have been completed without you.

Francisco Amangual, Trustee of the Presidio

Introduction

On March 30, 1808, Capt. Francisco Amangual (1739–1812) left San Antonio de Béxar with an expedition of two hundred men and traveled for nine months to Santa Fé, New Mexico. As a former commander of the Segunda Compañía Volante de San Carlos de Parras, a mobile cavalry unit, Amangual likely included some of its members for the journey. Among the several goals of the thousand-mile expedition, none was more significant than establishing a safe passage between two frontier outposts of the Spanish-Native-French borderlands, reaffirming peace with the region's many indigenous polities, exploring the Red River and the Oscura Blanca and El Sacramento mountain ranges, and, finally, returning to Texas. Part of this study focuses on Francisco Amangual's career as his presidio's paymaster and his role as a functionary of the Spanish imperial apparatus, while another portion examines the various teams of soldiers comprising the *compañías volantes*, or flying squadrons, of the colonial frontier. Amangual's role as a soldier in the saddle includes his captaincy of the San Carlos *volantes*. The flying squadrons emerged as a type of at-the-ready mounted response charged with surveilling the Provincias Internas.[1] New Spain's so-called Far North (Septentrión) encompassed a vast territory including military headquarters found at the presidios of San Antonio de Béxar, Monclova, Coahuila (Nueva Extremadura) in northern Mexico; Santa Fé in New Mexico; and Tucsón in Arizona, among others. Scholars of colonial borderlands history are familiar with Amangual's journey to Santa Fé, his peregrinations across the region, and his residencies at several garrisons in Texas.[2]

While Francisco Amangual emerges in Spanish colonial military history as the leader of an expedition from Béxar to Santa Fé in the waning years of the era, it was his multiple roles as a presidio soldier (*presidial*), a paymaster (*habilitado*),[3] and, subsequently, captain of a flying squadron (*compañía volante*) that shed light on one soldier's experience in the context of everyday life. Original sources document the career of Amangual, and the focus of this book traces the trajectory of his ascension in the ranks via his participation in convoys, skirmishes, and primarily the routine of company interaction.

This is not a birth-to-death biography. Instead, the main thrust of my book considers Francisco Amangual's tenure as a borderlands operative from 1770 to 1808. In this capacity, he served as his garrison's fiduciary, responsible for managing the general accounts of debits and credits of the Béxar company's personnel and the inventory of its material supplies while ensuring the accuracy of his own work. This undertaking was chiefly important because the company payroll and expenses would eventually come under close examination and, if approved, satisfy his superiors, including the captain of the presidio and other officers as well as the *comandante inspector*. The paymaster administered the individual accounts of each soldier and was responsible for admonishing spendthrift members of the unit to restrict their expenditures to absolute necessities. He oversaw having a sufficient reserve of "every type of item," and he was to ensure that the presidial storehouse's supplies conformed to official specifications.[4] As this book will show, Amangual's performance in the roles of both *habilitado* and soldier not only impacted the careers of the garrison's troops but also conditioned their accessibility to material resources. Documentation of fiscal business and the day-to-day interplay he generated on behalf of his company allows readers to become familiar in intimate ways with military life by way of the human players within the presidio walls.

By centering my research on Amangual's endeavors as a soldier and as his company's fiduciary, I argue that his work as an administrator structured interactions with, among others, frontier soldiers within his own company and from outside; indigenous groups encountered as visitors, friends, and fugitives; and non-Hispano migrants into the province of Texas and beyond. But I find that actual administrative pattern and practice, apart from the publication of ordenanzas, reglamentos, and dictámenes, has gone insufficiently examined in colonial military history. Scholarly efforts have largely ignored the correlation between duties in the field and work behind a desk, both within and outside of an interdependent presidio network. Portions of Francisco Amangual's career, including the 1808 expedition and his command of a flying company in the last five years of his life, appear briefly in archival sources as do sporadic episodes from the historiography of the *volantes* and their presence across Native homelands. Prior to this project, only one other book-length study of a single presidial soldier's career has specifically targeted the wide range of social give-and-take, including infighting, collusion, and other complicated scenarios that transpired *within* the colonial garrison. Though Fay Jackson Smith's book strongly presents as its key topic a "history" of the Fronteras presidio, its content more emphatically spotlights the escapades and outrages of its captain, Gregorio Álvarez Tuñón y Quirós.[5] Other studies have divulged individual personality traits

Introduction 3

of soldiers as participants in conflict-and-resolution incidents in the frontier, but they have focused attention on better-known commanders and higher-level administrators in the broader colonial system.[6]

The present study shows that as socioeconomic realities played out within the ranks of the presidials, the asymmetries of power triggered by these complex interactions often gave way to an imprecise adherence to orders and regulations issued by commanders, governors, and even the viceroy himself. Moreover, documentation by Amangual of the daily grind and its impact, often deleterious and sometimes criminal, on heretofore unacknowledged men fulfilling the royal service advance our understanding of life in the *Comandancia General*, essentially an emphatically militarized reimagination of the Provincias Internas.[7] Given the historiographical prominence of men like Brig. Gen. Pedro de Rivera, Cmdr. and eventual Viceroy Bernardo de Gálvez and the first Cmdr. Gen. of the Comandancia General Teodoro de Croix and other better-known functionaries in the militarized borderlands, compared with the relative obscurity of others among their ranks, my inquiry steers in another direction. It focuses on the lesser-known Amangual and his contemporaries within the hierarchy of the army over a period of forty years. Tracking his conduct through correspondence has simultaneously cast light on many of his colleagues and their professional relationships with him as either subordinates to his authority or as his commanders.

In the chapters that follow, I show how he and other soldiers carried out their duties to varying degrees by adhering to—or, just as often, resisting—the prescribed course of conduct dictated by the various regulations that emerged between the years 1729 and 1786. I assess Amangual's apparently unequivocal acceptance of his responsibilities as the presidio's duly elected paymaster. However, the position of keeper of the company funds proved to be an obligation fraught with controversy. Original sources show how the customary functions of his office came under attack from his fellow company members when he was accused on at least three occasions of misappropriation of funds or merchandise. These allegations required ongoing rebuttals on his part. Similarly, illicit activity by the troops in his own company complicated Amangual's tasks, as did the ebb and flow of funds from several large and important accounts. From these unfortunate circumstances, the personalities and eccentricities of individual soldiers, merchants, and others tied in one way or another to the borderland's economic operations reveal the personal motivations and often criminal inclinations of certain key players in garrison life.

Francisco Amangual's periodic task of executing often substantive inventories and regular documentation of gifts for the various Indian nations[8] constituted a significant aspect of his job requirements. His work as an accountant has been mostly ignored by writers until now. The array of social interplay that devolved from the ordinary paperwork documenting so-called peace by purchase in the interest of Native polities by presidial commanders and merchants remains little examined in the historiography. This is remarkable given that the sources for various textual communications—military service records, legal proceedings, censuses, ledgers, inventories, and correspondence—are extensive. This book contributes to an understanding of how individual soldiers and commanders, unsung in the historiography until now, across a multitude of garrisons, vendors, civilians, missionaries, indigenous peoples, and military governors, interacted with one another across large swaths of the borderlands. Since these encounters often involved illegal transactions, unsubstantiated accusations, and severe punishments that could derail career advancement or even lead to exile, they contrast especially so with military operations that garnered praise, promotions, and monetary and titular rewards.[9]

Occasional system-wide acknowledgment and subsequent broadcasting of outstanding individual achievement and collective performance among one detail of troops counteracted embarrassing conduct by another. By analyzing the seemingly mundane commercial interactions alongside interludes of personal conflict and resolution structuring presidial life, specialists and students alike will come to understand at many levels the thought processes and emotional responses of soldiers to often precarious conditions in a life where insubordination had consequences.

The secondary organizing principle of the book's two-pronged investigation examines the development of the flying squadrons (*compañías volantes*), understood as a kind of at-the-ready military force in the *Provincias Internas*. The *volantes*—referred to variously as *cuerpos volantes*, *escuadra volante*, or *tropas volantes*—evolved in tandem with the emergence of the fixed presidio network and served as a posthaste cavalry charged with defending New Spain's far northern regions. Persistent concerns by viceregal authorities about foreign incursions from multiple points on the compass and grumblings in the trenches by commanders facing Native hostilities led to heightened security.

Broadly surveying the presidio and its function within the colonial state, Max Moorhead noted that when new military bases emerged, some of the older presidios were in turn suppressed. With infantry and cavalry to protect established towns and even new communities of armed civilians, garrisons appeared at strategic points, usually in more remote locales, distant from population strongholds.[10] Fated to be inconsistent, the process of concretizing a visual presence of authority proved to be of strenuous

Introduction 5

complexity given its merging of pragmatic experiments with psychological considerations. Formidable consequences followed the stunning aftermath of the Pueblo Revolt of 1680. As Moorhead notes, when officials abolished Chametla and San Hipólito, both located in western Nueva Vizcaya (today Chihuahua and Durango), four new presidios—El Pasaje, El Gallo, Conchos, and Casas Grandes—took their place. During this period, Janos emerged and the garrison at Casas Grandes dwindled to a mere post, eventually becoming the headquarters for a *compañía volante*, or what Moorhead describes as a "roving company" of forty men. In 1693, with no "systematic coordination" planned for the several presidios in the war zone, and with governors and commandants unable to visualize an overall strategy, military personnel of varying rank and administrators began to offer new approaches to the presidial line of defense.[11] A colonial observer of the time, Agustín Herbante del Camino, suggested that the soldiers of the "newly erected" presidios have multiple tasks to include moving constantly in one body, sometimes separated and in different places and based on the "demand of the occasion," weather permitting.[12]

Such an expectation is difficult to imagine given the reality of circumstances on the ground. Camino himself acknowledged his own conceptual overreach in considering not only the extent of the territory to be defended and upsurges in rebellious Native populations but also the practicality of securing a "roving" company to operate in different districts at the same time. Frontier events prompted the usual reactionary Iberian assessment of the treatment of indigenous peoples and the creation of a new policy of defense to include the *compañías volantes*. Reviewing the literature on the colonial military apparatus, historians of the northern borderlands have over the past several decades documented the *volantes'* presence while occasionally noting the substitution of the flying squadrons for stationary presidial garrisons.[13]

From one unidentified source, the viceroy received a suggestion that he dissolve the lately created presidios of Conchos, El Pasaje, El Gallo, and Casas Grandes and then consolidate their forces into a single *compañía volante*.[14] In theory, the proposal envisioned a flying company, presumably an exceptionally large impermanent force, providing protection for both travelers and merchandise along the roads. This cavalry outfit would have the ability to deploy rapid assistance to any place under attack in Nueva Vizcaya. Permanence in contrast to mobility has, over time, become normalized across much of the historiography in delineating whatever differences existed between a presidial company and a flying squadron. From his perspective in the late 1960s, Moorhead used a specific example to clarify those differences, indicating that by 1692 the fighting unit at Coro de Guachi (Fronteras) in Sonora had not been "formally established," and was, therefore, still considered a *compañía volante*. Moorhead describes the "presidial company" as "authorized," suggesting its official designation and recognition by administrators in Mexico City. At the same time, he alluded to its eventual conversion into something *pro forma*, that is, according to protocol or developed organically from its troop strength.[15]

On orders from the viceroy with instructions to carry out a comprehensive report, in 1693 Field Marshal José Francisco Marín suggested three proposals to remedy the situation. First, Marín recommended that the aforementioned presidios *not* be consolidated into a single flying squadron but, rather, that each be retained for the present; second, he proposed that the new squadron of Sonora be converted into a presidio and that stabilizing efforts coordinate with those at Janos in order to stem Apache invasions and Pima rebellions. Bordering Sinaloa and with Sonora to the north was Presidio Janos and a flying squadron that could help with any setback, despite their great distance.[16] Finally, Marín insisted that several presidio companies dispense with prioritizing convoy or garrison duty and instead unite from time to time in "large scale offensive operations." Marín's logic behind these proposed changes was that "the waging of continuous offensive war on the enemy tribes" placed resistant Native populations on the defensive and left them no opportunity to plan and execute raids on frontier settlements.[17]

In times of both conflict and peace, expectations fell short. By the time Pedro de Rivera completed his inspection of the presidios in 1728, the dubious viability of the *volantes* became plain. In his *Proyecto*, their function and organization are conceptually delineated in black ink. Thus, the actual performance of the flying squadrons witnessed by Rivera clashed with his expectations. In his report, he described in no uncertain terms what he found in several companies. The inspector grappled with the flying squadrons' ambiguous operations in the homelands in stark contrast to the fixed position and more precisely described function of regular presidial cadres stationed at fortified garrisons. Moreover, there is the sense that Rivera was deeply troubled by the *volantes'* presumed specialized status. As his concerns unfold in chapter 1 of this book, Rivera's recommendation for reform of the presidio apparatus involved careful planning, the close management of local resources, and entrusting his best officers with carrying out beneficial changes.

As the foregoing summary shows, modifications across time and within military prerogatives underscored the element of transformation characterizing the squadrons' bifurcated function: maintaining sporadic movement and site-specific permanence.[18] The most cynical way to understand their

Introduction 7

history is to see inconstancy as a defining element of the *volantes*. That frame of reference emerges most forcefully among administrators with reform on their minds and ink in their quills. It can also serve as a key point of departure for thinking broadly about all the military units associated with the *presidio/misión/ranchería* complex. And so, questions emerge. How are we to explain discrete variables that differentiated one cadre from another so as not to blur the intended objective of each of the units and their relationship to the civilian community? Additionally, in the administrative areas of task and purpose, was it possible that overlap held fast between and among the various armed forces—cavalry, artillery, infantry—and, especially within the culturally-inscribed spaces of the borderlands? Communication in the time of Francisco Amangual often made indistinct, if not highly questionable, the prescribed mission of not only the *volantes* but also that of other military operatives protecting settlements through periods of war and appeasement.[19]

This book draws on the foundational work of Max Moorhead insofar as contextualizing the on-the-ground processes of compromise and constancy that structured not only armed defense in the aggregate but also the socioeconomic dynamics of the presidio ecosystem at the microlevel. Long-standing jurisdictional fluidity in these peripheral spaces served as an impetus for the most opportunistic, if not guileful, among colonial inhabitants to manipulate to their own advantage the organization of life. For some, it mattered not if their actions contradicted bureaucratic directives to that effect. Moreover, existential realities necessitated the cross-positioning of tasks (officially sanctioned or otherwise) among and between military units and civilian localities of different formulations, adding another layer to organizational motility where it concerned law and order. In the first example, we will see how *contrabandistas* and other brigands within the ranks of the military resisted the dictates of the various *reglamentos* and follow-up orders from local commanders. Corrective measures specifically targeted misconduct and lawlessness at the presidios during the long period leading up to the promulgation of the *Ordenanzas de Intendencias* and the Gálvez *Instrucción* of 1786. In the second, in the matter of strict adherence to military protocol, career opportunities existed for those individuals tractable enough to respond to orders from administrators operating out of Mexico City or from their commanders in the next room. How ever impractical or shortsighted, intermittently issued regulations shaped the contours of presidio life by attempting to cover all aspects of a soldier's service.

Troops who fulfilled their obligation to duty in the hopes of finding favor with viceregal authorities and local commanders comprised the no-nonsense adherents to military regulation. Others resisted injunctions from above through engagement in illicit activities, dereliction of duty, and even desertion. Somewhere in between the multilayered interplay of soldiers, indigenous and civilian populations, opportunities surfaced to make frontier life tolerable and military service workable. Where the rise and fall of economic and social circumstances animated life in the militarized borderlands, at intervals the seizing of opportunities by soldiers through extralegal means and usurping authority by rejecting official mandates entailed straying from honorable behavior. Among some men garrisoned across the Commandancy, slogging on according to organizational strategies prescribed by authorities in the metropoles and enforced by commanders in country frequently lost its relevance.

In the context of the soldiers' stakes in the frontier, that substantial investment of doing right and playing by the rules impacted work obligations and often left them, individually and collectively, the recipients of relatively fewer rewards than their counterparts in the urban spaces of the empire. Did a soldier's devotion to duty serve as enough of a positive motivator to maintain blind obedience to commanders and to comply with official precepts that might, potentially, result in career advancement? Military powerbrokers across the centuries championed much of the same kind of speculative ideal in evolving regulations and instructions. Given the harsh realities of carving out what must have seemed like nothing more than mere existence, were even the most circumspect troops willing to occasionally partake of more extreme acts of disobedience and even outright criminality in order to ensure survival?

My findings show that questionable scenarios transpired in myriad ways among the key players to the extent that the deeply human dimensions of presidial life become all too apparent. Deviant ways among soldiers often translated into more tempered responses by superiors, like using the advantages of negotiation and accommodation through a deliberate bending of the rules. Archival sources reveal multiple documented episodes of work-related ruptures in the more intimate spaces of the presidio. Transcripts of official proceedings project onto the historiographical stage the voices of litigants, complainants, and the accused. Many of these actors' experiences in New Spain's borderlands have rarely penetrated the field of late colonial military history in any extensive study to date. Moorhead's scholarship functions as an investigative catalyst for this book by building on that scholar's focus on the presidio network's bureaucratic substrate. Going further, I chart how social interplay among lesser-known stakeholders conditioned the political calculus of the army and reshaped the character of the periphery.[20]

Introduction 9

Over the past four decades the flying squadrons' subsequent disappearance from scholarship of the speculative Cowboy West from the nineteenth century forward betrays an incipient marginalization of their presence within the historiographical frontier. But colonial-era documentation of their activities requires a rethinking of not only how a tactically inclined unit operated in the sociopolitical culture and militarization of the borderlands, but also what influence, if any, did their history have on later cavalries. To that end I locate common strands between the *volantes* and members of other presidial units as a method of ascertaining their disparate responsibilities in the colonial army hierarchy. In the case of Francisco Amangual, those tasks were manifold. This book treats the fighting forces as integral to the borderlands' socioeconomic arena since its commanders' professional objectives aligned with the larger project of maintaining imperial authority in New Spain's *Septentrión*.

The frontier army's methods of command and control extended widely and often in covert ways but were negligible at best. Given the army's chronic shortages, a stark reality presented itself: true dominion of the region resided with the Comanche, Wichita (Kitikiti'sh, Kirikirish), and other First Nations.[21] Capitulation to Spanish colonial authority among the more, or less, pacified indigenous groups was usually haphazard as was that of non-Iberian interlopers like the English, French, and Anglo-Americans, individuals and groups that more persistently emerge during the twilight of the empire. With hostile Indians, the mechanisms for soldierly containment of the enemy ranged from avoidance to clever manipulation, and from nonstop harassment to utter extermination. Encountering resistance by powerful Native groups including the Ndé (Apache), and acquiescence on the part of the Spanish military population, including the flying squadrons, proved to be best practice and downright necessary to shore up the possibility of peace, an objective rarely taken for granted. No matter how much officers-in-charge, like Amangual, chose to convince themselves of their success in the name of viceregal enterprise, tactics involving accommodation and tolerance gave commanders in trouble spots at least a semblance of control.[22]

Much like their appearances across the colonial frontier, imagined by some as a ubiquitous cavalry unit coiled and poised to spring into action at a moment's notice, the *volantes* emerge in the documentary record in short historiographical bursts. Mingled into the scholarly detritus, their activities unfold for brief periods only to recede into the archival record once other, more substantively documented military cadres arrive to occupy larger page counts in borderlands literature. Nonetheless, my findings indicate that there indeed exists a more expansive context for the *volantes* as important players in colonial history given their multiple, if diffused, appearances in the archival record. Though chronicled in the historical record, interludes of daring escapades on horseback through the wide-open spaces of the Comandancia and punitive forays across that landscape do not form a preponderance of the original documentation relative to the flying squadrons' actual experiences.[23] Those adventures are not the focus of this book.

Rather, there does exist in primary sources a more conventional record of the *volantes'* (and fixed soldiers') activities as found in the inventories of company storehouses, including those authored by Francisco Amangual; registers of soldiers' belongings and military service records (*hojas de servicio*);[24] the army's surveillance of the *despoblado*; and, more remarkably, the flying squadrons' and presidials' shortcomings as effective containment detachments. Drawing on military historian Juan Marchena Fernández's work, but with a geographic focus on the American outposts rather than its urban spaces, my research has uncovered incidences of both compelling significance and workaday drudgery. My book reinserts the flying squadrons' presence into the larger context of presidio-centered contributions to regional history.

In his study of garrison life emphasizing a world of routine (*"un mundo de rutina"*), Marchena Fernández highlighted the "absolute monotony" of daily service experienced by soldiers, a recurring element given the defensive nature of the work involved. Duty reshaped prevention (against enemy assaults) into routine, and routine into monotony.[25] Borderlands historian Odie Faulk described the "most severe trial" facing boots on the ground in Texas was "overcoming the monotony which confronted them year after tedious year" with the demoralizing effect of loss of initiative and personal freedom.[26] The latter reality was, historically, countered by protracted absences if not permanent departure—that is, desertion. Apart from their specialized functions as described in the official record, remarkable commonalities existed between assorted military operatives that straddled diverse ethnic, social, and geographic boundaries. Furthermore, mutual objectives of containment fluctuated even as these anecdotal borders were often unified, if only temporarily, and once more undone in the face of danger, intrusion, and by the defensive strategies of managing the frontier.[27]

Inquiry into the steady stream of official pronouncements directed at military personnel circumscribes the subject matter in this book. My study of the *reglamentos, ordenanzas,* and viceregal instructions led me to interpret key differences and subtle inflection points emerging from their content. Among the colonial inhabitants and the military personnel affected by the mandates, I am mainly concerned here with contextualizing the language within this array of texts about officially sanctioned behavior in the interpresidio setting, which also encompassed civilian spheres of contact.[28]

On the other side of the administrative spectrum, opportunities to upwardly advance in the royal service existed from time to time. Now and again, this was true for principled men keen on carrying out orders by superiors operating out of Mexico City and from commanders in proximity to the northern provinces. For example, archival sources suggest Francisco Amangual's unshakable deference to authority. But, as it will become apparent, in certain instances otherwise incorruptible soldiers saw as unquestionably necessary to ensure survival the advantages of negotiation, accommodation, and even deliberate manipulation of official statutes. The stories that follow in this book provide the essential narrative of how the exigencies of military life reached their conclusions.

New conditions for not only violence and warfare but also transregional economic opportunities and increased settlement across the Ibero-American colonies arose after the Seven Years' War (1756–63) with decisive repercussions for the military. Yet again, multiple ordinances found use as organizational frameworks for instituting desperately needed upgrades. The former pattern of governance, based on the Laws of the Indies and deemed outdated and inflexible by changing demographics and urbanization, was ripe for renovation. After two centuries of mutations, the intention now to deploy progressive, rational-based ways of thinking, galvanized both the Iberian Peninsula and the North American continent. Frontier soldiers in theory adhered to regulations specific to their location in New Spain. Lyle McAlister's text brings to light the troop rage for privileged status conferred by the *fuero*, its value as an instrument to avoid penalties for misconduct, and so makes the *Real declaración* of 1767 relevant to this study. Similarly, Lillian Fisher's analysis is useful for its discussion of the 1786 Intendant System's Department of Finance's articles referring to expenditures for the military, its personnel, and for the revenue gained from tobacco distribution.[29] In its various manifestations, this singular plant was a source of litigation and focus of intrigue involving many *presidiales*, including those who abused their office of supervision over this valuable resource. For a soldier like Francisco Amangual, in 1796 he will be one among some entrusted with conducting an important inventory of the commodity.[30] The Department of War's articles specifically addressed inventories, accounts, computations, and merchant transactions and comprise another significant component of New Spain's reorganization of capital.

However, for the purposes of this borderlands microhistory, the intendancy's fiscal methods energize to a lesser degree my discussion of

Introduction

Amangual's responsibilities as a fiduciary. This is due to the presidios having separate governance in the form of the Comandancia General which emerged as part of a two-prong plan of Viceroy Croix and Inspector Gálvez to include establishment of the intendency system,[31] and discrete financial oversight from that of the regular army in New Spain.[32] From the perspective of viceregal authorities in Mexico City, the presidios' rebounding meant that deteriorating conditions might improve for a while, but backsliding was fated to persist at some localities. As matters stood, some of those shortcomings stemmed from the failures of certain garrisons to fulfill their missions effectively, thereby requiring cyclical issuances of regulations by dint of hard-pressed commanders.

Five decades before this study, Max Moorhead analyzed the several *reglamentos* that functioned as reference material for the commanders and their subordinates stationed at the frontier's many garrisons.[33] However, this book reevaluates much of the content of three *reglamentos*, namely, those of 1719, 1729, and 1772, as well as the Gálvez *Instrucción* of 1786. Since fact-finding tours generated diary content that preceded these mandates and other directives intended for system-wide issuance and given their eventual publication in English and Spanish publications across decades, I dwell less on day-to-day recording of events and discoveries. And slightly less attention is paid to long-standing and occasionally overlapping royal *ordenanzas* directed at Peninsular and Viceregal armies.[34] Successive regulations and instructions officially spelled out punishment for transgressors, but much of it was strangely tepid when compared to harder-hitting royal edicts.[35] In part, the content of three manifestos (excluding that of 1719) representing first person inspections by Rivera, Rubí, both Gálvez, and Croix, specifically addressed troop discipline in the *frontera*. Therefore, my focus is intentionally focused on the reformist outcomes spawned by their issuance. Doing so allows me to tease out from the official doctrines the social ramifications for soldiers and their contemporaries affected by their content. What becomes evident over and over is that intra-presidio crises stemmed from soldiers acting out their rejection of bureaucratic protocol and procedure. I have confined my research to the period roughly conforming to Francisco Amangual's years in the royal service while expanding those years slightly to include the time frame of the *volantes'* presence as disclosed in original documentation. Thus, the trio of official directives at intervals structure sections of this book's narrative by providing a bedrock set of reference materials for the sweeping guidelines to which soldiers and their commanders were expected to conform.

In furtherance of the more aggressive policy of defense proposed by Marín in 1693, one historian argues that by the time the Royal Regulations of

Introduction 13

Presidios appeared in 1772, a more formal organization of the *volante* units emerged. And even it was subject to change over a span of several decades. Andrés Tijerina contends that, in Texas, it was composed of local volunteers, mostly Tejanos trained by professional officers.[36] They served longer terms of duty and engaged in extensive *campañas* (offensive maneuvers) across the borderlands. Landowners in the *frontera* initially organized soldiers on horseback as "flying companies" to thwart on a moment's notice indigenous incursions. The most significant change, as reported by Tijerina, was that now the *compañías volantes* maintained offensive strategy against intruders rather than simply defending the home front.[37] Alternatively, a standardized system of colonization implemented by representatives for private-interest groups led to the settlement of Nuevo Santander, a segment of the uncultivated *Seno Mexicano*. For his part, the Conde de Sierra Gorda José de Escandón formed a group of prominent investors hankering for militarized government across the entire jurisdiction.[38] The region's financial backers were equally desirous of replacing what they considered an antiquated mission-presidio administrative structure of clerics and full-time soldiers with a large civilian population. Making the process almost completely transactional, Escandón reorganized the militia corps in the back country of Nuevo Santander. In 1787, one of the landed elites of the region José Florencio Barragán, a wealthy merchant of Rioverde and heir to an immense fortune, created, armed, and directed a *compañía volante* from the villa of Santa Bárbara. Barragán provisioned the eighty-man flying company with food, gunpowder, and bullets, and even led campaigns against the hostile Indians of the region.[39] Escandón and Barragán's efforts at mobilizing a militia and a flying squadron and arming the citizenry of the Santander jurisdiction were not entirely innovative enterprises during this period of intense militarization of the borderlands.

If compared with Moorhead's discussion of the presidio system, my study casts light on the logistical or operational activities carried out by lesser-known, if not historically obscured, military personnel and the ways in which they responded to a cascade of official mandates. As a case study, readers become acquainted with not only Amangual but many other individuals animating the "bastion of the Spanish borderlands" as Moorhead described the frontier garrison writ large. In the pages that follow, my characters emerge as principals more forcefully. I employ a two-pronged tool of analysis by (1) evaluating in the aggregate higher-authority directives aimed at tracking presidial soldiers' and commanders' comportment among themselves and outsiders and, in the earlier chapters, by (2) characterizing how discrete mandates tethered the *volantes'* actual purpose with the greater objectives of a reliably reactive imperial program. As it pertains to the

Lino Sánchez y Tapia, "Soldado Mexicano Presidial." Courtesy of the Gilcrease Museum, Tulsa, Oklahoma.

Introduction

second prong of the study, scrutinizing chapter and verse in the historical record will enhance understanding of the *volantes'* (im)precise function in the colonial borderlands. Hewing closely to available documentary sources uncovers those areas of martial performance where the squadrons fell short and, conversely, what tasks set specifically for these cavalry units merited praise. The necessity for such an approach has not crystallized in studies by other historians who have overlooked standing order delimiting soldier behavior. In the case of the flying squadrons, the general conclusion is that their haphazard positioning as an armed force and their visibility in multiple capacities complicated their presence as military personnel with ambiguously prescribed duties. Contemporaneous documentation records their lived experience as residents, community law enforcement, patrol detachments across the Comandancia's broad expanse, and, undeniably, as neglected *soldados del Rey*. If, and when, they adhered to protocol as a collective endeavor, the *volantes* enhanced surveillance of large open spaces beyond the presidio. How they engaged with local populations and their methods of restructuring authority within their own ranks problematizes their status as a borderland's management unit.

In service to the empire, they negotiated the closely interwoven activities of capturing and detaining lawbreakers (outside the presidio), distributing gifts for gain, and fostering productive interpresidial relationships with local societies. As if this profusion of tasks were not enough, the squadrons had to maintain cohesion within the unit itself by setting examples of both proper conduct inside the garrison and mindfulness of the civilian population outside. While highlighting the *volantes'* sporadic appearances as woven throughout each chapter, the principal objective of this book pinpoints the character of contact by identifiable presidio soldiers with each other, their commanders, merchants, and indigenous groups. Thereafter, I contend with episodes wherein military personnel either acceded to or deviated from mandated responsibilities. With Amangual as the central protagonist soldiering on as both paymaster and officer, what surfaces throughout his workaday activities and interchanges with others are matters of pattern and practice, of conflict and resolution, with much of it enacted within the intimate spaces of the garrison. Archival sources record the uneasy navigation of complex, if often overwhelming, bureaucratic waters by Amangual and others from the military and civilian arenas.

Imperial inclinations fueled expansionism in the form of hostile takeovers that set into motion the development of peripheral communities. Detailed narratives of life among individuals affiliated with the colonial state's military comprise pages upon pages of documentation. The prolonged course of intrusion, penetration, and occupation in New Spain's

16   Introduction

Comandancia involved violence and asymmetric warfare, disordering indigenous planes of existence and consequently delaying and even laying waste to outsiders' machinations. The socioeconomic apparatuses that shifted from the earliest colonial practices deep within Mexico's interior to the viceroyalty's outposts included the deployment of time-tested, if uneven, settlement patterns among civilian, ecclesiastical, and military communities. The entirety of this process, well documented in a historiography too vast to include here, dislodged Native people from ancestral homelands. However, in the eighteenth-century "Texas" borderlands, multiple indigenous societies used accommodation, manipulation, and strategies of domination to orchestrate systems of spatial control to their advantage. Their resistance to intensifying pressures of change, in turn, fomented trespassing by the exponential presence of missionaries, soldiers, civilian immigrants, and their followers. Military society, imagined so, can provide a framework for interpreting mechanisms of social control used by colonial enforcers, however ineffective, against powerful Native groups. Fueling the patterns of military encroachment was an overarching imperial agenda administered from a distant metropole insistent on buffering presumably isolated regions from trans-Atlantic rivals equally determined to gain a foothold in new economic and political realms.

Soldiers enlisted in the various flying squadrons and other troop units chronically faced the fluctuating nature of upholding aggressive defense of the presidio and its surroundings while cultivating productive relationships with groups perceived to be subjugated by imperial force. Even when that notion proved to be unrealistic, documentation nevertheless records such indigenous contestants as "Friendly Nations." And, in the case of Texas, pragmatic commanders accepted that polities like the Comanche—a regional power wielding enormous control over local resources—ought to be appeased. Borderlands historiography makes public that ceaseless hostilities with the Ndé led to elaborately designed strategies of supervision including deception on the part of both sides.[40] That Francisco Amangual juggled the weight of maintaining fiscal propriety while regularly providing for Native visitors speaks to his ability to multitask within closely related spheres of responsibility. Further, he did so within the context of managing, when calculable, intricate social relationships among the presidio's various clientele.

This study is a microhistory that contributes to and expands on the prevailing *meta*discourse of borderlands history, or, to use its other well-worn descriptor (and used, too, in this book), frontier studies. However, that type of description will not make this book unique or a departure from its

Introduction   17

predecessors in the historiography, except in one rather significant way described below. Nor is it likely that this book will be ascribed to the realm of revisionist scholarship except where it spotlights individual military men whose literal, if often abridged, voices emerge from testimonies where episodes of conflict, resolution, and continuity underscored the everyday tasks of soldierly life. Scholars of the Ibero-Indigenous borderlands have heard some of these voices before in other contexts. Similar narratives dependably appear in stories of contention and crisis, resistance and acquiescence, and usually involve settlers, citizens, adventurers, Indians, and soldiers and their commanders.[41] My reliance on archival sources to highlight what to others may appear as the most banal circumstances in a workday will not disappoint a documentation-focused audience. But I will try to convince other readers that, taken all together, presidio-generated paperwork and related ephemera brought to pass an extraordinary body of official discourse.[42]

Given that the original testimonies interwoven throughout this study for the most part attest to an apparently compulsory if not obsessive pattern of documentation, it follows that these types of narratives reflect the inner workings of presidio administrative life. Tedious though such texts may appear to some, official communication required the substantiation of even the most innocuous action taken in and around the garrison, with an emphasis on the activities of individual companies. Notwithstanding the volume of primary sources, often incomplete, from multiple archives, what is left preserves the decontextualized fragments of a once cohesive documentary milieu. Ink to paper expedited means of communication in the frontier, transmitting oral disclosures that found a way into the textual record. Extant data preserve a kind of historical authenticity articulated from the vantage point of those who had the power to memorialize and transcribe. Written observations recovered from various repositories and from among a broad range of participants can be something more than merely a veneer for emerging perspectives on the colonial borderlands. Instead, neglected voices reflect the thoughts, feelings, and actions of the usual groupings of frontier protagonists—soldiers, traders, clerics, provincial administrators, Indian chiefs[43] and their followers—all within the spatial boundaries, imaginary or otherwise, of an often-unforgiving territory. Voices long silent within these texts have passed through a process of official filtration that leaves the researcher with a distillation of narratives that some would prefer to see minimized, annotated, or otherwise textually marginalized. This study is not one more iteration of the so-called *big man* scenario or another latter-day monumental history. The focus of its content draws mostly from documents exchanged between lesser-known but, as it turns out, just as significant actors, the majority of whom were enlisted men, their indigenous counterparts, and merchants of all stripes.

Other historians have called for deeper levels of social insight, particularly as narratives spelled out the slow walk of empires, conquest, and rapacious power-brokering throughout the colonial Atlantic world. As Eliga Gould indicates, "entangled histories are concerned with 'mutual influencing,' 'reciprocal or asymmetric perceptions,' and the intertwined 'processes of constituting one another.'"[44] As the colonial state's symbolic marker of oversight and surveillance on the frontier, the Spanish enterprise's complex of presidios, though physically spaced apart to disadvantageous effect, were created to make conspicuous a barrier to intruders. Counted among that number were rivals, hostile to and indignant over the viceroyalty's dual objectives of domination and religio-economic development as the homelands grew increasingly militarized. The onward march of soldiers with weapons, of horse herds and gear, and the construction of garrisons intensified mutually influential and reciprocal exchanges between competing societies. Between fulfillment and disappointment, these closely aligned groups—military, ecclesiastic, Native, and civilian—struggled for dominion when and where that was possible. In an often-repeated scenario, some interactions with rare exception recast malleable, if shaky, relationships between ancestral peoples and immigrants from other empires.

This book contributes to the study of intra-presidio relations through the military's interplay with a wide array of borderlands polities. Documented instances of troop disunity emerge with enough force to identify spaces of contention among those working collectively as agents for the colonial state. As a focal point for making sense of misconduct and insubordination within the ranks, reports by commanders chart the organizational context of bringing resolution to arenas of conflict involving subordinates. More than an indistinguishable mass of gun and powder–toting fighters both on foot and on horseback, individual soldiers provided a significant human resource for colonial policy making in New Spain and in its frontier theater of operations. Nurturing cohesion among the troops served the interests of a secularizing authority, and by the late eighteenth century that vehicle for provincial oversight was often at its most vulnerable in the most distant reaches of the viceroyalty. Commanders in the trenches and royal administrators in Mexico City and Madrid were keenly aware of the need to appease the Septentrión's military force. Their numbers included men who half-heartedly performed their assigned tasks, those who readily complied with superintendence despite meager rewards across expansive territory, and some soldiers only too eager to abandon the military complex in its entirety. Whether or not those in positions of authority acquiesced to the dereliction and grievances of these burdensome actors plaguing the presidios and as documented in voluminous paperwork shapes the contours of this book.

Into these treacherous outposts and onto this platform of frontier discourse European adventurers and intruders materialize, bringing with them cultural practices, personal aspirations, and economic objectives. Their entrances, exits, and prolonged stopovers triggered apprehension—and even more documentation—from colonial stakeholders maneuvering within a complex social arena. Added to this cultural fusion are several names, like Vial, Croix, Gil Ibarvo, Nolan, Ashby, and de Mézières, that will be familiar to scholars engaged in studies about the American West and its geographic and historiographical antecedent, the colonial *Ibero–Franco–Anglo*-Indian borderlands. Moreover, regionally centered gamesmanship put socioeconomic factors in play and politically advantageous maneuverings to work. Advancing an agenda out of step with decaying Bourbon Reforms, their collective momentum in shrinking whatever was left of imaginary borders would soon become the customary reference points for thinking about the Far North and its place in later US–Mexico relations.[45]

Challenges to the Imagination

My study explores the processual dimensions of bureaucratic regulation in pattern and practice by dint of the black letter of the law. As a socially dynamic hub of sorts with its perpetual flow of humanity into and out of its walls, the presidio served as the locus for its documentarists to construct a distinct type of written matter. Military service records, monthly company reports, and correspondence between commanders, subordinate officers, and provincial administrators created the channels to accomplish two opposing but closely related goals, at least on paper. Written injunctions could cohere disparate communities, though that actuality was as often imaginary as it was real. Its content recorded cleavages, both transitory and permanent, among individuals and like-minded groups cohabiting common and segregated spaces alike. Across the ethnically diverse borderlands, official discourse set out to delineate a kind of communal if also hierarchically-inscribed territory while conforming to the overarching objectives of the imperial apparatus. In doing so, the process sought to fix the parameters of well-defined social spaces that functioned to legitimatize an ideological climate initiated by the military presence. Ethnic taxonomies in focus, the effort spent in cementing group cohesion among imported civilian and indigenous populations, and within *hispano*-dominant garrison populations, required thoughtful documentation.[46]

From the vantage point of a postcolonial discursive context with a view toward one individual soldier's career and one specialized cavalry unit's function, then, my study reorients the reading and interpretation of borderlands patrol and defense, both mechanisms deployed by a bureaucracy seeking to harness often chaotic territory. Since portions of the secondary sources root the presidials in a kind of fabled past that minimizes their less-than-virtuous presence, this study will be a deviation from earlier prototypes by exposing on-the-ground occurrences, some undeniably commonplace, from across a wide array of primary sources. Throughout the research for and writing of this book and given that entrenched ways of imagining the frontier pervade some aspects of borderlands military historiography, that is, its projection of armed and mounted operatives occupying the Septentrión amid hostile working conditions, resistant civilians, and inconstant Native peoples, one challenge persisted while I constructed the narrative.

My earliest attempts at making sense of the documents by mapping my own subjectivities onto the existing historiography surfaced from just such a framework of *a*historical imaginings, ruminations, and long-held beliefs about the frontier. That process of analysis and interpretation almost succeeded in distorting—if not ignoring outright—the lived experiences of the actual protagonists having varied rank, virtue, and status. Within the archives, what I found more often than not was prosaic, if sometimes tedious, and usually tendentious. By releasing once and for all the notion that I would find a glut of audacious acts of heroism and unrelenting bravery across the hallowed confines of various repositories, I yielded to a course of action that prioritized the mundane facets of presidial life and administration. Through a careful exhumation of sources, that endeavor involved several colonial paymasters conducting inventories; preparing monthly company reports, and, in this book, Amangual's (and his cohorts') perpetual counting of expenditures for the Indians. These types of habitual activities circumscribed the boundaries of my research and structured the main thrust of my argument. Because the inclusion of the flying squadrons' operations across the borderlands has rhythmic parallels to the trajectory of Francisco Amangual's career and even forms a subcategory of analysis in this study, it follows that the discursive architecture is set largely by the extant documents from multiple archives at my disposal.

Introduction

Overview of Chapters

Chapter 1 interweaves the military career of Francisco Amangual with the historical emergence of the compañías volantes. By charting his ascension within the Iberian army as a dragoon, followed by his travel overseas to Nueva España, military service records (*hojas de servicio*) and other documents from 1779–1786 trace his interactions with a key figure in colonial borderlands historiography, Gov. Domingo Cabello. From official observations made by inspectors like Pedro de Rivera and the Marqués de Rubí, the Regulations of 1729 and 1772, respectively, had ramifications for the presidials. So too did Amangual's election as paymaster of the Béxar garrison. Transformative elements, like population increases and environmental realities, impacted the development of military stations within the presidio-mission complex. The flying squadrons, too, had to meet those demands, and competing factors often blurred the site-specific purpose and function of these "roving" companies.

Chapter 2 addresses the presidio ecosystem's method of staking out borders and its efforts at managing disparate societies within ambiguous demarcations. The Royal Regulations of 1772 informed that practice, which, like precedent reforms, affected the lives of soldiers in the borderlands. A section of the chapter considers the offensive and defensive maneuvering used in strategizing campaigns to enhance control and subordination, efforts that relied on the willingness of company commanders to accept orders from and comply with superior directives. In some cases, like that of Cpt. Juan Cortés of Presidio La Bahía, realities as they existed forced presidio captains' refusal to conform to orders from above. Their expertise with and jealously defended knowledge of frontier terrain could supersede mandates from officials unfamiliar with local conditions. Broadly preserving stability, imaginary or otherwise, across the borderlands had its challenges, as it did more intimately within the ranks of the garrisons. One example involved two veteran officers, José Rubio and Juan María de Ripperdá, whose conflictive interactions demonstrated the sensitive nature of relationships forged from the official business of running the military. Compounding their difficulties meant contending with less-than-exemplary job performances on the part of functionaries in the colonial bureaucracy. Twenty years hence, workplace animosity erupted in a 1792 lawsuit involving two soldiers from the rank and file of the Béxar presidio force, Sgt. Manuel Rodríguez and Lt. Amangual, with other soldiers lined up as witnesses. The testimony included in this chapter has never been published in any form and is enlightening, given the insight provided from the perspective of original voices from the period. Soldier and civilian depositions from this entanglement tell us as much about the moral character of and obligation to duty of certain individuals in particular as it does about military legal proceedings in general.

Chapter 3 presents the conclusion to the Amangual–Rodríguez slander case, and then moves into a discussion of attributes demanded by superiors for prospective soldiers. When they failed to meet standards of good conduct, intra-presidio conflicts were mitigated by disciplinary efforts targeting misconduct. Some aspects of individual identity emerge from examining the military service records (*hojas de servicio*) of select soldiers. The formatting itself of the records feature multilayered dimensions that say much about origin, class, status, and ethnicity in the military ranks. Personal attributes of soldiers, Native people, and civilian settlers also found expression in the Gálvez *Instrucción* of 1786 but, since his invective underscores the content, the focus in this chapter turns to the viceroy's singular nemesis, the Apache. Colonizer José de Escandón emerges, too, as a key powerbroker in his role as governor of Nuevo Santander in the Río Grande Valley prior to his eventual promotion to interim governor of Texas. The narrative returns to suspicions cast yet again upon Accountant Amangual in a case involving questionable balances in the Béxar *Habilitación* Fund. The chapter unites the gutsy Cpt. Juan Cortés and the beleaguered Amangual in yet another proceeding aimed at soldier insubordination. This time it involved contraband charges among troops traveling from Natchitoches, Louisiana, to Nacogdoches, Texas, in the summer of 1792.

Chapter 4 delves into the conventional practice of accommodating with provisions and favors Native visitors to the presidio, a manifestation of the colonial mechanism of "peace by purchase." As a staging area for goodwill and gift-giving, military installations drew representatives from the Tancague, Guichita, Lipan, and Comanche nations, among others. Into that widening mix came the enterprising Frenchman and *soldado distinguido* Andrés Benito Courbiére, an individual who appears throughout this study in a variety of contexts. Recurrent soldier misbehavior necessitated another inventory for Amangual, this one involving contraband brought by Toribio Durán and his men from Nacogdoches to San Antonio. Like other lists of commodities trafficked through smuggling operations, material goods in commercial transit suggest the buying preferences of individuals navigating malleable socioeconomic spaces in the colonial borderlands. The same can be said of property belonging to French residents and passersby of the presidial environs. Census and biographical data of foreigners within these

Introduction

regions provide a focal point in the chapter for understanding the frontier's growing mixed demographic during the early 1790s.

Chapter 5 notes how tracking foreigners continued to be a concern for viceregal authorities and now, more than ever, Anglo-Americans moved into the sphere of suspicion. However, the unending necessity for keeping peace with indigenous nations proved to be an imperative requiring constant reiteration, from distant authorities to local commanders. As presidio finances demanded stricter oversight to ensure accuracy, substantive documentation of expenditures for "friendly" Indian nations continued unabated. The style of leadership and response to episodic challenges of meeting Native exigencies brought together a skittish Cpt. Espadas, the Lipan leader Canoso, Governor Muñoz, and Interim Escandón.

Chapter 6 in part presents the vehement rebuttal by Amangual to discrepancies in his bookkeeping alleged by the Superior Accounting Office in Mexico City. Yet again the paymaster was put on the defensive and, once more, we see how other aspects of military life remained unchanged: based on compliance with authority, soldiers faced both punishment and promotion. Increasing Anglo-American presence meant intensifying vigilance over all matters, military and civilian, reinforcing the exponential militarization of the Comandancia. The *compañías volantes* resurface through their activities and those of their relatives, with Amangual's ascension to the rank of captain of the flying squadron of San Carlos de Parras marking a significant milestone in his career.

Chapter 7 sees more unwelcome incursions into the Septentrión even as the frontier army welcomed the enlistment of Amangual's son into its ranks. The subject at issue in this final chapter is that most frequently referenced episode from the career of Amangual, the 1808 expedition he commanded from San Antonio de Béxar to Santa Fé, New Mexico. Amangual kept a remarkably detailed diary of the nine-month-long journey, and portions of his narrative are herein summarized and aimed at shedding new light on significant aspects of the excursion. The exploration diaries of the Frenchman Pierre "Pedro" Vial and his companion, the retired corporal José Mares, who traversed the same route in multiple trips between 1786 and 1793, have served as points of comparison for Amangual's 1808 diary. In this chapter, the content of two translations, that of Mattie Hatcher, who translated the Amangual Diary in 1934 for the Béxar Archives, and the Noel M. Loomis and Abraham P. Nasatir rendition that appears as an entire chapter within their 1967 publication, provides reference material for discerning comparable elements within the collective texts.[47] There are slight differences in the latter two translations, and these tell us as much

Introduction

about interpretations by past scholars working on colonial texts as they do about the sequence of events and key players within the historical narrative as told by those same actors. Viewed from the perspective of researchers, highlighting the daily activities of the 1808 expedition team allows for disentangling social interactions never before given voice but reported by members of Amangual's squadron and local groups they encountered along the way. Indians, foreigners, Mexicans, Anglo-Americans came forth, some identified by name and others unknown. Drawing from a variety of sources and Amangual's own handwritten descriptions, the chapter includes original documents that have never before appeared in other texts mentioning the journey.

ONE

❦

Presidial Units, *Volantes*, and Amangual in the Frontier, 1680–1786

Soldiers were always in short supply in New Spain's Far North. Recruitment for armed forces there met with unique challenges given the region's harsh environmental conditions, doggedly resistant Native inhabitants, and its constant privation. When men performed admirably despite these hazards, their value to the empire elevated its status on the global stage. A premium was placed on youth, as it is in today's armies worldwide, where it involved getting bodies to serve in the fighting forces. The lure proved tempting enough for fourteen-year-old José de Herrera Britdale from Mexico City when, on October 20, 1797, he entered the service of the king. Along with his tender age, he brought with him "noble" status and robust health, qualities that boded well for his future as a good subaltern officer in the *compañía volante* of Punta de Lampazos. Though he had not served in any campaigns or actions of war, his commander Capt. Simón de Herrera described him in more favorable terms than some of the older, more experienced fellow soldiers of the company. José's military service record reveals nothing of the attributes that roused Captain Herrera enough to extol his potential as a notable cadet, only that the youngster had served three years, two months, and ten days as of December 31, 1800.[1] Since the documentation ("filiación") does not list the names of his parents as do those of other soldiers deployed throughout the borderlands, it can be safely assumed that young José de Herrera was the son of Simón. With cadet status regulated in 1768, a boy of twelve could indeed enter the military, but only if that recruit met one key criteria: he had to be the son of an officer.[2]

Though his youthfulness accentuates the actuality of one soldier's entry into frontier service, it is the description of José's performance-to-date found in his service record that makes his appearance in the documentation that much more remarkable. As far as his apparent good conduct and adherence to proper comportment contrast sharply with that of several older colleagues in his flying squadron, it is almost certain his father wrote the glowing report. Or, perhaps, parental pride coupled with a healthy dose of nepotism intensified Captain Herrera's positive assessment of the child cadet serving in one of the many units of the frontier fighting force.

Several of those units were the *compañías volantes* identified in the extant historiography and primary sources. Some background information specific to this study is necessary here. As a specialized cavalry force, the flying squadrons developed in tandem with the physical arrangement of the presidios, and each of its regional units was charged with defending the *Provincias Internas*. Garrisoned forts to protect established towns and even new communities of armed civilians first emerged in strategic positions in more remote locales, distant from population strongholds. Accelerating Spanish incursion into Native ancestral lands fueled a series of rebellions carried out by groups like the Xixime, Acaxee, Tepehuan, Tarahumara, Concho, Chiso, Suma, Manso, Jano, Toboso, and Julime nations.

In the aggregate, localized insurgency presaged a punitive tide of reaction also from the Pueblo nations of New Mexico.[3] Demonstrably upending to such a degree that it panicked settler communities, the desperate sought refuge after expulsion. It cannot be overstated that this *first* American Revolution, in 1680, remote beyond compare from Lexington and Concord, galvanized the Peninsula, shuddered the viceroyalty, and launched a new policy of frontier defense. From 1599–1700 intermittent revolts by Native polities surfaced with the goal of severing Iberian dominance from the central corridor of the northern frontier. As Hadley and Naylor describe it, the central corridor constituted territory contained within a single, gigantic province, Nueva Vizcaya. At the beginning of the eighteenth century, this stretch of land encompassed the contemporary Mexican states of Chihuahua, Coahuila, Nuevo León, Tamaulipas, and portions of Durango.[4]

One of the first implementations of the Bourbon Reforms targeted the widely held belief that the presidial configuration was woefully inadequate and in no small measure a factor in the Pueblo Revolt of 1680. Persistently reactionary, administrators in the metropole called for supplementary protection throughout the presidial line of defense across the sweep of the Septentrión. More generally and related to the economic and political ecosystem of the colonial period, the viceregal government considered the *volantes'* nascent presence a variation of the regular presidio soldier. As the centuries passed, authorities envisioned all military personnel, including those in the borderlands, as essential to preserving order during the so-called twilight years of the Spanish colonial state. Commanders everywhere understood, differently, especially when they ascended to the role of viceroy, from the distant civilian bureaucracy the flying squadrons' role as itinerant agents of the frontier.

Discrepancies in the chronology of the squadrons' emergence, continuity, and sustained presence in colonial history come to light. For example, Andrés Tijerina discussed their origination in 1713 when Viceroy Duque de Linares ordered landowners in the *frontera* to organize "flying companies" to thwart indigenous incursions on a moment's notice. In 1749, Antonio Ladrón de Guevara, commander of one of José de Escandón's expeditionary forces, founded the villa of Nuevo Santander and, after surveying the region of the Bahía de Santander, formed a *compañía volante* for the protection of settlements and roads in the new colony.[5] Tijerina writes that by the 1770s a more formalized organization composed of local volunteers, mostly *Tejanos*, and trained by professional officers developed in the *provincia* of Coahuila y Tejas.[6]

International intrigue and desperate financial woes triggered Spain's return of the Louisiana territory to France, which, in 1800 gave rise to the burgeoning threat of an American invasion. Given its significance as a borderlands community, San Antonio de Béxar's chief security came from a small group of its presidio's soldiers. Thereafter, a *volante* detachment from Coahuila's Álamo de Parras was one of several reinforcement efforts. With the secularization of the mission at San Antonio de Valero, a walled enclosure and factory (perhaps an *obraje* to produce woolen goods for the indigenous locals) was subsequently abandoned.[7] But in 1801 the Álamo de Parras company reoccupied its location and remained there until 1813.[8] As seasoned veterans, the men ramped up protection from predatory Indians and significantly reduced the theft of livestock and the introduction of contraband. As a mounted contingent, they served at times as couriers and escorts for the Spanish governor. Alongside the main protagonist in this book, the Parras squadron will fill in the ranks of the 1808 expedition to Santa Fé.

In place of the company's long name, a shortened one, La Compañía del Álamo, or more simply El Álamo, became commonly used. Knowles argues that through this association, Mission Valero came to be identified and henceforth remembered as the Álamo.[9] Because of its association with the popularly venerated and historically contentious Texas landmark and given the site's hallowed status for many who study American history, the Segunda Compañía Volante de San Carlos de Parras garners some attention in Texas historiography. Elsewhere, the Parras company emerges in a document by Pedro de Nava indicating the year of their

28 Chapter One

creation, 1781, and their force of one hundred soldiers under the direction of Capt. Juan Fernández Carmona.[10] However, it will be during the final years of Francisco Amangual's career that the Parras squadron's association with the veteran soldier and paymaster will more sharply come into focus. An extensive discussion of the *volantes* will follow in the next chapter especially, but throughout this study their presence is ubiquitous. The Parras unit will emerge more forcefully in chapter 7 as an auxiliary force headed by Amangual, but for now we examine the early years of this soldier's engagement in the frontier.

Moving Up in the Ranks: Amangual's Transformation 1780–1786

The organizational maneuverings of better-known commanding officers and viceregal administrators absorb most of the ink in official documentation held in repositories across the world. The result is repetition in borderlands historiography pertaining to the presidio, its armed forces, and the *compañías volantes*. Owing to primary source material, an opportunity to descend the military hierarchy toward its rank and file makes it possible to illustrate a noteworthy expression of soldierly rectitude in the face of senior leaders. This happened by way of an unusual encounter between lower-level troops and an important commodity traversing the Texas borderlands. We take up the story of Francisco Amangual's early service vis-à-vis Gov. Domingo Cabello's opinion on matters related to the province, since the latter's authority still constituted the de facto final verdict. In most cases and for subordinates undertaking decisions about potentially volatile circumstances, that required authorization from above. In March 1780 while on detached service at Fort Cíbolo in present-day Big Spring, Texas, Amangual and a party of timber cutters under his command discovered a substantial cache of tobacco. Rather than covertly distributing this precious find among his fellow soldiers or otherwise disobeying protocol, Amangual asked Cabello how to deal with the commodity. Weighing the package to ascertain its value proved a challenge since he had no scale.[11] But Amangual was unwilling to deviate from regulations dictating precise measurements of quantities of goods. In fact, that unswerving diligence on his part will emerge repetitively throughout his career.

Found in a tangle of tree branches on the shore of the El Cleto arroyo, the bootleg tobacco consisted of eleven *manojos*.[12] Given its perishable nature, Commander General Croix directed Cabello to have Amangual deliver it to the tobacco inspectors at the revenue branch dedicated to consumer goods. There, its "consumable quality" and salability was to be determined by qualified persons in the *estanco*; in this context, the *estanco* can be understood as a monopoly goods store. The store experts determined the tobacco's value as profitable, priced at two and one-fourth *reales* per pound, and thereafter the proceeds would be distributed among all the soldiers. Since he was one of those beneficiaries, Amangual probably drew certain conclusions about navigating operations in the field.[13] In all likelihood, the El Cleto contraband incident left Amangual with a memorable happenstance to be shared with new recruits well into his old age. Perhaps he recounted the story as a way to quash fear and inspire confidence in fidgety troops. But scanning widely across the first six years of his life on the frontier, Amangual will undergo both monotonous tasks and exhilarating events shaped by success, embarrassment, and vindication.

As one method of bolstering the presidio system of surveillance, we have already seen how detached service to outposts could be financially advantageous for soldiers if serendipity and smuggling also factored into the assignment. However, its implementation could also bring about precarious conditions that made something like the precise measuring of tobacco weight seem like just another ordinary (and clearly safer) task for soldiers. Months after the El Cleto smuggling affair Amangual, still on detachment in Cíbolo, reported that one of his company's two interpreters, Julian Rondein, was killed. Amangual informed Captain Cabello that eighty Comanche spotted that day were responsible for Rondein's death. At approximately two o'clock in the afternoon on the day before, Pvt. José Miguel Sánchez and two other soldiers from the Béxar presidio's *tropa ligera* were surprised by seventy Comanche who surrounded them. In a harrowing episode of frontier aggression, Sánchez was able to escape the Indians' pursuit by spurring his horse into the woods. There is no indication of what happened to the other two men.[14] Good fortune that day favored Sánchez and others at Fort Cíbolo, but destiny's random presence likely accounted for other narrow escapes from tragic consequences.

No such luck surfaced for Amangual with the advent of a New Year that found him at Fort Cíbolo, gravely ill, making it imperative to request relief from his post so he could return to Béxar. The irony here is that First Alférez Marcelo Valdés was also ill and thus Manuel de Urrutia, first sergeant of the Light Troop of the Béxar presidio (and a soldier who will cause embarrassment to Amangual a decade hence), made haste to Cíbolo to fill Amangual's vacancy. His illness, acute according to Cabello, and his departure for Béxar may very well have saved his life. A horrific event at Cíbolo in early February 1781 saw the deaths of six *presidiales*, all of whom were under the command of the afflicted alféreces Valdés and Amangual, absent during that calamity.[15] As the rest of the year passed and dispatches

30   Chapter One

got worse, it would be the highest ranking general who determined that the site should be forsaken, so desperate had conditions there become.

Monthly reports of the cavalry division of Béxar presidio in 1782 detail Amangual's routine obligations and, in at least one unnerving episode, he saw piles of bones from cattle killed by Lipan (*Ná-izhan, Ipa-n'de, Sejines, Tindi*) raids.[16] That was enough evidence to set off Amangual, a coalition of troops, and residents from the presidios of both San Antonio and La Bahía on a mission to dislodge the Lipan from their camp on the Guadalupe River. Further, when First Alférez Marcelo Valdés was sick, again, throughout September and October 1782, it fell to Amangual to lead a campaign of fifty men against the Comanche. They drove them into the wilderness flanking the Pedernales River, an area just thirty leagues from Béxar. He and his men killed eight of their foes, with the gruesome aftermath of their heads brought back to the presidio. Once the Comanche retreated and Amangual and his men could no longer penetrate the underbrush, they gathered up equipment left behind by the Indians, took seven horses, and even confiscated arrows. Considered prizes all by their captors, the booty went to auction with the proceeds, including five *reales* apiece, divided among the soldiers. By early December 1782, Amangual was on his way to the banks of the Medina River, the site where pre-incident indicators of the February 1781 events resulted in a loss of soldiers to the Lipan. He went there to scout for Comanche spotted happenstance by Béxar residents gathering walnuts in the area. Finding it necessary to reinforce the horse herd guard with twenty troops, Amangual dispatched Indian scouts to explore the Medina's tributaries.[17]

Reconnaissance sorties lingered into the next year, as did the weekly grind. Amangual set out on January 24, 1783, with fourteen privates and one sergeant in a semicircular sweep (*recorrido*) of the western circumference of the Béxar presidio. There, the reality of a hostile winter became clear by the sparseness of grass and extreme aridity of the fields. His surveillance, intended to locate sworn enemies at the usual entry points, yielded no such evidence. The following month, Amangual made four additional *salidas* against the Comanche, the first on February 12 spurred on by fresh tracks discovered by a resident of the Béxar presidio. Two days later, again notified of Indians afoot, he ventured out in heavy rain with a sergeant and twenty men. By the end of the month, when alerted by an Indian from the Valero mission about a recently killed unbranded horse, Amangual and his soldiers made haste to reinforce the herd guard conducive to warding off threats of confiscation. Throughout 1782–83, monthly reportage by Cabello of the presidio's cavalry division blamed stampedes and theft as the cause of most shortages of horses and mules. Vanished animals propelled the search, too, for missing or dead residents and soldiers, a burden that became as routine as looking for lost horses. In one particularly heinous episode of disappearance, Amangual headed a search party for two youths who had gone missing after looking for teams of oxen; prior discovery of a dead servant boy of Sgt. Manuel de Urrutia catalyzed this new search. All three boys came up dead, scalped, undressed, and with multiple stab wounds. After committing these atrocities, the perpetrators took the boys' clothing and horses.[18]

Eventually, Amangual and his team located two horses stabbed to death like the boys who went to retrieve them, but the search party failed to apprehend the killers and returned on March 21. Ten days later, on an unrelated excursion, Amangual set out with troops and two Indian scouts (*rastreros*) under new orders to cut across all the outlying areas of missions including that at San Juan Capistrano. The goal now was to find Karankawa warriors bent on carrying off women of their nation held at Capistrano. Coincidentally, on April 9 Lipan leaders Agar and Zapato Zas brought for interrogation by Governor Cabello a Comanche prisoner taken at the Pedernales River. The captive admitted that on March 19 he witnessed the murders of the three youths from Béxar presidio.[19]

Retribution lingered into the summer of 1783. No longer incapacitated, both Valdés and Amangual led sorties in pursuit of Comanche while the presidio's indigenous scouts traversed even greater distances tracking human and animal footprints.[20] Once in the field, soldiers' efforts led to the discovery of tracks and, occasionally, an inability to keep pace with fleeing enemies. Their departures, along with those of fellow presidials on escort duty and horse recovery, left the Béxar garrison undermanned and vulnerable to attack. This was a consequence of troop deficit and, also, a perennial complaint of Béxar captain Domingo Cabello. Moreover, until the end of the year conditions in general did not improve. Intermittent appearances and questionable sightings of presumed hostile Indians prompted reconnoitering of the territory surrounding Béxar and La Bahía. In some instances, investigatory forays proved impractical because of the lack of soldiers thereupon left to hold down the forts. But by December 1783, Cabello received a message from General Neve hailing an attack on the Karankawa made by Alférez "Antonio" de Mézières. With Neve's encouragement, "similar operations" would continue until the enemy's "well deserved ruin."[21] However, almost three years later a planned expedition against the "Carancaguaces" was not possible because of the usual shortages, including a workforce of "canoes and paddlers" from Louisiana.[22]

Frontier manpower or the lack thereof was not all bad news. In 1786, upon the retirement of First Alférez Marcelo Valdés, Governor Cabello

32   Chapter One

endorsed as his successor Francisco Amangual. Cabello cited Amangual's "most senior" status and his "good qualifications" among the soldiers at both the Coahuila and Texas garrisons.[23] His experience unrivalled by any other officers of the Béxar company upon the retirement of Valdés, the forty-seven-year-old Second Lieutenant Amangual was best qualified to move upward in rank.[24] As the monthly reports show, tracking the miscellany of his experiences over the course of six years affords some insight into the wide-ranging assignments faced by some of the most upward-bound men in the ranks of the Comandancia General.

Compañías Volantes:
Early History and Transformation

To provide context for the myriad interactions chronicled by Amangual and other border bound soldiers, I turn attention back to a specialized unit of the presidio fighting force, one of which Amangual will lead in his later career. The fixed presidial company was a colonial entity comprised of troops who were neither Iberian regular soldiers, nor members of a militia or, even, civilians occasionally mobilized for military service.[25] Cantoned at strategically placed forts in hostile territory, the frontier supplied local men willing to enlist for one or more terms of ten years. Juan Marchena Fernández specifies that what he calls "American militias" were the only solution for the defense of the Indies considering the impossibility of ensuring the safety of the entire continent with peninsular, veteran, regular, or fixed contingents. But the militia was not a "substitution, but the creation of a reserve [available] only when necessary."[26] By contrast, the *companias volantes* were ambulant, autonomous cavalry troops ready to respond expeditiously to crises across localities. Or so their commanders imagined their function in the broadest sense. Moorhead notes that both *volante* and presidio (fixed) soldiers followed orders issued, initially, from a commandant inspector, then by the specific region's commandant general,[27] followed by their company's captain and, thereafter, the viceroy. Periodically issued regulations separate from *ordenanzas* governing the regular army circumscribed the many moving parts of frontier troop life and its hard obligations.

The king himself clarified in 1772 frontier-specific mandates applicable to almost everything military except "obedience and penal laws."[28] Deployment of these specifications ensued to varying degrees of compliance since armed forces besides the *volantes*, such as the *compañías veteranas* (longest serving army companies) and *compañías milicianas* (militia companies), often performed similar services including surveillance.[29] However, even

Presidial Units, *Volantes*, and Amangual in the Frontier   33

that task focused on adjacent terrain and solely for the purpose of intercepting invading groups or individuals.

In all cases, preserving tranquility throughout the region proved to be tenuous at best for presidials. Soldiering on with assigned tasks, the men of these companies were expected to display physical fortitude more than fighting effort in order to stymie attacks by Native communities.[30] Soldiers meeting those expectations confirmed their adaptability to the rigors of presidial life by accepting the unique challenges of inhospitable terrain. Just as often, troops utterly failed to reconcile the hazards of life on the frontier. Seeking to escape lives of deprivation and debt brought on misconduct, desertion, and sometimes, death.

Among the many variations of military companies deployed across the borderlands, it is possible to confuse cadres of troops and their prescribed functions. When and where a presidial unit transformed into a flying squadron, as change over time would indicate, or just the opposite, alludes to the adaptive capabilities of its human participants. One specific case involved the garrison of San Juan Bautista de Río Grande, established in 1701 among a cluster of missions. Originally a *compañía volante*, it became a fixed garrison, that is, a presidio two years later situated on the Río Grande's southern bank.[31] In a July 1700 letter, the fiscal José Antonio de Espinosa conveyed his concerns to Viceroy José Sarmiento y Valladares, Conde de Moctezuma. According to Weddle, Espinosa's chief misgivings centered on the establishment of the Bautista presidio and its twofold importance: First, its presence was necessary to ensure the safety of the Río Grande missions. Second, and equally crucial, its soldiers might quell encroachment by French settlers. Rumors provided by Native informants intimate with a friar named Marcos Guerena had incursions occurring above the Bay of Espíritu Santo.[32] In other places besides Bautista and Bahía and worrisome to all combat personnel in the *Septentrión* was the spread of firearms among the Indians of Louisiana and Texas, an activity "entirely in the hands of the French." As Schiltz and Worcester argue, the Comanche "received French guns through trade with the Taovayas and [Wichita] and through warfare with the Pawnees [*Chahiksichahiks/Chatiks si chatiks*]." Among the Caddo (*Kadohadacho*) in eastern Texas, "a very profitable trade developed" in which they supplied the French with horses in return for guns and ammunition.[33] Imperial officials had every reason to be nervous about saddled-up Frenchmen and their Native coconspirators and to fear for the safety of missionary envoys. The ensuing documentation generated from both the metropole and the frontier testifies to the urgent need for soldiers with the skill and mettle to perform specialized duties.

34 Chapter One

The viceroy's response on March 28, 1701, regarding the Bautista presidio was unambiguous: he ordered the creation of a "flying company without station or form of a presidio" and its establishment designated by missionaries and an officer. The company was to consist of thirty men led by Capt. Diego Ramón with the initial task of assisting the mission of San Juan Bautista del Río Grande del Norte in Coahuila. Its objective required fortitude: to "free the missionaries and inhabitants from the invasions of the barbarians." The latter did not include the "Tecocodames," a "populous nation" waiting to congregate near Bautista.[34]

A few more men made up the other requirement. Viceroy Sarmiento emphasized the need for soldiers from Coahuila to assist the *compañía volante*, and from this company three squads of ten men each were to take form. Two of these squads, along with the *presidiales* from Coahuila, were to "travel continually over all the land," conducting manifold surveillance while protecting the religious. Further, the *volantes* were to maintain vigilance over the settlements, activities, and maneuverings of the French, incursions already documented by the religious. Sarmiento directed the remaining company of ten men to be "always in company" with the missionaries, and to avoid "losing them from sight." The goal here differed not in the slightest: to defend the padres against hostile indigenous groups. On May 4, 1701, Ramón, stationed at the presidio of San Francisco de Coahuila, received orders to form a new *compañía volante* of the Río Grande del Norte. Toward the end of July in the same year, he left with his company to establish headquarters for the flying squadron at San Juan Bautista. However, after only a brief time, the squadron gave way to a formal presidio with Diego Ramón still in charge.[35]

Given the chronological discrepancies found in the historiography I describe above, it is no surprise to see the squadron's emergence coming a decade earlier. Consequently, inconsistencies appear as it specifically pertains to the development of the *volantes*. In February 1691, Governor Pardiñas made it known that the presidio in Sinaloa would be better situated somewhere between there and Sonora. Several officials supported his recommendation, including Francisco Marmolejo, auditor-general of the Junta de Guerra. Marmolejo favored the creation of a *compañía volante* composed in part of soldiers from Sinaloa. Then, around July 1691, a *junta de hacienda* resolved to create a flying company under the captaincy of Francisco Ramírez Salazar with instructions like those advising the Coahuila-based *volantes* led by Capt. Diego Ramón. The squadron was to "constantly patrol the provinces of Sonora" after dissolution of the garrison in Sinaloa. However, that arrangement drew protest from the Sinaloa presidio's Capt. Manuel de Agramont. He asserted the importance of main-

Presidial Units, *Volantes*, and Amangual in the Frontier   35

taining his presidio given the drawbacks of supplying troops to the flying company of Capt. Ramírez Salazar. Agramont's opposition found support from two Jesuit provincials and the rector of the College of Oposura.[36]

A portent of things to come, by the beginning of 1693 Ramírez Salazar still commanded forty-three *volantes* at Sinaloa, but in an apparent spirit of generosity he dispatched seven of his soldiers to Sonora. Whereas Ramírez needed even more boots on the ground, Agramont did not share Ramirez's benevolence and so urged the viceroy to return the seven men. He feared the presidio's diminution would result in the loss of Yaqui and Sonora country. Also, when Field Marshal Marín left for El Parral on February 20, 1693, he possessed an order by the viceroy to ascertain whether it would be best to unite the forces of the presidio and form yet another flying company. Charged with evaluating the state of the province, the character of the presidio forces, and to chastise the hostiles, Marín was to also establish peace for the inhabitants and to avoid any discord that might impair good administration.[37]

In his reply to the field marshal, the *fiscal* Augustín Herbante del Camino argued that when operations were weather conducive, soldiers of the "newly erected presidios" should move constantly as a flying squadron, sometimes in one body, sometimes separated, and in different places according to the demands of the occasion. Whether or not Herbante was willing to formally declare the unit a flying squadron is unclear. However, he cited the immensity of the territory to be defended from "barbarous Indians and the rebels who join them" as a key factor in the *volantes*' importance to neutralizing attacks on many fronts and in many different places.[38] Given the obvious preoccupation of Marín with budgetary concerns and saving the king's money at almost any cost, the reality of borderlands armed conflict and provisioning a fighting force to address this existential threat clashed with bullheaded stinginess even on the part of commanders in the Septentrión. Reducing the number of presidials while at the same time enlisting "Indian friends" to save costs added to the main issue at hand. Incredibly, a plan of action by the field marshal to police the distant frontier was supposed to materialize even as enemy units recruited rebels, thereby increasing Native numbers. As we will see, in some precincts the king's soldiers had to parcel out defense forces.

On December 15, 1693, Marín suggested to the viceroy that the fifty men in the flying company under Domingo Jironza should establish a headquarters and supply base at "Teuricache." Fifteen soldiers were to remain there, and the balance were to answer the most urgent calls for aid. These thirty-five soldiers had to consolidate their efforts with the people of Janos for "the success of any operation that should give a lesson to the Indians."

Four and a half years passed before the *fiscal* Herbante finally answered the recommendations in their entirety. He agreed that the *volantes* should remain in place to prevent Indian raids. But the rest of the flying company had to "move constantly about" as one method to squash opportunities for attacks. Doubtful that indigenous resisters could be pacified, officials in Durango advised the king on a surefire way to accomplish this goal: create a flying squadron at each presidio and supplement it with a company of twenty-five Indian allies. The coalition was to be paid six thousand pesos from a war and peace fund.[39] By April 1698, the *fiscal* of the Council of Indies endorsed the retention of Nueva Vizcaya's existing presidios with thirty supplemental "field" soldiers (*compañia de campaña*) and fifty *volantes* under the command of Captain Jironza.[40]

Structured by revisions to the content of military injunctions demanding from the squadrons both sporadic movement and permanence, sequences of transformation and division recur in the history of the flying squadrons. Contextualizing these multilateral swings is a key point of departure for thinking about the special forces of the presidio/mission complex and help to explain the *volantes*' mutable character. Taken altogether, the elements differentiating the units were not so distinct as to harden the prescribed function of each and, by extension, soldiers' accountability to commanders and civilians. Moreover, as the documentation shows, overlaps in objectives and implementation existed between and among the various military companies, *volantes*, and the rest. It is not difficult to imagine the borderlands beyond the presidio–mission complex as a liminal space more readily accommodating to soldiers' ambivalent feelings toward embracing the rule of law in exceedingly difficult circumstances. Across the spectrum of frontier experiences, it may have been just as easy to rationalize away transgressions and choose defiance when it meant survival.

The Rivera Inspection

Disappointment by those determined to organize and ensure troop compliance with authority was inevitable. So, too, was the indignation felt by the troops. In his much-documented 1724–1728 inspection tour and report of the *Provincias Internas*' presidios, Brig. Gen. Pedro de Rivera pinpointed problems garrison by garrison. In doing so, he produced official observations about the flying squadrons that revealed more than any other work to date. He credited Sarmiento, viceroy from 1696 to 1701, with creating a flying company in 1698 at the insistence of Coahuila's Gov. Francisco Cuervo y Valdés and the missionary fathers. Rivera reviewed the company of thirty-two soldiers and its captain. Their purpose was to defend the missions along

Presidial Units, *Volantes*, and Amangual in the Frontier

the Río Grande, a point that clarifies the *volantes'* presence during this time and, more specifically, in Coahuila. It should not be remarkable, then, that it was the missionaries who determined where the company was to be cantoned. It may have been either concern for the well-being of the neophytes or an overt gesture to signify ecclesiastical authority over the military that a barrack built so close to the mission of San Juan Bautista allowed the soldiers to hear the Indians praying. Foreshadowing the destitution experienced by presidials and, in this case, the *volantes* throughout the colonial frontier at various times, Rivera described the barracks as constituting the entirety of what the flying company could call their own since the missionaries denied them both land and even water from the nearest stream. With motives both hidden and in plain sight, the missionaries jealously defended that which they believed belonged to the Indians, resulting in the soldiers' lack of access to basic means of survival. Resentful of the padres' apparent unwillingness to share resources, the troops eventually made known their grievances in a memorandum to Rivera. However, he took no action since the company was (or so he claimed) the responsibility of the missionaries, and thus Rivera deflected toward Viceroy Casafuerte to resolve the matter. Therefore, it is unclear the outcome of the Bautista mission situation, but Rivera concluded, perhaps in exasperation, that Bautista could "do without soldiers." [41]

The intricate paperwork generated by the Rivera inspection evolved into something quite compelling as official observations based upon a fact-finding tour. After nearly two months spent on the inspection of the presidio at Nayarit, the Rivera entourage returned to Zacatecas for five weeks before moving on to Durango.[42] Rivera's earliest report of a flying company occurs in the *primer estado* of the 1729 *Reglamento*. He characterized the comportment of the fifteen *volantes* detached from the garrison of Valle de San Bartolomé, located to the north near Parral. They were there

> *for the security and protection of* [Durango], *governed by the capitulares* [members of the Durango *cabildo*, or town council]; *and since* [the detachment] *had the name/title of "flying squadron" and was without a determined place for its assignment, the soldiers wandered about always dispersed, except when the town council members employed them for their own interests, lest the soldiers waste their time in personal affairs. The soldiers spent little time on their assigned jobs unless necessity impelled them to discharge their duties; then, when they did, they never gained favorable measures against the enemy.*[43]

This same squadron then transferred to the presidio at Mapimí and came under the direct authority of Sgt. Maj. José de Berroterán. Since there was no corporal to command the soldiers, each man did as he pleased. They wasted their salaries, their debts increased since they paid inflated prices for required goods, and they became victims of profiteers. Rivera lamented the absence of an armorer for the soldiers' weapons and other equipment needed to defend the presidio, such was the "unhappy" condition in which he found the Durango squadron. Besides all this, Rivera spent time wresting the unit from the Mapimí and relocating it to a new site near the city. He remained in Durango until October 8, 1725.[44]

In early 1726 after his disappointing visit to Durango, Rivera and company made their way to San Bartolomé where they encountered thirty soldiers and the captain of its presidio. Entrusted with guarding the passes within its vicinity, the *volantes* lived dispersed throughout the settlement of more than two hundred people but, unlike the soldiers at Durango, the Bartolomé unit housed themselves. Not surprisingly, most of the members of the flying squadron worked for the governor as couriers of his documents, doing so for the sake of paying back the many debts they owed him. The truth was simply that for many years the *compañía volante* functioned only to provide escorts from San Bartolomé to that of Cerrogordo.[45] By the end of 1727, Rivera reached the presidio of Río Grande del Norte, staffed with a flying squadron of thirty-two soldiers and their captain. It must have been cold comfort for him to discover that when the soldiers were not assisting the missionaries at both the San Juan Bautista and San Bernardo missions, they conducted exercises like waging punitive expeditions against hostiles, engaging in scouting patrols, and providing escort for travelers through the "dangerous region."[46]

When Rivera finished the inspection of all the presidios and having reached the third stage of his comprehensive report, he was prepared to offer suggestions for the future status of each locale. Having witnessed the disarray of the San Bartolomé flying squadron, he stressed in no uncertain terms that its soldiers were unaccustomed to military service, unlike soldiers of other presidios, and their laziness roused only indulgence in vices. Furthermore, a mounted force established *not* to actually protect the town but, instead, to reconnoiter and surveil the surrounding area did nothing to mitigate its failure to execute their assigned mission. The paradox here is that during those times when the company was excluded from the town proper, the area experienced no harassment by Indians. Still, Rivera believed that the flying company's status and disregard for its responsibilities over the previous fifteen years could find remedy.[47] He proposed disbanding the company and using its members to establish a presidio at Atotonilco, located about fourteen leagues from San Bartolomé.

Presidial Units, *Volantes*, and Amangual in the Frontier

It is odd that Rivera would want to recycle apparently useless soldiers, even officers, for a new garrison. Rather than allow the governors of the *provincias* to appoint and dismiss captains as they saw fit, Rivera recommended that a captain, named by the viceroy and confirmed by the king, command the presidio in the manner accomplished elsewhere. Human inadequacies aside, the location itself was well suited for two reasons: its abundant pasture for herds and its potential to stymie enemy invasions.[48]

The problems affecting the Bartolomé *volantes* and those endured by their counterparts at Bautista had roots in the usual trifecta of strained relationships forged by ecclesiastical, indigenous, and military competition for local resources. Rivera reported that when the flying company first developed and ten of its soldiers went to assist the missions of San Juan Bautista, San Bernardo, Del Peyote, and Punta de Lampazos, it was because he discovered the missionaries living in total solitude. That situation changed only when many Natives arrived to accompany them.[49] Rivera does not specify which indigenous communities represented the most recent arrivals or whether they sought peace, but he reveals the small number of soldiers comprising the *compañía volante*—thirty-two men— and stressed the necessity for their return, rather than remaining with the missionaries. Also, Rivera was quick to point out that it was crucial that the *volantes* remember their duties and to never forget their service and obedience to the king. Even if their commanding officers were at some distance the troops had to satisfy their obligations.[50] Rivera's long history of interactions with legions of fighting men may have shaped his tolerance for even flagrant noncompliance among his subordinates. It is possible, too, that the adversities of frontier life inspired in him a compassion for enlistees, which may explain his optimism about correcting those willing to serve in demonstrably strenuous conditions.[51] His composure pushed to the limit, however, payback manifested as cutbacks straightaway impacting soldier pay.

In separate articles of the Third Status of his *Proyecto*, Rivera describes the conditions leading to the creation of the flying squadrons. He highlights the disparities between what the units did from day to day and what their assigned tasks were at the time of their emergence in the borderlands. For instance, in Article 51 Rivera states, "At the time that the flying company [defending the missions along the Río Grande] was created, the royal treasury had some shortages by what they came up with in all the presidios that existed then; the wages of each one of the soldiers, up until the current ones, stationed at all the presidios were divided proportionately so that the necessary funds were available to pay each soldier of the flying company

300 pesos and its captain 500 pesos. In this way, members of the company have maintained and continue to maintain themselves and they lack not one thing for their necessities."[52]

Wanting to give precision to purpose, the descriptor "flying [*volante*]" proved inappropriate to Rivera's thinking about this specific company. In one of the most remarkable entries in the *Proyecto*, he provided compelling reasons for the word's unsuitability for describing actual soldiers based on what he witnessed at San Juan Bautista. Going further, Rivera suggested several ways to ameliorate the dilemma produced by that specific nomenclature. Sharpening his focus, he centered on land use and the ways in which the soldiers charged with protecting territory could carry out His Majesty's orders.

His propensity for practicality ever in mind, Rivera sought to facilitate governance of the presidio system. In theory, Article 52 stressed the significance of land as the locus for achieving control and social cohesion among the frontier's inhabitants. As an instrument for strengthening order among the troops it had, like the rest of the articles, the potential to redirect their efforts toward carrying out the wishes of the king rather than aiming for personal gain. Rivera wrote that, besides the name *volante* itself being improper and "tarnishing the armies," the term had nevertheless rendered so much force, presumably in word and deed, that the name was congruent to actual practice. Therefore, the soldiers literally wandered incessantly since they had no specific destination for respite and recovery. Rivera recognized that the *volantes* were meandering from here to there but, in doing so, they fulfilled none of their core responsibilities. Their task was to defend the missions and pacify the land, ridding the area of enemy Indians.[53] It is possible that in the main Rivera conceived the flying squadrons as a *less* mobile protective force than did his predecessors. Still, some frontier administrators remained convinced that the *volantes* were to travel continually or move constantly in patrol as their predominant task.

Determined to eradicate dysfunction in the military, Rivera called loud attention to the customary waywardness of the flying company, an apparently directionless unit, and he did so by exposing the lack of discipline among its members. However, even if the *volantes*' conduct was unintentional, he perceived something akin to confusion as they attempted to reconcile the demands of the missionaries who oversaw their activities with their assigned duties. Since the company's captain gave Rivera a report addressing these very issues, it may have seemed less confrontational for befuddled soldiers to simply appease the missionaries in the meantime. Nonetheless, that meant failing to adhere to their chores as enumerated in an original order from the viceroy. But as we shall see, the missionaries

Presidial Units, *Volantes*, and Amangual in the Frontier   41

abused their authority by requiring the soldiers to do much more than guard duty. What is truly remarkable is that Rivera found that the company lacked nothing in the way of necessities and, though landless, somehow managed to live off their subsidy.[54] At least, this is what he documented as an official observation.

Rivera went as far as to suggest to Viceroy Casafuerte that it would be a good idea, from that moment forward, that the label "*volante*" *not* be applied to the company but, instead, "presidio," like the rest of the other garrisons. Moreover, in terms of its soldiers' remuneration, Rivera suggested that widely publicizing the fact that their salaries were paid by the royal treasury would quell any notion that funding came by petition or commission as so many believed.[55] Rivera took his argument one step further by indicating to Casafuerte that if he ordered the governor of Coahuila to appoint a qualified person to mark the boundaries of the missions on their eastern borders—given the surplus of land harnessed by ecclesiastical orders there—the soldiers could then be assigned lands to the west and north of the river. Potability would be of no concern since lands would include water from San Juan Bautista mission's spring without any malevolence toward the religious. Stressing the element of landholdings, Rivera reasoned that because the missionaries had ample natural resources from Nogales at their disposal, the soldiers would similarly have land and water to supply *their* needs. Rivera's final comment on the issue acknowledged the quandary tolerated by the flying squadron in this locale: once said and done, the *volantes'* land, in fact, belonged to the king and no one else.[56]

That competing economic goals and a challenging environment made reliance upon the land a shared but precarious reality pointed to the often-contentious relationships between the military and the missionaries. Limited farming opportunities also adversely impacted the character of their contact. Still, the rank and file came first. As De la Teja argued, what little market economy existed in colonial Texas relied heavily on meeting the needs of the presidio. For example, soon after the Canary Islanders arrived at San Antonio de Béjar in 1731, they complained to the viceroy that presidio commanders and missionaries were conspiring to prevent the sale of Isleño corn to the garrisons. Thereafter, a viceregal order forced the presidios to purchase the Islanders' crops as opposed to that from the missions; in turn, the missionaries were successful at preventing the settlers (a group that included many former soldiers) from gaining access to indigenous labor. Civilian ranchers also grumbled about the missions having appropriated excessive amounts of land as a means of preventing settlers from establishing viable ranches. They even accused the church fathers of laying claim to the descendants of animals originally brought to the province by the

42 Chapter One

colonists. Further, even if their ancestors had been *vaqueros*, soldiers in the king's service were to remain just that and nothing else.[57]

Rivera had another thought about the padres. In two additional articles of his *Proyecto* Rivera noted that each of the four missions, including two at San Antonio, employed two soldiers of the flying company as overseers. Since this type of work was inappropriate for soldiers and because the king should not pay soldiers inattentive to service, Rivera encouraged the viceroy to correct the abuse. Furthermore, Rivera affirmed that sufficient Natives remained at the missions who could perform the same task, and if the missionaries griped about the loss of the soldiers—fearing their absence would result in loss of control of the neophytes and even the missions—the viceroy should pay no attention to their rumblings. But Rivera was certain that any number of people in the area and, more specifically, poor men could work as overseers if given a piece of land on which to plant their crops.[58] Undoubtedly, practical concerns, however narrowly focused, marked the religious communities' belief that the perpetually horse-bound *volantes* were indeed the best employees for farming exigencies.

Anticipating a rebuff from the missionaries, Rivera devoted Articles 54 and 55 to responses directly aimed at abuses committed by the religious orders against the flying companies. Ever conciliatory, at least to a point, Rivera acknowledged that the padres might vigorously argue that their four missions should have two soldiers apiece, as did those at Los Adaes and "Texas."[59] But those latter two missions were isolated, and no Indians lived there. Hence, Rivera concluded that the missionaries required protection by two soldiers only. However, he could not extend the same privilege to the two missions near the San Antonio presidio for one important reason which he readily enjoyed reminding any religious in his line of fire: up to the time of the inspection the *volantes* served the padres as overseers, a task that violated their duty to the Crown and, even more seriously, to the army.[60] While the most compelling reason for his messaging to the viceroy was to ensure that the soldiers were fulfilling their true assignment, it seems he also wanted to convey his awareness of the church fathers' collusion.

The realization that fighting forces were usurping their obligations to the Spanish Crown must have been at the forefront of Rivera's thinking after his inspection of the presidios. He was certainly familiar with the *Reglamento de Habana* of 1719 and the king's opening statement in that document expressing dissatisfaction with the garrison's preparation for action. For that, His Majesty blamed the lack of proper order required by military discipline.[61] Yet in its first twenty-five articles, the 1719 Regulation mentions not a word about soldiers' personal conduct on or off the battlefield.

Presidial Units, *Volantes*, and Amangual in the Frontier   **43**

Rivera continued to insist that the eight soldiers employed at the four missions under scrutiny should rejoin the 1701 Sarmiento-conceived flying company, which assignment would fill out the ranks of a unit having only thirty-two men. Rivera reiterated that their transfer entailed the soldiers performing their duties without forgetting the service and obedience owed to their officers even when distance separated them. But those intervening miles likely provided a fighting chance for the missionaries to make their move on their presumed subordinates. While Rivera conducted his inspection, he noticed that one of the *volantes* of the Sarmiento company spent a year and a half at the mission of Punta de Lampazos located in Nuevo León, fifty leagues from the Río Grande. Proving his point, this soldier's furlough symbolized yet another reason Lampazos should not have been assigned two soldiers. Rivera took special note of the fact that the missions of La Candela (located forty-four miles east of Monclova) and Santiago (twenty-eight miles southeast of Monterey) had no soldiers to assist them, yet they managed to survive anyway.[62]

Or, perhaps, allegiance to God and good was just fiercer at the Texas missions. There, and at the presidios of both La Bahía del Espíritu Santo and San Antonio de Béxar, attacks by Native warriors were of such regularity that it became imperative for reinforcements to come from other nearby presidios. In one instance the governor, the municipal judge, council members of the *villa* of San Fernando, and even its presidio's soldiers expressed their fears to the *comandante general* about Apache incursions upon the horse herds and mission. Because the Apache *rancherías* were "warlike and numerous," the community's leaders stressed the presidio's insufficient manpower to repel attack. The auditor of war Oliván Rebolledo agreed with the governor and suggested that the San Antonio garrison, consisting of only forty-three soldiers, needed to scale up its force by twenty-five men, possibly mustered from La Bahía.[63] Another option was that reinforcements come from soldiers at Los Adaes, with that presidio's sixty men serving only as a barrier force against the French in nearby Louisiana.[64]

As we have already seen from events in Sonora and Sinaloa in 1691, augmenting forces from either nearby or distant garrisons became a recurring dilemma for the borderland's presidios. But escalating combatants often met with resistance from commanders only too eager to convey their disapproval to higher authorities of the chronic lending and borrowing of their men. Across time stopgap measures surfaced. As one example, Capt. Joseph Urrutia brought to bear his extreme familiarity with the Ndé and their lifeways from seven years of experience living among them. That made him the best candidate to seek a peace treaty with the nation as an alternative to

Chapter One

farming out more troops.[65] In his case, the expertise and potential influence of one valuable soldier may have mitigated the brokering of troop forces. Even for the flying squadrons, the likelihood of transfers and exchanges drawn from their numbers remained a real possibility, too. In all cases, the search for competent military men committed to the ideals of empire and service remained an open-ended process. In much the same way as Pedro de Rivera navigated the Far North in his effort to repurpose the army's longstanding inadequacies, and Captain Urrutia used his resourcefulness with a perennially intractable Native population, others further down the hierarchy would emerge to professionalize garrisons long festering in what had become obsolete pattern and practice.

Francisco Amangual: From the Iberian Peninsula to Colonial Mexico

Ten years would pass from the time of the promulgation of Rivera's *Reglamento* of 1729, based on a chronicle of discovery and recovery for New Spain's Septentrión, to the birth of Francisco Amangual on an island in the Balearic Sea. And more than eighty years after Rivera's inspection, Cmdr. Gen. Nemesio Salcedo would choose Amangual to head an 1808 expedition stretching from one garrison to another further afield in the borderlands. Amangual would receive orders for the expedition from Gov. Antonio Cordero y Bustamante of Texas who, in the previous month, ordered a reconnaissance through territory along the Texas–New Mexico boundary.[66] Sixty-nine at the time, Amangual was the officer considered most fit for the journey, possessed with unmatched leadership and authority, and a man by then deemed capable of enduring the rough terrain of both wilderness and *llano*.[67]

Tracing Amangual's military experience can advance our understanding of one presidio soldier's navigation of life in the frontier and his embrace of a strict sensibility forged from desk duty within garrison walls to piloting a cavalry squadron late in his career. Considering his interactions with Indigenous communities, early historians note that Amangual was "no novice around Indians" since he recognized the signs of their presence: stampedes, strange riders on hilltops, strange visitors in camp for no particular reason.[68] A precautionary approach circumscribed his comportment in the field. He used his scouts effectively since he understood the value of Indigenous guides and the same apperception extended toward members of his squadron. He had troops inspect their firearms and initiate target practice, and he even rescued some of them from their own misconduct. As captain of a *volante* unit late in his career, his responsibilities included informing his

Presidial Units, *Volantes*, and Amangual in the Frontier   45

soldiers of the laws and penalties for infractions. It is not overreaching to think of Amangual as a loyal defender of the colonial regime even as that apparatus began to erode during its twilight years. Granular consideration of his military career during his enlistment allows for better insight into not only how that experience shaped his approach to all things presidial, but why his stint in the Comandancia solidified his role as a functionary of the viceregal administration.

Briefly, then, Francisco Amangual was born on the island of Mallorca around 1739 as the son of a farmer,[69] entered the army of Carlos III toward the conclusion of the Seven Years' War, and then served in the rank of private and corporal for nearly twelve years. Fragments of his military service are known to earlier scholars of borderlands military history. Amangual served two years in the Batavian Regiment of Dragoons and then served fourteen years in the Spanish Regiment of Dragoons. Once arrived in New Spain, he distinguished himself as a cavalryman in the Sonora Expedition of 1767–71 and attained the rank of sergeant on May 30, 1774. Having proved himself a warrior, he transferred to the northeast frontier in 1779, the year marking his arrival in the Texas borderlands. In September of that same year, as a second lieutenant (alférez) he served at the presidio of San Antonio de Béxar, engaged in punitive strikes against the enemy, killed twenty-six Comanche, and confiscated horses and spoils. In 1788 he assumed responsibility as paymaster of that same company.[70]

The earliest documentation of his presence in Texas records the journey of forty-year-old Amangual accompanied by Policarpo Prada, both men former sergeants in the "Dragones de España," traveling from Coahuila to San Antonio in 1779 to begin new assignments.[71] Another former member of the same dragoon regiment, Mariano Ureña, joined Prada and Amangual. Prada would later become the second alférez of the *tropa ligera*[72] at present-day Goliad's La Bahía del Espíritu Santo[73] whereas Ureña became first sergeant at Béxar under Amangual, now a second alférez. On September 16, 1779, Prada and Ureña were joined by Francisco Borra and Felipe Ferrero, the latter—a native of "Turín," in what is today Italy—appointed second corporal (*cabo*) to Presidio Béxar.[74]

From the start all the troops, including Amangual, experienced heightened debt due to several factors underscoring the principal themes throughout this study. Privations across military life surfaced for all soldiers irrespective of their unit designation or assignment locale, and frontier service offered no quick remedy to chronically harsh conditions. Amangual's active-duty history shows this simple truth. For example, on November 11, 1779, deductions from his pay transpired. But the reasons for the withholdings—probably for repayment of debts owed—are not clear when compared to those subtracted

46   Chapter One

from the salaries of two other company members. Third Sgt. Mariano Ureña had a charge of fifty-five pesos and Cpl. Felipe Ferrero, eighty-three pesos, four *reales*. A December 26 letter written by Croix to Capt. Domingo Cabello pointed to overarching reasons for the arrears; the *comandante general* cited the "state of bad government" under which he found the troops, noting their "continued hardship and [...] proportional decrease in assistance," in contrast to the "abundance of provisions in the province under Cabello's command."[75] Amangual, Ureña, and Ferrero had arrived on October 30 and then, on the following day, took their respective positions as delineated in articles three, four, and five of *tratado dos*, *título* 25, Book 1 of the 1772 Royal Regulations. Cabello described being "astonished at the obligations of these men," and while specific reasons for deductions to Amangual's pay do not emerge, those of the other two men are carefully noted.[76] Transferred from Nueva Vizcaya all three men were almost certainly victims of unscrupulous paymasters or administrators, the fiscal conditions in that province notoriously bad for troops.[77]

In this same letter to Croix, Cabello acknowledged that it was "necessary to furnish Sergeant Ureña a coat, trousers, and hat to complete the uniform worn by these troops." Ill-equipped even for combat, Ureña needed "a sword, for he had none, not even a saber. [78] For his part, the forty-one-year-old Torinese cutler Ferrero had signed his affiliation papers, documented his understanding of the requirements and penalties associated with his duties, and agreed to be bound by its terms.[79] While it is true that the black letter of the law obligated Ureña and Ferrero to be prepared for action, so too did its content apply to their superiors. The Regulations of 1772 required the company captain to hold regular inspections of the soldiers' uniforms. It was his responsibility to provide soldiers with any articles of clothing should the need arise. The captain looking after Ureña must have overlooked him. The newly minted position of paymaster, a role performed by officers only and one Amangual would eventually assume, oversaw having a sufficient reserve of "every type of item." He was to ensure its conformation to the previously mentioned specifications.[80] Cabello ended his letter by stating that with these expenses, the debts of Ureña and Ferrero would "increase even more."[81]

Casting blame on soldiers for falling out of line or for deficits beyond their control did little to alleviate indebtedness and doing so failed to tell the complete story. Overt greed by corrupt captains undoubtedly spiked fiscal liabilities and put troops on a carousel of year-round debt. Not unlike a deeply bewildered parent might do, Cabello ordered that the two soldiers receive no more than two *reales* a day in pay plus rations as anyone with the rank of private might expect.[82] Since this form of reprimand did not extend to Amangual, whose officer status likely positioned him in these kinds of circumstances above that of his traveling companions, it is safe to conclude that he escaped the embarrassment of official punishment.[83]

Troops needed supplies, salaries, and supervision. The 1772 Regulations went further, spelling out in deep relief the parameters for conduct, compensation, and composition of each unit. Its Title Two concerned things that mattered most to its audience: "Footing, Pay, and Gratuities of the Presidial Companies." It made clear that each of the presidios would consist of a captain, lieutenant, ensign, chaplain, and forty-three soldiers including a sergeant and two corporals. Recruitment included ten Indian scouts, from which one would serve as corporal.[84] During this period, the presidios at Béxar and Santa Fé did not figure into the so-called line of defense. The end of the Seven Years' War (1756–63) altered the "borders" across North America and further established the northern provinces of New Spain as an independent bureaucracy and proto-militarized entity, the *Provincias Internas*. Eventually, governance became the responsibility of a commandant general reporting directly to the Council of the Indies in Seville. Therefore, key personnel in New Mexico and Texas included a captain (who, at both presidios, was also to be the provincial governor), two lieutenants, an ensign, a chaplain, and, in Texas at Béxar, seventy-seven soldiers. By contrast, New Mexico's unit included seventy-six soldiers (one fewer than in Texas), but both provinces had two sergeants and six corporals.[85]

Title Two also stipulated that each of the fifteen presidios form the corridor of the frontier and the *compañía volante* of the colony of Nuevo Santander (present-day Tamaulipas) was to remain in the same configuration; that is, its status corresponded to the same level as other units with its perennial privileges continuing unabated.[86] However, the main difference between the presidios in Texas and New Mexico as described in the *Reglamento*, concerned the person selected as captain of the flying company at Nuevo Santander. He retained the same salary but now performed his job in the capacity of first lieutenant, and the provincial governor assumed the role of captain.[87] Differences in allotments of horses, between the *volantes* and the *tropa ligera*, surfaced from the soldiers themselves when the required number of horses and mules necessary for meeting their responsibilities did not match the expectations of superiors.[88]

Even so, in the colonial borderlands the practicality (at least from the perspective of fighting men) of having enough horses seemed questionable for administrators of the viceroy, some of whom had no actual experience with warfare of any stripe, much less rapid response to emergencies. Subsequently, official inquiry from above required a critically informed, respectful reply from presidio captains in country. This happened in November 1780 when Col. Cabello scrutinized twenty articles of a new plan developed by Teodor de Croix outlining the system of maintaining the quota of horses for use by the frontier troops. In it, Croix proposed a method for corralling horses and mules at the presidio's stables.[89] During this same time, the fifth and six articles of Title Four of the *Reglamento* of 1772 still governed mounts and their maintenance.[90] Commander General Croix had sent an official letter on April 3 of that same year, a document that did not demand adherence but asked only that Cabello be impartial in his assessment. In his answer Cabello, assuming the utmost if not exaggerated deference to his superior, confessed his failure to comprehend so important a matter. He apologized for the "limited talents" preventing his ability to convey a definitive opinion to the general since, as he wrote in self-effacing prose, he lacked the means "and other qualifications" necessary for his opinion to prevail. Stopping just short of obliterating his own capabilities in the eyes of his commander, Cabello subtracted nothing further from the political calculus at hand by, finally, answering the general's question: Regarding their internal management, could all the presidios be governed by both general or specific rules for the greatest economy and effectiveness?[91]

Perhaps feeling he had deferred sufficiently enough to his supervisor and reckoning that by showing his appreciation and respect for the discretion demonstrated by Croix in adhering to system-wide regulations governing the Texas presidios, a thus emboldened Cabello offered his opinion on changes to the horse maintenance program suggested by the *comandante general*. Croix had offered but two proposals for Cabello to consider: the first, whether to grant permission to all troops to retain seven horses and one mule; the second, whether it was possible to keep two horses and one mule at the presidios' stables. Cabello argued that by conserving the former method, the *provincia* would survive for years. But the alternative option—by which the soldier would have only two horses and one mule at his disposal—would result in the total collapse of the presidio. He reasoned that too many hostile Indigenous groups perpetually imperiled the frontier, and only the complete extermination of their number would allow for conditions in which the troops would need only two horses and one mule. Barring that approach, he contended that depleted herds would leave the citizens entirely exposed and that all property, land, cattle, sheep, horses, and mules, would be completely helpless in the face of enemy rapacity.[92]

Pressing the matter further, Governor Cabello deemed inadequate such a small allotment of animals needed by each soldier to alleviate the "fatigue" caused by defending the province. Stacking hard numbers at his superior, Cabello disclosed bewildering data about horse allocations associated with the military *and* civilian population. That figure lay somewhere between

1,742 and 1,780 animals. In fact, he wondered if the same attacks on and wholesale slaughter of provincial citizens might also be perpetrated against troops along the sequence of forts. The total troop force defending the presidial line during this period numbered 2,266 men. This tally appears in Croix's plan and regulation "at the end of the sixth article [out] of thirty-five in the new project." Cabello asserted that the "lack of people" is what allowed aggressors—and he specifically identified the Comanche—to make what progress they did by predations. Moreover, he argued that if the presidio populations expanded by twofold, then provisions for three horses and no mules could go into effect. Cabello was certain that troop escalation would frustrate incursions by the hostiles and, from a fiscal perspective, negate the triple cost expenditure required for the purchase of mules. Cabello noted the number of riding animals at Béxar presidio was 568, with 1,742 additional kept at citizens' ranches and counted in the allotment from July through November 1780.[93]

Cabello witnessed firsthand even more scarcities by soldiers not having the requisite weapons for defense, besides horses, of the commingled region. Wearisome this conversation must have been for both governor and general. Two years prior Croix realized that the *tropas ligeras* at La Bahía and Béxar lacked essential armaments causing him to petition the king for help. In the interim, he requested that Cabello locate guns in good condition. Since functional guns were unavailable, Croix wrote that he would move forward with another plan to acquire weapons. He also knew that in the storehouses of San Luis Potosí new pistols awaited the troops of Coahuila. He conveyed this information to Cabello so that once informed, the paymasters of both presidios could, while collecting funds for their respective soldiers, ask for the proper decrees from treasury officials who could then supply new guns.[94] As if a shortage of weapons was not bad enough, only two years earlier it was Croix who suggested a reduction of horses and protective gear to presumably enhance agility for the light troops. Over and above supply shortages, the human deficit in fighting power continued to factor into the usual privations in the borderlands.

So depleted was the availability of horses by February 1785 that it took Commander General Rengel to intervene on Cabello's behalf in pursuance of fresh remounts. Predictably, selfishness or self-preservation reigned at the highest level of command. The governors of Nuevo León and Santander imperiled the survival of civilians and soldiers when they refused to fulfill both the Coahuila and Texas companies' desperate requests for horses so that war operations might continue.[95]

The scarcity of horses intensified their value as a commodity for not only presidials like Ureña and Ferrero, but their adversaries and trading allies, too. That stark reality became obvious by the bewildering if often self-serving conditions described above. In fact, the status of tobacco as a vendible object would similarly continue the trend of intensifying product desirability among frontier communities competing for resources. When military obligations required soldiers like Amangual to be on detachment from their homebase, that service came with risk. On balance with commodities, good order and discipline ramped up the value of certain soldiers in the king's service to their commanders.

TWO

❧

"Truly elected" Paymaster, Civil and Military Administration, and Service to the King, 1781–1793

Cabello's interaction with his superior likely convinced Croix of his expertise with the overriding challenges at hand and further showed his genuine concern for the troops under his command. Once a fledgling himself, Cabello impressed Croix to the degree that the general credited him in his 1781 Report for an astute analysis of Texas' "sad situation" from the time Cabello was an infantryman, so often had he solicited aid in the form of increased troops.[1] Since a poverty of manpower existed across the borderlands, several inducements to ascend the military hierarchy took effect. Commanders like Cabello with the authority to advance careers had other considerations to contend with in accordance with the king's orders. Vertical movement in rank at most stages followed a pattern. For example, second alférezes, whether presidial or *volante*, had to have the most seniority in their class and in the province they served. Nevertheless, this type of ascension in rank could not occur without an order from the commandant general on prior notice. Also, second alférezes who by higher station ascended to the first alférez position in companies other than their own would have to secure dispatches in other posts. Repositioning career soldiers for service in the frontier relied on a hierarchical structure intended to facilitate the nominating of subalterns for the rank of officer. When vacancies occurred, the governor of each province sent to respective company commanders the scale of seniorities with a statement about the merits of those officers chosen as candidates for a position. [2]

Seniority had its benefits. Long-term service impacted pay scales and put into effect the distribution of funds in the following manner. In August 1781,

Carlos III decreed that all soldiers who had the ability to continue serving in their same units, preferring active duty to retirement, would enjoy the pay for which they qualified and would also be considered for a pay increase in their current posts. According to royal decrees of October 4, 1776, and January 20, 1767, troops must have earned the pay of ninety *reales de vellón* per month and to have served twenty-five years in the infantry, thirty in the cavalry and dragoons, or had received 135 *reales* at the rank of officer and completed thirty-five years total.[3] Outside of a lucrative marriage, no borderlands soldier amassed wealth while serving the viceroyalty, and unscrupulous deductions from salary for supplies and expenses ensured that outcome. Like so many before and others still to come, Amangual and his traveling companions Ureña and Prada discovered that hard, ugly truth. The best any soldier could hope for in the immediate sense was an incorruptible paymaster. Even then, length of service guaranteed nothing in the way of compensation for loyalty.

However, there were incentives for staying the course. Aside from the king's ruling, extending service constituted a high priority for imperial officials. They encouraged commanding officers to not only submit the respective qualifications but also to certify the merits for issuance of pay raises. A further requirement dictated soldiers themselves petition for these rewards. Moreover, pay increments would cease when three conditions existed: the moment soldiers scored promotions to more highly paid posts in the regiments; on becoming officers in service in those regiments; or, upon entering the royal infantry guard at the rank and benefits designated for the most senior sergeants by its special ordinance. In these cases, soldiers would not retire with a lesser salary than what they had already earned.[4] That great irony lay in the fact that the king offered the same pay for retirement as for sustained service. But, even if retirement afforded a predictable avenue out of military life, as a career move it was not without peril.[5] With the passage of time, borderlands soldiers might even see their careers cut short by physical incapacity. A few years earlier in a circular sent to Presidio La Bahía, *comandante inspector* Rubio advised Governor Ripperdá that the king would no longer support any soldier incapable of performing military service. Rubio's letter included twelve blank licenses for completion by individuals of Ripperdá's company, at both Béxar and La Bahía, who might have become so disabled as to preclude a military career. In a pointed last line of the letter, Rubio advised Ripperdá to "always remember [:] do not let their strength decline."[6] Months later, Ripperdá responded that he informed the captain at La Bahía of the king's order, and that one of the enclosed licenses had been filled out by a trooper stationed there. Though

"Truly Elected" Paymaster and Service to the King   53

the disability is unspecified, soldiering on was no longer possible for this unnamed individual.[7]

Rewards for outstanding service and bravery in action remained powerful inducements for many soldiers. Having succeeded Lt. Col. Hugh O'Conor,[8] newly minted Inspector José Rubio relayed a message from Carlos III to Governor Ripperdá confirming honors granted to Alférez Narciso de Tapia and his Third Compañía Volante. Garnered for their successful engagement against enemies at Las Bezerras *estancia* in April 1776, Tapia received not only the rank of lieutenant of the infantry but also its compatible salary, with each of the thirty-one *volantes* who survived the skirmish compensated fifty pesos. Even the widows of those who died were to receive a monthly stipend of eight pesos.[9]

Feeling decidedly generous to even those leaving service, the king granted Manuel de Villa his retirement with the salary of three hundred pesos a year and the rank of captain in the army's cavalry.[10] Other retirees, identified by Ripperdá as worthy of those promotions, could look forward to judicial posts, and even their children and relatives might ascend to honorary positions. The governor was responsible for recommending individuals whom he felt were most deserving of highly valued appointments in post-military careers.[11] By October 1777, several veteran soldiers resigned and received congruent salary, and for some officers that included honors conferred by the king. To name a few, Capt. Vicente Rodríguez of the presidio at San Juan Bautista, Capt. Manuel de Villaverde of San Carlos, and Capt. Francisco Vellido of the San Elizario presidio all received an annuity of 1500 *pesetas*, as did Lt. Joséf Camilo at Monclova. Others, like Capt. Bernardo de Urrea of the presidio at Santa Gertrudis del Altar, retired with the same salary as the soldiers above, but with the added prestige of achieving the rank of lieutenant colonel. Unexplained in the documentation, Joséf Castilla ascended to the rank of captain upon his retirement with half of his active-duty salary.[12]

During his career, Francisco Amangual would similarly achieve a measure of these benefits and honors via his decades of experience. Fortunately, he rose to seniority status in two locales, Coahuila and Béxar, in what was becoming an increasingly militarized frontier. If official documentation is any indicator, it was his administrative role as trustee for his company's finances that not only solidified his significance to borderlands commerce but also sharpened his attentiveness to in-house practicalities.

The role of the paymaster was an important one and its responsibilities constituted the entire content of the fourteenth and final "Title" of the 1772 *Reglamento*. Stressing the communal trust expected of soldiers toward the fiduciary, the first obligation of each potential candidate was "to be worthy of the confidence placed in him by the company in the management of its interests." In theory, the *habilitado* had to be capable of carrying out this assignment with "integrity and honor inseparable from his profession." Title Fourteen implies that one determinant for presidio soldiers' presumed esteem for the paymaster would be their recognition of his "honest[y] and zeal."[13] Stepping into a new role, Amangual won election as paymaster of the Béxar company in 1788, becoming responsible for keeping the general accounts of debits and credits and ensuring their accuracy. This was markedly important since the payroll and expenses were examined and approved by the captain and other officers, as well as the *comandante inspector.* The paymaster administered the individual accounts of each soldier and was responsible for admonishing spendthrift members to restrict their expenditures to absolute necessities. Outwardly, the forty-nine-year-old Amangual performed competently as a fiduciary, and the skillful execution of his duties may have enhanced his reputation as a circumspect, detail-oriented leader. In time, however, his standing among the troops would come under question.

At this point in his career, Amangual's bureaucratic efficacy probably had more impact on stabilizing unity and reducing friction among his underlings than had his battlefield exploits. Indebtedness so eroded military morale that all parties, from the most timeworn veterans down to the freshest recruits, suffered from the incessant privations worsened by a life on the frontier. However, even in this regard on-the-ground conditions mediated Amangual's dedication to his responsibilities and, specifically, his management of the pay setup. Moorhead argues the presidial payroll neither stimulated the frontier economy nor solved slashes to soldier pay given the multitude of deductions and extortions that almost never covered their service and personal expenses.[14]

In some ways, the social and economic milieu of San Antonio de Béxar during this period did not deviate much from that of other military installations elsewhere and especially as it concerned form and function. As the units were differentiated in chapter 1, presidial companies were not regular army units even though each classification saw troops like Amangual gain experience by serving in both and in different territories. Filling their ranks chiefly depended on inhabitants of the frontier who, in return for their willingness to defend the outposts might gain opportunities to participate in the establishment of a permanent settlement (colony). Some soldiers took families to their new posts, but if young men who arrived as bachelors remained garrisoned for some time, the likelihood existed of marrying into a socially prominent, economically secure family in a civilian neighborhood like San Antonio.[15] Even before the arrival of women and

"Truly Elected" Paymaster and Service to the King 55

children to the presidios, the locations of El Gallo, Cerrogordo, Conchos, and Casas Grandes (re)emerged as civilian communities not long after their use as military outposts. By 1760, all but one of the twenty-three garrisons in several frontier *provincias* had settlements that averaged thirty-seven civilian *vecinos* to each company of fifty officers and men. If the troops' families factored into the statistical data, the nonmilitary population was even larger.[16]

Civilian settlement was a top priority of the viceregal government and specifically addressed in Title Eleven, "Political Government" of the 1772 Royal Regulations. Deploying somewhat vague descriptors for the civilian populations, the viceroy warned against deterring people engaged in "good life and habits" from settling within the vicinity of the presidio.[17] But families entering the garrison had to be accommodated. If the campus itself was not large enough to contain incoming families, one section of it was simply expanded with work done as a communal effort since, ostensibly, it would benefit all inhabitants. The Regulations instructed captains to distribute and assign lands and town lots to those that requested these properties and, in turn, assignees were expected to cultivate them. Furthermore, they were to keep horses, arms, and munitions for use in expeditions against enemies when necessary. However, soldiers that had served their ten-year enlistments held sway when land was apportioned, and preference extended to retired sick or elderly troops as well as to the families of those now deceased.[18]

But getting troops in the first place was not so straightforward. Recruitment and sustenance for both soldier and citizen proved to be challenging for colonial administrators, and this would be persistently true for those two demographic sectors of the Spanish-French-Indian borderlands. In a 1759 letter to Viceroy Amarillas, Gov. Martos y Navarette of "Tejas" responded with practical suggestions for a proposal to encourage settlement. In effect, soldiers at the presidio of San Agustín de Ahumada willing to serve for six years would remain as "*vecinos*," and lands and water would be distributed to them and to fifty others who would establish a villa.[19] This never materialized but, presumably, if it had, the villa would have been given the preestablished name of the presidio and mission complex, Orcoquisac.[20] The governor informed the viceroy that should the soldiers remain citizens along with fifty civilians and even receive a subsidy from the Royal Treasury (as ordered by the viceroy in a March 30, 1756, dispatch), there would still be elevated production and abundant harvests.[21]

While this would appear to be an advantageous result, Martos y Navarette reminded the viceroy that the villa's citizens would have no market for their products. Furthermore, he doubted whether the populace could maintain themselves in the region without the additional and necessary income achieved by selling to the governor and captain of the presidio. Martos affirmed that there were no other buyers because the distance was so great between presidios in this region of the borderlands where this small number of inhabitants could support themselves.[22] One must wonder whether during this time period Governor Martos contemplated his own economic vulnerability and, if so, whether that uneasiness inspired his overcharging the soldiers at the Los Adaes presidio, an accusation that would emerge as a lawsuit a decade hence.[23]

At the time of the original order Jacinto de Barrios y Jáuregi was governor of Texas. He had received instructions to send a qualified individual to assemble twenty-five "Spanish" families and twenty-five "Tlascalan" families, to purchase livestock, and to supply the fifty families with rations. But in a telling statement three years later, Jáuregi's successor Governor Martos declared to Amarillas that there was no one whom he considered qualified for this important commission. Martos added that if the viceroy ordered the villa established, he must ask Amarillas to absolve him of the responsibility and confer the duty upon someone else for its fulfillment. Martos simply could not entrust the duty to anyone else and, more specifically, to any of his immediate underlings, so great was his fear that their ineptitude would reflect an unfavorable impression of *himself* to the viceroy. However, to prevent any discord Governor Martos did agree to make the entire distribution after the livestock and the merchandise arrived.[24] Whether or not Martos himself could be trusted with the task is suggested by his reluctance to accept such an undertaking. It is also possible that he already planned to sew up fiscal gold through less than savory ventures involving his own soldiers. Embarrassing for all concerned, incompetence on balance with enemy encounters constituted the bigger threat to the empire's goals of peopling its far-flung provinces with stable, law-abiding subjects.

While the deficiencies of others were enough to cause concern for one's own reputation even at the highest levels of borderlands administration, social tensions arose when military personnel became embroiled in disputes with the local citizenry. This was conspicuously true when disagreements stemmed from dubious commercial transactions and the consequent lawsuits by individuals representing merchant interests and the supplying of the presidials. The 1772 Regulations expressly forbade soldiers from accosting merchants selling goods and other non-prohibited provisions, nor were artisans to be impeded in their establishments, sales, or transient labor. In his dual role as presidio commander and governor of the civilian settlement, responsibility fell to the captain as final arbiter in these communal matters.[25] In one particularly contentious episode that will shortly emerge, a citizen merchant named José Macario Zambrano accused paymaster Francisco

Amangual of unilaterally breaching a contract for the sale of corn to feed the soldiers.[26] Misunderstandings with civilians aside, a presidio paymaster's purchase of merchandise could be as diversified as the customers he served.

An invoice of April 14, 1788, shows Amangual brought supplies to the Béxar presidio consisting of several pieces of cloth and textiles along with cords and thread, all presumably to construct clothing. Over three *varas* of hemp cloth were intended for overcoats. He listed the following items: 75 hats and 12½ *arrobas* of iron plates, with the rest of the inventory consisting of six reams of paper along with boxes, nails, and leather pouches used to carry money.[27] Amangual's notation on the invoice states "Por mi comision[sic] á 2 por ciento" amounting to fifteen pesos, six granos.[28] That privilege of taking a share of the profit from sales was precisely the prerogative that saw so much abuse during the colonial period by countless borderlands *habilitados* and the companies they so often dishonorably served. Even though he had not yet ascended to elected paymaster, Amangual was designated by his predecessor Bernardo Fernández, with support from officers and the sergeant of the Béxar presidio, as an interim to transport these supplies and the company payroll from San Luis Potosí. What makes this April 1788 transaction interesting is the fact that Amangual's emergence as custodian of the company funds stemmed in large part from his adherence to official mandates and his superiors' early confidence in him as a capable administrator.[29]

At the beginning of the eighteenth century, viceregal policies then in place aimed to improve what was historically erratic compensation of soldiers that resulted in substantially defrauding them of their salaries; in charging exorbitant prices for any commodities acquired; and, ultimately, asymmetrically benefitting presidio captains. Ingrained practices like these came at the expense of the presidials' salaries, usually with large amounts illegally deducted from their already exceptionally low pay. The pervasiveness of that demoralizing reality had become almost institutionalized by 1723, but in 1724 Juan de Acuña y Bejarano—Viceroy Casafuerte—instructed Brig. Pedro de Rivera, inspector of presidios, to investigate these pernicious practices. As it appeared in the previous chapter, Rivera's recommendations for improving the state of the frontier garrisons resulted in the *Reglamento* of 1729, a uniform code intended to, inter alia, restore salaries in the form of cash payouts; make the purchase of clothing an option for the *presidiales* (since heretofore half of their salaries had occasionally been paid in clothing); and, to establish maximum prices for commodities at the provision stores of the presidios.[30] But Rivera's altruism had its limits. Alternately disgusted and appeased by what he found on his 1724–27 fact-finding tour, he determined that pay cuts were one way to punish apathetic soldiers who cast aside their military obligations.[31] Still subject to ongoing pecuniary abuse, though, it is difficult to understand how reductions in salaries might inspire men to become more circumspect in their duties, much less devoted to supporting the goals of an empire willing to shortchange many for the mistakes of a few.

Excessive profiteering and price gouging by presidial captains continued unabated even after the king himself became aware of these conspiracies. Whether moved by compassion for the troops and their families or persuaded by the suspicion that his overseas realms could disintegrate by criminality in the military, the king finally responded. He enacted severe and public procedures intended to punish those already guilty of fraud and inclined to perpetuate the same prohibited activities in the future. This type of malfeasance caught the attention of other members of the local population. During the 1760s, Fray Juan Sanz de Lezaún described the absurd cost of poor-quality clothing the troops in Santa Fé were forced to pay while being double-charged the current price for local produce. Across the consumer spectrum, a wide range of inferior commodities from horses to clothing for family members continued to form the basis of supplies intended for the troops. Some captains even went so far as to appropriate the best horses for their own use while selling the worst to their men at regulation prices, even when some of these superior animals had been part of each soldier's own herd of remounts.[32] Other unscrupulous commanders charged inflated prices for food, including corn and beef, but even minor items like soap, cigars, and blankets presented another opportunity for them to price gouge the soldiers by as much as tenfold. In July 1767, the Marqués de Rubí sought to alleviate the gross irregularities within the presidios by ordering captains to issue corn, beef, beans, chili, brown sugar, and even shoes at prices prescribed in the 1729 regulations.[33]

Relief appeared imminent when in 1778 *comandante* Croix received opinions from then-Governor Ripperdá and Luis Cazorla, the captain of Presidio La Bahía, about adjutant paymasters and quartermasters handling presidial companies' interests. Almost one year before, Croix's adjutant inspector Antonio Bonilla enumerated the overwhelming hardships, including hunger, experienced by the troops from paymaster abuse of the provisioning system. Even after all these abuses came to light, Croix reiterated a *bando* declaring not only the extent of powers given by companies to their paymasters but even the method by which the election ballots for candidates were to be handled. Ballots were now to be remitted in advance by the presidio captain, subordinate officers, and one representative for the troops.[34]

"Truly Elected" Paymaster and Service to the King 59

Put bluntly, his declaration truly accomplished nothing more than to reconfigure slightly the articles within the *Reglamento* of 1772 and its provisions for the duties of the paymaster. Relatively quickly, Croix secured the consent of Governor Cabello that any "future uncertainties" would be avoided by following the redesigned method for electing *habilitados* for both presidial and *volante* units.[35]

Soliciting opinions, acting on them, and getting compliance from one's subordinates rooted Croix's expectations, but disappointment was inevitable. A significant irony of the opinion rendered by Luis Cazorla to Croix about fiduciary obligations to troops was that only two years later Cabello compiled charges against Cazorla himself. Cabello launched the investigation because of an inspection review passed on the Bahía company in January 1780. The charges were severe in scope and potentially damaging to Cazorla's reputation but, as we shall see, not necessarily hazardous to his career. The first charge made against him was for excessive prices charged to his troops, amounting to 100 to 200 percent higher than prices set by the 1772 *Reglamento*. The second charge was more stupefying: he supplied troops with items consisting of "lustrines, satins, pekins, and ribbons," merchandise not only costly but also inappropriate for the soldiers' rank.[36]

As if this type of provisioning did not cast enough of a cloud of deep suspicion over Cazorla, a third charge specifically addressed documents related to the "list and note of effects" procured for his troops but unaccounted for by him. The absence of paperwork thereby left the captain ignorant of what goods he had delivered or even of their quality, price, or appropriateness for use by or service to his soldiers. Worse still, when the inspection targeted Cazorla's *cuaderno* consisting of a "detailed record and account of receipts, issuances, consumption, and remaining supplies of powder" belonging to the paymaster's office, it found all the entries were illegal and unsubstantiated. In fact, the entire mess called attention to the inappropriate method of the cuaderno's form and substance.[37] Zealous documentation in the form of reports, inventories, official proceedings, and fiscal recordings was the sine qua non of presidial administration. Thus, a study of borderlands oversight would not be complete without attention paid to the stockpile of written matter Cazorla, Cabello, Rivera, and Amangual among others produced in their collective roles as operatives for an empire obsessed with corroboration.

Recording stores of merchandise was not the only facet of commerce engaged in by *habilitados*. Away from their desks and inkwells, they were entrusted with cold cash being physically transported from metropolitan treasuries to and from expansive and dangerous territory. For obvious

60   Chapter Two

reasons, the task required commanders to be singularly diligent toward those charged with this extremely sensitive responsibility.

Where Cazorla fell short in his responsibilities, others excelled. In November 1788, interim military and political governor Rafael Martínez Pacheco reported to Gen. Juan de Ugalde that Alférez Amangual had satisfactorily returned to San Antonio from San Luis Potosí with the company payroll. Accompanied by a corporal and five privates, the assets appeared without discrepancies. Distance and discretion prompted Amangual's due diligence; the trip covered over five hundred miles and despite privations, the alférez and his cohorts did not tamper with the funds. One week later, assuming a dramatically different role for his company, Amangual headed up twenty-eight soldiers, two civilians, and one mission Lipan to follow the tracks of horse thieves, successfully returning two days later. No coin in tow, this time he brought back seven "Taguayaz" prisoners and eighteen stolen animals.[38] His luck at work would change, however, since only one month later, on December 24, Martínez Pacheco answered the *cabildo* of San Fernando (Béjar) regarding a complaint filed by a Joaquín Menchaca against Amangual. It is unclear what were the precise circumstances surrounding the conflict between the two men, but the episode did demonstrate that, though trustworthy in his collection and care of the presidial funds and successful in the pursuit of bandits, Amangual was perfectly capable of committing an "oversight." When mixed with a dash of vitriol, it required correction. It seems the soldier, who apparently started the dispute, betrayed some disdain toward Menchaca in their confrontation. Martínez Pacheco defended his admonition to the alférez by making him aware of the situation so that "it might serve as a guide in the future" to Amangual and to his company.[39]

Though it may have been a source of embarrassment for him, the Menchaca-Amangual conflict was not so severe as to hinder First Alférez Amangual's successful election on December 30, 1788, to company paymaster. His colleagues at Presidio Béxar evidently considered him the "most appropriate for the handling of the [financial] interests" of all the soldiers of every rank there. Amangual's initial tenure was to last from 1788 to 1792. This event, which further invested Amangual with power of attorney, was memorialized in a letter signed by Martínez Pacheco and involved several other witnesses. These included First Lt. Bernardo Fernández; Second Alférez José Xavier Menchaca; and Sgt. Andrés del Valle, men who will reappear in later chapters. Prudencio Rodríguez, commander of the horse herd, and Amangual himself were present. Two witnesses, Vizente de la Cuesta and José Melchor Yámez, appeared as witnesses to the occasion. Documentation

"Truly Elected" Paymaster and Service to the King 61

of the proceedings lists the chaplain and the second lieutenant as absent since at that time both slots were vacant.[40]

As a "truly elected" *habilitado,* Amangual's responsibilities included appearing before the lord administrators of the main treasury in San Luis Potosí to collect the soldiers' salaries, a task he had previously accomplished as interim. He was to adjust and liquidate the accounts for his three-year term and those left pending from 1788, receiving the balances from both the current and the former, and he was to pay the debts that the company incurred during that same period. Moreover, Amangual was responsible for receiving, collecting, paying, and issuing receipts, letters of payment, quittances, concessions of rights, and waivers of the laws of nondelivery. All these responsibilities would have come as no surprise to Amangual since they replicated the workload described in the 1772 Regulations. However, what emerges in the correspondence of the period is the company's trust in Amangual who was by this time fifty-years-old and a seasoned military man.

Advancement and greater responsibility came quickly. By March 14, 1789, Amangual received a promotion from first alférez to second lieutenant after the retirement of José Antonio Músquiz.[41] Power of attorney had already been conferred upon Amangual but now Commander of the Armies for Texas and Coahuila Juan de Ugalde approved the designation on April 11, 1789.[42] With the imminent arrival of new recruit Juan de la Cerda approaching, Amangual must have been reminded of his own arrival in the Texas borderlands ten years earlier accompanied by Mariano Ureña and Policarpo Prada. Now it was he who received instructions concerning the incoming soldier's lack of outfitting from Ugalde and forwarded to him by Martínez Pacheco. The directive specified necessities like "defensive and offensive arms, eight horses, a good saddle, three changes of linens," all required for Cerda to be able to rendezvous with the rest of the company, first at the Río Grande garrison, and then at Paso de Longoria on July 31, 1789.[43] Fully equipped and with his official orders and status report, Private Cerda departed on July 20 to meet his commander Lt. Pedro Nolasco Carrasco at Río Grande en route to the upcoming campaign.[44]

Amangual: Funding the Presidio and Correcting Accounts

Gearing up soldiers entailed shepherding money and effecting transfers of funds. In December 1790, *comandante* Pedro de Nava arranged for seventy pesos from Gov. Manuel Muñoz and the *alcaldes* Pedro Flórez and Francisco de Arocha of the villa of San Fernando to be delivered from the *Mesteñas*

Fund to Amangual.[45] Then Amangual was to forward them on to Second Lt. Juan Cortéz at the Valle de Santa Rosa. Cortéz had used them as payment for shipping gifts consisting of twenty-eight *cargas* of goods destined for the peace-abiding indigenous groups of that province.[46] Amangual's attentiveness to the potentially volatile *Mesteñas* Fund presented open-ended challenges to his daily tasks as fiduciary and leaves unquestioned its significance as the primary source for the Béxar presidio's accounts receivable and payable.

The importance of the *Mesteñas* Fund to borderlands military society is indisputable and further explanation contextualizes its ramifications for civilians and soldiers alike. As its name suggests, its development stemmed from profit-driven management of big animals running loose across the frontier. In 1778, Croix developed a five-point plan for the fund specifically intended to avoid the complete destruction of unbranded livestock and the liabilities that could potentially impact individuals like farmers and ranchers in the vicinity of the Béxar presidio. He voiced his concern about branded animals that had been killed and left to rot in pastures by their owners, or other unscrupulous types, with nothing of the carcass utilized but the fat stores, valuable for use in the manufacture of soap. Croix ordered that no person of whatsoever quality or condition—a pointed reference to inhabitants' ethnic admixture or socioeconomic status—could go out, round up, kill, or otherwise confiscate wild or unbranded animals in the entire district of Texas and its frontiers. This constituted an unlawful act that would result in forfeiture of animals taken; the payment of a four-peso fine for each head of cattle; or two pesos for horses taken, and eight days imprisonment in the public jail on the first offense. The fine would double as would the term of incarceration for a second offense. A third offense meant a strikeout with even more serious consequences: the repeat offender faced the same doubled fine plus exile for four years of hard labor, for rations only and without salary, and assignment to whatever royal or public works deemed appropriate. To face charges for these penalties, no proof was required other than confiscating the animals in the offender's possession.[47]

The Croix proclamation further prohibited any citizen or rancher from taking from the province any herd of cattle or horses, even if domestic, or branded, or of the citizen's own breeding stock, without first getting a license from the magistrate. Like the one obtained by Joaquín Menchaca, the license was issued in writing free of charge, without carrying any other duties other than those of sealed (official) paper or, in its absence, other qualified paper. As we shall see, issues concerning paper products for official documentation

"Truly Elected" Paymaster and Service to the King   63

of civic and presidial matters were an invariable point of contention in the borderlands. Licensing was intended to show the number and breed of animals to be removed, by which persons, and their respective territories, and their owners' identities. Those who disobeyed the license restrictions were subject to equally severe penalties that included: for the first offense, the loss of the branded animals removed; for the second, the loss of the animals and payment of a four-peso fine for each head of cattle and two pesos for each horse; and, the third offense would result in the aforementioned penalties plus a two-year exile of hard labor in the same capacity and reimbursement (rations only, no salary) as the first point of the proclamation.[48]

By the time Ripperdá left the governorship of Texas, the small sum left in the Fondo de Mesteñas was fourteen pesos, an accumulation woefully inadequate in the opinion of the incoming Governor Cabello.[49] However, he cited the six *reales* duty imposed against each horse caught as the reason why *vaqueros* were uninterested in catching them, along with the fact that in order to do so it was necessary to use a good, swift horse (*"un buen caballo corredor"*). But since some animals became crippled and therefore unusable after one of these chases, the profit to be gained from capturing any mustang was simply not worth it. According to Cabello, people did not consider it worth the work entailed nor the risk to which they would subject themselves or their mounts. The governor believed that if the six *reales* duty imposed on captors was reduced to two *reales* it would expand revenues for the fund, and folks would be more disposed to catching the wild horses. But Cabello wanted others to get busy, too. He asked Croix to mandate that the missionaries adhere to the same conditions regarding the mustangs since, at the time of his letter, church personnel did not devote themselves to catching them.[50] With the *Mesteñas* Fund looming large as a revenue source and economic vector in the Comandancia General, gathering and then documenting livestock had its limitations, inconveniences, and a fair share of unique challenges.

Given the hard circumstances of a soldier's life in the frontier and the long-standing misdirection of funds by other presidio paymasters, one could assume that Amangual might have himself absconded with funds from *Mesteñas* assets. Having spent over a decade in the Spanish army on the Iberian Peninsula, he could legitimately contrast that life with his new one and that of his subordinates in the *frontera*. Cash here was hard to come by; indeed, presidial salaries by the late eighteenth century and early nineteenth were paid in specie but only after substantial deductions and service charges—often illegal or greatly inflated—cut into the net amount a soldier took home. Amangual knew all of that.

64 Chapter Two

Whatever outside ambitions motivated his decision Amangual may have now seen, with an insider's view, his own reflection in the plight of fellow soldiers, themselves dependent on *his* incorruptibility. Besides, he had his own reputation as a stockman to uphold.[51] In April 1791, he contacted Governor Muñoz, yet again. But this time the petition was not to reimburse acquiescent Indians but, instead, to provide for his own soldiers. He needed two thousand pesos from the *Mesteñas* Fund. Amangual had appealed for the same amount somewhere between the time of the "Friendly Nations" arrival and the April request to acquire remounts for the company. He wrote up his intention to reimburse a total of four thousand pesos upon his return from San Luis Potosí on a trip planned for July 1791. Later in the year, the same two officials of the villa of San Fernando involved in the December 1790 repayment to Cortéz, *alcaldes ordinarios* Francisco Arocha and Pedro Flores, acknowledged receipt of two hundred pesos as payment toward this large obligation. Whether or not Amangual had made other payments or whether this December remittance was the first on the original July loan is unclear. Nevertheless, driven by a desire to prepare for every contingency, Amangual was forthright in his repayment obligations.[52]

However, when those obligations involved one of his superiors, the chain of correspondence shows that complications could quickly arise. On July 23, 1791, Amangual requested reimbursement from his immediate supervisor Governor Muñoz for over 739 pesos from the Mesteñas Fund due and owing to his *habilitación* from the Brig. Gen. Juan de Ugalde. While Muñoz acknowledged receipt of the accounts forwarded to him by the Adjutant Inspector Juan Gutiérrez de la Cueva in an official letter of May 23, the governor advised Amangual that Commandant Gen. Pedro de Nava had told Muñoz that the *Mesteñas* Fund was the source for food provisions for the Friendly Nations.[53] Therefore, Muñoz reasoned, he could not reimburse Amangual since a prior order from either the *Comandante General* Ramón de Castro or Viceroy Conde de Revillagigedo II was not only mandatory, but acting otherwise would constitute Muñoz's failure to obey their orders. Fueled by indignation, Muñoz let Amangual know that he had explained this same situation to Capt. Martínez Pacheco, who was the recipient of the provisions paid for by the loan, and he also upbraided Martínez Pacheco for not having applied for reimbursement from the royal coffers [in San Luis Potosí]. Muñoz made it clear that orders from royal administrators should have been issued indicating what fund was to have provided the monies in the meantime.[54]

Ultimately Muñoz informed Amangual that Martínez Pacheco had not only ignored a call to action regarding his obligation to pay back the loan, but he had also disregarded an order from Muñoz himself. Preoccupations

"Truly Elected" Paymaster and Service to the King

or premeditations aside, Martínez Pacheco similarly ignored a request placed by Amangual, which included copies of the accounts of the provisions that were delivered by the latter.[55]

Trouble in the Presidio: Negotiating Bad Behavior and Unscrupulous Deeds

Nagging fiscal discrepancies, overlooked directives, and any complications that arose from provisioning and receiving reimbursements were part and parcel of the presidio paymaster's daily routine. Some bothersome incidences were beyond the control of the *habilitado*. But in an equally important task Francisco Amangual often took testimony from his subordinates as part of exercising authority over troublemakers within the company. While suspicions might on occasion incline toward his performance as company paymaster and that may have provoked surveillance, Amangual's reports to his commanders document his compliance with regimentation and service to imperial authority in the wake of his own managerial missteps.

In one telling episode, two soldiers raised suspicions about a fellow company member to Amangual. Andrés Benito Courbiére, an interpreter for the Friendly Nations of the North,[56] and the interpreter for the Comanche and "Taguayaz" Francisco Xavier Chávez, let slip that Alférez Manuel de Urrutia[57] struck up a close friendship with two young Comanche braves among the residents of the Béxar presidio. Insofar as that interaction was not unusual, the soldiers' concern arose since Urrutia cohabited with an unnamed Ute Indian woman in an uneasy relationship that must have included violence since Urrutia faced jail sentences several times. The tipoff was that Urrutia's interactions with the two young Indian men evolved as a way to rouse others to prevent the woman's impending departure, most likely fueled by a clearly exasperating liaison with Urrutia.[58] What followed in the summer of 1791 was a remarkable series of events set off by a breach of protocol on the part of one soldier's error followed by his immediate supervisor's response to that breakdown in discipline. Moreover, the disruptive episode spotlights the interplay between soldiers and civilians, commanders and subordinates, Spaniards, mestizos, and Native peoples within the confines of the presidio.

As told from the perspective of Amangual, one late afternoon while the "Capitan Cumanche" Ojos Azules and the Ute woman sat in the plaza of the presidio, the soldier-translator Chávez, acting upon the orders of the governor, told Azules that he should return to his lodging and take the Ute woman there as well. Urrutia, witnessing the trio's interaction, attempted to detain Chávez so he could interpret on Urrutia's behalf to Azules. However, it did not take long for the interpreter to recognize the drunken state of Urrutia, and Chávez did not obey his superior. Chávez then quickly instructed the capitán to avoid saying a word to Urrutia, since the latter was too intoxicated to even comprehend his warning.[59]

At this moment, an unidentified private under the direction of Amangual physically attempted to remove Urrutia who, in turn, ordered Chávez to tell the Ute woman how ungrateful she was and how much it had cost him to rescue her. Again, Chávez did not comply, and the Comanche leader took the woman to his lodgings where, as Amangual told it, he had always treated her like a sister. Then, during the night, Ojos Azules came to Chávez's house with his weapons and his wife, his sister, and the Ute woman in tow, all fleeing from Urrutia who was now menacing them with a bow and arrows. With that, Chávez told Azules to take shelter in his own house and not to worry; he assured the refugees of late that if Urrutia were to arrive there, Chávez would chase him away with threats of punishment from the governor. Furthermore, Chávez instructed the sentinel on the presidio parapets that in case he encountered the drunken Urrutia in the plazas, he was to order him to leave and to advise him of the governor's awareness of his harassing behavior.[60] And that was not a good thing.

As if it could not get even more bizarre, one day prior, Urrutia's nephew Clemente Arocha reported to Amangual that on the previous evening his uncle had circled the capitán's house with a quiver and arrows—and the confiscated saber of Sgt. Mariano Rodríguez—issuing taunts, once again, as a way of coercing the Ute woman out of the residence. Wanting to avert a potentially deadly situation, Arocha encouraged Amangual to apprehend the drunken Urrutia so that Urrutia's mother should not have to suffer the shame of his violence. At this point, Amangual made a confounding decision to put the erratic Urrutia in charge of the presidio's guardhouse and, incredulously, further made him responsible for dispatching patrols at their designated time. Perhaps thinking it would help, Amangual then secured a promise from a presumably still intoxicated Urrutia that he would not abandon his new post. Not surprisingly, Urrutia disobeyed the order and for the remainder of the evening wandered about the presidio, apparently still under the influence. Amangual admitted to his superior, Governor Muñoz, that had he recognized the inebriated state of Urrutia, he never would have assigned him to the sensitive post of supervising the guardhouse and lining up patrols.[61]

The next day, Squad Cpl. José Manuel de Castro accompanied fifteen Comanche, including four women, Ojos Azules, his sister, and the Ute woman to Urrutia's house to bid their farewells. Without warning, Urrutia grabbed a lance from Azules, turned it in reverse, and hit Castro with its

"Truly Elected" Paymaster and Service to the King 67

shaft. Even though the assault likely caused him pain, Castro's objective was undeterred: he got off his horse, took the lance from Urrutia, returned it to the Comanche leader, and pleaded with his superior to get himself under control ("*le rogue al* [Urrutia] *se contuviese recogiendose*"). Castro then remounted his horse and left with the party in his charge, intent on completing his assignment. Clearly Ojos Azules was highly offended and even told Castro that had other Indians been present they could very well have wounded Urrutia with arrows or just killed him. Castro attempted to assuage the leader's outrage by assuring him that Urrutia was drunk, and that no attention should be paid to what he was doing, his dishonorable conduct spurred on by the adverse effects of alcohol.[62]

When Amangual read the report of June 12, the day after the incident when Corporal Castro returned from his trip as escort, he expressed his concerns to Governor Muñoz. Amangual had contacted Alférez Urrutia's brother Francisco, a private in the company, to ask him whether he knew anything about his brother and one of the Indian youths he befriended, a mute Lipan. Somewhere along the way, he had enlisted the aid of the boy in his troubled relationship with the Ute woman. Private Urrutia corroborated the account given by Corporal Castro, verifying that the mute Lipan was serving his brother in collaboration with another Indian, named Mariano, from the same tribe. Amangual confirmed to the governor that Private Urrutia and his mother experienced tremendous embarrassment from Alférez Urrutia's acting out, especially his torment over the Ute woman and from interference by the Lipan youth.[63]

From this protracted episode of a drunken soldier breaking rank, it appears that Amangual was as capable of misidentifying the outward characteristics of someone deeply troubled—behavioral markers that surely would have precluded this individual from assuming tasks and responsibilities of grave importance—as he was of choosing an ineffective person, the unnamed private, to intervene on his behalf. Amangual's misjudgment of character flaws, even as he preserved his commitment to soldierly chores and paymaster obligations for the benefit of his company, muddled his career accomplishments since he had to explain his reasoning. The Urrutia debacle was an embarrassment for Amangual even as he sought methods to encourage the goodwill of not only his fellow *presidiales* but also the garrison's adjacent communities.[64]

Not much changed by the following month. Amangual reported to Muñoz that on July 10 Urrutia notified him that he had withdrawn from a detachment in compliance with the governor's order. By that evening Urrutia, again drunk, went to the house of Ygnacio Pérez, where his wife was waiting. He attempted to physically set her atop a horse to force her return, but she refused given his inebriated state. Urrutia then aimed his lance at her, but it made no contact. With that, a nephew promptly ushered him out of town. Amangual, perhaps sympathetic—or just tolerant, and maybe supportive, to a fault—went out to search for Urrutia. He found him on the banks of a creek, on horseback, with all his weapons, the lance in his hand, and very drunk. Amangual transported him back to Urrutia's sister's house where he fell asleep. The next morning, Urrutia went to his mother's house, and by noon the presidio's corporal reported that the troubled alférez had gone out, alone, and without orders to rejoin the horse-herd detachment. Amangual sent Pvt. Antonio "Martines" posthaste with a demand from Captain Muñoz for Urrutia to return immediately. Urrutia refused, ignoring the command but allegedly telling Martines to let the governor know that he was not coming back because "I am naked and wet and I am going to fulfill my duty (*digale á el Señor Governador que no boi porque estoi en cueros, y mojado, y que boy á complir con mi obligacion*/sic passim)."[65]

One could interpret Urrutia's sodden determination to complete his obligation as, on some level, strangely admirable. That news prompted the departure of Lieutenant Fernández to the detachment, taking into custody a now readily obedient Urrutia, who complied "without the slightest hesitation" and who was jailed upon arrival at the Béxar guardhouse.[66] As this study will show, Urrutia's debauchery would reemerge time and again. So, too, would Amangual's intra-presidio woes, a trend destined to continue throughout the coming years.

Zambrano's Corn—The Lawsuit

In fact, Amangual's troubles did not so quickly diminish since there unfolded that same summer of 1791 yet another interpersonal conflict, but this time related to commercial entanglements. This one involved a presumed agreement regarding the sale of corn. Only one month after the drunken Urrutia subverted the better judgement of Francisco Amangual, the merchant Macario Zambrano, having identified himself as a thirty-years-long citizen of the villa of San Fernando and a soldier of the Béxar garrison, attested to Amangual having appeared before the *alcalde de primer voto* and likewise custodian of funds Francisco Arocha. Making his case, Amangual demanded a sum of three hundred pesos.[67] Zambrano acknowledged the debt but questioned the receipt of information that he provided regarding the payment sought by the *habilitado*. Making matters worse were the setbacks and losses of his plantings consequent to the suit. Thus, Zambrano found out his petition had no validity, and he should repay Amangual. Otherwise, he would be apprehended for noncompliance.[68]

"Truly Elected" Paymaster and Service to the King 69

When Zambrano verified his petition's content and presented it to the *cabildo* so they might certify the document as true and thereby enter it as an official proceeding, its members could not accommodate him. They argued that they were prevented from doing so and threatened with severe punishment by the governor if they performed official acts on any day other than Thursdays. Or so Zambrano claimed. Further, Zambrano declared that there was a strict condition that the *cabildo* required at least one day's notice beforehand so that Governor Muñoz could preside over the matter. Clearly, Zambrano was mistrustful of the governor since he believed that everything that had happened to him was done with Muñoz's approval and direction. Consequently, Zambrano reached out to the commander general himself, Ramón de Castro, in the hope of finding justice. He grounded his demand for fair treatment on his assertion that he and Amangual had agreed upon a certain price for his grain. He even alleged that there existed a viceregal order that decreed those citizens receive preference over the missions for the favored price of three hundred pesos.[69]

Zambrano's deposition was riddled with inaccuracies, or so it appeared from the reaction his petition received from Governor Muñoz. He repudiated Zambrano's claim that he had given orders to prevent the *cabildo* from holding assemblies at the times and on the days they found best. Muñoz unleashed more. No members of the *cabildo* were prevented from, or intimidated with penalties for, holding official proceedings on any day other than Thursday or, for that matter, with the strict condition that he, as governor, be notified the day beforehand in order to preside over the meetings. And, the *alcalde* Arocha had not asked for guidance from the governor, nor had he seen Zambrano's petition presented in his court regarding the claim for three hundred pesos made by Amangual. Equally determined to prove his point, Arocha was willing to certify the latter and by doing so demonstrate that Zambrano was lying.[70]

This is where the report becomes unusually interesting. Zambrano stated that, in contemplation of paying three hundred pesos to Amangual, he had from the beginning of the harvest fifty *fanegas* of good-quality corn to take to Presidio La Bahía to sell. In fact, Zambrano's *wife* went to seek a permit from the governor, who refused to grant it. However, the governor had just taken office and had not yet issued any permits at all for the export of grains until he could get a report on the amount harvested for supplying the citizenry and the presidial company. Only then could he ascertain what was left over for La Bahía. Significantly, the governor had taken these measures attentive to the scarcities that the region had suffered up to that time. But no permits had been withheld for the export of grains after verifying sufficient stores of the commodity. For that matter, if Zambrano or a representative of

70 Chapter Two

his had requested it, there would have been no reason to withhold it from him or any other petitioner.[71]

Room enough lingered for a new angle in the controversy to emerge in the form of Zambrano's relationship with yet another future litigant against Amangual. Apparently, the presidio had received thirty-two *fanegas* of corn from Zambrano's son-in-law, Sgt. Mariano Rodríguez, a soldier who would himself come forth in the following year to lodge a formal complaint against Amangual: he will accuse the paymaster of misappropriating funds. Rodríguez's corn was part of that which Zambrano's wife had wanted to send to La Bahía. He was paid three pesos, four *reales* for it in September 1790 and its value was intended to pay the merchant Juan Martín Amondarain.[72] Zambrano claimed that his agreement with Amangual was premised on the latter's having asked him how many *fanegas* of corn he could sell him. The governor himself knew that Amangual did the same thing with all the other farmers because they had put the word out that the harvest was going to be exceedingly small. Mindful of keeping expenses low as the presidio's fiduciary, Amangual would have indeed inquired as to who would most cheaply sell him corn for his soldiers.[73]

Without further information it is unknown how arbiters in the corn deal resolved the matter. It is known that only two months later while Amangual was away from Béxar, *comandante* Castro ordered Governor Muñoz to sell the corn in question before it deteriorated.[74] As an agent for his company's interests, Amangual made efforts to become well informed of current market prices for basic commodities. Even when his patience was tested, Amangual responded with business-minded acuity. In doing so, he managed to enhance his relationship with some in the merchant community while alienating others in the military establishment. As we shall see, from the perspective of Sgt. Mariano Rodríguez, the Zambrano episode for future reference conveniently created a cloud of suspicion around Amangual. Settling a score fueled resentment that would soon harden into outright accusations of wrongdoing and consequently inspire official action.

In more positive interactions, official correspondence with Commandancy personnel chronicle Amangual's resolute efforts toward concretizing productive relationships with the local indigenous communities. This would be as crucial in the multi-demographic Béxar ecosystem as it would be during the long expedition that he would eventually lead in the final phase of his career. Listing gifts of superior commodities was but one method of carrying out the Spanish empire's continuing policy of peace by purchase, or, as Gálvez plainly put it, "peace by malice (*paces por dolosas*)."[75] The broader point to emphasize here is that just as important for the efforts directed toward enhancing mutually beneficial exchanges among locals while gaining administrative traction with superiors was the documentation of that interplay.

Armed with his ledger, on March 27, 1792 Francisco Amangual ordered four pesos of cigars—a highly significant commodity—to be delivered to Comanche captains Sojas and Soquina. In turn, Governor Muñoz ordered Amangual to document this expenditure for the Native leaders as proof of sustenance provided by the presidio.[76] One month later, Muñoz again ordered the delivery of four more pesos of cigars, but this gift was intended for the "Tancague" Nation and thus noted on the expenditures account for that group.[77] The very next day, ten Comanche men departed from the presidio, necessitating a charge on the expenditures account for these same Indians since, as Muñoz documented on what appears to be a scrap of paper, they were being sent off with one peso of cigars.[78]

In fact, April 27, 1792, was a significant date for Amangual. He produced a ledger to show funds received from the royal treasury at San Luis Potosí for payment of salaries through December 1791 to officers and others in the

Accounting records of Amangual, April 27, 1792, e_bx_006653, The Dolph Briscoe Center for American History, The University of Texas at Austin.

Béxar company. He also noted the amount introduced in tobacco with an inventory of that commodity up to 1792 as well as provisions for the troops congruent to various other charges related to mail. Details of the content in each fund and quantities on hand could be found in the coffers and payment orders circulated within the first semester of 1792.[79]

With receipt of an official letter dated January 25, a plausible reaction from Amangual could have been astonishment when an order directed him to cease issuing requests for payment from loans due in that first semester of 1792. He also had to stop paying drafts issued by him up to that time without prior review and authorization from Muñoz. Apparently, an examination of the tobacco department funds triggered an inquiry, and Amangual swore prompt obedience to the letter's demands. The document conveys, both, Amangual's sense of urgency and strict deference toward his commanders with his acknowledgment that it was his responsibility to account for a "few cigars" placed in the Béxar store. Upon their sale and receipt of payment, he was to furnish the security mentioned in an earlier letter. He was to comply without departing from a single point called for in the official letter. Fulfilling the orders, Amangual executed the immediate retirement of all promissory notes issued by him and, instead, charged them to the troops' year-end accounts. The imperative here was to clarify the good or bad state of the debts under his responsibility. Since his cashier José Bustillos was "seriously injured" during this period, it is possible that Amangual may have simply been annoyed with Muñoz's directive to find another individual to settle the company's accounts. Interpersonal animosities aside, that may have been the usual method of summarizing the Béxar presidio's store-house.[80]

The charges recorded by Amangual against the account included thirty-five thousand pesos allocated by royal officials at San Luis Potosí for salaries of the Béxar company's officers, sergeants, corporals, privates, and others for fiscal year 1791. Amangual's next entry, which constituted the next high-est charge—4,999 pesos—was for tobacco sold during the same year.[81] After these two highest charges, subsequent entries in the ledger show much smaller amounts; for instance, two thousand pesos were on hand in the form of deposits for the construction of El Cíbolo's fortress. Amangual also issued a payment order requiring reimbursement during the first semester of 1792. Another thirty-eight hundred pesos provided by the *Mesteñas* Fund was for horses, provisions, and supplies for the troops.[82]

Amangual's calls for reimbursements to the *Mesteñas* Fund got the atten-tion of the paymasters of the presidios in the Eastern Provinces (Coahuila y Téjas, Nuevo Santander, and Nuevo León), which collectively delivered 2,031 pesos. These were subsequently expended on the urgent needs of his

"Truly Elected" Paymaster and Service to the King   73

own company. This document, signed by Amangual on April 27, 1792, was witnessed by several people including—and this is significant—the sergeant of the company *de cuera* at the Béxar presidio, Mariano Rodríguez. All the troops, including Rodríguez, concurred: the amount received by their company paymaster was complete, without any questionable withdrawals whatsoever.[83] That certitude would soon be tested. Sgt. Rodríguez will reemerge shortly in another role: that of slanderer against Amangual, accusing him of misappropriation of funds, a serious charge that had the potential to deleteriously impact the paymaster's career.

In the meantime, more money came his way. Amangual received from the governor and the *alcaldes ordinarios* of San Antonio a repayment of 245 pesos. This represented an amount withdrawn by the magistrates to pay individuals who had furnished support specifically intended for the "Friendly Indians of the North." These groups, probably Tancahue, entered peacefully into the garrison from May 22 to July 5, 1792.[84] Then one month later, on August 14, Amangual issued yet another receipt for almost 1,012 pesos that the same officials expended for the same reasons but for an extended period since the previous July 5.[85] By December of the following year, Amangual produced documentation for Governor Muñoz to answer a query from *Comandante General* Pedro de Nava as to whether a deposit of 2,842 pesos, delivered by Capt. Martínez Pacheco, had indeed flowed into the *Mesteñas* Fund.[86]

In reply, Amangual sent certified copies of payment orders amounting to almost 2,032 pesos given to him by the adjutant inspector (as proxy for Brig. Gen. Juan de Ugalde) Juan Gutiérrez de la Cueva.[87] It appears that Amangual placed these payments into the supporting funds of his office, an entry previously balanced on July 26, 1793. Further, Amangual informed Muñoz that he had also in his possession over seventy pesos delivered to him by Alférez Tomás Gonzáles Huerta (of the Lampazos *volantes*) with the two entries combined totaling almost 2,103 pesos. Amangual notified Muñoz about his bookkeeping so that if the governor wished to update Commander Nava on amounts received, he could do so. Amangual's copies show that Inspector Gutiérrez de la Cueva tallied up the receipts—some involving myriad units of flying squadron troops, Amangual himself, and four other paymasters—and itemized the payments in the following way:

> One payment order against the *alférez* of the *compañía volante* of La Punta de Lampazos, Don Thomás [sic] Gonzales Huerta: 520 pesos, 5 reales, 1 5/8 granos

> Another against *alférez* Don Francisco Vásquez, *abilitado* of La Bahía del Espíritu Santo: 156 pesos, 5 reales, 9 granos

Chapter Two

Another against *alférez* Don Joaquín Vidal, *abilitado* of the third *compañía volante* of La Colonia, in Laredo: 596 pesos, 1 real, 3 7/8 granos

Another against Vidal, that he received from the first *compañía volante* of La Colonia: 156 pesos, 2 reales, 3 granos

Another against *alférez* José de Rávago, *abilitado* of the company of La Bahía: 307 pesos, 4 reales, 3 granos

Another against *alférez* José Miguel del Moral: 138 pesos, 3 reales, 3/8 granos

One receipt from Lieutenant Francisco Amangual: 156 pesos, 2 reales, 9 granos

And, finally, what was delivered by the *abilitado* Alférez Thomás Gonzales Huerta: 70 pesos, 5 5/8 granos.

The inspector originally compiled this account in September 1791.[88] Since Amangual made certain to include this information in his December 18, 1793, letter to Muñoz, presumably in order to validate the *Mesteñas* Fund's accounts receivable, he was following best practices to ensure his reputation as paymaster remained beyond reproach. Further, he had already endured two accusations made against his character—from Zambrano and Menchaca—during the previous five years. But as we shall soon see, Amangual had particularly good reason to anticipate that his accounting procedures might be questioned. He would confirm those suspicions once he identified the inquisitor. This time, would it be a colleague within the presidio or an upper echelon administrator in the viceregal capital?[89]

Amangual: The Accused

In the nine years spanning his arrival in the Septentrión to his ascension as Béxar presidio paymaster, Amangual experienced the highs and lows and especially the middling moments of any soldier's military career. He sought advice from his superiors about processing contraband, received promotions for good service within the ranks, collected payroll, made demands for reimbursement, and presented invoices of supplies he provided for his company. As a dispute involving a fellow soldier unfolds in chapter 3, Francisco Amangual's effectiveness as company fiduciary came under scrutiny from his expenditure of funds and receipt of commodities. Having enough of an assault on his character and honor to instantaneously go on defense, by early 1793 Amangual will write to his superior, Lt. Col. Manuel

"Truly Elected" Paymaster and Service to the King 75

Muñoz, requesting a more appropriate punishment for the sergeant of the same company, Mariano Rodríguez, who in the previous year had slandered Amangual for misappropriation of presidial inventory. Though Amangual will acknowledge that the proceedings conducted via judicial examination of the merchandise in question resulted in the full exoneration of any mismanagement on his part—an investigation pursued by Amangual himself, who continuously reasserted his lawful conduct with the inventory under his charge—he conveyed exasperation over Rodríguez's lack of jail time. As documented, Amangual appears expressly annoyed that his accuser was not assessed any other penalties and that the information was not immediately brought to his attention.[90] Moreover, Amangual will voice deep concern—perhaps internally experienced as raging indignation—about the leniency extended toward Rodríguez and that its potentiality would be the sergeant's future abuses of the law.

What is most telling in the letter to Governor Muñoz is Amangual's couching his concerns about Rodríguez's dishonorable conduct by admitting long experience with the "rowdy character (*bullicioso genio*)" of the sergeant. Making clear his awareness of military protocol, Second Alférez Amangual will argue that the honor of the military superiors, presumably self-evident to the lowest ranking soldiers, was principally based on the upper-ranked officers' greater service to the king and the unswerving discipline of all the troops in common. As the documentation unfolds, Amangual is especially perturbed over the message that the Rodríguez incident—and the perpetrator's subsequent escape from serious punishment—might convey to the troops.[91]

As a rebuttal, Muñoz attested to his receipt of a January 26 order from the Commandant Gen. Ramón de Castro y Gutiérrez that the latter *not* be informed of the case and, therefore, he was disinclined to relay this information to Amangual.[92] This news very likely irked Amangual, compounding his fury over Rodríguez dodging sanctions for his infractions. Indeed, correspondence between he and Muñoz suggests a civil, if somewhat strained, relationship between the two men. Setting aside any ill will, Amangual will acknowledge to his superior that he received a certified copy of the instruction of principles concerning various points of discipline sent by Castro. In closing, Amangual will express his intention of scrupulously observing the instruction, following Muñoz's order that he do so.[93]

As the particulars of the lawsuit that pitted Francisco Amangual against Mariano Rodríguez emerge in the next chapter, Manuel Muñoz officiates an intra-presidio case that mixed slander with deception and linked commodities with questionable conveyance. Testimonies by both soldiers and others during a two-month investigation of accusation and repudiation provide a glimpse into one garrison's internecine conflict. Delving further into never-before-published documentation reveals a predicament instigated by a single culprit who sowed disinformation while mustering a widening conspiracy among superiors, subordinates, and even outsiders.

THREE

❧

"The Detachment Cannot Be Effective and I Will Not Be Responsible"

The *Reglamento* of 1772, Situational Strategies, and Slander

Twenty years prior to Amangual's promotion and the emergence of his legal entanglement with a subordinate, large-scale and distinctly militarized transformations recontoured New Spain's northern frontier. Considered broadly, the Bourbon Reforms sought to strengthen the imperial system by centralizing authority and making it more efficient. Accomplishing that goal meant weakening the political and administrative dominance of the viceroy and building a permanent defense force with a standing army and civilian militias to include indigenous auxiliaries. Formalizing protection involved organizing strategies for irregular warfare and creating an orderly chain of garrisons to assert by deed and presence Spanish authority and control (however imaginary or tenuous) over a wide swath of territory.

Front-line realities caused policy makers on the Peninsula to expect a "much greater degree of professionalism" from frontier troops.[1] Using a conceptual approach when it came to territory out of bounds from direct, immediate viceregal supervision, administrators established the Interior Provinces, an expanse consisting of Nueva Vizcaya, Sonora, Sinaloa, California, New Mexico, Chihuahua, Coahuila y Tejas (formally unified as one large state in 1824),[2] Nuevo León, and Nuevo Santander. The main thrust of the Bourbon-forged *reglamentos* aimed to magnify the northern Mexican frontier's shift from a religious-based effort to a military one.[3] Through mutual collaboration, the visitor general and the viceroy prepared a plan to create a General Commandancy in January 1768, with the adoption of its establishment by late 1769.[4] Having signed their *informe* on June 22, 1771, Visitador Gálvez and Viceroy Carlos Francisco Croix would have to wait until May 1776 when Spanish administrators formally authorized the Commandancy. What this maneuver accomplished was essentially to sever the Interior Provinces from the jurisdiction of the viceroy, effectively mitigating power from that royal administrator. As Donald Chipman argued, "Its creation as a separate viceroyalty in every aspect except name" portended significant changes across the borderlands. Shortly after its creation, Carlos III designated the Viceroy's nephew Teodoro de Croix as the Commandancy's chief administrator (Comandante General) of the now-severed *Provincias Internas*.[5] Extensive in scope, revisions to defensive mechanisms enacted by the Croix administration provided the basis for the evolution of the presidio into a two-pronged apparatus geared for managing its civilian and military populations. With respect to the first point, the presidio took on new significance as a base for military offensives directed at resistant indigenous communities, including the Ndé; with the second, the presidio was envisioned as a sanctuary of sorts for the growing number of Native people who ostensibly sought peace.[6] The content within the 1772 *Reglamento* makes clear its status as a legal instrument that drew heavily on its antecedent, the *Reglamento* of 1729, but with the intention of standardizing all aspects of presidio form and function. Naylor and Polzer argue that while the 1772 regulation was significant and influential, what it did was unprecedented: its content set the character of military history but for only the last half century of Spanish presence in the *Provincias Internas*. Before its issuance, peninsular interest in military and economic reforms had already preoccupied Felipe V enough to order an inspection of the presidios in the Northern provinces.[7]

The preamble by Carlos III to the 1772 Regulations left no question about what sparked reorganization, what he considered to be the real threat and the price of that threat, and the goals he hoped to achieve as enumerated in a September 10 *cédula*. The king wrote, in part, "As the interior presidios were erected and are maintained at great cost [...] it seems that the number and the boldness of the hostile Indians increases every day, and the ravages of those provinces multiply."[8]

Reconfiguring the frontier through administrative imperatives and with cost saving at the forefront had three key objectives. The first entailed a strategic plan to relocate some presidios for more effective defense; the second sought to vary the economic management of the garrisons and the troops; and, finally, the king conceived the office of commandant inspector as a method to "direct and arrange [the presidios'] expeditions and services."[9] Stepping into the breach created by swindlers and grifters at headquarters,

Reglamento of 1772, Strategies, and Slander

steering the fiscal administration of the presidios eventually involved the services of a paymaster (*habilitado*), a role fulfilled by Francisco Amangual and one that would spawn professional dilemmas for him and others entrusted with the same task. Oversight by a commander inspector satisfied the king's unflagging push toward offensive operations against hostile Native populations and, in theory, presumed fealty by soldiers to authority. But, often, that came at the expense of (mis)understanding local conditions. Nonetheless, realities at the outposts and the more immediate concerns of commanders frequently proved to be at odds with imperial strategies from afar of subjugation and control, notions persistently suspended in a tenuous state across New Spain's Comandancia General.[10] Unofficially, the king and his commandant inspector usually acquiesced to the expertise of operatives in the field who had firsthand knowledge of frontier warfare and its challenges.

Upon the departure of Croix as commandant general in 1783, Felipe de Neve, commandant inspector of the *Provincias Internas*, ascended to his new role, assumed the same authority that Croix had exercised, and expressed his complete confidence in his predecessor's policies of reform.[11] Regarding the military, Neve had been broadly impressed with the discipline of the troops, officers' instruction and training, and the efficiency of supply availability. This seems odd since, having been an Inspector, he must surely have known, root and branch, that some aspects of military preparedness had glaring weaknesses in derelict troops.[12] Nonetheless, on October 1, 1783, Neve transmitted a royal order from Viceroy Matías de Gálvez that reflected not only the purported stability of the presidial state-of-affairs and his characteristic loyalty to Teodoro de Croix but also the outgoing commander general's efficient maintenance of the soldiers and citizenry of New Spain's frontier. Gálvez credited the king with recognizing that hostilities had ended, and peace had been established in his overseas domains. However tenuous the ceasefire, calm in the provinces brought about the cessation of a one-time monetary contribution for maintaining defense of the Crown.[13] In all likelihood, however, the enemy here had merely retreated momentarily to replenish both supplies and stamina to reignite guerrilla attacks that were imminent. Reverential loyalties aside, Neve certainly knew that instability permeated asymmetric warfare, with obverse reactions persistently sparked by some soldiers' waywardness and prone to change quickly.

A peculiar reversal in military complexities was such that, though the king now exempted his subjects in the Indies from donations to the royal war chest, offensive operations ramped up against the Ndé across the borderlands. As matters stood at the very top of the chain of command, a 1782 royal order obligated Commander General Neve, as it had his predecessor Croix, to renew campaigns each month against the enemy. Further, the order required troops to rotate offensive and defensive strategies so that at any one time a third of the frontier force was in constant pursuit.[14] In practice, sustained campaigns against hostile indigenous groups demanded the same kind of well-planned partitioning of soldiers where they were most needed. In a manner that was both expeditious and productive, troops on campaign were to circle the area near watering places conducive to hiding the enemy.[15] In 1782, Neve grouped the presidial companies and the flying squadrons into divisions, each consisting of one-third of the soldiers from two or more companies. Sonora had four divisions with a total campaign force of 268 troops; Nueva Vizcaya had four, also, with 328 troops; there were two in Coahuila with 170; and one division in Texas with fifty-six. By 1784, Sonora counted two companies of Opata soldiers as auxiliaries with one of their own as its captain.[16]

Apportioning bodies across regiments had ramifications for all troops, and that included the *compañías volantes*. A little more than a month after the moratorium on donations, Captain Cabello received word from Neve that he was to continue in the same capacity in rank and duty as Croix originally authorized. Thus, Cabello would continue reviewing the troops and complying with all orders and instructions pertaining to presidio inspections until a new *comandante inspector* arrived. As part of the piece-meal process that circumscribed all military exploits, Cabello compiled and then remitted the general review reports to Neve so that those could be forwarded to the Royal Treasury in San Luis Potosí.[17] Documentation was a significant aspect of a presidio commander's job, and in Cabello's case, much ink was spilled over the course of eight years as he corroborated a variety of activities that took place at the garrison. When pressured to send his men out on campaigns, Cabello's piercing commentary about troop shortages and concern for his presidio's safety made it difficult if not impractical to accede to any higher authority's orders. That might include attacking sworn enemies or otherwise engaging in offensive maneuvers.

When it was necessary, repositioning soldiers like pieces on a chess-board went beyond the rank and file to include officers. Much like boosting punitive campaigns while simultaneously waiving local donations for war, the process led to confusion. In November 1783, Neve notified Cabello of his decision to promote Lt. José Menchaca of Presidio San Juan Bautista del Río Grande to commander of the Aguaverde presidio, even though Neve's predecessor Croix had prearranged for Lt. Pedro López to take on that assignment. Menchaca's vacancy was subsequently filled by Juan Antonio de Arce, formerly of the San Elizario presidio, due to the death of its Capt. Juan Antonio Serrano.[18] The broader point to underscore in these types of operational reconfigurations is that, clearly, Felipe de Neve had intimate knowledge of his soldiers' competencies, almost certainly gleaned from years of side-by-side frontier soldiering and reviewing military service records. That familiarity gave him enough insight to install those judged sufficiently talented in specific appointments at garrisons across the borderlands. Unquestionably, in his role as top commander, those prerogatives were his to exercise. Neve's opinion of a soldier's worth in this specific instance superseded that of an immediate supervisor, here, Cabello, and therefore he could override even a provincial governor's distaste for that same soldier. Notably, however, a resourceful soldier, jittery about forced displacement elsewhere, could in desperation directly petition the commander general as one way to safeguard career stability.

A clear example of this access to higher authority occurred in November 1783 when Capt. Luis Cazorla appealed to Neve to continue service in the borderlands despite a negative critique of his job performance by his superior. The disparaging remarks, discussed in chapter 1, stemmed from an inspection review of Presidio La Bahía del Espíritu Santo conducted by Gov. Cabello earlier that year. As further evidence of Neve's powerful sway in more localized spheres of engagement, the decision came down to transfer Cazorla back to his captaincy at La Bahía after the king himself had already granted Cazorla assignment to the dragoon regiment in Mexico City. In an effort to appease Cabello in what may have come off as a dismissal of his low opinion of Cazorla, the commander general assured the governor that the reinstated captain would make honorable satisfaction with respect to the charges leveled against him.[19] Since these types of logistical maneuvers between commander and commanded had but one objective, the maintenance of a superior–subordinate hierarchy, their expediency in mitigating disruptions to interpresidio relations further shored up colonial authority in the Comandancia General.

But by late 1784 the next *comandante general*, José Antonio Rengel, perspicacious but unsettled, noticed that, in general, soldiers on punitive forays returned to their presidios (or locations from where they decamped) as soon as they had dealt any blow to the enemy, even after only seeing a few days in action. Though the 1772 *Reglamento* mandated incessant war against hostile Indians, nowhere in its content appears a compulsory duration of engagement by troops on campaign. Consequently, Rengel found it necessary to remind Governor Cabello of previously issued directives for soldiers to remain out for a month, a period suitable for implementing the best service to the king. Rengel detected a flaw in the prevailing belief that since hostile forces had spotted the troops, dealing them a second blow was

82   Chapter Three

improbable. Further, to overcome hesitation on the part of the soldiers and, more practically, to obscure from the enemy any route taken by the presidials, Rengel suggested that commanders of detachments on maneuvers choose the direction deemed most practical. Built into Rengel's strategizing of campaign outcomes was the hope of sending back with soldiers the spoils of battle. Once adjacent to a populated area, these troops would determine a convenient location to rejoin the rest of the company.[20] Or so went the general's reasoning.

Naturally, Governor Cabello had his own ideas about military preparedness that took into consideration what he knew all too well: the never-ending deficiency of troops. In fact, on February 16, 1785, Cabello presented compelling reasons for the extreme difficulty his Texas companies would experience by leaving the presidios for a month or more per Rengel's orders. In what must have again required delicate handling of an acutely sensitive topic, Cabello reminded Rengel that the latter's predecessor, Felipe de Neve, became well informed about the troops' extended absences when he visited Béxar in May and June 1783. Apparently, the matter was discussed at length. The conclusion reached at that time was that Neve left for Cabello's discretion the conducting of sorties and sweeps (*"salidas y cortadas"*). These maneuvers correlated to the same terms that had existed up to the period of Rengel's official observations and were still in effect. Stressing the fiscal challenges routinely faced by his soldiers, Cabello explained to Rengel that it was not possible for presidials at Bahía and Béxar to leave on campaigns for periods of one month or more. Once detached, the small number of troops remaining heightened the fort's vulnerability to attack. Aside from the consequences of absent soldiers, when trouble lurked and called for general sorties it was essential to make use of the citizenry—and even Indians—from the missions of both presidios. However, these groups, auxiliaries in effect, similarly could not defray the costs of being away from home for even a month given the expense to equip themselves with supplies and horses necessary for that length of time. An exasperated Cabello argued that it was "impossible" to make sorties with the troops alone because of their slight number. Therefore, in making customary sweeps, success was attainable only during those times when residents and mission Indians appraised as adequate for military exercises could supplement and reinforce the company.[21]

Even with extensive preparation Cabello lamented that increasing troop strength in punitive campaigns could never exceed one hundred men. Going after various hostiles, campaigns were generally unsuccessful since the enemy, specifically the Comanche, arrived in small parties and then split up. Jockeying to evade detection, they headed for hilly areas where virtually all the presidial horses lost their footing. Similarly, after committing hostilities the Karankawa, a group established on the northern Gulf coast, fled in small boats to their settlements. In hot pursuit to the beach, the troops witnessed the Karankawa mode of escape, using large canoes easily accessible. With the chase effectively thwarted, the soldiers gave up.[22]

Given these and other challenges to favorable military performance, Cabello, from a sensible perspective, spelled out to his commander various failed retaliatory strategies. Throughout the tense years 1782 to 1785, his monthly reports from Béxar bluntly registered his desperation about inadequate troop numbers. Indeed, the most compelling part of Cabello's argument in defense of short-term campaigns by Texas *presidiales* was his assertion that it was more appropriate for his men to sweep around the outskirts of the immediate locale rather than planning campaigns too far in advance. His alféreces Amangual and Valdés did so many times. His rationale was practical and sounded familiar, if not repetitive: with few remaining troops left at the presidio, there would be no soldiers to relieve the guard or the horse herd detachment, let alone men with which to form convoy service for the mail pouch. The lack of neighboring settlements at both Béxar and La Bahía put the troops and their ability to provide even the slightest assistance to each other at great disadvantage. Given not only its distance but also its being under the command of a different governor, the presidio at San Juan de Bautista del Río Grande presented the greatest challenge for the Texas troops' front-line response.[23] Where it concerned Amangual and Valdés, it is clear Cabello could routinely depend on these two men to carry out orders with competence. Whether they knew it or not, having the good will and trust of Cabello at this point in their careers must have buoyed the morale of both men as they negotiated not only the military pecking order but also the very real challenges of service in the borderlands.

"The Detachment Cannot Be Effective and I Will Not Be Responsible"

Opinions about soldiers seesawed among those with the authority to effect change and determine the course of careers and, as we have seen, ulterior motives and conciliatory measures impacted those decisions. In some instances, preferential treatment of soldiers may have occurred because of ancestral notoriety or military standing of one's parental lineage. Doubtless this was the case of the young cadet and *volante* candidate José de Herrera Britdale noted in chapter 1.[24] Factoring out special favors, nepotism, and familial bias, it is conceivable that assigning troops to offensive

Chapter Three

campaigns while accommodating a superior's orders placed commanders at high risk when it involved making decisions to ensure troop safety and presidio security. This was evident in the Cabello–Rengel dispute about the duration of campaigns by Texas presidials. Apart from the established hierarchy of the army's ranking system, strained interactions with higher-ups compelled presidio commanders to invoke their military acumen for determining what was best for the local environment. This had the other effect of military leaders devising strategies to either acquiesce to or refute orders from above.

Much of this situational strategizing proved decisive for presidio captains chiefly in Texas and it involved maintaining respect, at least outwardly, for a commander's seniority while being adamant about treacherous matters at hand. One familiar scenario emerged in August 1791 when Capt. Juan Cortés unequivocally declared that he would have no personal responsibility for the anticipated disastrous results that might come to pass if he gave up troops. When Gov. Manuel Muñoz ordered the transfer of twenty-five troops from Presidio La Bahía to a site called Paso de los Caballos, the move was intended to engage the Apache. Cortés balked. As he documented the interaction, he was appropriately respectful toward Muñoz, even acknowledging the wisdom of the governor's strategy. If we are to believe his words, Cortés understood Muñoz's order as one aimed at providing the best service to the king and to the welfare of the empire's subjects.[25]

Nevertheless, like Cabello in his earlier exchanges with both General Rengel and Inspector Neve, Cortés held firm in his belief that fulfilling the governor's order would jeopardize the force left to protect the garrison under his command. Surely, he planted his tongue firmly in cheek when he asked Muñoz to specify what strength in numbers the horse-herd detachment would have left once his soldiers transferred out; how many troops would then form the security guard of the presidio; and with what would the company respond, given the multiple incidents likely to occur after the troops departed for Paso de los Caballos. Cortés was unambiguous in declaring that a loss of twenty-five soldiers, even if only temporary, could be potentially catastrophic. He spelled it out this way: his remnant force could not be effective at their current numbers. He went further, insisting that the detachment would not leave until Governor Muñoz detailed assignments for the Bahía presidio.[26] No doubt Cortés knew no answers would be forthcoming from Muñoz.

By contesting his superior's directives in a way that pointedly conveyed his trepidation about fulfilling the request, Captain Cortés showed his lack of confidence in Governor Muñoz's proposed detachment of Bahía troops

Reglamento of 1772, Strategies, and Slander   85

for a maneuver that, fundamentally, left vulnerable the fort back home. In the end, Cortés' nervy counterargument achieved its goal. The governor offered an alternative that upheld *his* plan's "reasonable aim" of reinforcing the troops in a campaign and other operations that he considered indispensable against adversaries who sought to attack his jurisdiction. However, acknowledging the validity of the looming crisis Cortés saw coming, Muñoz cancelled his orders regarding the Bahía detachment. Thereupon he made other plans to punish the indigenous troublemakers in their own territory and *rancherías*.[27]

Cabello's wrangling with Rengel concerning Paso del los Caballos can be broadly conceptualized as a contrast of principle and practicality. Here was a soldier who clearly had no hesitation about conveying to his superior the crux of his argument about the defense of each of the presidios under his command and even those beyond his purview. Similarly, the Cortés–Muñoz exchange provides yet another glimpse into the complex relationships forged in the colonial garrisons during times of conflict and in an atmosphere of apprehension about potentially deadly conditions. The surviving documentation of military life allows scholars to explore aspects of soldiers' identities across the professional hierarchy of the frontier army. What makes the archive of presidio interactions such compelling commentary are the methods by which individual commanders strategized the work of the armed forces and how those processes shaped the entangled realities of life and career for their subordinates. Though fragmentary, filtered, and viewed from the perspective of assorted witnesses, the borderlands army's official observations are critical to understanding the complex social milieu that surfaced within the garrison's workaday ecosystem.

In this context the medium of documenting and categorizing the combat experience of individual soldiers by those higher up the pecking order contributed to a unique form of literature found not only in the military service records but also in the requisite monthly reports authored by presidio commanders about each garrison. Official army reportage allowed for no more than a truncated narrative featuring the actors and events deemed most significant by those in charge. Among the extant fragments of soldier work history within routine paperwork is the recording of personal qualities considered indispensable for service to the king, troop movements during campaigns, reconnaissance sorties, and escort duty. The irony here is that each commander's subjective remarks about individual troop encounters with civilian populations and civic administrators reveal as much about the reviewer as they do about the soldiers profiled in the military service records.

Hojas de Servicio: Military Service Records and Formatting the Borderlands Soldier

Much of what little we know about the identities of borderlands armed forces personnel stems from the military service records (*hojas de servicio*) of each soldier within a company or squadron. The formatting of the one-page, often preprinted template that functioned as a soldier's work history gives the individual's name and age and lists their *pais*, or place of birth. The record attempts to clarify social status by use of the term "*calidad*," and in most cases this information equates to ethnic composition. But whether self-identified by the soldier or described with veracity or inaccuracy by the commanding officer, ethnic admixture is still uncertain. Finally, the condition of their health (*salud*) with rare exception shows up as "*robusta*."[28] The heading of each template specifies the "services and circumstances" of each soldier with formatting that includes the initial date of the soldier's service and his job, or rank, when he first enlisted. What follows is a chronological record of quantitative data registered by the years, months, and days of each soldier's tenure in successive companies, activity that demonstrates across time an ascension in rank. All service records culminate in a running calculation of time served in the military and up to the end of the year profiled.[29] Directly beneath the tally of each soldier's service the form then shows the regiment and company in which the soldier served, followed by his participation in campaigns and military operations or acts of war. This section of the service record provides the most obvious shift in the template's strict formatting of vital information.

Thereafter, the documents show the most personalized aspects of individual career summaries, which, although truncated and narrowly focused, highlight each soldier's accomplishments on the battlefield. Moreover, this largest section of the service record plays up engagements with various indigenous groups. In the Comandancia General, commanders attempted with uneven success to develop an offensive strategy for securing the presidial line's fitful impenetrability. To that end, soldiers came into frequent contact with numerous Indian nations, including Comanche, Apache, and others. Under orders from various officials, the killing and capturing of the Ndé (Apache), especially women and children, and the recovery of horses are conspicuous in the service records.

Finally, in the lower right-hand corner of the template appear the handwritten notes of the presidio captain or an inspector that uncover intriguing insights about each soldier. It is safe to say that the importance of substantiating military performance within the four corners of a one-page official instrument of the colonial army required sensitivity and perception,

Reglamento of 1772, Strategies, and Slander   87

although personal biases almost certainly shaped commanders' impressions. Gathering and disseminating qualitative summaries in authorized documentation make public individual soldiers' identities, behavioral tendencies, and social statuses.[30] Like pages torn from a roster of actors without faces, the martial exploits of the king's frontier corps fill the constricted space of the service record's rigid formatting. Within this context a range of modest biographies emerges, and what follows here are a few representative pages of this type of archive with an emphasis on several men appearing in this book.

One of the older soldiers already discussed in this study, First Sgt. Mariano Rodríguez, was fifty-seven years old at the time of his report, had his country of origin listed as the "presidio de Béxar," his status as "honrrada," and his health described as good. As far as his service, the record states: he served in the cavalry company of the presidio of San Antonio de Béxar for thirty-three years and had also served in an unspecified *compañía volante* until December 1797. Rodríguez participated in engagements that cost forty-two Comanche their lives, with two taken by Rodríguez himself, and the capture of 119 horses, leaving few dead animals ("*despojos*"). However, under the notes of the inspector, unidentified in the report, the following sentence appears: "*deve correxirle y si no se le separará.*" In describing his valor, only one word is written: *tiene*. And, perhaps making plain the reason behind the admonition to any future superior reading the remarks about Rodríguez, his conduct is described as "bad."[31]

After thirty-three years as a cavalryman with one of the flying squadrons and, more significantly, as a *cuera* first sergeant stationed at the largest presidio in Texas, it seems doubtful that Rodríguez would have been unfamiliar with the burdens of his rank. In fact, the Regulations of 1772 prescribe responsibilities that included knowing "from memory" all the duties of the soldiers and corporals, and curbing noncompliance such as "prohibited conversations" and incidents leading to disobedience.[32] But something bent Rodríguez toward resisting authority. As we shall see, events in February of 1792 proclaim that his tenure as a career soldier entailed infighting with his colleagues and unmitigated disorder that prompted legal action from his superior Francisco Amangual and others.

Another veteran soldier discussed in later chapters, Second Lt. Don Manuel Menchaca, forty-two years old, from Monclova, whose status is listed as "honrrada" and his health described as "robust," served for over twenty-five years and was a member of the "[Compañía] Volante de Santiago del Saltillo." Menchaca cantoned at the presidio of Monclova and, subsequently, at Béxar where he, too, worked alongside Amangual. There he continued his service, won election as paymaster, and was eventually

88   Chapter Three

promoted to first alférez. He participated in seven campaigns, the last one on orders from Lt. Col. Miguel José de Emparán, governor of Coahuila, where he participated in five engagements with the enemies and various "*mariscadas*" in their pursuit.[33]

First Alférez José Gervacio de Silva, forty-seven years old, from Querétaro, who shared the same status—*honrrada*—as Second Lieutenant Menchaca, served twenty-six years in both the provincial cavalry of Querétaro and as a sergeant in the *compañía volante* of "Nuevo Reyno" de León. Thereafter, he continued with the flying squadron of San Juan Bautista de Lampazos until he gained promotion to alférez of Presidio Béxar where he served over four years. He participated in various pursuits of enemy Indians, capturing two and retrieving ten sheep. The Inspector described his valor as "it shows," and, under notes de Silva is described as a "regular officer of the company."[34] During his long career de Silva will also assume the role of paymaster.

Second Lt. Juan de Urrutia, twenty-six years old, from Sevilla, had his status listed as "hidalgo"[35] and his health described as robust. He served as a cadet from July 25, 1789, for over six years and as second lieutenant for only twenty-one days, for a total of six years, ten months, and ten days. Urrutia served in the cavalry of the Presidio del Príncipe (active 1778 to 1804)[36] as a cadet, and in the Fourth Flying Squadron as a second lieutenant. As of December 1795, he saw action in nine campaigns and six *correrías* (forays) in which he killed eighteen Natives, both males and females, took prisoners and horses, and accomplished all of this with "valor."[37]

The 1796 military service record of Lt. Miguel Meza, from "the town of Babonoyaba" (Chihuahua), records his status as "Spanish," his health "robust," and forty-five years old with twenty-five years of service. His career began on August 1, 1770, steadily ascending the ranks as a corporal, sergeant and, finally, as lieutenant. Throughout his military career, he served in the Second and Fourth flying squadrons of Nueva Vizcaya, and in campaigns and various *corredurías*[38] in which he took several prisoners, three captives, and many horses. He distinguished himself in combat by sustaining an attack with twenty men against sixty of the enemy, presumably Indians, and killing one of them.[39] Meza crops up again in an inspection review conducted by Antonio Cordero in July 1793 when he served as second lieutenant in the Fourth Compañía Volante of Nueva Vizcaya. Cordero described him as having proven bravery and good performance in war, but a soldier not suitable for the handling of funds.[40] Apparently, not much had changed in a decade's time. His commander at the Compañía de San Carlos de Cerrogordo, First Lt. Blas de Arramburu, doubted Mesa's "fitness to command" but he, too, noted his bravery and ability in the field.[41]

By December 1796, the forty-four-year-old Second Lt. Juan Truxillo's career spanned twenty-three years in capacities ranging from soldier, to corporal, to sergeant, and second lieutenant.[42] During that time, he served in several unspecified flying squadrons of the Army of Nueva Vizcaya. In eight campaigns and various *correedurías* he had, with his hands, killed four *gandules*[43] and one woman, and his squadron even culled quite a few *piezas*.[44] We learn that Truxillo was successful three times in battle, being quite the warrior and performing well as a fighting man. Curiously, however, a handwritten sentence appears in the lower right of the service record: "little can be expected from this officer." Given Captain Maynez's evaluation of Truxillo's bravery as "regular," his dedication as "the same," his capacity as "medium," and his conduct as "good," the report's low estimation of Truxillo is perplexing. With its single-page formatting, the military service records in all cases are out of necessity compressed. Therefore, the discrepancy in this case, with one section of the record praising the accomplishments while another section seems to negate even the possibility that Truxillo could achieve future success, adds to its peculiarity. Without further information that might illuminate such a seemingly incongruous opinion about this soldier, we must assume that his commanding officer anticipated that Officer Truxillo would retire from the force.[45]

Time and again the *hojas* evince an amalgamation of social identities and ethnic composition within the ranks of the Commandancy. Their overall content intimates a key element in intra-presidio dynamics whereby submission to authority and general compliance among the troops were expected but not consistently realized. In one document from the period, Adjutant Inspector Juan Gutiérrez de la Cueva described the daily routine of a flying squadron that he inspected in September 1790. In his summary, Gutiérrez de la Cueva made the following observation that provides an albeit narrow window into the ethnic composition of presidio society: "*everything is of good form, and the company has the agility and robustness required for this war; an exact subordination is observed* [since] *half of the troop is Spanish, and the other of various castes*."[46] Inspector Gutiérrez's remarks concerning "exact subordination" strongly suggests that a routine by-product of the squadron's Spanish composition among the officer class, and a larger presence of various castes filling the lower ranks of the company, was strict compliance based less on rank and more on adherence to New Spain's systemic social hierarchical divisions.

According to Juan Marchena Fernández, a "tremendous gulf" existed between the officer corps and the regular troops due to the Crown's exportation of military leaders from the Peninsula destined for the Indies. These men, ambitious without end, predicated the possibilities for augmenting

Chapter Three

their diminished economic position on continually justifying their noble origins, lineage, and high birth. For their part, native-born (criollo) men, in need of social recognition otherwise precluded by their lesser economic status, also turned to the army as a serviceable rung in the ladder toward upward mobility alongside the peninsulares. As much one as another used the military as an avenue for economic and social ascension, with the troops as a "huge force that made everything possible."[47]

Documentation in its entirety, by way of terse service records and official correspondence, expressed the pattern and practice of relationships forged between superiors and subordinates. Unfolding as a singular brand of literature, presidio history serves as a point of entry for understanding military operations in the frontier. But words on paper told only part of the story of soldier readiness for irregular warfare.

Superiors, Subordinates, and Shortcomings

As a first step toward fulfilling military obligations, natural aptitude and basic preparedness for action varied widely among the troops. Though the process had its flaws, composing the military records allowed commanders to assess each individual soldier's comportment and attitude toward their chores, the two characteristics intertwined to reflect a soldier's response to instruction and drills. The Regulations of 1729 and 1772 specifically addressed soldier discipline and training in *números* 27–72 of 1729, and Title Seven, Article 1 of the 1772 Regulation. But indoctrination in all things military aided each soldier but only to the extent where, for example, the utmost skill and accuracy in shooting became obvious. Put simply, success at intimidating the enemy hinged on marksmanship. Another crucial factor related to tactical prowess was the judicious use of provisions, necessary for troops working in the frugal edges of the empire. Stepping slightly back in time, in 1729 six pounds of gunpowder—reduced to three in 1772 and distributed in cartridges with bullets—constituted the presidio soldier's yearly dispensation. His target practice in 1729 had to be conducted in the presence of the company's captain, officers, and others, but not at the expense of leaving the presidio and its precinct unguarded.[48]

By June 1777 Inspector *General* José de Rubio found it necessary to remind Texas governor Juan de Ripperdá of the useful effect of shooting exercises to prepare soldiers for the functions of war. Rubio knew that expertise depended on the men being well instructed in loading and aiming their weapons quickly and correctly. Allegedly, target practice at two Texas presidios had been ignored as had the stipulation in the *Reglamento* of 1772 pertaining to its importance and value to the borderlands troops. Rubio

Reglamento of 1772, Strategies, and Slander 91

further advised Ripperdá that the gun powder annually apportioned for each military post and its auxiliaries was intended for practice so that the "advancement" of the troops might continue.[49]

Official pronouncements and systemic stinginess aside, not long after he sent his letter Rubio felt compelled to contact Governor Ripperdá, yet again, with a reminder to engage the troops in target practice. Likewise, Rubio instructed Ripperdá to encourage the same routine for the soldiers at Presidio La Bahía del Espíritu Santo. This second communication is striking in two ways. First, Rubio adopted a far more solicitous tone with Ripperdá, assuring the governor that his admonitions of enforcing target practice were not to cast aspersions on Ripperdá's efficacy as the garrison's captain. Offering up conciliation, Rubio indicated his future directives would not duplicate the first letter's rather presumptive approach. Second, Rubio made plain not only that he valued the governor as a military leader but also that he wanted to prove that his "affection and sincere friendship" were just that.[50] What the inspector general alluded to by way of mutual respect between the two men was a quality esteemed by Rubio and that Ripperdá had demonstrated thus far: dedication to duty.

That same faithfulness to military obligations extended to the certainty that Rubio must have felt when he codified methods for weapons training of the presidial and flying companies. Only two months after the nuanced exchange between Rubio and Ripperdá, the importance of target practice and specific, achievable goals reached by repetition emerged in a twelve-page instruction that included remarks on the "school of marksmanship." Whether or not Rubio felt that Governor Ripperdá could drill his men in the use of arms is suspect, and the commander's directions are obvious if not condescending. For example, in Rubio's document the soldiers are reminded to direct their aim to the middle of the target so that the impulse of the bullet, forced by ignited gunpowder to propel either up or down a line of fire, could hit the right spot. To that end, the troops were to always be careful and become familiar with the sound of gunfire to prevent any suspicious perceptions (*aprehensiones recelosas*) that might cause them to turn their heads and alter their firing position. Rubio cautioned the troops under his command that anxiety could induce misunderstanding about how a bullet always moved forward and its trajectory was impossible to change.[51] In this and other official correspondence, the inspector projects a paternal demeanor, enumerating the key points of his orders as a caring father or uncle might do toward adolescents in need of guidance. This same heedful approach typically emerges in Rubio's documented exchanges with high-ranking personnel, but with Ripperdá it may have manifested as something far more sardonic.

Chapter Three

As we will see throughout this study, adherence to regimentation had the potential to temper the thornier dimensions of military life. Or so the constant stream of ordinances and regulations would suggest, and commanders would have their soldiers take to heart. Conversely, the neglect of elemental military imperatives, like order, discipline, and conformity, had severe consequences for not only the rank and file but also for commanders.

One particularly devastating example of the negative effects of troop disorganization and noncompliance occurred during the late summer of 1775. Prompted by a misstep in strategy, Viceroy Bucareli bypassed Rubio and took it upon himself to scold Governor Ripperdá because of the lack of discipline among the Texas troops. Proof came in the form of an event that cost the lives of several soldiers at the hands of Natives duty-bound to seize an opportunity where they found it. Having received a damning report from then–*comandante general* Croix, Bucareli found out that troops had disregarded fundamental precautions and failed to obey the regulations. What made the event, and its aftermath, even more appalling was the stark reality that the Comanche had fewer fighters than the presidials but caused great losses among the frontier forces. Bucareli believed two reasons contributed to the debacle: first, the troops had not received proper training and lacked discipline. Second, the Natives had firearms ("armas de fuego"), a fact recalling the viceroy's echoing that official orders had been issued to prohibit trading between Texas and Louisiana. Had Béxar's troops followed those orders, Bucareli argued, and if peaceful Indians had been barred from the presidio, the Comanche might have been defeated. During the attack, the Comanche were successful at forcing back the presidials. He warned Ripperdá that all responsibility for further setbacks caused by perceived glitches would fall upon him.[52] Predictably defensive, but likely unmistaken, Ripperdá made it known that even after a year had passed, his soldiers still lacked useful weapons and a shortage of replacement arms existed in the presidio's supply of provisions.[53]

If he was not incompetent, it is at least possible that Ripperdá was hardheaded. As if condemnation from the viceroy was not bad enough, two years after Bucareli's reprimand even Commander Inspector Rubio found it necessary to castigate Ripperdá for the soldiers' dismal efforts in battle. Rubio placed the blame for these misfortunes on the disorder with which the troops had executed their maneuvers and in full view of the enemy. Rubio reasoned those mistakes often occurred when a more spirited soldier ("*el soldado más alentado*") moved out ahead of the company to assail the enemy, unleashing a course of conduct that caused other soldiers to scatter in great confusion. In their haste, troops did not wait for orders from the officers, sergeants, and corporals in command. Rubio cited the wholesale slaughter of the party led by Capt. Antonio Casimiro de Esparza; the "enemigos" took advantage of the presidials' lack of cohesion and proceeded to pick off the soldiers one by one. According to the reports, their bodies were scattered at considerable distance from each other, implying that throughout the ordeal pandemonium doomed the men.[54]

Rubio's solution was to issue an order on April 24, 1778, to all the commanders of the presidios at San Elezario, Príncipe, El Norte, San Carlos, San Sabá, Babia, Monclova, Agua Verde, Río Grande, Béxar, and Bahía del Espíritu Santo, locations that he or his scribe listed in the margin of the document. Commanders were to counteract the disorder witnessed in the Esparza debacle. Further, they were to inform all troops that if any sergeant, corporal, or soldier should advance without orders from a superior to whom he was subject, that individual was to be punished for serious insubordination. The "blindest obedience" to superiors, dictated in the Royal Regulations by the king himself, was to hold sway in all presidial interactions and during engagements with enemies in the field. Ripperdá certified his receipt and thus his knowledge of Rubio's order on June 26, 1778, and, presumably, his were the last hands to receive acknowledgment from all other commanders. It is likely that he would have then forwarded the final comprehensive document to the *comandante inspector*.[55] It is no coincidence that the Esparza tragedy figured into a much larger resolutions package created from a notable *junta de guerra* in 1778 attended by top officials in the periphery.

In the well-documented military conference Commander General Croix assembled a bevy of familiar names from the annals of colonial borderlands history: Brig. Gen. Pedro Fermín de Mendinueta (former governor of Nuevo México), Col. Jacobo Ugarte y Loyola (governor-elect of Sonora), Lt. Col. Felipe Barri (governor of Nueva Vizcaya), governor-elect of New Mexico Juan Bautista de Anza, and Pedro Galindo y Navarro, the auditor general of the Commandancy at the first Council of War. Capt. Antonio Bonilla, as assistant inspector of Presidios, served as the Council's secretary with documents bearing instructions for the meeting.[56] Since Croix had reports describing the Provincias Internas as deplorable, he focused his discussion first on the most distant ones, Coahuila and Texas, where he had previously held *juntas* with Galindo y Navarro in attendance. Seated at the conference in order of rank and seniority the voting members submitted their opinions, and the majority determined the Junta's resolutions. The minutes of the previous two juntas were read, as well as reports from Lt. Athanasio de Mézières, governor of Fort Nachitoches, and that of Texas governor Ripperdá. Over the next two days, in the villa of Chihuahua the second junta transpired, and former governor of Sonora Colonel Francisco

94   Chapter Three

Crespo and the Intendant Gov. Pedro Corbalán submitted reports from that province. Croix's previous report from November 20, 1777, was read as well to provide information that would leave the attendees sufficiently instructed in the regional historical context. The conclusion reached at this third council was indisputable. As "declared enemies," the Apache had successfully waged war over the course of forty years without interruption and, adding urgency to the matter, with even "incomparably greater" gains in just the previous five years.[57]

Bonilla's notes are dispositive of the commanders' unified concerns and show that the placement of the presidios on the present frontier line occasioned the greatest damage. Enduring losses might have been avoided had the presidio line of separation entailed shorter distances from the settlements since many of the outposts were situated on lands with little water or pasture. In short, the presidios were few and far between (*raro*) from where the founding of a settlement was critical and convenient. Once moved at distances of more than 150 leagues from the settlements, both presidio and settlement were unprotected from continuous assaults by the Apache. Victories bolstered their audacity, pride, and daring and made them experts in the operations of war. In fact, Secretary Bonilla documented the provinces' suffering in war as "harder and bloodier" than that of previous years. Spanish deaths were squarely attributed to Apache attacks, the spoils of which included the captivity of children of both sexes who, consequently, became members of the nation. The council even speculated that kidnapped children were the ones who did "the greatest harm" to Spaniards and their military forces.[58] We must assume this meant once the separated youngsters were old enough to fight, to acquire skill with weapons, and after thorough inculcation with Apache ethos and identity.

The council attempted to estimate the Apache population and its associated tribes—the Lipan (upper and lower), Mescalero, Natage, Lipillanes, Faraon, Navajo (*Diné*), and Gileño—but Mendinueta and Bautista de Anza both believed it exceeded five thousand men. Those disparities caused a measure of discord among the voting members. Compounding their concerns was that both men were also convinced that to this an equal number of women had to be added since, even if they did not wage war in the same manner as men and despite whatever action the Apache undertook, women formed a de facto reserve corp. In battle strategy, they did their part by scattering the horse herd while the men attacked the troops. New Mexico's two representatives believed that even when women were of no other use except to amplify the bulk of the parties, the enemy managed to intensify their objective: making themselves feared exponentially more by their adversaries. To the thinking of Spanish commanders like Mendinueta and

Reglamento of 1772, Strategies, and Slander   95

De Anza, that enterprise was a "well-founded idea."[59] This is not to say that the Apache had no avowed enemies.

To the east, the Ndé counted the "Tavoayaze" Indians and the Nations of the North as their unappeasable foes, a conclusion shared by both councils. Added to that number, the Apache had the Comanche as bitter opponents whom they feared because of their cruelty in war tactics. Brigadier Mendinueta noted the Utes had always been friends with the Gileños and Navajos until 1775. Crediting his own trickery (*"maña"*), Mendinueta had convinced the Ute people to wage war on the latter two groups. He did so because he was certain that if all three nations united, the province of New Mexico would be irrefutably lost. Eventually the Ute made peace with the Navajo and even maintained it. But their movements had constantly to be scrutinized since Mendinueta's experience taught him that any trust offered by all three tribes was negligible given the Native populations' persistent disloyalty. Thus, the voting members resolved that in none of the provinces could the Apache be peacefully admitted since their friendship always produced "dismal effects." Experience proved it so and especially in recent events implicating the Gileños. Under the guise of friendship, they showed up at the presidios of Janos and San "Elicario" and at the settlements of El Paso and Albuquerque.[60] Even voicing their expectation of gifts appeared suspicious.

Doubts concerning the reliability of peace by purchase as a preemptive strike seemed to be well founded. Consensus held that the process of appeasement turned out to be a "fruitless waste of money," given the serious damage committed at the very places the Indians sued for peace, a clear reference to garrisons and settlements. Further, when their numbers diminished or when demoralized by events detrimental to success, the Apache in their various manifestations would then feign peace or a desire for reduction. Forbidden to grant a truce to the Apache not already established and secure, any yielding on the part of the troops and their commanders might be interpreted as weakness and, accordingly, a harder stance prevailed. War against all Apache tribes was to continue. For all that, pursuit of the Lipan halted until the army could overcome that other unremitting hurdle: there had to be enough troops in the province to execute the operations of war. The council considered very urgent an escalation of forces to keep the Lipan, the "right arm of the Apache realm," from quickly bringing about the ruin of the provinces.[61]

Aside from the Apache threat, a scarcity of troops continued to plague the borderlands throughout the late eighteenth century. Worsening the predicament, desertion from the ranks among garrisons in Coahuila–Texas did nothing but undermine most conclusions reached by the various juntas.

96 Chapter Three

The blind obedience called for in the 1772 *Reglamento* was hardly a part of the grindstone calculus for any soldier who saw flight from the army as a better choice overall. As a rule, mass desertions from the presidios were uncommon. Imperial officials in Madrid, including the king himself, knew that applying measures to arrest deserters was a difficult if not pointless task. In 1726, an *ordenanza* from five years earlier regarding desertion was reissued to address the growing problem among the troops.[62] In light of that sobering reality, it was unforeseen that five decades later concessions again had to be made. *Visitador* Gálvez received an order to publish an *yndulto* in the king's name that would, incredibly, benefit deserters who returned to their respective garrisons and completed the required service in their regiments for six years.[63] So desperate were staffing conditions in the borderlands that the king was clearly willing to overlook infractions of a serious nature and even allow incentives for return to duty by defectors. Defensive hurdles, like insubstantial evidence of dereliction or commanders arguing for rehabilitation of wayward soldiers, impeded a direct route to condemnation. Therefore, punishment occasionally gave way to leniency for a presumed fugitive.

Private Méndez Goes to Church

In one instance, the military inspector of Béxar and Coahuila Luis Cazorla requested clemency for an exceptionally despondent soldier. In April 1779, while taking refuge in the church located at Presidio La Bahía, Pvt. Manuel Méndez was summoned to surrender by then-commander Lt. José Menchaca and, later, by Cmdr. Eugenio Fernández. The sad truth was that since August 1778 Méndez had alternated between incarceration and asylum, the latter by order of the commander at that time. Having heard a rumor that superiors sought a replacement to complete his term of enlistment and that the resultant credit for his service-to-date was to be rescinded, a dejected Méndez emerged and acknowledged his offense. He made known the misdeed attributed to him by his immediate supervisor was insubordination.[64]

According to the beleaguered soldier, he suffered bodily injury from a sword attack by Joseph González, the acting corporal who held rank over Méndez. The latter claimed that he thought Corporal Gonzáles was joking since the two were friends and that, after the alleged attack, they even sat down together to have dinner. At least, that was his version of the truth. Nevertheless, Méndez felt compelled to flee from what he perceived to be unwarranted punishment from the corporal. With that, Gonzáles further imposed his irregular authority over the wounded soldier by declaring

Méndez a prisoner. He then sent word to his superiors, where presidials took Méndez into custody and put him in shackles.[65]

Inspector Cazorla received notice of these matters by Lieutenant Menchaca and Alférez José Aguilar, both of whom verified that Méndez sat imprisoned in the mission for insubordination toward Corporal Gonzáles. However, Cazorla expressed incredulity to General Croix that Méndez withstood such severe punishment, the trio of superiors having thrown the book (*"le echavan toda la ley"*) at the troubled soldier. Further, Inspector Cazorla believed that there was no justification for "one who commands"— in this case, the acting corporal—to be horse-playing with a subordinate nor to impose punishment at the first disagreeable word. Inflexible about his own reputation as a compliant officer, Cazorla insisted to Croix that during his tenure as captain he had maintained the highest degree of discipline within the Bahía company. However, Cazorla had noticed an atmosphere of gradual deterioration at that garrison due to what he suspected was a lack of discretion by those now in command. As its former leader, Cazorla regretted the dramatic backsliding by troops given his expenditure of so much effort putting the company on solid footing at the time of his departure.[66]

In his petition to Croix, Cazorla confirmed the abused soldier was now in his care, and that he was keeping him at his own expense and out of pure charity. This was not surprising given his unflagging empathy with his men, and Mendez's dilemma was no case of malingering. Cognizant of the system-wide dearth of manpower, Cazorla's ultimate request was for Croix to pardon Méndez and order him back into service; he believed doing so would benefit the royal service.[67] However, as it will soon be evident, Cazorla may have had another objective besides magnanimity for preserving enlistments, especially when doing so might prove beneficial if personal financial gain was within reach.

By the summer of that same year, Méndez presented himself at Santa Rosa, which prompted Croix to order Governor Cabello to resolve the matter.[68] Unable to commit one way or the other, Cabello responded that Cazorla had apprised him of the situation, but that the latter had sent Croix the *causa* concerning Méndez. Taking advantage of a way out, Cabello would not form an opinion and make a final determination of the matter. Toying with insubordination, Cabello's dodgy stance meant the commander general now held responsibility for the private's fate.

Ever the conciliator, or perhaps fearful of retribution, Cabello capitulated. He asked Croix to have the *causa* forwarded to him and if that was not possible, Cabello would nevertheless take testimony and decide the matter as Croix so commanded.[69] Eventually, Croix ruled that the royal *yndulto* of 1776 would apply to Méndez on two charges of misconduct: as a deserter and by insubordination to his commander Corporal González. As if that were not enough consolation, Croix granted clemency to the beleaguered private by allowing him to both continue serving the period of his enlistment without any objection and to retain intact his years of service.[70] Without further information, we must assume that Cabello adhered to the commander general's directive and that Méndez completed his enlistment term. Perhaps, because of Cazorla's kindness and Croix's empathy (or unvarnished practicality), Private Méndez acquired a certain amount of emotional stability that had for some time eluded him during his career. For its part and at least for now, the empire hung on to one more man to bear arms.

He was not the first deserter, nor would he be the last. The 1776 royal pardon for desertion by lower-ranking soldiers like Manuel Méndez and the subsequent doctrine of penalties for desertion by officers clarified imperial decisions concerning acts of insubordination by individual wrongdoers. Whether still potent or now perfunctory, the intent of the Regulations of 1772 was to cast a long shadow over garrison interactions and generally define the boundaries by which soldier discontent and dereliction could reach resolution. One intriguing part of its content encouraged subaltern officers to assist the presidio's captain in cementing order and control, by stating, "[Besides the] principle of subordination to their superiors and the exact observance of how much is instructed in my ordinances and established thus with what is mandated by their chiefs, it is also the obligation of these officers to contribute inasmuch as it is on their part to the completion of the captain's orders and in his absence, they will take care of the company left in their command with the same responsibility and diligence. Furthermore, they must know by memory that which is provided in this regulation and in the penal laws in order to punctually observe and enforce them."[71]

Stringent adherence to military governance had some palpable benefits for borderlands soldiers. In documents to Governor Ripperdá, Inspector Rubio mandated policies to award military men for bravery and patriotism while acknowledging Ripperdá's expertise in warfare. Rubio had fair intentions (*"justo mira"*) as he urged troops of the *Provincias Internas* toward acceptance of and compliance with their respective obligations by observing the rules of subordination called for in the king's *ordenanzas* for the army. Conformity might lead to favorable opportunities during their service. By projecting his own reflections onto mandates issued from the Peninsula, Rubio hoped that those musings would not merely hover in theory but instead harden into practice. And if his deliberations became public knowledge among military personnel across the borderlands, then all the better. Appealing to his troops' presumed avidity for military acclaim by addressing only subalterns and soldiers in the presidios and those riding with the flying squadrons, Rubio made an overt reference to forces overseas. He exhorted "all good warriors" to honorably emulate the acquisition of glory that had made famous the armies of Europe.[72] His assumptions about his men and the combatants they faced in the Far North seem astonishing for an experienced commander. Even if the Comandancia's soldiers had Continental experience with guerrilla hostilities, fighting Native people here in the frontier was an entirely different affair.

Notwithstanding that harsh reality, officers had to impress upon their soldiers that both respect and subordination were achievable by strict adherence to the rule of law. Military men were to exercise perseverance, blind obedience, and "unimpeachable honor" while in service, whether in command or commanded by others. Convinced his aspirational goals were shared widely, Rubio argued that an illustrious military career induced those who professed a desire for it to find glory alongside other noble, ambitious men. He believed soldiers could advertise those qualities in no better place than in the very public operations of a campaign. In that contested space valor, talent, and skill were crucial for engaging the enemy and for avoiding all confusion in the field.[73]

At the same time, Rubio was clearly aware of some soldiers' disenchantment with active duty. He admonished Ripperdá to discourage conversations among the troops that in any way discredited the militia, whose numbers included veteran soldiers endowed with honor and great pride (*blasozón*).[74] Given his own lengthy career in the army, his experiences with deserters, and his fatherly disposition, one senses that Rubio had a keen understanding of the soldiers' occasional immaturity and inclination to gossip. But by upholding the personal qualities of conduct and valor as decreed in 1772, servicemen would gain the attention of Rubio through in-person monthly reviews of the presidio and its personnel.[75] In turn, he could then recommend select soldiers to the *Comandante General* Croix, a military man "supremely fond of justice, equity, and good men," and who would subsequently pass this insight on to the king. Situated at the apex of the chain of leadership, it was Carlos III who had the ultimate authority to dole out rewards to the troops.[76]

Whereas the Royal Regulations mandated monthly reviews by presidio captains of their company, it was the commander inspector or his assistants taking on yearly appraisals of the presidios. The inspector assessed the conduct and reputation of the officers and reported his findings to the viceroy. He took note not only of the companies in their entirety but also the quality and aptitude of the soldiers, the condition of their weapons, their conservation of gunpowder, and the dexterity of soldiers and Indian auxiliaries in handling arms and horses. Given the Crown's obsession with any depletion of the royal coffers, the handling of finances was under constant scrutiny. Not surprisingly, troop irresponsibility with money surfaced as it had before and would continue to do so as it did in June 1777 involving a *compañía volante* in Texas. Inspector Rubio reviewed the Third Flying Squadron and informed Governor Ripperdá that despite some of its soldiers having accrued large balances, there were enough funds to pay them in cash. Rubio suggested that if most men had excessive balances verified by computations formalized through December 1776, solving the issue would mean docking their pay by a small percentage every month. Thus, the accumulated interest could be repaid. Ever the realist, Rubio was quick to add as "indisputable proof" that soldiers who responsibly managed their accounts could still not endure with their salaries alone whatever charges they accumulated.[77]

Given the perennial fiscal hurdles that figured into royal service, monies earned by soldiers to care for their families with some measure of ease also came with a certain amount of anxiety. Coaxed by Rubio to a plan that might put the company in a state of equilibrium, Ripperdá was to follow certain procedures based on efficient governance, enthusiasm, and the reputation (*crédito*) of the officers. Using ample tact toward this occasionally fitful officer, Rubio requested punctual observance of these steps. He encouraged Ripperdá to take prudent measures so that during the next inspection he would find the soldiers well maintained and free of debts that could not be repaid.[78] Two months later came Rubio's ten-page instructions aimed at improving the internal management of all presidial and flying companies. Attentive to frontier realities but tuned in to personal sensitivities, Rubio ordered Ripperdá to distribute certified copies to every one of his subaltern officers. The expectation was that the governor-captain would get compliance from his subordinates. Further, Rubio insisted that, in favor of achieving the best possible result from his instructions, Ripperdá was to immediately put content into practice and get due diligence from his men's strict adherence to the new policies. Soldiers who failed to comply were to receive serious reprimands for their disregard of the mandates.[79] Those who excelled in the performance of their duties could ascend the military ranking system by promotion, provided all other obligations were strictly carried out as decreed in Rubio's instructions.[80]

Even so, the practical concerns of defense in the use of arms and the deployment of innovative battlefield technique did not constitute the highest priorities enumerated by the Inspector in this remarkable document. So important to Rubio were the fiscal concerns of the presidial and flying companies and their respective paymasters that he made them the focal point of his instructions. As straightforward in his approach as an unyielding parent, Rubio simplified the matter: for servicemen to get a positive critique from an official inspection, they had to pay special attention to the *economic* interests of the government. To that end, soldiers were to be vigilant about preventing anything that might short-circuit the "well founded" precautionary measures implemented by the paymaster. Doing so infused honor all around, distinguished by the *habilitado*'s reliability as he managed those interests.[81] The specific reference to insulating the paymaster from disruptions by the rank and file makes clear not only the significance of the chief financial officer's tasks within the presidio but also how his responsibilities served the career interests of the troops. Rubio appears to encourage at least a tolerant if not dispassionate approach by soldiers to the company paymaster's work to mitigate their suspicions about the officer controlling their money. This may have partially stemmed from long-standing abuses over time by men unwilling to act as fiduciaries for their garrisons.

Money Management and the Soldiers

Commander inspectors like Rubio, stationed in faraway Chihuahua, held no responsibility for managing the collective funds of the presidio troops.[82] Liberated from their debauchery since captains in chorus lost the job in 1773, the obligation belonged now to elected paymasters. Title Twelve of the *Reglamento 1772* urged the commander inspector to ensure prompt receipt of soldier pay and rations. Peninsular methods of accounting and payroll shaped Rubio's decision to settle accounts at the end of each four-month period. Optics mattered, too. Anything concerning the interests of the army must be made public so troops would be well informed about their allowances and duties. The potential benefit to the paymasters was that soldiers would be less likely to allege doubt about or dispute over balances and debts.[83] Given the recurring issue of presidio bankruptcy and fraudulent transactions in the past, it is logical that the rank and file would have every reason to question the slightest discrepancy or oversight detected, or suspected, in their company paymaster's accounting practices.[84]

Scrupulous dedication to task by the paymaster would, to Rubio's mind, make it possible to supply the troops without preferential treatment given to a particular entity or individual. After all, he reasoned, soldiers had to seek out goods where they found them with relative ease.[85] Though the paymaster's duties were enumerated in the *Reglamento*, Rubio prefaced his instructions by reiterating the important task of managing company

Chapter Three

funds by the officer chosen to provision the men. Assisting the paymaster was a sergeant or a corporal, and two soldiers. Collectively, all four soldiers examined and certified the transparency and objectivity (*de la pureza,* y *desinterés*) of the process. Provisioning was expedited in a manner intended to ensure the satisfaction of all soldiers, including absentees. The expectation of full disclosure during distribution meant that once returned from their duties, soldiers would be convinced of the faithful conduct with which those responsible had managed the company's assets. The paymaster and three assistants were to receive from the provisioner a copy of the bill of sale, the entire process officiated by a responsible supervisor present at the time of the transactions.[86]

The totality of these duties was not without challenges, and Amangual's experiences prove this simple truth. The intricacies of fulfilling the paymaster's responsibilities as described in the 1772 Regulations also required the added skill of carefully negotiating soldiers' needs while upholding fiscal accountability. Withholding a substantive amount from soldiers in debt constituted a critical aspect of presidial economic affairs that had to be complied with "unalterably." To be fair, soldiers could retain monies needed for daily expenses. As Rubio made clear in his directive to Ripperdá, the reserve fund was supposed to reach the sum of one hundred pesos. In theory, six pesos were withheld in the reserve each month, and five pesos were for a soldier's personal affairs. This procedure was to continue until one hundred pesos accrued for soldiers cantoned at a presidio; in the case of those serving in the flying companies, the requisite amount was fifty pesos.[87]

As it usually does with hard copies, and especially those that show evidence of tampering, the optics of practice and procedure also mattered. Rubio stressed to Ripperdá that accounting books with various transactions had to be clear and without blots or amended items. Entries should have brief, but comprehensive, explanations to ward off any doubt, contradiction, or complaint. Full settling of the accounts was to take place in each four-month period (*quatrimestres*) and the money that each soldier received in hand would be the balance of his wages due after his debts canceled out. These cash amounts became the soldiers' own to employ at their discretion and for the well-being of their wives and family. In at least two cases from 1778, monetary care extended to children under the custody of their fathers, men stationed at various presidios.[88]

By April of the following year Rubio found it necessary, yet again, to issue another order to Ripperdá. Its content steered toward the commanders of the presidios routinely in need of soldier discipline and retraining. But he now focused on ensuring the correct rendering of fiscal accounts since

Reglamento of 1772, Strategies, and Slander

enactment of the 1772 Regulations. Officers received directives not to charge any other amounts other than those included in a document which contained purportedly fixed rules. Rubio reiterated to Ripperdá that no reasons existed for charging outlandish expenses and, furthermore, all expenses which had depleted the presidial fund were to be reinstated by reversing those expenditures to either the company or whoever was responsible for their remittance.[89] Rubio limited the expenses that could be charged against the common fund (*fondo de gratificación*) of the presidios in the following manner:

repairs of walls and balustrades, but not those of churches and houses; the latter expenses were to be met by each concerned party, and the former by the common troops and citizens by way of a work detail

Wine for mass, wax for church, and flour for the host [Eucharist]

Ornaments, sacred vessels, adornments for the altar, missals, and the holy oil

Paper for cartridges, lead for bullets, and flint

Debts of the deceased or deserters, those of the latter restored should they present themselves or be apprehended

Prisoners' rations and gifts to Friendly Indians; of this latter expense, however, with an account kept so that the amount could be restored to the fund by the treasury to which it corresponds

The light which the guard corps require [presumably for the guard-house].

The cost of the safe (*caja*) within which the fund was kept, as well as the freight costs of everything carried and charged thereto.

And, in a section called "Notes":

The anticipated cost of equipping recruits is not expressed, because of the nature of reinstatement.

The freight cost of powder should be supplied by the agency or administration from which it comes.

Ripperdá knew that each captain was to extract a certified copy of Rubio's order and his attachment. Further, the paymasters at each presidio were to comply with its instructions.[90]

From such an onslaught of correspondence, Governor Ripperdá had every reason to feel the sting of incessant policing of his administrative service.

104   **Chapter Three**

The seemingly endless notices to Ripperdá from both Commander General Croix and Commander Inspector Rubio appeared to be a calculated effort to spotlight every blunder or bureaucratic oversight made by Ripperdá during his tenure in the dual role of governor and presidio captain. A decade prior, having achieved the governorship, Ripperdá made it known to top officials at the Villa of San Fernando of his satisfaction. By dint of a letter at that time, he hoped to attain "accomplishments"—which he does not specify—for the benefit and public good of the villa. Moreover, his desire to manifest his aspirations is poignant for its sincerity if not demonstrative of his failure to identify the vaguest provisions for doing so. One might wonder whether Ripperdá's altruistic civic concerns at the inception of his governorship were still intact after interminable streams of pesky orders coupled with supervisory forewarnings and after almost nine years on the job.[91]

Dealing with the Indians: Gifts, Warfare, and Escorts

As it turned out, only a few years after his appointment Ripperdá had ample opportunity to justify his worth as a borderlands commander. Viceroy Croix's successor, Antonio María de Bucareli y Ursua, advised Ripperdá to carefully ascertain the degree of peril that antagonists presented to the territory. While waiting at Los Adaes for the arrival from Nachitoches of its Lt. Gov. Athanasio de Mézières, who was bringing multiple tribes pledging peace, Ripperdá expressed concern about potential Apache depredations. Bucareli suggested that since the governor of Texas was closest to Coahuila, a region where Apaches engaged in relentless pillaging, certain outcomes could be expected by their "treachery and barbarism." He warned Ripperdá that when conditions demanded war against the Apache in Coahuila, he would have to do so if he wanted to scare them off (*"debe ejecutarlo por si se logra escarmentarlos"*). Bucareli acknowledged the governor's discretion and knowledge of the territory, but suggested Ripperdá use as much discretion to achieve the desired effect: seeing the Apache leave the province in peace.[92] As these disparate strategies unfolded, the most recent iteration of regulations purporting equity and advantage had not yet been issued.

For a while it seemed Ripperdá's efforts panned out. During the spring of 1773, a state of precarious tranquility reigned over Texas.[93] Viceroy Bucareli received word from Ripperdá to that effect, but Bucareli found it necessary to admonish him to practice vigilance. Inasmuch as favorable reports streamed into the viceroy's offices to the degree that stable relationships with the indigenous communities in Texas continued without incident, ambivalence lingered. For instance, Bucareli cautioned that if residents of the region's settlements and missions insisted on going out to chop wood and hunt bison, Ripperdá was to grant them escorts. Nonetheless, protection by soldiers was possible only if they could do so without leaving vulnerable the presidios and adjacent territories. Without question, assigning bodyguards to civilians, or not, created tension between commanders and their superiors. Predictably, the result was diminished security at the garrisons, thereby increasing the danger to personnel.

If borderlands troops remained convinced of the duplicity of everyone Indian, the viceroy was certain that at least there was no need to fear the Karankawa escaping since he considered their character "weak and cowardly." In fact, Bucareli viewed Ripperdá's measures to apprehend the indigenous ringleaders (*cabecillas*) as wise. However, he encouraged the governor to draw others into the fold of the missionaries with leniency and cleverness, with the help of the religious orders but without the use of force. When manpower was available, punitive tactics were to be used only as a last resort.[94] The situation in Nueva Vizcaya and New Mexico was quite different. One historian describes Spanish authorities' numeric calculations from 1771–76 that told a harrowing story for that stretch of territory. Mounting losses precipitated shifts in imperial policy.[95]

Across the decades, defining the murky boundaries between estrangement and civility proved challenging for administrators. The Regulations of 1729 prohibited governors and commanders from waging war against non-baptized Indians maintained in friendship or against the neutral communities. Native inhabitants were not to be agitated but, instead, attracted to conviviality with pleasure and in a good way ("*con agrado y buen modo*") so that the affection shown to them by soldiers served as a prompt for their settlement.[96] However, by 1778, any belief on the part of the viceroy, commanders in country, or settler societies that the Karankawa were an ordinarily docile group averse to committing hostilities of any sort quickly diminished. The same commander who safeguarded the refugee Private Méndez and who would eventually appeal to Pedro de Neve to resuscitate his military career so as to earn the rank of presidio captain, Luís Cazorla, advised *Comandante General* Croix that the Karankawa had become aggressive. Unfortunately, in punitive forays Cazorla's troops had failed to operate at the highest level. Given, too, their unsuccessful reconnaissance expeditions, Indians from Misión El Rosario ran off. In their haste, they left women and children behind. Given the hardship of relocating to the San Antonio mission, it is no surprise the most vulnerable could not accompany the fugitives.[97]

Despite all that, Viceroy Bucareli's trust in Ripperdá apparently captured the attention of the commander general, too, and in a baffling move Croix ordered Ripperdá to maintain scouting expeditions by La Bahía forces.

Chapter Three

Further, while General Croix was aware that the Karankawa may very well have sought safety on the Texas coast—perhaps on Isla de Culebra[98]—he believed that the planned course of action to retrieve fugitive tribe members could be achieved with additional forces composed of inhabitants of La Bahía, the villas of Bucareli and San Fernando, and the presidio of Béxar. Once subdued, Croix instructed Ripperdá to advise him of the best location to resettle the escapees and their families. The governor's decision would in fact make little difference. Whether reunited with the women and children at the San Antonio Mission, removed completely from the province to distant sites, or reduced and then set free from San Antonio, the Karankawa would likely return to the coast.[99]

In the meantime, Croix encouraged Ripperdá to undo the new alliances forged by the Karankawa with the Orcoquiza through skill and caution (*"con maña y prudencia"*) but, with the Coco, by gentle means.[100] Conversely, the Apache and the Comanche represented a far greater strategic challenge to presidio personnel and thus Croix's very different approach to aggression by these two groups. In the eyes of the Spanish, a sure-fire tactic utilized by the Comanche was to retreat through certain sites in an attempt to fool their pursuers. A practice long in use, this kind of maneuvering served to project a false identity. The most obvious and habitually used impersonation was that of the Lipan. Upon receiving word of the death of Cayetano Travieso, attributed to the Apache, Croix discovered from official communications conveyed by de Mézières that the Comanche had in fact caused it. In response, Croix's strategy regarding defiant Indians followed Ripperdá's lead in that it was directed at both containing and punishing the Comanches with a two-punch method: by preventing a coalition between the Apache, the Tejas, and "Bidais," and by aiding the town of Bucareli with troops and munitions.[101] Ripperdá had, at least this one time, successfully won the commander general's approval for his proactive answer to enemy nuisance.

Conciliation figured into peacemaking, too. Providing gifts to the Indians was an imperial lever calibrated by local administrators in the Comandancia to maintain productive if often strained relationships with Native polities. Well before Francisco Amangual's accounting records show his presidio's regular outflow of material support to petitioners, the *Reglamento* of 1729 referenced the complex powerplay between presidials and their indigenous cohabitants. When Rivera made his inspection of the presidio of Texas in November 1727, he denounced the garrison as deserving no such honorable name since it consisted of only a few huts of sticks and grass (*"chozas de palos y zacate"*) and very poorly constructed dwellings at that.[102] Rivera condemned the soldiers there for being fooled by the Indians' docility, posting no guards or sentinels, and for doing nothing else (in the form of cautionary watchfulness) but assisting three nearby missions.[103] On the other hand, once he reached the presidio at La Bahía, Rivera noted that the surrounding Indians—"Cocos, Cancaraquases, Coapites, Cujanes, and Copanes"—were so few in number they also posed little threat to the ninety soldiers presently cantoned there. Further, Rivera believed that fifty soldiers were excessive for the Bahía presidio since the "Tacame, Araname, Mayaye, Pampopa, Pastia" and other Indian nations of the area lived in isolated *rancherías*. So convinced was Rivera that these groups were cowardly enough to pose no real trouble, he rationalized that its original forty soldiers were sufficient to garrison La Bahía.[104] But Rivera's conclusion may have only been a veiled excuse to relocate surplus troops to more vulnerable stations across the borderlands.

The passage of time reversed all of that. When the Regulations of 1772 were issued, the presidios at La Bahía and Béxar housed detachments that were expected to provide mutual aid. Since both presidios were located more than one degree of latitude outside the proposed line of defense, the king declared Béxar as the garrison most exposed to the raids of various warlike tribes of the north pursuing their abhorred enemies, the Lipan Apache.[105] Inconstant cohabitants, the most reliably menacing indigenous groups now had to be routinely appeased through a reinvigoration of peace by purchase. Transactional to the degree that its purpose must have been obvious to Native leaders, the process involved the participation of paymasters like Amangual, merchants, artisans, and consumers in a comingled exchange of goods and services. Into the mix came conspirators animating the presidio and the polities in its orbit as a dynamic hub of commerce and cultural interchange. While efforts to placate the rebellious inclinations of Native people continued, during this same period displaced soldiers had yet to receive overdue salaries and still waited for goods owed to them. Throughout the late 1770s and well into the next decade, restrictions for them seemed lopsided by comparison since they were not only barred from trading horses and armaments (even when theirs were defective) but, also, deprived at the dinner table: soldiers could not eat meat and fish at the same meal or during the same day.[106]

In fact, more than a decade after the 1772 *Reglamento*'s affirmations, gifting Native communities with all manner of provisions accelerated. From September 1786 to October 1787 utilitarian items in bulk made their way to the Indians at Béxar. For instance, the Comanche received 542 awls, 655 shaving blades, 542 knives, 53 hoes, 106 axes and hatchets, 94 pounds of wire, 37 pounds of vermilion, 53 pounds of beans, 284 pounds of bullets, 142 pounds of powder, 34 rifles, 10 staves, 7 pairs of trousers and an equal number of coats.[107] Provisioners supplied the Comanche with hundreds of *varas* of cloth, including *indiana*[108], wool, and cotton, combs, mirrors, and "worms" (gun worms or patch worms for cleaning the barrels of guns). The Lipan also acquired a good share but not the large yield collected by the Comanche. Their people got only about half as many items and sometimes even less, often only one quarter-percent of the Comanche haul and mostly clothing, tools, and dyestuffs. Other groups, including the "Tahuacanes, Tahuaias, Guichitas" (Wichitas), Orcoquizas, and the Vidais, received gifts at different times of the year.[109]

By the mid-1780s, gift-giving and customer service constituted relatively effective socio-economic practices by the Commandancy superstructure to thwart aggression. Its efficacy toward creating (co)dependence by indigenous communities upon presidial largesse proved ambivalent; it may have seemed to some troops that provisioning the empire's occasional rivals was more of a priority for commanders than doing so for the king's own frontliners.

Across the borderlands, operatives did their part to stimulate the economy while stifling combativeness. For example, on September 18, 1789, José Antonio Bustillos and the ubiquitous Andrés Benito Courbiére purchased items from Amangual at the Béxar presidio. Some of the materials were used to create clothing for indigenous visitors and are described below from an accounting of goods supplied by Amangual.[110] Undoubtedly the indigenous communities had among their number individuals capable of performing the work of turning lengths of cloth into usable forms like clothing or bedding. Whereas the presidials' sartorial preferences were dictated by ordinances and regulations issued from the peninsula, Amerindian populations close to the frontier garrisons had more of a free hand in what they wore and what merchandise they demanded for their attire. But, because deficiencies in the supply train often triggered resistance to weakly enforced ordinances, soldiers regularly did not conform to costuming requirements.

Too, it was not uncommon for certain services to be available to Indians whose intentions were peaceful and for those willing to recast key aspects of their identities in accordance with Spanish taste. Ready to accommodate them was Juan Antonio Romero, the master tailor of the Béxar presidio company who performed work for indigenous folk with a penchant for bespoke styles. In March 1789, he made two suits and eight waistcoats, adding ruffles to one of them, and then made nine shirts. He charged a total of twenty-nine pesos, one *real* for his customers. Later that same year, Romero made four coats, fourteen waistcoats, and fourteen shirts, charging almost forty pesos. For the remainder of the year and into February 1790, Romero continued to fashion clothing for "pacified" Indians, making trousers and lapels, and even adorning hats if requested by his customers.[111]

Meanwhile, by August 1790 Amangual had a *Mesteñas* Fund sum of 3,438 pesos from which to deduct allowances for the maintenance of and gift-giving to various indigenous communities. He documented over two hundred pesos spent on the maintenance of 225 Comanche, Tancague, Guichita, and Lipan Indians from August 14, 1790, to December 31, 1792. Amangual noted this amount originated from the *Gratificación* Fund but was then reimbursed from the *Mesteñas* Fund on orders from Cmdr. Gen. Ramón de Castro.[112] When expenses for Indians prompted higher authorities to draw from these accounts and even that of the payroll, the consequent confusion and misunderstanding created a dilemma for Amangual. Such was the contentious Amangual-Muñoz-Ugalde reimbursement scenario from the summer of 1791. Throughout the often-messy financial allocations of 1790–1792 Viceroy Revillagigedo ordered Amangual *not* to allocate funds from the royal treasury for any purpose other than supplying the troops. However, by the time Amangual received the directive, Muñoz had already invested the monies elsewhere.[113] These expenditures are unspecified but very likely gone by way of the high-stakes gamble of peace by purchase. A recurring aspect of borderlands administration was the contributory failure of viceregal oversight to cast its long shadow successfully enough to grasp both local conditions and solidly constructive relationships.

Transactions could get complicated with frustration inevitable for a meticulous paymaster like Amangual. When changes to and modifications of financial affairs required verification, transfers from multiple accounts helped to ensure the provisioning of servicemen. At least, that is how the process was intended to function. Bookkeeping generated a body of paperwork unique in borderlands history with content elastic enough to offer insight into other spheres of garrison life. Allocations like those for Native people entailed a process of debits and credits necessary to ensure fiscal equilibrium while conserving basic supplies and merchandise for the presidials, a dual-pronged effort and, itself, transitory at best.[114]

Money in flux streamed to all corners of the Commandency. From January 6 to April 1791, almost three hundred pesos were disbursed for the maintenance of forty-three Guichita, Tancague, Comanche, and Lipan Indians. Tangible largesse came in the form of a shipment of goods destined for the "Friendly Indians of the North" from Presidio Santa Rosa in Coahuila to the Béxar presidio.[115] One year later, Amangual produced a report on goods furnished to Gov. Manuel Muñoz as provisions needed to clothe the Indians of Misión El Rosario. Stressing their scarcity, Amangual made it clear that these items, representing a wide array of finished products and yardage of cloth, were unavailable in San Antonio. Amangual's total expenditure for the merchandise was over 352 pesos.[116] (See appendix 1.)

110 Chapter Three

Throughout January 1792, Comanche and Taguacana (Tawakoni) representatives appeared at the presidio seeking gifts. Mariano Menchaca provided twelve cattle, bought at four pesos apiece, and salt at three pesos, four *reales*. Similarly, Antonio Rodríguez Baca sold corn and other provisions to this same group of Indians, and Amangual paid him for his services.[117] Amangual continued to fulfill his obligations and received over 340 pesos from the storehouse guard José Antonio de Bustillo y Cevallos. This amount from the *Mesteñas* Fund reimbursed Amangual for paying individual merchants who provisioned the "Friendly Indians of the North."[118] The aforementioned Menchaca and Rodríguez Baca circulated throughout Texas as did Joachim de Amezqueta, a militia captain in Sonora, and Joaquín de Ugarte in Chihuahua. Purveyors maintained close associations with the presidials and often communicated among themselves about their clients.[119] All of these men, from merchants to paymasters, represented frontier residents taking on the provisioning of the presidios with a view, however refracted, toward promoting the regional economy. One of them, Amangual, did so in the service of the colonial state, while the others worked from the perspective of local interests and personal financial gain.

Budgeting for upkeep could be tricky. By late 1790, Amangual found himself having to ask Governor Muñoz which fund was to be utilized for maintenance of the "Friendly Indians" recently come to call at Presidio La Bahía. It was Gen. Pedro de Nava who issued the final word: the *Mesteñas* Fund was to bear all costs associated with provisioning them. Nava insisted on the greatest possible economy toward that effort and petitioners were to have accommodations for the least possible number of days. Conciliatory to a point, Nava directed soldiers to send the "Yndios" on their way as soon as their business concluded, but with skill and good manners (*"con arte y buen modo"*). Gifts, utilitarian in all probability, already consigned for one year are unspecified in this episode.[120]

Amangual's receipt of reimbursements dribbled in from borrowers who had extracted monies from the *Mesteñas* Fund. Some of these debtors had done so to supply provisions for Indian allies from the North who entered garrisons from January through February 26, 1792. It is fair to say that Amangual must have felt a sense of relief at having been reimbursed since it is clear the *Mesteñas* Fund, with its fluctuating income and outflow, was the resource of choice for monies earmarked for expenditures at the presidio. For example, the paymaster of the Bahía presidio Manuel de Espadas, on orders from Capt. Juan Cortéz, contacted Governor Muñoz to request five hundred pesos from the *Mesteñas* Fund to settle the accounts of five privates who, after a review inspection, were being discharged. Espadas asked the governor to deliver the urgently needed funds to Cpl. Hermenegildo Gómez, carrier of the mail pouch who, with a substantial escort, could bring the funds to Bahía. Responding on March 2, Muñoz replied that the *Mesteñas* Fund was devoid of cash because sums supplied from it to the Béxar presidio had not yet been reimbursed. That was not entirely true, however. Nevertheless, Muñoz was unable to fulfill Espadas' request to relieve Bahía's shortage since his own presidio was in the same condition.[121]

Amangual vs. Rodríguez—Slander at the Presidio, 1792

Fiscal shortfalls within the two main sources of garrison provisioning created aggravation for and explanations from an intricate network of associates within the presidio. Viceroys, inspectors, and supreme commanders all gave input, but often the resolution of such conflicts fell to the individual with preeminent authority as the arbiter of localized frontier governance. Among the many duties that Manuel Muñoz performed was that of governor, lieutenant colonel of cavalry in the royal armies of Carlos III, subdelegate of the royal treasury and ministry of war of Texas, and captain of the cavalry company of Béxar presidio. Over and above these army-related tasks, he served as presiding judge of *expedientes* (records/ case file) brought to court from civilians as well as military personnel. From within the thicket of presidio economic transactions, occasional discord seemed preordained among some soldiers. One such case found expression as a lawsuit pitting Lt. Francisco Amangual against Sgt. Mariano Rodríguez.

On February 29, 1792, Amangual accused Rodríguez of defaming his character in an action that involved two civilians: a merchant from the area and the master tailor of the company. It seems Rodríguez told the soldiers of the guardhouse that Amangual had extracted loads of clothing and subsequently taken the merchandise to the house of the merchant Ángel Navarro. Equally troubling was that two colleagues overheard this remark: Alférez Manuel Urrutia (resident troublemaker, abusive suitor, and drunk) and Béxar presidio tailor José Arreola.[122] The *autos* requested by Amangual were fulfilled and thus Urrutia, Arreola, and the two soldiers on guard duty that day, Andrés del Valle and José Manuel Granados, received summons to appear before Muñoz on March 6 to provide testimony about the charges.

Urrutia was the first to be questioned by Governor Muñoz, who asked: From whom had Urrutia heard it said that *tercios* (loads or packs) of goods had been taken from the *habilitación* of the Béxar company? Urrutia described the encounter thus: "One morning in February when it was raining, when I was warming myself at the fireplace in the guardhouse, Sergeant

Chapter Three

Mariano Rodríguez was there and told me, that he was 'amazed at having seen the store of the merchant Don Ángel Navarro looking abundant [*rica*] this morning when it was meager [*pobre*] last night.' However, on the previous day he saw that [the store] had no more goods than two bolts of blue and crimson chintz and calico and that he had also seen many *brettañas*, cambric, scarves, and stockings, and other fabrics that correspond to good stock [*buen surtimiento*]."

Asked whether he knew (or, had heard it said) from where or how the aforesaid goods came into Ángel Navarro's possession, Urrutia replied that Sgt. Rodríguez said he had asked Navarro where he acquired the merchandise. Navarro responded, telling Rodríguez he brought them from Mission San José. Navarro added that he still had other unopened *tercios* and what Rodríguez had seen was nothing. Rodríguez said he did not believe it. Rather, what he did believe was that the aforesaid goods were from the *habilitación* because, they told him, during the night Sgt. Andrés del Valle had extracted goods in bundles and taken them to the house of Cpl. José Manuel Granados. From there the merchandise made its way to Navarro.[123]

When Muñoz asked who was present when Sgt. Rodríguez provided this information, Urrutia replied that the tailor Arreola was present. Asked to whom Urrutia repeated what the sergeant had just said to him, Urrutia declared: he had heard Rodríguez say the same thing two days prior. Asked whether he had anything else to say, Urrutia replied that there was nothing else to add to his testimony. However, when Urrutia asked the sergeant from where they had extracted the goods, Rodríguez was astonished that Urrutia would even ask that question. Urrutia himself knew that there was no problem ("*no havia ningun incombeniente*") extracting provisions from behind the paymaster storehouse.[124]

Questioning now turned to the presidio's master tailor José Arreola. Once Amangual's *expediente* was read to him, Arreola provided his recall of the events of the previous month, stating:

> On the morning of February 19, when I was with Alférez Manuel de Urrutia in the guardhouse and seated on one of the stone seats, Sergeant Mariano Rodríguez arrived and Urrutia asked him: "Is it true that the paymaster's store has run out [of provisions]?" Rodríguez replied: "It is true that the goods in the *avilittación* are all gone, because they have all been taken to the house of Ángel Navarro," and for this same reason he had not seen in any year such a well-stocked store. Further, Rodríguez knew quite well what Navarro had brought in this year since Navarro had no more than two bolts of chintz—one blue, the other crimson—and other items of little value. By the next morning Rodríguez saw that Navarro had many

bretañas [cloth imported from Brittany, France], knitted cloth [*pontibíes*], girls' scarves, and other fabrics that he did not have [in stock] before. And Rodríguez claimed to know the persons who had taken them from behind the *avilittación* and [then transported them] to Navarro's house.

Asked if he heard Rodríguez say which individuals had taken the merchandise from the paymaster's storehouse and carried them to the house, Arreola replied: "Rodríguez said that Sgt. Andrés del Valle and Cpl. José Manuel Granados had taken the goods from the *avilittación* and carried them to the house of Navarro, and that this was [expedited] by the *habilitado* Amangual because the prices set by the Commander General were very low. Furthermore, in order not to suffer so much loss Amangual had moved [the goods] to the house of Navarro."

Asked whether he had anything else to say, he replied, "no," and that he was honest under oath.[125] Arreola's statements were conflated with those of Urrutia in the original documents filed by Lt. Amangual and were subsequently relayed to Sgt. Andrés del Valle, the next soldier to be questioned about merchandise removed from the paymaster's office.

Muñoz asked Sgt. del Valle: On what day and in the company of which individual did he take bundles from the back of the office? And where did he take them, and on whose orders? He replied: "I did not see, nor did I extract, any materials from any place in the circumference of the storehouse to take to any house whatsoever except for those materials that I bought for use by my family. And they cannot prove otherwise against me."

So went del Valle's terse defense, whereupon he ratified his deposition, gave his age as fifty years old, "more or less," affirmed his testimony by signing his name, and spelling his surname "Balle."[126]

The foregoing testimony of Amangual, de Urrutia, del Valle, and Arreola was repeated for Cpl. José Manuel Granados. He was subsequently questioned so as to ascertain whether he had gone with Sgt. del Valle to take goods by the rear door, from the paymaster's office, carry them to his own house, and from there to that of Navarro, or, to the house of Arreola. Granados articulated a rebuttal, but with a pronounced defensive tone:

At no time or on any occasion whatsoever did I see or accompany Sergeant Andrés del Valle or any other person, to take materials from the *habilitación*; whether they were taken from the front or the back of it, to the house of any citizen, nor any other individual with the exception of those materials that I purchased for myself and my family. And nothing contrary to what I have said can be proven against me. But I have heard

114   Chapter Three

> it said by the soldiers that Sergeant Mariano Rodríguez told them the
> same thing about whether I had participated in removing and taking the
> aforesaid materials to the house of Ángel Navarro. That allegation has
> been hurtful to me because it impugned my honest ways and honorable
> status with a highly denigrating shortcoming.[127]

Asked if he had anything else to say, Granados could think of nothing to add to his testimony. This was the truth he swore to under oath.[128]

Though Urrutia, del Valle, and Granados may very well have anticipated tedious interplay with their commanding officer, the three *presidiales* and the master tailor Arreola weathered a military inquest involving a repetitive process of questioning that, ultimately, structured the entire official testimony of the proceedings. Nonetheless, Lieutenant Amangual's chief concern was that both Navarro and Rodríguez also receive summons in pursuance of proving the charge for which they were accusing him. Naturally, Amangual's reputation among his troops and superiors and even those beyond the presidio was important to him. The notion of his subordinate Rodríguez accusing him of theft of property was so denigrating to his honor and position (*"y siendo esta calumnia tan denegrativa á mi honor y empleo"*), that he was eager to have all individuals with knowledge of this tawdry episode, or participants in slanderous behavior, brought in as deponents. If cleared of all charges and freed of the defamation he withstood, Amangual prevailed upon Governor Muñoz to punish the perpetrator Rodríguez according to army regulations. Hoping to avoid the possibility of Rodríguez agitating the company with lies and provoking them into sedition, Amangual encouraged Muñoz to remove his accuser from the post he held as a deterrent to any future episodes of this type.[129]

Captain Muñoz agreed to at least part of Amangual's request. He summoned Sgt. Mariano Rodríguez and expected him to support with evidence the charge that resulted from his having damaged Amangual's "good reputation and lawfulness" in managing the affairs of the company.[130] What is striking is that the summons appeared to have a built-in verdict since the deposition professed that justice might be satisfied and serve as an example to the other troops to abstain from conversations detrimental to the honor of their officers. Muñoz's thinking as found in the subpoena more generally referenced the rank of sergeant since disreputable conduct among its conferees was especially serious for this reason: it exposed subordinates to disobedience and caused other disturbances against the royal service.[131]

Aware now of Amangual's attestation and Muñoz's *auto* since both documents had been issued on the same date, on March 6 Rodríguez responded.

Reglamento of 1772, Strategies, and Slander 115

In doing so he introduced two new names into the cast of players on the morning of February 19.

> It is true that while I was at the stone benches of the guardhouse, I reported to Alférez Manuel de Urrutia that I had been told by a truthful individual that I was wearing a blindfold if I did not know that the materials from the paymaster's office had been removed to the house of Ángel Navarro. But my statement was motivated by the fact that the *señor* priest of this villa, Francisco Gómez Moreno, had informed me of this in clear and understandable language at the time that I went to make payment for the burial of my father-in-law, José Macario Sambrano.[132] It was in the following way: "You people are wearing blindfolds, because I know that the goods from [Amangual's office] have been removed to the house of Ángel Navarro, and if they ask me I will prove it."

At this point, Sgt. Rodríguez was asked whether he told Urrutia which individuals had taken the goods in the *habilitación* and from where? Had he seen the inventory of Ángel Navarro depleted at nightfall but then well stocked the next morning? Rodríguez indicated that, on both counts, he had said nothing of the kind. Asked who was with Urrutia when he spoke about the situation, Rodríguez replied: while he was talking with Urrutia, the master tailor José Arreola arrived. Apparently unconcerned, he continued discussing the removal of the materials from the paymaster's office to Navarro's house. However, and this will be significant, he did not mention the priest.[133] So concluded the first round of interrogation with a respite now of several days.

Having reviewed in total the statements from Urrutia, Arreola, del Valle, Granados, and the consequent reaction from Rodríguez—a reply that neither absolved Amangual of the charges made against him nor proved what Rodríguez stated in the presence of Urrutia and Arreola—Muñoz resummoned Rodríguez to appear on March 15, 1792.

Upon arrival Muñoz asked Rodríguez whether everything documented in his March 6 deposition was true. The response was predictable. Rodríguez issued a course of rebuttals that not only expose his desperation in recalling his testimony of the week prior but also gave rise to an inquiry more specifically targeting the array of merchandise in question. For example, he denied having told Urrutia that del Valle had taken the materials from the paymaster's office to Granados' house and, from there, to Navarro's store. Then he denied having told Urrutia that he was "astonished" at the amount of merchandise in the store on February 19, 1792, when it was empty the night before. Asked whether he had told Urrutia that the store had no more than two bolts of blue and red calico and canvas (*yndianillas angaripolas, azules, y encarnadas*) on that night, but that he had seen many *bretañas*, cambric, scarves, stockings and other materials by the next day, he denied having made the statement.[134] When Rodríguez was asked whether Navarro had told him from where he had brought the materials (he himself having asked the very same thing) and, furthermore, why he asked him that question with everything else that he knew, Rodríguez supplied information that further implicated a religious participant in the lawsuit:

> When I went to find some white ribbon at the store of Ángel Navarro for the coffin of my father-in-law, José Macario Sambrano, (which Navarro did not have [in stock]) I asked Navarro for a *vara* of *pontiví*. Because Navarro asked seven *reales* for it, I asked him why he had previously offered it for five and six *reales* but now wanted seven? To this, Navarro replied that he was asking seven *reales* because, for that quality, he had no supplier and that among the goods that he had on hand, their quality did not match what others had brought. At that moment I told Navarro that the padre of [Misión] San José would have the charity to give him these goods to earn those greater profits. To this, Navarro said that he did not need friars to obtain what he had. But I said none of this to Urrutia.[135]

At this juncture in the interview Muñoz asked Rodríguez why he denied having informed Urrutia that the merchandise was taken from the paymaster's office to Navarro's house. In fact, in his earlier deposition he had confessed to having done so. Rodríguez explained: "I did not want to expose the priest Don Francisco Gómez Moreno, the one who gave me the information, until the present case came around because I told Urrutia that a truthful individual had told me that they [had] blindfolds on, and that he clearly knew they had moved the materials from the paymaster's office to the house of Ángel Navarro."[136]

Asked whether he had said anything to officers, sergeants, corporals, privates, or citizens regarding the transfer of goods to Navarro's house, Rodríguez denied saying anything at all to anyone *except* Urrutia. Then, when asked whether he knew that he had to substantiate the slander aimed at Amangual, Rodríguez affirmed: "I know that I am obligated to substantiate the slander uttered against the lieutenant and paymaster, but since my informant was the priest, I will seek from him a document to substantiate the charge, as requested by Amangual."

After the deposition was repeated to him, Rodríguez declared its content as true, that he had nothing at all to delete or add, and gave his age as forty-three years, "more or less."[137]

On this same date Muñoz recalled Urrutia and the tailor José Arreola. For what was about to ensue, Rodríguez was also retained from his interview.

Convened as a trio under scrutiny, the men swore to the oath of truth.[138] But first, Arreola was asked to leave so that Urrutia could counter the allegations by Rodríguez in his depositions of March 6 and March 15, the sergeant having already contradicted what appeared in the deposition given on that first date by Urrutia. After this testimony, Rodríguez was asked to respond with everything that might disprove the charge against him, and he replied: "It is true what Alférez Manuel de Urrutia states in his deposition inasmuch as I might have told Urrutia that a truthful individual told me that they were all wearing blindfolds because Padre Gómez Moreno clearly knew that they had removed merchandise from the paymaster's office and then taken it to Navarro's house."

Asked whether Rodríguez's reporting was consistent with his foregoing reply, Alférez Urrutia said: "The sergeant's reply concurs except for his having mentioned the truthful individual that he refers to."

Now the interaction between the two soldiers became adversarial. Sgt. Rodríguez, instructed to offer proof to the denial by Urrutia, replied: "I have no one with whom to prove what I have declared, and [I have] my word."

Asked whether he had anything to say regarding key points mentioned by Urrutia in his deposition, Rodríguez replied: "Everything that Urrutia states about the materials having been taken by Sergeant Andrés del Valle from the *habilitación* to the house of Corporal José Manuel Granados, and from there to the house of Navarro, including the transfer of merchandise from San José by Navarro, is untrue."

Urrutia countered Rodríguez, insisting that when the sergeant told him about the removal of goods from the paymaster's office, Rodríguez had not said to him that he had been given that information by the "truthful individual" that he now referenced. However, everything else communicated by Sgt. Rodríguez was true. At this point in the testimony, Urrutia was ordered to withdraw, and Arreola was called into the room. His deposition was read in the presence of Rodríguez, who responded: "What is in the deposition of José Arreola is true only [insofar as] I told Urrutia, with Arreola present, about the removal of the materials from the *habilitación* to the house of Navarro. [I did so because] I was told this by a truthful person, and not that [goods] had been taken by Sergeant del Valle to the house of Corporal José Manuel Granados."

Asked to respond to the objections made by Rodríguez to his deposition, Arreola replied: "Although Rodríguez may make objections and corrections to his deposition, I cannot change it because everything that I stated in it is the truth. Furthermore, I heard Rodríguez say the same thing that Urrutia said. And, I did not hear Rodríguez say that he had heard it from a truthful individual."

118 Chapter Three

Moreover, to prove everything stated in his deposition as accurate, Arreola reminded Rodríguez of what he had said to Urrutia in his presence: that he knew which individuals had removed the materials and from where they had come; that a private had told him Corporal Granados had a stock of chintz fabric; and, during a dark, snowy night the materials were removed from the paymaster's office. Rodríguez was now asked for his response to Arreola's testimony. He replied that everything that Arreola said about the removal of the materials on the snowy night was reported by Urrutia and *not* by him.

In turn, Muñoz asked Arreola what he had to say about Rodríguez's statement. He countered by saying he did not hear Urrutia say the things that Rodríguez now claimed, adding that Urrutia asked Rodríguez only one thing: what persons had removed the materials from the *habilitación*?[139] As reported by Arreola, Rodríguez responded by identifying del Valle and Granados. Rodríguez was then asked to respond to Arreola's ratification; he confirmed Arreola's statements as matching those of Urrutia.

Overstrung nerves now lay bare. Arreola challenged Rodríguez, saying that the same thing that he ratified he heard from the mouth of Rodríguez but not from that of Urrutia, and that what he had divulged was "nothing more than the truth." Furthermore, if Rodríguez denied that which was real, then he will deny as unclear that which is in plain sight.[140]

As the face-to-face confrontation between Arreola and Rodríguez and between Captain Muñoz and his subordinate ended, Rodríguez was asked to reply to Arreola. Other than what he had already said, he had nothing more to say. Having taken testimony from Urrutia and Arreola, Muñoz informed Rodríguez that he had not convinced these two witnesses, and, in fact, they had made objections to his reporting during their individual exchanges. Consequently, Muñoz ordered the testimony read aloud to all three men. Upon its completion an intransigent Rodríguez reiterated that he had told Urrutia and Arreola that merchandise had been removed from the paymaster's office and taken to the house of Ángel Navarro, the veracity of which stemmed from his being informed of this by a "man of truth (*un hombre de verdad*)." Equally adamant, both men again refuted Rodríguez's testimony, denying that he had learned the news from the so-called truthful man and saying nothing more than what they had already affirmed. Muñoz asked Rodríguez for his response to the two soldiers' identical depositions. Like his fellow company members, he, too, swore there was nothing at all to add to his testimony.[141]

The Inventory: Accounting for
the Goods in Question

With the conclusion of testimony, the slander suit advanced to the next phase of the inquiry. Rodríguez now had a deadline to substantiate his accusations against Amangual: four days. On March 17, Governor Muñoz further ordered the opening of the company's coffer and the accounts therein balanced, a move authorized for the sake of determining fiscal discrepancies, if any, in the bookkeeping practices of Amangual. Discovery there might confirm wrongdoing. Both activities were to be conducted in the presence of officers, one sergeant, one corporal, and one private appointed by the company as its agent. Thus, Lt. Bernardo Fernández, Alférez Urrutia, Sgt. Prudencio Rodríguez, Squad Cpl. Juan Antonio Urrutia, Pvt. José Alexandro de la Garza (representative for the company soldiers), and the governor proceeded to balance the accounts and examine the supplies on hand for the troops. The irony surely evident to presidio insiders was that, even as he defended his reputation from a fellow soldier's accusation that cast him in the role of crook, Amangual's expertise as paymaster remained indispensable but, at least during this ordeal, imperfect. Though he himself apparently counted nothing, Amangual placed all the items on display including account books, along with active and inactive debts of various funds and of private citizens, to certify their legitimacy.[142]

Apart from the economic significance of the material objects of presidio life and their status as commodities for both provisioners and consumers within and outside the garrison walls, inventory and display of evidence represented more than suspect merchandise. Their tangible presence spoke to the global context of politico-economic inclinations forged by the intake and outflow of merchandise by frontier folk. That process had ramifications for Spain's trans-Atlantic colonies. Historian Juan Marchena Fernández notes that the collateral reforms of the Bourbons were destined to maintain the military component as it related to royal finances, administration, and trade policy of the Spanish empire. By means of a series of deregulatory steps Carlos III liberated the policies of commerce, an effort conducive to stimulating trade between the American colonies. That began in 1765 and reached a climax in 1778 with the promulgation of the *Reglamento de Comercio Libre*. These measures stimulated legal trade and widened the entry of taxes derived from the same procedures.[143] In his 1778 proclamation, the king conceded that he had come around to freeing up (*he venido en libertar*) for ten years all the duties and excise taxes (*arbitrios*) upon exit from Spain's warehouses (*almoxarifado*) and, upon entrance to the Américas, all manufactured goods of wool, cotton, and linen.[144]

Chapter Three

In fact, American affairs relevant to trade, navigation, or fisheries constituted 134 items brought before the Junta by the minister of finance between 1788 and 1792. Jacques Barbier has argued that the "economic aspects of the reforms were pushed forward vigorously" during this period. Further, the "Spanish government wished to secure the economic benefits of colonialism without having to confront an American insurrection." Whereas liberalized trade policies were in effect elsewhere in the empire, they were now to apply with full force to previously excluded areas such as New Spain and Louisiana.[145]

Several background points clarify the process. Allan Kuethe has described the government of Carlos III as having recognized that New Spain, with its strong economy, suffocated the development of the weakest economies found in its peripheries and, by extension, weakened the growing capacities of its military. Still, American defense was more important than the volume of commerce between Spain and its colonies and, even, achieving maximum peninsular prosperity.[146] Having it both ways was never going to work. Whether encompassing or discrete, when peninsular policies reached the Comandancia General, the exigencies of frontier life required compromise and even improvisation in economic interactions between presidio personnel and the non-military populations in their orbit. As we have seen and will continue to see, getting troops in the first place for defense, having the will to unleash money for supplying those same troops, and mitigating dereliction of duty by desperate troops, all too frequently took a back seat to other priorities and expenses.

As matters stood in the Amangual–Rodríguez undertaking, the conflict among its key players was not that unusual as an intra-presidio event. However, in the context of its potential for embarrassment, disruption, and impediment to individual career advancement, the organization, description, and documentation of the inventory as evidentiary support functioned as part of a compulsory process of legitimizing transparency in legal proceedings. Once archived, the written matter activated by the slander suit, including that of the stockpile in dispute, was available for perusal by a limited number of personnel in the frontier bureaucracy. Made plain during the inventory inspection is a fascinating log of the material wealth held at the garrison. Indeed, the international origin of some items reinforces the notion of the presidio's storehouse as a showcase for the influx of merchandise from across the world with this inventory's heavy emphasis on cloth, utensils, and hides.[147]

The first items listed in the storehouse inventory included blue cloth from Castilla, yardage of blue serge from England, and twelve bolts of "royal Silesian linen" amounting to 494 pesos. Other products related to garment

Reglamento of 1772, Strategies, and Slander   121

making included chintz, calico, and eight bolts of mother-of-pearl and green ribbon from Genoa; thirty-five silk handkerchiefs with a sun motif in all colors; buttons for dress coats, including five gross of gilded buttons for uniforms; three dozen pairs of fine scissors; and one thousand needles. From Mexico came six pounds of twisted "Misteca [Mixtec]" silk in all colors and one bolt of red Querétaro cloth; thirty *rebozos* and four bolts of striped cotton duck from Puebla; eighteen hats from San Luis (Potosí); and other equally interesting items. Almost two pounds of musketeer's braid with five strands appeared in the list, and one hairnet; four reams of superfine paper; and five bolts of Chinese burlap. The sum of this extraordinary array of items amounted to 2,072 pesos.[148]

The last section of the inventory lists items intended for the soldiers; the merchandise reveals select costuming elements of the presidials and members of its cavalry force. Other items related to horse riding gear rounded out the stockpile. (See appendix 2.)

Incapable of completing the inventory until the next day, the inspection committee described that day's duties as having listed in the "greatest detail and to everyone's satisfaction" the measuring, counting, and weighing of the contents of fifteen baskets of soap, munitions, lead, general merchandise, weights, and measures. The inspection staff on March 17, 1792, consisted of Cpt. Muñoz, Lt. Bernardo Fernández, Alférez Manuel de Urrutia,[149] Squad Cpl. Juan Antonio Urrutia, Sgt. Prudencio Rodríguez, and Pvt. Alexandro de la Garza. Having painstakingly documented all goods accumulated over time and from across the borderlands' economic territory and beyond, the men noted the merchandise as being the same items that were on hand in the paymaster's office. The truth now made manifest, the staff admitted their findings into the proceedings.[150]

The next issue requiring further investigation was the inspection and recording of the goods held in the possession of the tailor Arreola. That event took place the next day and included inventory like buttons, large and small, and metal buckles with straps, that one might expect to find associated with a clothier. However, Arreola's inventory had other items like blanketing, *morinillos* for beating chocolate, copper bowls and kettles, a weight scale, a Mexican brass weight standard, corn, beans, and even cash amounting to seven hundred pesos. The latter entered the coffer containing the required three keys of the *fondo de gratificación*. On March 18, 1792, the combined grand total of the goods and other accessories separated, counted, and measured by the officers, sergeant, corporal, and the private representing the company, amounted to almost 5,700 pesos.[151]

The inventory conducted at Amangual's office must have been a time-consuming, tedious endeavor. In fact, the official record of the event suggests that by late afternoon the process of listing all the merchandise held in stock had become an exhausting chore necessitating a reprieve for all involved. However, the itemization was instrumental in upholding the charges forming the crux of the slander suit instigated by Lieutenant Amangual against Sgt. Rodríguez. Once officially designated by election as paymaster, Amangual obligated himself to ensuring the strict maintenance of the general accounts of debits and credits with the greatest clarity and justification. He did so in anticipation of his recordkeeping being examined and approved by the captain and other officers, including the *comandante inspector*, at the end of the year.[152] Whether Amangual stumbled now in this his most significant responsibility held by any presidio's fiduciary, and whether his culpability alleged by a subordinate was definitively established in the slander suit, will be discussed in the next chapter.

FOUR

❧

Managing Soldiers, Questionable Accounts, and a Case of Contraband, 1792

Surviving colonial writings make plain that a presidio paymaster's daily responsibilities incurred challenges that added to the inherent strain of military life in the borderlands. Documentation by the *habilitado* of these tasks exposed other routine interactions apart from monetary concerns within the walls of the garrison. Still, safeguarding fiscal accuracy, provisioning his fellow servicemen, and ensuring the legitimacy of daily accounting responsibilities determined the context of the paymaster's work. That, in turn, evoked innumerable reactions from the troops.

One month would pass before any other documentation surfaced regarding the slander case brought on by Francisco Amangual against Mariano Rodríguez. Nonetheless, the usual work of fiscal intricacies continued apace. On April 19, Amangual presented a statement signed on the same date as the Arreola inventory showing goods distributed among the Béxar company workforce totaled over 8,628 pesos. The amount dovetailed with company funds. According to the account received in August and recorded by the Royal Treasury, these monies arrived as salaries from San Luis Potosí during the second semester of 1791. In fact, they were used to purchase the inventory reported and examined by Gov. Manuel Muñoz and his team, entries of items which were read to both Sgt. Rodríguez and Pvt. José Manuel Pérez and from which both benefitted. Now both men were under arrest because of the slander suit.[1]

All individuals present during the March inventory expressed satisfaction with the goods received and recorded in their accounts with the exception, perhaps anticipated, of Rodríguez. He declared that he was not in possession of a bolt of wide *bretaña*, ten *varas* of *pontiví*, one peso of soap,

124 Chapter Four

but that their total value of over fifteen pesos was credited to him in the company ledger. Likewise, Pvt. Francisco Antonio del Río also demanded three *varas* of *jerga* fabric previously paid to him in cash. Even the soldiers who were sick or otherwise indisposed acknowledged their respective accounts, for which purpose the inspection committee went to those soldiers' lodgings for verification of recorded transactions. As a final piece of evidence, Amangual was ordered to submit a general report showing the funds in accounts under his management. These included presidial salaries, general stockpiles, debts owed by the paymaster's office, the Cíbolo fund, deposits for contraband, and *gratificación* reserves for the men.[2]

The total value of the goods on hand in the storehouse of the Béxar *habilitación*, consisting of what was provided to the troops, from November 15 through December 31, 1791, and from January 1 through March 18, 1792, amounted to over 14,727 pesos. This total appeared in the ninth and tenth entries of the general account signed by the inspection committee members and headed by Governor Muñoz with a congruent explanation.

The conclusion, reached on April 27, 1792, was unambiguous: the funds received at the royal treasury by Béxar's paymaster Amangual were untouched. There had been no removal of any goods by Amangual as alleged by Sgt. Mariano Rodríguez. Of this outcome Rodríguez was convinced and satisfied. He expressed as much in the presence of the committee, at which point he then asked for forgiveness from Amangual. It seems he had made the allegation because the priest Francisco Gómez Moreno had told him so, a contention Rodríguez asserted throughout his testimony and in all his ratifications. However, knowing now that the priest misspoke, Rodríguez asked for a pardon. When asked if he was appeased by the sergeant's response, Amangual replied: he was not. Heightening the tension further, he declared that Rodríguez now had to perform his garrison duties wherever it might suit *Amangual*.[3]

At approximately 3:15 p.m. on that same day, Pvt. Alexandro de la Garza appeared in front of Governor Muñoz as the representative for the sergeants, corporals, and privates of the Béxar company. He swore that in fulfillment of what Rodríguez had promised in the previous proceeding, the sergeant had spoken to Lt. Bernardo Fernández, First Alférez Manuel de Urrutia, Second Alférez José Xavier Menchaca, and lower-ranking soldiers. He said, "Gentlemen, I have come to retract what I said [*vengo adesdecirme*] about the gentleman paymaster Lieutenant Don Francisco Amangual [...]."

He admitted this because, as he had insisted all along, he made the accusation in the first place only after the priest Francisco Gómez Moreno had disinformed him. With that, Governor Muñoz's response revealed his

Managing Soldiers, Questionable Accounts, and Contraband   125

conciliatory nature while at the same time suggesting an outwardly tepid relationship between himself and Amangual. Muñoz stressed the remorse conveyed by Sgt. Rodríguez to Amangual—in the form of an appeal for forgiveness from the paymaster—and the sergeant's confession to the company that his allegation was based on the disingenuous report given by the irksome padre. Whether he meant to show mercy or not, Muñoz rehashed, as the additional indignity suffered by Rodríguez (but certainly known to his comrades), his one month and eighteen days of confinement sustained from the day of his arrest until April 27 in the presidio's guardhouse.[4]

Nevertheless, sympathy from Muñoz played no part in conveying the grievances of Mariano Rodríguez. For his part, the sergeant may have expected a different result following the testimony in the slander suit and after all the interviews with multiple witnesses. Some of them, his long-time presidio companions, he had faced during depositions where his veracity was openly contradicted in the presence of his commander Muñoz. On April 26, the day before Muñoz reached his conclusion, Rodríguez appealed to the commander to set him free from confinement. In his petition he pleaded

> Since the fifth of March, I have been in public confinement, exposed to insults and disgraces that I have not [before] experienced, for no more cause or reason than [it came] after the slander that I am accused of having raised against my lieutenant and paymaster Don Francisco Amangual. [It] was discussed openly in such a way that the public attorney of the illustrious town council of this villa divulged it in the presence of the guardhouse squad of this royal district long before my arrest, what had not been witnessed before the integrity of Your Lordship with regard to my having been deprived of all dealings and communication with other people[.] Similarly, I could not take the most minimal recourse. By virtue of this, and of the great shame caused to me by the outrages and mistreatment I am receiving to this day, as well as the dishonor that my aforesaid lieutenant has created for me with his petition—labeling me a liar, ringleader, and trouble maker [*el desdoro que dicho mi Teniente ha originandome con su presentacion, tratandome de falsario, cabecilla, y enrredador*]—when I never have given cause to incur such an accusation, as is proven by the authentic certifications that I keep in my possession. Because it is clear that were it true, I never would have been given these [certifications] by my previous superiors—I beseech the benign mercy of Your Lordship to please order that I be freed from my shackles and confinement so as to be able freely to answer my afore-cited lieutenant, giving him [Amangual] full justification of how

126 Chapter Four

and in what circumstances I [described as] gossip (let us say it like that) has been spread in public. In doing so I will receive mercy with justice [*que en hazerlo asi recibiré merced con justicia* (sic/passim)].[5]

Rodríguez implored Muñoz to grant his request since it was in his "best interests." He asked the governor to accept his petition, written on plain paper because the proper kind was, apparently, not used in this district of the frontier. This detail is peculiar in view of the exhaustive inventory that occurred over several days. With its stockpile of items representing international trade and transregional commerce, it is difficult to imagine that this "proper" paper for official documents was not available in the Béxar *habilitación*. In fact, "four reams of superfine paper" was one of the commodities listed in the suspect inventory. However, as Rodríguez himself admitted, these were the customary limitations in the colonial frontier.[6]

Muñoz's response was immediate. Improper plain paper or not, that same day he accepted Rodríguez's petition and insisted that it be considered when the inventory of the paymaster's office was completed.[7] In the final passages of the forty-three-page slander suit, Muñoz disclosed his approach to ending the matter: "I have decided to admonish Rodríguez that henceforth he must refrain from making such allegations about the conduct of the paymaster officer, as well as the other officers and members of the company, with regard to [the fact] that he, as first sergeant, should keep his soldiers under control and admonish them to carry out their duties, restraining them from improper conversations. And should he become aware of any other defects in the management of the [company's] business or matters of the service, he is to report it with all due subordination to the captain of the company so that he might apply the remedy that is consequent to his responsibilities."[8]

Muñoz made Rodríguez aware of his decision, and once the sergeant understood it, he said he would obey it and comply with the decision completely. Rodríguez apologized for having made the accusation against Amangual. At this point, Muñoz released Rodríguez from confinement and reiterated that the written complaint made against the paymaster be done. However, Rodríguez "beseeched the Governor" not to insist upon the necessary document (validation by a certain padre) because it was "not the best thing for him." Shamed into submission, he asked that it be torn up or suppressed by the governor's authority.[9] That seems prudent since, from the beginning, Amangual demanded "proof and substantiation" of Rodríguez's charge against him. Undoubtedly, Muñoz knew the dispirited sergeant could not corroborate any of it nor provide any documentation

Managing Soldiers, Questionable Accounts, and Contraband   127

from the "truthful" Father Gómez Moreno, a claim Rodríguez made when confronted with the rule of law.

Then, on April 27 Rodríguez now asked Muñoz to cancel his strange petition from the day before. Without asking why, Muñoz simply entered the last affidavit into the record which was signed by attestants José de Jesús Mansolo and Vizente de la Cuesta.[10] Why Rodríguez made this request is speculative. It is possible that Governor Muñoz advised the sergeant that settling the petition would accelerate the finality of the slander suit and put an end, once and for all, to the entire matter. Then, too, seeing the process terminated may have been a condition for Rodríguez's release from jail and facilitate his return to his responsibilities.

The question remains as to how Béxar presidial relationships continued to function past the point of the final verdict by Muñoz and once the investigation was over and certain conclusions were reached. Several answers are possible. As we have previously seen, out of necessity and given the realities of survival in the remote reaches of the empire, military personnel pledged (with or without conviction) to maintain some semblance of communal equilibrium within the confines of the garrison. In fact, Amangual and Rodríguez would soldier on as they had done before. The rest of the year's rosters divulge this version of reality, which is not to say that such reports are infallible. Monthly company reports could be construed in ways to achieve administrative traction while claiming in black ink the upper hand in policy making, whether factual or imagined. Requests for transfer often led to soldiers' departures with the dual intention of maintaining the general well-being of multiple companies and mitigating hostilities that may have existed between one individual and another. However, one indisputable truth remained: every presidio was woefully understaffed, some so vulnerable as to cause sleeplessness and exasperation to those left in command and often without any soldiers as backup. We recall the unfortunate, if not disturbing, circumstances of Capt. Domingo Cabello at Béxar in the 1780s and, more recently, the dire actuality faced by Capt. Juan Cortés at La Bahía. Moreover, the 1783 royal *cédula* granting sweeping amnesty to deserters willing to resume duty was likely a response to embarrassing shortages in military staffing across the king's purported dominions.[11]

All wounds do not heal with time. Amangual's indignation over the results of the investigation stung bitterly and especially so where it concerned the punishment of Rodríguez. In his opinion, it was far too lenient and would require further angling on his part to achieve a more desirable result. But the Amangual–Rodríguez episode was an intra-presidio conflict predicated on the expectation that its protagonists would, at least at the official level,

128   Chapter Four

maintain a certain decorum based upon seniority, rank, and obligation to
duty first. All assumptions aside, that also required a disciplinary effort at
once fair and impartial and intended to curb the disobedient impulses of
any recalcitrant soldier.

The Work of the Presidio Continues

At times, this sort of infighting, stemming from ignorance or outright
malice, involved the very people entrusted less so with inculcating martial
prowess but instead with tending to the spiritual needs of the frontier population. In the presidio setting, the severity of certain situations embroiling
members of the clergy may have appeared less contentious and therefore
beyond the bounds of aggressive prosecution given the hallowed status of
some of the accused. Ancillary evidence from the Amangual–Rodríguez
slander suit shows that a petition was drawn up and signed by several citizens in an apparent unified denunciation of the original troublemaker in
that feud: Padre Francisco Gómez Moreno. He was the "truthful individual"
who had, perhaps intentionally, supplied Sgt. Rodríguez with disinformation about the illicit transfer of goods from the paymaster's office. Apprised
of the complaint now made against the parish priest by members of the
San Fernando *ayuntamiento*, on February 27 Governor Muñoz sent the five
fojas útiles comprising the original petition to Commandant Gen. Ramón
de Castro. As we shall shortly see, Castro by experience must have felt more
than a little exasperation with the Béxar padres.[12]

Despite grappling with the dysfunctional inclinations of some garrison
personnel and even ecclesiastical staff, Francisco Amangual stayed the
course throughout the Rodríguez ordeal. In fact, some of the business-
as-usual approach of Governor Muñoz toward the paymaster appears in
extensive documentation of gifts for the Indians during this time frame. For
instance, on March 16, 1792, Muñoz wanted Amangual to tell Andrés Benito
Courbiére (the successful merchant and esteemed interpreter discussed in
the previous chapter) that he, Muñoz, had delivered to the tailor José Arreola
(one of the deponents who had figured so prominently in the slander suit)
a quantity of cloth and thread for a waistcoat and trousers intended for
the son of Comanche intermediary Soquinas. Muñoz directed Amangual
to provide Arreola with the lining and buttons and pay for the work, all of
which were charged to the expenditure accounts for the Indians. A little
more than a week later, Muñoz had cigars delivered to Comanches led by
Soquinas and Sojas, again instructing Amangual to charge their account.
One month later, Muñoz issued a promissory note to Amangual for cigars
for ten Comanches visiting the presidio on April 11 and 15.[13]

Managing Soldiers, Questionable Accounts, and Contraband   129

Contemporaneous records including inventories show European-styled clothing, tobacco products, and even armaments intended for high-level Comanche leaders made up the material efforts of peace by purchase. One week after sending his short note to Amangual regarding delivery of the tailor's supplies, Muñoz received an order from Cmdr. Gen. Ramón de Castro to deliver to the same Comanches, Soquinas and Sojas, and now to include the man who withstood the drunkard Urrutia's outrages, Ojos Azules, twelve of the muskets he had sent for this purpose. The objective of this dispatch was for the three leaders to distribute arms as they thought best among the individuals of their nation. Castro further instructed Muñoz to give an amount of powder and bullets considered appropriate by the governor. As he had always done up until that time, Castro recommended good treatment of the Comanche and the so-called Friendly Nations of the North. Castro's reasoning was unambiguous. He told Muñoz that "abrasiveness and excessive economizing" were not instruments to fortify a close friendship that must be preserved with indigenous inhabitants. Putting a finer point on the matter, Castro stressed that the king himself commanded goodwill at all costs.[14]

Feeling much differently about the Apache, General Castro did not extend that same magnanimity to them and now, even less so, to the Lipan whom he declared as sworn enemies of the region and of humanity. As if to compound the general's frustration, yet another episode emerged of ecclesiastical prerogative supplanting martial authority. Once again, a member of the clergy would contest or otherwise short-circuit the military effort of castigating an enemy, this time specific bands of the Apache. Castro took Muñoz at his word when the latter informed him that during the previous months three Lipan appeared at the mission of San Antonio even though it was Muñoz's impression that the Indians had *not* come in good faith. Muñoz informed Castro that they had not asked for peace, but that Fray José Francisco López had given them food and a *manojo* of tobacco anyway.[15] Padre López then failed to deliver a timely report to Muñoz so that the Apache could be apprehended consequent to superior orders, the latter most likely emanating from the viceroy himself. A plainly exasperated Castro minced no words expressing his dissatisfaction with the entire event and fired off a salvo to eviscerate one of the missionaries usurping his command. He wrote, "There never fails to be someone who will shelter the declared enemies of religion and humanity while the King is employing vast sums and the power of his arms for the purpose of exterminating them. I have said several times that under no pretext should any Indian of the Apache race be admitted into our presidios until [they] are forced to sue for peace in good faith, if that is possible in their treachery."[16]

Chapter Four

If Castro's disgust with the religious orders is only thinly veiled in the opening paragraph of the letter, by his last words to Muñoz he was unequivocal: "This you will make understood for a second time in the jurisdiction under your command, and especially by the missionary p[*adres*] of the far-too-many missions that I think exist in the province. You will express to the aforementioned [López] how unpleasant such pretenses are to me [*lo desagradables que me son tales disimulos*], and that I will report even to the King himself if a second complaint of this nature should come to me."[17]

Clearly relationships between the military and the Lipan had changed over time, and it was not for the better. The most cynical way to assess the situation was that at least, for now, interplay between soldiers and clergy maintained the status quo. In fact, only a decade earlier and even after José de Gálvez's expeditionary forays into the borderlands, a royal order of June 27, 1782, called on Cmdr. Gnl. Teodor de Croix to renew offensive operations against the Apache. Croix's successor, Felipe de Neve, carried out the order and grouped the presidial companies and the flying squadrons into divisions. Each one consisted of a third of the personnel of two or more companies deployed in relentless pursuit of the enemy via monthly campaigns.[18]

By November 1783, Neve had also completed an extensive inspection of the presidios of Sonora, Nueva Vizcaya, and Coahuila y Téjas. When he died unexpectedly in 1784, his replacement, Commandant Inspector José Antonio Rengel, came vested with the same powers possessed by Croix and Neve. Rapid changes came, too. In April 1785, the autonomy of the Commandancy General of the Interior Provinces ended when its management became subordinate to viceregal authority. As Moorhead explains, in this the twilight era of the Spanish colonial regime, what made the new viceroy different from those previous was that now the role was filled by a soldier with considerable experience, knowledge, and ability in dealing with the peculiar military and political problems of the Septentrión. That man, Bernardo de Gálvez, had served as a captain of a Chihuahua *compañía volante* just as Amangual would later do for the flying squadron stationed at Béxar.[19] Gálvez had also been military commandant for both Nueva Vizcaya and Sonora from 1770 to 1771 and governor of Louisiana from 1777 to 1783.[20]

Given the military acumen of the new viceroy, conditions seemed favorable for maximizing stability and cohesion in the borderlands by way of a 1787 transformation by separation when the *Provincias Internas* split into two distinct military districts. From out of the ranks to govern the region came two military commanders, the aforementioned Juan de Ugalde in the East, and Jacobo Ugarte y Loyola in the West. José Rengel would remain

Managing Soldiers, Questionable Accounts, and Contraband   131

comandante inspector.[21] Though the inauguration of high-level soldiers gained administrative traction in the metropoles, in many areas the de facto upper hand of authority belonged to Indigenous groups resisting the empire's first responders. Native rulers ran much of the show by intertwining tactics of sheer aggression, acute perception, and rickety compliance.

"A lesser number of good troops is worth more than a multitude of useless men"

As operatives carrying out separate but closely aligned duties in the farthest reaches of the frontier, soldiers like Amangual, Sgt. Fernández, the tailor Arreola, and even General Castro's irritant (by way of Apache benefaction) Fray José Francisco López, all fell under comprehensive jurisdiction. A plethora of ordinances repurposed the vast region from the perspective of enlightened governance. If, as Elizabeth John has described, Enlightenment thought was characterized by a process of "system and analysis," then, an equivalent approach manifested in documentation of presidio administration.[22] The body of literature created by soldiers in the literal and metaphorical trenches has gone unacknowledged as equally vital to understanding colonial iterations of rationalism and progressive thought.

One topical focus of this book is to analyze more closely the bureaucratic machinery of supervising the Comandancia General, its garrisons of soldiers, and ubiquitous *rancherías*. If it is true that a regionally specific character developed in the borderlands by melding ecclesiastical, military, indigenous, and civilian communities in flux, regular episodes of dissent and compromise had at the root a common element: the invariable stream of de jure house rules meant to superimpose a veneer of uniformity to the periphery.

Policy makers in distant places, whether in Madrid or Mexico City, generated pages of regulations and ordinances intended to set the parameters for its military across its incohesive empire. No study to date has sought to contextualize the *Reglamentos* of 1729 and 1772 in comparison to the main thrust of the Gálvez *Instrucción* of 1786. Though the audience for all three documents varied but slightly, the content of each directly impacted civilians, indigenous polities, and military personnel. The kind of broadly conceived monograph provided by Max Moorhead is the bedrock to understanding organizational mechanisms for defense, like a series of garrisons dotted across a combative landscape, necessary for sustaining, more or less, Nueva España's *frontera*. From a confluence of interests, assorted directives issued from the imperial center impacted the bureaucratic calculus of the presidial ecosystem. Given the complexities encountered in this niche of colonial administrative commentary, it is not hard to imagine those spaces emerging as hubs for international encounters among local inhabitants, soldier interactions with civilians, and interpresidio affiliations stretching from Coahuila-Texas and Louisiana to New Mexico.

Bernardo Gálvez drew up his *Instrucciones* upon receipt of a royal order from Carlos III. The viceroy's mandate was specifically directed to Cmdr. Gen. Jacobo Ugarte y Loyola as guidance for and timely observance by this senior officer and his immediate subordinates.[23] Gálvez prefaced the 216 points in the Instructions by declaring the "unhappy state" of the frontier but acknowledged the efforts of his and Ugarte's predecessors as they attempted to alleviate the evils from which the provinces suffered. Gálvez credited the borderlands soldiers' perpetual sacrifices in all operations of war, though certainly he was aware of the troops' less than stellar performances in the field. Across the horizon of possibilities, outsized ambitions underscored the corps' commitment to or repudiation of their military obligations even as they drew salaries and swore allegiance to their commanders and king.[24]

Unlike Rivera's regulations of 1729, early on into the preamble of his Instruction Gálvez invoked the name of *God* when he shared his certainty that the desired pacification of the borderlands offered even greater difficulties than those historically experienced in the region. Convinced that these challenges to peace appeared even more insurmountable in the calamitous mid-1780s, Gálvez imputed divine intervention for the provinces having been endowed with the "fair proportions of mild climate, fertility, and wealth."[25] Furthermore, he insisted that God would "use His mercy, restoring to them health and abundance" while at the same time consecrating the Spanish military offensive in its "operations of war." Expressing in black letter the customary benevolence toward soldiers altogether, Gálvez surely tempered his aspirational impulses by an awareness of the troops' occasional resistance to authority. In some instances, their comportment was more akin to that of the enemy. Leaving aside paternal instincts, the messaging of the Gálvez endeavor was wholly oriented as an exhortation to only one highly ranked soldier, Ugarte, a man expected to be attentive to the key precepts of a complex but explicit injunction. Unquestionably, the viceroy was aware that his *puntos generales* were but one part of overhauling the borderlands forces. At minimum, all publications aimed to inspire appreciation for and prima facie compliance with various other official mandates. The 1786 Instruction proposed to improve and standardize the army's governing machinery.[26] Throughout the empire, implementation of policy required commanders like Rivera, Gálvez, Ugarte, and on down the chain of command to be willing to put content into play.

Managing Soldiers, Questionable Accounts, and Contraband 133

Elsewhere, global conflict reached the Comandancia by way of action through documentation. Adding another mandate into the mix provides not only context for the significance of these late eighteenth-century directives but also reveals how they shaped frontier life during the colonial period. Doing so provides in highly abbreviated fashion a methodology for delineating key differences and subtle changes that emerged from the issuance of viceregal edicts. The existential impact of the Seven Years' War (1756–1763) reinvigorated large scale upgrades to the Spanish colonial superstructure by applying the inner workings of Peninsular bureaucratic reorganization. Financial and military systems constituted focal points for improvements, and increased centralization of the viceregal government provided a template for its application elsewhere. The Ordinance of Intendants, finally promulgated in the same year as Gálvez's Instruction (1786), had as one of its overarching objectives the creation of militias, a move on the part of reform-focused administrators to support local merchants and augment district-level bureaucracies with a visible paramilitary presence. The reconfiguration of the colonies into intendancies was a process which today one might refer to as redistricting but, here, minus suffrage. Since one of the Ordinance's other key goals was to replace the long-standing bureaucratic hegemony of the *alcaldes mayores* with a new set of agents for the empire in the persons of intendants and *subdelegados*, the ramifications were several. Lillian Fisher described a mercantilist philosophy that evolved from the issuance of the Grand Pragmatic of Free Commerce, or *libre comercio*, in 1778, a policy of free trade carrying the stipulation that interchange occur only within the official boundaries of the empire. According to one historian, once the conquest-era practice of *repartimiento* was abolished in 1782 and taxation ramped up revenues, the colonial tobacco monopoly took flight.[27]

As it was subsequently established in New Spain, the ordinance system replaced four departments of government: justice, general administration (*policía*), finance, and war. This meant relief for the viceroy from functions connected with the division of finance. Moreover, the intendants fulfilled the role of assistants to the viceroy with regard to the other three phases.[28] Since strategizing a ground game in times of conflict was not its focus, the Ordinance of Intendancies took a far more tepid approach to indigenous communities in general (quasi-abolition of repartimiento), and hostile ones in particular. Conversely, the Gálvez Instruction was explicitly militaristic in its content and aimed at eradicating what the viceroy saw as the Native menace to the frontier. This is not surprising, given that its content specifically exhorts to action a veteran scrapper like General Ugarte, assisted by the utterly pugnacious Juan de Ugalde. Since Gálvez had experience in the

134   Chapter Four

trenches, he could be as warlike as the Apache he fought as a young man. This was true, even now, in his messaging as the king's representative in Mexico City. However, his directive was tempered by a willingness to forgive if contrition was aboveboard.

In the previous chapter, I discussed the implications of the Instruction for the *compañías volantes* and, more specifically, for soldiers who demonstrated both a single-mindedness to the duties of military campaigns and an aptitude for avenging Indian predations. Article 91 of the Instructions encouraged Ugarte to immediately prepare to eliminate unfit men from presidial companies, flying squadrons, dragoons, and volunteers, and replace them with those more suitable for offense. If the feckless included officers, Article 92 required Ugarte to separate them immediately no matter what their rank and to consult with Viceroy Gálvez about the future these men would face. Subsequent articles concern selection of officers for vacant positions within the presidial hierarchy. Articles 99 through 103 are far more precise. These address the qualities needed in warfare and especially against Indigenous combatants.[29]

Given that soldiers were always in steady demand in the borderlands because of miscalculations, mismanagement, and poverty, attention will now turn to the Apache and their wavering relationship with the forces of occupation during the 1790s. Offensive military action in whatever form was predicated on monitoring the machinations of those considered hostile to the army. Disparate bands of Apache roamed the arid mountains and valleys along the entire frontier from Texas west to the Gila River (in present-day Arizona), but they were not a consistently united force and frequently sparred with one another. Worcester indicates the Mescalero lived in southern Texas, along the Río Grande, and targeted Coahuila and Nueva Vizcaya; the Lipan and Natagé invaded the settlements of southeastern New Mexico and El Paso del Norte, while in the mountains west of the Río Grande the *mimbreños* roamed. Northeast of New Mexico were the Jicarilla, with Nueva Vizcaya, Sonora, and New Mexico menaced by the Gileños, ensconced near the headwaters of the Gila River.[30]

Looking back, acrimony in the mid-eighteenth century Septentrión convulsed to the degree that decisive measures needed enactment. Max Moorhead wrote that by 1748 Apache depredations had reached such serious proportions in Nueva Vizcaya that Viceroy Francisco Revillagigedo I issued a formal declaration of war against the nation. Things would only get worse. Ordered to produce a report on conditions in the province, Conchos presidio captain Joseph de Berroterán complied and told the ugly truth.[31] From 1749 to 1763, Spanish estimates had Apache warriors killing more than eight

Managing Soldiers, Questionable Accounts, and Contraband   135

hundred people and destroying approximately four million pesos worth of property, principally targeting a two-mile radius of Chihuahua. Some raids came dangerously close to the city itself. Donald Worcester cited much higher numbers in the decade that followed when Apaches killed about 2,000 people, depopulating 116 ranches and settlements in the process.[32]

Gálvez grappled with the usual hazard worrying Spanish administrators in Monclova and Mexico City and corroborated by borderlands' military personnel in direct contact with the Apache. But Article 20 of his instruction was direct and unequivocal; war was to be waged without intermission in all the provinces against the Apache who declared it. Like commanders Rivera, Nava, and Cabello, who were attuned to rapprochement, Gálvez tracked with best practices, making Article 24 equally unambiguous: if the Apache groups sued for peace, concession would be made to them immediately. The truth cut deep. Gálvez acknowledged the martial wherewithal of the enemy against that of the Spanish forces; he noted their ability to surprise and ravage the presidials in the mountains and plains by managing their own forces with dexterity. He equated Apache skill on horseback to that of the Spaniards, and he even believed it surpassed that of the frontier cavalry. However, he also recognized that a cessation of hostilities was possible. To prove his point, Gálvez argued that all the Nations of the North were at peace in Texas; so too were the Lipan in Texas and in Coahuila. New Mexico's Jicarilla, Navajo, Ute, and the Comanche remained placid. He credited the Apache for having achieved amity with the town of El Paso in 1771, just as the Gileño had done with the presidios of both Janos and Fronteras. Further, the viceroy attested to Mescalero pacification in Nueva Vizcaya.[33]

Article 52 of the *Instrucción* may provide the most telling of all Gálvez's beliefs about the Apache. It makes clear that he ascertained a certain vulnerability in various factions of that nation.

> *I do not believe that the Apaches will submit voluntarily* [since only] *God can work this miracle, but we may contribute to the means of attracting the different factions of this tribe, making them realize the advantages of rational life, which should please them. They should become accustomed to the use of our foods, drinks, arms, and clothing, and they can be part of the greediness for the goods of the land. Even if in the beginning we are not successful in achieving these ends, as they require much time, this course will put us on the path to eventual success.*[34]

By the 1790s, conditions on the ground with some Native peoples were such that the Gálvez directives manifested in stabilized, if tenuous, rela-

136   Chapter Four

tionships and in form at *establecimientos de paz,* or state-run reservations of compliant Ndé groups.[35] In certain other forms, like Ndé farming and even ad hoc soldiering, the avenue to success he conceived in black ink for system-wide implementation, was already long in use. It found expression in the courting of Indians through gifts, diplomacy, and trade.[36] And for those, like the Mescalero, who refused to comply with these ostensibly benign mechanisms of command and control, Gálvez kept his word; he ordered his agents to wage continuous war. Far to the north and following the death of the leader Cuerno Verde, who likewise insisted on unceasing war on the Spaniards, more conciliatory members of the Comanche signed a peace treaty with the governor of New Mexico. In San Antonio, a similar treaty was signed by eastern Comanche, though that peace would never be as firm with Texas as it was with New Mexico.[37] When it worked, peace by purchase continued to be an indispensable tool for forging and solidifying diplomatic and interpersonal relationships between assentive Indians and the military. Bolstering the colonial troops, the Comanche agreed to help deficient Commandancy forces defeat the Apache. During this time, some Ndé fighters and their families sought protection at the mission–presidio complex or fled to established *rancherías.* Gálvez's mandate played out to some success.

In time, a "new era of security, growth and prosperity" emerged in New Mexico and Texas. DeLay saw peace between New Spain and indigenous communities in the borderlands as a triumph for colonial administrators. By financing frontier defense and infrastructure, by centralizing command, and by acting respectfully toward Native allies, bureaucrats from afar and military personnel in-country understood that New Spain's preservation depended on the security of their thinly populated northern frontier. That security hinged on good relations with the Apache (achieved, occasionally, with the Lipan), Navajo (*Diné*), Wichita, and the Comanche, described by DeLay as, collectively, very much "the real masters of that vast, difficult realm."[38] For all that, even this "new era" of optimism was marginal at best. Witnesses to a peninsula financially wrecked by war and immobilized by persistent stinginess toward its overseas frontiers, managers of the royal coffers rarely adopted a fiduciary approach to enhance the lives of the empire's outliers.

Gálvez had a solution for expenses saved by redistributing "unneeded" troops: take the money for their upkeep and apply it to "gifts for the peaceful Indians."[39] Presidial administration writings tell a quite different story of the consequences of shortchanging soldiers and neglecting infrastructure, with disobedience to authority and outright criminality as an inevitable if not preordained outcome.

Nuevo Santander, Escandón, and the Bustamante Victory

Breaches in security were inevitable. Following the issuance of the 1786 Instruction, resistant Indian groups hellbent on carving out spaces of domination managed to prevail in several pockets of the borderlands. The pursuit of the enemy ranged extensively, and punitive campaigns dipped far into south Texas. By March 17, 1792, Cmdr. Gen. Ramón de Castro received a report from the governor of Nuevo Santander José de Escandón, the Conde de Sierra Gorda, of week-long bloodshed across a swath of borderlands territory involving soldiers, civilians, Indians, and one notorious chief. Given the paucity of eyewitness accounts of these types of protracted violence, this rare, detailed narrative from the hand of Escandón is included here in its entirety.[40]

On the 6th day of March, I arrived at this villa without any incident. On the 10th at midday, I received a note dated the 9th from the lieutenant of the villa of Reynosa in which he tells the lieutenant of the villa of Camargo that at the moment he was fighting in that villa with the enemy Indians [not specified], who already had killed two of its citizens and an Indian auxiliary. He [Camargo lieutenant] continued on to Mier and Rebilla [sic], whose lieutenant Don Miguel de Cuellar tells me he was getting all the citizens together and was awaiting my orders. The promptness of this report provided me the ability to take timely steps. I instantly sent an order to the aforesaid lieutenant to leave the villa with competent reinforcements, cross the Río del Norte, and await [the arrival of] Captain Don Ramón de Bustamante. I ordered the horse herd brought in to provide extra mounts for the troops, and shortly before the prayer, I ordered the aforesaid captain to march with 30 men to join the aforementioned Lieutenant, and according to reports from the other villas, to pursue the Indians to teach them a lesson [(*ha de*) *escarmentarlos*]. On the 11th, with the aforementioned captain now joined with the citizens of Revilla, they continued their march straight to Paloblanco, where at about 7 in the morning of the 14th, they caught up with and killed one captain [and] 14 Indians, and took from them a captive, as Your Lordship will see in the report and diary that I enclose. If the dead *capitán* is, as they say, Zapato Sax, and two of the dead his sons, this has been most fortunate because, according to what I heard, he was one of the most famous captains. According to what the captive says, they intended on the way back after leaving here to attack the horse herd at S[an]ta Rosa, for which [reason] the aforesaid captive is being sent to inform Your Lordship about the places where their Rancherías [...] are located, as well as the intentions that he perceived from them.

I am sending the head and foot of the aforesaid chief, fifteen pairs of ears, and an equal number of genitals. All the plunder listed in the report remains here at Your Lordship's disposition and is not being sent now so as not to delay the soldiers.[41]

So significant an episode in borderlands armed conflict did Castro consider the events of March 9–14, 1792, as related to him by Escandón, that he asked—but did not order—Muñoz to circulate the report among the companies under the general's charge. His reasoning was that the news might serve to glorify Captain Bustamante's success and become a psychological stimulus to other officers and troops. Castro considered Bustamante company's undertaking to be of the greatest honor to the army and of benefit to the *Provincias Internas*.[42]

What amounted to a bonus of sorts with this victory was confirmation of the death of the "cruel and warlike" Capt. Zapato Sax; this assessment about the headman is known from depositions taken in the lower Río Grande Valley and in Laredo from individuals who knew him, including the one who was his captive. Castro's urgency that news of the battle be relayed immediately compelled him to send the letter to Muñoz so that Bustamante would have the satisfaction of being officially recognized for his enthusiasm, spirit, and efficacy in the service of the king. He wanted to make known how praiseworthy such glorious action was for all the provinces. Willing to prove it, Castro expressed to Muñoz how highly he would commend the Bustamante campaign to superior authorities, presumably in Mexico City, as he would do for all those who similarly distinguished themselves.[43]

Though six years separated Gálvez's instruction to Ugarte and the Bustamante victory, the counsel and the commission taken together represented the fulfillment of one key point as they specifically applied to Nuevo Santander and the region's only "declared enemies," the Mescalero Apache. Gálvez made clear in his Instruction that all the "barbarous" Indians were to be treated with distrust. Employing deception, the hatred between the "Nations of the North" and the Lipan, who still preserved their former peace with Texas and Coahuila, was to be "promoted with much skill and discretion." That meant no overt action in any provocation between the two. For the time being, however, Gálvez wanted it both ways so that his "combined plans" could have the desired effect: "friendship" maintained between these same two groups.[44]

What is known of the Bustamante achievement at Paloblanco discloses a remarkable, but uneven, network of coordination and cooperation among presidial troops in safeguarding civilians while accomplishing the goals of a punitive expedition. Both deeds were intended to set an example to

Managing Soldiers, Questionable Accounts, and Contraband 139

enemies of the empire. Sierra Gorda's account of defending Revilla's citizens by troop reinforcements demonstrates not only single-mindedness in gaining the upper hand but also, by mutilating Native corpses, an overt messaging of Spanish savagery. As it often appears, sections of the original documentation can obscure subtleties in closely aligned objectives such as the deployment of troops for offensive assistance and protection. As real-time conflict played out, the lines of function among the various military cadres often blurred in times of desperation and indecision. The same may be said about how motives within superior directives figured into juggling interwoven relationships among Native groups while suppressing hostilities. Going up against battle-scarred adversaries set the playing field for how enmity and amity could be manipulated to achieve these goals.

As we saw in the previous chapter, the parameters for using military escorts across the northern frontier are explicitly described in the *Reglamento* of 1729.[45] In one case, sixty-three years after the 1729 mandate and in the month prior to the Bustamante escapade, Sierra Gorda requested security from General Castro for a trip to San Antonio. The business at hand dealt with matters related to superior orders authored by Viceroy Revillagigedo. Upon receipt of the request, Castro ordered Governor Muñoz to prepare a convoy led by an officer from Béxar with an additional fifty men. They were to proceed as soon as possible to the presidio at Laredo since by the following week Sierra Gorda would arrive, ready for the journey to San Antonio.[46] What is telling in this episode is that from scratch Castro expected Muñoz to cover the absence of the troops with citizens from Laredo until that presidio's troops forming the Sierra Gorda contingent returned and resumed their duties.

One month passed before Muñoz complied with Castro's order for escorts. He informed Escandón that he had arranged for a party of fifty men headed by Alférez José Xavier Menchaca to march to Laredo, supplied with provisions including munitions for a month. Quick to defend his tardiness, Muñoz explained to the governor that Castro's order had not come to his hands until March 16.[47] That delay was not his fault. Muñoz assured Escandón that Alférez Menchaca knew to speed up his march so that he could arrive as soon as possible. Without further information, it is unclear when Menchaca and his fifty men finally arrived to accompany Escandón to San Antonio. Rankling things even further, on or about the same day Castro ordered Governor Muñoz to prepare the escort for Escandón, Alférez Menchaca apparently suffered a lance wound to the arm from two Apaches spying on the Béxar presidio's horse herd. The content of Muñoz's original letter of February 13 is known, secondhand, from a short note by Revillagigedo who, learning of Menchaca's bad luck, wondered why the

140 Chapter Four

troops accompanying him did not come together against the attack; who questioned the measures taken by Muñoz to pursue the two Apaches; and, of the problems that prevented that pursuit. Perturbed, the viceroy asked what precautions Muñoz had taken to avoid Indian attacks in the future.[48]

Whether accompanied by Menchaca or not, on April 9 Escandón arrived in San Antonio and received clearance by Muñoz to undertake the tasks assigned to him by the viceroy. By the end of May, Escandón assumed the role of interim governor of Texas and on July 1, 1792, produced his first review of the cavalry company stationed at Béxar presidio.[49]

As we have seen, deficits and vulnerabilities surfaced when escort duties took troops from their garrisons. The more recent *Instrucción* of 1786 dictated that defense of the provinces required frontier troops to be excused from "useless escort duty" and to instead facilitate operations of "incessant warfare." Gálvez knew that abuse occurred often enough to warrant prevention. Even six years later, Muñoz must have anticipated that, too. When he issued his mandate, the viceroy urged Ugarte in Sonora to avoid taking any measures, "either contrary or favorable," with the Yumas and other tribes of the Río Colorado since assaults against those groups, the Seris, and Tiburones, along with unrelenting attacks upon the Apache, would result in "nothing [being] accomplished."[50] But cessation of presidial aggression there might allow for convoys of protectors elsewhere.[51]

Missionary success in Texas, achieved by the recruitment of converts, came with calls for military escorts but stalled for the usual reason: presidio commanders' reluctance to sacrifice soldiers for convoys. Almost fifty years prior to Muñoz's release of soldiers headed by Menchaca, missionaries exulted over their success at attracting Indian people to the banks of the Brazos and San Xavier rivers (present day San Gabriel River) for settlement. They pointed to the "fitness of the lands for sowing, the advantages of the river for irrigation, and the abundance of its waters" as proof of their need for establishing missions. However, those aspirations depended upon troops for protecting not only the neophytes from Apache attacks but also the Spanish settlers who might join them in soil cultivation and cattle raising. In the words of Morfi, "this last proposal altered the attitude" of the region's military commanders like Gov. Juan Antonio Bustillos and Presidio La Bahía's Capt. Joaquín Bazterra in 1746. They dreaded, "and justly so, that the guard would be formed with troops from their respective presidios." Thus, they were quick to "discredit the advantages of the site selected on the banks of the San Xavier." So great was their aversion to losing soldiers while providing security for civilians, including the religious, that any justification, however wild-eyed or fallacious, was fair game for commanders in country. Another concern was foreseeable: the quality of soldiers available for security purposes. In one case, Padre Benito de Santa Ana Fernández, the missionary in charge of Misión Concepción and president of the Querétaran missions in Texas, complained about the "practically useless" soldiers supplied by Cpt. Costales of La Bahía to guard the religious structures.[52]

Whether ineffectual or a good fit, presidial troops' function as escorts, if only occasional, did not necessarily involve traversing long distances. Further, these duties did not exclusively involve members of the flying squadrons. Even in times of peace, precautions were necessary to ensure the safety of frontier residents and the *Reglamento* of 1729 was quite specific apropos of protectors. Because guard service for private individuals outside of the regular schedule was a burden and detriment to the soldiers insofar as that caused them more work, the provincial governors and the presidial captains were admonished to refrain from providing any unnecessary services. When soldiers were employed as guardians entering or leaving the provinces, they were to do so only at predetermined times and at assigned places so that travel concluded while under convoy.[53]

However, the transregional nature of soldiering in the Comandancia was consistent with an often-impermanent status characterized by sustaining productive, if often tenuous, relationships with other battalions and even adversaries. Troops carried out assignments in one place to ensure security in another. Operatives like Bustamante, Menchaca, and Francisco Amangual experienced all these things across the reach of the army's scattered international frontiers. Often, what it meant for soldiers in the saddle or seated at a desk involved both physical mobility and diligent bookkeeping as tactical maneuvers to enhance the flow of commerce for the sake of brokering peace.

Amangual: Questionable Accounts, Incorruptible Accountant

In the meantime, if Béxar presidio's *habilitado* thought the aggravation stemming from his slander suit against Sgt. Rodríguez that he endured for some two months had come to an end, he was wrong. About two weeks before Escandón assumed the governorship, Amangual would find himself again having to answer for his bookkeeping, but this time based on suspicions from on high. Representing the Superior Accounting Office of the Royal Tribunal of Accounts in Mexico, José del Cavo Franco issued a document in May 1792 inferring "questionable balances" against the *habilitación* fund of the Béxar presidial company. The inquiry sought a review of the accounts and examination of expenditures for gifts intended for the maintenance of peaceful relations with Native inhabitants. It specifically

142 Chapter Four

targeted bands that had presented themselves in peace from December 3, 1786, through August 15, 1790.[54] Though Amangual is not mentioned in the Cavo Franco inquiry, the term of the questionable balances corresponded to, at least partially, his tenure as paymaster while the bulk of the period in question belonged to his predecessor Bernardo Fernández. Moreover, though volatile Apache groups might only be placated by private traders using "peace by deceit" to make them dependent on provisions supplied by the Spanish (a strategy Gálvez promoted in his Instruction), surely even their numbers arriving in spasmodic peace at the presidio were taken into account by Amangual and other paymasters.[55]

The Cavo Franco inquest is presented in a series of numbered "notes" preceding a column of "reports," and numerically ordered but not inclusive. A portion of the report's content and formatting is duplicated here because of its significance to the creation of inventories, a complex task within the scope of all paymasters' duties. Itemizing stockpiles necessitated due diligence from colonial administrators in ensuring accuracy when reporting product intake and outflow. This chapter, and those previous, treat the subject of preserving mutually conducive relationships with the indigenous communities through the wobbly practice of peace by purchase. Handwritten ledgers, often difficult to decipher, reveal the expenditures of frontliners and other agents of the empire and even list the preferences of their clientele—Native and otherwise—in a standardized and chronologically expressed format. Military accounting practices provide evidence for the kinetics triggered by inter/intra-presidio transactions and exchanges of goods during the late colonial era. Much of the documentation comes from Amangual and his contemporaries and further illuminates the day-to-day activities that presidials and others engaged as participants in the imperial economy. Likewise, the Cavo Franco compilation establishes that commercial activities in New Spain's Comandancia were closely monitored by bureaucrats in the metropole whose interest in expenditures for the Native populations persisted and thus required justification. Herein lay its granular content

NOTES[56]

1st...The dated entries in the aforesaid accounts, dealing with salaries for servants [*mozos*] employed in preparing food for the Indians and in attending to them, and with the rental of pots and other utensils (from which came the afore-mentioned doubtful balances), lack the corresponding statement, because in general they refer to the time covered in each account, from which it results that in order to balance or examine the amount of each one of the aforesaid entries, it is necessary

Managing Soldiers, Questionable Accounts, and Contraband 143

to do so for the days that passed during the aforesaid time to which the accounts refer. For this reason, one notices repeated errors, and some of importance in that category.

2nd...This same repetition and seeing that neither the servants nor the owner or owners of the pots protested such errors (since there is no evidence of such), causes one to believe fundamentally that, in reality, they did not exist and that [the errors] consist of [the fact] that no explanation is made in the aforementioned entries.

3rd...It is not easy to arrive at a fixed point in discovering the cause upon which differences [of the entries] are based, which can consist in that during the time included in each report, the men would not always be employed, nor even the pots be used, and that the aforesaid servants and the owners of the aforementioned pots would be credited only for their days of service, and those [days] only would be paid to them, being the amount put forward in the expressed entries that seem to be incorrect.

4th...This notion is verified by the fact that in the 6th entry in the account of expenditures for maintaining the Indians that is enclosed with report No. 20 that ran from July 11 to August 13 of 1790, and includes thirty-four days, there are entered for the service of two men only eighteen days, and it says clearly that this one time they were employed in preparing the food and attending to the Indians. And even in the other accounts in which differences are found, there is no similar expression made, [and] the same thing could have occurred, even though they include the number of days in each one, the servants would not be employed in all of them, nor [would] the pots [be] in use.

5th...For these reasons, it has been judged appropriate to deal separately in these documents with the afore-mentioned entries in which a difference is encountered in the area of questionable balances, [and so] the governor of Texas is appropriately prepared to clarify this point and to reply on what happens.[56]

The latter report, No. 32, had combined expenditures of servant salaries and rental of utensils, and prompted Cavo Franco to insert a note that read

[...] only nine pesos are entered, with the statement that it is for the salary of the afore-mentioned servant and for the rental of pots. It is not possible to distinguish how much corresponds to, or how much was paid for, the aforesaid rental, nor [is it] easy to state the difference that exists with the aforementioned salary, [since] nothing is entered here in the margin; and this explanation is given solely for the record.[57]

Chapter Four

At this point in Cavo Franco's document, there appears to be a discrepancy in the numbering of the reports, or it may be that those reports from succeeding years simply reused the same numbering sequence. However, a note on the document indicates that "up to here runs the 1st report" presented by Lt. Bernardo Fernández, "and the second one follows, from the agent José Antonio de Bustillos y Zevallos." The information deviates little from the content of the previous reports.[58]

As explored in the last chapter, Amangual's performance as his garrison's manager of funds had already come under scrutiny to the extent that accusations by a fellow company member against him led to a slander suit. However, that was an intra-presidio annoyance borne out of mischief and instigated by a troublemaker who, also, happened to be a mission padre. Here, in this new assault on Amangual's integrity, the investigatory entity represented a formidable bureaucratic arm of the viceregal government. Notwithstanding his unwavering adherence to protocol, three years would pass before Amangual gave his response to the Cavo Franco allegations of discrepancies in the expansive report of 1792. His predecessor as paymaster Bernardo Fernández would do the same, as we shall shortly see.

In the meantime, in an ironic twist of circumstances and only two months after his own altercation with an accuser, Amangual found himself as caretaker and inspector of newly discovered contraband allegedly in the possession of the captain of Presidio Bahía, Juan Cortés. Out of necessity, perhaps, Amangual postponed his reply to the Superior Accounting Office by explaining this new obligation as an unavoidable interruption caused by immediate, more pressing concerns. Nevertheless, he ignored none of it—answering for discrepancies found by Cavo Franco, and now housing someone else's alleged bootlegged goods in *his* office—even as his own troubles only recently deescalated.

Beyond its emergence as one more legal embroilment for presidials engaged in economic operations, the Cortés contraband inquiry of June 1792 is significant for another reason. Across time and space that peculiar form of misconduct by the army's operatives had historically been an incessant obstacle to not only maintaining order in frontier commerce but also cementing honorable conduct within the ranks.

Soldiers Testify in Texas: The Cortés Contraband Case

In the summer of 1792 *Comandante General* Ramón de Castro ordered the Interim governor of Texas José Escandón to investigate a contraband charge against Capt. Juan Cortés, his men, and outsiders during a trip from

Natchitos, Louisiana, to Nacogdoches in East Texas. Escandón initiated the proceedings even though he had refrained from arresting the accused captain. Further, General Castro required Escandón to place in safe storage the goods in question, whether they turned out to be smuggled or not. Ultimately, the viceroy would render the decision as to whether the goods were to be delivered to the interested parties.[59]

But first, the alleged contraband followed the usual process of inspection and tabulation. Amangual itemized all dubious goods as part of the investigation, something he had not carried out for his own slander suit but one with which he had long familiarity. Another irony here is that twelve years earlier, as alférez of the Béxar company, Amangual—on detached service at Fort Cíbolo—headed out under orders to the rancho of San Francisco with a group of men to intercept suspected co-*contrabandistas* Felix Menchaca and Juan de Ysurieta and to subsequently escort them back to the presidio. Amangual and his men were to seize any goods found in the pack train originating from Louisiana. That included any boys as servants that might be accompanying the merchandise. The more remarkable twist to this most recent incident of smuggling was that Cortés had very recently acknowledged receipt of a viceregal *bando* pardoning smugglers trafficking in prohibited beverages.[60] Perhaps now he visualized a stroke of fortune whereby a pardon might extend to include non-liquid merchandise should that circumstance arise.

As documentation of the Amangual–Rodríguez slander suit appears in this book, the original testimony from the recorded depositions of the Cortés case follows with minor annotations in order to maintain the tenor of the relevant voices. The legible manifestation of the inquiry similarly progresses along a chronological timeline. The associated inventory provides a fascinating view into the types of merchandise soldiers and vendors desired to trade in or bring home as their own. Taken together, this method of exposition makes plain the bureaucratic processes underscoring military inquiries into dereliction of duty and chiefly where and when it involved frontier commerce.

Part of the intrigue surrounding any investigation of alleged smuggling are the actual items in question. Interpreting the significance of contraband to all parties suspected of involvement in that enterprise adds to its mystique. Like the inventory earmarked in the Amangual–Rodríguez slander suit, animal hides constituted the bulk of the merchandise confiscated, with ironware and tobacco now thrown into the mix. Amangual's inventory of the items found in the baggage of Cortés and his cohorts lists the suspects' names next to an itemization of those articles they were accused of taking illegally. (See appendix 3.)

Chapter Four

Several citizens, including women, the commander general himself, and the former adjutant inspector of presidios, find their way into Amangual's official documentation. He added the following short paragraph and the list of animal hides (see table 1) to his inventory:

> Also found in the baggage of the aforesaid Sergeant Treviño was a package that he was carrying by order of Nicolas de Lamatth to deliver to Dona Maria Concepcion Henriquez, which upon being examined contained one fine silk kerchief, two contraband card decks, two ivory toys, fourteen single cards for various individuals of this community, others of a similar category for Señores Don Antonio Bonilla, Don Bernardo Bonavia, and Don M [?/MS torn] Mexía, a double for the Señor commandant general of these provinces, and another single same for his secretary, Don Juan de Aguirre y Morales, all of which on today's date I have forwarded to their respective destinations [sic passim].[61]

The formatted list ends here. However, Amangual added a final caveat regarding the inventory. He pointed out that Capt. Juan Cortés carried with him four black slaves—a husband, wife, their son, and a girl "belonging" to his brother-in-law José de Jesús Alderete—as well as nine mules and horses, all property of militia captain Antonio Gil Ibarvo. It seems Ibarvo was eager to receive Sgt. Treviño's deposition as well as those of the other soldiers listed in the inventory. In fact, he was more interested in the depositions of "Mariano Basques" and "José Basques" since Ibarvo specifically wanted answers to the following questions: Upon whose order were the men acting? And, from whom came the money that they paid? Finally, with what monies did they purchase the chamois and buffalo skins in the Indian nations? And since Ibarvo from his declaration self-confessed that "at no time will they be held responsible for anything," Ibarvo perhaps hoped that his soldiers, as men who were not part of the regular army and despite evidence to the contrary, would be found innocent or, at least, less culpable given their militia status.

One additional note was appended: according to Sgt. Treviño, hostile Indians had carried off four bundles and two horses from those listed in the report.[62] The inquiry began with the customary aggregate of questions directed to five soldiers including Sgt. Treviño, Corporal Maldonado, and the privates Gómez, Trexo, and Rodríguez. What kinds of commodities did the soldiers see? By whose orders were the loads delivered, and to who? How were the goods paid for and who were they from? What funds were used to purchase or what goods were traded for chamois skins from the Indian nations?

Table 1.

Name	Buffalo Hides	Chamois (white)	Chamois (colors)	Deerskins, with/without Hair
Capt. Juan Cortés	3	5	2, dyed touchwood (yesca)	
Sgt. Antonio Treviño	1	4		1, without hair
Cpl. Hilario Maldonado	0	1		4, without hair
Soldado Distinguido José de Jesús Alderete[a]	4	36, +2 (for the *padres*)[b]	8, dyed touchwood, 4, black	1, with hair
Private José de la Garza	0	6	2, dyed touchwood	
Private Antonio Gómez	1	4		
Private Salvador de Cierra		5		
Private Juan José de la Garza		2		
Private José Trexo	1	2	1, dyed touchwood	

[a] Commander General Pedro de Nava described the soldado distinguido to Governor Muñoz, advising him that these soldiers, categorized with this term by either the circumstances of their birth or from being the sons of officers, were exempt from all manual labor (like sweeping the plaza or barracks) and to be employed only in military duties. Nava to Muñoz, instructing him not to demand manual labor from distinguished soldiers, BA February 9, 1791. The Spanish military historian Marchena Fernández (1983, p. 126) adds: "This variable will include, only in some geographic zones, those persons that had requested the filing for Hidalguía, and are in general of known quality [by birth], but always arbitrating a title of nobility, or already possess it, or are close to having it. On several occasions we have encountered titled noblemen included in that classification while in others it is only specified that their noble title is pending."

[b] Cortés...smuggling, BA June 16, 1792. Amangual's notation here is "in which were items obtained for the padres."

148 Chapter Four

Table 1. *Continued*

Name	Buffalo Hides	Chamois (white)	Chamois (colors)	Deerskins, with/without Hair
Private Cristóbal de Higuera		5		
Private Joaquín Galán	1 (worn)	6		
Private Antonio del Río	1	4		4, without hair
Private Pedro Grande		4		

The Depositions, September 10, 1792

When asked what items he saw introduced by the Frenchmen coming from "Nachitos"[63] to Nacogdoches, Sgt. Treviño verified seeing tobacco, two kegs of liquor (*aguardiente*), gunpowder, bullets, large knives (*veldúquez*), beads, vermillion, two casks of lard, and one sack of beans. Treviño counted seventeen loads and stated that he knew nothing else about other items the men had brought. Then, when asked if he knew by whose order or to whom the loads were delivered, he said that they were all delivered to "Nicolas de Lamate," who received them at his home. Asked if he knew how the goods were paid for and whom they were from, Treviño said that he only knew that his commander Cortés gave a Frenchman named Gaspar Friola some two hundred deerskins. He also stated that these skins came from the Ibarvo seizure. Questioned about the funds used to purchase chamois skins from the Indian nations, Treviño said the ones in his possession were given to him by Lamath, and other soldiers brought them in trade for tobacco and knives. But he did not know what monies were used to buy skins from the Indian villages.[64]

Immediately after the Treviño deposition, Cpl. José Ylario Maldonado testified, claiming no knowledge as to what Luis Belame, Mariano Vásquez, and José Vázquez were carrying in their loads. The latter two soldiers' depositions were under serious scrutiny by Ibarvo. Corporal Maldonado also stated that he heard that the goods would end up at the home of Lamate. Further, he did not know from whom they came or how they were purchased. As far as the deerskins, he did not know that any amount was paid out. Of the chamois skins, Maldonado responded that these were bought in trade for a little tobacco from what was supplied to him for trading—a large knife, one *candonga* and one bridle—by order of his captain. Unknown to him was what the skins were traded for in the villages. The corporal affirmed that another Frenchman, Luis Arman, brought tobacco, lard, salt, corn, and sugar into Nacogdoches.[65]

For three lower ranking soldiers, similarities prevailed in what they witnessed during the transaction. For example, Pvt. Antonio Gómez's testimony differed slightly from his predecessors', in that he had been guarding the horse herd and thus did not see any more than three loads come in, one of them containing *aguardiente*. He stated that he would not have seen other loads appear once he was relieved of his guard duties. But he surmised that if by chance others had been introduced, their arrival came by way of the Frenchmen he saw in Nacogdoches. However, he confirmed, as did Treviño but not Maldonado, that goods unloaded found their way to Lamath's house. He could not say with what the goods were paid for or from whom they came, but only that he witnessed Frenchmen from Nacogdoches exporting a quantity of deerskins and buffalo tongues to Nachitos. Gómez said that his chamois skins were traded for a cinch and a large knife, but that the ones bought in the villages were purchased by Cortés, or the others.[66]

Though Pvt. José de Trexo confirmed that Luis Belanze and both Vázquez men had in association with the French trafficked the alleged contraband into the Nacogdoches presidio, the items he saw brought in were fabrics for clothing, aguardiente, gunpowder, lots of bullets, a great deal of tobacco, blankets, and large knives. Since they arrived in three batches, he never learned of the total number of loads. The first deponent to specify a precise location of a home delivery, Trexo saw some goods unloaded in "Lamate's" parlor. He evaded specifics about from whom the merchandise came (that is, from their original point of departure in Natchitos) or how it was purchased since he could not, or would not, say. Of the deerskins, he could remember seeing several in the possession of the Frenchmen who supposedly traded with everyone. Trexo added that since the French were trading gunpowder, bullets, tobacco, large knives, cloth, and blankets, chamois skins were purchased by the *presidiales*. Trexo himself traded a bridle and some biscuit for his chamois, but he could not say what Cortés exchanged for his skins.[67]

While Pvt. José Antonio Rodríguez witnessed loads taken into Lamath's house, he did not know the exact number. However, he helped open one keg of gunpowder, a sack of bullets, and two *hachos* (bunches) of large knives; he also found out that the other loads contained tobacco. Additionally, Rodríguez was the first deponent to confirm knowing the goods belonged to Lamath because Lamath had sent them to Patates, Arralde, and Abalanché—who were in Nacogdoches—to bring them to him in Natchitos. Since Rodríguez did not know how the goods were purchased, he could claim ignorance regarding the deerskins, but admit that he knew a "Monsieur Davi" had more than two hundred of them. Nevertheless, Rodríguez did not know the supplier. He did verify that the major item of contention, the chamois, were bought by the soldiers with tobacco, large knives, and even a vest he saw traded. Unable to confirm what Captain Cortés had traded for the chamois he acquired, Rodríguez overheard an unidentified Indian say that Cortés had given him half a *manojo* of tobacco for some chamois, and that Pvt. Pedro Grande traded a three-footed pot for three chamois skins, and a *jorongo* for another one. Like Gómez and Trejo before him, Rodríguez did not sign his deposition because he could not write.[68] All three of these men self-identified as "Spanish," and all were in their twenties.

Summoned to the capitol on August 15, the accused Cortés informed Governor Escandón that Alférez Antonio Treviño would be traveling to San Antonio with the rest of the individuals mentioned except for José Trexo, who was in San Luis Potosí and "Christobal de Yguera," who was already in San Antonio. Cortés also let the governor know that he himself would not be going due to a ruptured tumor in his left arm—an injury he claimed prevented him from riding a horse—and his heavy workload on an audit for the outgoing *habilitado*. The latter task included forwarding the results of the audit to the incoming paymaster since, presumably, the latter would need it during the transition of duties.[69]

From the information specified in the inventory including Amangual's caveat and where it concerns Cortés' brother-in-law Alderete, it cannot be assumed that the items gathered for the padres were necessarily requested by the missionaries in collusion with the soldiers. Without further information, we can only guess as to why Amangual included this additional descriptor—"in which were items obtained for the *padres*"—for the two chamois skins and what they contained, presumably, hidden within their folds. If Amangual was tasked with performing a no-frills accounting of the suspicious merchandise, overseers of his assignment and its results may have paused to contemplate his comment regarding the religious. All the same, firsthand observers of the Cortés intrigue likely experienced no astonishment whatsoever to the annotation especially considering the appalling Padre Gómez Moreno factor in Amangual's only recently concluded slander suit. In any case, it seems attention to detail guided his course of action and, in depositions requiring ratification by his commanders, Amangual testified with little hesitation.

Managing Soldiers, Questionable Accounts, and Contraband 151

Since the Cortés investigation now consumed his work schedule and with his prior bookkeeping just then under a cloud of suspicion from the Royal Tribunal's inquiry, Amangual slogged on with the inventory at hand. He surely set aside any concerns about his culpability in flaws detected by administrators in Mexico City. After almost four decades in the army, he had achieved a certain measure of foresight and wisdom. Having put these qualities into practice in all things military, he could confidently claim expertise and thus inspire trust from his superiors.

As noted in chapter 1 of this study and as Max Moorhead argued, the day-to-day workload of a presidial company's paymaster was invariably suspect.[70] Unsurprisingly, from the previous century into the present, un-principled individuals took up fraudulent activities when provisioning soldiers. Transgressions occurred. Intermittent mishandling of financial affairs for the companies staffed with *habilitados* constitutes one of the best-known aspects of borderlands military history. Whether duly elected by fellow soldiers or serving in an interim position, the frontier paymaster faced enormous challenges in his role as fiduciary of garrison funds.

Similarly, complex interactions, like infighting among presidial soldiers over bureaucratic mandates and misunderstandings about fulfilling basic obligations, often engendered an imprecise adherence to the various orders and multiple regulations issued by commanders, governors, and the viceroy himself. The social kinetics and the asymmetries of power brought on by frontier exigencies often short-circuited obedience among the troops, in turn causing some—like the periodically hard-headed Juan Cortés—to stray from the presumed codes of honor, subordination, and devotion to duty expected from soldiers. Matters were not helped by collusion among dishonest merchants, self-indulgent commanders, and errant local padres, among other cheaters who opted for abusing soldier pay and provisioning for much of the past century. Various reforms enacted across the periphery were meant to curb pernicious practices but did little to alleviate troop indebtedness and supply shortages. Not infrequently, soldiers across the borderlands conspired with *contrabandistas* within their ranks, causing the invariable ebb and flow of goods into the colonial garrisons to occasionally fall under suspicion and face official scrutiny.

While it is true that Amangual's accounting efforts continued to be questioned by some, what becomes evident is an uninterrupted reliance by principals on Amangual's experience. At this point in his career, he had achieved senior status as an officer of long tenure and had acquired con-sistent upward mobility on the military ranking scale. The same could be

152 Chapter Four

said of Juan Cortés, an officer never reticent about expressing his opinion, even at the risk of appearing insubordinate, if not downright nervy, toward his commanders.

Cortés Comes to Testify—September 10, 1792

On September 10, Escandón reported that Captain Cortés was in San Antonio de Béxar and could now be deposed. The first question to Cortés was one not asked of the other deponents: Why did he dispatch Sgt. Treviño and another soldier to Nachitos? Cortés replied that Treviño had asked him for permission to go there with another soldier since Treviño told him that he was going to collect a debt. Asked why Treviño departed, yet again, for Nachitos, and with whom, Cortés replied: Nicolas "Lamathé" had asked him for Treviño's accompaniment to Nachitos, to which Cortés replied that if Treviño wished to go, he could; if not, then he would stay. Thereafter, Cortés claimed knowledge of only two or three loads brought into Nacogdoches by the Frenchman "Blanz," but he knew nothing about Mariano and José Vásquez. Cortés knew about what went to Lamath's house; however, the merchandise mostly consisted of tobacco, scarlet and blue cloth, vermilion, glass beads, knives, mirrors, gunpowder, and bullets. He alleged that all these items constituted gifts to seven or eight distinct groups among the Indian nations visiting him at Nacogdoches where even more gift-giving ensued.[71]

Cortés insisted that all this activity was in accord with the intentions of Cmdr. Gen. Ramón de Castro to whom he reported everything and who, in turn, approved of his efforts. Betraying a lack of attentiveness to expenditures, Cortés stated that he was unsure as to the cost of these gifts, whether it was four hundred or five hundred, or so, a sum still due and owing until Castro's decision.[72]

During the deposition, Escandón reminded the captain of superior orders issued again and again to commanders in Texas prohibiting trade of all kinds with the French. In fact, the only products that could be introduced into this sector of the borderlands were fabrics and goods brought in through the port of Veracruz and others authorized by the king. In what must have provoked incredulity from Escandón, Cortés replied that he was unaware of orders addressing this issue in the archives at Presidio La Bahía. He insisted that if such directives existed, he was similarly unaware of how he had disobeyed them.[73] It is not difficult to imagine the scrappy Cortés, hackles raised, positioning ignorance, probably feigned, as a defense mechanism, when in truth it may have only raised further suspicions about his negligence and, even, further established his complicity. What does

Managing Soldiers, Questionable Accounts, and Contraband   153

strain the imagination is the possibility that Cortés, if interrogated, might push this same defense in the presence of the frontier army's supreme commander, Gen. Ramón de Castro.

At this point in the interrogation, the primacy of certain objects as instruments of barter, procured legally or otherwise, becomes clearer as does their importance to the indigenous communities. Contextualizing the items as social signifiers in the seesaw rhythm of trade diplomacy explains the ramifications for several groups' inaccessibility to some commodities across the Commandancy. Far more than scarcities coveted by both soldiers and Native populations, some items took on added significance as those perilous to military discipline and trade protocol during the process of peace by purchase. The defendant Cortés was asked whether he knew if any persons (their status as either civilians or soldiers is not shown) might have taken items, including tobacco, playing cards, and fabrics, from the cargo introduced from Nachitos. He responded that he knew of no other seizures other than ten *manojos* of tobacco that he took to the people of the Nations of the North on his journey through Indian "pueblos." A portion of this tobacco was left over to him since he had not yet passed the "pueblo of the Taguayaces," and because most of the Quiches and the Tahuacanes were out hunting buffalo. Otherwise, the entire quantity would be expended.[74]

Environmental conditions, even hypothetical ones, and personal property factored into the testimony. Cortés proposed that had the rivers been high, he would have found it necessary to barter with the Indians for corn, beans, and beef in exchange for tobacco. It seems flooding was not a concern since the seizure included Cortés' own tobacco, an item given to him for his own personal use because there were neither cigarettes nor cigars at Nacogdoches. Also confiscated were four pieces of cloth, out of five purchased, for a doublet he commissioned but ultimately, or so he alleged, ruined by a tailor. Cortés had three or four decks of cards with which to play in the privacy of his house, or so he claimed, but these were taken from him because, like the tobacco, there were none available in the entire province. Seized, also, were two kerchiefs, one bolt of chintz, and a set of buttons for a coat, all of which including the tobacco cost him thirty pesos or so. Unquestionably, Cortés knew from troops in his unit that merchandise intended for their families was confiscated from them, as well. That revelation steered the inquiry toward even more personal matters.

Family culpability may have crossed Escandón's mind based on relationships noted in the Amangual inventory. Suspicious without end about questionable tobacco and fabric, Escandón asked Cortés about their presence in the seizure. Cortés professed to know nothing of any tobacco other than what he had mentioned. However, his brother-in-law Alderete's baggage contained clothing (his own), and cloth given to him by another relative, Padre Bernardino Vallejo, one or two cuttings of skirts for his wife, and thirty or forty chamois skins obtained by Alderete at the request of Cortés. These were needed for the repair and construction of a few *cueras* (protective leather jackets for troops), and this was the maximum amount Alderete could amass, even though Cortés had asked for more. When asked what quantity of tobacco and goods Sgt. Treviño and his attendant soldiers brought, Cortés could not say what the sergeant had in his possession. Finally, Cortés pointed out that none of the goods mentioned was purchased in "Nachitochis" but, rather, in Nacogdoches.[75]

The Ratifications, September 25, 1792

The testimony presented by Cortés, Treviño, and the others concluded on September 10. Two weeks later, Governor Muñoz issued an *auto* indicating that the ratifications of testimony were to be expedited with a special urgency, since calls for Cortés by the Lipanes necessitated his presence back at the presidio. Thus, his immediate ratification was necessary, as was that of the other deponents in the alleged smuggling case.[76] Or, was it that Muñoz had received a terse directive from Castro to continue the proceedings until a ruling had been made, despite the governor's opinion that the entire contraband case was unworthy of consideration?[77]

After being read his September 10 testimony from beginning to end and then asked to confirm its content as the same one he gave on that day, Cortés replied that nothing needed to be deleted from his deposition. However, he did add another piece to his statement. Besides what was confiscated from him, he traded five chamois skins for a *cuera* and two for some boots, a medium size pot for his kitchen, and a little coffee.[78] One must wonder if Cortés had an epiphany about this heretofore unreported transaction or, perhaps, some deep-seated guilt loomed large about events in Nacogdoches and Nachitos that induced him to own up to this extra merchandise.

When it was his turn to ratify his deposition, read to him from beginning to end, Alférez Treviño affirmed its content as true and valid and the same information he gave to Escandón on June 20. Emphasizing the testimony's veracity, Treviño stressed that he would ratify it once, twice, and as many times as might be necessary since he had nothing at all to add or delete.[79] The insistence of repeatedly validating one's defense against charges of contraband may have been common performative practice among soldiers

Managing Soldiers, Questionable Accounts, and Contraband   155

under investigation. On the other hand, for a bald-faced liar it might just as well serve to deflect suspicion of wrongdoing during interrogations.

In Cpl. Ylario Maldonado's case, however, there was additional testimony that he offered Governor Muñoz on the day of his ratification. At that time, the entries in the Amangual inventory of confiscated goods were the same ones, including the chamois and deerskins, he had transported while in the company of Pvt. Joaquín Galán. Further, even though he had a buffalo hide, that item emerged among those of the *soldado distinguido*, Cortés' brother-in-law José Alderete. Maldonado's additional testimony concerned one specific commodity: he reiterated that Luis Arman, a regular dealer of pack animals, had supplied him with tobacco by order of Cortés.[80]

That comment inspired more pointed interrogatory of Maldonado by Muñoz. The governor asked the corporal how long he had been in Nacogdoches and what amount of tobacco he had received from Arman. Specifying a timeline of the journey, Maldonado set out on February 9 from La Bahía with Captain Cortés, they arrived at Nacogdoches on March 6, and returned to Béxar on June 18. In Nacogdoches, he received for his own use four *manojos* of tobacco with estimated weight of twenty pounds; whether out of necessity or magnanimity, he gave a portion to his female cook who then bought food with it. The last of it he traded to the Tahuacanes for a chamois skin. Asked where, and with what, had he purchased the *candonga* mentioned in his deposition, he admitted to winning it in a game of *malilla* in Nacogdoches from a citizen named Gavino Menchaca.[81] Since Cortés was asked about the prohibition of imported goods into Texas and, especially, playing cards, Maldonado made clear he knew tobacco and cards were contraband, as well as uncut cloth!

Then Muñoz asked him if, in order to gloss over the contraband and thereby attract no attention of any kind, he had ordered the cutting of the skirts that were seized from him. Maldonado clarified he had ordered the *making*—not the cutting—of the five skirts. When asked about what he, along with Galán, used to purchase the twelve entries ascribed to him in the Amangual inventory, he affirmed it was with tablecloths, one shawl, a set of buttons, a silver cigarette box, and the saddle he gave with Cortés' consent. Did Cortés know about the purchase of the confiscated goods and their shipment? Maldonado replied that Cortés could not have been unaware of it since Cortés gave him the saddle to sell. With that, Maldonado upheld his deposition.[82]

Though it was now Pvt. Joaquín Galán's turn at ratification, it must have come as a surprise that he had yet to be deposed, effectively grinding the process to a halt. Confirming his presence at Nacogdoches with the troops

Chapter Four

escorting Cortés, he could not say with certainty the length of his stay there but asserted that he was not dispatched anywhere outside Texas. Asked to account for the foreign goods he purchased while in Nacogdoches, Galán admitted he bought two pairs of skirts of silk and scarlet *polonesa,* others of chintz, and one silk doublet from an Englishman named "Don Phelipe." Galán confirmed having Cortés' permission to make these purchases. Other items confiscated included a dust cloth, a three-footed pot, nine chamois skins, a buffalo hide, and a deck of cards. When asked if he understood these items as contraband in Texas, Galán admitted he knew the bolts of fabric, the tobacco, and the card decks were illegal, but that the precut and used skirts were not. Just as he had done with Treviño, the governor asked Galán whether he had had the skirts made to protect himself from charges by passing them off as trade items. Galán said he purchased the skirts as newly cut, being neither made nor used, just like those of silk and polonesa. Not so easily persuaded, Muñoz wanted one contradiction explained: Why did Galán say that the skirts were cut from fabric when earlier he indicated that they were fitted? Pressed to the point of confession, Galán clarified that indeed they *were* fitted. In order to purchase the smuggled items, he admitted using the value of three horses (one of which he offered with permission from Cortés) while the other two he assumed permission for; that is, he took for granted their availability for sale.[83]

Furthermore, by order of Cortés, the dealer Arman supplied him with one pound of tobacco. Then, at the Río Neches, he received the fourth part of a *manojo*[84] given to him by Sgt. Treviño and one amount by order of his captain. When questioning turned to the cargo coming from Nachitos to Nacogdoches, Galán answered the same questions posed to his fellow soldiers. He overheard that there were five or six loads brought by Mariano Vásquez from Nachitos, including a keg of liquor and another of gunpowder. All these goods entered the house of Nicolás Lamath, and Galán saw them through the window of the house. However, he did not know who had sent the goods or under whose order.[85]

Galán probably anticipated playing cards would be included in the merchandise. Tricks of the hand proved reliable for presidials in need of supplies. The game of *malillas*, from which a win garnered a *candonga* for both Treviño and Maldonado in Nacogdoches, similarly resulted in a prize of chamois skins for Galán in the same town. At La Bahía, he traded a peso worth of cigars to "Juan Bosque" for yet another chamois. At the Tahuacan village, he traded two *candongas* to an Indian and a soldier—unnamed in this deposition—and received two chamois skins, and to another Tahuacan he gave an old waistcoat and a cloth for two more. At the *ranchería* of the same Indian group, another cloth and old waistcoat got him two more chamois skins, and with a resident of the *ranchería* he traded a *zarape* for a buffalo hide. Galán must have been proficient at the game of *malilla*, and the turf for displaying his dexterity with cards mattered not: at the Guadalupe River he won another chamois from Pvt. Juan José de la Garza. When these goods were confiscated from Galán, he lost six of his hard-won chamois skins and the buffalo hide. With the remaining ones, he paid for what he owed prior to the seizure, probably debts festering on his account at the provisioning store at La Bahía. Muñoz asked Galán if he knew that tobacco and playing cards were in the baggage of the troops. Here, the private claimed no such knowledge except that Captain Cortés brought both.[86]

Muñoz then asked Galán whether Cortés was traveling with the intent of inspecting the confiscated goods at San Antonio or if Galán knew that the captain had arranged to send them to Presidio La Bahía. Galán claimed he heard people were coming from San Antonio to meet them in accordance with Cortés' request, prompting the captain's travel to the capital. Moreover, he ordered Sgt. Treviño to take the *camino real* to La Bahía, and from there Lt. Bernardo Fernández would accompany the troops and the baggage to Gov. Escandón. Galán was asked several other questions regarding the *candongas*, and if he had seen gunpowder, bullets, and tobacco distributed to the Indian nations. If so, from whose hands did he acquire these commodities? He confirmed he had seen tobacco distributed but would not name specific individuals, and he estimated the number of Indians representing the Orcoquiza in Nacogdoches at about fifty.[87] Finally, asked if he had anything further to say regarding the interrogation, he addressed the sources of the fabric: the cuttings of *polonesa* and the silk skirts came from the "Englishman Phelipe," and those made of chintz, and the doublet, were from Nicolas Lamath.[88]

Judged by Galán's reticence at naming specific individuals in his testimony, it seems Governor Muñoz did not press the issue and instead moved on to ratifying Pvt. Antonio Gómez's deposition. On September 26, Gómez swore that his June 20 testimony was correct with nothing to delete. It did occur to him that the *aguardiente* mentioned by Cortés in his deposition arrived in only one keg, and he never deduced the contents in the other keg brought on the trip. When Muñoz showed Gómez the June 18 inventory of confiscated goods processed by Francisco Amangual and that of hides seized on June 20, the governor asked Gómez whether his were any of the goods. Gómez confirmed his transport of the items on both lists from Nacogdoches. Asked to name the person who supplied him goods, what method of payment he used for the purchase, and if Cortés knew about it, he identified "Nicolás de la Mathé" and citizens of Nacogdoches. Gómez gave twelve pesos to Lamath, then added that he received no prior permission from his captain to make the purchase.[89]

When asked if he knew whether any individual troops went to Nachitos, on whose orders did they go, and for what purpose, Gómez explained that Alférez Antonio Treviño, who was a sergeant at the time, went on orders by Captain Cortés to Nachitos along with Private Juan José de la Garza. Gómez learned from an unidentified source that Treviño was going to collect a debt owed to him by a "Santiago de Mecie[res?]." Questioned further as to how many loads of cargo he saw or even heard about and introduced by the French or Spanish into Nacogdoches and then shipped from Nachitos, Gómez knew of four loads more than the ones he declared had come with the French from Nachitos. Additionally, he saw rifles, lard, and soap at the house of Luis Arman, the tobacco supplier to Corporal Maldonado, Private Galán and, as we shall see, Private del Río.[90]

The interrogation proceeded apace. Had he seen, did he know, or had he heard that any of the items brought from Nachitos were carried into Lamath's house? Gómez admitted seeing three bundles of cargo unloaded there: one load of fabrics, another of kegs, and the remaining one filled with coffee, mirrors, beads, and other things. Concerning the tobacco and its introduction into Nacogdoches, Muñoz asked him: By whose order and into whose hands was it delivered? Gómez said that a Frenchman, identified as "Pedrito," sent a quantity of tobacco to Lamath that Cortés intended for the Indians; he added that Luis Arman had delivered a pound every two weeks to the soldiers on orders from Cortés. In fact, Gómez knew that the fabrics, tobacco, playing cards and other goods brought from Nachitos were prohibited, a revelation that prompted Muñoz to ask if he knew that Alderete, the brother-in-law of Cortés, bought the goods seized by Escandón. He admitted knowledge of that activity and added that the fabrics were bought from citizens of Nacogdoches. However, Gómez was unaware of prior permission from Cortés to purchase hides and other confiscated goods along with bridles, scarves, used clothing, and large knives. He noticed, too, that two soldiers arrived without bridles on their mounts.[91]

Allegedly, Gómez witnessed tobacco, playing cards, and cloth removed from Cortés' trunks. Therefore, one final question remained: Did he know his captain may have given an order that his baggage and that of the troops be sent to La Bahía but, instead, that his directive was not carried out and that all the cargo went to Béxar? Gómez claimed no knowledge of that news but confirmed that Lieutenant Fernández went to escort them to San Antonio and Governor Escandón.[92]

Managing Soldiers, Questionable Accounts, and Contraband   159

Pvt. Antonio del Río answered a similar question regarding the baggage brought to San Antonio: For what reason and by what order did he inspect the goods of Cortés and his fellow troops? He did not know the reason why the baggage had come to the capital. However, he saw Fernández accompany merchandise to Escandón's home. And Del Río heard from other soldiers that Lieutenant Fernández counted the cargo and ordered none of it disappeared. Though he knew that tobacco and playing cards were prohibited, he also knew that merchandise including fabrics brought from Louisiana had been seized from Menchaca and Galán. At this point, Muñoz asked Del Río why he and the other men transported the goods if he knew that certain of them had been seized from these two soldiers. The private insisted that he purchased his items, convinced that they were not contraband because he had brought them from the citizens of Nacogdoches. Further, while he was unaware of how other soldiers paid for their goods, the ones he bought for himself were in payment for horses owed to him by a "Nepomuzeno de la Zerda." Like Galán and Maldonado, he received one pound of tobacco from Luis Arman by order of Captain Cortés. And he knew Cortés' baggage contained *manojos* of tobacco, but he was unable to confirm their weight in pounds nor how many existed in total. Finally, asked if he knew from where the tobacco came and if it went to Nacogdoches, to both questions Del Río professed his ignorance.[93]

That response apparently troubled Governor Muñoz, who then asked the deponent to restate his name, his place of birth, and with what company he undertook military service. His name was José Antonio del Río, he was born at the heretofore abandoned presidio of Los Adaes and began his career at La Bahía del Espíritu Santo. Asked at what age he left Los Adaes, and did he know how far that was from the Natchitoches post, he replied: he left at the age of seven for the presidio of Orcoquiza but did not know the distance from Los Adaes to "Nachitos." He had been there twice before, the first time as a citizen and the other as a soldier of La Bahía. That answer prompted Muñoz to ask the question that initially provoked his annoyance: having been in Nachitos and to the other presidios, how could he *not* know from where came the seized tobacco? Private Del Río responded: the tobacco came from that harvested by the French. As we have seen, this regional variety of the plant was the type preferred by the presidials.[94]

The answer must have satisfied Muñoz, who quickly moved on to the last questions. What had Del Río used to purchase chamois skins? He traded a blanket and biscuits. Did he know whether other soldiers might have traded weapons, gunpowder, or bullets to the Indians for chamois? He did not. Private del Río answered two questions specific to Sgt. Treviño: Why

160 Chapter Four

did his superior go to Nachitos? When Treviño returned to Nacogdoches, did the individuals who brought the cargo into that town come with him, or later? To the first question, del Río replied that Treviño went to collect a debt from "Atanasio de Mezieres," obviously a correction to the misinformation provided by Gómez. To the second, he affirmed that soldiers who brought cargo into Nacogdoches preceded Treviño's arrival, and these same men left from Nacogdoches for Nachitos before Cortés and other troops arrived. Finally, del Río answered a question not posed to any other deponent in the proceeding: Had someone with whom he might have spoken regarding the confiscated goods coached him to answer in a certain way? He declared that he had not. Like his predecessor Gómez in the proceedings, Antonio del Río was unable to write, and, like Gómez, he ratified his deposition by making the sign of the cross in testament to the truth.[95]

How the King Dealt with *Contrabandistas*

The Cortés case and the responses of its deponents say as much about the limits of state power over its agents in the borderlands as it does about the manipulation of royal policy by those same human resources. Several background elements help to provide an administrative context for the frontier realities of survival and endurance, and by extension, the extra-legal activities deemed appropriate by some military personnel to ensure, at best, a meager livelihood. Investigations into French clandestine trade alarmed royal administrators and got the attention of the viceroy in early 1751 and thereafter by certain goods from Natchitoches confiscated during the mid-1760s. Illicit commerce persisted into the 1780s.[96] It is no surprise that Juan María de Ripperdá, the beleaguered Texas governor regularly in need of oversight by his superiors, received instructions on how to proceed with smuggling cases in the 1770s. As a rank-and-file soldier in the king's army and prior to his election as presidio paymaster, Amangual had confiscated illicit tobacco in Texas in 1780. Later, thinking visual deterrents might work up a modicum of respect, in 1785 the king ordered the royal banner flown on ships as a method to ensure both the security of the royal revenues and the suppression of contraband.[97] The purely symbolic gesture may have been effective along the coastal regions, even though at the time of its issuance the king acknowledged that there were no vessels employed for that purpose. However, there is no question that overt displays of royal authority were somewhat successful in curbing illegal trade on the ground and away from the sea. Cattle, tobacco, and cloth all constituted regularly bootlegged goods. The latter two especially crisscrossed New Spain's Comandancia with unfettered ease even while colonial adminis-

Managing Soldiers, Questionable Accounts, and Contraband 161

trators conveyed their concerns to superiors on the Peninsula. Ongoing episodes of lawlessness, carried out even by mail couriers, demonstrate both the porous nature of institutional regulation of commerce and the pervasiveness of resistance to state superiority by operatives of all stripes in the king's domains.

By 1791, Carlos IV had developed criteria for the investigation of seizures of contraband. During the reign of his father, the Council of Indies had proposed in a report of July 6, 1761, that the General Accounting Office divide cases of confiscation and their circumstances and perpetrators into five categories for greater clarity:

> those involving a considerable amount with the culprits present.
>
> those involving a considerable amount without the culprits present or known.
>
> those involving a small amount with the culprits present and capable of bearing the costs.
>
> those involving a small amount without the culprits present or known.
>
> those involving a small amount with the culprits present or known, but poor or incapable of bearing the costs.[98]

Thereafter, the accounting office proposed what litigation could proceed as it pertained to each of these circumstances. Apprised of everything discussed thirty years prior at the Council of the Indies including the opinion of his *fiscal*, Carlos IV concluded that cases of confiscation in the first three categories should continue to be substantiated according to methods stipulated by law. He did so for two reasons: (1) there was no reason to change it, and (2) its observance contributed to correction of the *corpus delecti*, that is, the physical evidence of the crime and of its perpetrator (*autor*). Upon hearing the smuggler's exculpation or exoneration in the prescribed manner, these methods surfaced to ensure the correctness of the measures appropriate to one or the other. Too, that left no risk of the proceedings being rendered null based on a pretext of "defenselessness or some other substantial defect."[99]

The king argued against anything superfluous in the proposed formula. Confiscated goods must be inventoried, inspected, and guarded in the proper place to prevent their loss. These procedures were to transpire in a timely manner for those involved, as in the Cortés case and as carried out by Amangual. With respect to the fourth category of cases involving small amounts of contraband but with the culprits absent or unidentified, the circumstances called for repairing for the present what was ordered

Chapter Four

by Article 22 of a follow-up royal *cédula* of July 22, 1761 (issued for matters concerning the provincial revenues of the Spanish kingdoms) and based on the clearest evidence made against the goods incurred.[100]

The abandonment of bootleg constituted a clear indicator of guilt, as did the failure of its actors to relinquish goods to authorities. Both deeds were tantamount to a formal confession of their illegal transport, the certainty of their poor quality, or fraudulent trade. The king's decree unscrambled any doubt that this fourth category corresponded to the "proper management and government" of tobacco revenues in the *Américas*.[101]

The fifth category of circumstances served as a springboard for conclusions to the *autos* used in civil matters and without admitting any other kind of proof or allowing further delays. In cases where the accused had not yet confessed, confessions from culprits were but one expectation along with a brief period for the preparation of a defense. However, if the guilty parties did confess, the process anticipated the rendering of an immediate sentence and a punishment commensurate with the degree of the charge and without delays of any kind.[102] In yet another irony of an accused soldier carrying out prescribed responsibilities while, at the same time, being shadowed by the specter of suspicion, it became the responsibility of Capt. Juan Cortés to make a copy of the royal decree for the archive at La Bahía.

The Amangual inventory of confiscated goods seized from Cortés, Treviño and other soldiers provided the essential master data for corroborating the testimony of military personnel involved with the alleged incident. Following the itemization of the merchandise listed in the Cortés proceedings, Amangual coordinated a public auction of the contraband. While Viceroy Revillagigedo acknowledged the decision by Escandón to sell the confiscated tobacco at the *estanco* of the presidio, he also agreed that Amangual should retain the surplus goods. Moreover, the viceroy credited Amangual with the foresight to recognize that the bulk of the inventory, the chamois and hides, had a wide variety of uses and were common trade items in the *Provincias Internas*.[103] One wonders why the viceroy would think that such an acknowledgment was necessary. After all, soldiers and civilians alike since time immemorial made prolific use of animal skins.

Those commodities were to return to their owners except for the skins belonging to Cortés and his brother-in-law Alderete. Revillagigedo blamed these two because they were the "culprits in this contraband" traversed between Natchitos and Nacogdoches in the summer of 1792. However, the viceroy implicated one other individual in the unsettling affair: it seems Croix's "emissary of confidence," Nicolas de Lamath, had received some of the booty into his own house. Private Galán had witnessed that event and

Managing Soldiers, Questionable Accounts, and Contraband   163

testified to it. Revillagigedo ordered Muñoz to eject Lamath from Nacogdoches and steer him toward San Antonio or some other location less likely to harbor ill-gotten goods. The governor himself was to remain vigilant about Lamath's conduct.[104]

The viceroy's final instructions to Muñoz, and subsequently conveyed to Amangual, entrusted the paymaster with the proceeds. All sums were to be handed over to him, then sent to Muñoz for certification of the amount raised from the auction and, finally, submitted to San Luis Potosí. Documentation of the process was to be sent there for the intendant to deduct it from the allocation corresponding to the Béxar presidio. According to the guidelines for confiscated materials, the sum would thereafter be recorded in the royal treasury and afterward forwarded to the central treasury for distribution.[105]

The Cortés trafficking proceedings, like those of the Amangual–Rodríguez lawsuit, represented the commingling of presidio soldiers, clergy, and Native merchants in troublesome episodes of misadventure, charges and countercharges, and dishonorable behavior that had serious implications for the military. Confiscation of black-market goods had a long history in the Septentrión, as did occurrences of soldiers accusing one another of misdeeds, or the suspicion thereof. This pattern was to continue over time and involve other players from the same occupational sector and similar socioeconomic status. Amid this flurry of less-than-productive activities, other communities entered the military garrison's sphere of accommodation and accusation, a slippery social dynamic that anticipated compliance and cohesion through a narrowing of spatial relations. Likewise, when Native populations made forays into the presidio complex, or when soldiers penetrated indigenous domains, their benign meanderings were defined by reciprocal efforts intended to cement loyalties among presumed friends. Countervailing forces, like raiding and retribution, made those relationships permeable and uncertain. The business of preserving such shaky alliances stayed relatively intact, and operational practices in times of unrest defaulted to economic dealings. Formal treaties of peace were but one method to promote adherence to prescribed modes of behavior for and reconcile contests of dominance by competing factions. The predictable outcome was that other endeavors involving the usual actors required just as much diligence along with the customary, if usually copious, documentation.

FIVE

— ❧ —

Further Accusations, Considerable Numbers of Apache, and His Majesty's Assurance

Promoting commercial interests in the borderlands ensured economic interplay among rivals, which, in turn, often reached further than proximate communities. Commodities in transport, even those routed extralegally, usually fostered reciprocal relationships of trust, cohesion, and productivity. Gov. Muñoz's accounting records show a mutually advantageous, if sometimes uneasy, relationship with the French-born merchants Nicholas Lamath and Andrés Benito Courbiére. If the paper trails of either of these men reached his desk, Amangual was privy to their transactions and especially as it impacted indigenous visitors to the presidio.

In accordance with payment orders generated by Colonel Muñoz, the prolific Courbiére accounted for his expenditures for the Taguacanos (Tawakoni), Taguayas, Tancagues (Tonkawa), Guichita (Wichita), and Comanches. By accommodating one hundred members of both sexes from these nations, Courbiére spent over 106 pesos for their stay at the Béxar garrison from May 22 until July 4, 1792. Recipients got eighteen cattle, *fanegas* of corn, *almudes*[1] of beans, thirteen cartloads of firewood, and a quantity of salt. The report shows that Courbiére provided corn and *piloncillos* to Presidio La Bahía for the Indians of Rosario Mission, costing twenty-one pesos to transport these provisions from San Antonio. The coastal-based Karankawa received only corn. Courbiére also provided cigars, gunpowder, and bullets to Indians from the nations above who arrived in peace, with rifles and blankets given to the agents for the Taguacanos, "Menchaca" and "El Mudo," and cloth for a waistcoat intended for "Jasinto." Buttons, silk, a hat given to leader Cojo of the Comanches, and

Accusations, Apache Encounters, and Assurance

one pair of spurs (possibly intended for "Cojo" or someone unidentified in the report) brought Courbiére's expenditures in total to just over 203 pesos.[2]

Apart from Menchaca, El Mudo, Cojo, and Jasinto, the names of other high-status individuals appear in Courbiére's accounting log. "Capitan" Sordo of the Comanche received a portion of six doublets of *queretano* cloth as did two nephews of Ciscat of the Taguacanos and the son of De la Malla of the Comanche. Cloth went to the Tancagues on May 30. Final items consisted of buttons for the doublets; four *almudes* of biscuits; payment to a "Master Pobevano" for the repair of three bridles and seven rifles of the Indians; with cloth, silk, thread, and buttons used in the making of a waistcoat and pair of trousers for "Cap.n" Cojo. The grand total for Courbiére's accounting report was over 245 pesos.[3]

Courbiére completed his report on May 22, 1792. In a peculiar twist of events, Lieutenant Espadas reported only three days later, at a place called La Tortuga near the Guadalupe River, the Comanche had accosted people rounding up cattle for the herd of Padre José Camarena.[4] All twenty-five of the *vaqueros*—most likely civilians—had been provoked into a bout, but the men tolerated the Comanche insults and saw the situation as being dire enough for Espadas to report the Yndios' misdeeds ("*fechurías*"). In his dispatch to Governor Muñoz, Espadas must have conveyed the same desperation by Domingo Cabello in another setting from ten years prior and from other commanders since time immemorial: he did not know what to do since the Comanche had not declared war. This, despite the robberies that the Bahía personnel expected from them, and even when Espadas noted the Comanche had stolen two horses from that same presidio. Espadas was above all apprehensive since his garrison was, of course, short of men and the horse herd detachment had only twenty-two soldiers. He suspected that one of the ten "*gandules*" that had remained at the presidio (after an almost weeklong visit) was only there to observe which animals he could confiscate, for which reason Espadas could not explain.[5]

Muñoz's response came the next day. When he received Espadas' report, a party of twenty-one men set out for Tortugas so that, once arrived and informed of the antagonism between the *vaqueros* and the Comanche, the soldiers could respond in ways so as not to project resentment toward the Indians. Muñoz sent Manuel de Urrutia, one of the deponents in the Amangual–Rodríguez suit from the month before, with instructions for Espadas to detach a private from his company at La Bahía, and one from Béxar. Espadas was to put in place preventive measures to curb further damage caused by the Indians.[6] However, weighty responsibilities often unnerved Espadas

Chapter Five

and episodes of his skittish reactions to frontier challenges surface more than once in the documentation. But, at least on this occasion, he acted with apparent resolve once it was determined that *his* ruling would be the final word.

It did not take long for the pragmatic Muñoz to surmise that the Tortugas agitators could have been Comanche since thirty-six of their number had departed from the Béxar presidio for the express purpose of tracking down the Apaches. After receiving a different report about the discovery of footprints, Urrutia set out as far as Los Olmos and discovered that those were in fact from the same Comanche avengers. Nevertheless, Muñoz cautioned Espadas to exercise the greatest care since all Indians were "inconstant" and little able to maintain allegiance. After all, he reasoned, loyalty from them was negligible. However, from Muñoz's vantage point, Spaniards had to overlook Comanche imperfections because they restrained other nations from terroristic behavior.[7] Muñoz urged Espadas to somehow convince the non-indigenous population to look upon them with favor, a challenge that likely made the young lieutenant cringe. Citing the intervening distance between himself and Espadas, Muñoz made it clear that he himself could give no explicit order as to how to proceed. He left that responsibility to Espadas, a presidio captain with only the slightest self-confidence and, at that, his certitude easily undermined by divisive issues troubling civilians or soldiers.

Muñoz's instructions to Espadas directed the unidentified private detached from Bahía along with his equivalent from Béxar, Pvt. Antonio Aldape, and the rest of the men to travel to Las Tortugas, the site of the cattle roundup for Padre Camarena. Alférez Urrutia was in turn to receive from Espadas the orders conducive to carrying out something akin to retribution. Muñoz prevailed upon Urrutia to avoid provoking the Friendly Nations and to conduct himself with the "greatest prudence" as he endeavored to determine the causes for the conflict between whatever Natives were involved and "civilized people (*gente de razón*)." Since it was Urrutia who detected the tracks at Los Olmos, Muñoz hinted at the identity of the yndios as he had to Espadas: they were quite possibly those who had departed in search of the Apache. Therefore, Urrutia was to avoid creating tensions.[8] However, curbing that ancient hostility must have seemed highly questionable even to Commander Muñoz and just plain ridiculous to a veteran (and reliably unbridled) soldier like Urrutia.

When Espadas received Muñoz's official letter, he did what he was told: two privates went to Las Tortugas to meet Alférez Urrutia. They had Espada's instructions to Urrutia about what was to be done with the Indians and ascertaining if they were friendly or hostile so to prevent any further

Accusations, Apache Encounters, and Assurance

discord between the military, the civilian settlement, and the Comanche. Though Muñoz harbored doubts, the usually diffident Espadas had none whatsoever identifying the instigators at Tortugas. Based on reports by the *vaqueros* working for Padre Camarena, they were Comanche.[9] More specifically, he was certain their leader was Ojos Azules and his people. Espadas knew Azules had angrily departed from La Bahía, but he was unaware of the reason for his agitation. Nothing of what Azules and his people wanted was denied. His nerves undoubtedly frayed, Espadas regretted that until the Comanche received everything they asked for, they simply were not satisfied. What he interpreted as unreasonable demands by the Indians could never be consummated in any manner to their liking.[10] Now his certainty about who provoked the Tortugas incident was about to be proven wrong.

For about a week, if Espadas was left feeling helpless about conflictive Indian interactions, there was little comfort from on high to calm his fears. Indeed, the outgoing Governor Muñoz distanced himself from Espadas with every expectation for Bahía's commander to fend for himself and his troops. For troublesome situations, he only needed to contact the *interim* governor of the province Manuel de Escandón, Conde de Sierra Gorda. Then, on June 2 Espadas received news that a citizen of La Bahía had been sent by leader Canoso (*not* Ojos Azules) with a message for the First Alférez of the Bahía presidio, Francisco Vásquez, to meet with him, alone, in the area where *vaqueros* were rounding up cattle for Padre Camarena. Canoso claimed that his people (Lipan, *not* Comanche) meant to do no harm but, instead, sought peace. Indeed, because of their numeric superiority, his fighters could have already finished off the cowboys, but their restraint ostensibly proved their desire for conciliation. However, Espadas did not consider combat with them a remote possibility, but he understood that the *vaqueros* had, in the same spirit of conciliation (or, to fake appeasement), remained at the site of conflict as if they were hostages until Vásquez arrived.[11]

Again, mindful of his lesser rank and perhaps hoping for intercession from just about anyone, a clearly flustered Espadas declared that it was not his decision to permit Vásquez to go to the meeting. But he did inform his substitute supervisor Escandón that he had suspicions that there might be others in Canoso's group capable of committing atrocities against the Camarena party and the soldiers there. Espadas took the opportunity to enlighten Governor Escandón about the sobering reality at Bahía: the garrison had no more than eighteen men to guard the horse herd. And, to underscore his predicament, he let him know that citizens willing to help were but few and they lacked reliable weapons. For all these reasons, Espadas justified his inaction in deciding which approach might best be geared toward Canoso's prickly request.[12]

168 Chapter Five

Several events occurred that may have eased Espadas' trepidation in dealing with all things Indian, and one welcome piece of news arrived the same day as Canoso's request. On June 2, the viceroy informed the governor of Texas that a November 12, 1791, order of 117 muskets was filled, sent to San Luis Potosí, and was ready to be transferred to San Antonio for its poorly armed citizenry. Of those inhabitants, only seventy-four could afford to pay for them upon immediate receipt; the remaining forty-three were to be paid off within two months of delivery.[13] Governor Escandón most certainly knew that the news would shore up the spirits of Lieutenant Espadas and since the viceroy's decision was conveyed by *Comandante General* Castro (the highest ranking official in closest contact with the presidios and their commanders), we can assume that Espadas felt an even greater sense of relief. But Escandón had even more news for the jittery lieutenant, although it may not have been information that would have allayed his fears.

On June 16 General Castro wrote to Governor Escandón about having received Espadas' report regarding Canoso's solicitation for peace—which Castro pronounced as deceitful, as always (*"dolosa como siempre"*)—and that of the instruction given by Escandón to Béxar Lt. Bernardo Fernández. Castro approved the governor's decisions about the proposal Fernández would make to Canoso, although he reminded Escandón that the peace offer made by the lately murdered Zapato Sax—who raided in Nuevo Santander but whose efforts were spoiled by the unidentified captain at Laredo—came from *the Lipan*. These same Apache had menaced Reynosa, with one in their group killed and another taken prisoner by the citizens of that villa and of Camargo. Stressing the urgency of it all, Castro warned that continual attacks, never suspended during times of relative peace, were occurring at the time of his letter. In fact, according to the commander of the Río Grande presidio, on June 12 the Lipan had stolen horses.[14]

Castro acknowledged Escandón's assertion that the Commandancy had never experienced loyalty or good faith from the Lipan. But ever the peacemaker (except, in general, to other Apaches and the missionaries who indulged them), Castro added that at present they were, at least, behaving in good faith. Since Viceroy Revillagigedo's opinion on Indian relations constituted the final decision, Castro instructed Escandón to distract (*entretenga*) Canoso until the viceroy disclosed his recommendations. Put in a hard place, Escandón was prevented from allowing the chief to enter any presidios since that would create great displeasure among the Comanche and other Nations of the North. From his perch in Santa Rosa, Castro's final words to the governor tendered reassurance: "their friendship is very useful and important to us, and we must preserve it at any cost because without their help we could not achieve anything."[15]

Accusations, Apache Encounters, and Assurance   169

Castro's placating of Espadas may have missed its mark. A visit by two *Lipanes* on the afternoon of June 18 was enough to send Espadas running back to his inkwell. He informed Escandón of the deep concern expressed by the Indians about Alférez Francisco Vásquez's failure to appear as they had requested two weeks earlier on June 2. Grasping for some kind of explanation while awaiting an order from the governor, Espadas assured the visiting Lipan that travel would commence once Vásquez, and his party, had permission to go. Insomuch as his message to Escandón had been sent just three days earlier and not having yet received a reply, Espadas was proactive in his approach to the Indians: of his own volition, he decided to send the Indians away under the pretext of concern for their well-being. However, one of the two reasons for his doing so was covert. He told Governor Escandón that he made the decision to dismiss the Lipan pair so that they would not become suspicious and, as he told them, to ensure their safety so as not to be harmed by their enemies.[16]

By midsummer, mutual suspicions had little changed between the presidials and the Lipan. On July 4, a representative named "Jacinto" went to the Bahía presidio under the banner of peace accompanied by two *gandules* from the same nation. They were eager to know what results came out of their request for peace. Unfortunately, the recently accused Capt. Juan Cortés could give no reply other than the swollen Río Grande had made it impossible to allow crossing by the soldiers. This troop carried the recommendation that Governor Escandón would make to General Castro regarding Lipan signaling for peace. As a consolation prize of sorts, Cortés gave the Jacinto trio a few boxes of cigars and sent them on their way, bound for their *ranchería* located at the "Old Mission on the Guadalupe River."[17]

Prior to the recent investigation of his alleged wrongdoing, Capt. Juan Cortés is remembered not only for his unswerving commitment to the safety and well-being of the La Bahía troops under his command but also for securing the presidio itself. Up to that point in his career, he showed himself to be a soldier of a completely different stripe than the sheepish Espadas,[18] especially in his ability to create the type of situational strategizing necessary when coping with absentee or disaffected superiors. Aside from his alleged participation in clandestine activity, which made him a controversial figure, Cortés had been, outwardly, a leader of great military acumen. Nevertheless, as we saw in the previous chapter, his is yet another example of a personality flaw allowed to fester and, ultimately, overwhelm deference to duty.

Only one year before, in the summer of 1791, when then-governor Muñoz ordered a detachment of troops from La Bahía, Cortés absolved himself

170   Chapter Five

of any responsibility for a loss of fighting power that would hamstring his garrison and invite disastrous results. Balancing respect for his commander with an itemization of plausible scenarios that might befall his command and jeopardize the force left to protect the Bahía presidio, Cortés asserted his thoroughgoing understanding of the local environment and the constraints these realities imposed on a commander's strict compliance with authority.[19]

Now, five days after the appearance of Jacinto and two young warriors seeking peace, Cortés conveyed to Governor Escandón the satisfaction experienced by Canoso for the good treatment—in part, feigned, according to Cortés—given to Jacinto on July 4, 1792. This time, and with the same purpose as his vanguard, Canoso arrived with an even larger contingent: 148 *gandules* and women of his nation. In view of recent Lipan overtures for peace, Cortés disclosed to Escandón that, having no rules to guide him "in the particular," he told Canoso how pleased he was with his offers. In the form of a gentle reminder, Cortés let him know how satisfying conciliatory efforts would be to the governor if Canoso fulfilled what he promised.[20]

Only one week after the Lipans' arrival and subsequent departure, a "considerable number" of Apache men and women, band unidentified, arrived at La Bahía. Though that group left the same day, Jacinto reappeared with three *gandules*, stayed, and reasserted their desire to travel to Béxar for a meeting with Escandón. Cortés warned them of the presence of "many Comanche" there, and even managed to get the four men to delay for six days. Presidial solicitude aside, an undeterred Jacinto stressed that a conference with Canoso, "all his people," and Escandón at the Colorado River was imminent.[21]

If Cortés thought his diplomatic proposals toward the Apache and subsequent reporting of those efforts to the governor might mitigate Escandón's approach to his contraband debacle, that strategy went to waste. By August 1792 Muñoz was restored to his post as governor of Texas and captain of Presidio Béxar, leaving Escandón free of the responsibility of dealing administratively with the multiple occurrences of scandal at that garrison.[22] With Escandón gone and having earned the approval of Governor Muñoz for his response to an unspecified circumstance involving the Xaranames and the Lipan, Cortés got a bit of wind in his sails and redoubled his efforts at proving his worth as a commander. He stressed his determination to use every means necessary for all nations to openly declare themselves enemies of the Lipan, and have the latter return the favor. According to a report by Cortés, perduring turmoil between the Vidaes, the Orcoquizacs, the Karankawa, and the Lipan virtually guaranteed hatred from these groups toward the latter. He assured Muñoz of his warning to El Canoso

Accusations, Apache Encounters, and Assurance   171

that slaughtering cattle located at the Guadalupe River was contrary to the peace that his people had promised, making repercussions inescapable.[23]

Communication between Mexico City and the Comandancia concerning the Lipan Apaches was as unrelenting as ever. In the summer of 1792, the trend continued when Viceroy Revillagigedo sent a short note to Escandón asking whether expenditures at the San Antonio de Valero mission remained untouched for the maintenance of the Lipanes. They had been sheltered there since 1786. Further, he was curious to know why they were not working in agriculture after being there for so long. Revillagigedo's reasoning was, as ever, to remove unnecessary demands on the royal treasury. Specifically, he wanted to know why the Lipanes could not subsist by the fruits of their harvest and with some cattle raising directed toward that effort?[24]

Revillagigedo's curiosity may never have been satisfied. Indian good will, expressed as conciliatory overtures and petitions by the Lipan for things like long-term stopovers by specific soldiers in the months leading up to increasingly restrictive economic policies, seemed unconvincing to authorities. Mingling with merchants and military personnel by Native groups accomplished little from the perspective of higher authorities. Clearly the Comandancia's relationship with the Lipan was a complex affair. It entailed arguably petty concerns about gift-giving and the dubious nature of peace by purchase via deceit. For example, the usually imperturbable Muñoz ordered the merchant Courbiére to make a report on the number of cooking pots and the variety of cooking utensils from the distant past and up to the present, used to prepare food for indigenous visitors to Texas presidios.[25] Revillagigedo approved of, both, Muñoz's decision to prohibit the slaughter of *mesteña* cows on pasturelands at Mission La Bahía and his endless gifting of trifles like cigarettes and short knives ("*velduques*").[26] Naturally, the viceroy admonished Muñoz to reserve more expensive gifts for the Nations of the North, the military's "friends and allies." He found it necessary to remind Muñoz to be ever circumspect of Lipan movements across the borderlands. Putting a finer point on the matter, on those occasions when Lipan warriors went marauding into Coahuila, Nuevo León, and Nuevo Santander, Revillagigedo conveniently justified his soldiers taking Native families as prisoners.[27] Another idea mechanically thrust into deliberations was simply moving the Lipan to Coahuila.

The frontier's top commander had seen enough. Gen. Pedro de Nava imposed penalties upon those who improperly traded or dealt with the Lipan.[28] Not yet convinced of submitting to military rule, the Lipanes proved unwilling to move to Coahuila. Accordingly, Nava instructed Muñoz to abandon the idea for the time being and until more of their number

172   Chapter Five

were established in peace. He pressured Muñoz to remind the Lipan of the good faith with which the troops treated them as a group, a notion he believed they undoubtedly knew very well. Thus, Muñoz would be able to make the Lipan see the advantages that would follow with their transfer to Coahuila.[29] Acquiescing to relatively mobile *rancherías* within Texas was one thing; wholesale uprooting across a swath of the central borderlands was quite another. Besides, the Apache in general were unlikely participants in what they knew to be underhanded designs by the empire's agents on the ground.

   Nava and Muñoz may have been irked by the persistence of the Lipan itinerant lifestyle since no amount of persuasion could dislodge their number from one settlement to another. Without question, the prospect of their attachment to any mission appeared inconceivable. Even in the context of compatibility between Spaniard and Apache, it was imperative for military men to effectuate the Commandancy's 1786 peace establishment policy. Back then the rationalization for commanders was that by making the Lipan dependent on foreign largesse by way of incentives in the form of subsidies, goods, and ammunition, their communities would benefit if they agreed to settle near the watchful eye of the presidios.[30] Yet, four years earlier, even after several Mescalero bands had gathered at Presidio El Norte, Commander General Ugarte postponed the conclusion of a formal peace with them until he had achieved similar arrangements with the Lipan in Coahuila.[31] By April 1794, Nava forwarded a copy of instructions issued on October 14, 1791,concerning the treatment and management of and assistance to friendly Apache established in settlements in Nueva Vizcaya and Sonora. Nava was particularly interested in the character of the *Lipanería* and told Muñoz that if members of the tribe requested sanctuary (he was convinced they would) and if they established *rancherías*, Nava wanted notification of their submission to Spanish entreaties.[32]

   All these efforts toward appeasement may have convinced both Nava and Muñoz that maintaining vigilance, and a healthy dose of patience, over the movements and activities of indigenous people was a far easier task than the alternative. Be that as it may, perhaps nothing compared to the heap of administrative stamina required by top brass to be ever attentive to routinely difficult soldiers falling out of line. When warranted, and even when devotion to duty was needed most, otherwise honorable troops came under suspicion by committing transgressions. And it all required documentation.

   Cleared of misconduct and declared free of all charges, Manuel Muñoz formally reassumed the governorship of Texas, even though it is clear he had never actually curtailed his responsibilities.[33] Nevertheless, in what would be one of his last acts as governor, the following month it was Escandón who

Accusations, Apache Encounters, and Assurance 173

generated a roster and summary review of the soldiers at the Béxar presidio. The seven-page document shows commonplace activity and a familiar workforce. Muñoz remained captain, Bernardo Fernández stayed put as first lieutenant, and some of the other protagonists from the Amangual–Rodríguez litigation reappeared. Last seen at Las Tortugas receiving Espadas' instructions from two privates dispatched for that purpose, the irksome First Alférez Manuel de Urrutia (the soldier who had successfully embarrassed Amangual during a drunken tirade) was now accompanying the Indians of the North. Amangual's other nemesis Sgt. Mariano Rodríguez guarded the horse herd along with corporals Francisco de Sosa and Juan Antonio Urrutia; and carrying the mail pouch, Cpl. Facundo Mansolo, Cadet Eusebio de la Garza, and José Maria "Olibarry."[34]

In September 1792, Amangual traveled to San Luis Potosí for the payroll accompanied by José Manuel Granados, Marcelo Borrego, José Leandro de Sosa, and Francisco de los Santos.[35] Only one month after his return to Béxar, Amangual's expertise with counting and recording, very recently questioned by a high official from the Superior Accounting Office of the Royal Tribunal of Accounts in Mexico, launched another investigation at the presidio. On this occasion, however, he was not the suspect of wrongdoing.

Old Reliable: Yet Another Inventory

In October 1792, Amangual got the call, once more, to inventory contraband brought by a soldier named Toribio Durán. The list of goods described by Cmdr. Cristóbal de Córdoba consisted of sixteen pots with three feet; four pounds of beads; and one *garro* and three cloths. However, Amangual enumerated items differently than tallied by Córdoba. He found three iron pots with six feet; seven iron pots with four feet; one of the same but with three feet; nine small cotton cloths with various designs, probably embroidered; and fourteen and one-quarter *varas* of superfine *indianilla* cloth in two pieces.[36] The remainder of the materials consisted of much of the same (see appendix 4). Amangual completed this inventory on November 12, almost one month after Córdoba's initial, and substantially smaller, count and description of the goods. When Durán appeared before Muñoz that same day with Córdoba's letter in hand, Muñoz ordered First Lt. Bernardo Fernández to go out and meet the loads transported by the suspect. Muñoz then inspected the haul and cross-checked the goods in Amangual's list. Next, he ordered Amangual to take custody of the goods until the viceroy's decision to either hold the items as illicit cargo, or hand them over to another entity. After three months, the viceroy did just that; he forwarded the case to the intendant of San Luis Potosí.[37]

174 Chapter Five

The coincidence by which alleged contraband narrowly missed detection, once again, via another imprudent soldier, led Muñoz to take these measures. His colleagues were still finishing the auction ordered by the viceroy of commodities seized from Cpt. Cortés in June 1792. To Muñoz's mind, had he not acted, the implication would have been to further encourage the unlawful importation of goods the military was attempting to curtail. In fact, all parties accepted that the pots and chamois skins belonged to Manuel de Verasady, an employee of an unnamed parish priest of San Antonio. Deepening the mire of controversy, Muñoz informed the viceroy that, having extracted a letter from those carried by Durán, Verasady appeared in front of Amangual. There, he made statements before the *habilitado* that lacked any decorum toward the governor.[38] Though it is unverified in the documentation, one wonders whether the unabashedly boorish Verasady worked for or was mentored by the "truthful" Padre Gómez Moreno, the instigator of multiple instances of chaos.

Once remitted to the *fiscal* of the royal treasury, Ramón de Posada y Soto, Viceroy Revillagigedo ordered Amangual's inventory of Durán's goods to be added to the proceedings associated with the earlier Cortés case. Whether doing so was to establish for the prosecution patterns of misbehavior among the rank and file is debatable. In both cases, it appears the viceroy's directive was an effort to show that soldiers, out of convenience or desperation, seized upon ignorance of ordinances as a defense for wrongdoing.[39] One month later, Posada provided more information for Revillagigedo. In accordance with Article 240 of a December 4, 1786, ordinance, issues of trafficking and seizures were the jurisdictional purview of intendants of the respective provinces working with the lieutenant *asesor ordinario*, and no one else.[40] Since the territories of the Commandancy General had no functioning intendants, the governors of Coahuila and Texas were considered subdelegates of the intendancy of San Luis Potosí in cases involving the treasury and economic issues of war.[41]

Once received, the acting counsel of the intendancy, Vicente Bernabeu, received word from the public prosecutor that the goods listed in "note number two"—the Amangual inventory—were not those of illicit trade, that the property was of very little importance and, even according to Muñoz (in his opinion of November 19), Durán himself was transporting the cargo without concealment. That conclusion mitigated nothing. Since Durán failed to list all the merchandise in the *guía* he had transported, he incurred a fine. He got a warning, too: if he repeated the offense, he would face severe punishment.[42]

Though his tenure as Béxar paymaster ended in December 1793, Francisco Amangual's name is the very last shown in the final documentation for the

Accusations, Apache Encounters, and Assurance

Toribio Durán case. However, Muñoz's injunction that Durán pay for all the goods seized, valued at eight pesos, and remit a fine of twenty pesos, was fulfilled by the company's current *habilitado* José Gervacio de Silva. He was also the Béxar company's First Alférez and a former member of two *compañías volantes*. Since Amangual inventoried the merchandise during his tenure as paymaster, he also became a recipient of certified copies of the proceedings. These included the opinion of the *asesor* of the intendancy of San Luis Potosí and the decree of agreement by the intendant. Merged with other documents and the Muñoz instruction, the entire cache went to the "abilitado of the company [at the Béxar presidio]" for which the paymaster created a receipt. Thus, it was Amangual, and not de Silva, who complied on February 22, 1794, a period during which he was no longer the presidio's paymaster.[43]

More, or Less, Accused: Bernardo Fernández, Juan Cortés, and Contraband

The legal ramifications of transporting contraband generated copious documentation by military personnel. Archival records show that "Indian" expenditures also had the potential to cause presidial paymasters to stumble from, or, in some cases, to incur blame for, their accounting efforts. Or so it may have appeared to their immediate supervisors and top-level administrators in San Luis Potosí and Mexico City. We have now noted the settlement of the Durán case, and we learned the outcome of one soldier's accusations of mismanagement directed at his presidio's paymaster in chapter 3. We shall see the resolution of yet another fiscal conflict by the end of this one. The Durán contraband case quickly followed the Cortés contraband inventory, and it was Governor Muñoz's reliance on Amangual's expertise for those two proceedings that took the *habilitado* from the obligation of answering the Cavo Franco inquiry of May 1792. There was but little time for presidial commanders and their subordinates to catch their collective breath before yet another inquiry from on high descended upon headquarters. On March 19, 1793, Viceroy Revillagigedo sent to Governor Muñoz five pages of new objections made once again by the Royal Tribunal of Accounts' chief communicator, the daunting José del Cavo Franco. These related to expenditures made in Texas for maintaining harmony with Native people. Referencing the same document awaiting answers from Amangual, this time Muñoz summoned the now-accused José Antonio de Bustillos y Zevallos to answer similar charges.[44]

Having no word from Bustillos, Muñoz sent another official letter on March 28 in the hope of getting a reply from him. Again, none was forth-

176   Chapter Five

coming. So, Muñoz went in person to the San José mission where he found Bustillos ill and bedridden, his poor health having prevented his departure for San Antonio. Bustillos promised to do so at the first relief that "God might grant him," and after a few days he was moved to San Antonio but, a short while later, died without being able to respond to the matter.[45]

With Bustillos' death, the weight of responsibility for a satisfactory response in one way or another for the Royal Tribunal's objections now fell upon First Lt. Bernardo Fernández. He also happened to be the former *habilitado* of the Béxar presidio preceding Amangual and was, therefore, summoned by Muñoz. Fernández's reaction was immediate: since he was familiar with it, the paperwork should be turned over to him to make appropriate answers.[46] Fernández received the cache on December 24, 1794, and rather quickly returned them on January 16, 1795. Ten days later, the five documents of objections reached Second Lieutenant Amangual who similarly asked, after being briefed on their content, that they be handed over to him in order to digest the materials more fully.[47]

Asked to testify in response to the charges retroactively ascribed to him, Fernández addressed several of them. One included a payment listed in the third document and made to the "*peones*" who prepared food for the yndios with charges for that service; in the fourth document, fifteen pesos were paid to the surgeon who tended to the Indians at the garrison; the fifth document listed a charge of sixty-six pesos given to a captive, Francisco Cháves, for a suit, and nine pesos to the notary. Charges for burial shrouds for several yndios appear, with the last one of these—colored linen for two burial shrouds for two deceased—entered by Bustillos, and the first charge said to be by Fernández. That prompted his immediate declaration of innocence; and the ninth document consisted of eighty-two pesos for the purchase of seven horses for the Comanche.[48] The conclusion of Fernández's testimony is included in its entirety and from his own pen:

> So far, I have set forth the charges resulting against me, made by the Señor auditor of the Royal Tribunal. From the [charges] that he would have encountered in the aforesaid accounts, I admit that they would be just, and that I would be obliged to reimburse them to the royal treasury, according to what the aforesaid Señor auditor aims for. But were this minister aware that for my part I had no hand in this agency, nor have I [had responsibility for] any part of it at all, I believe with no little basis that he would exonerate me of them and for the reasons that I shall discuss.
>
> At the time that the aforesaid accounts were drawn up, I was engaged in the duties of paymaster for this company, and I devoted the greater

Accusations, Apache Encounters, and Assurance

part of the year to them in trips back and forth [*en las marchas y contra marchas*] to the city of San Luis Potosí and to the villa of Saltillo, to the latter to stock up on supplies for the company, and to the former to pick up the funds corresponding to the salaries enjoyed by its troops. And for this reason, I had no other participation than to write my signature on the accounts and in the place indicated on the form that was sent by the aforementioned Señor Don Juan de Ugalde to Governor Don Rafael M[a]r[tíne]z Pacheco. The truth established, it would be doing an injustice to me were [the auditor] not to realize it and therefore hold me responsible for paying for the results of the mishandling displayed by those managers in the expenditures for Indians during the period indicated in the afore-cited documents.[49]

His defense fully focused, Fernández drew attention to the signatures that appeared on the accumulated papers. He signed his name with "characteristic sincerity," convinced the same earnestness would be observed by those who signed their names below his. Fernández then made a pointed reference to "the one who with his own hand was requesting directly from Governor Pacheco the payment orders" for the resources that he needed to feed the Indians who came to visit. The identity of the person to whom he was referring emerged instantly:

> Beginning in the year [17]81, appointment was given to Don Andrés Benito Courbiére as *soldado distinguido*, and his salary began to run on November 6 of the afore-cited year of 1781, with the duties of lodging the yndios, maintaining them, and serving as interpreter. To those ends he was employed by the governor of this province, Don Domingo Cabello, and he continued during the term of his successor, Captain Don Rafael Martínez Pacheco, until the latter submitted the accounts about which we are speaking. Although in the past year of 1788, the afore-mentioned Señor Ugalde, with the consent of Don Rafael Pacheco, gave investiture as warehouse keeper to Don José Antonio Bustillos—the cashier that I had for company issues, and no others. Not for this reason did Don Andrés Benito Courbiére fail to handle the purchases and expenditures for the supplies that he considered [necessary] for the maintenance of the yndios, which likely I can prove with the copies of the afore-cited documents.
>
> From all this, it seems that the mismanagement [*mala versación*] of increasing expenditures on corn, beans, and the rental of pots came from no other hand than that of the manager, Don Andrés Benito Courbiére, who, if he sought to exonerate himself of charges (of this nature, which only he should absorb and reimburse to the royal treasury), should have made it known to Governor Pacheco so that he might remedy this

178 Chapter Five

problem. But since he kept silent about these disorders, it can be seen prudently that he was taking advantage of [personal] interest in their management.

In this, he would have continued taking advantage had not the Most Excellent Sr. Viceroy Conde de Revillagigedo issued a call to undertake efforts to eliminate all mismanagement, in which the officers and other members of this company were questioned, along with some citizens, from which the royal treasury has reaped no little savings, as will have been seen from the accounts submitted by the present government, which same have gone out under my hand, not for having managed or distributed the goods for maintaining [the Indians], but rather under the circumstance that appears in the decrees, and seeing that the gift items are delivered to the Indians. If in these there is some objection, it corresponds to the present governor to absorb them, since by this own [hand], without Courbiére having the despotic management that he had before, and had it been monitored, that what is consumed among the same Indians is what is gathered for them. If former Governor Don Rafael Martínez Pacheco had exercised similar management, all the efforts made by the most excellent Señor Viceroy and the Royal Tribunal of Accounts would have been spared.

It is an established fact that the one who manages a thing is obliged to make an accounting of it, and since I exercised no management in the first place, but rather the afore-mentioned Don Andrés Benito Courbiére, he is the one who should absorb the charges, as I have set forth and he will not deny them, because in this case, it will be confirmed with copies in his own hand, and it will come to light how much of the truth I have exposed: I appeal to the Royal Tribunal to take this as sufficient, heeding the sincerity with which I have given my response to the charges made against me.[50]

Having asserted his innocence, Fernández urged the committee to acknowledge his noninvolvement in any of the accounting miscalculations. He was unequivocal in placing blame directly on the *soldado distinguido* and merchant Courbiére and, by casting his net wider, he also implicated a former governor.[51] He came by his righteousness with clarity and competence. Though it was promulgated years before his birth, Fernández likely knew the penalties for committing perjury from Article 121 of the *Reglamento* of 1729. It required soldiers to be wary of its presence and specified the consequences of outlawed behavior.[52]

No other documentation has been found to suggest further complications for him or that any other action was required from him to the Cavo Franco charges. Since Muñoz confirmed a "solution" of some kind as of January 16, Bernardo Fernández resumed his duties at the Béxar presidio.

Accusations, Apache Encounters, and Assurance 179

By February 2, 1793, he was able to preoccupy himself with much the same type of socioeconomic matters involving Native populations; he recorded appearances by the Comanche, the Taguacan, and the arrival of two notable names among others, including the Lipan intermediary "Bautista." The latter reported that his people had killed a Comanche and captured another and a woman on the banks of the Colorado River.[53] Ten days later, Fernández generated the weekly report of arrivals and departures made at the Béxar presidio by, among others, members of the "Los Yndios Amigos de las Naciones del Norte" from February 4–12; a Comanche, one Taguacana who had remained at the presidio since the previous month; and even dependable Capitán Sojas arrived with six of his people including two women. On February 8, gifts went to three Comanche, and in the evening of that same day, the same three ran away after stealing three horses quartered beyond the adjacent plazas. However, no pursuit ensued in consideration of the fact that among the fugitives, one was a brother of Sojas and another, his brother-in-law.[54] As usual, irony and amnesty figured into the frequently baffling process of peace by purchase, and especially when it was used as a preemptive strike. Borderlands forces could often anticipate the outcome of linking their collective beneficence to what they perceived to be ungratefulness on the part of their indigenous co-habitants. For Lieutenant Fernandez, though, the familiar routine of deskwork may have been welcome relief from a concurrent investigation of his bygone responsibilities.

It becomes clear from documentation that Sojas was an individual among the various nations that regularly appeared at the presidios and whose presence required judicious handling, given the sensitivity of his position among the Comanche. Periodically, touchy matters complicated the prescribed duties of military personnel. Without fail, those of paymasters, dead or living, were no exception. During the time he was held responsible by Ugalde for the presumed miscalculations by the now-deceased Bustillos and then had to explain himself to Cavo Franco, Lieutenant Fernández tackled presidial tasks. They were usually mundane, sometimes atypical, and occasionally tricky, the latter when dealing with visiting Indians. For example, when Lieutenant Colonel Muñoz instructed Fernández to send three privates provisioned and supplied with remounts for two months, Fernández complied. He let Muñoz know that the soldiers were taking fifteen pesos of cigarettes, ten pesos of *piloncillos* (sugar loaves), a musket, and a three-footed copper pot (which came with a note about exercising care in its handling). The trio was to arrive by that weekend at the presidio—unspecified—where Muñoz was located.[55] After the soldiers departed, there was a proliferation of activity at the Béxar presidio. Lieutenant Fernández reported that Comanche people appeared and withdrew, including the omnipresent Sojas and, on the

180 Chapter Five

evening of February 20, a drummer of the Third Flying Company of Nuevo Santander showed up at the garrison lacking any documents. The youthful musician-in-training admitted to Fernández that his captain sent him to learn "to perfection" the cadence of military ordinance.[56] It fell to Francisco Amangual to provide the unanticipated *volante* drummer with what was strictly necessary for his subsistence.

In this strange but animated episode of presidio activity, one other confluence of interests involved cloth and two accused paymasters who thought "very good" the lining of their soldiers' capes with scarlet flannel ("*bayeta*"), a task to be done with urgency and with the hope that there would be enough for the entire troop.[57] Without further information, it is difficult to know whether the fabric choice and its use was meant to provide additional warmth for the troops that might wear the accessory, or whether the flannel was intended to color-code by way of costuming the identity of a particular presidio.[58] It may seem insignificant to document such an seemingly trivial episode in the daily chores of these two soldiers even when it involved a prized commodity. However, some minor affairs take on new meaning in light of the larger issues impacting the lives of these two administrators. In this case, both Fernández and Amangual operated under clouds of suspicion stemming from intra- and interpresidial disputes. Bewildered, but undeterred, both men persevered in their responsibilities at a moment in their careers when even their workplace ethics came under question. And if that meant addressing issues related to drummer boys, deceased paymasters, and making decisions about fabric for uniforms, both men did so with apparently little fuss. For that matter, so did Juan Cortés, a soldier still under investigation during this same time for purported confiscation of contraband. Generating his own pile of paperwork, Cortés detailed the structure and strength of his company at Presidio La Bahía, with distinctions made by ranks of and salaries paid to its officers and troops. Missing from Cortés' report was the service record of one sergeant who achieved both higher rank and an escape from scandal while stationed at Bahía.[59] That sergeant was one of the Cortés contraband deponents, then-first sergeant and now newly promoted Alférez of the Lampazos *volantes*, Antonio Treviño.[60]

With more substantive affairs and flying squadrons to attend to, Fernández reported troops, detached and encamped at Los Encinos stream with the horse herd, having witnessed eleven of the twenty-six Comanche (who had set out to find the Lipan on February 11) slaughtering breeding cows ("*chichiguas*"). Subsequently, the commander of the horse herd reported that an "*escuadra volante*," unit unspecified, set out to sweep the vicinity and discovered Indian tracks. The *volantes* followed the trail and soon found

Accusations, Apache Encounters, and Assurance   181

the suspects. Even the recently exonerated (but not forgiven by Amangual) Mariano Rodríguez surfaced in the report as the brother-in-law of a woman who owned one of the slaughtered cows. Living animals might substitute for the losses of dead ones, and a likely remorseful Cortés himself offered fifty tame riding horses to Muñoz.[61]

The mundane continued to mix with blood and thunder. On July 14, 1793, superior orders convened, once more, three recently embroiled soldiers. Lieutenant Fernández, First Alférez Manuel de Urrutia, and Second Alférez Amangual reported to Governor Muñoz that Béxar's master blacksmith José Francisco Pobedano had prepared to fire the burners of five cannons brought up the Trinity River to San Antonio. According to Amangual, only four of the cannons were functional while the fifth had many defects. He, Fernández, and Urrutia stored the four working cannons in the Guardia de Prevención.[62] Earlier that year, Muñoz informed the viceroy that after the residents of Bucareli and Pilar withdrew to Nacogdoches, he took certain measures to transport six bronze artillery cannons abandoned at the Trinity River. Revillagigedo instructed the governor to keep Cmdr. Gen. Pedro de Nava informed so as to receive future orders from him rather than the viceroy. And, if this was not enough to keep Muñoz busy, Nava fixated on the conduct of Urrutia and expected reports about him to flow from Muñoz's pen.[63]

Alférez Manuel de Urrutia's erratic behavior crops up in chapter 1 of this study. He had faced jail sentences several times because of occurrences of domestic violence and public drunkenness. Thereafter, as highlighted in chapter 2, while in custody he was an equivocal deponent in the Amangual–Rodríguez lawsuit. Urrutia's tribulations only worsened. When the Commandancy General was still a dual entity, Ramón de Castro received a directive from Viceroy Revillagigedo to order Urrutia's withdrawal from a "Taguacane" village and present himself to the viceroy in Mexico City. Cleverly planned and carried out by Governor Muñoz under the pretext of a forthcoming new commission or assignment, its intent was to ensure the appearance of the troubled First Alférez. His whereabouts in early 1793 were known from very recent news by company member Pvt. Josef María Hernández confirming his physical location. Castro encouraged Muñoz to meet the viceroy's demands with all possible subtlety so that neither Urrutia nor anyone else would see through the ruse.[64] Wary of keeping his cover, Nava directed the governor to withhold employing the alférez in any service that took him far from the presidio, nor demand much from him in his individual performance.[65]

Whether or not the accusatory circumstances piled on Amangual, Fernández, and Cortés triggered the memo is unclear, but Nava instructed

182   Chapter Five

Muñoz to restrain Urrutia and his "excesses of indulgence and drunkenness" while Nava waited on records held in Mexico about his bad conduct.[66]
In the meantime, Muñoz was to fall back on other measures to discipline
the unruly alférez. It did not take long for the viceroy himself to learn of the
Urrutia situation, and on the same day that Nava contacted the governor,
Revillagigedo also contacted Muñoz with the same instructions. With
that, the state of affairs had reached a point where Muñoz arranged to
have Urrutia return from his stay at the pueblo of the Taguacanes, travel to
Mexico City, and appear before the viceroy.[67] For some reason, Nava must
have felt compelled to direct a separate letter to Muñoz on this same day,
but its messaging addressed military performance among all the presidial
soldiers and specifically those stationed at Béxar and La Bahía.[68] Singled
out in his superiors' four-months-long communication loop, Manuel de
Urrutia may have been a favorite of the Tawakoni, but among his fellow
presidials and his commanders the sentiments bore no resemblance. It may
have surprised no one that the trajectory of his arrogant ways would curve
toward a predictable conclusion via severe punitive measures.

Misbehaving Troops: The King Responds

By mid-1793 several Comandancia soldiers highlighted in this study had
experienced a substantive dose of apprehension stemming from accusations of abuse of privilege and power in their work-related responsibilities.
From administrators in his overseas dominions, the king himself learned
of vexing circumstances undermining the primary obligations of those
in his service. Apart from intra-presidio dissonance, he understood how
these situations intertwined with the livelihoods of civilians and especially
merchants across the frontier. On February 9, a copy certified by Muñoz
of royal orders sent from Aranjuez to the Conde del Campo de Alange
placed civil cases involving military personnel under the jurisdiction of
military courts. Hardship, low pay, and difficult working conditions contributed to the realities of garrison life, and the king acknowledged the
considerable shortages experienced by his army. One factor came by way
of the extraction of 12,000 militia men in 1770. The absence of that much
manpower coupled with the general drafts (*quintas generales*) in 1773, 1775,
and 1776 could be attributed to the abolition of the *fuero* in many cases and
the privileges that had been granted to the military by his predecessors
Carlos I and Felipe II.[69]

    As this long century was ending, Carlos IV recognized that protracted
delays in both punishment of the guilty and absolution for the innocent pre-

Accusations, Apache Encounters, and Assurance

sented "serious damages" to the state and therefore affected the discipline of the troops.[70] Some of these entanglements arose from the thicket of ambitions pitting soldiers against one another in circumstances across multiple jurisdictions while royal administrators fashioned decisions. Sporadic lags in the judicial system had severe ramifications not only for servicemen but for the king's ministers and *fiscales* of the superior tribunals, occupying a great deal of their time that might have been better spent on other duties. Change from on high was inevitable. Therefore, it is helpful to consider the language of the royal orders as it pertained to administrative parsing of soldier misbehavior.

Aiming to "sever at the root all jurisdictional disputes," Carlos IV decided that military justices should hear solely and exclusively all civil and criminal cases in which the accused were members of the army. The only exceptions pertained to instances of primogeniture in possessions, properties, and the distribution of inheritances. Some of these cases might not have stemmed from testamentary resolution by military personnel themselves, without which there could be no filing or jurisdiction admitted by any tribunal or justice under any pretext. However, the king made known that any filings deemed pending, be they civil or criminal, were, in effect, concluded. He further insisted that when these cases arrived before justices and tribunals, they were to forward consequent *autos* and proceedings to the proper military jurisdiction. There they might proceed to congruent duties according to the ordinances.[71]

Offenders faced arrest by prompt order of the ordinary royal jurisdiction, which would then proceed to file charges and send perpetrators to the nearest military justice. No matter what had previously been called for in any rulings, royal resolutions, orders, *pragmáticas*, *cédulas*, or decrees, the king now revoked. However, punishments imposed by these statutes were to remain in "force and vigor" but were to be imposed upon the troops by military justices.[72]

Royal orders of assigning civil cases of military personnel to the jurisdiction of military courts formed the statutory instructions of aiding soldiers by having their legal struggles appropriately deliberated. On the same day Carlos IV issued his orders plainly acknowledging the quagmire impacting troop discipline and by extension its impression on the whole-of-government, he also generated another letter. In this short dispatch specifically extending the legal rights of his men Carlos conveys a slightly different tone, one marked by patriarchal benevolence that assured his troops of their "satisfaction" with its content. [73] Undeniably, the king's special goodwill toward those in the military had the potential to decisively alter the lives of soldiers like Amangual, Fernández, Cortés, and others. Positioned at the apex of authority, His Majesty's conclusions affected the outcome of any proceedings linked to their alleged misdoings and those of others.

With that in mind, by mid-1793 it is doubtful, for example, that Francisco Amangual would have reached out to the king to resolve his disenchantment with the final verdict of his slander suit against Sgt. Mariano Rodríguez. Almost exactly one year after the initial charges materialized—for which Amangual was fully exonerated of any culpability—the absence of any serious jail time for his accuser justifiably irked the paymaster. Amangual was keenly aware of military protocol. He knew that the source of high esteem, that is, honor, was one presumably aspired to by officers of integrity, qualities Amangual no doubt felt he wholly embodied. He voiced concerns that his personal honor and even that of others holding his same rank would be tainted by one disreputable soldier having escaped any serious consequences for his actions. For his part, First Lt. Bernardo Fernández urged those conducting his proceeding to acknowledge his noninvolvement in any of his predecessor's bookkeeping errors. Similarly, Capt. Juan Cortés awaited the outcome of charges leveled not only against him for transporting contraband but also for his family's complicity in his alleged illicit activities.

What military reports the Conde de Alange did receive out of the Comandancia General were not all disheartening. For example, from one inspector he discovered that the Third and Fourth *compañías volantes* of Nueva Vizcaya maintained a rather moderate-in-quality state of instruction, discipline, and governance. The Third Flying Company covered the district of Pilar de Conchos (Chihuahua) under its Capt. Manuel Rengel with other positions filled by two lieutenants, two alféreces, a chaplain, an armorer, and a drummer. Lt. Col. Antonio de Cordero hoped that by sending to the king's representative in Mexico the reviews of his inspection of the two *volante* cadres, in return he would receive decrees of *Ymbálido* and awards for those worthy individuals within the ranks. It was men like sergeants Antonio Griego, Ignacio Sotelo, Lucas Domínguez, Pedro Quiñones, and corporals, carbineers, and soldiers of Conchos who most impressed Cordero. Their robust size, agility, fierceness, and singular integrity complemented their strict subordination and apparent talent with firing and handling weapons. Cordero had himself instructed a few of the cavalry members, the group he was least impressed with, but praised the performance of the company's Captain Rengel, a leader he described as useful in all areas of service.[74] Documentation from the period makes evident the king's paternal attitude to his subjects, especially those carrying arms, and that consideration extended to soldiers in the Américas.

Accusations, Apache Encounters, and Assurance

Carlos IV grounded his compassion for the troops in his willingness to be "ever ready to dispense as many favors as possible" to his subjects, and especially to those who, by "postponing with generous spirit their comforts and their own lives," devoted themselves to the defense of the state. In pursuing the "glorious career of the military," the soldiers of the royal army occupied a "special admiration and distinguished place" in the king's "magnanimous heart." Thus, he saw fit to expand the basic tenets of the urban *fuero* so that military personnel involved in frontier court cases would have only to answer to "their own logical leaders" and, presumably, receive more expeditious administration of justice.[75] Dereliction of duty punctuates enough narratives from the Comandancia General to confirm its pervasiveness. For practical reasons the King's benevolence and the quick conclusions of some episodes of insubordination may have helped propel perennially outnumbered soldiers back into their saddles sooner than later.

Across the contested borderlands, archival records from 1792–93 documented accusations of contraband and mishandling of presidial finances. Soldiers in key positions of authority became suspects with reparations to make to not only their fellow company members and superior commanders but also to the viceroy and the king himself. It meant, too, that those same men might heavily scrutinize job performances by defendants in their midst. By summer 1793, First Alférez Manuel de Urrutia, esteemed by the Tawakoni and the Lipan as one of their own, had from the perspective of Spanish military superiors become a repeat offender based on his reckless behavior.[76] In January 1792, six months after his last jail sentence, Urrutia was arrested for insubordination stemming from a drunken rampage. This time his fury was directed against Lt. Bernardo Fernández.[77] And even though the troubled Urrutia time after time proved to be more than a minor annoyance to several of his superiors during this same period, colonial and peninsular administrators saw the need for consolidating their power toward eradicating criminality at large.

Much of the dogged misconduct cited so far in albeit isolated incidences had become so pronounced that corrective action was unavoidable. As distracting as was the willful comportment of a demonstrably alcoholic soldier repeatedly charged with dereliction of duty, the viceroy's outlook widened considerably. It was his responsibility to convey the king's concerns about insubordination as it occurred among individuals engaged in collective transgressions. Disruptive to the extent that it involved investigations, convening witnesses, and taking depositions, impropriety by soldiers had the potential to cause economic imbalances. Untoward behavior impacted regional and global commerce. Amangual knew this to be all too true as

186   Chapter Five

evinced by his elevated workload with tangible evidence in the form of cataloging contraband.

Correction and compassion figured into resolving systemic corruption. In the summer of 1791, Revillagigedo communicated the royal order of clemency granted on March 18 by Carlos IV to *contrabandistas*. Special, even exculpatory, conditions formed part of the criteria for the king's general pardon. While acknowledging the harm caused to the state and to the royal treasury by subjects engaged in clandestine trade, the king could not look with indifference upon the sad fate of the families affected by these offenders. Accordingly, he resolved to grant a general pardon for the crime of contraband to all of those, even deserters from the army or navy, who had not also committed homicide. If located in the province of their garrison and within a two-month period of abandoning their unit or if away without leave for four months and outside their province, defectors could present themselves with impunity to their respective companies to serve out the term of their enlistments. Other smugglers, presumably civilians like Toribio Durán, had to appear before the subdelegates of the royal treasury having jurisdiction in their cases and to comply in those courts with the royal decree's formalities.[78]

Evidence of the king's extraordinary, if abstruse, generosity became clear in his desire to extend the general pardon to the furthest reaches of the *frontera*. Now, amnesty accommodated smugglers who *had* committed homicide.[79] So long as the act was not premeditated or evil-intentioned, the king granted this class of smugglers not only a pardon for the crime of contraband but also a pardon in commutation with the requirement of a pardon *de parte* pursuant to the laws. However, repeat offenders were to be adjudicated as soon as they were apprehended and, without further investigation, given the penalty of ten years in prison (*diez años de presidio*)[80] or public works, according to the degree of their offenses.[81] The special conditions in the king's orders included the following:

> Smugglers were to turn themselves in to the subdelegates and hand over at the same time the tobacco, arms, or other type of illicit commerce.
>
> Smugglers were required to sign an obligation and post a bond of two hundred pesos *fuertes*, according to the capabilities of each one, not to return to the contraband trade, and to return to the towns of their residences and to devote themselves to honest work to support themselves and their families.
>
> If one, or some, of the smugglers could not post the bond and if that impossibility was substantiated, they would be relieved of it but still sign the obligation.

Accusations, Apache Encounters, and Assurance 187

Smugglers in jail while their cases were pending or with sentences not yet in effect were to be pardoned as well; those individuals were to follow the requirements of the newly accused with no difference whatsoever. They were to be set free, as were any soldiers imprisoned for the crime of fraud, so that the latter could present themselves to their unit in order to serve the time remaining of their military obligations.

Smugglers could not leave the places where they had established residences for other places without stating the reasons for doing so to the justices in their jurisdictions. With legitimate reasons for leaving, justices could grant them permission, indicating the time that they could remain away; if the pardoned individual could not return in time or was notably overdue, the justice could determine whether there was a justifiable reason for the tardiness or if the individual had gone to suspicious places; in the latter case, the justice could proceed to punish the individual.

Subdelegates of the royal treasury were to send to the justices in the town of the smugglers' residences a copy of their signed obligation and the bond that they posted to not return to contraband trade and to devote themselves to honest work, so that they might be held to their obligations by justices overseeing their conduct. If pardoned smugglers engaged in fraud again or abetted that behavior, justices were to arrest them with a *sumaria* against them. They were to send both prisoner and paper to the subdelegate of the royal treasury in their district so that a case might be made against the accused, act against their posted bond, and impose the punishment stipulated by the royal decree.[82]

To check compliance, all sides of the equation were under surveillance. Justices had to enforce the royal orders, and dereliction of duty from their cabal could result in a heavy fine (four hundred pesos) for the first offense and double the amount for the second, paid to the subdelegates of the royal treasury. These same subdelegates charged inspectors of tobacco and other revenues with the same task as corporals and lieutenants completing the rounds of their respective jurisdictions: they must exercise diligence in discerning where the pardoned smugglers might go and whether justices were carrying out their duties. Even with potential fines and assorted punishments levied against dishonest justices, the most damaging result would be the displeasure of the king himself once informed of their misdeeds. Contrabandists who did not turn themselves in as prescribed by the decree were to be pursued with "the greatest vigor" for their apprehension and subsequently receive the corresponding punishment.[83]

188   Chapter Five

The subdelegates of the royal treasury were to send to the justices a copy
of the decree and the instruction when these saw publication in the provincial capitals. Thereafter, functionaries entered these two documents into
the *ayuntamiento* records. These were then read by scribes to the *alcaldes*
at the beginning of each year so that its leaders might know the obligation
imposed upon them. Even the scribes could be assessed a fine of three
hundred pesos (pesos *fuertes*) if they were remiss in their responsibilities.[84]
The paradox here is that, by the very scope of its generosity and equanimity,
a specter of suspicion effectively surrounded the pardon, such was its potential for abuse. With its radius widened and extended to the perpetrators,
now essentially its main beneficiaries, it makes one wonder if the king, his
assistants, and even borderlands administrators questioned the wisdom of
its issuance in the first place.

It will become clear if the mercurial Capt. Juan Cortés reaped benefit
from the royal pardon, too. It will be a matter unsettled if fundamentally
obeisant officers like Bernardo Fernández and Francisco Amangual were
better informed about the consequences of misbehavior while on duty.[85]
As we shall see, officer status and long tenure soldiering on in the Comandancia did not necessarily signal unfaltering allegiance to protocol. Nor
did sustained service preclude the possibility of those in the army's upper
echelons committing crimes against the state.

Amangual and Cortés: Self-Defense and Defending the Defendant

By December 1793, Amangual had given thirty-one years to military service. His immediate supervisor Manuel Muñoz described him as a soldier
possessing valor, with good conduct but limited skills. What precisely those
skills were that Amangual had in short supply is unknown. The service
record notated by Captain Muñoz concedes many admirable qualities
in Amangual, and it is conceivable that certain of his skills described as
limited in a general sense were similarly lacking among other presidials.
Therefore, by comparison, Amangual was no exception.[86]

Archival sources expose a not so unusual strict formality in the correspondence between Amangual and Muñoz, their professional distancing
the result of not only long-standing abstemious interactions but perhaps
also from the superior status conferred by multiple appellations held by
the captain who was also serving as governor of the *provincia*. One short
exchange between the two men and written by Amangual demonstrates
the stratified protocol circumscribing textual interactions between those

El Segundo Teniente D.n Francisco Amangual, su edad 5 años, su Pais Isla de Mallorca, su Calidad, hijo de Labrador, su salud buena, sus Servicios y circunstancias los que expresa.

Tiempo en que empezó á servir los Empleos.				Tiempo que ha que sirve, y q.to en cada Empleo.			
Empleos	Dias	Meses	Años	Empleos	Años	Meses	Dias
Soldado y Cavo	" 3.	Dia.re	1762.	Soldado y Cavo	" 11.	" 5.	" 27.
Sargento	" 3 o.	Mayo.	1776.	Sargento	" 3.	" 3.	" 1.
Alferez 2º	" 1.	Sept.re	1779.	Alferez 2º	" 7.	" 2.	" 21.
Alferez 1º	" 2 2.	Nov.re	1786.	Alferez 1º	" 2.	" "	" 3 o.
Teniente 2º	" 15.	Nov.re	1789.	Teniente 2º	" b.	" 9.	" 15.

Total hasta fin de Diziembre de		1793			" 30.	" 9.	" 1 b.

Reximientos, Presidios y Compañias Volantes donde ha servido.

El Reximiento de Dragones de Batavia 2 años, y 2 dias, del que pasó á el de España, á el tiempo de su formacion, en que sirvió 16 años, 8 meses, y 26 dias, hasta que fue ascendido á Alferez de la Compañia de Cavalleria del Presidio de Bexar, en que ha que sirve 3 años, 3 meses y 1 dia.

Campañas, y acciones de Guerra en que se ha hallado.

En la Expedicion de la Sonora desde el año de 1767, hasta mediado del de 1771, hallandose en 6 funciones: y en este Presidio ha echo varias salidas, mandando Partidas para castigar los insultos, y hostilidades de los Indios Comanches, con los que se le han ofrecido quatro funciones logrando matar á 26 de ellos, apresandoles 2 vivos, y cogidoles cinquenta Cavallos, y otros varios Despojos.

Man.l Muñoz

Valor ....
Aplicacion ....
Capacidad ....
Conducta ....
Estado ....

Amangual military service record, e_bx_010604, The Dolph Briscoe Center for American History, The University of Texas at Austin.

190   Chapter Five

dissimilar in rank: "As a consequence of your order of June 1, 1794 and the letter included by Capitán Juan Cortés of the Presidio de La Bahía del Espíritu Santo, in which I am informed that I have been named by the soldier who is being prosecuted, Juan José de la Garza, as his defender: I have arranged to transfer immediately to that presidio in order to take the oath and witness the rest of the directives that he prepares; that which I inform you of is for the record."[87] More practically, a no-nonsense approach toward the paymaster of the company was likely a priority with Muñoz. He could hardly be blamed for his aloofness given the awkwardness potentially surfacing from anything less than orthodox within the garrison's workspaces. None of this would have aggrieved Amangual. Years earlier a paymaster election at the Béxar presidio details Gov. Domingo Cabello's urging the "due formality" required for convening officers to determine the ultimate result of the voting process.[88]

Distinctions in rank and formalities aside, it is apparent that when he was not defending his own work as company fiduciary, Francisco Amangual answered the call to defend suspected wrongdoers in other garrisons. In the excerpt above, yet another ironic convergence of former and current accused soldiers materialized on paper. It was Capt. Cortés who had requested permission from Governor Muñoz to allow Amangual's travel to La Bahía in order to defend *soldado* de la Garza. His crime was particularly heinous: the alleged murder of his fellow company member Cpl. Vizente Serna. De la Garza is familiar as one of the deponents in the Cortés contraband case. Amangual's presence was crucial, not only to confirm the ratifications of the witnesses but also to establish the defense of an unfortunate soul who was putting all hope for acquittal in him.[89] The verdict came in due course.

Accusations of murder form a unique category in frontier documentary literature. When it occurred, imperial authorities issued formal responses apart from ordinances directed at military personnel. For example, a February 28, 1794, royal *cédula* declared that those accused of committing homicide would not have access to immunity since the act was not accidental or in self-defense.[90] And yet, the July 1791 royal decree referenced above pinpointed the fact that smugglers were exempt from punishment for homicide so long as it was unpremeditated or evil intentioned. In three years, something had changed. Insofar as that rule of law further confounds the issue of a consequential charge associated with death, it does prompt the question: What types of extenuating circumstances linked illicit commerce and its perpetrators?

One answer is possible. When he extended the legal rights of his soldiers, the king believed that the *fuero* was still relevant for stiffening the loyalty of his otherwise disenfranchised troops. Few, if any, would have disagreed.

Accusations, Apache Encounters, and Assurance 191

However, presuming his men's ability to recognize what he and other like-minded administrators felt was a "glorious career in the military" may say more about the king being out of touch with the realities of life in the Septentrión despite his compassionate overtures. The notion of achieving glory commensurate with long years of service may not have resonated so much with men facing chronic privations as part of life in a needy army. Further, it mattered not whether hardship occurred in the more populous regions of the empire, which it did, or in its outlying spaces.

As Amangual and his ward, the accused De la Garza, faced the outcome of their separate allegations, so, too, did Capt. Cortés. Having similarly awaited a final verdict in his own contraband proceedings, Cortés received word from Commander General Nava regarding the outcome of the Garza murder charge. The auditor of war advised Nava that for a period of three years, on rations and without pay, Garza was to labor in the public works at Presidio Béxar. Cortés was to arrange for passage and delivery of the indicted soldier to that location. The urgency and apparent finality of the order meant that Garza was to leave immediately, that is, on the day following the auditor's directive.[91]

Since he was not a convicted murderer but, instead, a suspected contrabandist, Cortés had already won a better outcome in his own legal entanglement. Months before the Garza final verdict, Nava reported his receipt of five notebooks concerning repayments to the Tribunal of Accounts that satisfied charges incurred by Cortés. Further, Muñoz received news that existing deposits delivered by Cortés to the *gratificación* fund of the company in question were deducted from the deficit by the tribunal.[92]

Correspondence trekked slowly in the borderlands. In Nacogdoches interim commander Christóbal de Córdoba confirmed Muñoz's letter from Nava dated December 6, 1793, indicating that Escandón had taken Cortés into custody that June with his illicit merchandise. Since protocol demanded that subordinate officers reiterate their compliance with and understanding of any instructions within an official document, Córdoba did so. He added that monitoring this issue was "very important" and it was necessary to be vigilant about banning forbidden goods into the province.[93] In turn, Muñoz affirmed that some things indeed were prohibited according to the "spirit of the order." To correct these types of excesses Muñoz added that passports must be checked at Béxar before reaching La Bahía.[94]

Misconduct by the commission of murder, harboring bootleg, and other forms of outright insubordination proved to be the impetus for penalizing soldiers plagued by chronic dereliction of duty. Clamping down on the necessity of accurate paperwork or intensifying drill work for soldiers and staff likely gave commanders the semblance of extracting discipline from their underlings, thereby strengthening cohesion. Given the archival evidence for undiminished transgressions by its military strength, however, disciplinary efforts by presidio officers also registered self-serving interests. But how else to convince viceregal superiors of their relevance to localized strategies of defense? On July 17, 1794, Nava sent instructions to Muñoz about another notebook, this one of exercises, formations, and cavalry movements that the general had forwarded to Assistant Inspector Juan Gutiérrez for use in training. For this instruction to be put quickly into practice, Muñoz was to confer a suitable officer to muster the troops of Béxar along with those under the direction of the besieged Lt. Bernardo Fernández at La Bahía. Nava further advised Muñoz to make a subaltern officer available to take part in the new training drills. An assembly of twenty-four men, if possible, was required. Troop strength being what it was, even sixteen or eighteen would suffice. Nonetheless, this was to include the entire troop, including soldiers exempt from duty in the company.[95] Once Governor Muñoz dispatched copies of the notebook, Fernández acknowledged his compliance with the instructions and promised to put them into play with little loss of time once his troops showed up.[96]

By November, Fernández considered the troops fully instructed in the new cavalry drills. Because *his* men did not know the exercises, however, Bahía's Captain Cortés did not have a single officer to send to the assembly. Cortés asked if Muñoz could, if he saw fit, retire the only lieutenant who half-understood the drills but who was now gravely ill.[97] It is no surprise that, in the final years of fading empire, higher status in the military hierarchy carried no weight where it concerned training for and then securing competent horsemanship in battle.

Finding Soldiers for the Borderlands: Training for a Career in the Frontier

The rise and fall of socioeconomic dynamics in the borderlands finds expression in the context of viceregal policing of all things military as officially documented by commanders on the ground. The entire process of company evaluations and individual soldier appraisals comes into focus by surveying the late career of Francisco Amangual. Despite at least two allegations of wrongdoing as company paymaster, his services as an accountant and especially his talent with executing laborious inventories were still in demand. His ability to testify in legal proceedings of a serious nature, and by providing testimony for a defendant charged with murder, speaks to his status as a creditable officer in the presidio ecosystem. And his regular engagement with the more mundane tasks associated with the

Accusations, Apache Encounters, and Assurance 193

responsibilities of a frontier soldier continued unabated despite multiple entanglements involving both civilians and military staff.

Whether it was recent events involving paymaster inaccuracies, or accused *contrabandistas* scurrying among the troops, or convicted murderers within the ranks, or a persistent and glowering French and Anglo presence in the borderlands, comandante general Nava stayed informed and had good reason to send the usual reminders to Texas. Ascertaining the abilities of enlisted soldiers was of the same old concern to viceregal authorities and demanded skilled personnel more so than the opposite. Though Nava is unambiguous, the tone of the letter is attentive to the long career and experience of Governor Muñoz:

> Your being responsible for individuals in the company the king maintains under your command to be useful for all circumstances, you should be particularly acquainted with the conduct of each one in order to request the dismissal of those that are useless or detrimental. You have to place the utmost care in the internal and economic governance of that company, and it will be an ongoing test [of that care] that the troop is presenting itself with [as] good order as possible for which you have its corresponding retention fund [*fondo de retención*]; and, above all, equipped with what it needs for war, in which [the troop] understands the good condition [for war], of the shortcut, the worth of campaigns and the rest. Prepared for departures [for campaigns from the presidio]: make yourself available so that the company is provided with anything it needs for such an important objective and, in that which their capabilities do not accomplish, that needs to be shown to me so that you can take the steps [to improve their performance].[98]

A little more than a month later, Nava contacted Governor Muñoz yet again. This time the general felt the necessity for what was essentially a refresher memo concerning the complexities of war in the borderlands. Nava insisted that commanders were not the only ones that needed to practice reconnaissance exercises, when possible. Whether or not he picked up on Cortés' plea to Muñoz for help with officer training, Nava demanded that drills continue without interruption by officers, sergeants, and corporals so that surveillance improved. Likewise, there had to be a proportionate effort to repeat maneuvers again and again and out toward the greatest possible distance. Since the weather had always to be kept in mind, honing skills might be possible only during times when strong rains or snow did not threaten.[99]

Though he referenced his June 1793 instruction of tactical maneuvers, Nava merely repeated mandates from almost a decade earlier. Among its emphases, the Gálvez *Instrucciones* of 1786 outlined stipulations to reconnoitering the frontier as a useful mechanism against hostile Natives. When first communicated to his intended audience of one—*Comandante General* Ugarte—the viceroy warned that if reconnaissance exercises were deployed at the same time and over the same lands, those efforts would produce nothing but predictable results. By that, as seen in Chapter 4, he meant negative. When Indians observed troop movements, they simply followed the soldiers' trails to interior country, made their raids, and then retreated to their *rancherías*. All of this they accomplished without the troops' ability to prevent any of it.[100]

At this point in the game, Nava stressed the importance of an indisputable truth: the type of war carried out in the Interior Provinces required thoroughgoing instruction. That meant anticipating the type of ground the troops had to pound, using their knowledge of or guesswork about all advances made by the Apache and studying the entrances, exits, and watering places to ascertain how far on horseback one could enter. An engine of many moving parts, this training entailed a battery of techniques comparable to understanding the mountain ranges and slopes found in the interior.[101] Clearly, the safety of the horses and his soldiers' equestrian skills were on Nava's mind since he stressed the need for certain maneuvers by the cavalry, doubtless essential for the *compañías volantes*. During horseback exercises or when Muñoz and other presidio captains were able to assemble a proportionate number of troops, the latter were to rehearse by hiding in the closest gorges ("*desfiladeros*") and canyons as a first step in cutting off avenues of passage.[102]

Parallels between Nava's instructions and those of Gálvez are undeniable, especially where troop safety was involved. In the latter, article 23 of the 1786 Instructions stressed the importance of allowing complete freedom of action, unlimited by any restriction, for commandants of detachments or independent forces on campaign such as the flying squadrons. Since Gálvez's article functioned as an indicator of the effectiveness of a forces' operations and its commanders' usefulness or not, Nava was likely conjuring article 23's forewarning to avert any waylay. Past performance showed that some detachments experienced being caught off guard on a regular basis because of mismanagement and having little confidence while traveling.[103] Nava emphasized these types of maneuvers as necessary so that neither the commander nor the commanded was taken by surprise in any circumstance. Rewards in frontier skirmishes were few but, in these moments, the spirited, the swiftest, and those who most distinguished themselves were to be praised; in effect, these were the soldiers to be taken care of insofar as it was possible.[104] Finally, Nava believed that instruction by the numbers would give a clearer idea of how many officers and troops should operate in campaigns rather than in any other type of drill. Just the same, he was quick to point out that not for that should "simple" exercises, practiced as much on foot as on horseback, be ignored by commanders. The importance here was to streamline and then drill for improving skill in asymmetric warfare.[105]

Soldier Ineptitude in the Twilight of the Eighteenth Century

In some places across the borderlands, some troops did more damage—if they did anything at all—than they did that which was of any use to anyone, anywhere. For example, Gálvez in his 1786 directive let Ugarte know that, as Commandant General armed with special instructions for Nueva Vizcaya, he had the power to act upon a request from the local ranchers. They wanted to be excused from annual excise taxes allocated for military purposes. Attentive to their vulnerability to enemy attack and equally protective of their own economic interests, the ranchers asserted a presumptive autonomy to vocalize dissatisfaction with soldiers responsible for protecting their corner of the frontier. That these same cattlemen had offered to sacrifice themselves in their own defense and that of the province betrays an incontrovertible focus on exposing the uselessness of two flying companies, those of Anaelo and Pueblo del Álamo.[106]

Settler stakeholders fixated on cost, security, and efficiency. But, if inept soldiers were mixed in, that also demanded self-preservation by civilians. Financing the restless borderlands and its military operatives was an interwoven affair, complicated further when its personnel came under fire for wrongdoing and fiscal irresponsibility. When Gálvez presented his 1786 instructions to Ugarte, the very deep concerns of civilians about their annual excise taxes incurred for military purposes were substantial. But now, in Gálvez or through his frontier surrogates, the ranchers of Nueva Vizcaya could count on a sympathetic ear for their complaints. The Instruction's article 142 stated that: "The general fund for excise taxes for military purposes of Nueva Vizcaya today must maintain three flying companies whose annual allocation costs more than seventy thousand pesos; but if the royal treasury is taxed with them, and accordingly with the regular increase which should be possible, with salaries and supplies of subordinate officers and troops of these provinces, the new costs would rise to an inordinate sum."[107]

It seems Gálvez had not quite expended all the ink in his well by conveying his dismay with the martial capabilities of the region's *volantes*. Balancing his concerns for the fiscal well-being of civilians with the undy-

196 Chapter Five

ing objective of tightening the belt on the king's money when it concerned wasteful expenditures, Gálvez's articles 143 and 144 do more than just censure the flying companies. They explain not only the financial risk that these specific squadrons represented but also the possibility that some of their individual troop members were incompetent and thus increasing the drain on the Royal Treasury.[108] Giving troops the benefit of the doubt, the viceroy encouraged Ugarte to find out whether other civilians, including the miners, merchants, and traffickers of the province, were of the same opinion as the ranchers. If there was consensus among all these settlers, Gálvez wanted to know the causes of the *volantes'* inutility.[109]

Presidial documentation at intervals establishes the king's beneficence to his soldiers across the great reach of the Comandancia General. Similarly, it corroborates the patriarchal, and often perceptive, approaches that some frontier commanders took toward their subordinates and, even, proximate civilians. However insignificant the rewards for good conduct and productive service to the Crown may seem, given the unique challenges of life in the empire's hinterlands, these forms of remuneration had value to troops within certain garrisons. Inasmuch as acquiring meaningful financial support was arduous and bewildering for its austerity, let us briefly recall some of the key issues that emerged from the 1786 *Instrucción* concerning fiscal management of the Comandancia's forces during the final decades of the century.

Since it was apparent that the ranchers in Nueva Vizcaya determined as "useless" the *volantes* of Anaelo and Pueblo del Álamo, Gálvez proposed that if these two forces were not necessary to defend the province, then they were to be reorganized immediately. He was convinced that this approach would end the primary cause for the exaction of onerous taxes.[110] Without hesitation, Gálvez had been in communication with one of the two men charged with assisting commander general Jacobo Ugarte. Col. Juan Ugalde, the colonel of the infantry, who also bore the title of Commandant of the Armies ("Comandante de las Armas"), as did Commander Inspector José Rengel, had already proposed a plan to repurpose the flying squadrons of Anaelo and Álamo. Hinting at his known hawkishness, Ugalde offered to defend the districts of Saltillo and Parras with the troops which he requested for the garrisons of the four provinces—Coahuila, Texas, Nuevo León, and Nuevo Santander—under his command.[111] The next series of articles from the 1786 Instruction specifically concern the contentious taxes required from the citizen settlers of Nueva Vizcaya. Their resistance to the tax caused the uproar sparked by the dismal opinion held by those citizens about the *volantes*. Most importantly, the articles in part engaged with the most expeditious manner of bringing about renovations that would not disrupt the delicate balance of stabilizing the royal treasury while preventing competent soldiers from being shortchanged. Urgent measures were necessary to avoid inciting potentially rebellious civilians and it was clear that the "private interests" of the *hacenderos* was a priority for Gálvez.[112]

Similarly, if soldier incompetence was due to some being unsuited to defend that region's population, Gálvez believed this class should be eliminated altogether. He argued for substituting for them others who had the necessary qualifications. Finally, if the real issue was that the companies were ill-placed in both locations—if there was a scarcity of pasture for the horse herds, or, because the greater number did not assist in defending the territory and making war on the enemy at their *rancherías*—then the alternative solution was to transport out those companies to more advantageous posts.[113] It is curious to consider how a change of venue would transform an otherwise indifferent soldier into an aggressive fighting machine. But Gálvez the itinerant administrator was also an experienced, proven scrapper.

He had a slew of ideas about controlling Native populations that form the crux of his deliberations. Gálvez calculated that the Comandancia had a force of 1,359 soldiers. But he wanted Ugalde to reduce that number to 969, regrouping the two hundred men of the two deadbeat flying companies, as well as 190 of those from Nuevo León and the Colonia de Nuevo Santander, presumably also *volantes*. Since change of any kind—structural, theoretical, or fiscal—governed Gálvez's reforms, Ugalde was to apprise the viceroy of how the presidial and flying companies of the four provinces under his charge would take shape.[114] Likely concerned about having to rely upon even more flat-footed troops, Gálvez disclosed that the collection of excess taxes from the militias of Nueva Vizcaya was on the verge of suspension.[115] Multiple layers of tax collection enhanced the province's "very valuable" status.[116] As with other top-tier operatives in frontier administration, fiscal alterations hinged on Gálvez's consideration of the entirety of reports generated by Ugalde, Rengel, Ugarte and their subordinates.

The suspension would supposedly relieve the burden on the contributors of these taxes, and Gálvez was certain the relief would be greater if some of the troops of Sonora, Nueva Vizcaya, and Nuevo México could be "reformed." Ever mindful of the slightest threat to His Majesty's money, Gálvez remarked that if increases of salaries and assets ensued in all presidios, flying companies, dragoons, and volunteers, upsurges could not be detrimental to the royal treasury.[117]

Gálvez went a step further by focusing on the necessity for restructuring the military ranks and by targeting certain members of the troop collective, even the non-Spanish soldiers. By allowing both Ugarte and Inspector

Segesser II Hide Painting (detail) 1720–1729. Courtesy of the Palace of the Governors Photo Archives (NMHM/DCA), Neg. # 158345.

Rengel to propose new formulas for upgrades or greater economy in assembling the presidial and flying companies of the three provinces, Gálvez showed a willingness to take advice from both men. One can imagine that his suggestion that an effective *Indian* auxiliary could replace the venerable leather-jacketed soldiers (*cueras*) elicited astonishment from his generals. However, the implication there suggests the degradation of that frontier mainstay in this moment.[118]

In the same breath, he was convinced that some corporals, sergeants, or subordinate officers could be excised from other companies with beneficial results gained from an increase in the number of "ordinary" soldiers

Accusations, Apache Encounters, and Assurance

(*plazas sencillas*).[119] Moreover, he may have had Native troops in mind for these positions. Where it pertained to Sonora and its "frequent" presidial campaigns against the Gileño Apache, he shared his preference for the Opata companies of Bavispe and "Bacoache," and the Upper Pimas at San Rafael de Buenavista.[120]

Apart from the pessimistic critique of the *volantes* he had received from ranching constituents in Nueva Vizcaya, Gálvez apportioned the 1786 Instructions in a way that cohered his thinking about funding, soldier training, and geography. From this outcome one certainty remained, and it was foreseeable. At some point prior to his 1786 Instrucción, Bernardo de Gálvez was so much less impressed with the *soldados de cuera* comprising the ranks of the armed forces to the degree that one of his proposed solutions, unapologetically, was to indeed muster Indian auxiliaries to supplant these specialized units. However, this may not appear so remarkable considering the eternal tensions between Lipan and Comanche communities and the chronically understaffed Comandancia.

But by mid-1795 it became clear that commanders were willing to accommodate the special preferences of their indigenous allies even when it came to supplying weapons for defense. This might even explain the attraction for the Indian auxiliaries as competent replacements for otherwise slacker soldiers at the presidios.[121] In May, Pedro de Nava received word from the governor of Texas that the "Friendly Indians" valued rifles over shotguns—presumably because of their more precise aim—and so he acted on that information. He ordered the governor of Coahuila, Lt. Col. Miguel de Emparán, to send to Muñoz the eighty rifles available in Monclova as a gift for their allies.[122] Undoubtedly this was one method of appeasing the Indians in the orbit of presidial commanders and their subordinates.

To that end, certain regions needed improvements specifically addressing the shortcomings associated with those territories. Whereas the Gálvez critique focused on Native peoples, the 1724–28 inspection by Rivera (which resulted in the 1729 *Reglamento* of Viceroy Casafuerte) had instructions for each of the presidios and the captains of their companies. The governors of New Mexico, Texas, Sinaloa, and Coahuila had specific orders to follow its content. While issued as yet another coercive edict envisioned somewhere between Rivera's bewildering critique and subsequent recommendations and the hard-nosed instructions of Gálvez, the 1772 Reglamento differed in its reception. Tracking across the bureaucratic hierarchy toward publication, these latest mandates presented the conclusions of the dual Marqués de Rubí-José de Gálvez inspections and were mulled over by the outgoing viceroy, then met resistance by the incoming one, and were, ultimately, promulgated by the king.

200   Chapter Five

Maintaining the semblance of peace with Native populations by issuing them guns and other gifts and issuing regulations and instructions to soldiers was one thing, but handling increased European migration into the Comandancia was another. Accommodating the French was now an entirely different matter of concern. As noted in earlier chapters, the Seven Years' War spurred on transmutations across the Spanish-Franco-Indian borderlands that decisively affected Texas and its closest nonindigenous neighbors. With the acquisition of Louisiana via the Treaty of 1763, Carlos III enjoyed further license to welcome colonizers across the board to his overseas dominions.[123] Mattie Austin Hatcher examined fiscal prerogatives of the king's enterprising administrator Gálvez, who had access to a select fund to encourage immigration, develop commerce, and to cultivate "friendly relations with the Indians." Its assets also helped to welcome beleaguered Acadians eager to take refuge among the Spanish populations in Louisiana.[124]

Routine documentation, crystallized in monthly company reports, divulged garrison strengths and new or unusual occurrences, including Europeans in their midst. They reveal personal narratives that show not only the growing French presence in the Texas presidio populations but also the grit and resilience of individual actors moving across and within Spanish-Native spaces. They were among many excursionists who accepted the challenges of life as it was, doing so to carve out an economic niche among military personnel and indigenous folk within and outside of the Septentrión. Historically, that effort sought to integrate the widespread *rancherías*. Some of these previously unvoiced outsider experiences emerge from reportage required by the presidio to gain entry. Often, the data reveals the petitioner's eagerness to establish new roots through sacrifice and commitment to service.

Pedro Joséf Lambremón, a native of New Orleans, deserted from there to the Béxar presidio in 1786 where he supported himself as a tailor. He was married for six years and had one four-year-old daughter.[125] Similarly, Juan de Mouy ("Demui") came from Mobile, province of Louisiana, and went to Natchitoches and entered its militia where he served as a second lieutenant. He served there until he earned a dispatch of second lieutenant; he received a passport to Béxar, owing a "Alexandro Dupon" a debt for this passage. He was married and had a four-year-old daughter.[126] De Mouy planned to return to his post once he collected the funds to repay his debt.[127] For his part, Alexandro Dupont was an individual who, at the turn of the century, began working as a surveyor in the mining industry.[128]

Pierre Chalis, baptized in the cathedral of Somer in the province of Anju, departed for Louisiana somewhere between the ages of eighteen and twenty. During the first three years of his life in the Américas, he supported himself as a barber and thereafter served in the military corps of the French king. Subsequently, he accompanied Gov. Jacinto de Barrios to Coahuila. Pressing on toward Béxar, Chalis supposedly stopped at Los Adaes. He married twice, and from his first wife he had two children, and from the second, three. He documented to the governor that he had been in Texas for a total of thirty-three years, living entirely in San Antonio.[129]

Ángel Navarro came from the island of "Córzega" in the province of Ayacho but left there in 1762. Against his parents' desires, he left home at the age of thirteen or fourteen and went first to Génova. He sailed to Barcelona and on to Cádiz, continually seeking employment as a servant. Once arrived in the Américas, he found work at the Real de Vallecillos (Nuevo León) under the tutelage of Juan Antonio Aguilar where he worked for eight years. From there, he came to San Antonio's presidio as a merchant, remained a bachelor for six years before marrying in 1783, and had two children.[130]

With a safe passage passport, foreigners met the requirement to demonstrate to the Texas governor what form of permission they carried, from where they came, and their reason for coming to the province. In April 1792, Viceroy Revillagigedo ordered Muñoz to send an accurate report of the outsiders living in his jurisdiction, be they married or just housed there, and those who were travelers, traders, or identified under any other pretext.[131] Muñoz complied with a report of that demographic indicating the name, country of birth, marital status, number of family members, and occupation. Ángel Navarro, Chalis,[132] and Courbiére are by now familiar to the reader of this study. But the census undertaken by Muñoz counts a Nicolás Lemé from the island of Re, province of Aunis, who came to the Béxar presidio in 1779. He subsequently enlisted as a cadet where he remained for thirteen years. In August 1792, he rose to second alférez of the presidial company of Aguaverde.[133] Muñoz also described Lemé as a bachelor and trader. Another native of New Orleans (but not a deserter like Lambremón), Antonio Connar, "alias Laforé," entered Texas for the purpose of building a church at La Trinidad. Since this did not happen, he went to Béxar in 1778. There he married and as recorded in the Muñoz census, had no children. Connar was a carpenter by trade and, apparently, even practiced medicine.[134]

In a few short sentences, the past and present merged in an official document generated by Muñoz. Its content was based on the evaluation of a specific sector of Texas' population with the result destined for administrators in Mexico City. One remarkable entry describes Pedro Miñón, a native of Boforte, located in the province of Aldas. From there he went to New Orleans

202   Chapter Five

as a private, and after he deserted, he entered the presidio of San Marcos.[135] Thereafter, he gained the status of *ymbálido* in the Béxar company but this time as an artilleryman by order of Viceroy Carlos Francisco, the Marqués de Croix. He married for a second time, from which union he had two sons (one, a soldier) and two daughters, and including his wife the family numbered six.[136] From this brief synopsis we learn that a Frenchman, formerly a low-ranking soldier in New Orleans, deserted like Pedro Lambremon. Apparently, that infraction cost Miñón little since he successfully moved on to join the Béxar garrison as an artilleryman and even got the viceroy's approval. His children bore none of the usual taint of their father having defected since one of his sons eventually became a soldier as well.

At Presidio La Bahía, the census lists Francisco Bontan, a native of France, "old and blind." He was married, supported himself as a carpenter, had children and grandchildren. Since the number of the descendants was unknown based on an incomplete profile, the presidio's Captain Espadas simply calculated his family as five persons. Antonio de Mézières, the son of the intrepid Athanase de Mézières, was a native of Louisiana, married, had ascended to first alférez at Bahía but was apparently unemployed at the time of the census.[137] Lorenzo René was a native of Marseilles and a widower. Caught with tobacco contraband in the mid-1780s, for a time he became a target of scrutiny where it concerned money matters.[138] He worked as a shoemaker and was receiving a stipend of three *reales* per day granted to him by the king during a time when Lt. José Curbelo went out to round up bison.[139]

Unmatched by that documented at the two Texas presidios, much less personalized data emerges from Nacogdoches. Muñoz's comprehensive report reiterated quantitative data while highlighting one of the French individuals routinely appearing in this study and in the context of merchant interactions with borderlands populations: "In the vicinity of this town are congregated 29 foreigners, 14 of them married, with 31 children and ten slaves, and currently present in [the town] are Don Nicolas Lamath and Juan Bosque. Altogether, they total 86 individuals, including 17 bachelors."[140]

Across the Red River in Natchitoches, Commander Luis DeBlanc contacted Texas governor Muñoz about Louisiana governor de Mézières' unsurprising revelation: the entry of Anglo-Americans into the French region from the Mississippi River was contrary to what the king had ordered. Further, DeBlanc claimed that under no pretext would they be allowed into the district under his command without a proper passport, and that he would have the Indians plunder the Anglos who encroached on their nations. He stressed obedience to his commander De Mézières' orders but added a caveat. When the intruders learned of this order, they entered covertly into Nacogdoches without his being able to prevent their movements. Additionally, DeBlanc discovered that they found safe harbor with Indians long-settled in the vicinity of Natchitoches post and in the *"dependencia"* of Nacogdoches. There, the Anglo-Americans managed to slaughter cattle for their sustenance, steal horses to be sold at posts far away from Natchitoches, and apparently did whatever pleased them.[141]

In the final analysis, the Muñoz census of May 1792 listed 125 foreigners of all ages, categories, and both sexes in the province of Texas.[142] The viceroy gave the same order to the governor of Nuevo Santander, admonishing him to not mistreat newcomers but to have them arrested anyway to avoid their escaping. Foreigners employed in the presidial companies and those who were married or had a fixed residence were not to arouse suspicion simply by their good behavior. Therefore, discussion had to be limited, if not sidestepped completely. It is no surprise that the viceroy singled out the plucky Alexandro Dupont, an entrepreneur who had captured Revillagigedo's attention a few years earlier. This time, however, the viceroy sought information pertaining to Dupont's seeking permission to work mines, and his proposal for subduing the Lipan with help from the Nations of the North and sharpshooters (*"cazadores"*) from Louisiana.[143]

Over and above the French diaspora and Anglo-American ingress, an acute focus on Nuevo Santander's foreign population was not the only worry for Revillagigedo during this time frame. By early 1793, he contacted Gen. Ramón Castro to request reports from Governor Muñoz about four missionaries who transferred to Texas accompanied by an escort from one of the Laredo companies. The missionaries had apparently overheard claims made by the Lipanes of El Canoso's *ranchería* that caused the viceroy uneasiness. Now, Castro was to secure formal depositions from the servants of the padres as well as from a San Antonio citizen who accompanied the Indians rounding up *mesteñas*. In the meantime, while Revillagigedo determined the best approach to getting answers to his multiple inquiries, he encouraged Castro to make use of whatever information the depositions of the corporal and private from the Laredo company held so as to frustrate any offenses by the Lipan. As we shall see in the next chapter, the Laredo *volantes* proved to be an essential unit of defense since even Gálvez pointed out their potential usefulness in his *Instrucción* in the decade prior to existential threats from many quarters.[144] And where Revillagigedo attempted to absorb the numerical calculations of borderlands populations and thereafter sought to discern the specific ambitions of individuals within these demographics, the paymaster Amangual had now to concern himself with past accounting tabulations under suspicion from on high.

SIX

❧

Defending the Numbers, a New Century, and Forty Years of Service

I rony and inquiry colored military life in the borderlands if we are to believe narrative history as preserved in the archive. After having sought redress from an accusation of theft by a subaltern and then, in a striking turn of events, finding his expertise with problematic inventories sought after by commanders, Amangual could reasonably expect turmoil. He was now expected to respond to a series of questionable balances found in the Béxar presidio *habilitación* fund by the Superior Accounting Office of the Royal Tribunal of Accounts in Mexico City.[1] Three years after receipt of the inquiry (issued in May 1792) into his expenditures favoring peace-seeking Native people, Francisco Amangual finished examining the objections by the auditor of the Royal Tribunal. He could now provide an explanation for the charges leveled against him.

Whereas his predecessor Bernardo Fernández provided a timeline for mismanagement of the purchases and expenditures made on behalf of indigenous visitors to the presidio, Amangual had a slightly different approach to resolving his dilemma. His defense targeted the actual objects of use in question and certain individuals, including the ubiquitous Pedro Vial, linked to apparently unnecessary expenses. Amangual's vast experience with inventory lists surely framed that perspective and almost certainly sharpened the focus of his argument. Amangual's response to the charges and his conclusion, heretofore never published, is presented here in its entirety.[2]

> The Second Lieutenant of this presidial company of San Antonio de Béjar Don Fran[cis]co Amangual having been informed of the content

204

of the five pages that the *Excelentisimo* Señor Viceroy [Branciforte] sent to you [Governor Muñoz] with the order of November 19, 1792 of the objections and charges that the Señor Accountant of the Royal Tribunal of Accounts surrendered to then Governor Rafael Martínez Pacheco, by way of then Commandant General Brigadier of the Eastern Provinces Juan de Ugalde, of the expenditures laid out [*erogados*] for the maintenance of the Indians that presented themselves in this district from Dec 3, 1786 until the end of the year 1788.

Said papers are numbered from one to five. In this last page, I notice two points that call for targeting [*conspiran contrayendose*]; the first, of the objections made for the superfluous expenditure by Pedro Vial and his four companions in the exploration of the road from the presidio of Santa Fé to San Antonio de Béjar, as well as for the considerable time they stayed in [*mansionaron*] this Presidio, that for more than seven months they were making individual expenditures like the one for the quantities that they requested and that were supplied to them at Nachitos and the town of Nacogdoches; in the first by Mnsr. [Monsieur] Requier [Mézières?], and in the second by the militia Captain Antonio Gil y Barbo in addition to the expenditure of twenty-five pesos that they paid to the young man Juan José Medina who came to serve them from Nacogdoches to Béxar without expressing with what order furnished them these sums, nor enclosing a notice of the outlay of the 181 pesos that were received by both, Vial, and his companions, nor if this quantity, and the 25 pesos of the servant [Juan José Medina], was taken by some indication they brought along with them etc.

The second consists of the objection that is made for an expenditure for more than was spent in the renting of houses, lights and maintenance for José Mares, Alexandro Martínez, and Juan Domingo Maiz. And from October 8, 1787 until January 18, 1788 by his having been able to apologize for the objection that they each lived in a separate house and having reduced them to three living in one house, when it was found inconvenient for them to be lodged in the barracks with the soldiers.[3]

I am equally unaware of the reason that is made for not making amends for the excessive costs that the renters generated for pans, vessels, and the rest of the utensils that were used for making food and other services for the Indians, but I ought not to respond to charges that resulted from the malfeasance [*la mala versación*] that provoked them. With respect to that, I did not have the slightest involvement in them since I did not do anything as paymaster of the company than provide what was needed, by order of the Governor Rafael Martínez Pacheco since I integrated and signed the accounts and receipts that I owed elsewhere because of not having it in the payroll office in my charge, for supplying it in the same way as when I reimbursed these quantities, and the rest that I supplied as gifts for the Indians and other things to that end.

To manage this, I did with sincerity that which is typical of me and only to certify here in some and in others that the named accounts and receipts that showed the aforementioned quantities were the same supplied and then paid to me. And it seems clear that said involvement and knowledge for determining and laying out the expenses they offered to this office has been reserved and restricted precisely for that very reason by the Governors, under this concept. It appears that I will be unable to, nor can I, give a reason for the motives for the excessive malfeasance and disorder like that [found] in the useless data [which is] like the odd style of the preliminary investigation of accounts. Because, in reality, I was nothing other than a lender of that which was ordered to be supplied by the Governor [*en realidad, yo no era otra cosa que un emprestador de lo que se mandaba ministrar por el Señor Gobernador*].[4]

Of everything there is to know or find out, I could give plenty of reasons as to why I am convinced that since José Antonio Bustillos was guard of the warehouse, but bearing in mind that he is already deceased, and in the duties of the *distinguido* Andrés Benito Courbiére, who was the one who helped him to set up the accounts, how to handle and distribute, what corresponded to the department of the former; this second one [Courbiére] is able to know in terms of everything, and the reason for which they were observed and managed in that method since it is normal that he knows it, assuming that he was at his [Bustillos] side and carried out all his functions. And if the aforementioned [Courbiére] does not provide the information, Don Rafael Martínez Pacheco as Governor will offer a report on everything about the province. I did not have a hand in anything other than what I have related. This is all [the information] I must explain concerning the objections above: [thus] I appeal to the Royal Tribunal of Accounts for my part, to have [this testimony] as enough and satisfactory.[5]

Amangual concluded with essentially the same rebuttal as First Lt. Bernardo Fernández: Courbiére was the one to blame for the accounting mistakes. No other documentation surfaces concerning this protracted, unsubstantiated (by the accusers) mélange of business following Amangual's testimony. Ironically, Governor Muñoz reported to Nava that the matter had been satisfactorily resolved and he did so on April 15, the day before Amangual's own response.[6] Given the outcome of the slander suits that had plagued Amangual before, Muñoz may very well have anticipated Amangual's exculpation in this most recent suspicion of wrongdoing.

Defending the Numbers and Forty Years of Service 207

But Nava was not similarly convinced. According to him, the accounts of expenditures made in Coahuila with the allied Indians from 1786 to 1792 did not exist in the General Commandancy, which explanation formed the report not yet remitted to him from Mexico City. Thus, it was impossible to clarify, whether found or not, overcharges of almost 740 pesos in the 1790 account distributed by Brig. Juan de Ugalde among his company. Having found a rough draft of the report in the Chihuahua archive, Governor Muñoz was to send Nava a copy of it, informing him of what he, Muñoz, knew of the subject. Thereafter, on August 1 Muñoz conveyed the Nava directive to Amangual.[7]

The paymaster's reaction was swift. As in so many of his formal responses archived in the administrative record, Amangual deviated not from his penchant for granular repetition of shared knowledge. He followed orders to deposit 209 pesos into the *Mesteñas* Fund, with an additional 2,842 pesos to follow.[8] Subsequently, Amangual accounted for provisioning the Friendly Nations of the North, from May 1 to August 16, 1795, by relinquishment of funds (*libramientos*) ordered by Muñoz. In May, the "Tancague" received gunpowder and bullets for Captain Cabezón and forty-one of their people. They received an extra ten pounds of cigarettes as did the "Tahuacame" and Comanche nations. On two different occasions later in the month, more of the same went to all these communities, as did gunpowder and bullets in June. However, the "Guichita" received only bullets.[9]

During the period covered in this book, presidio accounting records told a story of relentless gift-giving as the transactional mechanism by which a truce might, literally, be purchased. Almost 740 pesos remaining from the original Mesteñas withdrawal complemented the amount Ugalde gave as expenditures for "enemy" Indians that helped in his campaign. This was true as well for what Juan Gutiérrez charged for gifts to allied Indian nations and with resolution of the report requested on June 18, 1795.[10] Documenting the outpouring of gifts amounted to multiple pages of expenditure reports for indigenous visitors to the Béxar presidio from January to April 1796. All this beneficence came from Second Lieutenant Amangual and regular provisioners Antonio Baca and Luis Menchaca, men who fitted out a staggering 800 individuals representing the Comanche, Tancague, Tahuacame, and Lipan nations.[11]

However, even by mid-1795 the governor and his presidio commanders may have wondered why all these expenditures were made after all. It seems that incipient threats loomed from other quarters, and a summary of frontier geopolitical conditions creating this backdrop is helpful here. Concerns from places and people closest to the most northern of Indian nations must have provoked enough consternation at the highest levels of the viceroyalty to warrant a wholly different kind of investigation. On July 24, Escandón received disturbing news from Viceroy Branciforte that American colonists (*"colonas"*) planned on sending emissaries to New Spain—and, presumably, its borderlands regions—to verify some unspecified uprising. Too, Americans themselves wondered whether the governor of Louisiana had put the region in a state of defense out of fear of a general conspiracy brewing specifically among blacks inhabiting the province.[12] Though unvoiced in the July 24 correspondence, authorities in the metropole were likely on edge about the serial Haitian slave rebellion, persistent agitation in Cuba, and the impending relinquishment of Hispaniola to the French.[13]

Similar rumblings prompted Escandón to urge Muñoz to maintain with the utmost vigilance the security of Texas by not permitting or introducing settlers, foreigners, or any person that aroused suspicion. If verified as true, they were to be apprehended with notices forwarded to the viceroy. So it was fitting that Escandón opened up correspondence with Coahuila and Texas in order to communicate his warnings and, in case it was necessary, to aid each other in this joint effort.[14] In one message pinpointing the delicate circumstances of preserving harmony between the leaders of the Nations of the North, Escandón suggested that Muñoz evaluate the northern frontier of Nuevo León and, if necessary, reinforce the Laredo company with flying squadrons, to make ready the militias, and to forewarn residents so they could deploy to all points of contention.[15] Through the prism of defense preparations and readily available manpower, it appears that the *volantes'* expeditious presence was at the forefront of Escandón's mind. Given his seminal mobilization of a militia in Nuevo Santander, urgent military assistance across the borderlands could never be far from his in-country strategizing. That was especially true where, through acquiescence, resistance, and duplicity, contested terrain came largely under the control of indigenous inhabitants.[16]

For all that, though, American encroachment put the entire borderlands on high alert, including Gov. Simón de Herrera of Monterey who established communications with Branciforte, Nava, and Muñoz.[17] The situation had apparently been enough to unnerve Nava who, like Escandón, pressed Muñoz only one week later to be circumspect with people passing through Texas. If entering the United States via its borders with Louisiana, they just might be the "emissaries" intent on provoking an uprising among the region's inhabitants. Then another bizarre threat ensued with news suggesting that the governor of Louisiana, Brigadier General Baron de Carondelet, was acting in a hostile manner toward the "greedy" townspeople of the western states. And, if all that were not enough to alarm the *comandante general*, Nava then relayed news to Muñoz of internal movements in Texas among black communities living there, and in Louisiana. Nava's intention was for Muñoz to warn the lieutenant governor of Nacogdoches, Bernardo Fernández, to capture foreigners, in general, and that Fernández could even apprise allied Indian nations of those maneuvers. He informed their principal headmen ("*jefes*") of these events so they might be well versed in the direction to take in these matters. Pressing the issue, Nava counseled Muñoz that Fernández should cautiously inquire about events occurring in Louisiana and especially about social unrest that might sabotage frontier security.[18]

Sensitive to the perception of the Louisiana–Texas border as a liminal space commingling outsiders and citizens, an apprehensive Nava was likely unconvinced that Muñoz understood that dispatches regarding intrusions by "foreigners" were not difficult to know by way of Nachitoches. He assured the governor of the ease of acquiring that information there but, nevertheless, encouraged Muñoz to convey any news of importance.[19]

Transgressions by newcomers, both real and imagined, doubtless preoccupied officials in the metropoles. Unsurprisingly, French ability to arouse Spanish phobias in the borderlands was never extraordinary news to any presidio commander if events from a century earlier were any indication. As it is well known, in early 1685 the French established Fort St. Louis near the mouth of the Lavaca River. The founder, La Salle, abandoned the fort in 1687, and the last French soldiers were ejected in 1689.[20] Forty years later, Spanish anxiety about that trespass remained intact. Articles 40–44 of Rivera's frontier inspection report specifically concerned the French menace to frontier communities. As if to safeguard its significance in the historical record, Rivera called to mind the expedition diary of the Marqués de San Miguel de Aguayo. In it, Fray Juan Antonio Peña disclosed the founding of the presidio at La Bahía as one method for preventing foreign nations from occupying and colonizing the area. But Rivera was here more concerned with the region's indigenous populations and thereupon convinced himself that the surrounding Indians posed little threat since, according to him, they were not like those of known bravery in that they did not have the "martial spirit of others."[21]

Indigenous hazards aside, by mid-1795 several global events further unhinged the imperial government, disordered as usual about outsider encounters in its alleged territories. Spanish policy imperatives on American trade and settlement in the frontier focused on maintaining that glowering entity's minimal presence, but the French Revolution scrambled that perspective. The Pinckney negotiations of 1795 successfully reoriented Spain's diplomatic position on foreign navigation of the Mississippi River, which, by

210   Chapter Six

extension, enabled broad-spectrum settler societies to continue their efforts
at westward expansion. Prior to the Treaty of San Lorenzo, military officials
in the borderlands remained wary of foreign encroachment. The region
between Louisiana and Texas was a hotbed of suspicion for commanders
and their soldiers, besides being a springboard for clandestine activity
among the most daring.[22]

In fact, an earlier royal order gave explicit instructions for detaining the
French in Mexico with that operation then shifting to the empire's periphery. When Nava sent the January 6 order to Governor Muñoz, its content
left no doubt that vendors had special privileges requiring consideration.
Among the perks given to French merchants was their exemption from
incarceration. Further, their material wealth was spared seizure or disposal
since, whether from compassion or fiscal considerations, they were to be
"confined" to their residences or places of business until the rendering
of some new decision. That verdict included assurances for the safety of
their persons and their goods.[23] One week later, Nava instructed Muñoz to
apprise him of changing conditions in Louisiana due to looming war with
the French.[24] Suspicions aroused, on January 29 Nava circulated orders for
guarding Nacogdoches and the coast in anticipation of potential hostilities
from both the French and the Americans.[25] Prejudice intensified. French
citizens and even those born in Louisiana and Mobile continued to be
investigated and jailed. That reality unfurled to include soldiers like the
distinguido Courbiére and the *ymbálido* Miñón; ironically, the two men
were still entitled to their salaries.[26] As was the custom, Francisco Amangual's signature, along with that of others, documented his presence at
proceedings involving those suspected, however unwarranted, of wavering
loyalties.

Five months of mutual mistrust and economic shortfalls must have
seemed an eternity to French merchants and their patrons but, as these
kinds of scenarios often played out, certain discomforting things met
with quick resolution in the Comandancia. By May 1795, Andrés Benito
Courbiére was set free, along with other soldiers and citizens detained as
French nationals, by Nava who then ordered Muñoz to reinstate all these
men back into service.[27] Courbiére wasted no time requesting funds he
considered his but not yet remitted. In April 1796, Coubiere sought to
ameliorate his losses while in charge of goods destined as Indian gifts.[28]
As a merchant of many years' standing, Courbiére's presence dominated
economic transactions in the borderlands. However, a year would pass
before his career would resume. When it did, Nava ordered Muñoz to
send Courbiére to the Nacogdoches detachment, or on trips to Saltillo, or

Defending the Numbers and Forty Years of Service 211

wherever else he might be needed.[29] Within two years, Courbiere's loyalty to the empire would pass a test that others never had to endure.

In another part of the frontier, the French situation proceeded altogether differently. Though he had received orders to do so by both Nava and Governor Muñoz, the indefatigable Capt. Juan Cortés made a startling claim: he never had to set free any Louisianans at the Bahía presidio since he had never imprisoned any of them. As he described it, their conduct, in general, had not warranted such serious action.[30] By November, all French prisoners were ordered released by Nava since no charges turned up and nothing had been established to incriminate the French.[31] Nava received a royal order of September 8, 1795, indicating that reconciliation with France came in a treaty definitively concluded between Carlos IV and the French. Muñoz notified all inhabitants of the province of a "solid and dignified peace" that would reopen communication and perhaps, more importantly, lead to reciprocal treatment from both countries.[32]

The flurry of communication between commanders and subordinates scattered across the Comandancia General targeting French populations chronicles the ways in which frontier realities were shaped by events in distant places. The speed by which the French roundup and release played out was remarkable for its temerity but, in the context of broadcasting events overseas, the process itself broke no new ground. However, the documentation of global interplay during wartime, in the aftermath of ceasefire, and rebuilding communal trust constitutes some of the most historically significant records involving competing politico-cultural identities. Distilled within the recesses of frontier archives, the everyday paperwork of presidial comings and goings surface from a morass of testimonials about the eighteenth-century borderlands. International occurrences aside, the daily grind of provisioning military forces and gift-giving to Native polities continued unabated by garrison staff.

Though he had proven himself capable in other arenas of military service and even after his tenure as Béxar's trustee supposedly ended in 1793, Amangual was still producing bookkeeping reports throughout 1795. Less interested in collegiality than in fiscal accountability, his reports on commodities transported to peace-seeking indigenous people and his staunch questioning of the competence of other paymasters persisted as before.[33] In the first week of 1796, Amangual received an order of payment for his purchase of gunpowder and for bullets intended as gifts for eighteen Comanche. This entry from the inventory is provocative, not so much for its noting of purchases and allocation but for the description of Amangual as "abilitado." He is described that way in all the inventory's pages, which show

212 Chapter Six

that as a supplier of munitions, he again purchased bullets and gunpowder on January 21. The pattern of gift-giving by purchase against Amangual's account continued in February when he bought ten pesos of cigarettes for the Comanche, Tahuacan, and Lipan.[34] On January 4, Muñoz certified a two-page document concerning the inventory at the Tobacco Office ("estanco") at Béxar and acknowledged the five *libranzas* given by Amangual, the sum of which amounted to 2,043 pesos received and delivered.[35]

Two other names, those of the aforesaid Antonio Baca and Luís Menchaca, appear recurrently in the inventory as presidial benefactors for the indigenous communities visiting the Béxar garrison. Their presence is no surprise in the archival record, and neither is that of the master tailor and slander suit deponent José de Arreola. He reemerges in an entry of March 13 as having been paid four pesos, two *reales* for his work on three *chupas* (waistcoats), one pair of *calzones* (breeches), and one shirt of *manta* made for Comanche captains Sojas and Manco, and the latter's son. Arreola needed money owed since he submitted a bill for his work completing clothing and accessories on April 30, 1796.[36]

The frequency of Amangual's purchases on behalf of Native allies and his interactions with a cadre of provisioners becomes clear since the Béxar inventory was subdivided by days of the month but not formatted here in the customary manner. The document appears to be a compendium of purchases over five months that Amangual probably excised from a ledger or similar register. It likely had categories for recording dates of transactions consistent with the formatting of a military service record. Aside from his dealings with merchants and other presidio personnel, it is intriguing to see Amangual described as the paymaster. Moreover, only later will it become evident that somehow, whether through election by his fellow company members or by superior designation from the governor, he reassumed his fiduciary role but, it seems, now with interim status.

Election for this important position was not without controversy. In one case, Governor Muñoz's response to Béxar presidio Capt. Gutiérrez de la Cueva lay bare a certain irritation precipitated by delays in the election of the company's paymaster.[37] Having very likely slipped Muñoz's mind, only two months prior Bernardo Fernández acknowledged to Muñoz that Manuel Menchaca had entered the Béxar company as its second alférez and was also his choice as its paymaster.[38] But, even after the election, documentation shows Amangual's purchases continued: he bought two *almudes* of biscuits for unspecified Indians and then supplied gunpowder and bullets to eleven Comanche.[39] Perhaps Muñoz strong-armed his preference for the tried-and-true fiduciary.

Defending the Numbers and Forty Years of Service 213

Whether elected or assigned, paymasters and presents factored into achieving the universal good, however fleeting or imaginary, of the provinces. The necessity for maintaining accord with indigenous nations proved to be a policy imperative requiring constant reiteration, dispatched from commanders to seasoned presidial leaders, and documented by soldiers like Amangual, Cortés, and Fernández. Its regional significance to borderlands communities doubtless overshadowed concerns about French and American incursions into New Spain's Septentrión and despite news of détente with France announced in Nacogdoches on February 7, 1796.[40] Rectifying localized conflict took precedence. Cmdr. Gen. Pedro de Nava never hesitated to reprimand (or, at least, remind) his subordinates about the necessity for unquestioned adherence to long established strategies for quelling indigenous troublemaking. As he found himself admonishing Governor Muñoz: "One of the maxims that should be observed on our part with more care, [and] with respect to the Indian nations, is to let them make reciprocal warfare since achieving this means the diminution of their forces; by invigorating the hatred between each other; and by avoiding a union and alliance between them, this will bring about that which is more consistent in our friendship, where they find assistance."[41]

However, Nava's advice was quickly followed by derision. Allegedly, when the Tahuacanes made restitution to the Lipanes for stolen horses, that action "conformed [very] little" to Nava's commands. His directive served to remind them of and obligate them to the shortage *they* incurred when they apparently stole merchandise transported by the merchant Juan José Bueno. [42]

Peace by purchase proved to be not only a tenuous strategy but something of an enigma in navigating socioeconomic interactions. Ironically, its deployment was often hindered by punitive measures carried out with alarming regularity to essentially achieve the same effect as gift-giving. Success, even the mere semblance of it and measured in terms of a protracted truce, also evolved from combat victories and then occasional stretches of communal goodwill. And when forces on the battlefield triumphed, that too found wide broadcast in the frontier.

In one rare document describing a skirmish in detail, Nava reported a win by soldiers over "la Yndiada" near San Elizario on May 5, 1796. A detachment under the command of Alférez Nicolás Madrid from Presidio San Buenavista set out for San Elizario to locate the enemy. Having passed the night of May 4 in and around the Sierra Cornuda, by early morning Madrid dispatched a small party to reconnoiter and detect a trail. Shortly after losing tracks, the soldiers in the camp felt live gunfire that compelled the

214   Chapter Six

commander and his regiment to reconvene with the detachment. The latter group fought the enemies and even recaptured nineteen pack animals.[43]

Positioning themselves aloft in a cave, the Indians entrenched at a place called Hollow Hill. There, the advantage of terrain and their greater number emboldened them enough to destroy the detachment. Madrid, trusting his expertise and that of his troops, took to the ground and divided the men. The presidials maneuvered with such bravery and perseverance (*con tal vizarría y constancia*) that, despite resistance by the Indians and a barrage of arrows and bullets from the cave, the adversaries retreated. With nightfall they crept out by way of an almost inaccessible precipice but within earshot of cries from the wounded. Proof of their major setback was nine dead *gandules* (young male warriors) and pools of blood indicative of the large number of those carried off.[44]

Convinced that news of the Hollow Hill victory should be shared with the troops, Nava endorsed the skirmish as an example for the army writ large to use skill and bravery to similarly attain battlefield success. Copies of his report circulated to the commanders of the presidios of La Bahía and Nacogdoches. Manuel Menchaca read the news in front of the Béxar company on June 26, 1796.[45] In lockstep with commanders, Capt. Juan Cortés extoled the distinguished action of Alférez Madrid and his *presidiales*, doing so to inspire his own troops at La Bahía.[46]

Good Soldiers, Bad Soldiers, and Getting Even

The Hollow Hill encounter and the 1792 Bustamante victory in South Texas are but two instances of presidials caught up in battle, negotiating strategies in the moment among troop units while, at the same time, safeguarding citizens. Apart from these very real clashes played out on the ground, some embattled soldiers who braved assaults not only on their lives but also on their reputations, continued to fight for personal victories in the workplace. Whether high profile or obscured by time, the range of obligations faced by serving as an officer in New Spain's frontier is surely one of the most fascinating and recurrent features in tracing military careers by dint of the documentation.

Francisco Amangual's stretch of professional misfortunes was, for the time being, quelled. Though a cloud of suspicion may have stalked him as he too persevered in his role as paymaster, it was the myriad concerns both away from and within his office space that buoyed his career in the final years of the century. Setting aside the professional hurdles he had overcome, the exonerated paymaster forged ahead with the mundane tasks of his profession. He handled the customary paperwork associated with stockpiles, duty taxes, and stipulations for grants of clemency. For example, on July 1, 1796, Amangual generated an inventory report of the Béxar presidio's Tobacco Office, confirming his inspection of the totality of goods on that day. It included the warehouse's supply of cigarettes, cigars, gunpowder, card decks, and sealed paper.[47]

But by the end of the same month, Nava sent to Muñoz a copy of a document of a completely different stripe that was to be made public throughout San Antonio. It was a general pardon for prisoners whose crimes fit the parameters for forgiveness described in two royal decrees from December of the previous year. In September 1796, Amangual carried out the king's order by posting copies of the document in the capitol's plazas and streets.[48] Perhaps one of the misdeeds qualifying for the king's pardon included vandalism. If so, its documented occurrence in presidio archives may have touched a nerve with Amangual based upon allegations of theft leveled against him in his slander suit from four years prior.

Throughout the Commandancy, soldiers misbehaved to varying degrees by dishonorably acting out because of missteps, misappropriations, and inaccurate fiscal calculations in multiple contexts. They did so, too, from just being plain misinformed. Here in the closing years of the eighteenth century, some presidials faced severe ramifications mostly stemming from their rejection of the garrison's imminently constrained way of life. Consider the thorny circumstances shared by Fernández, Muñoz, Amangual, Cortés, and Antonio Gil Ibarvo and the avenues to resolution that each man took to minimize career-sabotaging fallout.

We have seen how Amangual's colleague Lt. Bernardo Fernández's reputation had come under fire because of violations perpetrated by his predecessor. Caught in the usual bureaucratic crosshairs, Fernández followed protocol to access the necessary documents for preparing a defense against accusations of financial mismanagement. Fernández forcefully argued for his own exoneration by making his case to the auditor in San Luis Potosí. Without further information, it remains uncertain as to the outcome of the proceedings instituted against him in 1792. However, by the middle of 1796, it was evident that his stature as a soldier of distinction remained untouched; in fact, he rose to the position of captain of the Third Flying Squadron of Chihuahua. Pedro de Nava specifically cited Fernández's "good merit" and seniority in service and ordered Muñoz to find a qualified individual to replace Fernández in Nacogdoches, thus freeing up the lieutenant to move with his family to Chihuahua.[49]

However, a new development in Nacogdoches would complicate his taking immediate command of the *volantes* in Chihuahua. Though never accused of swiping others' property, Fernández had dealt with vandalism among his soldiers and the civilians in his jurisdiction. In the previous chapter's investigation of suspected contrabandists Juan Cortés and Toribio Durán, which involved inventories completed by Amangual in 1792, the name "Antonio Gil Ibarvo" also fell under the glare of suspicion. At the same time the United States declared its independence from Great Britain, Gil Ibarvo served as the captain of the militia and *justicia mayor* of Nuestra Señora del Pilar de Bucareli. Over the next few years, he garnered praise from Croix for the prosperity and development of the town.[50] Adhering to official protocol like a good soldier, Gil Ibarvo had confiscated pirated cloth and tobacco in San Antonio and Nacogdoches coincident with Amangual's discovery of abandoned tobacco on the banks of Arroyo El Cleto in 1780. Throughout the next two decades, Ibarvo, like Amangual and so many other operatives in the Commandancy, carried out an array of responsibilities requiring substantial documentation. Decision-making by these officials impacted soldiers, friendly and hostile Indian groups, and foreign traders including the ubiquitous Pedro Vial and even Nicolas de La Mathe, the chief nemesis of Ibarvo. In his role as lieutenant governor and apart from questionable confrontations with civilians and criminals, Ibarvo continued to accrue positive recognition for his achievements spanning central Texas to the Louisiana border.[51]

But by the mid-1790s, greed, gullibility, or gall and too many years in the difficult frontier must have gotten the better of Ibarvo. In September 1796, Pedro de Nava rendered several decisions in a serious case concerning the veteran soldier. What came to light was Gil Ibarvo's attempt to conceal contraband and, therefore, Nava had ultimately to conform to a *dictamen* issued by the auditor of war: Ibarvo's military service was over. And it fell to Governor Muñoz to make the unlucky man understand the decision. That meant the governor was to deliver all the goods that had been seized from Ibarvo so that the items could be placed where suitable.[52] That same day in a separate letter, Nava ordered that upon its receipt Muñoz was to halt Ibarvo's salary since there was no need to continue burdening the Royal Treasury. In effect, the commander general unilaterally retired the soldier.[53] So great was the disgust that Nava had for Ibarvo that, only two months after his ignominious departure, he ordered Muñoz to prohibit the disgraced soldier from establishing residence in Nacogdoches.[54] For some military personnel, situational strategizing by frontier commanders clearly had severe consequences. Ibarvo's scrapes had a ripple effect. For others, it meant the usual confusing circumstances with the potential to impact career mobility.

Days after Ibarvo's forced retirement, Nava ordered Bernardo Fernández, who had only gotten as far as Saltillo, to have his wife remain there until the

Defending the Numbers and Forty Years of Service   217

right circumstances developed for him to "comfortably" take her along to Chihuahua.[55] Subsequently, Governor Muñoz assigned the Nacogdoches post to Cadet José María de Guadiana instead of Amangual, who may very well have been the initial candidate for Ibarvo's replacement but who had assumed Muñoz's duties because of the governor's infirmity. Cadet Guadiana surely convinced Muñoz that he was well informed enough about Nacogdoches and, therefore, well qualified to assume the post. With his directive, Muñoz further ordered instructions about Fernández's destination—presumably, his May 20 appointment as captain of the Third Flying Squadron in Chihuahua—to be handed over to Amangual so that the latter could take over that assignment. Fernández could then return to Béxar.[56] On October 24, Fernández not only acknowledged his receipt of Muñoz's directive but also that he had already given the command of Nacogdoches to Guadiana the week before with departure the next day to the capital.[57]

A piecemeal approach to Fernández's transfer to Chihuahua and subsequent travel to San Antonio predictably figured into cut-and-dried shuffling of soldiers from post to post. As in other interludes of filling empty slots, doing so functioned as part of the larger project of safeguarding the empire's frontiers with what bodies were available. More practically, it was a method of recycling dependable men to places where they were most needed as in the case of Courbiere. There is no question that Ibarvo's indiscretions circumscribed the transfers of Fernández, Guadiana, Amangual, and other personnel spanning volatile zones from Nacogdoches to Chihuahua.

From an operational perspective, so went the (re)positioning of key players in the borderlands resulting from misconduct on the part of one senior officer, Ibarvo, who made the unfortunate decision to engage in and then attempt to conceal criminal activity. The irony of these staffing alterations was that, during the week prior to Nava's order that Ibarvo not be allowed to establish residency in Nacogdoches, it would be Guadiana who would inform Muñoz that Ibarvo was to have his property returned after all.[58]

Leniency among commanders toward delinquent soldiers blew hot and cold based on complex circumstances that, above all else, prioritized manpower in all forms over any security void. It was in no way unusual to see the king's benevolence to his subjects in the Comandancia General emerge by way of general pardons. But what self-indulgent soldiers forthwith had at their disposal was more specifically oriented. A few years after the broadly inclusive 1796 pardon, a copy of yet another royal *cédula* appeared that now favored *contrabandistas* and even those who had committed homicide while engaged in this type of criminal activity. The document's content left little doubt about the king's inchoate tolerance of inappropriate, even murderous, behavior from his frontier soldiers. But that compassion had

218   Chapter Six

its limits. Those men who pursued the crime of procurement (*lenocinio*) were to be dishonorably discharged with the revelation widely broadcast among the commanders of the Texas companies.[59] As disproportionate the consequences for turpitude surely appeared even to killers, more dramatic changes lay on the horizon for irksome soldiers. The fickle nature of discharges and forced retirements in the military corralled everyone including those seemingly undeserving of proscription, some highly esteemed and of long tenure in the presidio, and others only recently arrived.

In the previous month, General Nava had directed that Andrés Benito Courbiére be assigned to service corresponding to his rank and previous experience. But after the Ibarvo debacle, Governor Muñoz must have felt similarly disinclined to further engage the services of the *soldado distinguido*. Having only recently been set free from what was essentially house arrest for having had the audacity of being French, Courbiére remained vulnerable. By the following month, Muñoz homed in on the long-time merchant and soldier, requested the necessary license giving him the authority to be rid of Courbiére, and Nava sent it.[60] What Ibarvo did was shameful. What Courbiére got was lopsided by comparison. What both veterans of frontier service shared in the end was the same: dismissal.

But for others in service to the empire, forced retirement was likely too humiliating a circumstance to bear. Having presided over the sacking of Ibarvo and Courbiére and the shuffling of officer assignments that relocated Amangual, Fernández, and Guadiana across the borderlands, whatever illness that played havoc with Muñoz's capabilities as a leader finally led him to quit. He informed Nava that he had taken certain measures to hand over authority of the Béxar presidio to Juan Bautista de Elguézabal. For all that, signs of an imminent transition became evident in September: Muñoz had already forwarded the Bexar company's monthly reports to the man who would succeed him, perhaps temporarily, but, potentially as a permanent replacement.[61]

Fortunately, Nava's willingness to mollify potential disruptions to presidio function and efficiency permitted him to accept Muñoz's transferring authority to another commander.[62] However, clarity came veiled not in confidence, but with concern. Having been advised by Amangual that Muñoz had suffered an unspecified accident, Nava wrote the governor to ascertain if his disability impeded the prompt performance of his duties. If true, Nava was prepared to install some other responsible person in Muñoz's position while the governor recuperated.[63] Without question, Amangual's disclosure peeved Muñoz. Answering Nava, the governor refuted Amangual's suggestion that, somehow, he had lost the ability to do his job. In a letter dated June 20, 1796, the usually circumspect Amangual had taken the unusual (or

Defending the Numbers and Forty Years of Service 219

premeditated) step of disclosing Muñoz's fragile condition to Nava. Going one step further, Muñoz stated, "It does not seem necessary to me that this officer [Amangual] should pass such information to my superiors," claiming that he had been carrying out his obligations in all matters. He even offered to prove it.[64] Fleshing out the contours of his character, it can be reasonably concluded that Amangual was capable of being petty and small-minded when perturbed by the target of his disdain.

In response Muñoz may have sought retribution by not only denying Amangual the Nacogdoches captaincy but also by compelling Amangual to pinch-hit for him by covering the Béxar presidio's responsibilities until a suitable replacement could be found. His ire heightened, Muñoz may have let Amangual know that he, still the superior officer, could choose whether to endorse the seasoned paymaster for the job. Across the 1790s, Amangual's relationship with this commanding officer had been complicated and often contentious. Now given his stony indignation over the mild punishment meted out to his slanderer Mariano Rodríguez, an embittered Amangual at this point may have been little concerned about potential hazards associated with publishing his observances of Muñoz's mental vulnerabilities and physical ailments.

Whereas Amangual had over the years likely inured himself to retribution of any kind and from anyone, susceptibility to formal rebuke had far-reaching consequences for others less senior in the borderlands. Commands from on high targeted already apprehensive soldiers, and even family members took on some of the associated grief of misbehavior by troops under scrutiny. When in November 1796 the captain of La Bahía Juan Cortés received a royal ordinance establishing penalties for officer mismanagement of company funds, a wave of regret must have fallen over him. The directive may have further shaken the only recently accused Cortés who had apparently not yet been successful at extricating himself from allegations of carrying contraband from Natchitos to Nacogdoches.[65] He would have almost one year to absorb the content of His Majesty's ordinance and perhaps return to a temporary state of emotional equilibrium while he grappled with the ramifications of his misguided, ill-conceived, and noticeably short border crossing from Louisiana to Texas.

Fully aware that some form of condemnation was afoot, Cortés must have then felt a measure of relief knowing that his commander recognized the necessity of the embattled captain's retention of his weapons and horses in order to continue in the armed forces. But the tentacles of punishment reached far beyond the intimate spaces of the presidio's walls, and now, even his wife's jewelry and other goods were to be sold off. His corruption advertised widely, those interested were alerted to the date of the auction.[66]

Adding to the irony, the newly installed captain of the Nacogdoches presidio Bernardo Fernández, himself once accused of misappropriating presidial funds, was to bring about the sale. Muñoz had orders to facilitate any aid Fernández might require.[67] And, finally, ensuring that Cortés received the maximum penalty for his misdeeds and to reimburse what he owed, the house he shared with his wife Catalina de Urrutia was to be auctioned off. Since it was his authority to have the final word in the proceedings, Nava instructed Muñoz to keep Cortés at Béxar pending further orders.[68] If that were not enough of an embarrassment, it would not be long before things were going to go terribly bad for him.

Four months after being subjected to near-complete liquidation of his family's property, Cortés, the itinerant officer unafraid to speak his mind and most recently convicted of transporting contraband, joined the list of forced retirees like Courbiére, Ibarvo, and soon, Muñoz himself. Still, he would exit military service with an annual salary of one thousand pesos.[69] We must assume that Fernández successfully and, perhaps, with a bit of bluster carried out the Cortés auction. That personal satisfaction was short lived since news arrived that he was to steer his own family in yet another direction. Since Fernández's flying squadron assignment in Chihuahua was now in the hands of someone besides Francisco Amangual, he was forthwith a candidate for another new position: captain of Presidio La Bahía.[70] With Cortés out, that important vacancy had to be filled with someone of long experience and slightly less encumbrances as a defendant.

Following the ignominious departures of a few of the Comandancia's key powerbrokers, it must have seemed like more of the same old routine for some in the king's army that, now, an array of ostensibly stricter codes of conduct hardened the parameters for correcting malevolent behavior. Those measures also carried a range of penalties—including forced sales of personal property, even that belonging to a spouse—across several spheres of engagement. Even so, issues of financial negligence, like those that had undermined if not doomed the careers of officers and impacted the lives of their family members, continued to plague the armed forces well into 1797. As money matters got the better of men working throughout the military, several new names came forward to compete with the tribulations of Cortés, Courbiére, Muñoz, and Ibarvo.

In one instance where bookkeeping discrepancies spanned months and even years, Elguézabal had collected and put into the coffers of the Bahía company funds that Alférez Antonio Cadena had improperly paid out to several individuals using allocations (*situados*) from the previous year. Cadena returned from Saltillo to Presidio La Bahía with the total amount in cash from an order of payment (*libranza*) submitted by Domingo de Outon

Defending the Numbers and Forty Years of Service

to Elguézabal. These funds constituted an amount for debts originating in 1795 from the easily spooked Bahía paymaster Manuel Espadas but then disbursed haphazardly the following year by his shoddily trained successor Cadena.[71]

Fiscal mismanagement proved costly for Espadas, the originator of the snarl, but in the eyes of his commanders the solution was practical. He would pay for his misdeeds with his freedom. The disgraced Espadas, having lost his post due to bankrupting presidial funds, had already been incarcerated at Béxar where he was to remain until he repaid the shortfall.[72] General Nava informed Governor Muñoz that Espadas' promissory notes would be paid with funds from the sale of Espadas' assets.[73] At least in this case, the one who helped make the mess was forced to clean it up.

Doubtless feeling more like the frazzled parent of reckless adolescents, Nava perhaps savored some relief that the ever-dependable Elguézabal had expressed a desire to stay on at La Bahía. Given the mysterious decline in Muñoz's health along with the Espadas–Cadena blunders, he urged Inspector General Elguézabal to put all the points of his commission into regular order, presumably in anticipation of reassignment. But to execute it so, Nava agreed to allow Elguézabal to stay put if he so chose.[74] Even when those who should have known better exercised poor judgment in their job performances, things in the chain of command often had to move quickly to conclusion. By January 1798 Nava gave Elguézabal the final instructions for the payment of Espadas' debts and, further, ordered Elguézabal to turn over the command of La Bahía to Lt. Joseph Francisco Zozaya.[75]

If nothing else, strategically repositioning presidio staff because of work-related distractions, disturbances, or outright incompetence likely made commanders the equal of Nava feel a certain gratitude for men pledged to simply doing their job, like Elguézabal. The same obligation to compliance fueled Amangual. And though he had made his share of administrative gaffes and faced accusations of mishandling company funds, his documentation of fiscal affairs carried on as before. Though it seemed he was headed to the captainship of a *compañía volante*, from January to August 1798 Amangual submitted the customary report of costs associated with aiding the Nations of the North.[76] He generated yet another report covering the next four-month period of dispensation to visiting "Yndios de las Naciones del Norte," including funerary expenses for one of their number.[77]

What is pertinent here is that taking care of visiting indigenous communities and seeing to the needs of susceptible soldiers were but two of the multitude of responsibilities for presidial commanders, a dual effort that depended on a number of circumstances that often overlapped to the detriment of one or the other. As we have seen, an entire body of official

S.n Antonio de Bexar 1.° de Maio de 1798.

Relacion de las subministraciones hechas por su Abilitacion para obsequio de los Yndios de las Naciones del Norte desde 1.° de Maio hasta fin de Agosto de 1798. A saber   Pesos R.s G.s

Maio en 8. para Zigarros .... 008.0.0.0.
Junio en 23. para idem .... 010.0.0.0.
En D. 29/6.° de Paño Queretano à 17 r.d. 2 3/4 v.° de
Sarga à 11 r.d. 8 g.r.° 2/3 v.a de Pontivi à 7 r.d. 2 g.r
3 r.d. de Hilo, 1.a tt.a de Sera à 17 r.d. 4 g.r, 2 d.za
de Coeta à 4 r.d, 6 r.d. para Velas de Sebo 4 r.d.
à los Enunios y 2 r.d. de Papel y p.a VVacia, todo
para mortaxa y entierro de una Yndia 016.4.0.3
Agosto en 31. para Zigarros ---------------------- 020.0.0.0.
Ydem pagados à D. Vicente Michels por seis
Dozenas de Cuchillos à 3 p.s y quatro Libras de
Vermellon à 4 p.s 4 r.d. para el repuesto des-
tinado al obsequio de los Yndios ------------- 036.0.0.0.
Ydem de lo subministrado à los Yndios en el Pueblo de Nacodoches segun manifiesta la Cuenta
de aquel Comandante comprehensiva desde 1.°
de Octubre h.ta 31. de Enero ultimos ------ 041.3.6.0.
Ydem ciento setenta y ocho pesos cinco y medio
reales importe de los efectos que para obsequio
de los Yndios, compró el Abilitar en el saltillo
el año de 1795. cuia cantidad havia sufrido esta
Compañia por equivoco y se le satisfizo en la ul-
tima revista de Ympeccion ------------------ 178.5.6.0.

                                    Total ---- 310.3.0.3

S.n Antonio de Bexar 31. de Agosto de 1798.

                        Fran.co Amangual

Francisco Amangual's [...] articles supplied to visiting Indians, BA August 31, 1798, e_bx_012388_001, The Dolph Briscoe Center for American History, The University of Texas at Austin.

Defending the Numbers and Forty Years of Service

discourse in the form of ordinances, regulations, and presidial reports of the type generated by viceroys, commanders, and trustees like Amangual dictated how that burden manifested in the official record. Before Christmas 1798, Amangual set out with escorts for Saltillo in the company of Alférez Manuel Menchaca, both of whom are listed in the monthly report as paymasters. Ten days later, Amangual compiled yet another list of gifts intended for the Nations of the North and covering September 1798 through the year's end.[78] Seated on a saddle or at his desk, Amangual arranged the tasks at hand and simply got on with it.

Over time, military superiors had unswervingly relied on Francisco Amangual for his expertise with itemization and tabulation of presidial accounts. While it is true that their confidence would be placed with and expected from almost any presidio paymaster in the execution of his duties (including Cadena), Amangual's role as trustee for his company is significant in view of the incompetence externalized by outright illegal transactions of disreputable *habilitados*, like Cadena, in the past. Recalling chapter 4 of this study, the Amangual inventory of the confiscated goods seized from Cortés, Treviño, and other presidio soldiers indexed the essential master data of official investigation for two key purposes. The first was fundamental, to document eye-witness accounts of alleged contraband; the second consisted of gathering subsequent ratifications of testimonies by troops involved in suspected criminal activity. In the Cortés incident, the merchandise in question traversed two points of engagement during the summer of 1792. Now, in the last two years of the century, Amangual's facility with numbers once again rectified the errors of others.

He probably spent all of the last day of 1798 fulfilling the same tasks that had dominated the latter part of his career. As one might expect, he was called on to catalogue the inventory of the Tobacco Department managed by the unfortunate Juan Timoteo Barrera, chosen four years earlier as interim paymaster of the Bahía presidio by the collector Juan Ignacio de Arispe. On December 31, Amangual found crates of cigarettes, cigars, loose tobacco, decks of cards, gunpowder, and sheets of sealed paper; this latter commodity's presence was likely celebrated throughout the presidio because of its annoying scarcity. Amangual also counted a substantial number of pesos and old currency of all types. He certified all this information with Gabriel Gutiérrez and Gabriel Gonzales as witnesses present on January 4, 1799.[79]

Three weeks later, perhaps sensing his son's impending doom, Barrera's father inquired about the possibility of examining Timoteo's accounts in order to find a deficit in some quantity of *reales* that would not have to be repaid.[80] Unquestionably feeling the sting of having placed an amateur in

Chapter Six

such an important post, Arispe contacted the retiring Governor Muñoz, asking that Barrera return the tobacco in his possession to the Béxar paymaster. Since he could not pay the sum he owed the treasury, Arispe requested documentation of a 50 percent discount that Amangual was due during the second half of 1799.[81] A reply eventually came when Arispe received a letter from Elguézabal reporting not only Luis Galán's appointment as administrator of the Tobacco Department of Béxar but also approving Barrera's detention until his accounts were settled.[82] Both men must have been hopeful, if not downright ecstatic, that Barrera left for Lampazos in a junket intended to collect debts so as to pay off the deficit in his accounts.[83]

Eventually, the raw truth of Barrera's debt emerged in an amount over 5,420 pesos.[84] That damning information clarified much of the financial predicament of the misguided Barrera–plays–Paymaster episode, but things got even worse. By the end of January 1800, stewards of Monterey's Santa Ygnacia Cathedral, Antonio Ramón de Canalizo and Juan Ysidro Campos, charged Barrera, "vecino y diezmero [citizen and tithe collector]," with embezzlement of their cathedral's funds. Canalizo and Campos alleged that over the course of eight years Barrera, even after being reprimanded by the pair, had never returned the funds.[85] Consequently, when Barrera made good on reimbursement of three thousand pesos, which he offered to verify upon arrival at the Béxar presidio, he requested an additional three months' leave in order to completely satisfy the balance of his overdraft.[86]

Examined through the lens of socioeconomic motility, the Barrera debacle foregrounds the cadence by which money circulated through the borderlands insofar as it explores transactional relationships between military personnel and colonial *vecino* populations. Recouping losses and pursuing debtors illustrate how jurisdictional boundaries structured these interactions, especially when disputes involving regional commerce ensued. For Amangual, the entire mess must have made him not only conscious of his own value to the proceedings by way of his accounting expertise but also grateful that at least this time it was not *his* job performance under scrutiny. Though Barrera's family attempted an alternative strategy to mollify their son's incompetence, which, ultimately, had such a disreputable conclusion, in other controversies involving soldiers and civilians, administrative bulwarks took the sting out of circumstances that might otherwise have been career ending.

Chronic (re)adjustments to army protocol and procedure as decreed by royal ordinances were symptomatic of the process of bringing organization to ground forces while maintaining societal alignment within the larger apparatus of dominion. The entire course of action trended toward

Defending the Numbers and Forty Years of Service 225

controlling the efficacy of those orchestrating the complex ambitions of such an unwieldy bureaucracy. The foregoing developments lay bare the fissures inherent in state building, some of which existed before obvious ruptures exposed paymaster misbehavior and presidial bankruptcy and therefore necessitated a reordering of military administration. This meant confronting the reality of illegal trade in commercial ventures, creating intendancies and a stand-alone military bureaucracy, and prosecuting criminal behavior.

Periodic episodes of soldier waywardness are not surprising in the context of a waning empire. Habitual transgressions on the part of borderlands operatives underscored a significant part of the historical trajectory of the Comandancia's army. Especially now, in the closing years of the eighteenth century, persistent attempts at reform and even forcing conformity within the ranks continued unabated. As we have seen throughout 1795–1799, mitigating the worst offences preserved an ambivalence between the commander and the commanded in a type of uneasy alliance among those presumably bound by the attributes of honor, respect for authority, and restraint. Lyle McAlister commented on the burgeoning capacity of the military to create a very particular class consciousness during this same period, saying, "During the closing decades of Spanish dominion, the army, thus created, acquired prestige and power as the defender of the nation in the face of almost constant threats of war and invasion. By the very nature of its functions and constitution it was also a class apart and so regarded itself. The possession of special privileges enhanced its sense of uniqueness and superiority, and at the same time rendered it virtually immune from civil authority."[87]

When he wrote these words, McAlister referred to the military presence in New Spain's urban spaces. In the Provincias Internas, documenting the voices of its key players grappling with and working through contention and collaboration provides an interpretive lens with which to examine the limits of state power. Its granular effect exposes two of those limitations: first, persistent stinginess on the part of the Crown in providing financial support and, second, reactionary impulses from administrators falling short of grasping actual conditions on the ground. Taken together, the viceroyalty's distance in proximity to and de facto uninterest in the hinterlands had corrosive effects on a region in flux. Somewhere between this existential disadvantage trekked the king's army, carrying out orders issued from a distant, otherwise preoccupied, superstructure.[88] If we accept the conclusions found in both the "official" record and extant historiography, that well-staffed entity located in a palace built on grounds once occupied

Chapter Six

by the *Hueyi Teocalli*, was ostensibly invested in upholding military might, but less so materially than in theory, in its northern periphery. More so than ever, foreign aggressors, too, snarled imperial efforts toward supremacy, compliance, and continuity.

Twilight of an Era and Life Goes On at the Presidio

Historian Navarro García argued that by the turn of the century the historical development of the General Commandancy relied on several factors, the least of which was the role played by the Commandancy itself. International wars, changes in ideologies across economic and political ecosystems, and the growing tensions of nascent insurgency began to have repercussions of major significance for the Interior Provinces. Furthermore, Navarro García suggested this next period of transformation in the nineteenth century commenced with the cession of Louisiana to France and its subsequent conveyance to the United States. An international frontier was now a fact in Texas, and the consequences were immediate, including division of the Commandancy itself.[89] Ongoing tensions between Spain and the emerging world power to its north and beyond the Septentrión fueled a politically charged and thus volatile environment for the kingdom during what can surely be described as its twilight era. Here, a brief survey of the period's historical actualities and some of its well-known players provides a backdrop for New Spain's most compelling concerns.

According to Navarro Garcia, from the moment the United States purchased Louisiana from France in December 1803, an era of disagreements stemming from boundary disputes between the United States and New Spain hardened.[90] In fact, instances of suspicion and mistrust became quite pronounced during the latter years of the 1790s, but the culprits now were not French. The intrigues of Irish immigrant and mustanger Philip Nolan put Spanish garrisons and militias across the borderlands on high alert—in places like Texas, Nuevo Santander, Nuevo León, and Coahuila—since that individual's forays into frontier territory was considered a pretext for Anglo surveillance of the region east of the Mississippi.[91] Among those in American administrative spheres and in-between local commanders in the Texas–Louisiana borderlands, Nolan was considered by some to be as much a confidant as an interloper, an outsider to be minimally trusted and thus unrelentingly eyeballed. Interactions with Nolan had always been complex and, it seems, a significant measure of latitude in tolerating his maneuverings was consistently advanced toward the adventurer. By centering Nolan into the thicket of presidio intercommunications about

Defending the Numbers and Forty Years of Service 227

Anglo-American encroachment, I look now at vacillating responses to that threat in the northernmost reaches of the Commandancy.

Philip Nolan's name figures into several correspondences between commanders and subordinates regarding his closely watched activities at frontier garrisons. Documentation covers his search for wild horses; a passport issued to him so that he might deliver furs intended for the commander general at La Bahía; and several other events leading to his eventual apprehension. By late 1798, the itinerant Nolan reappeared at Presidio La Bahía requesting horses from the local population. With Nava's help and instructions to Muñoz to aid him in securing stock for Louisiana, Nolan quickly achieved his goals by the following year.

But the arrangement soured instantaneously. On Nava's newest orders of that same day, Muñoz was to now block Nolan's introduction of goods into Texas.[92] The Irishman's hustle served as a catalyst for blockades across the borderlands. Only two years later Brig. Gen. Sebastián Nicolás Calvo de la Puerta y O'Farrill (identified in the Béxar Archives as the Marqués de "CasaCalvo") stationed in New Orleans, assured Governor Elguézabal that he ordered "stringent measures" to obstruct French and American interlopers from penetrating Texas frontiers.[93] Riverways proved particularly alluring to intruders. By mid-April 1800, Miguel Moral sent to Elguézabal a copy of a more recent letter by Casa-Calvo who reported his attempts to prevent yet another episode of foreign aggression by both the English and the French, in league with Arkansas, Cherokee (*Aniyvwiya, Anigaduwagi, Kituwah*), and Chickasaw (*Chikasha*) warriors. Aggressors from their number were apprehended and brought to Nacogdoches for punishment. Casa-Calvo suspected that they were the "American" party that had evaded detection by movement across the territory. That left him no other recourse but to reissue severe orders to contain "whites and Indians," which was itself difficult because curtailing gift-giving might trigger hostilities.[94]

When American posts materialized along the "Rio Colorado," Casa-Calvo feared that all preemptive steps taken by the government were nothing more than "illusory." One senses a certain desperation on the part of the assentive Casa-Calvo from his having to contend with all these variables, not the least of which was the persistent Nolan menace. However, he reassured Elguézabal that he had done his part, and he promised compliance with orders from both the governor and the king. Casa-Calvo was smart enough to realize both commissions required "harmony and good correspondence" between Louisiana and Texas.[95] He must have felt a sense of relief when on November 8, 1800, Elguézabal reported Nolan's trip to Mexico and ordered his detention.[96] That same year, Elguézabal directed Lt. Amangual at La

Bahía to send troops to reconnoiter the coast in search of Nolan, and he even alerted Gov. José Blanco of Nuevo Santander to "the intended violation of [Blanco's] jurisdiction by the bold adventurer."[97]

Indicative of his growing concerns about the fiscal consequences of outsider movements across the borderlands, Cmdr. Pedro de Nava provided Elguézabal with an account of expenditures for the maintenance and travel expenses of the Spanish and Anglo-American companions of Nolan.[98] As Navarro García argues, the westward ambitions and expansionist views of President Jefferson were well known prior to and after Nolan's execution in 1801, and the subsequent pursuit of Nolan's friend Robert Ashley became a chief preoccupation two years later.[99] The hard truth was that gumptious Americans were moving rapidly in their quest to explore the interior of the continent all the way to the Pacific. Nava's successor Brig. Nemesio Salcedo ordered the governor of New Mexico to organize a small expedition that would accomplish two objectives: the first, to ratify a peace treaty with the indigenous communities, especially the "Pananas" along the Missouri River; and second, to covertly reconnoiter the land up to the shores of that river. For the purposes of updating knowledge of the terrain for reconnaissance efforts, in February 1804 Salcedo received a map of New Mexico created by Fray José María de Jesús Puelles who was stationed in Nacogdoches.[100]

When Casa-Calvo heard news of Meriwether Lewis receiving instructions from President Jefferson to make observations along the Missouri River, he alerted General Salcedo, who then ordered an interception on May 3, 1804. Fulfilling the commands, Gov. Fernando Chacón quickly dispatched interpreters and "friendly" Comanche with the dual task of affirming peace between the allied Indians and observing the movements of Lewis who, by that time, was already at the confluence of the Mississippi and the Missouri rivers.[101] History, indeed, has a way of repeating. Only four years later, Francisco Amangual got the call to carry out essentially the same objective when he set out with three hundred men on his well-documented expedition to Santa Fé.

Repetition persisted at the garrisons too. As the months passed and as international intrigues played out, the Béxar presidio's workaday tasks endured. As ever, fiscal preoccupations maintained as significant a place in the order of all things military as did preparedness for large-scale defensive planning. Revisiting the start of a year that would see efforts, often flimsily organized, at delimiting the shared borderlands, Governor Elguézabal listed activities, stock of supplies, and total troop force in place at Béxar during the previous month. Convulsed by ongoing cases of contraband movement, desertion, and mismanagement of presidial funds by agents throughout 1794 and 1795, soldiers' interactions with civilians required just

Defending the Numbers and Forty Years of Service

as much scrutiny now to avoid compounding impropriety. Susceptibility to misdoings was robust since the presidio lacked a captain and had seven soldiers marked "invalid," meaning that in one way or another they were unavailable for much service. In this new century, Béxar armaments were in good condition, and the reserve supply consisted of shotguns, pistols, and blades for lances.[102] At least, that is how Elguézabal officially recorded it.

Like the military service record and expedition diaries, the monthly report constitutes a ledger of sorts within the larger body of presidial literature. Functioning as an abbreviated history, the Elguézabal report, like those issued by other chroniclers, represents a microcosm of presidial life intended for a more intimate audience. By contrast, earlier diaries of explorations recounted events ultimately bound for a capacious number of analysts across time and newly trodden spaces. Even so, the activity documented in the December 1799 report is compelling for its recounting of both the unremarkable and the noteworthy, and especially so with each new arrival of indigenous visitors to the fort.

As the days passed, Native people representing numerous tribes appeared at Béxar with various objectives. On December 3, Lipan Apache headed by the well-known Captain Chiquito[103] arrived with one of their people wounded, telling the *presidiales* that the Comanche had killed two of their own including four women and, apparently, their entire horse herd. By December 5, eight Comanche including three women departed; the day before, four Comanche including one woman had arrived. Throughout the month, other indigenous groups came, including Captain Hoyoso ("pitted," probably a reference to a pockmarked face) with three of his nation, and later, a larger group consisting of "Taguacanes" (Tawakonis), "Taguallases," and "Guchitas" (Wichitas). During the last two weeks of the month, other Comanche also appeared at the presidio.[104]

The extent of activity that took place at La Bahía and Béxar suggests the Texas presidios' perpetual status as a kind of international hub of sorts for multiple interactions with people of useful talent, or none, representing many polities. Typically, soldiers from other presidios made stops at the Béxar precinct while en route to other places. As indigenous arrivals and departures were routinely reported by Elguézabal, so too was the return of the presidio's corporal and six soldiers carrying the incoming mail. Life was indeed "un mundo de rutina." The next day two men from the Bahía presidio left with a mail bag, and the Béxar troop conducted drills with seventeen men.[105] Three soldiers coming from Nacogdoches then left to complete their journey to La Bahía. If we take Elguézabal at his word, on most days nothing remarkable occurred given the recurrent "*sin novedad*" appearing in the documentation, and drills were conducted almost every day of the month.

Chapter Six

On the winter solstice, then-lieutenant Amangual left with one corporal and six soldiers for the *villa* of Saltillo on a religious holiday. A week later, Elguézabal indicated that the contingent returned with the mailbag, but it seems Amangual did not.[106]

However, the March 1 report showed Amangual returning to Béxar on February 3 with his company's funds, accompanied by the same number of troops that left with him in December, but perhaps not his original travel partners.[107] Troops in chronic transit across the Comandancia make obsolete the notion of a frontier marked by idleness and stagnation. As in other years and at other garrisons, routine tasks like those described above permeated military life during this period. Documentation as recorded by Amangual similarly reveals nothing particularly dramatic or alarming occurred at the presidio in the final months of the eighteenth century.

Amangual: Forty Years (and Counting) of Service to the King

Up to this point in his career and after two instances of accusations by his presidial comrades, Francisco Amangual had, nevertheless, distinguished himself in his duties as Béxar paymaster and in his capacity as alférez. His cavalry skills must have been just as reliable, since in October 1801 he went to pursue Comanche raiders who had intercepted a herd of contraband horses headed to Louisiana. Virtuosos as equestrians, he was unable to overtake the thieves.[108] By 1802, he had reached the rank of first lieutenant and had completed forty years in the royal service. When his commanding officer Elguézabal described Amangual's performance in his service record, he noted the lieutenant's bravery, sufficient effort, and honorable conduct. Elguézabal also credited Amangual with "moderate ability," and being skillful in his duties.[109] It appears that the first years of the new century were some of the finest for advancing his career.

Another promotion came quickly and once ascended in 1803 to the rank of captain and now in command of the *compañía volante* of San Carlos de Parras, it was Amangual's turn to produce a military performance report for Elguézabal. In it, he described some of his soldiers in ways that affirmed their suitability, or not, for service and he revealed personal attributes specific to martial exercise and the handling of official communication:

> *Lieutenant Dionicio Valle has plenty of valor, little intelligence for paperwork, much love for service, and a good disposition in command, capable of fulfilling the role of whatever commission that he is entrusted with. Alférez Francisco Adam [Adan] has been known for enough courage, he has the best conduct, he is suitable for command, has plenty of talent, and*

Defending the Numbers and Forty Years of Service

[is] *intelligent with documents; and capable of discharging other work higher than he* [now] *enjoys. First Sergeant José Mendes has plenty of courage and the disposition for command; no intelligence with documents, and capable of performing any commission except for the management of funds. The Second Sergeant Felipe Arciniega also has plenty of courage, aptitude for command, shows promise [and] enough hope by his zeal and love for military service, knows perfectly all the evolutions of drills and the fulfillment of his obligation, but has nothing suitable to take care [of] funds. The one from the same class, Vicente Tarín, has a lot of bravery, suitable to carry out whatever commission except that of funds; he is more intelligent than* [Arciniega] *with documents/paperwork, he knows with perfection the fulfillment of his obligation, precise in service, and he carries out with grace the drill of infantry and cavalry. The Cadet José María de Arze: his bravery is unknown; his conduct, medium; little application to service and nothing suitable for commanding parties [of troops], nor to take care of funds, and considering his dealings with the troops he wants the things of his youth.*
  San Antonio Valero 15 de enero de 1803 Francisco Amangual [rubric].[110]

The report voiced the professional opinion of one commander about his subordinates, remarks that may have paralleled his personal feelings toward these and other men in the unit. One might wonder which sentiment, the professional or the personal, took precedence among leadership in determining which soldiers should stay and which would go when transfers were necessary. Relocation was inevitable while strategic repositioning remained vital, and the San Carlos flying squadron's troop strength fulfilled both contingencies. On February 15, 1803, *Comandante General* Nemesio Salcedo deduced that thirty-three of the one hundred San Carlos *volantes* would transfer to Nueva Vizcaya, a task undertaken by Amangual. After the company's march to Texas, fourteen of their number left to various destinations. But Salcedo reasoned that these same men had also to be counted as part of the entire force and as though they were still in Chihuahua.[111] Combat effectiveness continued to be a preoccupation of commanders in the trenches, and chronic shortages had to be accounted for (or numbers had to be embellished), since such disadvantages had always to be explained to imperial authorities.

Compensating for cutbacks in the San Carlos volantes, seventeen more men were siphoned off from among those stationed in Coahuila. In this number and for this very reason Joséph Olguín, Nicolas Soto, Francisco Planes, and Nicholas Tomé, all of whom left families in the villa of San Gerónimo, received word to rejoin their people. Since the stated number of troops comprised a third of the total force, Salcedo calculated within that percentage three corporals. That would likely explain why he kept in mind that soldiers Rafael Soto, Santiago López, and Joséph Nava also had families at San Gerónimo.[112]

Ultimately, Salcedo recommended that Alférez Adán, one of only two San Carlos soldiers to receive exemplary praise from Amangual, should take charge of the troops destined for Chihuahua. Salcedo cautioned Elguézabal to make certain that Adán transported the money needed for the troops under his command. With his expertise in recordkeeping, it was natural that Salcedo also assign Amangual the accounts of the troops so he could generate a report on the horses, mules, armament, and clothing of each man.[113] But it is even more likely that the veteran Amangual had as much to do with shepherding Adán's compliance with Elguézabal's orders as when Salcedo initially endorsed him.

In this same letter to Elguézabal, the general gave the governor further instructions that reveal his concern for the well-being of the company on their journey: "The group that he brought to make the journey directly from the presidio at Aguaverde to the [presidio of the] North was insufficient, [and thus] I advise you that from the first of these stops ask Colonel Antonio Cordero for the route and, furthermore, in your journey settle upon the course that he gives you."[114]

As attested to by several commanders, when detachments went out the result was that insufficiencies were felt elsewhere. Even as these types of inconveniences occurred and given the heightened potential for attack and loss of life, officers and commanders strategized among themselves the ways to mitigate danger to the presidio and its inhabitants. Military superiors with any sort of defensive acumen counseled their soldiers in tactical maneuvers. They did so with the goal of eliminating fear or panic and to prevent indecisiveness that might arise during combat.

Decision-making shaped the contours of daily life in the presidio to the extent that all soldiers carried out routine tasks of varying degrees of difficulty or, sometimes, relative ease. Seen from the vantage point of a single operative's experience, Amangual's monthly responsibilities cut across the spectrum of intra-presidio interactions with troops and civilians. By 1803, his supervisory activities involved tracking Native and non-Native fugitives, providing a convoy for a missionary, and generating paperwork in a desertion case. We learn that Captain Amangual reported the Comanche theft of nine animals and killing of two residents—including a "Carancahua" named Patricio—from Mission Refugio; the perpetrators breached the corral of the horse herd.[115] He sent Alférez Antonio Cadena with a cadre of twenty troops and an additional nine *vecinos* in pursuit of the raiders. Though Amangual enclosed the diary of the event for Elguézabal, the

Defending the Numbers and Forty Years of Service 233

attack's outcome is uncertain.[116] When General Salcedo learned of the events at Refugio, he responded by deploying a reinforcement of the mission's company with eight men—most likely a detachment of the *volantes*—aimed toward pursuit of the Comanche. Since he now commanded Presidio La Bahía and was overseeing its flying squadron, Amangual issued the order for the chase.[117]

On March 3, Amangual again freed up three soldiers from Bahía to escort Father José María Sáenz to San Antonio, knowing that his men would be absent for eight days.[118] With desertion long afflicting frontier outposts, he may have experienced mixed emotions at their departure but perhaps, also, an unshakable belief in their return. His faith likely proved prescient but, then, overshadowed by the usual disappointment one week later. It found expression in Amangual's summary of the proceedings in the desertion case of the soldier Pedro Castañeda. Anticipating further instructions from Elguézabal, the one-page report was necessarily brief and thus incomplete. That same day, Salcedo advanced a decision against second-time deserter Manuel Flores, also from the Béxar company. It must have been more disheartening for Amangual to receive news the following month of the desertion of yet another soldier from the Parras company.[119] So went the unlawful exodus of men fed up with life in the saddle or otherwise encumbered with issues that could only find resolution by escape from the forces.

Not unlike other years during his decades-long career, it is evident that Amangual's daily affairs throughout the first half of 1803 ranged from the extraordinary to the humdrum. He exchanged correspondence with Elguézabal on a wide variety of occurrences, some so seemingly inconsequential as to appear hardly worth the documentation. However, his records illuminate the importance of not only chronicling everyday tasks but also memorializing a multitude of transactions involving troublemakers, like defectors, throughout the borderlands. Moreover, these types of testimonials linked much of the interpresidio web of governance and even reveal the socially charged variables within official communications. Proof found in the archives of the dual nature of soldiering and supervising becomes clear in a series of analogous interactions while discharging routine business. For instance, Amangual informed Elguézabal that eight men from Béxar escorted mules bringing grain seed for the company at La Bahía.[120] In turn, Elguézabal informed Antonio Cordero that the "current" captain of that presidio, Amangual, apparently in an interim position, had examined the presidial accounts.[121]

So went the enduring chain of documenting the mundane, but by midmonth the characters become more compelling and the circumstances more concerning. We find that Amangual assembled judicial records regarding

234 Chapter Six

forty-eight cargo animals implicated as illegally transported to Louisiana, seized from the "mulato Denis," and worthy of a confiscation penalty ("la pena de comiso")[122] that landed Denis in the presidio's jail.[123] On that same day, Amangual asked Elguézabal for a description of an unidentified fugitive priest who had arrived in Texas in 1801.[124] Subsequently, on orders from the comandante general, Amangual transmitted a census report of thieves circulating among foreigners and outsiders.[125] Finally, in what might have struck an all too familiar chord within the old soldier, an issue of contraband trade had supposedly occurred at La Bahía, which news Amangual communicated to his commander. In response, Elguézabal ordered an investigation into the report with a directive addressed to the former cadet in charge of the Nacogdoches post and now its alférez, José María Guadiana.[126]

This flurry of documentation had at its core an often-repeated scenario: illicit activity carried out by those who should have known better or by those hopelessly lost to criminality. One can assume that by autumn 1803 routine tasks prevailed over the extraordinary since in October Amangual was on his way to Saltillo to collect supplies for the troops.[127] Elsewhere, and especially further east, the boundary between Texas and Louisiana became the locus for scaled-up scrutiny. Documentation proliferated with the arrival of Anglo-Americans, thereby prompting a torrent of correspondence in late 1803 centered on intensifying vigilance over all matters, military and civilian.

Correspondence, Relocations, and Departures

Arrivals and departures at the Béxar presidio attest to its function as a hub of international dimensions. Its purpose represented a kind of way station for soldiers in transit as well as a philanthropic entity from where diverse indigenous communities might receive replenishment of supplies including food. Farther east, a report generated by Capt. José Joaquín de Ugarte reveals the similarly mixed regional composition of the detachment of Nacogdoches with its soldiers representing two presidial companies: Béxar (sixteen), Bahía (fifteen), and one *coahuilense* from the ranks of Álamo de Parras volantes for a total of thirty-two men.[128] Besides the intermingling of military identities, there are entries in Ugarte's report that are particularly compelling but for reasons far more ominous. Since the Texas–Louisiana borderlands represented a liminal space of opportunity for economic interactions and commercial development, buyers and sellers with little hesitation made headway into its volatile environment. The presidio complex was the fulcrum by which outsiders from points north

Defending the Numbers and Forty Years of Service

235

and farther east could jockey to gain a foothold toward transforming their own pecuniary interests.

As found in inter-presidio dispatches, the American presence energized communications related to trans-border business conducted at the Nacogdoches presidio. Circulating within this confluence of interests, "Indian Agent" Dr. John Sibley was one such individual under the eye of Ugarte. As Chipman and Joseph described it, from "his base in Natchitoches, Sibley missed no opportunity to move Indians toward a favorable view of the United States." Tenacious without end and driven by his acquisitive impulses, Sibley launched derogatory salvos at Spanish traders in Nacogdoches, claiming their "high prices" could not be blamed on the United States. As time passed, Sibley's resourceful tentacles reached other frontiers. Then, 1804 saw the inception of the Lewis and Clark Expedition as well as the lesser-known Dunbar and Hunter exploration of the Arkansas headwaters, a journey that never quite reached Texas territory.[129] Having foreigners at the forefront of his worries, Captain Ugarte would later describe news of the 1803 transfer of New Orleans as emanating from reliable information. But he then told Governor Elguézabal that the "Anglo-Americans" would receive the province from the French on December 25, not on December 15 as the "Irishman" (and defector from the American Army) Michael Bruno had reported. Spanish officials had for several decades at the close of the eighteenth century warned of the dangerous presence posed by lately independent Anglo-Americans.[130] Ugarte suspected that Americans would take possession of all towns in Louisiana and, furthermore, it would not be long before they would do the same thing in Natchitoches. Therefore, he planned to go there to witness the transfer since he had serious doubts concerning the dividing line between Texas and Louisiana.[131] That the American imposition of speculators across the board raised issues related to borderlands security and compounded military personnel departures only made things worse. Ugarte himself had soldiers heading for the exits, and American peregrinations likely underscored his anxiety over an increasingly porous frontier.

Acquisition of Louisiana territory by the United States or not, for some in the army their stint in the Far North had been quite enough and they wanted out. When presidials hankered to leave the service, they made their wishes known to Captain Ugarte as did those undaunted soldiers (or those out of options) wishing to reenlist. Men like Ignacio Pereda, José de la Garza, and José Luis Maldonado belonged to the former category, and each asked for a discharge. Similarly, Manuel Ortiz felt finished except for one piece of business. He asked only to receive credit for a horse charged to him from the remount (*remuda*) of wild horses, but which he claimed not to have taken. But others were ready for more action, including Francisco Galván who reenlisted for four years but petitioned for two months' leave. Juan de la Cruz Montalla reenlisted for three years and similarly requested two months' leave and with pay from the retention fund. Only Agustín San Miguel asked to be placed on the *inválido* list since his lameness resulted from a fall during his service.[132] Like other commanders before him, Ugarte must have had strategies for coping with attrition among his forces as well as methods of retention for the skeptics in his company.

Fluctuations in the Comandancia's garrison population continued through manifold tactics by soldiers requesting discharge and by others resorting to their own brand of unofficial exit including desertion. Nevertheless, for some soldiers channeled into service by either a sense of duty to the empire, or through ancestral associations, or for more practical concerns like providing for family, change within the ranks by men either freshly arrived or on their way out could be far less profound. Given the swings of both the mundane and the magnetizing in fulfilling responsibilities, fresh assignments for some might not have seemed worth the effort.

Managing the Flying Squadron of San Carlos de Parras: Imminent Expedition

Diversification of any kind in the militarized Provincias Internas came through administrative restructuring of the royal service. In the spirit of most things mulled over in the capital, changes even now were reactive rather than anticipatory. The progressively foreboding American presence aside, zoning modifications included the 1804 division (for the second time) of the ten *provincias* into two general commandancies of equal representation but distinguished by regional denominations. One became the West, the other the East.[133] Parceling territory normally meant partitioning of troops, and documentation of the San Carlos de Parras flying company emerges more forcefully via monthly reports of the Béxar presidio from 1803 through February 1804. January 1803's military report highlighted individuals commanded by Amangual and personnel changes within the company.[134] Four months after Amangual's description of his soldiers' attributes, Cmdr. Gen. Nemesio Salcedo directed Cpl. Yldefonso Galavés of the Parras company to take charge of leading the troops and families from the villa of San Gerónimo to San Antonio de Béxar. Essentially performing as an armed guard, Galavés was to carry out the departure with congruent "good order and arrangement," and to prevent anyone in the group from remaining in any of the towns along the way. The only exception was if someone took ill on the journey. Galavés had to document this type of mishap with certification from a justice in the place where it occurred. Stressing the gravity of the situation, the governor of Texas must be made satisfied with an explanation of the circumstances that obligated Galavés to leave that person behind. In effect, Galavés held responsibility for mistakes incurred by individuals under his charge and any punishment was to apply irrevocably.[135]

Unsurprisingly, the San Carlos de Parras company's activities in the month of February were equal parts mundane and treacherous, and ranging from money matters to Indian predations. Fiscal concerns held precedence when a corporal, six soldiers, and an unidentified paymaster returned from Saltillo with a half year's supply of payroll and provisions for the troops. A week later, Amangual sent over to Governor Elguézabal three thousand pesos, an amount representing the balance left on December 31, 1803, from the expense fund for the San Carlos company. Following instructions by the perspicacious General Salcedo, Sgt. Felipe Arciniega remitted the funds to Elguézabal, which were in turn deposited into the strong box at Béxar.[136]

Soldiers were back in the saddle by the end of the month but not for retrieving mail or company funds. This time it was for punitive measures after the theft of six horses from the Sambrano ranch by Native people. Sgt. Melchor Rodríguez, along with twenty men from the combined Béxar, Parras, and Bahía companies rode out in pursuit. According to the report, they witnessed the suspects scatter into the hills with the plunder. Flummoxed, the presidials were unable to follow their tracks any further because the hoofprints of wild horses run amok caused confusion. While the soldiers thought the crooks were Comanche, the presumed perpetrators outsmarted them again (this time without the incidental help of mustangs) by following a quite different route, unspecified, from that which was usual. Apart from this startling event with no documented conclusion, business as usual found a corporal and four soldiers detailed the next day from Béxar and the Parras unit to carry the outgoing mail.[137] Upon the return of both the corporal from the Béxar company and the paymaster of the Álamo troop, Elguézabal sent a notebook of the supplies issued to the latter company with the cost: almost 438 pesos to be disbursed by the royal treasury at Saltillo. Since the paymaster furnished the supplies, the payout would come from the allocation of the next half year's funds for the company.[138] It must have been no surprise to the presidio's soldiers that fiscal affairs had far more predictable reckonings than chasing after mounted thieves who intuitively knew the adjacent terrain better than they did. And so, it went as it always did and all in a month's work.

238 Chapter Six

This is not to say that balancing the books was dependably free of controversy. Provisioning the troops presented deeply rooted challenges for commanders and paymasters, with abuse and fraud and persistent royal stinginess as correlative factors in that troubled history. Meeting the demand of replacing troops for his company was an equally complex and often frustrating task even for a soldier of long tenure like Captain Amangual. In some cases, the soldier simply had to go, and two documented cases make this clear. In the first, when Miguel Pando petitioned for transfer from his company (perhaps the San Carlos squadron) to another, he must not have been entirely candid about his years of service. Reviewing the records, Amangual detected inaccuracies in Pando's claim; he had in fact served three years, nine months, and fifteen days. Not having any of it, Pando accused Amangual of prejudice based on a disparaging critique by a sergeant within the same company. Amangual responded with a fair amount of indignation. Insisting that Pando had no foundation for making such a claim, Amangual pushed back: the soldier had never endured any mistreatment from him, nor had he allowed any idea of it to even be imagined.[139] Furthermore, as Amangual stated in his message to Elguézabal:

> I have reprimanded [Pando] only mildly, and sometimes arrested him, not punishing him harshly but being lenient even when he shows a lack of subordination toward the sergeants and corporals of the said company. [I have done so] also because of his being guilty on more than one occasion of disposing of the animals and equipment issued to him and perhaps selling them or aiding other persons in the troops to [similarly] do so. Therefore, I will in no way oppose his transfer from this post if it be left to my decision.[140]

Three days after issuing his response to Pando's request for transfer and likely glad to be done with yet another antagonistic soldier, Amangual reported the desertion of José Arellanes from a detachment under the command of Lt. José Músquiz. Arellanes was assigned to Amangual's company but distinguished himself by absconding with his arms, his mount, his clothing, and a horse belonging to Ignacio López, a fellow presidial. It seems Arellanes was in debt to the company and thus inclined to escape his obligations. He had five horses and mules that were now in the custody of Amangual, who asked Elguézabal if, from proceeds of the sale of Arellanes' animals, he could pay for the one stolen from López.[141]

What the outcome was of the proceedings against Arellanes is not clear. What is indisputable is that, at the age of sixty-five, Francisco Amangual had experienced a wide array of both significant successes and bitter disappointments across his forty-year career in the military. Most of these experiences register his and other soldiers' stakes in the frontier community. Their adventures in the army reinforced the notion of personal and professional investment incurred from and even thwarted by the demands of a life that often left them the recipients of far fewer rewards than losses. Though the collective content of formal statutes, derived from ever-evolving *reglamentos, ordenanzas,* and other official mandates, was expected to be thoroughly absorbed by soldiers in real time, it is not difficult to make sense of the actuality that dedication to duty could be usurped by men like Urrutia, Cortés, and Barrera. Perhaps extralegal adjustments to protocol were perceived as necessary to temper the harsh realities of boots on the ground in the restless periphery. Further up in the hierarchy, rank fortified privilege. Demonstrably principled officers like Elguézabal, Amangual, Fernandez, and Salcedo had within their purview the political expediency necessary for negotiating, accommodating, and even deliberately bending the rules to ensure survival for themselves and their men.

It is entirely conceivable that staying the course in the empire's frontier while coping with officialdom's more restrictive elements triggered dissidence by some in the military. Personal inclinations and professional motivations often clashed with rules and regulations, and desperation rather than outright malice doubtless proved to be the impetus for supplanting the rule of law. Several justifications are plausible, but one overarching conclusion cannot be denied. Some indicators point to the possibility that, for several reasons, such seemingly counterproductive activity among the Comandancia troops had its advantages. Even as the colonial apparatus in the Américas and especially in its far-flung spaces was unraveling, the military as an institution had grown exponentially across the borderlands. As a policy move so wildly antithetical as to appear self-destructive, the king's extension of the military *fuero* and his extraordinarily benevolent pardons to wrongdoers hardened the expanding authority of the army, extending even to the frontier militias. In this era of impending governmental cleavages and social upheavals with repercussions that would traverse the Atlantic, some things remained the same.

That sameness no doubt lent itself to a certain predictability underscoring all things military across the vast colonial landscape. It was more intimately found within the confines of the presidio complex for soldiers on the hoof and when complying with orders from on high. This becomes clearer in scope where it concerned the repositioning of squadrons, individual unit transfers, and filling out the ranks of less fully fledged companies. Such strategic maneuvers likely fit the military prerogatives and bureaucratic exigencies conceived in the minds of frontier commanders. Tactical organization was predicated on the incessant challenges of soldiering on in the royal forces apart from whatever international protocol took precedence elsewhere in the empire. For Amangual, changes abroad were only incrementally experienced. Instead, the daily tasks of managing the San Carlos de Parras flying company, caring for his soldiers, and performing the routine procedures of his office continued unabated in the face of imminently larger transformations across the contested borderlands.

SEVEN

❧

Change of Command, the 1808 Expedition, and the Road Home

Soldiers on the move animate the January 1, 1804, monthly report of Béxar operations in the previous month. Among others, a corporal of the company of San Carlos de Parras along with the presidio's carbineer and soldiers from the Bahía and Aguaverde presidios, left for Nacogdoches to escort the wife of its Capt. Joseph Ugarte.[1] Only a week and a half later, Elguézabal's report indicates that Alférez Guadiana left for Monclova with a cadet named José María Amangual, and the pair were accompanied by four other soldiers. Cadet Amangual was the son of Capt. Francisco Amangual. What little extant information about the young man will emerge shortly that will shed light on the relationship of the father and son from the perspective of generational service in the army. By New Year's Eve 1803, Guadiana and the rest of the party, including José María, returned to the Béxar presidio.[2]

It is provocative to consider what might have been the elder Amangual's reaction to his son's enlistment in the colonial army and, even more so, to reflect on what the cadet's future might hold for him serving in the last years of the Comandancia. Amangual must have understood that his son would be subject to excursions across the borderlands and participation in campaigns against the enemy as the need arose. Given the alterable nature of the presidio population, it is certain, too, that the younger man knew of his father's loss of soldiers through reassignment, desertion, and death. By the middle of 1804 José María would have known of Pedro Castañeda's desertion and his father's *sumaria* of the case. The younger Amangual would also have known about his father's reporting of the desertion of two other soldiers from a detachment Amangual Senior would one day command.[3] He would have heard of the Spanish transfer of Louisiana to the French

Chapter Seven

and that empire's subsequent handing over of the province—indeed, the entirety of the territory constituting the Louisiana Purchase—to the Anglo-Americans on Christmas Day 1803. And he would soon know of those soldiers who wanted to reenlist in the army, as well as those who requested a discharge from further service. By April 1804, he likely learned of further attrition from his father's *compañía volante*. Cadet Amangual probably witnessed José María de Anze, serving as a cadet in the Parras company, ascend to the rank of alférez and transfer to the presidio at Aguaverde.[4]

Both senior and junior Amangual would have known of the diary kept by Lt. Miguel Músquiz during an expedition carried out to counter any harm by Anglo-American renegades who had presumably set out from Natchez. Músquiz described the lands he traversed and reported considerable losses of horses and clothing from his detachment.[5] Shortly thereafter, Amangual will be called on to provide a diary of his own experience leading an expedition that would carry him and a company of soldiers across a large swath of the Texas frontier into New Mexico.

In the meantime, the borders that ostensibly separated the United States from the Louisiana territory appeared to be daily more imaginary. During the time frame coinciding with the younger Amangual's entry into the armed forces, Meriwether Lewis and William Clark headed a secret expedition up the Missouri River to the Pacific. The practicability of an overland route to the great ocean was part of the goal of the two explorers working on behalf of President Jefferson. Bureaucrats in Mexico City had occasionally lost interest in the region but now things were different, with incidences of perceived or actual threats of aggression emerging in the Septentrión and its easternmost borders. Cmdr. Gen. Nemesio Salcedo warned the viceroy that precautionary measures must be considered since the political status of Louisiana had changed. Now that Louisiana was controlled by an aggressive foreign power, those circumstances leaned toward the very real possibility of future hostile advances against the security of Texas and so the need for the utmost vigilance.

Salcedo's seemingly apologetic assertion that he needed to train and mobilize the troops to respond to these dramatically altered conditions hews closely to other portrayals of his character. Unbending in his desire to furnish them with as good a choice of weaponry as that of their opponents, the burden of responsibility to instruct them in their use was his to share. Up to this point they were unaccustomed to anything other than the regular guns they deployed for war against indigenous nations. Salcedo informed Viceroy Iturrigaray that cannon of "ancient caliber" remained in the provinces of Texas and Coahuila, but none was in the proper condition.

Amplifying the destitution, the commander indicated that there was no one capable of training the soldiers in their use except for one artilleryman with strikingly similar capabilities as the artillery itself. That soldier belonged to the Béxar company but was incapacitated due to his advanced age of one hundred years and, besides that, he was completely deaf. Treading carefully with his superior, Salcedo requested the delivery of four or six mounted cannons to Monclova, accompanied by a corporal and four artillerymen.[6]

The commander's requisition to the viceroy was in no way arbitrary. Put bluntly, though his notification of post–Louisiana Purchase conditions in the borderlands evinced a peculiar mix of unflinching credibility and courtly tenor, the instinct to genuflect prevailed. Salcedo justified his needs thus: "By operating the number of cannon designation, the troops of these provinces can receive instruction in the art of handling and use of mounted cannon. There will be no disturbance or innovation, because they will be placed inland from the frontiers at Villa Monclova where there is a military school for cadets and young officers. Later, these soldiers can carry the instruction they have received to whatever post necessary in the aforementioned provinces."[7]

Salcedo's petition was to no avail. The viceroy's sobering response was just that: no such cannon existed in the quantity required by the commander. Iturrigaray merely encouraged Salcedo to take whatever steps he deemed proper in view of the situation in the region.[8] The viceroy's confidence in the general's perspicacity is not surprising. Practicality underpinned most of Salcedo's decisions and, given the on-the-ground constraints at this time, Iturrigaray recognized the need for placing unfettered authority, if not working hardware, in the grip of a veteran soldier like Salcedo.

On the other side of Texas, Gov. Casa-Calvo warned Captain Ugarte in Nacogdoches of impending expeditions from the United States. He also contacted Elguézabal after having been informed through reliable sources that President Jefferson was ready to send an expedition consisting of an officer, twelve soldiers, and a surgeon to each of the rivers: Colorado, San Francisco, and Arkansas. Potential tasks might include examining and exploring waterways from their sources to their mouths, with instructions to make maps, explore mining sites, and to form friendships with the tribes they encountered. From Casa-Calvo's perspective in New Orleans, it was imperative to immediately take all of it—steps, measures, any precautions— for the purpose of diverting and, even, destroying dubious expeditions if the integrity of the territory was to be preserved. In making his case to Elguézabal, Casa-Calvo declared that defensive action on the part of the frontier army would be justified.[9]

Chapter Seven

Warnings of foreign intrusion were nothing new for the governor. It will be recalled that he set off these same alarms in early 1800 and had at that time conveyed a certain dissatisfaction with the measures in place to prevent aggression from interlopers. Indeed, Casa-Calvo cautioned that individuals within the exploring parties should be stopped, have their papers and instruments collected, and treated in the most humane and generous manner before being sent back to their government. A complaint evoking an infraction of the prerogatives and rights of the Spanish king was to follow indicating that the explorers' tactics had disturbed the peace and "good feeling" that existed between the two nations. But Casa-Calvo's response was not that of an alarmist. His concerns about the erosion of borderlands security cropped up years before the Louisiana Purchase and he had forewarned his Texas counterparts, as he was doing so now, to be watchful of emissaries with what he perceived to be questionable intentions from the United States. He did not hesitate to convey this latest information to Elguézabal since he was complying with his responsibility as governor. As he described it, the steps he took were animated by his devotion to the best service for His Majesty and doing so in a timely manner.[10]

Captain Ugarte's answer to Casa-Calvo's admonitions followed protocol but predicated his sustained involvement on the geospatial boundaries of his commission. He stated that since the Colorado, San Francisco, and Arkansas rivers were in territory beyond the jurisdiction of Nacogdoches, he did not dare take any steps further other than to observe the Colorado River from the perspective of and with help by "Indian friends."[11] Covert machinations by others might work as a means of ascertaining if the Jefferson-backed expedition traversed that specific river. But General Salcedo's reaction to Elguézabal was more direct if not stoic. The orders he sent regarding the Anglo-American expedition were transparent enough. But so were all the other points constituting the principal duties of the government, citing those of September 13, 1803, and May 22, 1804, the contents of which Elguézabal was to always keep in mind. Pressing the matter, Salcedo indicated that his orders were sufficiently complete to cover Elguézabal's obligation as governor, and that there was no need to issue any new instructions to him. What Salcedo made clear to Elguézabal was that he was to observe instructions he already had in hand "carefully and precisely," and not to make any decision on account of information that he may have acquired through formal or informal methods. The aboriginal factor never out of mind, Elguézabal was to follow a prudent course to prevent any trouble among allied Native nations; he was to encourage the "Tahuayases" and the Wichitas to stave off any fear by vigorously resisting

Change of Command and the 1808 Expedition 245

any attacks from tribes in Louisiana. Salcedo was especially worried that attacks among ancient enemies might extend into Texas and metastasize to other tribes.[12]

Meanwhile, New Mexico's governor Chacón received the same news concerning the Lewis and Clark expedition. On May 3, 1804, Commander General Salcedo ordered him to organize a small expedition that would outwardly ratify the peace and reaffirm the friendship of the *Panana* (Pawnee) while secretly reconnoitering the region for signs of any Anglo-American presence. Named to commandeer the New Mexico–based expedition was none other than Pedro Vial, the itinerant traveler who will figure into the discussion of the Amangual expedition of four years hence.[13]

More than a decade earlier than Vial's 1804 Panana expedition, Amangual had, on February 7, 1791, responded to a letter forwarded by Viceroy Revillagigedo. The latter had instructed the intendant of San Luis Potosí to arrange for Amangual to receive almost 1,200 pesos spent on the expeditions for discovery of routes. These journeys were carried out by Mares in late 1787, then later by Pedro Vial with several companions, from the villa of Santa Fé to Béxar. The intendant was to send the sum at the first opportunity to reimburse the provisioning fund.[14] Having a long memory for the king's money, the viceroy asked whether or not the account included an entry for 491 pesos, enumerated by Field Marshal Jacobo Ugarte, that went to Vial and his entourage in 1788 by the Nachitoches commander, "Luis Blanc." Amangual verified the entry was not recorded in the accounts sent from the Béxar presidio and, likewise, he had received no word of an expenditure for Vial's company made by the Nachitoches presidio.[15]

Nomadic to his core, Vial was a frequent traveler across the borderlands. In 1784, he accompanied Juan Bousquet on an expedition to the village of the "Taboayazes [Taovayas]" in order to investigate a silver mine found nearby.[16] After completing a journey to the Comanche nation and fulfilling his mission there on behalf of the Spanish Crown, Vial offered to establish a route from Béxar to Santa Fé. Commander General Ugarte stipulated that it would have to be the most direct passage from any of the friendly Indian villages from the interior and, furthermore, Vial would put together an exact itinerary as he promised. Convinced enough to hire, the commander general approved Cabello's effort to commission Vial for the expedition.[17] Then, in September, Cabello transmitted Vial's response to one of Ugarte's questions: When could he undertake the journey? Vial answered: right away, immediately after he bought supplies with the three hundred pesos he had received as compensation for his expedition during the previous month.[18]

246 Chapter Seven

Pedro Vial's three principal trips in the closing decades of the eighteenth century included the 1786 to 1787 San Antonio to Santa Fé journey; the one lasting from 1788 to 1789, from Santa Fé to Natchitoches, to San Antonio and back; and the Santa Fé to St. Louis trip from 1792 to 1793.[19] As Navarro Garcia sees it, in August 1804, entrusted with another expedition by Governor Chacón, Vial set out in the company of interpreter José Jarvay[20] and a few Pawnee associates who were among the Spanish including ten *vecinos* and ten Indians from Taos. By September 3, they arrived at the edge of the Chato (Platte) River, and after failing to encounter the Clark–Lewis company, Vial's party received valuable information from French visitors to a Pawnee camp about *norteamericanos* and gift-giving, and afterward returned to Santa Fé on November 5, 1805.[21]

During this same time frame, another administrative decision from afar animated the Spanish borderlands in ways that must have seemed, if not futile, at least unfeasible to some in the army. Field marshals and chiefs-of-staff of engineers and artillery, Antonio Samper and Joséf Navarro, in a letter of April 22, 1804, explained that the viceroy, with the king's approval, had opted for a new system of governance in the Interior Provinces. In fact, the plan was not so new.[22]

The 1804 reorganization plan, an outgrowth from existing conditions, directed that command of the region be divided into two distinct governments identified as Eastern and Western provinces. The first consisted of Texas, Coahuila, the Bolsón of Mapimí, and the parts of Nuevo León and Santander situated between the Río Bravo and the Pilón River from across several points. The second division comprised the provinces of Sonora, Sinaloa, Nueva Vizcaya, and New Mexico. As described in its content, the order's principal purpose for partitioning the Comandancia was not unfamiliar: to increase and develop the population of Texas as a buffer territory by using military colonists and the local militia. One sad truth the order revealed was that since the essential human resources necessary for this goal were scarce, troops and colonists sent from Coahuila would have to alleviate that deficiency. But until that occurred, the reconnoitering, clearing, and distribution of the lands sited for initial settlement would begin.[23]

The viceregal subdivision of the Provincias Internas provided the impulse for collaboration from myriad sectors across the borderlands and beyond. Settlement was to commence on the coast, with boats and barges constructed to enter the Río Grande del Norte and the Colorado River, as well as the bays of Espíritu Santo, San Bernardo, and Galveston. The laborers for these public works were to come from Cuba under the supervision of the Navy Department in Havana. In proportion to the settlers' recurrent arrivals over time, the troops were to originate from the army of Spain

Change of Command and the 1808 Expedition   247

and the other two-thirds were to come from the Américas and its frontier presidios; all were to be organized one after another with the formation of a mounted artillery company. Officials for the administration of the treasury and justice as well as parish priests were candidates for inclusion in the process of organizing governance within the "new" jurisdiction.[24]

Amangual: Change of Command

Reorganization of the presidial forces, what I term "situational strategizing," by either plotting out defensive or offensive movements in real-time combat or understood as a system-wide schema for assault preparedness, figured into making universal the burgeoning militarization of the provinces. In July 1804, a superior order from General Salcedo directed former captain of the Third Flying Squadron of Chihuahua Francisco Xavier de Uranga to pass his current command of Presidio La Bahía to Capt. Francisco Amangual. In Amangual's absence, Lt. Dionisio Valle was to head the flying company of San Carlos de Parras.[25] Captain Uranga was then to proceed to Coahuila despite his unrelenting illness, an unspecified affliction.[26] Only four days later, Amangual reported Cpl. Diego Cadena was going to Nacogdoches with six men of his company, all fully equipped for the trip, to relieve a detachment of an equal number returning from that post. Then, on July 29, 1804, Amangual reported that, instead, he had received command of Presidio La Bahía from Uranga. Two weeks into his new assignment he found all too familiar conditions of scarce supplies including cloth for, perhaps, soldier uniforms, and replacements for guns distributed from a reserve supply in Nacogdoches and sent to the Béxar company.[27]

From Nacogdoches, Captain Ugarte reported that the general of the "Apalache" tribe, Luis Tinza, had not yet presented himself at the presidio. Ugarte reassured Elguézabal that he would obey the May 8 order by Salcedo, but that Tinza's new plan for settlement and selection of territory the tribe would occupy was still uncertain. Ugarte committed to vigilance over the Apalaches' conduct to avoid potential trouble ensuing from their settlement, and he suggested a chapel might be built and a priest appointed to minister to them.[28] An influx of Anglo-American traders and settlers with surnames like Davenport, MacFadden, Barr, Hesser, Hinso and Clark emerge in the documentary record in places spanning Nacogdoches to Coahuila.[29] By the first week of 1804, under orders from the viceroy, General Salcedo directed the Texas governor to prohibit any immigrants coming from Louisiana to enter the province. If they did, they were to be sent to Béxar or Coahuila, and presumably Monclova, under certain conditions.[30] By the spring of that same year, Salcedo received news of Robert Ashley's

248 Chapter Seven

band of Anglo-Americans having scaled up to 143 men bound for the frontiers of the "Tahuayas." Lieutenant Músquiz of the Nacogdoches presidio was to use the detachment under his command to apprehend Ashley, if possible. In April, Músquiz finished a reconnaissance of territory intended to prevent possible damage caused by a party of rogue Anglo-Americans, perhaps Ashley's contingent, rumored to have set out from Natchez.[31]

By September 1804, Amangual still retained interim captainship of the Bahía company, and promotions were awarded to members of his *compañía volante*. The post of second alférez was vacant because Francisco Adán had advanced to first alférez. Since Elguézabal also served as assistant inspector of troops for Texas, and because Amangual was away on special duty, he had the authority to recommend soldiers for vacant posts.[32] Having three prospects, Elguézabal endorsed the Third Sgt. Vicente Tarín. He had served for over twenty-one years and ranked a sergeant for over two years and until September 1804. In war, Tarín had set out on two campaigns in which he killed seven men, took twenty prisoners, and brought in sixty-one head of stock. He fought in a battle with the Tahuayases in which, single-handedly, he killed one and put two others to flight at the point of a lance. No less important were the intangible qualities considered necessary for all soldiers, allowing Elguézabal to justify Tarín's worthiness for promotion to second alférez based on his faithfulness, ability, and honor. And, since the governor wanted to fill the post with a person of courage, good conduct, and dependability, Tarín was his first choice despite his youth.[33]

Elguézabal's second choice was Juan Antonio Urrutia, third sergeant of the Béxar company and a thirty-year veteran of the army. He had held the rank of sergeant for over ten years, made various scouting expeditions and forays, and commanded various parties. In one battle, his horse was killed and in a recent battle, he killed nine Tahuayases.[34] The third, and final, choice for the position of second alférez was Felipe Arciniego, second sergeant for the *volantes* of Parras, who had served for over nineteen years as a private, corporal, and sergeant, the last rank held for over five years. Arciniego fought in a July 27, 1797, battle under Capt. Pedro Nolasco Carrasco.[35]

By the fall 1804, the monthly report of the military operations of the company of San Antonio de Béxar accentuated the law enforcement activities of the San Carlos de Parras *volantes*. When Ignacio Pérez discovered the dead body of a fellow servant lying on the road leading away from the presidio, forty-six soldiers—half representing the Béxar company, and the other half from Parras—rode out with Alférez Manuel Menchaca to find the perpetrators and punish them for the crime. Elguézabal reported that his initial suspicions were confirmed by the first *alcalde* of San Antonio: the dead man

Change of Command and the 1808 Expedition 249

was shot by "Yndios" from an unspecified nation. When Menchaca's party returned on September 4 after following the tracks of two men on foot and two on horses from the spot where the murder occurred, they continued to pursue the trail made by the horses. However, their tracking of the presumed criminals was disrupted by an encounter with two citizens, presumably *bexareños*, with forty horses traveling to Nacogdoches without permission. Menchaca seized the horse herd and brought the two people back to the capital.[36]

Without further information, it is unknown if the murderers were ever caught. However, it is perplexing that on September 4 the *volante* component of the search party was not sent out independently from the other troops of Béxar to continue the search or, at the very least, to determine the extent of the trail left by the horse tracks. It is difficult to imagine that Menchaca would have required all forty-six of the soldiers to manage the confiscated horses of the Nacogdoches-bound travelers. But curtailing the flying squadron is puzzling since these men were expected to roam freely while surveilling the frontier and policing thinly populated spaces. And while this episode confirms one of most widely understood tasks of the *volantes*, the documentary record also shows that by year's end, strict cohesion in the San Carlos de Parras squadron dissolved when some of its members went out on detachments or singletons performed as escorts. What it does verify, unsurprisingly, is that extraction of troops for specialized maneuvers occurred, thus proving that fragmentation within the *volantes'* composition was occasionally necessary. Though unspecified, in all likelihood some Parras associates accompanied Amangual during the 1808 expedition. Disunited more frequently than the historiography would suggest, the primary sources show that flying company inseparability was inconsistent. In fact, these troops often escorted the mail bag from one presidio to another, further invalidating the notion that the *volantes'* daily tasks did not correlate with the more mundane chores of regular soldiers. Their obligations encompassed more than, exclusively, patrol duty or reconnaissance on the open range.[37]

In any case, the reorganization plan of mid-1804 split up once more the Comandancia General, presaging an eventual demise. Further east, boundaries were reconfigured after contentious disputes among the usual competing factions. From Nacogdoches, Capt. José Ugarte reported to Governor Elguézabal that on December 27, 1804, Capt. Felix Trudeau conveyed news of the quarrels between the Spanish court and the Americans about borderlands demarcations. If the Americans retained the Floridas, the stretch on the western side of the Mississippi was to be Spanish territory with the river itself as the boundary. Ugarte also received news of

250   Chapter Seven

the English declaration of war against the Spaniards, but that the report was unconfirmed as of the date of his letter.[38] This news may have shaken Elguézabal enough to reach out for reinforcements. It is just as likely that Ugarte had anticipated extra troops might be necessary for the Texas capital. On January 6, two days after Elguézabal received Ugarte's news, soon-to-be-governor Antonio Cordero, having conformed to Commander General Salcedo's orders, arranged to have a fully equipped detachment assembled at the presidio of Río Grande. The assignment was simple: be ready to move out at an instant, present themselves before Elguézabal, and obey his orders. Lt. José Rávago was charged with the welfare and discipline of the troops, but all were to be under Elguézabal's supervision.[39]

Expeditions across the Borderlands: Antecedents to the Amangual Journey

On March 30, 1808, Capt. Francisco Amangual left San Antonio de Béxar with an expedition of two hundred men and traveled for nine months to Santa Fé, New Mexico. Along the way on the thousand-mile expedition he and his team were to establish a safe passage between two extreme frontier outposts of territory conjured as Spanish dominion and equally spoken for by the Comanche and Apache nations. While exploring the Red River (of the south) and mountain ranges in New Mexico, the overarching purpose of the excursion will become clearer through interactions with local indigenous bands and other assorted wayfarers.[40]

In light of events that transpired on the Iberian Peninsula in early 1808 and given, in terms of their appeal to outsiders, the ongoing issues that continued to bedevil New Mexico, Louisiana, and the presumed open spaces of the Texas plains, it is remarkable that imperial authority would call for yet another exploratory expedition across a well-worn path from San Antonio to one of the most remote haunts of the empire. However, as recently as 1803, the governor of Texas had received a *bando* from the viceroy on measures to be taken in accordance with the Superior Council of the Royal Treasury for the "development and happiness" of New Mexico.[41] With the mutiny at Aranjuez, the abdication of Carlos IV followed by the accession of his son Fernando VII and, then, the subsequent removal of both royals from the Spanish throne,[42] one might imagine it as a spooked response that Amangual had orders in February 1808 to lead what was essentially a reconnaissance during this month of decisive upheaval on the Peninsula. Even as far west as the outpost of Santa Fé, New Mexico, suspicions elevated to the degree that French interlopers and now even

Change of Command and the 1808 Expedition 251

Americans constituted an increased threat to territory claimed by the Spanish. As recently as 1805–6, Zebulon Pike had completed surveys of the Mississippi River from St. Louis to its source and then arrived in Santa Fé in March 1807. Events throughout 1802–06 caused enough jitters spanning Nacogdoches to Mexico City to warrant military reinforcements from Commander General Salcedo.[43] Enlistees within the military apparatus and bureaucrats in viceregal governance may have worried about indigenous populations of the regions west of San Antonio and La Bahía; had they been successfully wooed to fidelity by American interlopers during yet another cycle of expansionism? Or, even further toward the Pacific coast, perhaps Russian economic inroads emerged as enough of a menace that, even if it was nothing more than a perfunctory overture since it was certainly toothless, a presidio-launched expedition was necessary to reassert the Spanish presence in largely Comanche-controlled territory.[44]

Since what follows is in no way construed to be comprehensive and given that it is not the focus of this study nor the purpose of this section, I briefly summarize some of the most significant expeditions that occurred prior to those of Vial and preceding that of Francisco Amangual's westward bound journey through the Septentrión. However, most of these *entradas* initially headed east toward the land of the Tejas, some to search for the French colony of LaSalle and others to "pacify" the indigenous populations. Whether the journeys were intended to subvert the establishment of outsider communities or convert the Native people, in all cases the overarching objective of these expeditions was to establish a settler presence that would dissuade *other* foreigners from incursion into territory peremptorily staked out by the Spanish. The best that imperial agents on the ground could hope for in achieving that goal was that Native actors might take conciliatory measures and be cooperative enough to convince distant bureaucrats of the military's success at extracting loyalty. Some official documentation describes those efforts so, and day-to-day occurrences as recorded in travel diaries were expected to enhance understanding.

One expedition in 1689 not only aimed to find the LaSalle fort but also intended to project (with soldiers) Spanish hegemony, however elusive. Alonso de León returned in 1690 to lead a second expedition to present-day Matagorda Bay (which he had located and named the year before), followed by travel directed at establishing a mission near the Neches River in present-day Houston County. According to Foster, the caveat attached to this enterprise hinged on condition that this type of edifice was specifically requested by a Tejas chieftain. Yet another expedition emanated from the Presidio of Coahuila in May 1691, but this one differed from the previous two in that

Chapter Seven

the leadership was split between two men with closely aligned objectives, a missionizing agenda and a military one: the cleric was Fray Damian Massanet, and the soldier was future governor of Texas Domingo Terán de los Ríos. Thereafter, Gregorio de Salinas Varona, the governor of Coahuila and a co-expeditionary of both de León and Terán, set out on May 3, 1693, to resupply Massanet in East Texas.[45]

By the turn of the seventeenth century, expeditions continued into Texas but in an easterly direction. In 1709 military and missionary travelers from the new Presidio San Juan Bautista and associated missions for the first time headed past the Frio River and beyond.[46] In 1716, Cpt. Domingo Ramón's expedition with Fray Isidro de Espinosa (1679–1755) utilized the services of the French traders Saint-Denis and the Talòn brothers. Having earlier accompanied the expedition of Capitán Pedro de Aguirre into Texas, Espinosa was named president of the Texas missions which were to be established by friars from Querétaro.[47]

Foster writes that Alonso de León's 1689 expedition was the first Spanish *entrada* to venture from northeastern New Spain to beyond the San Antonio River. The expedition went no further than the west bank of the Colorado River and brought the Spaniards into contact with the Tejas Indians of east Texas.[48] Farther east, the French remained a threat in Louisiana and influenced the pattern and flow of Spanish expeditions throughout the last years of the seventeenth century and for more than half of the century that followed. During the early years of the eighteenth century, the Spanish stepped up efforts to seriously explore the outermost reaches of their ostensible empire.[49] In Europe, Spain experienced stiff competition from France, England, and the Dutch in their determined effort toward land acquisition. Because of unyielding challenges to Spanish hegemony in the borderlands of the "Greater Southwest," royal administrators found it necessary to produce current, accurate maps of their own, disputing the scope of its territory across the Atlantic as delineated by printed maps generated by their rivals.[50] In Texas, two missions had been founded among the Hasinai but were abandoned by 1693. However, the Franciscans did not forget Texas. From the region between Monclova and the Río Bravo, the missionaries carried forth the process of Christianization, which, in turn, the indigenous communities alternately accepted or rejected as relationships with outsiders fluctuated and as economic exigencies and dangerous rivalries demanded. Eventually, the padres managed to persuade the viceroy to reinvigorate the colonization of East Texas in 1716. When it finally got off the ground, Alarcón's expedition established Mission Valero but failed to recruit badly needed reinforcements there and at the Tejas presidio.[51]

Change of Command and the 1808 Expedition

Recording the Expedition

It is indisputable that accuracy in descriptions of the terrain and details of the changing topography provided a necessary counterbalance to other aspects of the expedition diary. Diaries were assumed to be the "primary and most reliable source" for determining expedition routes; they were official Spanish chronicles, mandated by the Crown, and usually signed under oath by the diarist and attested by at least two responsible members of the party.[52] Often, more than one expedition diary or account was kept, which gave additional means of verifying the route. In most examples, two notations were required: the distance in leagues traveled and then recorded in the entry itself, and, further, indicated in the margin of the page with at least one notation of directional travel each day.

Experienced travelers were familiar with the use of the compass and the astrolabe, and the distance traveled was affected by the condition of the terrain, the severity of the weather, and whether the route was one that had been used over and over or was newly created along a previously uncharted pathway.[53] The distance recorded was measured by a formula: diarists multiplied the travel time by an informed estimate of the speed of the march on that day. Foster points to experienced indigenous guides as essential to an expedition's success. And the 1772 *Reglamento* seemingly advocated for their value to such travel when, of all things, issues concerning exchange of prisoners occurred.[54] Indeed, the captains of all expeditions were to ensure Native scout retention at all costs. A leader's intimate knowledge of known indigenous trails was based upon the previous two centuries of Iberian expansionist efforts in the *Americas*. However, as Foster indicates, this meant that no new expedition routes would be created through previously untrodden wilderness. In fact, the ancient trails of the Native inhabitants represented the "best available" trade routes.[55]

The opening pages of the Ramón "trail diary" list the travelers, including the religious personnel who are described as representatives from various colleges along with the captain Domingo Ramón, twenty-five soldiers, twenty-two settlers—including French citizens—in a mule train, and eight married women. Having essential knowledge of the landscape and its hazards, indigenous scouts were expected to accompany the expeditions. In this regard, the Ramón foray was no different in that four Tejas Indians accompanied the party even though they go unmentioned in Espinosa's diary.[56]

Thereafter, the Espinosa diary follows the customary format prescribed by viceregal edict for all expedition travelogues as noting the day of the

254 Chapter Seven

week, month, and date, followed by descriptions of two key elements that repetitively appear in colonial documents of expeditions. The first of these required granular portrayals of the landscape, soil conditions, and locations of water sources; and the second feature deemed as necessary was the recording of all Catholic religious observances, including the obligations of mass, sermon, and feast days. Friendly encounters with Indians, celestial sightings, and the occasional animal stampede lend specificity to the many moving parts of expeditions including Amangual's venture. However, these events are fundamentally unremarkable in that colonial documents of this type are replete with assorted challenges to travel itineraries. Skirmishes with Native populations are noteworthy and magnify the reality of incessant danger to life and limb across the Comandancia. The final note on each entry of all expedition diaries is the number of leagues traveled, a distance roughly equivalent to two and six-tenths of a mile.

Historian William Foster tracked as precisely as possible the route used by eleven expeditions initiated by the de León expedition of 1689 to the Solís 1768 Inspection tour of the Zacatecan missions in Texas. He plotted the daily directions and distances recorded from some seventeen diaries (kept on the eleven expeditions throughout the 600- to 800-mile trek from Monclova and Saltillo in the state of Coahuila, to Matagorda Bay, East Texas), and in some instances on to Los Adaes, the colonial capital of "Tejas."[57] Giving meaning to process, the central purpose of this chapter is to compare the content of the Amangual diary as translated by Mattie Austin Hatcher in 1934 with that of the Loomis and Nasatir 1967 study of Pedro Vial. The latter included in a separate chapter the 1808 expedition diary in its entirety, with annotations and footnotes, and using the Béxar and the Guerra translations.[58]

These two sources are then cross-compared with the original diary of Capt. Amangual that is held in the Béxar Archives. I adopt this comparative approach since, among interpreters of this firsthand account, mostly minor similarities and differences exist in recording the route and associated events, some prosaic, others dramatic. Though I seek to identify the common threads of daily experiences on the trail of discovery across the borderlands/Apachería/Comanchería,[59] I dwell less here on the minute details of each day's activities and, instead, opt for drawing out encounters of some importance but not highlighted in Hatcher's Béxar translation and Loomis and Nasatir's *Vial*. Ascertaining incongruity between the two involved correcting translation errors in both.

Diario de las Novedades, y Operaciones ô Ocurridas
en la Expedicion que se hace desde esta Prov.ᵃ de
Fexas, ô la del Nuebo Mexico, de Orden Superior, Siendo Primer Comand.ᵗᵉ el Capitan D.ⁿ Fran.ᶜᵒ
Amangual, segundo el Capitan D.ⁿ Jose Agabo
de Ayala, en 30. de Marzo de 1808.

Dia 30 de Marzo

Obserbaciones y Novedades

Desde la Mision de S.ⁿ Ant.ᵒ hasta el Arroyo del
Novillo, donde Paramos, no hubo Otra novedad. si
no la perdida, de una mula, Cargada de Pilon
sillo, de la 2.ᵃ Comp.ᵃ de la Colonia. 2. leguas.

Dia 31

Este Dia amanecio sin haver Ocurrido novedad.
mas que la perdida, de un Macho en pelo de la
Comp.ᵃ de la Bahia, y haviendo Emprendido
Marcha, por Jerreno Piedroso guarnecido de
Poco monte Generalmente de Encino Prieto
hasta Llegar al Arroyo de Leon don't nos alo-
pamos sin Otra novedad: 8. leguas.

Dia 1.ᵒ de Abril

Este Dia haviendo amanecido sin novedad segui-
mos la Marcha por un Camino Plan, lo alto que
se devisan de hambos lados, son vien Piedrozos
pero Francitables, de buen Pasto aunque Estesil
y nos acampamos en el Arroyo del Sibolo
sin haver Jenido en el Francito. 8. Leguas

Dia 2

Este Dia amanecio una gran Jempestad acompa-
ñadas de orribles Jruenos y Relampagos con

256   Chapter Seven

Amangual's Story: The Expedition
to Santa Fé, 1808

By early March, Commander Salcedo informed the governor of New Mexico that a company of troops from the Texas garrison would cross the plains from San Antonio to Santa Fé with enough provisions for the trip outward bound.[60] Starting with his departure from Béxar, Amangual was to keep a detailed diary about the march, the distances covered, routes, and events that followed. With acute attention and care, he had to give a complete impression of his role in the important objective with which he had been entrusted. Furthermore, the document was to be carried each day so that once arrived at his destination he could present it to that province's governor.[61]

When Amangual set off from Béxar on March 30, 1808, his second-in-command Capt. José Agabo de Ayala was by his side. They and their group of 202 men consisted of twenty-five presidials from the Béxar Company (including some *volantes*), and Lt. José Antonio Cadena; twenty-seven presidials from the Bahía company, with Alférez Juan Antonio Urrutia, and the chaplain José Miguel Martínez. Gov. Antonio Cordero directed Simón de Herrera to send a detachment of 150 men,[62] which would include fifty men from the Cavalry Corp of Nuevo Reyno de León, including its Capt. Agabo, Lt. Felix Pérez, and Alférez Juan de Ybarra. Rounding out the Herrera detachment were one hundred soldiers from the Cavalry Corp of Nuevo Santander, including Capt. Cayetano Quintero, Lt. Miguel de Arcos, and the alférezes Manuel Alanis and Gregorio Amador.[63]

Having reviewed his men's weaponry, clothing, saddlery, and criminal status, plus the horse herd, Amangual recorded the supplies, contents of the strong box, and archives. Amangual indicated that all his soldiers had muskets, pistols, and shields except for three men who, robbed by deserters within the ranks, did not have lances. The missing items were inspected in accordance with orders left by the commanders. Seven shotguns and fourteen new pistols constituted replacements for weapons independent of those for Nacogdoches within that presidio's storehouse. The troops were to carry out several objectives: to maintain the dependency status of the Indian nations, particularly the Comanche, across whose lands they would transit; to cut off communication with whatever strangers to whom their people had been introduced; and to stymie American expeditions at a distance as far as possible from the territory claimed by the Comandancia.[64]

Further, the detachment was to thoroughly inspect the territory between Béxar and that closest to the source of the Red River in the vicinity of the present-day Texas panhandle. In the instructions to Amangual, the name used by others to call the same river "Colorado de los Cados" is included,[65]

Change of Command and the 1808 Expedition 257

as are the rest stops in different *rancherías* where two Comanche factions existed. The Spaniards gave names to each, with one in the east named "Cuchamica" and the other in the west, "Yamparica." Such designations regularly occurred even though other motivational urgings must have proved challenging in translation. For example, in their interactions with the chiefs of these indigenous groups, Amangual and his troops were to inspire fidelity and love for the Spanish king. For their allegiance, they were assured of the king's protection against any invaders of their territory.[66] The irony here was the invasion of the Iberian Peninsula and subsequent occupation of key cities like Barcelona and Pamplona occurring the week before these letters were composed.

During these last two days of March, the expedition made it as far as Arroyo Novillo[67] where their first loss of an animal occurred: a mule loaded with *piloncillo* belonging to the Second Company of Nuevo Santander. The loss of a stallion belonging to the Company of La Bahía occurred the next day. Clearly, this expedition would be no different from any other, including those that formed Vial's multiple peregrinations across the frontier, in that it included men, animals, and supplies from multiple garrisons. Given that the company's next few stops targeted arroyos as camp sites, it can be surmised that low-lying water flow would be ideal, as would any adjacent grassy areas for the horses. Stampedes by the horse herd plagued the expedition during the first week of travel, with animals skedaddling from the companies of Nuevo Reyno de León, Nuevo Santander, and a troop referred to simply as the "veteranos."[68]

Wrestling with the environment and happening upon wildlife consumed the expedition's major responsibilities from the second to third weeks of April. During that period, Amangual's men cleared vegetation with axes, crowbars, and shovels to cross marshes along a creek's banks; they killed a bear at the Arroyo de Chimal and spotted buffalo; and they continued through a region that Amangual described as extremely rough country, heavily wooded. They made it to the "very wide" Llano River on April 9, with wild onions growing on its banks and high, rocky hills. Curiously, there was no grass available until the group arrived at the San Sabá River where they found more herds of buffalo.[69]

Then on April 11, two Comanche from the *ranchería* of "Cordero"[70] came to the campsite while headed to Béxar. Amangual gives no further information on the pair, although it is likely that the two were men en route to the presidio to receive gifts. Here Amangual noted the extensive woods of pecans and other trees, many fish, turkey, bear, and all kinds of animals. Later that morning, accompanied by ten soldiers, he went to examine the presidio of San Sabá abandoned some fifty years before. He found a small

258 Chapter Seven

plaza enclosed on all four sides with a stone wall, partly destroyed, with evidence of bulwarks at each corner. At the north end, there was a ruined building, possibly of two stories. Water flowed east to west from a ditch or spring, used to irrigate an extensive plain extending from the hills to the river on the south. Amangual described land very suitable for all kinds of planting.[71] The next day, the expedition's Indian guide reported their proximity to the Cordero *ranchería*.

Two soldiers and an Indian were sent ahead to make the expedition's arrival known; a while later, a Comanche came running to inform the party that "Yndio Cordero" had moved his people to a place where there was good grass and plenty of water. Traveling through low hills, they could see the *ranchería*, which, as described by Amangual, looked like a city perched atop one of the hills near a beautiful plain. As the troops drew up in column formation, Cordero and his men approached, their bodies painted with red ochre, and dressed in various costumes. The presidials beat a march on the drums and went through various ceremonies to convey good intentions and fellowship. Amangual's company stayed at the Arroyo de Conchos to discuss the expedition with Cordero and to pasture their animals, described as very thin, in an area with good grassland to refresh them.[72] What transpired next conjures up a ceremonial staging of formalities intended to cement two objectives: reciprocal friendship and the multipronged commitment sought by Amangual in fulfillment of his orders.

On April 13, Amangual, escorted by two intermediaries, an assistant, and an interpreter, went to Cordero's lodge to present a walking cane and rifle sent by Texas governor Antonio Cordero. Though it is apparent that these intimations of philanthropy had as their intention to reassert the Comandancia's presence in the Comanchería and, further, signaled an expectation of Cordero to govern and defend his village, Amangual reported that Cordero received them "very cordially."[73] Assuming the diary's missing pages as further description, this event must have been carried out as a purely symbolic and even self-serving gesture, enacted by players on both sides of the equation. However, Amangual in his role as expedition leader makes no mention of the objects' representation of, in truth, the empire's long arm of the law according to viceregal concepts of dominance and assent.[74] Ceremonial displays of reciprocal fealty had great significance, but Amangual and his troops came with a specific course of action and, in turn, Chief Cordero answered all questions and offered to supply guides with experience, loyalty, and good conduct. As to whether his generosity was authentic or if he was simply playing along, the official documentation does not speculate.

Amplifying the goodwill, the next day Amangual made another overture of accord. Showing gratefulness and true affection, he invited various captains of militia, presumably Quintero and Agabo, Cordero, and other subordinate intermediaries from Cordero's *ranchería* to a luncheon. Though he does not say so, Amangual and his men seemingly stayed the night of the 14th and then pressed on just a short distance in the morning. The next two days were spent hunting buffalo and processing meat ("*carnear*") with their Indian friends and tending to an injured *arriero* of the company of Nuevo León. In an episode that would shortly turn bizarre, the soldiers even managed to bring back three live calves, one of them a yearling and, predictably, very wild.[75]

Despite camaraderie between soldiers and Indians, the Comanche guide who had accompanied Amangual and his troops complained with apparent cynicism that he had lost an iron chain, perhaps attached to a quirt. This concern prompted a search of the soldiers' belongings by Capt. Agabo de Ayala, the expedition's second-in-command. With suspicions aroused, confirmation of a theft was not long in coming. Soldier Matías Cantu found the chain in the possession of Faustino Lozano, the discovery of which led to the thief enduring twenty-five lashes with a thin stick inflicted by the company's corporal as punishment. Amangual tells us it set an example to the others. Now a prisoner, Lozano was sent to the guardhouse to await his fate.[76]

From April 22–26, Amangual reported crossing over country dotted with good grass but little mesquite. Though Amangual and his team found discourteous their treatment by villagers under headman Chiojas (Sofais), he nevertheless presented a small gift, unspecified, to its leaders in the same way as he had done with Cordero's chiefs. Along with that token, an interpreter's skills came into play. Amangual gave a lengthy speech about their arrival with the aim of inviting them to visit; to apprise the village of the love by their "king and father" (Fernando VII, briefly) toward them; and, as Amangual goaded his audience, the loyalty and fidelity that they in turn bore toward both their earthly and heavenly "fathers." Amangual discouraged the Indians under Sofais from trading with any other nation since, in his mind, the objective of those entities was to dismantle their allegiance toward the Spanish.[77] In response, a spokesperson for the villagers expressed being satisfactorily informed of everything presented by Amangual, affirming themselves as "Spanish," and professing their belief in everything communicated by the Béxar company. Amangual noted that this band had accepted nothing from any other nation. Or so they claimed. Sofais' representative added that they knew nothing of American entry into

260   Chapter Seven

their lands nor the establishment of a trading post.[78] Whether the impolite reception by the villagers as alleged by Amangual was nothing more than wariness on the part of its first responders is uncertain. One senses that Sofais' people were fully capable of and outwardly comfortable with messaging their skepticism about the military arrival. Even after piddling ceremonial displays, one of their commanders expressed, however insincerely, congeniality and acquiescence to his Spanish counterpart.

As before and across the miles, the tragic and the prosaic intermingled. Amangual requested guides for the expedition's continuance, emphasizing good conduct and loyalty as the preferred attributes for the task. Stamina and no underlying conditions might reasonably have been unvoiced requirements for all, whether Spaniard, Mestizo, or Native. When a soldier named Rafael Mansilla, from the company of Lt. Luciano García, fell ill complaining of pain in his side, the company's chaplain came to hear his confession. Two days later, he died and was buried. Without further information, the cause of his death or the state of his health at the beginning of the journey is unknown. Nevertheless, travel continued until the end of the month with further stampedes from the usual renegades, the horse herds belonging to the companies of Nuevo León and Santander. Soldiers crossed over very flat country with scattered hills as well as patches of mesquite trees, several arroyos, and numerous dry creeks. One of those arroyos, flowing into the "Almagre" River and Verde Creek, ran west northwest to east southeast.[79]

On May 1, Capt. Agabo de Ayala ascended a particularly high hill that provided a good view of the landscape. He saw nothing but other hills in every direction. The expedition party traveled through them and entered a small valley along the river. According to the Native guides, the accumulated riverways were branches of the Colorado. Amangual described rivers in this area as having large numbers of trees near them, good watering places ("*buenos abrevaderos*"), and abundant grass. He found the soil here to be the best thus far. The following week allowed for buffalo hunting, with animals so abundant that the soldiers could kill them near the camp. Nevertheless, the expedition team braved hailstorms, windstorms, and, despite all this rain, now a troubling scarcity of watering holes. Reconnoitering helped to clarify environmental conditions: no further water sources lay northward, which was the direction of their destination, and this dilemma caused the company to recast positions to reach northerly running streams so that the journey could continue. On May 3, in the first instance of Amangual's written expression of deep concern for the well-being of his men and, perhaps, fear for their survival, he wrote "God guide us."[80]

Alarmed by a scarcity of watering holes, Amangual issued orders to safeguard the animals, too, in the expedition. Out in the wide-open spaces,

Change of Command and the 1808 Expedition   261

a larger number of them required more protection since management was often compromised by stampedes, a recurring event documented in the diary. Each company was to take charge of its own *caballada* since keeping the herds en masse prevented them from grazing and drinking sufficiently. Thus, each division of horses and mules came under the care of a corporal and six soldiers.[81] By contrast, daily corralling at the presidios had animal stock guarded by only one, sometimes two, soldiers. To add to their workload, the team still had to contend with the three buffalo calves captured three weeks prior. While the party rested and cared for their animals, they waited for the arrival of the chief of the Yamparica, probably Quegue, whose *ranchería* was in hills only recently traversed. When he, Lieutenant Cadena, and four soldiers as escorts returned with another Yamparica named "Sanbanbi" and two companions, the Native men expressed their desire for friendship with Béxar's Spaniards and mestizos. Therefore, rather than return to their village, the Yamparica stayed the entire night in the expedition camp.[82] It is conceivable that the choice of Amangual as an intermediary from the Spanish army for encounters with indigenous policy makers across the borderlands was predicated not only on someone with long experience but also an operative with highly developed relational skills. At best, that competence would have required the ability to project a non-threatening demeanor and a high degree of discernment in demystifying the thorny process of meeting strangers.

Still, this kind of encounter was nothing new for Amangual. Twenty-three years prior, Amangual spearheaded an escort for visiting Comanche leaders that positioned them upon departure in the center of a processional battle formation. The gesture was not purely symbolic; its fundamental intention was to ward off while in transit a rumored attack by the Lipan.[83]

Quegue and Sofais were known to at least some of the expedition soldiers from previous junkets, and Amangual habitually delivered cigars to "Sojas," as he is sometimes referred to in documentation. Meeting the Yamparica leader and his people was productive, temperate, with no apparent volatility. In glaring contrast to Comanche cordiality, the following day Captain Amangual apprehended one of his own, Lt. Luciano García, an adjutant of the Nuevo Santander company. That disruption required Alférez Manuel Alanis of the same company to assume the administrative and fiscal affairs of the company.[84] For some reason García's crime is unspecified. And, notably, Amangual appears to have been far more concerned with recording troop interactions among indigenous people and, especially, the leaders of *rancherías* than dealing with an officer who should have known better. Nevertheless, Amangual persevered with the task at hand. Over the course of two days, expedition personnel distributed presents, promised protection,

Chapter Seven

and issued the customary request that the Yamparica disallow passage to other foreigners, that is, non-Spaniards. For their part, the Indians "showed a true and sincere willingness[85] and promised to be faithful in their friendship," to give accurate information about the country ahead, and to offer the company an extra guide to lead them toward abundant water. On May 9, Amangual admitted "a big difference," based on their own map, between what he had imagined about the land and what they in fact encountered.[86]

The maps, of course, could not have forecast weather conditions. Consequently, throughout the month of May the expedition team endured heavy rains and high water. The latter circumstance prevented visits from the Indians to the soldiers' camp. Once they appeared, however, Amangual indicates that his men could not eat or sleep, or do anything for that matter, because the Indians were curious, "intruding into the tents and among the soldiers."[87] Inquisitive behavior by the Indians was tolerated since, as it will become obvious, throughout the expedition to Santa Fé Amangual and his men relied on their Native guides. That dependence was not unusual since an international array of folks in the service of indigenous and foreign powers, operating as traders, explorers, spies, and periodically solo adventurers like Vial, were similarly keen on investigating unfamiliar spaces across the frontier. Watched closely by their rivals and by those they, too, hoped to placate, Native stakeholders did so for potential economic and political advantage.

This reliance on indigenous expertise crystallizes with an episode in mid-May when the guides told the expedition party that nothing more lay ahead. Armed with knowledge of the terrain superior to that of Amangual's troop, they forewarned that it was impossible for the expedition to get through during the day. The expeditioners determined to press on ("*cantiando rumbo*" [sic]) through an area the guides had carefully examined consisting of ravines with water, level ground with pasture, and mesquite wood. As soon as they pitched camp, the Indian guides straightaway headed out to locate water for the next day, such was their apparent devotion to the well-being of Amangual and his men as well as to Quege's promise of loyalty and good conduct.[88] However, reciprocity and accommodation between out-of-towners and Native people did not mean that trust and goodwill were bestowed impulsively or without certain reservations.

A few nights earlier, one Native man arrived at the camp and presented himself to the guards. When they reported the arrival, a lieutenant and an interpreter were summoned to interrogate the visitor. He replied that he was a dependent of the *ranchería* of another Yamparica leader[89] identified by Amangual ten days before, and that he was searching for an escaped horse

Change of Command and the 1808 Expedition 263

belonging to his commander.[90] It seems the soldiers feared that he might cause harm to their horse herd. Therefore, they suggested that it would be better for him to sleep in the guardhouse, and then he could continue his journey the following day.[91] The outcome of this encounter is unknown, but it anticipates another instance of the shaky underpinnings of reciprocal trust between outsiders and Native communities when, subsequently, Quege of the Yamparica and his followers promised to inform the Amangual party of any dangers in the region. As was customary, they proposed to the Gran Capitán their desire for yet another guide since illness emerged among those accompanying the expedition. More specifically, the *wife* of the most experienced guide for the explorers was seriously ill, and he was reluctant to go on. In fact, their other guide was also sick but, even if he were not, he knew nothing about the land or the water holes. Thus, he was, essentially, useless at this point in the journey.[92]

In response, the Indians declared that since the route the explorers wished to travel would entail many difficulties, not the least of which was the lack of water, those efforts would result in great losses to the animals. More protective than obstinate, Quegue told the party that under no circumstances would he provide any of his people as guides. The presidials, responding in chorus, proceeded to remind the Yamparica that they were allies of the Spanish, that the royal government had extended friendship to them, and that the Indians knew how well Amangual and his men had treated them. Quegue's reaction to all that rhetoric could be alternately interpreted as reasoned or paternalistic: through an interpreter he answered that he had no authority to force one of his people to act as a guide and that Yamparica laws were vastly different from those of the Spaniards. Furthermore, leader Quegue asserted that this was what he told his men. However, he added that if any one of them wished to go voluntarily, they could go, guiding the expedition as far as Santa Fé.[93] If Amangual and his troops expected loyalty and good conduct from their guides and given that they themselves had far less mastery of the terrain, it is difficult to fathom why they rebuked the Indians. One senses Quegue knew that his people better understood how expertise commensurate with restraint might accelerate a placid, orderly departure of the Comandancia's operatives from their territory.

As the dilemma unfolded, practicality over bullheadedness prevailed: the explorers remained in camp, making every effort to relieve the sick woman since, as Amangual states, it was not possible to travel without an experienced Indian guide. Marital devotion aside, the most favored guide promised that he would make headway the following day whether his wife recovered or not. Eventually, the woman improved enough to leave the *ranchería* where she had been taken for medical treatment.[94] The expedition soldiered on the next day.

From May 20 to the end of the month the journey forged ahead, having multiple interactions with Native peoples, that diversified group fulfilling their own individual and collective responsibilities to local communities. In an unidentified valley, a Caddo man returning from a visit to the Comanches to appeal for peace and where, in fact, his efforts found success, asked to travel with the Amangual party so that he would not have to travel alone. Through one canyon a small group of Indian men and a woman arrived disclosing their destination for a campaign against the "Lipillanos."[95] All carried lances and four had muskets. The suggestion here is that the woman was also a warrior since she too carried a lance, and of the four that had rifles, one of those must have been in her hands. Traveling across an expansive plain that descended to El Blanco creek, the expedition party encountered another Native man and two women who were hunting.[96] Like those headed for war, it is equally likely that these two women were also active participants in the hunt, possibly even combatants, and not simply tagalongs.

Environmental conditions confronted Amangual and his team, some old enough to remember the region when it was healthy. Now a barren landscape, it was wiped clean of grass by the onslaught of buffalo and drought.[97] By the end of the month and after traveling sixteen leagues and having almost reached the "Rio Rojo," they found trees, pools of water, seeping springs of permanent water, vineyards, and even "Castilian rosebushes." The last two days of May and the first of June 1808 found the expedition engaged in extremely hard manual labor, using pickaxes and crowbars, opening the way through very rough country—hills, creeks, bluffs, and precipices—by making a path up and then down for the train that progressed with great difficulty. When deep waters posed a challenge, it became almost necessary for the muleteers to carry the loads across in their arms. In fact, they yielded to countless detours looking for the best terrain to traverse until they came to the banks of the "Rio Rojo."[98]

On June 1, the party met a group of five men, and a Frenchman self-identified as "Don Pedro," all claiming to be residents of Santa Fé on a buffalo-hunting expedition. That afternoon, the men retired to their camp, but the Frenchman remained to spend the night with the Amangual company. He proved to be a source of valuable information. He described the surrounding territory as very peaceful; that the adjacent river had two names (*"este rio es el Colorado y por otro nombre el Rojo,"*) and that it did not flow past "Natitoches." Pedro spoke of a long distance from their present

Change of Command and the 1808 Expedition 265

location to where it joined the "Napeste" (Arkansas) River with both entering the Mississippi. He confirmed the river that the expedition had left behind on May 22 was the "Rio de Natitoches," and that they were at its source.[99]

The next day led them to another informant, Manuel Martínez, a "veteran soldier" and interpreter for the Indian nations, who was hunting with those of the San Miguel del Bado missions. The team had every reason to trust the word of Martínez. He and Lt. Facundo Melgares[100] had explored the river together and confirmed intelligence provided by the unnamed Frenchman: the river was not the one that flowed to Natchitoches, that its source was in the Sierra Blanca, and it was indeed impossible to travel on horseback. Subsequently, the journey continued by way of a level sandy plain along the river until they met up with an unidentified local from New Mexico. Fronting a party of 120 men, Martínez discussed the route and then returned to their camp. Veering along the river, Martínez and local Indians accompanied the Amangual party; the going was rough, and many horses and mules came up lame. Great care and special arrangements were necessary to avert further damage to the pack mules. The journey continued over hills, creeks, and dry ravines until the team reached some ditches, identified as the work of the Yamparica and dredged by them as a method of defense against the Quitaray.[101] Bad country consisting of deep trenches ("*fosos*"), hills, creeks, stretches of rocks along the river, and even a bulwark, made for unpleasant travel. Since there was no other crossing, the company was forced to ascend a canyon with many "high rocky bluffs" and with the unfortunate result of many injured horses and mules.[102] Almost daily heavy rains plagued the expedition by soaking the troops and supplies, effectively delaying departure. On June 6, Manuel Martínez accompanied a sick soldier to Santa Fé for medical attention.[103]

Throughout the middle part of June detachments of soldiers set out to look for water holes, inspect the ground for suspicious trails, and follow the flow of the river. For a few days, Amangual and part of the company remained stationary since separate parties of troops arrived while others were still out on reconnaissance. When all the soldiers reassembled, the news was not good from any point on the compass. The collective evaluation from Amangual's emissaries was that travel over the rough country, whether on foot, on horseback, or with a mule train, was impossible. Windstorms and rainstorms erupted, followed by calm. Then, Amangual issued one particularly intriguing order: thirty men and one lieutenant were to be ready at dawn on June 11 with supplies for three days.[104]

At daybreak, Amangual set out with an escort to reconnoiter the ground previously explored by patrols. Once gone, the remaining troops broke

Chapter Seven

camp and traveled over what he described as good country skirting along the creek. In a matter of a few hours, the two parties reconvened, traveled a short distance more, and then camped on a level elevation devoid of any kind of wood (*"palo de ninguna clase"*).[105] One might wonder if Amangual had lost confidence in the surveying abilities of his troops and simply decided to do the job himself. He does not mention his reasons for staking out the terrain of his detachments. What is clear is that his group, and the other one, encountered perfectly serviceable country to travel without major incidents. Deviating not from the routine of reconnoitering or waiting out a hailstorm, a rainstorm, or a sick soldier, and moving camp because of rising waters, mundane tasks continued until it was time to move on. Undeterred, they followed the riverway in the direction of the first mission they would find in New Mexico. An apparently relieved, if slightly ruffled, Amangual wrote in his diary

> Having concluded the expedition, and in order to fulfill the instructions of Antonio Cordero, Governor of the Province of Texas, we continued to travel over a level plain until we arrived at some small hills that form several cañadas and some low hillsides.

Second-in-command Captain José Agabo did what he was good at: he climbed one of the highest hills and sighted a range of high snow-capped mountains to the northwest. Following its elevation and windings, he and his party came to a small creek which eventually dumped out into the Gallinas River where they camped. After crossing flat country and entering a narrow canyon formed by the mountains, the expedition ascended and descended slopes until they approached the Pecos River. Ahead lay the mission San Miguel del Bado about three miles distant.[106]

June 16: Arrival in Santa Fé

After spending the night on the Pecos, Amangual sent forth to Santa Fé a corporal and ten soldiers with a message, adhering to protocol for reporting the expedition's arrival and for receiving any orders from the commander general: *"El dia 15 del corriente de haber finalizado todos los puntos de mi comision, he arribado a este Pueblo de San Miguel del Bado a fin* [?] *con la expedicion de docientos hombres* [con] *inclusos tres capitanes, siete subalternos y un capellán de mi cargo de provincia de Tejas* [sic passim]."[107]

Late in the evening of the next day, two soldiers conveyed back a letter from the governor and delivered by Capt. Dionisio Valle who had camped at the Pecos mission. Valle is remembered for assuming command of the

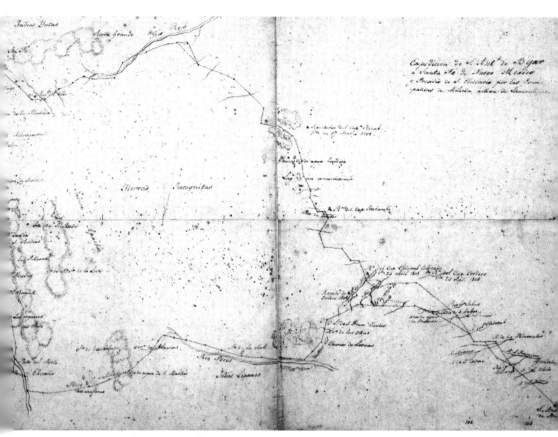

Map of the route followed by the active militia of Tamaulipas in their expedition from San Antonio, Texas to Santa Fe, New Mexico, and back via El Paso, March 30 to May 19, 1808. HM 2051, The Huntington Library, San Marino, California.

compañía volante of San Carlos de Parras when its captain, Francisco Amangual, took interim command of the Bahía presidio in 1804. Upon receipt of the letter, Amangual ordered that the march toward the city begin the next day. At dawn, the company crossed the Pecos River, traveling across rough country and skirting along a mountain range south of the Sierra Grande with spruce trees until they reached the Pecos Mission where they, too, camped. The next day, after covering even rockier terrain, the expedition reached the Sierra Nevada and a high point from which Santa Fé came into view. The squadron halted and a soldier galloped ahead to inform the acting governor of their arrival; the soldier returned at once with an order for the expedition to come to the capital.[108]

Eventually, Amangual's troops arrived at another large plaza with "very comfortable" congregate housing; two barracks were assigned to each

268   Chapter Seven

company, and the officers were allowed to select the best quarters available.[109] Amangual and his company remained in Santa Fé for three months, and then set out on the return trip, traveling through the presidios at San Elizario and El Paso. He set aside the diary during that time but resumed the narrative when the time came to push on.

Santa Fé to San Elesario

When the expedition party left Santa Fé on September 20, 1808, they traveled south until they reached the small settlement of Río Abajo. By four o'clock they passed the mission of Santo Domingo and one hour later were only about a mile away from the San Felipe mission. Amangual notes in his diary that "nothing unusual happened except the desertion of two militiamen of the first company of the Colony," a usual reference to Nuevo Santander hearkening to its initial naming as La Colonia de la Costa del Seno Mexicano. Throughout the diary, Amangual refers to the region, and its unit, simply as the *Colony*. He also indicated that two other soldiers managed to break their guns.[110] Perhaps, by this point in the journey, nothing surprised Amangual, and desertion was anything but unusual.[111] After such a lengthy stay in the capital he may have even wondered why the soldiers chose to abandon the company on the day the expedition left Santa Fé.

Amangual probably counted on the men returning at some point given the king's ongoing beneficence toward deserters from the royal armies. As per an 1801 royal decree, Carlos IV was determined not to deprive soldiers of bonuses they earned when, after being punished for their misdemeanors, they proved themselves worthy of forgiveness and had thereafter continued to act honorably and with loyalty.[112] The big difference leading up to the Amangual expedition was that Carlos was no longer on the throne, and even his son Fernando had been deposed and subsequently replaced by a Bonaparte. Besides, a communiqué from 1804 proved the king's paternal view toward transgressors, and the decree's fundamental premise of amnesty remained unchanged.[113]

Over the next two days the expedition made many stops, but Amangual did not provide nearly the amount of detail about the terrain and road conditions as he had while en route to Santa Fé. On September 22, one of the two deserters from the militia was found in the *caballada* at dawn, while one of the *arrieros* (muleteers) ran away from the Bahía company during the night. The next morning, the second militiaman who deserted on the day of departure from Santa Fé found refuge, literally, in the horse herd. There among the beasts he, too, got caught.

Change of Command and the 1808 Expedition   269

The land of enchantment undoubtedly has held a strange allure across time and space, because now even the expedition's music makers wanted out. Just the day before, Amangual indicates that two drummers, one from the First Company of Nuevo Santander and the second from the Company of Nuevo León, deserted. Maybe they caught up with the first two *Colony* deserters and the drummer boy. In the five years preceding the Amangual expedition, cases of second desertions and trials dealing with chronic defection constituted a significant part of military affairs in communications during the spring of 1803 and between General Salcedo and the governor of Texas. As we have already seen, Amangual had to occupy himself with dereliction of duty by at least three truant soldiers in April 1804. By November of that same year, he informed his commander about the desertion of four more soldiers.[114]

The same night as the desertion of the two drummers, another two soldiers, one from the First Company and the other from the Second Company of Nuevo Santander, took off. The next morning Amangual and his troops found the trail left by the pair, and it was obvious they had taken animals with them. Immediately, a captain, subordinate officer, and twenty-five men followed the trail and appraised it as that of two saddled horses and two mules. However, when their last horse became exhausted, they gave up the search and returned without having captured the two fugitives. Then, they discovered that a soldier of the militia, whose horse had been the first to give out, had climbed a tree to see if his companions were returning, fell, and broke his leg.[115]

Aside from bumbling deserters and escapees with nowhere to go, it seems that Apache raiders had stolen cattle on September 4. However, they, too, left a trail that the expedition followed eastward from Sevilleta until they had reached a level plain in the early evening. The party stayed the course on this type of terrain so the enemy would not notice any dust raised by the horse herd. Having left the exhausted mule team behind, when they finally arrived at Sierra Oscura at four o'clock in the morning the company was forced to make camp without water. They had traveled twenty-one leagues over seventy-two hours.[116] After only three hours of rest, they were back in the saddle. At eight o'clock in the morning, they found a pool of water and Amangual decided to wait there for the mules which finally arrived at eleven o'clock. The party traveled for eight leagues passing through the Cañon de la Piedra Parada, and by midnight they stopped because their mules were exhausted.

270 Chapter Seven

Bad Lands, Very Bad Lands

For the next few days, water was scarce. Choosing camp sites at the end of long days of travel depended on both accessibility to water and exhaustion, even if some places had no water. According to Loomis and Nasatir, the expedition had just crossed the "Jornada del Muerte."[117] On September 30, Amangual made a note after his daily summary of travel. He described the area as "bad country (*el mal país*)," running from north to south between two mountain ranges, the Oscura and the Blanca. The land appeared to be formed through its entire length by volcanos and was impassable except for trails made by the Indians. The rocks were melted by fire, and Amangual compared them to an iron mine. As if that were not daunting enough, he indicated that the trail by which his men traveled had horrible precipices on both sides and at every step.[118] When the terrain improved, the party remained circumspect about enemy movements, and that included their guides spying on some of the *rancherías* in view. Then, on October 7, one of the most remarkable episodes of escape and survival occurred while the expedition headed toward San Elizario. Described in detail by Amangual but clearly abbreviated, it involved not a soldier or an Indian guide but, instead, a child.

In the late evening, while the company was still on horseback, a boy of ten or eleven years old came out from a thicket where, apparently, he had been hiding. Amangual identified the child as one kidnapped by the Apache in Sevilleta on September 4. The boy told the company that he had run away from his captors five days before when they were rounding up horses to relocate their *ranchería*. Somehow the unfortunate boy miraculously escaped from the multitude of Indians. And, sadly, his body bore the most evident proof of the cruelty of the Apache, identified by Amangual as "savages" who mercilessly and without regard for his tender age beat the boy constantly.[119] His name was Juan Cristóbal "Padia."[120] Remarkably, throughout his five days in hiding he lived on nothing but *piñones* that he had gathered before emerging from woods in the Sierra de Nuestra Señora de la Luz.[121] This is the only information that Amangual provides concerning the child. He will write nothing more about the discovery of the boy nor provide any other information except for what amounts to a footnote ten days later.

Turning aside from an otherwise poignant narrative, Amangual goes on to describe reuniting with the reconnaissance party that had left the day before. They found fresh trails by suspected Yndios, triggering detachments in pursuit and further travel by the main contingent of the expedition. What followed was dearly welcomed downtime awaiting the return of various

Change of Command and the 1808 Expedition 271

units. Scarcity of water was still very much a concern.[122] On the morning of October 13, 1808, Amangual concluded that the Indians ahead of the troops were part of those that had committed the robbery—and kidnapping of the Padilla boy—at Sevilleta. He ordered eighty-nine men to select the best horses and leave the rest with the expedition under the command of the lieutenant; the search team was to follow the river to join the main train under the command of Capt. of Militia José Agabo de Ayala.[123] On October 14, the expedition caught up with the fleeing Indians running on foot up the highest part of the Sierra de las Pitacas[124] while driving their families and horses before them. Amangual ordered his men to dismount, and he and the troops went up the hill where the Indians were now out of sight. They pursued them as far as they could, but the Native warriors, lying in wait behind rocks, sent a shower of bullets and arrows upon the men. In the melee, a successful getaway (by outpacing Amangual's pursuit) played in the Indians' favor since they simply threw rocks down upon the soldiers from the hill's summit. Given the expedition team's unfamiliarity with the terrain, they were at considerable disadvantage, and after three hours of engagement, Amangual ordered a retreat. One soldier from the Nuevo León unit lay dead with six others wounded, including two veterans.[125]

Although the moans and cries of the Yndios were certain indications to Amangual and his men that many of their number had perished in the attack, Amangual could give no exact count of their losses. At one o'clock in the afternoon, the team retired in "good order," and having attended to the wounded and watered their horses, Amangual held a review of arms and ammunition. He found that a gun, lance, ammunition and cartridge belt, and a box of cartridges were missing; these belonged to the deceased soldier, Vicente "Hustaita."[126] Four lances belonging to wounded militiamen, two lances belonging to the veterans, and two guns belonging to José Benegas and Antonio Nañes, both also wounded, were missing.[127] By three o'clock in the afternoon, the expedition set out again and shortly thereafter made a dry camp.

Only two days after the battle on the hill, they encountered troops under the command of Lt. José [Arvio?] from the garrison of Santa Fé.[128] At two o'clock in the afternoon the expedition arrived at "Brasito"[129] where they were joined by the detachment that had gone out on campaign under the command of Cpt. of Militia Cayetano Quintero.[130]

Their stay in Brazito was unremarkable except for one event, outwardly insignificant since it appears almost as an afterthought in the diary: the boy Juan Cristóbal who had escaped the Apache and survived alone in the elements was returned to his father.[131] The next day, the expedition found the herd belonging to the company of San Elizario.[132] Amangual decided to leave there the horse herd of over six hundred animals with a guard of forty men under one officer. He continued traveling with only the loaded mule team and got as far as Paraje de las Boregas, where the company stopped to camp. Just before noon the next day, the expedition passed through El Paso and came to the edge of its fields. Finally, at 3:30 p.m. the Amangual expedition reached the Presidio of San "Elzeario" where the troops accessed their respective garrisons. However, Amangual had to arrange other accommodations for one of his men, an individual perhaps too long on horseback and fed up with the entire journey. The captain made this notation: "I arrested a soldier of the company of Nuevo Reyno de León, named Nepomuceno Martínez, for insubordination in service and for having drawn a short sword (*"belduque"*) which hit the cartridge belt of the *carabinero* Vicente Cabrera of the Béxar Company while under his orders."[133]

Insofar as the long journey had resulted in the loss of life of one soldier and the wounding of several others during a skirmish with Native people, and though the troops had, in the middle of nowhere, come upon a stray child physically marked with the signs of both cruelty and resilience, some expeditioners upon arrival at a safe place crumbled emotionally after having ridden out episodes of high drama and even death. There is no denying that tensions among Amangual's various subordinates had reached a level of volatility that, even after finding sanctuary following such an arduous experience and surrounded by men of their own kind, none of it was enough to mitigate the psychological toll extracted from a journey coming to its finale.

From San Elesario to the Capital of Béxar:
November 8 to December 23, 1808

Two weeks passed before Amangual, a sixty-nine-year-old soldier surely just as worn out as his younger counterparts, if not more so, took up his pen to continue the narrative of the expedition diary. This time, Amangual and his men set out with two Apache guides, perhaps Lipan, and headed southeast. That the Apache could be beneficial and not solely adversarial was indisputable as that deep-rooted inconsistency emerged even now. They crossed the Río del Norte at noon and camped at a watering place called San Antonio, remaining there the entire next day because troops had stopped to wait for mail coming from Chihuahua.[134] From the presidio at Elizario to the banks of the Pecos River the team traveled seventy-three leagues, a distance that took its toll on several horses and mules in the

Change of Command and the 1808 Expedition 273

form of exhaustion and even death. Throughout these two weeks, Captain Amangual records the availability of watering holes and the necessity of rest periods for the animals. But those intervals do not appear as regularly in his diary as do their being overcome by fatigue.[135] A militiaman of the company of Nuevo León fell off his horse, causing his musket to break. Whether his horse was suffering from extreme exhaustion or became frightened and thus threw the rider is not known. On this same day, however, Amangual documented the debilitation of twelve horses.[136]

When on November 29 Amangual and his party spotted three Yndios fleeing on horseback on the opposite side of the Pecos River, he sent out a reconnaissance team that reported finding a *ranchería* abandoned but with eight fires still burning. Later that evening, three of their number appeared at the expedition camp site and indicated that they were Comanche, followers of Cordero, on campaign against the Apache. Further, they promised to provide guides who would take them to their leader's village. They made good on their word the next day.[137]

By the first week of December, two mules from the Béxar company and two horses belonging to Compañía de Nuevo León died on the trail; during the two days prior to their deaths, the animals had traveled only five leagues and had rested the entire day before. The cumulative effects of the journey extracted a mighty cost from the animals since rest and refreshment were insufficient, as further proof will emerge. After the death of the four equines, the expedition remained in camp from December 5–6, 1808. So as not to lose them on the road, the company traded twenty-one of the most worn-out horses for four mules and four horses left in the care of Captain Cordero. Fortunately, at least for the animals, December 8 was rainy all day and so the expedition stayed in camp.[138]

For the remainder of Amangual's narrative, the entries are attenuated, as though he had decided with the journey's end in sight to provide only the most essential information for his superiors. The expedition reached the headwaters of the Río Verde, the creek of Nuestra Senora de Loreto, and the abandoned presidio of San Sabá. One week away from home, Amangual wrote that the poor, run-down, worn-out animals in the care of one sergeant and twelve men would travel in slow stages. He noted this procedure continued until they reached Béxar.

If the return trip did not physically exhaust to the point of death the expedition team, it must have at least broken the spirit of two more soldiers. Juan Govea of the First Company of Nuevo Santander was under arrest, charged with insubordination and aggression toward Cpl. Francisco de León.[139] Two days later Pvt. Faustino López of the Colonia company, too, met the same fate as Govea and was jailed for the same reason: breaking rank by intimidating with weapons the same object of abuse, the tormented Corporal de León. Since the other troops managed to hold it together long enough to get back home, the rest of the week is on record as uneventful except for one extremely sick horse finally breaking down. On December 23, 1808, at eleven o'clock in the morning the Amangual expedition, undoubtedly frayed to the point of unraveling, arrived at the presidio of San Antonio de Béxar "without further incident."[140]

Conclusion

The expedition to Santa Fé was the culmination of the military career of Francisco Amangual. The documentary record shows his relinquishment of certain duties tied to his administrative obligations just prior to his departure, like his transferring the management of the Béxar military hospital to Mariano Varela,[1] his being relieved as major of the Viceregal Militia Corps,[2] and the transfer of command of the *compañía volante* of San Carlos de Parras to José Antonio Aguilar.[3] All of these matters directly preceded his leadership of a team of soldiers, indigenous guides, a chaplain, and other personnel from the Béxar presidio to that of Santa Fé on March 30, 1808. Only two years after his return, Amangual's efforts did not amount to much. By the following year Comanche relations with the New Mexican military appeared to be one of sharing information about outsider threats including arrests of American invaders. A campaign against the Apache involved Comanche–Spaniard alliances, but by 1810 Comanches resumed raiding in Texas.[4]

For enlistees, life in the military was essentially undesirable, neither lucrative nor prestigious, until higher rank was achieved, for a wide array of reasons. But for some, enlistment anywhere in the viceroyalty equated to an income—of sorts—and for others, it provided an opportunity to ascend yet another rung on the rickety, colonial ladder of hierarchy. Answering the call to service in the treacherous, low pay borderlands equated to perpetual turns on an axis of both harrowing conflict and stifling workaday routine.

During the era covered by this study, challenges to life and limb retained some of the same force as in decades, and even centuries, prior. Spanish policy in the service of empire and across its frontier outposts utilized to wavering effect benign, but calculated, maneuverings like peace by purchase, accomplished through incessant gift-giving to the indigenous nations. In the same vein, royal administrators and operatives on the ground recognized the weakness of colonial instruments of control by their own acknowledgment of Native powerbrokers working within the domain of contested geopolitical spaces. Those regions included the Apachería, Comanchería, and other strongholds of Native communities. Outright failures

276 Conclusion

by and repositioning of missions and presidios to constrain indigenous polities and a determined resistance to those efforts by its targets made even centralizing command formidable as the *Provincias Internas* were cohered, split, and reconfigured many times. In the end, the Provincias outlasted the perpetually dismantled Comandancia. Permanent peace proved to be illusory in a place where dominion was at best imaginary. What seemed inevitable and, indeed, predictable was that soldiers usually came out on the worst side of a wholly lopsided deal.

Attacks by the Ndé and Nímᵾnᵾᵾ on each other, on Spanish soldiers, presidial horse herds, and cattle ensured that complete trust between polities remained hit or miss even when troops found redress from some of the difficulties associated with presidial life in New Spain's Septentrión. Even then, such modes of existence did manage to harden some men in other, less productive ways. As this study shows, soldiers devoid of a moral compass or made desperate by conditions out of their control reverted to outlawed behavior. Higher up the chain of command, men of some military stature fell under the sway of illegal activity, desertion, and addictions like alcoholism. Carving out a career, much less mere existence, through life in the militarized hinterlands was clearly difficult for many, even with the communal sense of duty anticipated by congregate living inside garrison walls or around its precincts. In an environment fraught with extreme danger, some troops succumbed to temptation given their relatively unfettered access to valued commodities like tobacco, cloth, hides, and paper. To recompense their guilt, some men attempted in other ways to fulfill their obligations to cross and crown. Armed with nothing but their troubled souls, they simply soldiered on, seemingly unmoved by their offenses.

A survey of the historiographical landscape and even a glancing review of the archival record makes it possible to identify multiple hardships endured by soldiers out on the open range or stationed at an adobe and wood fort. Like others in Spain's colonial army, Francisco Amangual faced elevated debt due to corrupt practices by paymasters, poor governance, scarce resources, and a decrease in assistance given the eternally skimpy and shoddy supply of provisions available. Privations in many areas of the army aggravated the lives of all soldiers, irrespective of their unit designation or attachment to specific companies. Compounding these realities, ascension in the ranks in the *frontera* offered no quick remedy to perennially harsh conditions. Amangual's military service record testifies to his enduring across thirty years hazardous, even potentially deadly, encounters in the field as he chased, apprehended, and killed enemies of the Spanish state in forays across the Comandancia General.

Conclusion 277

Identifying Francisco Amangual's position within presidial society and charting his career from among a host of other better-known names across the historical landscape of the Spanish colonial twilight era served two purposes. First, highlighting the everyday tasks and consequences of administrative procedures in the presidio setting, however mundane and unglamorous, allows for projecting onto the stage of borderlands history one soldier's role as an unapologetic navigator of the region's exceptional challenges. Since he worked for some time as his company's paymaster, substantive documentation by him and others in his orbit survives to reveal the career trajectories and core responsibilities of staffers at several garrisons and the immediate environs. Second, routine activities constituted the bulk of the chores carried out by presidio paymasters and thus deflect any notions of frontier life as a kind of peripheral theater for endless war enacted via heroic feats of daring by men on horseback, or, as a socio-politically-charged space wholly engulfed by gunshots, wild horse rides in the night, and bloody confrontations with obstinate Native populations. It is true that these conditions indeed existed across large swaths of the Comandancia and that the army's relationship with *lo indígena* fills the annals of regional history with source materials frequently marked by a paradoxical tenor. There can be no mistaking that such electrifying events permeated the borderlands and were even advanced by multiple factions for reasons chiefly related to survival, economic gain, and control of resources. Many involved the active participation of Native enlistees, acknowledged in black ink by commanders as reliable and effective, supporting the martial efforts of the presidials. Some have emerged in this book.

Further, this study shows that the testimonials provided by Amangual and his cohorts and found within the historical record put new focus on the overarching administrative functions fulfilled by the paymaster and others in the noticeably lettered frontier. The narrative herein may help orient scholars toward the significance of the empire's intermediaries documenting the more mundane activities of life in the presidio. In tandem with bookkeeping, inventorying supplies, generating and receiving mail, recording daily occurrences and producing monthly summaries, "official" reports (generated by those with the power and standing to do so) added to this compelling body of literature. Colonial instruments for regulating militarized zones extended to the management of the king's armies working in that massive space and reflected the system-wide policy of standardization implemented by post-inspection *reglamentos* detailed in this book. Communications between viceregal administrators and commanders on the ground undergirded the statutes of 1719 (Havana), 1729,

Conclusion

1772, and the Instruction of 1786, the latter two approximately coeval with New Spain's creation of the Ordinance of Intendants and the segregation of the Comandancia General. Though the borderlands troops were governed by discrete laws curated just for them, many of their number (including the illiterate) were certainly aware of the contentious *fuero militar* and its benefits to their counterparts in other regions of the empire. All these policies, brought to bear as they were in an effort to recast the aging and essentially obsolete Laws of the Indies, underscored the king's determination to centralize management of Spain's overseas colonies. Since that involved a cascade of paperwork that in turn generated copies intended for mass distribution, documentation of the period helps us assess the ways in which streams of official mandates circumambulated the Far North to achieve, more or less, a singular, cohesive effect: order and discipline across the armed forces.

To that end, declarations within the 1786 Gálvez *Instrucción* to Ugarte, Ugalde, and others, are unambiguous but nothing novel. Article 91 forewarned commanders to immediately eliminate unfit men from presidial companies, including the compañías *volantes* among others, and replace them with those more suitable for armed conflict. In fact, two articles within Rivera's 1720s *tercer estado* even questioned the appropriateness of the name "*volante*" to describe the actual and ongoing duties of this unit of the borderlands' army and how the term at the outset devolved upon the group. The nomenclature of that time implied that its troop members were to wander incessantly across the frontier since they secured no precise physical locale in which to permanently garrison. Corrective action there usually involved transfer elsewhere.

Across the decades, the terminology associated with nonstop movement on horseback demanded closer scrutiny. How else to achieve a more thoroughgoing understanding of the flying squadrons than by disentangling their place from among the various presidial units in the colonial borderlands. Working with original sources, this type of inquiry into the historiography in some ways perhaps reverses the trend of imagining the *volantes* as a spirited patrol force or even as a peripatetic, ever-at-the-ready cavalry against hostile enemies of the Comandancia. In the early decades of the nineteenth century, they may well have fulfilled that function; however, during the period covered in this study I argued that the *volantes* as a unit were a rather mixed lot, and their effectiveness as first responders in some localities across the frontier was seriously questioned by Pedro de Rivera and his team of inspectors. Seeing for himself how the *volantes* comported themselves in the field, if they ever appeared there, a resolute Rivera advised retraining, censure, and outright dissolution to establish orthodoxy

Conclusion 279

among this specialized cavalry. From a temporal and spatial perspective, what commanders could count on for success in combat were tactics that prioritized situational strategizing of the troops who had taken training to heart.

Administrative performance with money matters also proved to be a target for suspicion and denunciation. For well over a year, Amangual weathered accusations by presidio contractors including the merchant José Macario Zambrano regarding the supply of corn to the soldiers as well as a complaint filed in 1788 by Joaquín Menchaca against Amangual. No documentation emerges as of the publication of this book specifying the circumstances surrounding the conflict between the latter two men. What the event does demonstrate is that Amangual was quite capable of committing an oversight that required correction so that it might serve as a guide in the future to both him and his company. However, Menchaca's unknown grievances were not so severe as to hinder Francisco Amangual's successful election in 1788 to the post of *habilitado*. Four years later, the son-in-law of Zambrano, Sgt. Mariano Rodríguez, would make accusations against Amangual a family affair by launching one of his own that triggered a forty-three-page slander suit. As if these contentious episodes in his military career and in his duties as his company's fiduciary were not enough to cause anxiety, Amangual had an obligation to ensure the strict maintenance of the general accounts of debits and credits with the greatest clarity and justification. This was necessary in order for his records to be examined and approved by his superiors, including the *comandante inspector*, at each year's end. His was a kind of accountability subject to long hard looks from everywhere across the military, ecclesiastical, and civilian spheres.

Distressing circumstances with many moving parts surfaced over and over: as soon as one charge of wrongdoing terminated, always in Amangual's favor, another one emerged just as quickly. In May 1792, Amangual had to, once again, answer for his recordkeeping based on suspicions from on high. When the Royal Tribunal of Accounts in Mexico questioned his balances against the *habilitación* fund of the presidial company of San Antonio de Béxar, Amangual responded with fortitude and precision. Such a daunting notice coming from a colonial administrative authority in the capital must have shaken the confidence of the paymaster, since the tribunal sought a review and examination of the accounts of expenditures for gifts for multiple Indigenous beneficiaries covering a period of almost four years. Bookkeeping was routine for Amangual, and it is evident from the mass of documentation generated by the Béxar *habilitado* that clear-headedness prevailed, and the case was closed.

Conclusion

Then, just two months later, in an ironic twist Amangual found himself as the caretaker and inspector of more contraband (allegedly in the possession of another fellow soldier, the usually circumspect Juan Cortés) that was now to be housed in his *habilitación*. Amangual was called on once more to inventory goods brought from Nacogdoches to San Antonio. In the context of valuing both its troop strength and the talent of individual soldiers, upholding military objectives is dispositive of the stock his superiors placed in the work ethic of Francisco Amangual. Despite at least two episodes of allegations of wrongdoing as company paymaster, Amangual's services as an accountant, and especially his talent at handling laborious inventories, were still needed. His ability to testify in legal proceedings of a serious nature including a case for a defendant charged with murder speaks to his status as a trustworthy member of the presidial population. And his ongoing engagement with the more menial tasks associated with the work of a frontier soldier continued unabated. The day-to-day practices of a presidial company's paymaster were invariably suspect; across the decades there had been many unprincipled individuals trafficking in fraud when provisioning the troops. Whether elected by fellow soldiers or simply implicit in a presidio captain's responsibilities, the bookkeeper faced enormous challenges in his duties as the caretaker of garrison funds.

Confronting intermittent complaints of malpractice during his career, Amanual never met with even temporary removal from service as a presidial company financial administrator and soldier. His various commanders could very well have authorized that humiliating finale or even forced retirement especially after this most recent embarrassment of slander and self-defense. Moreover, though he complained that Sgt. Mariano Rodríguez's accusations had been "so degrading" to his honor and work, there is no evidence that presidio insiders looked on him as any less the professional he had proven himself to be, time and again, over the course of his service. Amangual's expertise continued to be highly esteemed, assuring his reputation remained unblemished even as he slogged through the tiresome slander suit proceedings and its aftermath. For their part, Manuel Muñoz, who oversaw the Amangual-Rodríguez litigation, and men like Elguézabal and Martínez Pacheco, carried on with the usual obligations of governors and garrison captains. Amangual served without interruption throughout each of these administrations.

The Cortés contraband proceedings and the Amangual–Rodríguez lawsuit represented the commingling of presidio soldiers and merchants in troublesome episodes of misadventure, charges and countercharges, and dishonorable behavior with serious implications for the Béxar garrison. Unrelenting incidents of contraband discovery and its confiscation had a

Conclusion 281

long history in the colonial borderlands. So too did occurrences of soldiers accusing one another of misdeeds, or the suspicion thereof, and friction would continue over time and involve other players from the same socioeconomic arena. Amid this flurry of dereliction in places like San Antonio and its garrison, like that at La Bahía, present-day Goliad, and into Nacogdoches in eastern Texas, civilian and Native communities entered and exited the army's garrisons. Into these complex networks of accommodation and accusation emerged a paradoxical dynamic that presumed compliance and cohesion through spatial relations within the orbit of the presidio. Once joined by reciprocal efforts aimed at self-preservation, the intent of those in command was to seal loyalties, if often permeable and uncertain, among presumed comrades. The business of maintaining rather shaky alliances was ongoing; formal treaties of peace were but one method of promoting adherence to prescribed modes of behavior in the professed best interests of all parties. As documented in black ink, the codification of ordinances and regulations was repurposed by indigenous negotiators, as well as their French, Anglo, and Spanish counterparts. Other endeavors involving the usual actors required as much diligence and, therefore, as much if not more substantiation. Archival records establish the king's beneficence to the soldiers across the great reach of the Comandancia and provide a window into the patriarchal, if not always perceptive, approaches that some commanders and their viceroys took toward their subordinates on the ground.

However insignificant to contemporary observers the rewards for good conduct and productive service to the Crown may seem and given the unique challenges of life in the borderlands, certain forms of fiscal and psychological remuneration were valued—payment in specie, commendable evaluations inscribed in *hojas de servicio*, appropriate and usable weaponry and supplies—by cliques within certain companies and among individual troops in the final decade of the century. For colonial administrators, this meant conceiving the most expeditious manner of bringing about upgrades that would not disrupt the delicate balance of maintaining the royal treasury. At the same time, their challenge was to avoid shortchanging competent soldiers, further antagonizing often dispirited civilians, and to allay the rightfully hostile inclinations of Native polities. Chronic adjustments to military protocol as mandated by royal ordinances and viceregal pronouncements were symptomatic of the unending grind of bringing organization to and procedurally aligning with the larger apparatus of increasingly faltering colonial rule. That meant controlling the behavior of the personnel that literally and metaphysically embodied such a burdensome superstructure. In the persons of Francisco Amangual and other presidials, much of that process found expression on the ground by work in warfare and in administration, thus legitimizing in some sense their internalization of allegiance to the empire.

The foregoing developments in this study revealed the fissures inherent in state building. Some vulnerabilities existed before obvious ruptures were exposed by paymaster misbehavior, presidial bankruptcy, (re)orderings of the military ranking system, and confronting the reality of illegal trade in commercial ventures and persistent guerrilla warfare with Native combatants. Unflagging episodes of soldier waywardness might not seem so surprising in the context of the twilight of the Spanish colonial substructure. Habitual transgressions on the part of the king's troops in the borderlands have formed a part of the historical trajectory of the Spanish army in its overseas dominions. In the closing years of the eighteenth century, ongoing attempts at reform included, at times, forcing conformity within the ranks of the military which did nothing more than maintain an ambivalence between the commander and the commanded. This resulted in a type of uneasy alliance of a society ostensibly bound by the attributes of honor, respect for authority, and restraint. But even as late as 1804 one well-intentioned cadet writing from his desk offered up a plan to reform the Commandancy's forces by addressing the deterioration of the troops. His efforts came to nothing. In that same year, the few cannons available for use in Texas and Coahuila were in the same poor condition. No others could be supplied, and no artillerymen existed anyway to train soldiers in their use.

And so went the daily grind of soldiering on.

As matters stood, the promulgation of *reglamentos* was functional only to the extent of borderlands commanders' willingness to enforce their content and their subordinates' compliance with those mandates. In the first years of the new century, events on the Peninsula induced other transformations of a type that would eventually ignite the call for independence across the Atlantic in regional spaces throughout México. In certain ways, life in the borderlands went on, too, in much the same way as it had over the course of many centuries, even though the colonial apparatus that had structured the lives of frontier inhabitants started its inevitable decline.

Epilogue

The historical record tells us that, following the 1808 expedition to Santa Fé, Francisco Amangual received permission to marry María Trinidad de Los Reyes y García in 1810. In the month before he left to lead the expedition, he wrote to the governor of Texas indicating that since December 1805, he had resided in a dilapidated one-room *jacal* (thatched, adobe hut) situated on the outer walls of "Valero" and that the unit was the property of the king. In fact, his own home was occupied as a military hospital. From Amangual's writings, we learn that the shack consisted of one room of eight *varas* and a porch; both buildings were used as a kitchen, the land was fifteen *varas* deep, not counting a narrow strip of public land adjoining the formation. Amangual's shack and porch, formerly occupied by an Indian woman named "Dolores," was one of those still standing when the mission was demolished.[1]

Amangual had personally done work on the unit and expended a large sum to repair the shack. Considering the expenses that he incurred and realizing that if he left the shack for any assignment—for example, the impending trip to Santa Fé—no purchaser would be able to afford to reimburse him for the expense. The main thrust of Amangual's letter was to request that the governor sell him the land and the shack (but, perhaps, not the porch) after its appraisal so that from its gross value a deduction could be made for the expenses incurred by Amangual. The captain made the renovations so he might provide a suitable home for himself and his baby girl.[2]

In his last will and testament of April 15, 1812, Francisco Amangual indicates that he owned a stone house in the capital that he used as a residence. He described it as having four rooms facing the street, on which the frontage was thirty-five *varas* in length with six rooms to the rear, running in depth to the river that flowed by the property.[3]

He stated that he provided well for the three children from his first wife, and he supported them until their deaths. Amangual added that his son, Cadet José María, received a soldier's salary but, nevertheless, Amangual paid for whatever he needed. When José left for Coahuila, his father completely equipped him with clothing, arms, munitions, and horses at a cost of 386 pesos. Later, Amangual sent his son forty-five pesos, none of which was ever returned to him after José's death because, as it is indicated in the father's will, his effects in total were sold to cover the shortage in his accounts for army equipment. The expenses for the funerals, burials, and associated costs for Amangual's first wife and his two daughters, María Antonia, and María Gertrudis, as well as prayers for the repose of José María amounted to 684 pesos. The son died owing 768 pesos, a debt that the father assumed.[4]

At the time of the writing of the will, Amangual had not paid off his son's debt, but he did provide in his testament funds for the remainder of the balance. On May 19, 1812, at 9:30 p.m. Francisco Amangual died, and his will and codicil unsealed the following day. He was buried in the Béxar Campo Santo on May 21, 1812.[5]

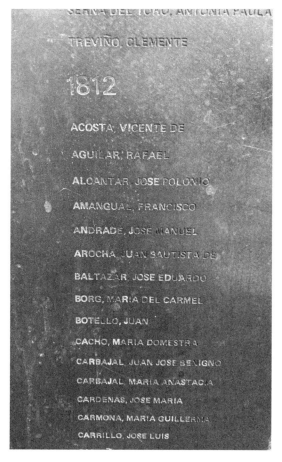

Plaque 1-3, column 2, line 7, Burial #437, May 21, 1812, commemorating original burial site of Francisco Amangual, Campo Santo (defunct), San Antonio, Texas. Photo by author (July 15, 2023).

Appendix 1

[...] seventeen documents [regarding] distribution of gifts to Indians, BA August 14, 1790 ["No.6, San Antonio de Béxar, January 13, 1792," signed Fran(cis)co Amangual].
Thus, he supplied

- 1 bolt of blue cloth in 37 ½ varas

- 6 pieces of *rayadillo*, because *bayeta* could not be found in these same stores

- 20 narrow pieces of *manta de Puebla*

- 36 pairs of calfskin shoes for men

- 12 hats [style not specified]

- 75 *varas* of rope strands, which Xabier [sic] Galán sold

- 2 grosses of similar buttons

- 3 rolls of blue *pita* [fiber thread] "that they call 'girl's' [thread]"

- 2 *conga* blankets

- 5 loads of burlap [*guancoche*] bags in which the goods are wrapped

- 7 lassos

Appendix 2

Slander suit, BA February 29, 1792 (Inventory of the paymaster's office, March 17).

- Thirteen short coats, incorporating cloth from Querétaro, 42 pesos

- One blue uniform coat, 7 pesos

- Thirteen ounces of blue twisted agave thread, 1 real 5 granos

- Seventeen blank notebooks [*libretas*] for the soldiers, 5 pesos, 2 reales, 6 granos

- Fourteen plain leather shields, 24 pesos, 4 reales

- Two bridles, 3 pesos, 4 reales

- Eight pairs of saddle irons, 12 pesos

- Six pairs of spurs, 9 pesos

- Thirty-seven cordons for sabers, 12 pesos, 2 reales, 8 granos

- Thirty-three sword scabbards, 41 pesos, 2 reales

- Seven [sets of] saddle trappings, consisting of saddle covering, saddlebag, skirts [*armas*], skirt holders, rear housing [*anquera*], and lariats, 49 pesos, 3 reales, 6 granos

- Twelve separate *anqueras*, 7 pesos, 4 reales

- Three saddle covers [*corazas*], 9 pesos

- Two pairs of saddlebags, 4 pesos, 7 reales, four granos

288 Appendix 2

- Eleven sets of cowhide stirrup leathers (strings?)/saddle trees (?) [*juegos de arciones*/arzón (?)[1]], 2 pesos, 6 reales

- Thirty-six rawhide harnesses equipped with their corresponding cinches, twenty-four headstalls, and twenty-four packsaddle covers, 220 pesos, 2 reales

- Eighteen muskets, 208 pesos, 1 real

- Thirteen and a half pairs of pistols, 156 pesos, 6 granos

- One lance blade, 1 peso, 6 reales

---

1. Arción is defined as: "arción (vulgarismo por acion). Tira de cuero de la que pende el estribo." See Leovigildo Islas Escarcega and Rodolfo Garcia Bravo y Olivera, *Diccionario y refranero charro, el caballo de raza Azteca en la charrería* (México, D.F.: Editores Asociados Mexicanos, S.A. de C.V., 1992), p. 29. One other valuable resource devoted to charrería and its associated terminology similarly defined the word as "Estribera. Nombre que los charros y jinetes del campo dan a la ación. Las arciones de la silla charra son anchas y algo gruesas; Las que llevan sudaderas son mas anchas en su parte inferior, junto al estribo." José I. Lepe, *Diccionario enciclopédico sobre asuntos ecuestres e hípicos* (México, D.F.: Editorial Porrua, S.A., 1972/1951), p. 31.

Appendix 3

Correspondence between Castro and Sierra Gorda, concerning case against Juan Cortés, BA July 14, 1792 [– September 9, 1792] (Amangual's inventory, June 18, 1792).

In the baggage of the aforesaid captain [Juan Cortés]

15 ½ varas of royal

7 varas of yellow silk lusurina [sic/lustrina, silk cloth possibly woven from alpaca hair]

10 1/3 varas of scarlet polonesa [polonaise]

7 cut [pieces] of silk armadores [possibly lining for sleeveless leather vests, or, cueras][1]

7 fine cotton kerchiefs

2 pairs of finished skirts, one of indiana and the other of angaripola [calico]

2 bolts of wool sashes

10 card decks

9 glass cups

4 tin pots

6 large axes

4 dozen large buttons de asa

5 [pounds], 5 [ounces] of coffee

2 medium pots with three feet

80 [pounds] of French tobacco in bundles and pieces

---

1. The brackets of this and the two previous entries in the inventory are my insertions; all other bracketing henceforth is as it is found in the original punctuation of Béxar Archives translators.

Corporal Ylario Maldonado and Private Joaq(uí)n [sic] Galán

7 ½ varas of blue lusurina [sic]

7 ½ same...same scarlet

7 fine cotton kerchiefs

1 same of chambray

5 1/3 varas of fine Indiana

6 same of scarlet polonesa

5 pairs of new indianilla skirts

1 silk armador

4 card decks

1 ordinary cloth

2 French blankets

6 medium iron pots with three feet

Private Antonio Gómez

5 varas of fine Indiana

2 kerchiefs...same

1 medium pot with three feet

[MS torn] of French tobacco

Sergeant Anttonio [sic] Treviño

11 varas of guinea

5 knives

7 ¾ varas of purple silk cloth

4 cut [pieces] of silk armadores

1 [pound] of thread de numeros

2 glass cups

13 2/3 varas of wide scarlet ribbon

1 tin pot

Appendix 3

3 dozen white buttons de asa

2 pairs of finished Indiana skirts

1 pot with 3 feet, and 3 [pounds], 2 [ounces] of French tobacco belonging to his servant Mig[ue]l Saravia

Privates Fran[cis]co Vázq[ue]z and Xpbal. Yguera

1 pair of finished skirts

3 fine cotton kerchiefs

2 card decks

Private José Trejo

6 [pounds], 13 ½ [ounces] of French tobacco

2 pots

Privates Antt[oni]o del Río and Pedro Grande

9 fine cotton kerchiefs

1 ½ varas of blue 2nd cloth

5 varas of guinea

7 ¾ varas of blue lusurina

3 ½ varas of Indiana

1 pair of skirts made from polonesa

4 white threads, garnet-colored [de granattes]

2 varas of scarlet cloth ribbon

Private Juan José de la Garza

4 varas of fine Indiana

1 fine cotton kerchief

4 threads, garnet-colored [de granattes]

Appendix 4

Case against Toribio Durán for contraband trade, BA Oct 19, 1792.

- 2 1/3 varas of blue limbriz cloth
- 4 varas of blue Guinea [cloth]
- 1 woman's jacket, finished and stained
- 6 ceramic dishes for coffee
- 1 pot of the same [material]
- 4 sealed letters
- 2 enameled metal boxes for powders
- 4 pounds of blue and white beads
- 86 chamois [skins]
- 21 deerskins
- 1 medium axe
- 9 ounces of coffee

Notes

Introduction

1. The Parras *volantes* were created in Coahuila in 1781 but were then based at Presidio La Bahía and other locations, including Presidio San Antonio de Béxar. From July to November 1782 the formation met with fits and starts because of paperwork related to the coincident creation of a Saltillo-based flying squadron. See "Expediente sobre la formación de las compañías volantes de Parras y del Saltillo y solicitud de despachos para sus oficiales," AGI, Guadalajara, 519, N.24. Some confusion persists as to the precise chronological origin of the emergence of the *compañías volantes*, which I discuss below. However, the first mention of a type of "roving company" — not necessarily intended to signify a flying squadron — in the secondary sources for the Spanish colonial borderlands appears in Moorhead's discussion of the origins and early development of the presidio. Moorhead elaborates only on the function of the unit, described as "a single company — a captain with thirty troops," that was but a remnant of the drastic reduction of the number of garrisons serving as strategic outposts for military personnel. The roving company could not seek out and destroy the indigenous nations comprising the *Gran Chichimeca*, since for several reasons that would have been improbable, but instead worked to attract them to peace by offering them material assistance. Max Moorhead, *The Presidio: Bastion of the Spanish Borderlands* (Norman: University of Oklahoma Press, 1975), pp. 13, 22. A process of pacification long in use would continue to form, however unworkable, the ideological substrate of controlling resistant Native populations for the next three hundred years. On the presence of the *compañías volantes* and their general function within the frontier military hierarchy, see also Robert S. Weddle, *San Juan Bautista: Gateway to Spanish Texas* (Austin: University of Texas Press, 1968); María del Carmen Velázquez, *La frontera norte y la experiencia colonial* (México, D.F.: Secretaría de Relaciones Exteriores, 1982); Regino F. Ramón, *Historia General del Estado de Coahuila* (Saltillo: Leonor Ramón de Garza, 1990); Fay Jackson Smith, *Captain of the Phantom Presidio: A History of the Presidio of Fronteras, Sonora, New Spain, 1686–1735* (Spokane: Arthur H. Clark, 1993); Andrés Tijerina, *Tejanos and Texans under the Mexican Flag, 1821–1836* (College Station: Texas A&M University Press, 1994); Diana Hadley, Thomas H. Naylor, and Mardith K. Schuetz-Miller, eds., *The Presidio and the Militia on the Northern Frontier of New Spain: A Documentary History*, vol. 2, part 2, *The Central Corridor and the Texas Corridor, 1700–1765* (Tucson: University of Arizona Press, 1997), hereafter Hadley, et al.; Charles W. Polzer and Thomas E. Sheridan, *The Northern Frontier of New Spain: A Documentary History*, vol. 2, part 1, *The Californias and Sinaloa–Sonora, 1700–1765* (Tucson: University of Arizona Press, 1997); Thomas Naylor and Charles W. Polzer, eds., *The Presidio and the Militia on the Northern Frontier of New Spain: A*

296   Notes to Pages 1–3

Documentary History, vol. 1: 1500–1700 (Tucson: University of Arizona Press, 1986); Thomas W. Knowles, *They Rode for the Lone Star: The Saga of the Texas Rangers* (Dallas: Taylor, 1999); Julio Albi, *La defensa de las Indias 1764–1799* (Madrid: Instituto de Cooperación Iberoamericana, 1987).

2. Spanish-language primary sources housed in repositories in the United States, Mexico, and Spain document not only the life and military career of Francisco Amangual and others in the borderlands but also demonstrate the *compañías'* investment in maintaining productive, if tenuous, relationships with the Comanche (*Nermernuh, Numinu, Нʉmʉnʉʉ, Numunʉʉ*), Apache (*Inde, Ndé, Ndee*), and other indigenous groups. At the same time, these sources reveal the squadrons' internal development, replete as it was with its members' often erratic adherence to military code, conflict resolution among various social groups, and accommodation to persistently hostile environmental conditions. Amangual's experiences in Native homelands figure most notably, if briefly, in several sources. See Tijerina (1994); Hunt Janin and Ursula Carlson, *Trails of Historic New Mexico: Routes Used by Indian, Spanish, and American Travelers through 1886* (Jefferson: McFarland, 2010). Amangual's career is outlined in Odie B. Faulk, *The Last Years of Spanish Texas, 1778–1821* (The Hague: Mouton, 1964), p. 44; in Carlos E. Castañeda, *Our Catholic Heritage in Texas, 1519–1936*, ed. Paul J. Foik, vol. 4 (Austin: Von Boeckmann–Jones, 1942); and in Thomas W. Kavanagh, *The Comanches: A History, 1706–1875* (Lincoln: University of Nebraska Press, 1996). See Noel M. Loomis and Abraham P. Nasatir's *Pedro Vial and the Roads to Santa Fé* (Norman: University of Oklahoma Press, 1967). The Loomis and Nasatir text is significant, chiefly for its translation of the original Amangual diary, written during the 1808 expedition to Santa Fé, and differs from the copy held at the Béxar Archives by small variations in the Spanish-to-English translation and in its brevity. Mattie Austin Hatcher, archivist at the Library of the University of Texas Department of Archives, translated the Béxar copy in 1934. Hatcher, "Francisco Amangual, *Diary of Operations and Events Occurring in the Expedition undertaken under Superior Orders from this Province of Texas to that of New Mexico by Captain Francisco Amangual, First Commandant, and Captain Don José Agabo de Ayala, Second Commandant beginning March 30, 1808*" (1808/1934), Center for American History, University of Texas at Austin (unpublished). For the original, see Francisco Amangual, *Diario de las novedades y operaciones ocurridas en la expedición que se hace desde esta provincia de Texas, a la del Nuevo México, de orden superior siendo Primer Comandante el Capitan Don Francisco Amangual, Segundo el Capitan Don José Agabo de Ayala, en 30 de Marzo de 1808.*

3. Spelling of the Spanish word for *paymaster* appears several ways. I use the various spellings as found in the primary sources and thus it manifests differently throughout this book. In all cases, the words mean the same thing.

4. *Reglamento e instrucción para los presidios que se han de formar en la linea de frontera de la nueva españa. Resuelto por el rey nuestro señor en cédula de 10 de septiembre de 1772, Título catorce, obligaciones y nombramiento del habilitado* [sic passim]; hereafter, *Reglamento 1772.*

5. Smith (1993), p. 13. For a summary of complaints against Tuñón y Quirós issued in 1718 by miners, farmers, and livestock breeders from the mining communities of Nacozari and "other places of defense," see Polzer and Sheridan (1997), pp. 277–301.

6. Donald Chipman and Luis López Elizondo, "New Light on Felipe de Rábago y Terán," *Southwestern Historical Quarterly* 111, no. 2 (Oct. 2007): 160–81; David Yetman, *Conflict in Colonial Sonora, Indians, Priests, and Settlers* (Albuquerque: University

Notes to Pages 3–5   297

of New Mexico Press, 2012): see especially chapter 1 for a discussion of Pedro de Perea and chapter 5 for the conflict between Father Guerrero and Captain Simón García in the mining town of Quimbunazorra. For a commander's rapport with his superior-ranking relative, see Félix D. Almaráz Jr., *Tragic Cavalier: Governor Manuel Salcedo of Texas, 1808–1813* (Austin: University of Texas Press, 1971). For insight into the ethnic composition of borderlands troops, individual soldier identity, and behavior toward and interactions with fellow administrators, see James M. Daniel and Pedro José de la Fuente, "Diary of Pedro José de la Fuente, Captain of the Presidio of El Paso del Norte, August–December, 1765," *Southwestern Historical Quarterly* 83, no. 3 (Jan. 1980): 259–78; for a lesser-known functionary who raised troubling concerns about troops and paymasters as late as 1804, see Jesús de la Teja, "Ramón de Murillo's Plan for the Reform of New Spain's Frontier Defenses," *Southwestern Historical Quarterly* 107, no. 4 (April 2004): 501–33; and for Morfi's description of another army hothead Colonel Carlos Benites Franquis de Lugo, see Fray Juan Agustín Morfi, *History of Texas 1673–1779*, trans. Carlos Eduardo Castañeda, vol. 2 (Albuquerque: The Quivira Society, 1935), pp. 285–86.

7. For summaries of the 1776 creation of the virtually autonomous Comandancia General, see among many, Moorhead (1968), pp. 64–86; (1975), pp. 75–94; Bobb (1962), pp. 143–52; Velásquez (1982), pp. 84–89; and Charles Cutter, *The Legal Culture of Northern New Spain, 1700 – 1810* (Albuquerque: University of New Mexico Press, 1995), pp. 54–63.

8. As it relates to Native polities, I use the term in the pages that follow just as the documentarists used it—in the broadest, general sense—as found in the original documentation.

9. As Kuethe and Andrien indicate, "Over the course of the eighteenth century, colonial officials also collected, summarized, and communicated large amounts of fiscal data more effectively than ever before. Although Crown treasury officials had compiled detailed accounts of income and expenditures throughout the Indies and from the sixteenth-century, accounts were assembled more consistently and became more detailed over the course of the eighteenth century, particularly with the application of double-entry bookkeeping in the 1780s. Reorganization of the fiscal bureaucracy in the Spanish Atlantic also allowed the Crown to understand and process fiscal data accumulated from the royal kingdoms more efficiently, leading to major increases in royal revenues. In the late eighteenth century, royal reports began summarizing large quantities of fiscal data in tables, which allowed royal officials to make sense out of the masses of financial information that previously might have been overlooked or lost." Allan J. Kuethe and Kenneth J. Andrien, *The Spanish Atlantic World in the Eighteenth Century: War, and the Bourbon Reforms, 1713–1796* (New York: Cambridge University Press, 2014), p. 9. However, Barbier notes that over the course of the central administration's Bourbon Reforms, the alterations made in 1787 and 1790 dispensed with some of Gálvez's innovations, including double-entry bookkeeping. In the post–Gálvez era, Barbier argues that there was a "continued drive for reform" that manifested in policy initiatives such as its economic components. In practice, the "Spanish government wished to secure the economic benefits of colonialism without having to confront an American insurrection." See Jacques A. Barbier, "The Culmination of the Bourbon Reforms, 1787–1792," *Hispanic American Historical Review* 57, no. 1 (Feb. 1977): 62.

10. Moorhead (1975, pp. 3–5, 7–11) argues the first presidios were established from the 1570s to 1600.

298   Notes to Pages 5–6

11. Moorhead (1975), pp. 20–23. A document by Antonio Bonilla (copy of a June 14, 1792, Nava to Revilla Gigedo nine-page, recto/verso letter), dated August 30, 1793, indicates the presidio of Purísima Concepción de la Monclova's establishment in 1685; San Juan de Bautista de Río Grande and San Bernardo (Sonora), both in 1687; Aguaverde (Santa Rosa del Sacramento) in 1736; Santa Cruz in 1742; San Agustín del "Tuquison" in 1753; San Antonio Bucareli de la Babia in 1773, subsequently relocated to the Valle de Santa Rosa in 1779; San Antonio de Béxar in 1718; and Bahía de Espíritu Santo in 1721. The earliest presidio, really nothing more than an outpost (Santa Gertrudis del Altar), was established in San Felipe to "defend the villa of Sinaloa" in 1596. See "Compañías Presidiales y Volantes. Provincias Internas" in Archivo General de Simancas (hereafter AGS), SGU, LEG, 7022, 16, images recto 5/9, verso 5/10, recto 6/11. For a monograph on Janos, see William B. Griffen, *Apaches at War and Peace: The Janos Presidio, 1750–1858* (Norman: University of Oklahoma Press, 1988).

12. "Don Augustin Herbante de Camino al Senor Maestre de Campo Don Joseph Francisco Marín, Parral 12 de septiembre de 1693." Since his identity is not specified by title or rank, we must infer that Camino was one of the twelve "most practical and experienced persons" of El Parral whose opinion Marín requested from the viceroy so that he might make his recommendations. See Charles Hackett, ed., *Historical Documents relating to Mexico, Nueva Vizcaya, and Approaches Thereto, to 1773*, Vol. I, II, III (Washington, DC: Carnegie Institution of Washington, 1923–37), pp. 72, 373–74. Hereafter, Hackett (various dates). See Naylor and Polzer (1986), p. 569. Precise territorial routes did eventually emerge in July 1777 in a lengthy missive from O'Connor to Croix. Donald C. Cutter, ed., *The Defenses of Northern New Spain: Hugo O'Conor's Report to Teodoro de Croix, July 22, 1777* (Dallas: Southern Methodist University Press, 1994), Articles 152–224, pp. 69–94.

13. Where the flying squadrons factored into actualizing a new military philosophy, Spanish policy makers saw units of "highly mobile mounted troops with the flexibility to respond quickly and efficiently" as vital to incidences of warfare. See Hadley (1997), pp. 3–4, 11–13; and Moorhead (1975), passim.

14. Five presidios had protected Nueva Vizcaya, but a royal order in 1751 called for their suppression and substituting a 76-man flying squadron and civilian settlements in their stead. Rotating presidial captains to stem their abuse of soldiers and price gouging of necessities constituted the reasons for closure and that of El Pasaje. (Hadley, 1997), pp. 141–52.

15. Moorhead (1975), pp. 22–24. A cursory examination of Hackett's (1926, pp. 71–82) section "Proposals for the defense and development of Nueva Vizcaya, 1693–1698" makes clear that the suggestion proposed to "Galve" has no identifiable source. But that proposal indeed spurred on Marín's inspection of the region and his seeking out the expertise of "the most practical and experienced" people in El Parral. The original collection of documents, *Testimonio de cartas y informes sobre los presidios del Reino de la Vizcaya escritas por […] el Maestre del Campo […] Francisco Marín*, is found in "Part III. 2. Documents relating to Nueva Vizcaya in the Seventeenth Century," and reproduced in both English and Spanish. Hackett (1926), pp. 364–409.

16. Hackett (1926), p. 446.

17. Moorhead (1975), pp. 23–25; for the detailed account, see Hackett (1926), pp. 384–408.

18. In his 1763 *informe*, Padre Ignacio Lizasoáin suggested that presidio-based soldiers could as a necessary means of enforcement act as flying squads, a strategy

beneficial to maintaining frequent communication for thwarting Apache attacks. See Polzer and Sheridan (1997), pp. 458, 473.

19. Hadley (1997, pp. 4–5) sought to disclose an array of attitudes expressed by the "major players" in the vast frontier, including "military officers, administrative officials, missionaries, large landowners, merchants, Spanish *vecinos*, and even indigenous peoples." The conversion of their disparate viewpoints into government policy "was as questionable as the implementation of any existing policy deemed inappropriate at the local level." Distance itself presented both opportunities and obstacles for communicators as documents followed a "temporal-spatial route" in circuitous journeys to deliver intelligence. See Sylvia Sellers-García, *Distance and Documents at the Spanish Empire's Periphery* (Stanford: Stanford University Press, 2014), p. 25.

20. For more on the putative changing character of the frontier, see Hackett (1926), passim, but especially pp. 391–99; Velázquez (1982), pp. 8–10; Eliga H. Gould, "Entangled Histories, Entangled Worlds: The English-Speaking Atlantic as a Spanish Periphery," *American Historical Review* 112, no. 3 (June 2007), passim; for the most comprehensive studies of soldier experience in urban settings, see Christon Archer, *The Army in Bourbon Mexico, 1760–1810* (Albuquerque: University of New Mexico Press, 1995), passim; and Juan Marchena Fernández, *La vida de guarnición en las ciudades americanas de la ilustración* (Sevilla: Ministerio de Defensa, 1992), passim.

21. Lafora recognized an apparent predominance of certain tribes in an August 30, 1771, map he created for the Rubí inspection. For example, he indicated in bold, enlarged text and across large swaths of his drawing territory marked as "Tierra de Los Cumanches," "La Papagueria," and "Provincia de Los Tejas," [sic passim]. Reproduced for Lafora and Kinnaird (1958), insert. In the third part of his "Views," Cortés described the "Naciones que en el Norte de la America Espanola" that constituted the groups most readily encountered by the Comandancia's soldiers. José Cortés, *Views from the Apache Frontier: Report on the Northern Provinces of New Spain*, ed. Elizabeth A. H. John, trans. John Wheat (Norman: University of Oklahoma Press, 1989).

22. For example, from 1774 to 1802 viceroys and commanders general communicated with various Texas governors about controlling diverse Indian uprisings. For a very small sample from among a multitude of documents electronically stored in the Béxar Archives (hereafter BA) and found online with the keyword "control," see Bucarely y Ursua to Ripperdá […] control Comanche uprisings, BA February 9, 1774; Croix to Ripperdá, […] control of Karankawa, Orcoquiza, and Coco Indians, BA September 15, 1778; [Elguézabal] to Uranga, […] control Karankawa uprisings at Refugio Mission, BA April 28, 1801; Nava to Elguézabal, […] detachment at El Cíbolo to control Indian uprisings, BA August 30, 1802.

23. Presidial chases after and engaging with the enemy is well documented in Mark Santiago, *A Bad Peace and a Good War: Spain and the Mescalero Apache Uprising of 1795–1799* (Norman: University of Oklahoma Press, 2018). Primary sources for this book are drawn from hard copy and digitized documents including military service records, correspondence, and related presidio material housed in microfilm depositories at the Archivo General de la Nación in Sevilla, España; the Béxar Archives in Austin, Texas; the Inventory of the Documents from the Archivo General de Indias and other related archives, 1505–1812, and Inventory of the Documents from the Archivo General de la Nación de México, 1520–1878 at the Center for Southwest Research at the University of

300 Notes to Pages 10–11

New Mexico's Zimmerman Library; El Archivo de Hidalgo del Parral, 1631–1821 at the University of Arizona in Tucson; and, the Inventory of the Spanish Archives of New Mexico II, 1621–1821 at the New Mexico State Records Center and Archives in Santa Fé.

24. A discussion of military service records follows in chapter 2 with a sampling of this type of narrative provided to illustrate its unique formatting.

25. Marchena Fernández (1992), pp. 193–219.

26. Faulk (1964, pp. 51–52) provides a San Antonio de Béxar presidial report from October 1778 as proof of the monotony of "the Spanish soldier's daily existence." However, the monthly circumstances included both the usual tasks and bizarre episodes of robbery and unexplained death and reprisals for stolen property. In its content, the soldiers investigated the death of an Indian man; delivered chewing tobacco to four Tonkawa headmen, a request made via a citizen of the presidio; replaced horses stolen from the Tonkawa by four Lipan Apache boys and included the subsequent pursuit of the property; and welcomed over fifty Tonkawa and found lodging for their number. The report indicates the arrival of Francisco Amangual and his escort of six soldiers with the company funds retrieved at San Luis Potosí. I admit to finding the summary compelling and, thus, I failed to detect the absolute monotony in the report as proposed by Faulk.

27. For an excellent discussion of the multiple units of troop divisions, see the first part, first chapter (*Primera parte, capítulo 1*) "El Ejército de América," and the section "Distribución de reglamentos territoriales" in Juan Marchena Fernández, *Oficiales y soldados en el ejército de América* (Sevilla: Escuela de estudios hispano–americanos de Sevilla, 1983), pp. 52–62. See further the section "Las armas en el ejército de América" and the charts on p. 63 with descriptions of individual units of the colonial army, pp. 64–69. In McAlister, see the appendices with tables indicating the names and numbers associated with New Spain's "regular" army, urban militia, and other units except for those in the *Provincias Internas*, that information contained in table 5. Governed by *reglamentos* specific to the frontier, these troops were not considered part of the regular army proper. From *Estado que manifiesta el en que se hallan los Cuerpos de Infantería, Dragones, y Compañías Sueltas que hay en el Reino de Nueva España . . . , 1758*. Kyle N. McAlister, *The "Fuero Militar" in New Spain, 1764–1800* (Westport: Greenwood Press, 1957), pp. 93–97, 98–99.

28. As Kuethe and Andrien (2014, p. 8) explain, "attempts to reform the Spanish Atlantic empire led to a heightened demand for information and the means to compile, summarize, and analyze it before making appropriate political decisions." Those systems of information gathering involved drawing reliable maps, ensuring the accurate counting of populations, and "writing reports on economic activities," thus allowing the provincial regions of the Spanish Atlantic to become "clearing houses for information" headed for the appropriate bureaucracy.

29. The Intendant System functioned as another mechanism by which the empire's administrative reconstruction might achieve success and, in effect, make obsolete the Laws of the Indies. Introduced in Spain in 1718 and later New Spain, its principal goals included fiscal reform and increased revenue. See Lillian Estelle Fisher, *The Intendant System in Spanish America* (New York: Gordian Press, 1969/1929), pp. 1–3. Even more relevant for the topical focus of this book, the system was proposed in tandem with the creation of the Comandancia General. See Velázquez (1982), 83–9; and Marina Mantilla Trolle, Rafael Diego-Fernández Sotelo and Agustín Moreno Torres, eds. *Real Ordenanza para el establecimiento é instrucción de intendentes de exército y provincia*

en el reino de la Nueva España (Guadalajara: Universidad de Guadalajara, 2008). For the urban setting and changing demographics affecting the military, see McAlister (1957), passim; and Marchena Fernández (1983, 1992); and Alan J. Kuethe and Juan Marchena Fernández, eds. *Soldados del rey, el ejército borbónico en América colonial en vísperas de la independencia* (Seville: Universitat Jaume, 2005); and, especially Christon Archer, *The Army in Bourbon Mexico, 1760–1810* (Albuquerque: University of New Mexico Press, 1995), passim.

30. As we shall see in chapters 1 and 3, the relationship between Amangual and legal circulation and containment of tobacco was always something of a contentious issue and predictably increased the workload of his already crowded schedule. For the development of the tobacco industry in New Spain, see Guillermo Céspedes del Castillo and Gonzalo Anes y Álvarez de Castrillón, *El tabaco en Nueva España* (Madrid: Real Academia de la Historia, 1992); for a comparative study with a focus on Peru, see Catalina Vizcarra, "Bourbon Intervention in the Peruvian Tobacco Industry, 1752–1813," *Journal of Latin American Studies* 39, no. 3 (Aug. 2007): 567–93. For a thought-provoking discussion tied to the metaphorical significance of the plant, see Fernando Rodríguez de la Flor, German Labrador Méndez, and Patricia A. Marshall, "Baroque Toxicology: Discourses on Smoke and the Polemics of Tobacco in 17th Century Spain," in "Cultural Studies in the Spanish Golden Age," ed. Elena del Río Parra, special issue, *South Atlantic Review* 72, no. 1 (Winter 2007): 112–42. The field of commodity studies is emerging, but currently has an emphasis on sugar in Cuba and other areas of the Caribbean. For more generalized texts with an emphasis on *Hispano*-America, see Arnold J. Bauer, *Goods, Power, History: Latin America's Material Culture* (Cambridge: Cambridge University Press, 2001); and Steven C. Topik, Carlos Marichal, and Zephyr Frank, *From Silver to Cocaine: Latin American Commodity Chains and the Building of the World Economy, 1500–2000* (Durham: Duke University Press, 2006). From an international angle but with valuable insight toward the metaphorical significance of the term, see Arjun Appadurai, ed., *The Social Life of Things: Commodities in Cultural Perspective* (Cambridge: Cambridge University Press, 1986).

31. See *Informe del Virrey y El Visitador General de Nueva España sobre la importancia y utilidad de que ahora se establezca la Comandancia General que S. M. tiene aprobada para las provincias de Sonora y Sinaloa, Californias y Nueva Vizcaya, 22 de junio 1771*, reproduced in Velázquez (1982), p. 85–89; Herbert Ingram Priestley, *José de Gálvez: Visitor-General of New Spain (1765–1771)*, vol. 5 (Berkeley: University of California Press, 1916), pp. 289–95.

32. Fisher analyzed inventories of the stock on hand of monopolized articles. This included tobacco and two other items that will emerge because of one's insufficient supply, stamped paper, and the other's forbidden, that is, irresistible nature: playing cards. Fisher (1969/1929), pp. 202, 208, 284–87.

33. Moorhead (1975), passim.

34. A bilingual version of the Regulation of 1729, sometimes referred to as the *Proyecto*, appears in Thomas H. Naylor and Charles W. Polzer, *Pedro Rivera and the Military Regulations for Northern New Spain, 1724–1729* (Tucson: University of Arizona Press, 1988). Hereafter cited as Naylor and Polzer but, when using Rivera's original language, as *Reglamento de 1729*, and for consistency when using Felipe V's earlier edict, as *Reglamento de 1719*.

35. See a summary of Croix's inspection of 1777–78 in Thomas (1941), pp. 27–53; 71–243.

302   Notes to Pages 13–17

36. Tijerina (1994), p. 79–80. The term *tejano* is an interesting one and relevant to this study. As Reséndez indicates, throughout the eighteenth century, "Tejanos had come to view themselves as the edge of the Spanish world deep in the heart of North America, the vanguard of Christendom and civilization. Their history had been one of hardship and tenacity in a hostile environment." However, as Reséndez claims, this ethnic group never used the term to self-identify. Andrés Reséndez, *Changing National Identities at the Frontier: Texas and New Mexico, 1800–1850* (New York: Cambridge University Press, 2004), pp. 21, 26. For two other perspectives on Tejano identity in the eighteenth century, see the collection of essays in Gerald E. Poyo and Gilberto M. Hinojosa, eds., *Tejano Origins in Eighteenth-Century San Antonio* (Austin: University of Texas Press, 1991); Jesús F. de la Teja, *San Antonio de Béxar: A Community on New Spain's Northern Frontier* (Albuquerque: University of New Mexico Press, 1996), passim; and Jesús de la Teja, "Spanish Colonial Texas," in *New Views of Borderlands History*, ed. Robert H. Jackson (Albuquerque: University of New Mexico Press, 1998), pp. 107–30.

37. Tijerina (1994), pp. 79–82.

38. For a short essay on peopling the Seno Mexicano, see Patricia Osante (Ned F. Brierley, trans.), "Colonization and Control. The Case of Nuevo Santander" in Jesús F. de la Teja and Ross Frank, *Choice, Persuasion, and Coercion. Social Control on Spain's North American Frontiers* (Albuquerque: University of New Mexico Press, 2005), pp. 227–47.

39. Rangel Silva writes that "Barragán had presented documentation of his merits and services [to the community] and requested the rank of colonel." Further, the "compañías volantes were created as a way of helping, in a rapid and effective manner, localities that were being attacked by Indians at the same time as the founding of Nuevo Santander." My translation. José Alfredo Rangel Silva, "Milicias en el oriente de San Luis Potosí, 1793–1813," in *Las armas de la nación, Independencia y ciudadanía en hispanoamérica (1750 — 1850)*, ed. Manuel Chust and Juan Marchena (Madrid: Iberoamericana, 2007), pp. 53–55, fn6. McAlister (1957, pp. 98–99) includes statistics for total enlisted strengths for the Nuevo Santander companies, regulars, and militia since these, like those of Nuevo León, were "directly dependent on the viceroyalty." The former amounted to 225 cavalry members and 1000 boots on the ground for the "frontier" militia.

40. Strategies of appeasement in dealings with hostile indigenous groups had utility for the empire's first responders in the hinterlands. A few pertinent examples include Pekka Hämäläinen, *The Comanche Empire* (New Haven: Yale University Press, 2008), especially pp. 20–21, for their emergence onto the southern plains; for the extent of occupation by Apache groups traversing the "Big Water Peoples' Country (Kónitsaahjj gokíyaa)," or "Gran Apachería," see Matthew Babcock, *Apache Adaptation to Hispanic Rule* (Cambridge: Cambridge University Press, 2016), p. 5; Thomas A. Britten, *The Lipan Indians. People of Wind and Lightning* (Albuquerque: University of New Mexico Press, 2009); Robert Weddle, *The San Sabá Mission: Spanish Pivot in Texas* (Austin: University of Texas Press, 1999); Max Moorhead, *The Apache Frontier: Jacobo Ugarte and Spanish-Indian Relations in Northern New Spain, 1769-1791* (Norman: University of Oklahoma Press, 1968), hereafter Moorhead (1968).

41. It is beyond the scope of this book to list them all but, from among many, see Yetman (2012); de la Teja (2004); Poyo and Hinojosa (1991); Ross Frank, *From Settler to Citizen: New Mexican Economic Development and the Creation of Vecino Society,*

1750–1820 (Berkeley: University of California Press, 2000); Julianna Barr, *Peace Came in the Form of a Woman* (Chapel Hill: University of North Carolina Press, 2007); Tijerina (1994); and Faulk (1988).

42. What Sellers-García describes as "elite" and "popular" forms of knowledge from various contributors is relevant here. Official documents indeed "depended on local informants," not just literate informants in the chain of command and should, therefore, be considered "composite productions" (2014, pp. 18–19). Indeed, subalterns in the form of rank-and-file soldiers, Native men and women, and civilians contributed to archival sources with content, firsthand knowledge, and historicity.

43. Though I use it sporadically in the context of historic Indigenous leadership as imagined by non-Native actors in the Comandancia General, I am sensitive to the use of the term "chief." I am persuaded to pay hard attention to the hypothesis put forth by Kavanagh when he suggests the word and its meanings might aptly fall into the category of "generalizations without particulars," and that the terms "spokesmen" or "intermediaries" with roles of "immediate interaction" as the situation warranted may be more appropriate (1996, p.15). Going forward, I will use Kavanagh's alternatives and "headman," along with their pluralized form. I use the original language as found in the documentation of the period when Spanish terminology describes certain Indigenous officials as "capitán," "jefe," or other titles indicative of authority.

44. See, for example, Jorge Cañizares-Esguerra, "Entangled Histories: Borderlands Historiographies in New Clothes?" *American Historical Review* 112, no. 3 (June 2007): 788–89; and see Gould's synthesis of imagining a comprehensive approach to the history of the Spanish- and English-speaking Atlantic worlds in the same issue (2007, pp. 766–69).

45. A useful entry point for outsiders wanting access to the most easterly part of colonial Texas, the "pueblo" of Nacogdoches and its jurisdiction of "all the ranches within fifty leagues" now had farmers, trade workers, and merchants representing the United States, Ireland, France, and Canada. Most had only been residents for about one year. See report of foreigners at Nacogdoches, BA January 1, 1805. This same area for socio-commercial interactions captured the attention of Rubí as he proposed to royal administrators in his Dictamen to Arriaga of April 10,1768. Convinced that the region near and around "the worthless settlement" of Los Adaes was being occupied only "in theory," or as it is written in Spanish and as I would translate it, "imaginarily," [que hoy ocupamos imaginariamente], and not in reality, by Articles 24 and 25 Rubi's conclusion left no doubt. The defense of the empire's "true dominions," situated more than two-hundred leagues from the "imaginary frontier [figurada frontera]," with its "imaginary mission [una misión imaginaria]," and the adjacent Presidio "Orcoquizá," staffed by its "very inept company [la ineptísima compañía]," required a barrier established "in a more respectable fashion" that would make difficult communication and transit by outsiders. Jackson and Foster (1995), pp. 59–60, 186, 195, 197; and Velásquez (1982), pp. 60, 70–72.

46. Donald Fixico's essay "Ethics and Responsibilities in Writing American Indian History," American Indian Quarterly, 20, no.1, University of Nebraska Press (1996: 29–39), has made me think harder about the absence of Native voices in Spanish colonial documents. So, too, have Joseph Marshall's *The Day the World Ended at Little Big Horn* (New York: Viking Penguin, 2007) and Colin Calloway's edited collection *Our Hearts Fell to the Ground: Plains Indian Views of How the West Was Lost* (Boston: Bedford/St. Martin's, 1996). The archives preserve the observations and subsequent

304   Notes to Pages 20–26

interpretations of people like Amangual and other soldiers as they engaged in commerce, peace by purchase, and hostile encounters with local indigenous people
within the walls of the garrison, and without. That said, while my study privileges
the imperial perspective and wants for the Native view on all things borderlands,
I cannot be an apologist for the Spanish documentarists. I can only interpret and
contextualize, albeit from a diminished, one-sided reading of archival sources. I do
so here on behalf of First Nations observers who certainly had their own universe of
discourse about centuries-long interactions with foreigners come to their territory.

47. I exclude Elizabeth John's investigation of the Vial-Cháves journey to Comanche
territory since that trek headed in another direction. However, because of his prominent role in Texas history John's insight into the governorship of Domingo Cabello
will be referenced in this study. See Elizabeth A. H. John, Adan Benavides Jr., Pedro
Vial, and Francisco Xavier Chaves, "Inside the Comanchería, 1785: The Diary of Pedro
Vial and Francisco Xavier Chaves," *Southwestern Historical Quarterly* 98, no. 1 (July
1994): 26–56.

Chapter 1

1. "Compañías Volantes de Nueva España," in AGS, SGU, Leg. 7277, 8, 10–31, recto.
See also Lt. Col. Simón de Herrera's *hoja de servicio* in AGS, SGU, Leg. 7277, 10–26,
recto; and his time served from 1763–1795 as Lieutenant Coronel in the compania
volante de Cavalleria de San Juan Bautista de la Punto de Lampazos, in AGS, SGU,
leg, 7277, 8

2. Juan Marchena Fernández wrote that the *Reglamento de Havana* of 1719 required
enlistees to be eighteen years old, but the sons of officers could be fifteen years old,
provided they had the height and sturdiness (*robustez*) of similarly qualified candidates. In other places, like Cartagena de Indias, the minimum age was sixteen. The age
criteria were not universal, and each garrison heeded only that found in regulations
and not the requirements of General Ordinances. Marchena Fernández (1983), pp.
275–76. However, Article 29 of the 1719 Regulation states that Spanish-born youths
must have reached the age of sixteen while *criollo* males had to be at least twenty years
old before enlistment. There is no provision in the Havana regulations stipulating a
different age threshold for children of officers. Naylor and Polzer (1988), p. 35. See
chapter 1, "Reorganización borbónica del reclutamiento," in Cristina Borreguero
Beltrán, *El reclutamiento militar por quintas en la españa del siglo xviii. Orígines del
servicio militar obligatorio* (Valladolid: Universidad de Valladolid, 1989), pp. 31–78. See
Antonio Cordero y Bustamente's entry into service at the age of fourteen as an "officer
cadet" in the Infantry Regiment of Zamora. He will be a future Governor of Texas,
a superior of Francisco Amangual, and a recurrent character in this book. Santiago
(2006), p. 371.

3. The best study devoted to most of the aforementioned groups and their resistance
to Spanish invaders is Susan M. Deeds, *Defiance and Deference in Mexico's Colonial
North: Indians under Spanish Rule in Nueva Vizcaya* (Austin: University of Texas Press,
2003). Three of the most recent sources for new perspectives on the Pueblo Revolt
include Matthew Liebmann, *Revolt: An Archaeological History of Pueblo Resistance
and Revitalization in 17th Century New Mexico* (Tucson: University of Arizona Press,
2012); Matthew Liebmann, T. J. Ferguson, and Robert Preucel, "Pueblo Settlement,
Architecture, and Social Change in the Pueblo Revolt Era, A. D. 1680–1696," *Journal of*

Field Archaeology 30, no. 1 (Spring 2005): 45-60; Joseph Aguilar and Robert W. Preucel, *The Continuous Path: Pueblo Movement and the Archaeology of Becoming* (Tucson: University of Arizona Press, 2019).

4. Immensely rich with mineral resources, the region was populated with indigenous groups who, from the conquerors' perspective, could provide an important labor pool for the mines. Viceregal officials were determined to protect the major trade routes that passed through a province with important requirements of communication and supply, all of which traversed some portion of Nueva Vizcaya. See Hadley (1997), pp. 3, 11-13. Hugo O'Conor was just as impressed with Nueva Vizcaya's profitability between 1707 and 1748 and its "contributing to the greater increase of the Royal Treasury [...] and giving rise to many riches in the Provincias Internas." Cutter (1994), p. 40-1. For noteworthy studies of the province, see J. Lloyd Mecham, *Francisco de Ibarra and New Vizcaya* (Durham: Duke University Press, 1927); Oakah Jones, *Nueva Vizcaya: Heartland of the Spanish Frontier* (Albuquerque: University of New Mexico Press, 1988); Sara Ortelli, *Trama de una guerra conveniente: Nueva Vizcaya y la sombra de los apaches (1748-1790)* (México, D.F.: Centro de Estudios Históricos, El Colegio de México, 2007); and Deeds (2003).

5. Tijerina (1994), pp. 79-80. For Guevara's exploits in the borderlands before his determined efforts to become the colonizer of the "Seno Mexicano," see especially chapter 2 in Armando Alonzo, *Tejano Legacy: Rancheros and Settlers in South Texas, 1734-1900* (Albuquerque: University of New Mexico Press, 1998). For his appointment as lieutenant general empowered to conduct the exploration and pacification of the region, see [...] Horcasitas' order to Governor of Texas [for assistance to Escandón for exploration] of the Seno Mexicano, BA September 3, 1746. See Guevara's report concerning the kingdom of Nuevo León in Hadley (1997), pp. 77-120. For its settlement by a Portuguese *adelantado*, see Samuel Temkin, *Luis de Carvajal. The Origins of Nuevo Reino de León* (Santa Fé: Sunstone Press, 2011).

6. Tijerina (1994), pp. 79-80. Knowles suggests the *volantes* were antecedents for "ranging companies," which, in turn, evolved into the law enforcement agency today called the Texas Rangers. Further, he highlights only one squadron in order to argue for that possibility: La Segunda Compañía Volante de San Carlos de Parras (Álamo de Parras). The company of one hundred Spanish lancers arrived in Texas in January 1803 from the pueblo of San José y Santiago del Álamo, near Parras in southern Coahuila. Under the jurisdiction of the curacy of the Villa de San Fernando and the Bishop of Nuevo León, they occupied the secularized mission of San Antonio de Valero. See Thomas W. Knowles, *They Rode for the Lone Star: The Saga of the Texas Rangers* (Dallas: Taylor, 1999), pp. 5-7.

7. The factory may have been intended for other locally developed products since, according to a report by Governor Elguézabal, by June 1803 the people of San Antonio had "never learned to manufacture textiles or rope, nor is there any raising of cotton." Owing to the relatively slight number of sheep living in the province at that time, very little wool was produced. Thus, vendors sent it to Saltillo to sell. Juan Bautista Elguézabal, "A Description of Texas in 1803," ed. Odie Faulk, *Southwestern Historical Quarterly* 66, no. 4 (April 1963): 513-15. See also Jack D. Eaton, *Excavations at the Alamo Shrine (Mission San Antonio de Valero)*, Center for Archaeological Research, University of Texas at San Antonio, Special Report 10, 1980.

8. Ramón (1990). After the Wars of Independence, the Álamo de Parras detachment withdrew and left abandoned, for the second time, the buildings and wall enclosures of the Valero mission. A late nineteenth-century study indicates the same: from 1793

306   Notes to Pages 27–29

to 1801, the mission of San Antonio de Valero remained unoccupied until the arrival of the Parras flying squadron in the latter year. See Adele B. Looscan, Julia Lee Sinks, and Lester G. Bugbee, "Notes and Fragments," *Quarterly of the Texas State Historical Association* 2, no. 3 (Jan. 1899): 243–47.

9. Knowles (1999), p. 5. Though Knowles cites not a single source in his book, Alessio Robles indicates that the Mission of San Antonio de Valero became known as "El Álamo" because it garrisoned for many years the soldiers from "El Álamo de Parras." See Nicolás de Lafora and Vito Alessio Robles, *Relacion del viaje que hizo a los presidios internos situados en la frontera de la America septentrional* (México, D.F.: Editorial Pedro Robredo, 1939), p. 208. Alessio Robles and Knowles may have referenced the 1899 "notes and fragments" cited above, as well as Marion Habig in *The Alamo Chain of Missions: A History of San Antonio's Five Old Missions* (Chicago: Franciscan Herald Press, 1968), p. 261.

10. Pedro de Nava, June 14, 1792 (copy: Antonio Bonilla, August 30, 1793), in "Compañías Presidiales y Volantes. Provincias Internas," AGS, SGU, LEG, 7022, images 16–5, 6; 16–9. The Parras company should not be confused with the flying squadron of San Carlos de Cerro Gordo, formed in 1774.

11. Cabello to Croix, requesting instructions [...] contraband goods confiscated by [...] Amangual (Amangual to Cabello), BA March 18, 1780.

12. Croix to Cabello, [...] auction contraband goods confiscated by Amangual and Ibarvo, BA June 9, 1780. Lafora mentions El Cleto's arroyo as a camp site for the Rubí expedition party in the summer 1767. The "rancho of San Bartolo" developed near the banks of El Cíbolo. See Nicolás Lafora and Lawrence Kinnaird, *The Frontiers of New Spain, Nicolás de Lafora's Description 1766–1768* (Berkeley: The Quivira Society, 1958), p. 161. Cabello's map, drawn in 1780, had "Cleto" as a reference point for ranch cabins in relation to Fort Cíbolo. See Jack Jackson, "The 1780 Cabello Map: New Evidence That There Were Two Mission Rosarios, and a Possible Correction on the Site of El Fuerte del Cíbolo," *Southwestern Historical Quarterly* 107, no. 2 (Oct. 2003): 202–16.

13. Croix to Cabello, [...] auction contraband goods confiscated by Amangual and Ibarvo, BA June 9, 1780.

14. Cabello to Croix, transmitting Amangual's report on Comanche depredations at Fort Cíbolo, BA September 19, 1780. According to one historian, Rondein spoke the Caddo and Wichita languages and he was one of the interpreters "so widely known and loved among Indians" that he could travel with only a light escort. Reputed to be brave and a good horseman, Rondein had qualities that, for good reason, impressed Cabello. See Elizabeth A. H. John, *Storms Brewed in Other Men's Worlds: The Confrontation of Indians, Spanish, and French in the Southwest, 1540–1795* (College Station: Texas A&M Press, 1975), p. 552. See Croix's report of incessant attack by Comanche bands, enacted as retribution for attacks initiated by misguided Spaniards, in Texas during the 1780s in Thomas (1941), pp. 72–82.

15. The entire episode is recounted in Robert H. Thonhoff, *El Fuerte del Cíbolo, Sentinel of the Béxar-La Bahía Ranches* (Austin: Eakin Press, 1992), pp. 61–63. See also the monthly report of the cavalry division of Béxar, BA January 31, 1781; February 28, 1781. The region of Fort Cíbolo must not have been too daunting since, two months after the loss of soldiers there, a group of San Fernando residents petitioned the *alcalde ordinario* of the villa Marcos Zepeda to go to the arroyo of El Cíbolo to bring back livestock for meat for the presidio. Included in the party were thirteen "young men [*mosos* (sic)]," even boys, or servants, accompanying their fathers, male relatives,

Notes to Pages 29–32   307

or employers. See [...] petition of [San Fernando residents] to bring stock for use at Béxar, BA April 21, 1781. However, Croix found conditions in Texas so hopeless that he recommended abandoning the Cíbolo outpost. He based his conclusions on the deteriorating relationships with the Comanche, Karankawa, and even those polities representing "friendly" Indians. See Croix to Cabello, [...] conditions in Texas and the promotion of peace with Indians, BA June 13, 1781. By January 1782, Amangual put the torch to Fort Cíbolo, an event that took place in March of that same year. See Cabello to Alcaldes of San Fernando [abandoning] Fort Cíbolo, BA March 11, 1782.

16. In the preface of his monograph, Britten provides a reconciliation of sorts when he considers the term "Lipan," and its several alternatives, to describe the people of his narrative and how these same people described themselves. Britten (2009), p. xiv.

17. Monthly report[s] of the cavalry division of Béxar, BA January 31, 1782; September 30, 1782; October 31, 1782; December 31, 1782.

18. Monthly report[s] of the cavalry division of Béxar, January 31, 1783; February 28, 1783.

19. Monthly report[s] of the cavalry division of Béxar, March 31, 1783. The murder and mutilation of young males — some perhaps mere boys — were apparently not that unusual. In the first week of April, yet another young servant of a presidio resident was found stabbed to death, scalped, and missing his nose and ears. He had gone one league distant from the Béxar presidio to burn ash to make soap, but never returned. However, his horse remained saddled and unharmed. Monthly report of the cavalry division of Béxar, BA April 30, 1783. For a concise description of the Karankawa and related Indian groups of south Texas and its Gulf Coast, see Barr (2007), pp. 116–17, 134; and, for a contemporaneous (1799) negative appraisal of the "Carancahuaces," see Cortés (1989), pp. 88–89. One of the earliest studies is Albert S. Gatschet, *The Karankawa Indians: The Coast People of Texas* (Cambridge: Peabody Museum, Harvard University, 1891).

20. Monthly report[s] of the cavalry division of Béxar, BA June 30, 1783; July 31, 1783; August 31, 1783; September 30, 1783.

21. Monthly report[s] of the cavalry division of Béxar, BA October 31, 1783; November 30, 1783; Neve to Cabello, approving attack on the Karankawa Indians, BA December 18, 1783.

22. Ugarte [...] to Cabello, postponing expedition against the Carancaguaces, BA August 3, 1786.

23. Cabello to Ugarte y Loyola, transmitting [...] Valdés' [...] retire from service [...] Amangual to succeed Valdés, BA August 24, 1786.

24. Cabello to Ugarte, [...] Marcelo Valdés [retirement] from service, and recommending Amangual to succeed Valdés, BA August 26, 1786.

25. Moorhead describes the "permanent military force" of the northern frontier as belonging to "neither [...] the regular Spanish army nor the colonial militia," and "somewhat inferior to the former and superior to the latter" in terms of pay and privilege." Moorhead (1968), p. 87.

26. Marchena Fernández (1983), p. 79.

27. As Moorhead explains, an effective pacification policy was "seriously jeopardized" by "repeated transformations," as when the Commandancy General was alternately divided and reunited by two viceroys: first, into two separate commands in 1788 (Worcester has the date as "1786"), but then reunited in 1790 (1793 according to Worcester) and divided again in 1791. The King then reunited in 1792 the two

308   Notes to Pages 32–36

divisions under Pedro de Nava, making the Comandancia once again independent of the viceroy as it had been under Croix. Moorhead (1975), pp. 111–12; Worcester (1951), pp. 23–24.

28. *Reglamento 1772, Título uno, artículo 6.*

29. Moorhead (1975), pp. 178–79, 194. *Reglamento 1772, Título trece, artículo 1.*

30. María del Carmen Velázquez, *El estado de guerra en nueva españa, 1760–1808* (México, D.F.: El Colegio de México, 1950), pp. 92–93.

31. Moorhead (1975), p. 29.

32. Weddle (1968), pp. 46–47.

33. Thomas Frank Schilz and Donald E. Worcester, "The Spread of Firearms among the Indian Tribes on the Northern Frontier of New Spain," *American Indian Quarterly* 11, no. 1 (Winter 1987): 2–3. Historians have subsumed the Taovaya, Tawakoni, and Waco into Wichita tribes in the aggregate and, similarly, as collectively referred to by the Spanish as members of the "Nations of the North." It should be noted that contemporaneous documentation verifies the term was in use ("el nombre genérico de Naciones del Norte") at the highest level of governance. See AGS, SGU, LEG, 7019, 36 — June 26, 1790, Revilla Gigedo to Valdes. A 1785 document of provisions lists the twenty-one "Naciones del Norte Amigas de la Provincia de los Texas." See AGS, SGU, LEG, 7019, 36, recto 17.

34. Weddle (1968), pp. 46–47. Thus, two historians, Weddle and Moorhead, argue for the initial appearance of the *compañías volantes* as, alternately, 1701 and 1713, the latter by a directive from Linares, albeit in two different places that in the modern era became two different countries.

35. Weddle (1968), p. 48. Besides the mission San Juan Bautista, it also protected two others: San Francisco Solano and San Bernardo. Hadley, et al. (1997), p. 468.

36. Hackett, vol. 2 (1923), pp. 23–24. Things must have been bad if the captain's argument had the backing of the Jesuits, who may have retained unpleasant memories of their benevolence gone unappreciated almost half a century earlier. In 1638, the college of the Company of Jesus in the villa of San Felipe demanded repayment of 5,708 pesos. The amount represented goods, including clothing and sustenance, dispensed from the religious to soldiers barracked at the presidio of Sinaloa. Their generosity to the troops left them "suffering great injury" since it deprived the Jesuits of their own food and clothing as well as what they needed for the "adornment of divine worship." Hackett, vol. 3 (1926), pp. 75–76.

37. Hackett, vol. 2 (1923), pp. 443; 429.

38. Ibid. (September 12, 1693), pp. 374–75.

39. Ibid. (April 2, 1698), p. 458. (April 1, 1698), p. 454. A decade prior, "Teuricachi" and two neighboring vicinities were hotspots for ongoing conspiracies among the Sumas, Janos, Jocomes, and Pimans. See Yetman (2012), pp. 108–21. By 1781, Lt. José de Tona commanded the Compañía de Yndios de San Miguel de Babispe, a presidial force of ninety *Ópata*; the following year, the *Ópata* de San José de Bacuachi was formed with the same allocation of men. In 1783, eighty-four Indians made up the Pimas de San Rafael de Buena Vista. See AGS, SGU, LEG, 7022–16 images 9–11, recto/verso; and Moorhead (1968), pp. 91–92. A diacritical mark over the first letter "O" in naming the Opatería people is as often used by scholars as it is not. This is true for much of the text included on the official website of the Opata Nation. For this reason, I use both as they appear in the sources cited hereafter. For Pima and Opata presidio service, dissent, and sacrifice in Sonora, see Cynthia Radding, *Wandering Peoples.*

Notes to Pages 36-40   309

Colonialism, Ethnic Spaces, and Ecological Frontiers in Northwestern Mexico, 1700–1850 (Durham: Duke University Press, 1997), pp. 256–63.

40. Hackett (1926), vol. 2, pp. 78–80. In a section subtitled "A Flying Company for Sonora," Fay Smith (1993, pp. 18–23) describes Jironza's leadership of the Sonoran *volantes* and the company's relationship with settlers and missionaries in the late seventeenth century.

41. Naylor and Polzer (1988), pp. 161–64. Weddle makes no mention of the padre's treatment of the soldiers but, instead, argues forcefully against Rivera's mandates. Weddle (1968), pp. 171–90. Rivera named the compilation of his three-and-a-half-year inspection tour of the provincial presidios *Año de 1728 Proyecto*, hereafter Rivera. In Spanish law, *Proyecto* had the connotation of a preliminary report or provisional policy that set down "the circumstances of a contract or treaty." The *Proyecto* is composed of three *estados*, or statuses. The first conveys the status of the presidios as Rivera found them; the second is a brief account of immediate reforms implemented by Rivera at each presidio; and the third essentially summarizes his recommendations for reform and conveys his expectations for each presidio's future existence. Compiled thus, the *Proyecto* inspired the thinking of Viceroy Juan de Acuña, Marqués de Casafuerte, and its content — especially that contained in the third *estado* — would underpin his eventual *Reglamento de 1729* constituting the expected result from the Rivera inspection. These regulations differed from the earlier 1719 *Reglamento de Habana* in that the ordinances governing military life in the Caribbean could not be so "easily rewritten to suit the needs of the mainland frontier." Rivera knew the territory by firsthand experience. Naylor and Polzer (1988), pp. 1, 8, 11–16; Rivera, *tercer estado, artículo cincuenta*.

42. Naylor and Polzer (1988), pp. 10–11.

43. Rivera, *primer estado, artículo dos* [translation: mine and authors'].

44. Ibid. Some historians credit Berroterán's expertise on Nueva Vizcaya as superior to that of distant authorities and make it clear that he had the upper hand where it concerned his management of the Conchos presidio. For his troubled relationship with higher authorities, see Hadley (1997), pp. 167–226.

45. Rivera, *primer estado, artículo siete*. For more on the founding of the presidio, see Naylor and Polzer (1986), pp. 335–67.

46. Rivera, *artículo diez y nueve*.

47. Rivera, *tercer estado, artículo trece*.

48. Ibid.

49. Rivera, *tercer estado, artículo 55*.

50. Ibid.

51. O'Conor was convinced "those who [were] recruited and enlisted" from the "lands of the Indian wars" would be able to adjust "with less difficulty" to the "extraordinary hardship" of this kind of warfare. In saying so, he may have had Native people in mind; the comandante inspector makes clear his preference for the Opata's "proven bravery as well as for their great knowledge of the land, sierras, and watering places." Cutter (1994), p. 88.

52. Ibid., *arículo cincuenta y uno*. From the perspective of political scientists, the links between law and practical concerns are profound in a theoretical sense. In one example, "it was apparently inconceivable for the monarch to have based colonial legislation on pragmatic grounds." But the reality for soldiers on the ground and missionaries, too, was such that "the laws Spain enacted for [her colonies] were

310 Notes to Pages 40–43

subjected to almost constant violation." See Frank Jay Moreno, "A Spanish Colonial System: A Functional Approach," *Western Historical Quarterly* 20, no. 2, part 1 (June 1967): 308–20.

53. Rivera, *tercer estado, artículo cincuenta y dos*.

54. Ibid.

55. Ibid., "charity or commission/ruego y encargo." The auditor Oliván y Rebolledo presented to Viceroy Valero on December 24, 1717, his "Fuerza y costo de los presidios" indicating the province, the soldier number, and the salary for all men stationed at newly created garrisons. Luis Navarro García, *Don José de Gálvez y la Comandancia General de las Provincias Internas del Norte de Nueva España* (Sevilla: Publicaciones de la Escuela de Estudios Hispano-Americanos de Sevilla, 1964), p. 64–65.

56. Rivera, tercer estado, artículo cincuenta y dos. The land may have belonged to the king, but on-the-ground realities guided soldiers in their quest for the availability of immediate resources and water surely constituted the most cherished. As Meyer wrote, when war broke out in the northern frontier "water availability dictated much of the military strategy." Further, military campaigns "were planned to coincide with [those periods of the year] when water was anticipated to be most plentiful." Meyer argues that shortages of water "limited the military activities of both Indians and Spaniards, but it seems to have had an especially negative impact on the Spanish troops, who sometimes refused to carry out expeditions in the desert [and in other places] if an adequate water supply was not assured." Michael C. Meyer, *Water in the Hispanic Southwest: A Social and Legal History, 1550–1850* (Tucson: University of Arizona Press, 1984), pp. 96–97. According to the *maestre de campo* Marín, the rainy season was the best time for making war on enemy Native populations since water would be available everywhere for both soldiers and horses. See Hackett (1926) op.cit., p. 435.

57. De la Teja (1998), pp. 120–21. Writing his opinions on a wide array of matters in April 1698, the *fiscal* believed immigrants from the Canary Islands constituted a more dependable community of settlers. Though there were more than enough people in Mexico's provinces, he considered them "not suitable" since "all in that kingdom are lazy and worthless." See Hackett (1926), p. 441.

58. Rivera, *tercer estado, artículo cincuenta y tres*.

59. Rivera, *tercer estado, artículo cincuenta y cuatro*. I presume he means the mission of San Francisco de los Tejas, itself associated with the presidio of Dolores de Tejas and founded in 1716, but temporarily abandoned in 1719 due to "French encroachment." Troops under the command of the Marqués de Aguayo reoccupied it in 1721, and it was suppressed in 1729. See Naylor and Polzer (1988), p. 85.

60. Rivera, *tercer estado, artículo cincuenta y cuatro*.

61. Naylor and Polzer (1988), p.25.

62. Rivera, *tercer estado, artículo cincuenta y cinco*.

63. Rebolledo's opinion […] attack by Apaches, […] Casafuerte's order to Urrutia […], BA July 18–24, 1733. More than a decade prior, dereliction of duty quickly followed a revolt by the Karankawa and the "inattention" of Presidio La Bahía's commanders, Domingo, and his son Diego, Ramon. (Hadley, 1997), pp. 465–71.

64. Rebolledo's opinion […] attack by Apaches, […] Casafuerte's order to Urrutia […], BA July 18 –24, 1733. Viceroy Casafuerte made it clear that once Capt. "Joseph" de Urrutia's duties were accomplished, he was to order the auxiliary soldiers to return to their own presidios without delay. Moreover, Casafuerte reiterated this provision twice in the same letter suggesting that he imagined the recalcitrant Apache would

Notes to Pages 43–45   311

quickly and efficiently be brought under control. The viceroy himself repeats this same instruction in [Casafuerte's order ... presidio of Béxar against Apache attacks], BA July 30, 1733. Jackson and Foster stress the significance of the auditor of war, Juan Manuel de Oliván Rebolledo, as a leading advocate of presidial reform in New Spain in the early years of the eighteenth century. As a judge of the Royal *Audiencia* and an influential member of the *Junta General*, he had cross-examined the French trader St. Denis when the latter appeared at the presidio–mission complex at San Juan Bautista. The Frenchman's testimony made Oliván acutely aware of how critical the defense of Texas was to the welfare of neighboring provinces. As such, Oliván outlined the potential for French intrusion and, from a broadened perspective, realized that the *frontera* was a "cohesive unit whose problems were interrelated" and, thus, required an encompassing approach in order to be corrected. By the end of 1715, Oliván's report to Carlos III was enough to solidify the decision to reoccupy Texas. See Jack Jackson and William C. Foster, *Imaginary Kingdom: Texas as Seen by the Rivera and Rubí Military Expeditions, 1727 and 1767* (Austin: Texas State Historical Association, 1995), pp. 6–9. For the auditor of war's varied responsibilities in viceregal administration, see Polzer (1997), p. 439, fn5.

65. For other historians' perspective on José de Urrutia, including his lengthy presence among Apache encampments in the region of the Colorado River, see Barr (2007), pp. 110; 313, fn1; Weddle (1968), pp. 39–40; and Anibal González, "The Legend of Joseph de Urrutia," *Sayersville Historical Association Bulletin* 6 (Summer 1985): 14–19. For documents related to legal proceedings concerning a dispute between Urrutia and a supplier to presidial soldiers, see [proceedings José de Urrutia vs. Gabriel Costales ...], BA April 27, 1735; Gabriel Costales vs. José de Urrutia [...], BA June 10, 1735.

66. Loomis and Nasatir (1967), p. 461.

67. Ibid. For a discussion of the officer corps and its middle-aged members, see Archer (1995), pp. 199–200.

68. Loomis and Nasatir (1967), p. 509.

69. Castañeda (1942, vol. 4); Muñoz, military service records of Francisco Amangual, BA December 1793.

70. Ibid. Castañeda indicates that Amangual became the Béxar presidio's paymaster in *1784*. This is incorrect since primary source material shows his election to that position in December 1788.

71. Croix to Cabello, [...] issuing commissions to Amangual and Prada [...], BA August 16, 1779; [...] arrival of Francisco Amangual [and Prada, Ureña, and Borra to] Béxar, BA September 16, 1779.

72. Moorhead describes the soldiers comprising the tropa ligera as essentially recreated in 1778 from Croix's disbanding of the Catalonian company of volunteers and two *compañías volantes* from Sonora. Bucareli authorized recruitment for the latter units, distributed thereafter as personnel among the presidios located in Sonora, New Mexico, Nueva Vizcaya, and Coahuila. The "light troop" differed from the traditional, heavily armed *soldados de cuera* (the so-called soldiers of leather, named for a particular type of leather-padded jacket designed to thwart arrow penetration) in that they were armed with only a musket, two pistols, and a short sword, forsaking the lance, shield and leather armor (a weighty hardship for the horses, as well) and specified in the *Reglamento 1772*. The light troopers needed only three horses instead of the regulation seven and, to save these for battle, they would perform long marches on muleback. In rugged terrain, and now minus the lance, they would dismount and

312   Notes to Pages 45–46

fight on foot. Moorhead (1975), pp. 82–83. For the Catalonian Volunteers' knowledge of Sonora and their reliability as fighters, see Sánchez (1990), pp. 107–9. For images and descriptions of presidial armaments see chapter 6 of Odie Faulk and Laura Faulk, *Defenders of the Interior Provinces, Presidial Soldiers on the Northern Frontier of Spain.* (Albuquerque: The Albuquerque Museum, 1988), pp. 58–74.

73. Roster of the cavalry company of the Royal Presidio of La Bahía del Espíritu Santo, BA December 1, 1780.

74. Croix to Cabello, […] arrival of Francisco Amangual [and Prada, Ureña, and Borra to] Béxar, BA September 16, 1779.

75. Croix to Cabello, [accounts of] Amangual, [Prada, Ureña, Borra, and Ferrero], BA December 26, 1779. Moorhead (1968, p. 31) argues that, in some cases, captains were loath to send troops out on campaigns if those same men owed substantially on their presidial accounts, a "major cause of the ineffectiveness" of the presidio's defensive capabilities.

76. Moorhead (1968), p. 31–32. Cabello to Croix, […] instructions for handling accounts [of] Amangual […], BA November 1, 1779.

77. In the early seventeenth century, soldiers in Nueva Vizcaya received "half of their salaries in cash and half in clothing," until the presidials petitioned the viceroy for their salaries to be paid entirely in money. When the change occurred, the soldiers immediately saw their salaries reduced by one hundred pesos, the amount saved by the modification. Moorhead (1975), pp. 202–3. The chapter in its entirety is still the most informative explanation of the workings of the presidial payroll, pp. 201–21. Croix describes as useless the troops in Nueva Vizcaya at the beginning of 1779 with the "worst situation" found among the two pickets of dragoons. Alfred Barnaby Thomas, *Teodoro de Croix and the Northern Frontier of New Spain, 1776–1783* (Norman: University of Oklahoma Press, 1941), p. 118–20.

78. Cabello to Croix, […] instructions for handling accounts [of] Amangual […], BA November 1, 1779. According to Title Four of the Royal Regulations, the weapons of the presidial soldier consisted of a broad sword, lance, shield, musket, and pistols. The sword, described as "the same size and style as that used by other mounted men of the king's armies," had a lance head measuring thirteen and one-half inches in length (32.48 centimeters) by an inch and a half wide. The shield was not to vary from those used at that time, with musket and pistols to include "Spanish-style locks" and reserved for "horsemen." Both weapons were to be .66 caliber with lock mechanisms of the "best temper" to resist the intensity [*violencia*] of the sun. *Reglamento 1772, Título cuarto, Armamento y montura.* For images of armaments described above, see Sidney Brinckerhoff and Odie B. Faulk, *Lancers for the King. A Study of the Frontier Military System of Northern New Spain, With a Translation of the Royal Regulations of 1772* (Phoenix: Arizona Historical Foundation, 1965), pp. 69–76; and especially Sidney Brinckerhoff and Pierce Chamberlain, *Spanish Military Weapons in Colonial America 1700–1821* (Harrisburg: Stackpole, 1972), passim.

79. Cabello to Croix, […] instructions for handling accounts [of] Amangual […], BA November 1, 1779.

80. *Reglamento 1772, Título catorce, Obligaciones y nombramiento del habilitado*; and see: Publication proceedings of Articles 5–14 on management of supplies for presidial troops and families, BA June 1, 1780. The Royal Regulations of 1772 mandated the uniform of presidial soldiers, consisting of a short jacket of blue woolen cloth with a small cuff, red collar, breeches of blue wool [*tripe*], gold button, a cloth cap of the

Notes to Pages 46–47 313

same color, a cartridge pouch, and a leather jacket. Significantly, each soldier was to wear a bandoleer of chamois embroidered with the name of the presidio in order to distinguish one from the other, a back kerchief, *sombrero*, shoes, and leggings. *Reglamento 1772, Título tercero, vestuario*. Twenty years later, uniforms must not have changed much since the same description is found in *Noticia de las companias presidiales y volantes veteranas de caballeria, de a pie y cuerpo de Dragones provinciales que hay en las Provincias internas del poniente de N. E. con expresion de su estado major, 30 de Agosto de 1793* [sic passim]. See AGS, SGU, LEG, 7022, 16 (11, recto).

81. Cabello to Croix, […] instructions for handling accounts [of] Amangual […], BA November 1, 1779.

82. Ibid. Corporals stationed at Béxar would have received 300 pesos annually, and a private 290. But, as a third sergeant making an annual salary of 350 pesos, it appears that Ureña, in receiving the same two reales as the corporal and private, was being humbled for his fiscal irresponsibility in spite of his superior rank. See *Reglamento 1772, título segundo, artículo cinco*. For all that, by the following year Ureña and Ferrero won high praise from their commander for their "excellent records of service" and for being "highly qualified" for instructing recruits, their training passed on to troops in two regiments, the *ligeras* and *cueras*. Cabello to Croix, [Ferrero's promotion], BA January 13, 1780. Domingo Cabello was a fifty-three-year-old army colonel when he arrived in Béxar and, according to Chipman, a man committed to Bourbon Reform policies throughout his eight-year term as governor of Texas. To his mind, no Indian could be trusted, not even those congregated for years at the missions. Cabello viewed "good will on the part of all Indians" as reliable only to the "proportional extent of the goods provided to them." See Donald E. Chipman and Harriet Denise Joseph, *Spanish Texas 1519–1821*, rev. ed. (Austin: University of Texas Press, 1992), pp. 207–8; for Cabello's waffling attempts at equity toward and preferential treatment of Native inhabitants in his jurisdiction, see Britten (2009), pp. 141–55.

83. Marchena Fernández argued for a sociological perspective as necessary to understand the ranking system of five sectors within the American army of the eighteenth century. Since Amangual was an officer, he belonged to the "highest military social group" vis-á-vis the regular units of the Royal Army. Disparities and similarities in socio-military hierarchy had a geographic component as well, best compared between officers from the Iberian Peninsula and those native born (*criollos*) serving in New Spain. See Marchena Fernández (1983), pp. 31, 78–79.

84. *Reglamento 1772, Título segundo, Pie, paga y gratificación de las compañías de presidios*.

85. Ibid.

86. *Reglamento 1772, Título segundo, artículo cuarto*.

87. Ibid. In one section devoted to reforming New Mexico's presidios, three documents explain the significance of strengthening alliances between the Spanish and the Native population by prohibiting abuses of *indios de rescate*, by punishing irresponsible soldiers and by better equipping and paying presidials. See Hadley (1997), pp. 281–329.

88. One prominent Mexican scholar differentiates between the tropa ligera and the 'regular' presidio soldiers but places more emphasis on the capabilities of the cavalry. See Luis Navarro García, "La expansión de las fronteras indianas en el siglo XVIII," in *Aportaciones militares a la cultura, arte y ciencia en el siglo xviii hispanoamericano* (Sevilla: Capitanía general de la región militar Sur, 1993), pp. 227–28.

314   Notes to Pages 49–51

89. Cabello to Croix, Report on plan to reduce army mounts [and keep horses] inside the presidio, BA November 1, 1780. Earlier in the year, Croix had ordered a review of the herds at the Texas presidios. Cabello to Croix [review of horse and mule herds at Béxar and La Bahía], BA January 12, 1780.

90. *Reglamento 1772, Título cuarto, armamento y montura, artículo cinco; artículo seis.*

91. Cabello to Croix, Report on plan to reduce army mounts [keep horses stabled] inside the presidio, BA November 1, 1780.

92. Ibid.

93. Ibid. The housing of horses in the vicinity of the presidio constituted yet another source of discord between provincial authorities and local communities. In one case five years prior to the creation of the Mesteñas fund, citizens of San Antonio de Béxar were ordered to remove certain of their horses from the *caballada* maintained at the presidio. In 1773 then–governor of Texas and colonel of the cavalry, Barón Juan María de Ripperdá, circulated an edict that the allowance ("*cituado*") of the horse herd had scaled up to 1,100 animals, sometimes more, with population spurts due to the arrival of citizens and troops from the recently closed presidio at Los Adaes. The transition proved to be fraught with danger for the animals. Injury to individual horses resulted from young animals bruising one another in the sorting rooms and relays which then stirred up the entire *caballada*. Owners had fifteen days to withdraw the animals or face the possibility of mares and colts being separated from the herd without their owners' knowledge, and "intact horses" being gelded. See Ripperdá's decree ordering [citizens' horses in] presidio's caballada to withdraw them, BA October 10, 1773. During the same year, in a much different scenario involving the same community, issues concerning horses were dispensed with in more accommodating fashion. Ripperdá received a response to a message he sent to Viceroy Bucareli informing him that *vecinos* working at a mine some thirty leagues away had discovered horses and mares which they recognized as belonging to four Lipan Apache. They followed fresh tracks but did not encounter them. Bucareli directed the Governor to alert the first Lipan individual that might appear to come and reclaim the horses. See Bucareli y Ursua to Ripperdá, ordering the return of horses belonging to Lipan Indians, BA December 8, 1773.

94. Croix to Cabello, distribution of arms to Béxar and La Bahía troops, BA December 18, 1778. Still a useful source for the development of the La Bahía presidio and mission but with an emphasis on secondary sources, see Kathryn Stoner O'Connor, *The Presidio La Bahía del Espíritu Santo de Zuñiga, 1721-1846* (Austin: Von Boeckmann-Jones, 1966). For images of eighteenth-century 69 caliber flintlock pistols and what one historian saw as difficulties experienced by soldiers in using firearms, see Faulk and Faulk (1988), pp. 68–69.

95. Rengel to Cabello, […] Rengel's order to governor of Nuevo León and [Santander] to allow Texas and Coahuila troops to secure remounts, BA February 5, 1785.

Chapter 2

1. Thomas (1941), p. 78. See Croix to Cabello, discussing conditions in Texas […], BA June 13, 1781.

2. Rengel to Cabello, [report explaining] differences in promotion of officers of flying companies and the presidial companies, BA September 15, 1785. A point of interest related to promotions in the hierarchy of military ranking further suggests

Notes to Pages 51–53 315

the specialized status of *volantes* vis-à-vis presidials. Rengel reminded commanders of a royal order of three years prior (May 21, 1782) indicating an "alternative" method when promoting officers in the *volante* companies as compared with those of presidios. If a captain of a flying squadron was a veteran, like others in the army, they were to receive preference in proposals for presidial companies over lieutenants with the same veteran status. Furthermore, there existed an inclination toward favoring *volantes* over first alférezes for lieutenancies of presidios. But first alférezes––whether presidial or *volante*––were to receive consideration without distinction between the two types and according to their ability and qualifications for lieutenancies. Second alférezes in both classes were to ascend to the rank of first alférez within their own companies and without the necessity of a nomination or dispatch just as Amangual did in August 1786 upon the retirement of Marcelo Valdés.

3. Neve to Cabello, transmitting royal order concerning merit raise for soldiers, BA December 19, 1783. "Vellón": made of billón, a fusion of copper and less than half silver; in other words, not a *real de plata*.

4. Ibid. Neve's letter conveying the Gálvez order of the king's decree includes a brief discussion of what today we might refer to as health insurance benefits. During hospitalization, the soldiers would "have two-thirds of their entire benefits discounted to them, being assisted as is appropriate to [their] designation [rank] which shall be at least that of sergeant." The king did not ignore the army's regimental musicians either: drummers, kettledrummers, fifers, and trumpeters were never to achieve the rank of officers, even if they had served thirty-five years. However, they would receive in pay 135 *reales* a month having the rank of sergeant. The king did not abolish the favors he had previously conceded to this class in royal orders of December 19, 1779, and February 17, 1780.

5. See Marchena Fernández's (1983, pp. 335–36) discussion of retirees in the Américas and the challenges of paying them half of their regular salary. Also, the inevitability of poverty dogged most retired soldiers in New Spain even as age took its toll on their bodies. See Archer (1977), pp. 199–202.

6. [. . .] Rubio to Ripperdá, concerning the dismissal of disabled soldiers, BA July 15, 1777. The commander inspector differed from the commandant general in that the former came under the supervision of the latter as described in the 1772 Regulations. However, if a Commandancy General had not been established (1776), the inspector would have remained under the direct orders of the viceroy. The inspector could not govern a province at the same time, nor could he be captain of a presidio since he was always to oversee the operations and management of all provincial governors and captains; in fact, he was required to change his residence if necessary. He was to hold annual reviews of the presidios and was, in the most general sense, expected to be vigilant about the military personnel's strict obedience to the requirements of the Regulation. *Reglamento 1772, Título doce.*

7. [. . .] Rubio to Ripperdá, concerning the dismissal of disabled soldiers, BA July 15, 1777. Another soldier from the company at "Béjar" also filled out a license for incapacity. In both scenarios, replacements were to be immediately available.

8. Hugh O'Conor, an Irishman in Spain's royal army, had served in the Regiment of Volunteers of Aragon and served in Cuba under his first cousin Marshal Alejandro O'Reilly. Following a special inspection assignment to Texas in 1765, he became provisional governor of Texas from 1767 to 1770. He then served from 1772–76 as *comandante inspector* of all the frontier provinces. Moorhead (1975), pp. 68–69; Bernard

E. Bobb, "Bucareli and the Interior Provinces," *Hispanic American Historical Review* 34, no. 1 (Feb. 1954): 22–36. In 1773, O'Conor was the subject of a mass distribution of information between the presidios following his promotion. Viceroy Bucareli ordered Ripperdá to inform troops at Los Adaes and those stationed at La Bahía of O'Conor's ascension into that new role. See Bucareli to Ripperdá, O'Conor's appointment as [Commander Inspector of] all interior presidios of New Spain, BA January 20, 1773. For other sources, see José Ignacio Rubio Mañé, "Nota Introductoria" in "El Teniente Coronel Don Hugo O'Conor y la situación en Chihuahua, 1771" and "Itinerario del Teniente Coronel Don Hugo O'Conor, de la Ciudad de México a la villa de Chihuahua, 1771," *Boletín del Archivo General de la Nación* 30 (1959): 355–91, 395–471, 647–55. Mark Santiago, *The Red Captain: The Life of Hugo O'Conor* (Tucson: Arizona Historical Society, 1994); Kieran McCarty and Mark Santiago, "The Founder of Spanish Tucson Petitions the King: Don Hugo O'Conor's 1770 'Relacion,'" *Journal of Arizona History* 39, no. 1 (Spring 1998): 85–98. For O'Conor's 1777 report to Croix, with a translation and photostats of the original document, see Cutter (1994).

9. Rubio to Ripperdá, confirming honors granted to Narciso de Tapia and his soldiers for bravery in action, BA June 18, 1777. For the complexities of retirement and the human dimensions of its eventuality, see Marchena Fernández (1983), pp. 335–36.

10. Rubio to Ripperdá, confirming honors granted to Narciso de Tapia and his soldiers for bravery in action, BA June 18, 1777.

11. Croix to Ripperdá, transmitting orders concerning employment of retired military men, BA March 30, 1778.

12. Rubio's list of frontier military men retiring with pay and honors conferred by the King, BA October 14, 1777. For more on retirement and disability, see chapter 3 of this study and especially my discussion of the *hojas de servicio* (military service records).

13. *Reglamento 1772, Título catorce, Obligaciones y nombramiento del habilitado.*

14. Moorhead (1975), p. 201. Recurrent themes in presidio history include the economic challenges to soldiers' pay and endless debt. But little has been written about troops conforming to, or not, the regulations that structured presidial life, or even about episodes of disunion that pitted one soldier against another. These types of interactions necessitated lengthy investigations that convoked stakeholders representing the military hierarchy across the colonial borderlands. I concur with Vicente Rodríguez García concerning the terms "bureaucrat" and "bureaucracy" in that I, too, advocate for sparing the terms from persistent status as pejoratives. Rodríguez García argues, somewhat cheekily, that the role played by the bureaucrat in the eighteenth century was of greater importance than that of today's bureaucrat, and that men in that role required a clear mind (*mente clara*) conducive to sorting out their work. Further, the bureaucrat of an earlier period had to possess not only technical knowledge but also a clear aim in the proper direction for all the issues that passed through his hands. Vicente Rodríguez García, *El Fiscal de Real Hacienda en Nueva España (Don Ramon de Posada y Soto, 1781–1793)* (Oviedo: Secretariado de publicaciones de la Universidad de Oviedo, 1985), p. 11, fn14. For the "special importance" of the fiscal in "all colonial central administration," see Pietschmann (1996): 80–81.

15. Jesús F. de la Teja, "Forgotten Founders: The Military Settlers in Eighteenth-Century San Antonio de Béxar," in Poyo/Hinojosa (1991), pp. 29–30. When the Alarcón-Espinosa expedition met the goal of establishing a mission on the San Antonio

Notes to Pages 54–57

River in 1718, it seems "few soldiers had brought their families" to foster stability in the region. Hadley (1997), p. 361. Settler numbers were slight, and recruitment from Coahuila was not promising as presented in Francisco Céliz, *Diary of the Alarcón Expedition into Texas, 1718–1719*, Fritz Leo Hoffmann, trans. (Los Angeles: The Quivira Society, 1935), pp. 21–25.

16. Moorhead (1975), p. 224.

17. *Reglamento 1772, Título once, gobierno político*; "buena vida y costumbres."

18. Ibid.

19. Martos y Navarette to Marqués de las Amarillas, BA December 16, 1759. Also, see *Reglamento 1772, Título trece, artículo cinco*. For a good, condensed essay on the system of recruitment for the Américas, see Carmen Gómez Pérez, "La recluta en el ejército de América," in *Aportaciones militares a la cultura, arte y ciencia en el siglo xviii hispanoamericano* (Sevilla: Capitanía general de la región militar Sur, 1993), pp. 79–84. For a thoroughgoing review of the recruitment process and the differences between mustering soldiers for service on the Peninsula and in the Américas, see Marchena Fernández (1983), pp. 263–74. For renovation of the recruitment system by Carlos III's *quinta*, a raffle by which one out of every five useful men should render service, see Borreguero Beltrán, (1989), passim.

20. Situated on the lower reaches of the Trinity River, Orcoquisac was established in 1756 with thirty soldiers to protect the missions for the *Orcoquisa* Indians. Moorhead (1975), p. 53. For other reactions to the "Orocoquisac" presidio, see Morfi (1935), p. 110; Herbert Eugene Bolton, *Athanase De Mézières and the Louisiana-Texas Frontier, 1768–1780* (Cleveland: Arthur H. Clark, 1914), pp. 29–30.

21. Copy of Martos y Navarrete's letter to Amarillas [soldiers serving in Texas remain as citizens], BA December 16, 1759. If the governor reviewed the 1756 petition presented by the friars of San Xavier, he might have felt a measure of guilt in their description of soldiers "continually naked, lacking weapons, and horses, unfit for Royal Service." José Porrua Turanzas, José Manuel, and Enrique Porrua Venero, eds., *Documentos para la historia eclesiastica y civil de la provincia de Texas o Nuevas Philipinas, 1720–1779* (Madrid: Ediciones José Porrúa Turanzas, 1961), p. 114.

22. Copy of Martos y Navarrete's letter to Amarillas […], BA December 16, 1759.

23. Proceedings [compromise] in the case of soldiers of Los Adaes vs. Martos y Navarrete, BA May 28, 1770. Whether Castañeda is an apologist for Martos or not, he argues that the Governor "was not as careless as Morfi makes him out [to be]." Referencing the Béxar Archives documents, Castañeda stresses the evidence found there shows that Martos "tried to do his duty." Morfi (1935), p. 413, fn52.

24. Copy of Martos y Navarrete's letter to Amarillas, [soldiers serving in Texas remain as citizens], BA December 16, 1759.

25. *Reglamento 1772, Título once, gobierno político*. Croix's 1780 instructions establishing a pair of settlements in the "Territory of the Yuma Nation" charged the paymaster at Presidio Altar, "for now," with the task and clarified that he was to provide "economically for the needs of all," including soldiers, residents, and workers. But when it seemed "more suitable" for a merchant to manage the money, the habilitado was to then stop collecting and providing supplies. Bringas (1977), p. 101. Paying the soldiers in specie proved to be just as challenging in New Mexico, but when it materialized "more money circulated in the local economy." Frank (2000), pp. 91–95.

26. Proceedings […] José Macario Zambrano vs. Francisco Amangual, BA July 30, 1791.

318   Notes to Pages 57–58

27. Ibid. 1 *vara* = 33 1/3 inches (846.67 mm), or 1 yard = 1.08 *varas*; 1 *arroba* = 25 pounds. In fact, Castañeda indicates that a half *arroba* is "about twelve pounds." Morfi, pt. 2 (1935), p. 425. Certified copy of invoices of supplies taken to the company of Béxar by Francisco Amangual, BA April 14, 1788. An early but still useful essay on Spanish colonial metrology is Manuel Carrera Stampa, "The Evolution of Weights and Measures in New Spain," trans. Robert Smith, *Hispanic American Historical Review* 29, no. 1 (Feb. 1949): 2–24.

28. Certified [. . . supplies taken to Béxar by] Amangual, BA April 14, 1788. More specifically, thirteen duties and obligations entrusted to the presidio paymaster appear in Title Fourteen of the Regulations, including the need for the paymaster to have enough provisions for the distribution of rations and for supplying the troops with clothing and equipment. And the paymaster had the right to collect from the captain, officers, chaplain, sergeants, and soldiers a commission of 2 percent for the "services and expenses" occasioned by his office. *Reglamento 1772, Título secundo* [sic], *pie, paga y gratificación de las compañías de presidios*.

29. Martínez Pacheco to Ugalde, reporting measures taken to send Amangual to collect payroll [. . .], BA March 12, 1788. The thirty-seven-year-old Bernardo Fernández had served in the Regiment of Dragoons of Sagunto before his promotion to lieutenant in the cavalry company of the Béxar presidio. See Affidavit [election of] paymaster of Béxar, BA August 1, 1776. Twelve years after having served as the presidio's paymaster, Fernández must have continued to excel as an officer. In his military service record under the section devoted to personal evaluations made by the presidio captain ("informe del"), the captain wrote "es acrehedor de ascensión [he is worthy of promotion]." When drawn from microfilm images at the Center for Southwest Research Library at the University of New Mexico, the military service records in this book are those originally archived in the Archivo de Simancas, Guerra Moderna, Legajos 7016, 7278, reel 62 (hereafter CSWR SAII). Military service record of Bernardo Fernández by Marcos Reañe, December 1795, CSWR, SAII. For more on the Sagunto dragoons, see José Ignacio de March, *Nociones militares, ó suplemento a los principios de fortificación del Señor Don Pedro de Lucuze: escrito para la instrucción de los caballeros de dragones de Sagunto* (Nabu Press, 2011).

30. Soldiers could be proactive toward their own interests, and especially where it concerned personal income. In 1702, forty-three troops from the presidio of Sinaloa in Nueva Vizcaya petitioned the viceroy for an increase to their salaries. See Polzer and Sheridan (1997), pp. 268–75. Similarly fed up with a lack of provisions and "no one to supply us," soldiers at Los Adaes directly petitioned the interim governor to alleviate their destitution. See Francis X. Galán, *Los Adaes, the First Capital of Spanish Texas* (College Station: Texas A&M University Press, 2020), pp. 93–94; and Proceedings [officers and soldiers of Los Adaes concerning supply], BA October 5, 1737. One soldier reached out to the Texas governor for help after his captain had exhausted hope in trying to feed and clothe his presidio company. See Córdoba to O'Conor, [soldiers without food and clothes], BA January 3, 1768.

31. Moorhead (1975), pp. 66–67. Soldiers serving at this time could not have known what frontier troops would endure in the way of further pay reductions by the time the Regulations of 1772 circulated in the Comandancia General. Polzer and Sheridan (1997), p. 12.

32. Moorhead (1975), pp. 202–5, 206 fn14; 207. See also Fray Lezaún's account of New Mexico's state of affairs in Hackett, vol. 3 (1937), pp. 468–79. In a case documenting

Notes to Pages 58–60   319

missionary benevolence by way of provisioning neglected soldiers while enduring economic sacrifice to themselves, see Fray Francisco de Ayeta's petition as ecclesiastical *juez ordinario* and *custodia*, in Hackett, vol. 3 (1937), pp. 290–93. Note how one general at the apex of authority in the Comandancia engaged in double-dealing when settling soldier debt to missionaries. Moorhead (1968), pp. 32–33. The soldiers stationed at Presidio de El Paso del Río del Norte complained about their captain Pedro de la Fuente's alleged malfeasance in interviews conducted by Lt. Joseph de Ibarra in 1766. See Duvall (2020), pp. 47–100.

33. Moorhead (1975), pp. 207–8. His full name was Cayetano María Pignatelli Rubí Corbera y San Climent, and the historiography covering his career is too extensive to be included here. Where his contributions to the Comandancia General are most significantly highlighted, especially his two- year inspection of the Eastern provinces, see Brinckerhoff and Faulk (1965), Moorhead (1968, 1975), John (1975); for the Viceroy's 1766 instructions to Rubí, see the English translation in Duvall (2020), pp. 19–27, and for Rubí's "Comprehensive General Statement" of April 3, 1768, signed in Tacubaya, pp. 245–46; and for the reproduction of the Dictamen signed in Tacubaya "10 de abril de 1768," see Carmen Velásquez (1982), pp. 29–82, and the English translation in Jackson (1995), pp. 171–207. For Rubí's itinerary, see the David McDonald translation in Jackson and Foster (1995), pp. 90–157; Foster (1999), pp. 177–93. For example, see the list of 101 items with price points and tables grouping presidios into nine categories in Naylor and Polzer (1988), pp. 282–86. In fact, the governor of Texas at that time, Ángel Martos de Navarrete, was aware of the impending *visita* by Rubí. Part of the inspection of all presidios included Rubí's review of the old price regulations in comparison with fluctuations of those same prices across time and space. See Cruillas to Martos y Navarrete, announcing Rubí's [inspection] of all presidios of Texas, BA February 27, 1766.

34. Croix to Ripperdá, […] proposed position for assistant paymaster for presidial companies, BA April 24, 1778. Independent contractors were not much better even though some of their lot came from the merchant guild of Chihuahua. See Moorhead (1975), pp. 214–17. As of this book's publication date, I have not located Croix's bando nor Cazorla's response to Croix's solicitation.

35. The ballots were to be sent sealed, then opened and published in the presence of a junta in the manner of Article 2, Title 9, tratado 1 of the General Ordinances of the Army, and in *Reglamento Instructivo de 13 de Noviembre de 1755* in Portugués, (Madrid: Antonio Marín, 1765), p. 34, número 36. See Croix to Cabello, giving instructions for the election of presidial paymasters, BA April 4, 1780; Croix to Cabello, […] regulating duties and powers of presidial paymasters, BA June 23, 1780; Cabello to Croix, acknowledging receipt of instructions regarding elections of paymasters, BA July 8, 1780.

36. [Cabello's] charges against Luis Cazorla after completion of review of La Bahía, BA August 21, 1780.

37. Ibid. Eight years prior, Cazorla's superiors called for a diary of an expedition that he was to have compiled. See Bucarely y Ursua to Ripperdá, requesting Cazorla's diary of exploration of the coast […], BA December 9, 1772. If his neglect of the requisite paper trail is any indication of his occasional inattention to administrative matters, Cazorla made up for it with notes of his exploration of the Texas coast. See Hackett (1931), pp. 392–97.

38. Martínez Pacheco to Ugalde, reporting the return of Amangual […], BA November 9, 1788. Military report, BA November 30, 1788.

320 Notes to Pages 60–62

39. Martínez Pacheco to the *Cabildo* [of San Fernando], discussing complaint filed against Amangual, BA Dec 24, 1788. Joaquín Menchaca was no stranger to financial crises; six years prior, he incurred a debt to the rector of San Fernando that also involved, according to Menchaca's wife Juana Delgado, the merchant José de la Santa. See Fray Pedro Fuentes vs. Joaquín Menchaca, […], BA May 29, 1782. Menchaca was eventually involved in cattle roundups and export, presumably to increase his livelihood. See License issued by Muñoz to Joaquín Menchaca for rounding up unbranded cattle, BA April 19, 1793; Petition of Joaquín Menchaca to Muñoz for an export license to take cattle out of Texas, BA August 18, 1793.

40. Reports on election of Francisco Amangual as paymaster of Béxar, BA December 30, 1788; Power of attorney to Amangual, BA December 30, 1788; Martínez Pacheco to Ugalde, [Amangual's election], BA January 3, 1789.

41. Ugalde to Martínez Pacheco, reporting the Viceroy's appointment of Amangual as second lieutenant, BA March 14, 1789.

42. Ugalde to Martínez Pacheco, […] power of attorney […] signed over to Amangual […], BA April 11, 1789. Two weeks later, Ugalde ordered Martínez Pacheco to allow Amangual to make only one annual trip to collect the payroll, and the governor was to inform Lt. Manuel Espadas to instruct the paymaster at La Bahía to accompany Amangual. See Martínez Pacheco to Ugalde [paymaster to make one annual trip to San Luis Potosí and Bahía paymaster to do the same], BA April 24, 1789.

43. Ugalde to Martínez Pacheco, instructing him to equip [Cerda] for an upcoming campaign, BA July 4, 1789; Martínez Pacheco to Ugalde, [receipt of his July 4 letter concerning] Cerda [order forwarded to Amangual], BA July 13, 1789.

44. Martínez Pacheco to Ugalde, [departure of Cerda fully equipped] for Río Grande, BA July 21, 1789.

45. Muñoz's certification of receipts for payments of transportation fees to Amangual, BA December 14, 1790. According to a 1778 proclamation by Croix, the Mesteñas fund had its origins in the wild, unbranded cattle and horses found in the *provincia* of Tejas and taken or destroyed by certain "vagabonds [*vagamundos*]" among the presidio citizenry. Croix believed their lawlessness encouraged discord among families and instilled a lack of subordination to and respect for the governors and other officials whose duties included the administration of justice. These "vagabonds" who lived off the goods, wealth, and cattle of more respectable citizens [*honrrados* (sic) *vasallos*] are not specifically named, but it can be assumed that they were part of both the civilian and military population. Croix made it clear that a contributing factor to their dishonorable behavior was the liberty with which many had authorized for themselves to build corrals and stockades, and subsequently round up, enclose, and take possession of wild and unbranded cattle and horses. The viceroy pronounced the animals in their entirety as belonging to the *Real Cámara y Fisco de Su Magestad* [Royal Chamber and Exchequer] for two reasons: first, they were strays and had no known owner; and second, because they were born and raised in unappropriated lands and not given in grants or alienated properties. See Croix to Ripperdá, […] establishment and management of mesteñas fund, BA January 11, 1778.

46. [Munoz's] receipts […] transportation fees to Amangual, BA December 14, 1790.

47. Croix to Ripperdá, […] establishment and management of mesteñas fund, BA January 11, 1778. The penalties for concealing captured animals to avoid payment of duties could be severe even if Governor Cabello mollified the amount imposed by

Notes to Pages 62–64   321

the commander general on October 27, 1779. See Proclamation reinforcing Cabello's decree [of] payment of mesteñas taxes, BA January 5, 1782. For an accounting of fines and duties imposed on civilians and soldiers for wrongful capturing of *orejano* cattle and mustang horses since January 1, 1783, see the Annual report of mesteñas fund, BA December 31, 1783. See also Jack Jackson, *Los Mesteños: Spanish Ranching in Texas, 1721–1821* (College Station: Texas A&M University Press, 1986), p. 9.

48. Croix to Ripperdá, […] establishment and management of mesteñas fund, BA January 11, 1778.

49. By the summer 1779, Ripperdá was under suspicion of wrongdoing to such an extent that proceedings were filed to charge him and the Béxar paymaster, Bernardo Fernández, with disregarding protocol while serving at the Texas presidio. See further Certified copy [of proceedings] against Ripperdá […] charged with mismanagement of affairs at Béxar, BA July 15, 1779.

50. The word *mesteña* is frequently misspelled — by Cabello or his scribe — "mesqueña" throughout the document, unless he meant to describe the horses as miserable (*mezquino*) or in otherwise bad shape. Cabello to Croix, reporting on mesteñas fund, BA April 4, 1779; and for documents concerning the collection of taxes for the fund from this same year, see Croix to Cabello, approving Cabello's measures for the collection of taxes for the mesteñas fund, BA September 16, 1779; Cabello to Croix, […] approving Cabello's suggestion [collection of tax], BA October 8, 1779; Publication proceedings [to the *Cabildo*, Justice and Regiment of San Fernando] of Cabello's decree relative to payment of mesteñas taxes, BA October 27, 1779.

51. By 1798, Amangual is granted a tract of land at the intersection of the "Adovitos" and San Pedro creeks to pasture his herd of cattle. He claimed, or was credited with, being "well known" from his efforts in raising cattle. *Concesión interina de terreno a Francisco Amangual, año de 1798*, Bexar County Spanish Archives, hereafter BCSA, 0167–0169.

52. Amangual to Muñoz, asking for a loan […] to pay troop salaries, BA April 20, 1791 [to 12/30/1791].

53. Amangual to Munoz, [payment from mesteñas fund], BA July 23, 1791. As it has already been noted, the "Friendly" nations are often not specifically identified. Muñoz uses the terms "amigos" and "Yndios de paz" in his response. Out of exasperation, one Texas governor a few years earlier did pinpoint as friendly by name, the "Texas, Tancagues, Mayeyes, Vidais, Cocos, and Orcoquizacs," to his superior. See Cabello to Rengel, [dealing with Lipans], BA September 19, 1785. See the "small nation" formed between the "Tancagües" and the "Mayeses," together with the "Yocobanes," in Cortés (1989), p. 83; and the neighboring nations of the "Orkoquisas, Vidais, and Texas," p. 86. See Chapter 1, fn 33 in this book. However, as a convenient descriptor for groups that frequented the presidios, a precise identification may not have necessarily been important to the upper echelons of military authority. Years later, when Nava instructed Muñoz to ensure that the friendly nations were "treated with the greatest affability by all government agents," he was specific in his mandates concerning food and its preparation: provide them daily with the customary ration of "meat, corn, beans" and furnish them with the "pots, firewood, and other necessary utensils to prepare their meals." Where these transactions concerned Amangual, Nava made it clear to Muñoz that this type of provisioning was to be "run by some intelligent individual who had managed those types of affairs in the past." Further, that person must understand that the Native recipients were to receive the same

322 Notes to Pages 64–65

rations as before, and they were not to be displeased by any tightening of the purse strings related to foodstuffs that had been consistently provided to them. Nava to Muñoz, discussing Indian relations, BA January 4, 1791.

54. Correspondence between Francisco Amangual and Muñoz, [...] sum owed by Ugalde, BA July 23, 1791.

55. Ibid. In late 1790, Muñoz found Martínez Pacheco to be in arrears to the tune of 13,458 pesos and one *real*. Once Nava became aware of this deficit, he was prepared to send documents to the *asesor* of the Commandancy General for his review. Nava to Muñoz, concerning shortage in Martínez Pacheco's accounts, BA February 9, 1791. But Martínez Pacheco was already under the bureaucratic radar. A few months earlier, he was the focus of a complaint filed by the Ayuntamiento of San Fernando that subsequently resulted in an investigation into apparent wrongdoing. Revilla Gigedo to Muñoz, [complaint] made by Ayuntamiento of San Fernando against Martínez Pacheco and ordering an investigation, BA May 11, 1790. For another perspective on the controversial captain, see the discussion about Martínez Pacheco's attitude toward the "Friendly Nations" in Barr (2007), pp. 273–76, 282–83, 285.

56. According to his own account, Andrés Benito Courbiére was a native of León, France, and came to Louisiana seeking a better life. He enlisted in the militia company of the Natchitoches Post, but then transferred to the Béxar presidio as part of a picket from the same company that was assigned to escort Lt. Col. "Atanacio" de Mézières. Courbiére attained the rank of "soldado distinguido" and subsequently petitioned to continue in the service of the Crown. Andrés Benito Courbiére to the Governor of Texas, [...] reasons for residing in Texas, BA May 12, 1792. Croix selected Courbiére to be an interpreter for those indigenous communities that frequented Béxar seeking peace. Documentation by numerous military personnel, including governor Domingo Cabello and cited throughout this study, verifies Courbiére's expertise as an interpreter. De Mézières attested to his ability to "read and write." See Bolton (1914), pp. 318–19. Courbiére's colorful presence as a reliable negotiator of intercultural (mis)understandings in the colonial borderlands appears in several studies, including Barr (2007), pp. 279–80; and John (1975), passim.

57. Manuel de Urrutia may very well have used alcohol to ease physical discomfort and emotional anguish. While he was First Sgt. at the Béxar presidio, Urrutia suffered a fall on the night of November 29, 1785, that caused considerable and recurring injury to his right shoulder. After multiple procedures to put the shoulder back in place, Urrutia lost the use of his right arm, causing him to be discharged. At that time, he was in line for the rank of Second Alférez of the cavalry company at La Bahía, based upon his "merits and good service." However, since his injury prevented his assuming the post, Governor Cabello advocated for Urrutia's status of 'ymbálido' with the rank of alférez so he could receive the corresponding compensation. Cabello to Rengel, [...] Urrutia's discharge from service [...], BA February 5, 1786; and for the high regard for Urrutia, holding the rank of second alférez at this time, by his commanders, see Ugarte y Loyola to Cabello, discussing discharge of Manuel de Urrutia, BA May 11, 1786; for the administrative conundrum that ensued, see Cabello to Cazorla, [official dispatch re:] Urrutia's appointment at La Bahía, BA June 10, 1786; for Urrutia's rise in rank even after his misfortunes, see Cabello to Ugarte y Loyola, [completion of orders regarding] Urrutia's appointment as second alférez of La Bahía, BA June 18, 1786.

58. Amangual to Governor of Texas, [...] incidents [...] Manuel de Urrutia, BA June 11, 1791.Things must not have changed much over the summer; the regidor

Notes to Pages 65–69   323

and interim alcalde of San Fernando de Béxar mentioned Urrutia's "amaseamiento escandaloso" with an "infidel" woman of the "Cumanche Nation." See Juan José de la Santa's affidavit [immoral character of] Urrutia, BA September 9, 1791.

59. Amangual to Governor of Texas [incidents] Manuel de Urrutia, BA June 11, 1791.

60. Ibid.

61. Ibid.

62. Corporal José Manuel de Castro to Governor of Texas, reporting incident with Lieutenant Urrutia, BA June 12, 1791.

63. Ibid.

64. Clearly Manuel de Urrutia suffered from alcoholism and his devotion to booze and its negative effects was confirmed by other presidials and commanders throughout his career. Only six months after the shenanigans with the Ute woman and the shame he brought to his own family, Alférez Urrutia was the defendant in a complaint filed by Lt. Bernardo Fernández. After the intoxicated Urrutia called his superior Fernández a "rotten coward" and a "good for nothing," he attacked his commander with a horse and grazed Fernández's clothing with the stock of his musket. See Bernardo Fernández vs. Manuel Urrutia, charged with insubordination, BA January 25, 1792.

65. Proceedings in the case of disorderly conduct of Lieutenant Manuel de Urrutia, BA July 11, 1791. In the same vein as "cuera(s)" is used to describe the customary clothing of the frontier cavalry, the term "en cueros" can be understood to mean "in uniform," since, apart from the specialized padded vest worn by the *soldado de cuera*, leather pieces constituted much of the soldiers' frontier outfit. Or, perhaps, a stupefied Urrutia meant to say, "*estoy encuerado*."

66. Proceedings in the case of disorderly conduct of Lieutenant Manuel de Urrutia, BA July 11, 1791.

67. Proceedings in the case of […] Zambrano vs. […] Amangual for breach of contract, BA July 30, 1791. The municipal junta consisted of an alcalde ordinario having the first vote of seniority and presiding over the council, as well as an alcalde *de segundo voto*. See Fisher (1969/1929), p. 123; and Cutter (1995), pp. 96, 100.

68. Proceedings in the case of […] Zambrano vs. […] Amangual for breach of contract, BA July 30, 1791. Whether in times of harvest or otherwise, cultivators were prohibited from selling their corn for a higher price than twenty *reales* for each *fanega*, and that whoever disobeyed would lose the grain. This *bando* applied to the missionaries and when so informed of its content, the *padre presidente* Fray Josef Rafael Oliva challenged it, citing Law 13, Title 25, Book 5 of the *Recopilación* [of the Laws of the Indies] that gave cultivators the right to sell wheat, barley, and other grains at the price they wished to set. See Martínez Pacheco to Ugalde, [no more corn from Béxar], BA January 10, 1789; [ibid,] fixing the price of corn, BA January 30, 1789; and the response in Ugalde to Martínez Pacheco, [dispute with Oliva] over the price of corn, BA February 14, 1789.

69. Several documents spanning almost sixty years related to distribution of the grain supply exist in the Béxar Archives. See especially Certified copy of proceedings […] rendering decision on other matters relative to the price of grain bought by troops from settlers […], BA January 24, 1736; Espadas to Martínez Pacheco, discussing the distribution of the grain supply, BA October 14, 1789; and the response, Martínez Pacheco to Espadas, […] equitable distribution of the grain supply, BA October 24, 1789.

70. Proceedings in the case of […] Zambrano vs. […] Amangual for breach of contract, BA July 30, 1791.

324   Notes to Pages 70–72

71. Ibid.

72. Ibid. Amondarain worked chiefly as a merchant and more specifically as an exporter of livestock. He was involved in several disputes with both ecclesiastical and military authorities. His life riven with controversy, he was alternatively prevented from and authorized to take cattle from missions and presidios in the Texas frontier. Perhaps the most compelling documentation of his life in the borderlands is his participation in a 1790 custody battle involving citizens from San Fernando that eventually resulted in Amondarain escaping as a fugitive from, apparently, a combination of his troubles. Cazorla to Martínez Pacheco, [...] exportation of cattle by [Amondarain], BA September 6, 1787; Cazorla to Martínez Pacheco, [...] reasons for preventing Martin de Amondarain from taking livestock, BA July 31, 1788; José de la Santa and Francisco Bueno vs. Amondarain, contesting his qualifications as custodian of children and their inherited property, BA October 18, 1790; Correspondence between [Fernández] and Muñoz, concerning escape of [Amondarain] and plans for his capture, BA December 20, 1790; BA December 24, 1790.

73. Proceedings in the case of [...] Zambrano vs. [...] Amangual for breach of contract, BA July 30, 1791. The case is briefly mentioned in Jesús F. de la Teja, *San Antonio de Béxar: A Community on New Spain's Northern Frontier* (Albuquerque: University of New Mexico Press, 1996), p. 90.

74. Castro to Muñoz, ordering Muñoz to sell Macario Zambrano's preferred grain before it spoils, BA September 10, 1791. By the summer of 1792, Zambrano was deceased, but Ramón de Castro sent the *expediente* of his case--presumably, his suit against Amangual--to Governor Escandón for his ruling. Castro to Sierra Gorda, [...] case of the late Macario Zambrano for judgment, BA May 19, 1792.

75. Artículo 38, in Bernardo Gálvez, *Instructions for Governing the Interior Provinces of New Spain, 1786*, trans. Donald E. Worcester (Berkeley: The Quivira Society, 1951), p. 101, hereafter *Gálvez*, 1786. Peace by malice or deceit can be interpreted as a method to gain the upper hand by *either* the Spaniards or the Apache.

76. Promissory note of Muñoz to Amangual [...] Soquina and Sojas, BA March 27, 1792. Sojas (Sojais) features prominently in John (1975), pp. 739–41, 743–44, 757–58, and, spelled "Soxay" in Moorhead (1968), p. 266; as "Sofais," in Kavanagh (1996), pp. 149–54; as does Soquinas (Soquina) in Barr (2007), pp. 283–85.

77. Muñoz to Amangual [...] visiting Tancague, BA April 26, 1792. The Béxar Archives lists the nation variously as Tancahue, Tancague, and Tonkawa in documents reflecting the range of spellings given to Native polities by Spanish military officials during the late eighteenth century and into the next. I use the assortment throughout this book.

78. Promissory note of Muñoz to Amangual [...] Comanche Indians, BA April 27, 1792.

79. Accounting records of the company of Béxar, by Francisco de Amangual, paymaster, BA April 27, 1792. The ledger has a header date of March 18, 1792.

80. Amangual to Muñoz, [...] financial management details of the company, BA January 26, 1792. This document is Amangual's response the following day. I have not located the "official letter" of January 25, 1792, with the original orders from Lieutenant Colonel Muñoz.

81. Accounting records of the company of Béxar, by Francisco de Amangual, paymaster, BA April 27, 1792. The production of tobacco in Texas and its accessibility caught the attention of Viceroy de Croix. He was principally interested in the quality, size, and price of tobacco crops produced in the borderlands. Moreover, he expressed concern

Notes to Pages 72–75   325

that prohibition of its sowing and free trade would make difficult the reduction of the hostile Indians and anger the Friendly Nations, including those established at missions and those not so effectively congregated. Creating profit for the Royal Treasury stood at the forefront of his thinking and thus his interest in two key issues: whether stores could be established in Texas and during what time periods did presidial captains and local merchants purchase the commodity. Croix to Martos y Navarrete, requesting full information about tobacco crops in Texas, BA December 1, 1766. For the relationship of the plant to frontier soldiers during this era, see: Proceedings concerning Croix's instructions to Governor of Texas for furnishing tobacco to soldiers of Texas, BA August 8, 1768; Rivera to O'Conor, [re: instructions for] shipment of tobacco received for the troop, BA September 4, 1768; Bucarely y Ursua to Captain of Los Adaes, [management] and distribution of tobacco in presidios, BA November 8, 1772.

82. Accounting records of the company of Béxar, by Francisco de Amangual, paymaster, BA April 27, 1792. Expenditures for presidio construction could be extensive and fiscal details for borderlands garrisons are rare. For efforts at reconstructing the Presidio at San Miguel de Horcasitas in 1750 and its subsequent investigation, see Polzer and Sheridan (1997), pp. 381–406.

83. Accounting records of the company of Béxar, by Francisco de Amangual, paymaster, BA April 27, 1792.

84. Amangual's receipt […] payment for items supplied to visiting Indians, BA July 6, 1792.

85. Amangual receipt […] mesteñas fund of expenditures […] visiting Indians, BA August 14, 1792.

86. Certified copy of Amangual's report to Muñoz, on Ugalde's account during military campaigns, BA December 18, 1793 [– December 22, 1793]. Having had previous arrearages, funds coming from Martínez Pacheco required extra scrutiny. See fn55 in this chapter.

87. Certified copy of Amangual's report to Muñoz, on Ugalde's account during military campaigns, BA December 18, 1793 [– December 22, 1793].

88. Certified copy of Gutiérrez de la Cueva's financial statement sent to Amangual, BA September 20, 1791.

89. Writing in 1522, the jurist Diego del Castillo stressed the importance of the account as a kind of "confirmation, *confirmacio* [sic], of a financial transaction" and even as a process stemming from "higher intellectual causes" showing "what [had] been received and in what manner expenditure or payment" was given. As Mills indicates, del Castillo "saw the account as fulfilling the same purpose in stewardship as did a witness' testimony in a court case, serving to separate the 'truth of what is received and justly spent from the false.'" In his view, "the most important formal bond between the administrator and his principal" was the account. I have found no evidence of any formal training outside of that acquired from his predecessor's experiences in the accounting practices of Amangual nor can I prove that he had read or was even familiar with del Castillo's writings. However, it is difficult to imagine that the conscientious Béxar paymaster did not similarly see his work as reflecting just such a relationship between himself and the company and captain he served. See further Patti Mills, "Financial Reporting and Stewardship Accounting in Sixteenth-Century Spain," *Accounting Historians Journal* 13, no. 2 (Fall 1986): 65, 70.

90. Amangual requesting punishment […], BA February 10, 1793.

91. Ibid.

326 Notes to Pages 75–78

92. Ibid.

93. [Amangual's] receipt of instructions concerning military discipline, BA January 7, 1792. The cache of documents apparently included instructions that required his acknowledgment. See Affidavit of [Amangual's receipt of papers] by Governor of Texas to the Viceroy, BA January 7, 1792.

Chapter 3

1. Naylor and Polzer (1986), p. 25.

2. From 1689–1690, governor of Coahuila Alonso de León extended his authority to include Texas. For his five expeditions into Texas, see Lola Orellano Norris and Israel Cavazos Garza, *General Alonso de León's Expeditions into Texas, 1686–1690* (College Station: Texas A&M University Press, 2017), pp. 13–28. He was succeeded by Domingo Terán de Los Ríos, who was appointed governor of Coahuila and Texas in early 1691. By 1693, however, Spain withdrew the Catholic missions from East Texas, and it was not until 1716 that Martín de Alarcón, appointed governor of Coahuila in 1702, reasserted control over Texas. When Alarcón's tenure ended, that of the Marqués de Aguayo followed, and his activities resulted in the separation of the two provinces around 1726, during the time of his successor Fernando Pérez de Almazán. Eventually, the provinces were governed separately with the capital of Texas at Los Adaes and that of Coahuila at Monclova. The Constitution of 1824 coalesced into one state the Mexican provinces of Nuevo León, Coahuila, and Texas. Nuevo León detached on May 7, 1824. Vito Alessio Robles, *Coahuila y Texas en la época colonial*, 2d ed. (Mexico City: Editorial Porrúa, 1978), pp. 1–14. For an account of the Aguayo expedition by the senior chaplain Juan Antonio de la Peña, see also José Porrúa Turanzas, José Manuel, and Enrique Porrúa Venero, eds., *Documentos para la historia eclesiastica y civil de la provincia de Texas o Nuevas Philipinas, 1720–1779* (Madrid: Ediciones José Porrúa Turanzas, 1961), pp. 1–86. For an English translation of Pena's account of the entrada, see Hadley (1997), pp. 398–464.

3. Brinckerhoff and Faulk (1965), pp. 6–7.

4. Velazquez (1982), pp. 84–89. Ignacio Del Río, *La aplicación regional de las reformas borbónicas en Nueva España, Sonora y Sinaloa, 1768–1787* (México, D. F.: Universidad Nacional Autónoma de México, 1995), pp. 64–65.

5. Chipman argues that because he was "authorized to report directly to [Inspector General] José de Gálvez or the king, Croix's powers made him virtually independent" of the viceroy's authority. Croix's ascension to this important post and his recommendations for alterations across the frontier undoubtedly generated conflict and resentment from his uncle's successor Viceroy Bucareli, and especially so vis à vis presidio defense. Chipman and Joseph (1992), pp. 198–99. Bobb makes the case for conflict, but his argument rests mostly in finding fault with Alfred Thomas' assessment of the Croix/Bucareli interactions and less with the historical figures themselves. Bernard E. Bobb, *The Viceregency of Antonio Maria Bucareli in New Spain, 1771–1779* (Austin: University of Texas Press, 1962), pp. 148–55. Babcock encapsulates Gálvez's royal order of 1779 to forbid Croix from settling the Apache in pueblos since nomadic tribes would in time covet Spanish commodities and subsequently embrace village life. Babcock (2016), pp. 86–87; Moorhead summarizes the order in (1968), pp. 120–23.

6. Moorhead (1975), p. 95.

Notes to Pages 78–79
327

7. Naylor and Polzer (1988), p.1. A series of royal decrees and orders from 1714–28 covered a range of military-focused topics including salaries, fugitives from the armed forces, recruitment of soldiers, and punishments for various crimes including bribery. See Joseph Antonio Portugués, *Colección general de las ordenanzas militares: sus innovaciones, y aditamentos, dispuesta en diez tomos, con separación de clases*, vol. 2 (Madrid: Imprenta de Antonio Marín, 1764). One suspects that royal directives apart from formalized Regulations confused the implementation of reform in the borderlands and therefore muddled communication since their content addressed individual issues as they arose.

8. Velázquez (1982), p. 93

9. Brinckerhoff and Faulk (1965), pp. 12–13.

10. In their efforts toward "control from a distance," bureaucracies produced "protocols of control over information," in the form of "recording, archiving, and retrieval." They relied "heavily on lower-level functionaries," to whom this kind of work was delegated. Kathryn Burns, *Into the Archive. Writing and Power in Colonial Peru* (Durham: Duke University Press, 2010), pp. 11–12.

11. The commandant inspector had the authority to determine the number, goal, direction, and time periods of the patrols and detachments required to inspect the countryside and terrain between all the presidios. Though he was expected to change his residence according to the demands of the army, he was to conduct only an "annual review" of the presidios, either personally or through one or two assistants with particular attention paid to the conduct and reputation of officers. See Reglamento 1772, Título doce, artículo uno, artículo cuatro. For a summary of Inspector Neve's performance, see Moorhead (1975), pp. 95–98.

12. In January 1783, the *alcaldes ordinarios* of the villa of San Fernando alerted Cabello to suspicious behavior by soldiers in activities with civilians. […] Alcaldes' petition […] to prevent gambling and other excesses by soldiers, BA January 24, 1783. By the middle of the year, one soldier's incompetence with recordkeeping and price gouging his troops had him pleading with Neve for continued service in the frontier. See Neve to Cabello, [charges against Luis Cazorla], BA May 18, 1783. However, on October 28, 1783, Neve issued instructions to commanders throughout the provinces to outlaw an activity widely believed to have a corrupting effect among the presidial troops. He deemed card playing as having the "consistent effect of distracting them [the soldiers] from duties to which their entire attention should be applied [giving] them cause to alienate their horses, uniforms, and riding equipment and to become involved in other bad practices which ought to be prevented." He further admonished the commanders to "set an example" for their subordinates, on the assumption that they would be held "strictly responsible for any permissiveness, tolerance, or disorder" that might result from gaming. Neve to Cabello, giving instructions to prevent gambling among the soldiers, BA October 28, 1783. Almost sixty years prior, gambling equated to disorder in the opinion of Texas governor Almazán, reporting his dismay that the insolent soldiers of Presidio La Bahía utterly disregarded the maintenance of all the provisions supplied to them in 1724. Hadley (1997), pp. 465–71.

13. Neve to Cabello, […] contributions for maintenance of war, BA October 1, 1783. The donation stemmed from a royal *cédula* issued on August 17, 1780, and consisted of one peso, from both "free" and "other" status people, and two pesos from Spaniards and nobles including "any distinguished persons […] in the Indies."

328   Notes to Pages 80–83

14. Moorhead (1975), pp. 96–7.

15. See Neve to Cabello, [instructions for Indian warfare], BA December 22, 1783; January 28, 1784.

16. Moorhead (1975), pp. 96–7. For militia and regular soldier numbers in Nueva Vizcaya, see Thomas (1941), pp. 62–3.

17. Neve to Cabello, authorizing Cabello to continue [. . .] as inspector of Texas troops, BA November 12, 1783.

18. Neve to Cabello, giving instructions for the fulfillment of lieutenant's position at Béxar, BA November 26, 1783. Three years prior, when Croix established two settlements of Spaniards and Indians in Yuma territory, Alferez Santiago de Islas, a corporal, and nine *soldados* were pulled from Presidio Altar to command both communities, along with a corporal and nine soldiers. Filling out the ranks meant bringing in Sgt. Juan de la Vega, two corporals, and eight soldiers from Presidio Tucsón and six more from Presidio Buenavista. The eleven Tucsón individuals were then to be replaced with three soldiers from Altar, one from Buenavista, and seven from Horcasitas. Bringas (1977), pp. 97–8. For more on the dizzying reconfigurations by Croix, Ugarte, and De La Rocha to concretize a more defensible line of presidios, see Moorhead (1968), pp. 52–54. De Arce is confirmed as captain of Presidio San "Elezeario" in 1792 in Nava to Revillagigedo, Junio de 1792, AGS, SGU, LEG, 7022, 16, image 18, verso 9.

19. Neve to Cabello, announcing the return of Luis Cazorla to La Bahía, BA November 27, 1783. Fifteen months later, with no other qualified officers to select from, Cazorla stayed on as the presidio's captain. See Rengel to Cabello, [royal approval to retain Cazorla], BA February 15, 1785. See chapter 1 for Cabello's charges against Cazorla after reviewing the Bahía presidio.

20. Rengel to Cabello, regulating duration of military campaigns against the enemy, BA December 9, 1784. See *Reglamento 1772, Título decimo, artículo uno* for treatment of "declared enemies" among Indians.

21. Cabello to Rengel, discussing difficulties in following orders concerning duration of campaigns by Texas troops, BA February 16, 1785. Elizabeth John provides a succinct character description of Cabello that suggests his acute preference for commanding from headquarters and especially with Native populations in the vicinity. See John (1975), pp. 698–700. John's assessment of Cabello spotlights the period beginning in 1786. Later studies challenge John's argument that Cabello only issued armchair directives. In fact, six years earlier he complied with an order from Croix and traveled to personally inspect the region near Mission Rosario after reviewing the cavalry at La Bahía. See Jackson (2003), pp. 202–6. After his nine-month stay at La Bahía, he traveled on to Fort Cíbolo to inspect it and the vicinity. See Thonhoff (1992), pp. 58–9.

22. Cabello to Rengel, discussing difficulties in following orders concerning duration of campaigns by Texas troops, BA February 16, 1785. For broad general studies of the Karankawa during the Spanish colonial period, see John and Wheat (2001): 560–76; Robert A. Ricklis, *The Karankawa Indians of Texas: An Ecological Study of Cultural Tradition and Change* (Austin: University of Texas Press, 1996); Thomas Wolff, "The Karankawa Indians: Their Conflict with the White Man in Texas," *Ethnohistory* 16, no. 1 (Winter 1969): 1–32; for an earlier study, see Albert Samuel Gatschet, *The Karankawa Indians, the Coast People of Texas* (Cambridge, MA: Peabody Museum, 1891).

23. Cabello to Rengel, discussing difficulties in following orders concerning duration of campaigns by Texas troops, BA February 16, 1785. Elizabeth John argued that by June 1785 Cabello found himself "under renewed pressure" from royal authorities

Notes to Pages 83–85   **329**

to "attain the peace with Comanches that had been a goal of imperial policy for two decades." In locating a willing negotiator for a peace offer to the Comanche, Cabello authorized a visit from Nacogdoches to the interior of the Comanchería, the result of which produced a report with the assistance of interpreter Francisco Xavier Chaves. See John et al. (1994), pp. 29–30.

24. In another example, Felipe de Neve directed Texas governor Domingo Cabello to place the two sons of Lt. Col. Athanase de Mézières in any vacant post of alférez, with the other as a cadet in either of Cabello's two companies. See Neve to Cabello, concerning military appointments of De Mézières' sons, BA Dec 18, 1783. The literature on Athanase de Mézières is extensive. He began his military career in Louisiana as an ensign at Natchitoches and later became the largest slave owner and tobacco producer in the region. As a result of his impressive network of allies among the Texas Native peoples developed through years of mutually beneficial trading, Mézières often served as an arbiter between the Spaniards and the Indians. By 1778, Commandant General Croix enlisted the expertise of Mézières after a council of war recommended that the Frenchman travel to Texas for a unified campaign by the Spanish and *norteños* (Kichai, Tawakoni, Taovayas, and Comanche) against the Lipan Apache. See also F. Todd Smith, "Athanase de Mézières and the French in Texas, 1750–1803," in *The French in Texas*, ed. Francois Lagarde (Austin: University of Texas Press, 2003): 46–55. For the seminal study of de Mézières' correspondence, see Bolton (1914); for a later treatment of his far-reaching presence, see John (1975), passim. For his role as a negotiator, see Barr (2007), pp. 212–60. Neve's predecessor, Teodor de Croix, had also encouraged Cabello to look after the French colonel since his rank, distinguished service, and especially his knowledge, experience, and acceptance among the Native inhabitants of the provinces rendered him deserving of attentiveness by the new Texas governor. See Croix to Cabello, discussing management of Texas, stressing the importance of […] De Mézières' aid, BA October 4, 1778.

25. Cortés to Muñoz, […] danger in leaving the presidio unguarded by sending troops on expedition against Indians, BA August 12, 1791. That same summer, the Adjutant Inspector Gutiérrez de la Cueva contacted Governor Muñoz concerning the serious situation with the Lipan and ordered him to attempt to attract the largest number of Comanche possible — as ad hoc soldiers for the king — for the purpose of diverting attention away from Nuevo Santander and Nuevo León. Gutiérrez de la Cueva to Muñoz, [serious situation with Lipan] and [recruit as many Comanches as possible for defense purposes], BA May 4, 1791; Correspondence between Gutiérrez de la Cueva and Muñoz, hostile activities of Lipan] and the wounding of the Commandant General, BA May 2, 1791.

26. Cortés to Muñoz, […] danger in leaving the presidio unguarded by sending troops on expedition against Indians, BA August 12, 1791. In the 1960s, John Phelan approached the study of Spanish colonial bureaucracy using a "conflicting-standards hypothesis" for understanding conflict and subordinate noncompliance with the law. Phelan's essay is broadly conceived and provides no specific examples for the main thrust of his argument. However, I can think of no better examples of the nature of conflicting standards at play in Commandancy exigencies than the Cabello–Rengel argument over campaign duration and the Cortés–Muñoz tensions over troop detachments. See John Leddy Phelan, "Authority and Flexibility in the Spanish Imperial Bureaucracy," *Administrative Science Quarterly* 5, no. 1 (June 1960): 47–65.

27. Cortés to Muñoz, […] danger in leaving the presidio unguarded by sending

330   Notes to Pages 85–88

troops on expedition against Indians, BA August 12, 1791. A few years earlier Gálvez himself insisted that troops seek out the Apache in their *rancherías* since that was the only way to punish them and secure pacification of the Far North territories. See Gálvez, 1786, *artículo 20*.

28. In a section devoted to "procedencia social," Marchena Fernández (1983, pp. 129–40) writes that no clear uniformity exists in the assorted social qualifications noted in the service records. Twenty variables comprise a table showing higher to lower social ranges with four groups of "titled" denominations. For soldiers in the Septentrión, the designations may not have differed much from those inscribed in regions closer to the viceregency's metropoles. In such places, "there may have been a fusion of caste and class status in defining one's social station" incorporating "combined biological, reputational, and occupational" identifiers into classification schema. See Ben Vinson, *Bearing Arms for His Majesty: The Free-Colored Militia in Colonial Mexico* (Stanford University Press, 2001), pp. 4, 240 fn9.

29. At times, military service records were unavailable on the frontier and an attentive commander with the responsibility of recordkeeping for his company might have to make inquiry of others, usually superiors, to access the materials. Given the documentation of his experiences as a *presidial*, it is no surprise that Capt. Juan Cortés was one such officer. In December 1791, he notified Governor Muñoz that the service records of the Bahía presidio troops were not in that company's archive. He needed those already sent to the previous governor, Martínez Pacheco, so that he could copy each one and then return the cache to the government. Muñoz responded with an enclosure of all the soldiers' service records requested by Cortés and for the years 1791 and 1790. Cortés to Muñoz, concerning format for military service reports, BA December 10 [–11], 1791. Two decades prior, Viceroy Bucareli insisted that then-governor Ripperdá have the service records of officers remitted annually to him so that the documents could then be forwarded to the king. Bucareli made the point to Ripperdá that he was to continue the practice without waiting for a reminder to do so. See Bucarely y Ursua to Ripperdá, concerning the service records of military officers, BA September 16, 1772.

30. I see the *hojas de servicio* as a type of account or tally for recording the fulfillment of official duties by soldiers active and retired. Though Patti Mills' study centers on the *libros de cuentas* of seventeenth-century transactions involving an administrator and bookkeeper, the same approach for recording the "content of entries" required details such as dates, names, places, and the "circumstances that gave rise to the transaction," can reasonably aid in the interpretation of the military service record. With the latter, a commander's aim was to contextualize a properly compiled set of records in such a way as to facilitate study and interpretation for the purposes of awarding promotions and making recommendations for career advancement. See Mills (1986), p. 70.

31. (You need to correct him and, if not, you will relieve him of duty). Military service record of Mariano Rodríguez, December 1796, MSS 841, CSWR reel 61 (hereafter CSWR, SAII).

32. *Reglamento 1772, Título trece, Funciones y facultades del capitán y demás oficiales, sargentos, cabos, soldados y capellán.*

33. Military service record of Manuel Menchaca, December 1796, CSWR, SAII. For his ascension in rank in Texas, see Fernández to Muñoz, [...] Menchaca as Second Alférez at Béxar [...], BA February 25, 1796; and his trips in Texas, see Correspon-

Notes to Pages 88–89　　　331

dence between Gutiérrez de la Cueva and Muñoz […] Alférez Menchaca to Laredo and Béxar or La Bahía, BA March 26, 1796. The term *mariscadas* is synonymous with "entradas" and "facciones" and translated by Navarro García as "incursions." Navarro García (1993), p. 228.

34. Military service record of José Gervacio de Silva, December 1796, CSWR, SAII.

35. The term *hidalgo* referred to noble status and had its origins dated to the Iberian Reconquest. In 1575, King Felipe II ordered that all those Spaniards who participated in the "pacification of the American Indies" would receive the title of *hijo dalgo* (a contraction of *hijo de alguien/algo*), literally translated as son of someone/something. Recipients of the title would enjoy the honors and privileges that corresponded to the customs and laws of Spain. John Nieto-Phillips, *The Language of Blood: The Making of Spanish-American Identity in New Mexico, 1880s–1930s* (Albuquerque: University of New Mexico Press, 2008), pp. 24–25. Marchena Fernández describes it as "los que están en posesión de un título de hidalguía." See further (1983), p. 126.

36. Charles Edward Chapman, *Catalogue of Materials in the Archivo General de Indias for the History of the Pacific Coast and the American Southwest* (Berkeley: University of California Press, 1919), pp. 62–63.

37. Military service record of Juan de Urrutia by Marcos Reañe, December 1795, CSWR, SAII.

38. The word *correduría* may be a substitution for or corruption of the word *correría*, a term used to describe raids, forays, short trips, or excursions. Hackett translated the word as "incursion." However, it might be that "correduría" is a contraction of the words "correría" and "duro/a," the latter signifying difficult or costly. The verb "durar" means "to last" or "to be durable." The Real Academia Española, hereafter RAE, defines the word as something unrelated to anything in this study: insurance mediation.

39. Military service record of Miguel Meza by Marcos Reañe, December 1796, CSWR, SAII. Lafora describes "Bobonoyaba" as a pueblo in Nueva Vizcaya, in the vicinity of the San Pedro River "inhabited by some civilized people and Tepehuanes Indians." Lafora and Kinnaird (1958), pp. 132–33.

40. Antonio Cordero, Extracto de la revista de inspección […] comp[añí] a que guarnece el quartel de Julimes, July 31, 1793, "Provincias Internas. Revistas de inspección," AGS, SGU, LEG, 7048, 5-1 (31/32 recto, verso).

41. "Extracto de la revista de inspección […] 19, 20, 21 de Septiembre de [1803], Revistas de inspección, Provincias Internas," AGS, SGU, LEG 7047, 26-14 (27, 28/144). First Lieutenant Arramburu's rank and his leadership of the *Third* flying company (as of 1788) is listed in *Gazeta de México, compendio de noticias de Nueva España desde principios del ano de 1784* […], Felipe de Zúñiga y Ontiveros, Calle del Espíritu Santo (Dec 31, 1784).

42. In the ranks of Spanish colonial military personnel, the alférez is the equivalent of an ensign, the rank below that of a lieutenant. Most of the presidios had a First (*Primer*) Alférez and a Second (*Segundo*) Alférez as well as a First Lieutenant (*Primer Teniente*), and a Second Lieutenant (*Segundo Teniente*).

43. In one colonial text, *gandules* are described as indigenous males, age fifteen or older, "braves," agile, and able to escape. De la Teja argues that the term derived from the Arabic *gandür*, "dandy" or "braggart," in medieval Spain, and could denote a member of a Moorish militia. By the eighteenth century, the term might describe someone who was a rogue, rascal, or vagabond. On the Spanish colonial frontier, the

332   **Notes to Pages 89–93**

term came to refer to an indigenous warrior. Jesús de la Teja and John Wheat, "Ramón de Murillo's Plan for the Reform of New Spain's Frontier Defenses," *Southwestern Historical Quarterly* 7, no. 4 (April 2004): 501–33.

44. Scalps. Blyth indicates the term could refer to an entire body, or pieces thereof, belonging to a Native casualty, or to describe captives or prisoners. Lance R. Blyth, *Chiricahua and Janos. Communities of Violence in the Southwestern Borderlands, 1680–1880* (Lincoln: University of Nebraska Press, 2012), pp. 90, 132, 134.

45. Military service record of Juan Truxillo by Marcos Reañe, December 1796, CSWR, SAII.

46. Extracto de revista de inspección […] a la tercera compañía volante, September 10, 1790, Nueva España, Extractos. AGS, SGU, LEG, 7299, 38–5, *recto*. Afro-hispano presence in New Spain's military forces amplifies the discourse on identity and ethnicity as found in Vinson (2001); and José Luis Belmonte Postigo, "El color de los fusiles. Las milicias de pardos en Santiago de Cuba en los albores de la revolución haitiana," in Chust/Marchena (2007), pp. 37–51. See also Peter Stern, "Marginals and Acculturation in Frontier Society," in *New Views of Borderlands History*, ed. Robert Jackson (Albuquerque: University of New Mexico Press, 1998), pp. 157–88.

47. Marchena Fernández (1983), pp. 306–7. Christon Archer noted the dominance of peninsulars among regular army officers in *Bourbon Mexico* (1977), pp. 192–98; for his discussion of the challenges of raising an army in New Spain and the "deep mistrust" held by Spanish officers toward the various *castas*, see pp. 223–31.

48. *Reglamento 1729, artículo 137; Reglamento 1772, Título séptimo, artículo uno.* See also Vito Alessio Robles, *Diario y derrotero de lo caminado, visto y observado en la visita que hizo a los presidios de la nueva españa septentrional el Brigadier Pedro de Rivera* (México, D.F.: Secretaría de la defensa nacional, Dirección de archivo militar, 1946), pp. 202–10.

49. Rubio to Ripperdá, enforcing target practice by soldiers, BA June 1777 [day of the month not indicated]. For summaries of Ripperdá's presence in the Commandancy, see Barr (2007), pp. 209, 218–19. Some historians have been sympathetic to the baron. Highlighting in his *Historia* the governor's attributes, Morfi depicts Ripperdá as the victim of San Antonians' ire and retribution, (1935), pp. 423–27. Similarly, Chipman describes Ripperdá as "especially committed" to the welfare of Texans and "service to his king" by his implementation of "wise and energetic" policies. Chipman (1992/2010), pp. 187–90, 202. For his approach to gun trade with Indians in Texas, see Schilz and Worcester (1987), p. 5; for Ripperdá's efforts at repairing the Béxar presidio, see James E. Ivey, "The Presidio of San Antonio de Béxar: Historical and Archaeological Research," *Historical Archaeology* 38, no. 3, *Presidios of the North American Spanish Borderlands* (2004): 111.

50. Rubio to Ripperdá, ordering target practice by soldiers, BA June 8, 1777.

51. Rubio to Ripperdá, […] instructions on management of presidial troops, BA August 16, 1777.

52. Bucareli y Ursua to Ripperdá, reproaching lack of discipline and training of Béxar troops, BA February 28, 1776. During the first few months of his administration, Bucareli had received dismal reports about Apache uprisings and the condition of frontier soldiers. See Bobb (1954), pp. 21–23.

53. Rubio to Ripperdá, discussing replacement of firearms at Béxar, BA May 12, 1777.

54. Rubio to Ripperdá, […] instructions enforcing order and discipline among

Notes to Pages 93–95   333

soldiers, BA April 24, 1778. As both a former lieutenant governor and flying squadron captain of Sonora y Sinaloa, Esparza filled the vacancy of captain of the Third Flying Squadron of Nueva Vizcaya. See *Expediente sobre el nombramiento de Antonio Casimiro de Esparza como capitán de una de las compañías volantes de la expedición de Nueva Vizcaya* in AGI, Guadalajara, 514, N.78, Bucareli to Arriaga, 27 de Diciembre de 1774 (after nomination by O'Conor, October 1774).

55. Rubio to Ripperdá, […] instructions enforcing order and discipline among soldiers, BA April 24, 1778 [Rubio to Ripperdá June 26, 1778]; "la más ciega obediencia," Reglamento 1772, título trece, artículo doce.

56. A handy administrator, Lt. Antonio Bonilla chronicled Texas affairs for the military in the mid-1770s. Viceroy Bucareli called on Bonilla to summarize the previous history of the province as a background report for a proposed *junta de guerra*. See the *breve compendio* in Elizabeth Howard West and Marqués de Altamira, "Bonilla's Brief Compendium of the History of Texas, 1772 (an Annotated Translation)," *Quarterly of the Texas State Historical Association* 8, no. 1 (July 1904): 3–78. Bonilla's work was questioned by Morfi, who called the lieutenant's opinions "undependable" since, according to him, Bonilla was unable to present "solid reasons" or "authentic documents" to back up his claims. See Morfi, pt. 2 (1935), pp. 322–23. For reference to the Bonilla report, see Moorhead (1975), p. 212, fn26 (*Apuntamientos sobre la creacion de empleos de Ayudantes Havilitados*, México, April 13, 1777).

57. Throughout this section explaining the Junta's findings, I use the original language and grammar as found in the documents to avoid the overuse of "sic passim." Moorhead summarized the trio of juntas held over the course of four months, but my discussion is aimed at bringing to light specific details regarding the indigenous offensive and its impact on the presidio line of defense. According to Morfi, Croix convened his first council of war in Monclova (Coahuila) on December 9–14, 1777, and followed that with his second council in San Antonio (Texas) on January 5–8, 1778. Curiously, Moorhead contends Croix convened a council of war March 14, 1778; John has him narrowly escaping an ambush in Nueva Vizcaya on March 1. Bonilla indicates the dates June 9–15 constituted the third council in Chihuahua. See the Certified copy [of the Junta de Guerra's minutes and resolutions] on proper frontier defense against Indian attacks, BA June 6, 1778. Moorhead (1975), pp. 80–84; (1968), pp. 46–49. John further condensed all three juntas and included the "formidable" questionnaire submitted to Croix's council for discussion. See John (1975), pp. 500–8. See Morfi, pt. 2 (1935), pp. 429–31.

58. Certified copy [of the Junta de Guerra's minutes and resolutions] on proper frontier defense against Indian attacks, BA June 6, 1778. According to a recent study, there were "too many fronts" for "Apachean distributions" of raiders across outsider settlements. See how the Apache could reasonably read triumph into the strategy of shifting the presidio line in Deni J. Seymour and Oscar Rodríguez, *To the Corner of the Province: The 1780 Ugarte-Rocha Sonoran Reconnaissance and Implications for Environmental and Cultural Change* (Salt Lake City: University of Utah Press, 2020), p. 194.

59. Ibid. Barr cites the same source of the 1778 frontier defense policy document, mentioning the Spanish official categorization of Apache women as the reserve corps of that polity's military force. However, Barr states that attitudes like this "put Apache women squarely in harm's way" vis-à-vis Spanish hostility and battlefield violence, a statement that suggests the inability of indigenous warrior women to be effective

334 Notes to Pages 95–96

defenders of their territory. Barr (2007), pp. 162–63. In fact, loss of presidial horse herds by stampede and theft by deserters was an ongoing reality for the army and only exacerbated Spanish failures to secure the borderlands.

60. Certified copy [of the Junta de Guerra's minutes and resolutions] on proper frontier defense against Indian attacks, BA June 6, 1778. According to Griffen, Apache fighters in 1774 engaged the *volantes* in the Janos jurisdiction. For nine hours, two bands totaling "seventy warriors battled the Third Flying Company" before retreating. In the end, one hundred Apache ambushed the Spanish who pursued them, killing Cmdr. Manuel Estéban Alegre and four soldiers. Griffen (1988), p. 32.

61. Certified copy [of the Junta de Guerra's minutes and resolutions] on proper frontier defense against Indian attacks, BA June 6, 1778. In fact, five decades earlier Juan Bautista de Anza complained about Apache duplicity even while he complied with Casafuerte's directives. His efforts at "bribing them" with whatever they demanded proved ineffective. Polzer and Sheridan (1997), pp. 305–10.

62. "Real Decreto de 16 de enero de 1726, expedido al consejo de Castilla repitiendo que se observe la Ordenanza de 20 de Noviembre de 1721 sobre desertores." This followed a royal order concerning desertion among the regiments of an unidentified garrison but with a reference to the Cuenca regiment. See "Real Orden de 9 de octubre de 1720, communicada circularmente sobre [. . .] la desercion [sic passim]," both in *Ordenanzas militares, tomo II* in Portugués (1764), pp. 668, 530.

63. Further, if repentant deserters did not complete the quota for the veteran corps, the commanders of those regiments upon orders from the king had the option of recruiting not only Spaniards but also "*mestizos limpios*" to actualize the required numbers. Certified copy of Gálvez's order to publish decree granting pardon for desertion, BA August 23, 1776. However, by the next month, Gálvez informed Commander General Croix that Carlos III issued separate orders for officers who deserted. He declared that any commander — officer, sergeant, or corporal — who left duty during wartime would face a death sentence. If these same men left during peacetime, they were to suffer dismissal from their job, expulsion from service, and a six-year jail sentence. If a private left during wartime, the sentence was death; if during peacetime, he would serve the same six-year jail term. Rubio to Governor of Texas, transmitting communication on penalties for desertion, BA February 26, 1777. Comandante General of Sonora José de Gálvez reaffirmed the King's 1773 declaration that no deserter, even those providing temporary service, could be reinstated in his army. See [. . .] Gálvez dispatch forbidding reenlistment of deserters, BA July 12, 1778. For the English translation of the King's designation of Gálvez as the Visitador-General, see Priestley (1916), pp. 404–17.

64. Cazorla to Croix, recommending clemency for soldiers of La Bahía charged with desertion, BA April 7, 1779. A royal order of September 10, 1776, called for the removal "with caution" of military offenders (*reos militares*) that took asylum in churches. The governor of Texas was able to give due compliance through orders passed on to the commander general. The governor was to order a detailed reason per the ecclesiastical jurisdiction for all causes involving such soldiers. See Rubio to Governor of Texas, [royal *cédula*] regulating arrests of military offenders seeking ecclesiastical asylum, BA October 14, 1777. Seeking refuge in a church entailed several conditions involving penalties for soldiers. See *Artículo 2, Título 17, tratado 2* [points 36–40] *de la Ordenanza* in *Recopilación de penas militares, segun ordenanza y reales* órdenes *hasta noviembre de 1806 con las obligaciones del soldado, cabo y sargento de infantería, caballería, y dragones,*

Notes to Pages 96–99 335

y otros particulares para instrucción de los mismos (Madrid: Oficina de D. Francisco Martínez Dávila, impresor de cámara de S.M., 1825), hereafter *Recopilación 1806*.

65. Cazorla to Croix, recommending clemency for soldiers of La Bahía charged with desertion, BA April 7, 1779.

66. Ibid. "*lo que me causa dolor por haverme costado tanto afan para ponerlo en el sobresaliente pie en que lo dexé*"/sic passim.

67. Ibid.

68. Croix to Cabello, [...] Cazorla's letter regarding Manuel Méndez of La Bahía, BA June 19, 1779. Lafora noted the mixed-ethnicity component of three small towns in Coahuila where 777 families of "Spaniards, mestizos, and mulattoes" included soldiers from the presidios of Monclova, Santa Rosa, and San Juan Bautista. Numerous Native families numbered 382. Lafora and Kinnaird (1958), p. 154.

69. Cabello to Croix, [...] case of Manuel Méndez, charged with desertion from La Bahía, BA August 14, 1779; Croix to Cabello, [receipt of records of] Manuel Méndez, accused of deserting San Saba [sic], BA September 16, 1779. However, there is no mention of San Sabá in this latter document.

70. Croix to Cabello, transmitting Manuel Méndez's pardon, BA September 25, 1779. Unfortunately, the one who may have suffered the most disappointment from this event was the unidentified recruit who had taken up Méndez's position in the belief that it was vacant. Mindful of this mix-up, Croix ordered that this man fill the first vacant position that became available. See also Cabello to Croix, [...] remittance to La Bahía of case against Manuel Méndez [...], BA November 1, 1779. Four years later, Carlos III granted a general amnesty to include army deserters of all stripes with generous provisions for returning to service, even after jail sentences. Certified copy of royal decree concerning pardon for military deserters, BA October 10, 1783.

71. *Reglamento 1772, Título trece, artículo nueve, Funciones y facultades del capitán y demás oficiales, sargentos, cabos, soldados y capellán.*

72. Rubio to Ripperdá, enclosing regulations to award military men for bravery and patriotism, BA May 28, 1777.

73. Ibid. The 1772 Regulations stressed "individual strength and valor" as the cardinal requirement in battle rather than uniformity among the troops. Cadence in the field might help, too. One New Mexico governor was convinced the company drummer was indispensable for instilling "valor in the soldier and fear in the enemy." Linda Tigges, ed., and J. Richard Salazar, trans., *Spanish Colonial Lives, Documents from the Spanish Colonial Archives of New Mexico, 1705–1774* (Santa Fé: Sunstone Press, 2013), pp. 554–57.

74. Rubio to Ripperdá, [...], BA May 28, 1777. The precise wording in the original document is "crédito y blozozon [sic]"; the latter word can be translated as either "honor" or "glory." Jealousy likely underscored soldiers' resentment of what was, in effect, the parttime status of the militias. When he gave his opinion on a host of subject matter related to Nueva Vizcaya, the *fiscal* Juan de Escalante y Mendoza clarified that "all the settlers [...] of those frontiers should be militiamen" and "all the prerogatives, exemptions, and enfranchisements of such, as well as freedom from all tributes, should be granted to them." See *Reply of the Fiscal concerning various questions relating to the war with the hostile Indians of the kingdom of El Parral which were raised by different reports of the viceroy of Mexico, the Count of Galve, and by the opinions of Don Gabriel del Castillo, governor of the said city of El Parral* [Madrid, April 1, 1698] in Hackett, v.2 (1926): 438–39.

336   Notes to Pages 99–102

75. *Reglamento 1772, Título octavo, artículo tres; noveno, artículos 1–4.*

76. Rubio to Ripperdá, [bravery and patriotism], BA May 28, 1777.

77. Rubio to Ripperdá, suggesting plan for keeping soldiers from running into debt, BA June 14, 1777.

78. Ibid. In the early 1770s, Ugarte reacted to debts accumulated by his officers (and owed to the religious) with maneuverings of his own to resolve financial encumbrances. Coincidentally, he profited from those entanglements. Moorhead (1968), pp. 32–33.

79. Rubio to Ripperdá, […] instructions on management of presidial troops, BA August 16, 1777.

80. Ibid. For more on promotion in the military and especially among the officer ranks, see Archer (1995), pp. 198–200.

81. Rubio to Ripperdá, [instructions], BA August 16, 1777.

82. However, the *comandante inspector* could act as a conduit between the king and viceroy for potential changes to obligations contained within the *Reglamento*. *Reglamento 1772, Título catorce, artículos doce, trece.*

83. Rubio to Ripperdá, […], BA August 16, 1777. Point #9 states that "Integro el fondo en los ajustes, quatrimestres la rresulta [sic] de alcances a favor del soldado […]." The time frame of the semester, a four-month period, is specifically indicated for officers in one of many *ordenanzas militares*: "[Yo el Rey] declaro ahora, que el referido semestre se ha de entender por quatro meses dentro de España, que han de ser los de Noviembre, Diciembre, Enero, y Febrero […] que la precision de executarlas no permita esperar a los referidos quatro meses." However, for officers outside of Spain ["los oficiales estrangeros, que tuvieren sus cajas, y dependencias fuera de España […] para los que las han menester para fuera de España"], this was a six-month period from October to March. See "Real adicion de 14 de junio de 1716. A las ordenanzas, y reglamentos militares sobre oficiales reformados graduados, inspectores, capitanes generales, consejos de Guerra, y otras cosas [sic passim]" (article 37), in Portugués (1764), pp. 172–74.

84. By the mid-1780s, the recurring circumstance of paymaster fraud had become so rampant that viceroy Gálvez warned his senior commander Ugarte to be watchful for it. Likely spurred on by allegiance to a scrimping king rather than imperiled servicemen, Gálvez insisted on a report detailing "*the delicate matter of managing the business affairs of the troops* […] *which up to now has not been found in the paymasters, who have incurred numerous bankruptcies,*" in Gálvez, 1786, *artículo noventa.*

85. Rubio to Ripperdá, [instructions], BA August 16, 1777.

86. Ibid.

87. Ibid. Almost one year after Rubio's instructions to Ripperdá, the aforementioned multiple Councils of War attended by borderlands notables like Ugarte, de Anza, and Croix, among others, grappled with the complexities of frontier provisioning for specific reasons. Where it concerned the paymaster's responsibilities, the final council determined that soldiers could not be governed well since [they] pawned their assets and created confusion on their accounts which led to the misuse of troop resources and even paymaster bankruptcy. Certified copy […] Junta de Guerra on proper frontier defense […], BA June 6, 1778.

88. Rubio to Ripperdá, [instructions], BA August 16, 1777. When extenuating circumstances prompted official intervention into the private lives of military personnel, disciplinary action from superior authorities exposed soldiers' neglect of responsible child rearing. In fact, one of the most intriguing aspects of the intersection of presidio

Notes to Pages 102–104 337

life with civilian family affairs was when it involved children at risk. Three instances of parental correction emerge during the period, although more examples surely exist. Acting on a directive from Croix, the governor of Texas Ripperdá ordered Juan Agustín Bueno to abstain from attending prohibited games — most likely a reference to gambling — once his children returned to him. Further, he was to give them a good education and set a good example; otherwise, Bueno was to be severely punished. That same day, following the orders of his commander, Ripperdá told "Christoval de Casías" that once they were returned to him, he was to raise his children protectively with love for his labor and by doing so, he would set a good example for them. Moreover, Casías was left with a warning: neglect of these instructions would similarly result in punishment. It is apparent that Croix had the welfare of children in mind on this day since he sent yet another order to Ripperdá. The governor was to immediately arrange to have María Juliana, a child held in custody, returned to her parents, Matheo Rodríguez Mederos and his wife. The couple was instructed to give her a good upbringing and to set a Christian example for her since they were obligated to do so as parents. Furthermore, Croix expected to receive word of Rodríguez' compliance with the order. These examples of frontier military authorities entangled with matters of great sensitivity involving domestic conflict, family interactions, and child rearing bring into focus the myriad tasks of the empire's top brass who wielded appreciable influence over the soldier and civilian societies in their midst. Without further information we must assume that Ripperdá found the mechanism or, perhaps, the most compliant subordinate, to carry out his commander's directives. See Croix to Ripperdá, granting custody of children to Juan Agustín Bueno, BA January 13, 1778; Croix to Ripperdá, granting custody of children to Cristóbal de Casías, BA January 13, 1778; Croix to Ripperdá, granting custody of child to Mateo Rodríguez and wife, BA January 13, 1778. For a brief discussion of children and education in 1820s San Antonio, see Jesús de la Teja and John Wheat, "Béxar: Profile of a Tejano Community, 1820–1832," in Poyo/Hinojosa (1991), pp. 1–27.

89. Certified copy of Rubio's instructions concerning presidial accounts, BA April 14, 1778.

90. […] Rubio's report on presidial expenses, BA April 13, 1778. The so-called common fund (*gratificación*) of the presidio, as opposed to the Mesteñas Fund discussed above, served as the source from which payment of general expenses occurred. It also functioned to anticipate the cost of rations for Indian prisoners, and those wanting to discuss treaties or sue for peace. The *fondo de gratificación* paid for the outfitting of recruits, an expense potentially recouped by gradual and prudent discounts. Monies in the common fund were safeguarded in a chest with three keys, each of which was carried by the company's officers. *Reglamento 1772, Título quinto, artículo cinco*.

91. Ripperdá to the Señor de Justicia y Regimiento de San Fernando, BA October 12, 1769.

92. Bucareli to Ripperdá, […] De Mézières and giving further suggestions on Indian relations, BA June 30, 1772. See Castillo y Terán's "Description of Coahuila, 1767" for predations by the Mescalero in Jackson (1995), pp. 159–69. According to Babcock, Mescalero Apache had capricious interactions with the military in the late eighteenth-century through the early 1800s, the period covered in my study. Babcock (2016), pp. 192–94.

93. For correspondence related to an uncertain peacetime in the 1770s with various indigenous groups and an undercurrent of suspicion about the military's relationship

338   Notes to Pages 104–106

with Texas Natives, see […] Bucarely y Ursua and Ripperdá, […] peace with Indians, BA January 6, 1773; for the viceroy's admonitions to Ripperdá to remember the peace maintained by the "Indians of the North" and even the Apache outside of Coahuila and Nueva Vizcaya, and to cease with his repeated entreaties to supply the "heathen Indians" with rifles, gunpower, and shot, see Bucarely y Ursua to Ripperdá, [threat of Indian alliance with] English in Texas, and disapproving plan to arm Indians, BA January 6, 1773; to heed the viceroy's warnings about discontinuing the trafficking of arms and munitions with inconstant Indians, see Bucarely y Ursua to Ripperdá, repeating recommendations to maintain […] peace with the Indians, BA March 1, 1773.

94. Bucareli y Ursua to Ripperdá, exhorting vigilance against surprise attacks by Indians, BA April 14, 1773.

95. In the six years between 1771 and 1776, Spanish estimates put Apache depredations at 1,674 people killed, 154 captured, more than 66,000 head of cattle seized, and more than a hundred ranches and haciendas abandoned. In New Mexico, Governor Pedro de Mendinueta recorded 106 attacks by the Comanche, 77 by Apache, and 12 by the Navajo with the totality of loss from these societies at 94 captured Spaniards and Pueblo Indians and the deaths of 382 others. Blame for part of these statistics rested with Spain's "inconsistent policies" and "underfunded military." It did not help that settlers' efforts toward enslaving, thefts, and aggression directed against Native populations contributed to this hostility. Brian DeLay, *War of a Thousand Deserts: Indian Raids and the U. S. Mexican War* (New Haven: Yale University Press, 2008), pp. 11–12. In November 1771, Jacobo Ugarte pleaded for more troops, a request met with cynicism from Viceroy Bucareli, who himself had called for more weapons for "civil defense." Ugarte was the Governor of Coahuila, the province separated only by the Bolsón de Mapimí from Nueva Vizcaya. See Moorhead (1968), pp. 28–33. Comanche and Apache interactions with each other, various Native polities, and the Spanish over the span of eighty years appear across chapters 7–18 in John (1975).

96. *Reglamento de 1729, Ordenanzas* […] *para el mejor gobierno* […], *número 41*.

97. Croix to Ripperdá, […] control of Karankawa, Ocoquiza [sic] and Coco Indians, BA September 15, 1778. In the original document, Croix spells the group's name, "Orcoquizás," while the English translation of the document has it as "Ocoquizacs." This communication acknowledges the five 1778 letters of March 27, April 7, June 11, July 22 and 29, written by Cazorla and sent to Croix, none of which are part of the Béxar Archives online holdings. Ripperdá informed Croix that the Indians from Misión Rosario took flight on July 13, 1778, aided by the Karankawa. They menaced the immediate vicinity of the Bahía presidio while a small number of women and children were transferred for safekeeping to "Misión de San Antonio." Eventually it fell to Fray Joaquín de Escovár to recover the women and children, return to El Rosario and then, grant a pardon to its fugitives. See Croix to Cabello, discussing flight of Rosario Mission Indians, BA January 14, 1779.

98. Probably Matagorda Peninsula, and not to be confused with Snake Island, in Town Lake (Lady Bird Lake), Austin, Texas.

99. Croix to Ripperdá, […] control of Karankawa, Ocoquiza, and Coco Indians, BA September 15, 1778.

100. Ibid.

101. Croix to Ripperdá, giving instructions on management of Comanche, Apache, Tejas and Bidai Indians, BA September 15, 1778.

Notes to Pages 106–109

102. Housing conditions way out west were apparently no different. For a comparable assessment of California's presidio campuses in 1792, see John Phillip Langelier, *El Presidio de San Francisco: A History under Spain and Mexico, 1776–1846* (Denver: US Department of the Interior, National Park Service, 1992), pp. 36–7.

103. *Reglamento de 1729, Tercer estado, artículo cuarenta.*

104. *Reglamento de 1729, Tercer estado, artículo cuarenta y dos.*

105. *Reglamento 1772, cordón de presidios, artículos diecinueve; viente.*

106. Croix to Ripperdá [money owed to] soldiers of Los Adaes, BA January 9, 1778; Croix to Cabello [decree forbidding trade] by presidial soldiers, BA June 23, 1779; Rengel to Cabello […] forbidding soldiers to eat meat and fish […] same day or meal, BA February 17, 1785.

107. Report of Indian presents made during 1786, BA September 20, 1787.

108. According to Nora Fisher, the term *"indiana"* can describe chintz, painted Indian cotton fabric of the Coromandel Coast and one of the most common cloths imported into New Mexico. "Indianillas" can be synonymous with *"indianas,"* a fabric mentioned in New Mexican church inventories of the period and used for altar frontals. Nora Fisher, "Colcha Embroidery," in *Rio Grande Textiles, Spanish Textile Traditions of New Mexico and Colorado*, comp. and ed. Nora Fisher (Santa Fé: Museum of New Mexico Press, 1994), p. 125.

109. Report of Indian presents made during 1786, BA September 20, 1787; for the best study, including a copy, of the English translation of the Comanche–Spanish Treaty of 1786, see Alfred Barnaby Thomas, *Forgotten Frontiers: A Study of the Spanish Indian Policy of Don Juan Bautista de Anza Governor of New Mexico, 1777–1787* (Norman: University of Oklahoma Press, 1932), p. 329. For a useful discussion of an inter-tribal treaty, see John R. Wunder, " 'That No Thorn Will Pierce Our Friendship': The Ute–Comanche Treaty of 1786," *Western Historical Quarterly* 42, no. 1 (Spring 2011): 4–27.

110. Most of the items consisted of cloth and costume accessories, including four *varas* of ribbon; a quarter ounce of silk; one-third *vara* of scarlet *chalona*; sixteen *varas* of *rayadillo*; twelve *varas* of *queretano* cloth; eight and one-quarter *varas* of *bayeta*, bought from a "Luiz Menchaca"; three pairs of spurs at twelve *reales*; and a bridle and a set of saddle tools. See Account of the goods purchased from the paymaster's store and stores for Indian gifts, BA September 18, 1789 [to August 13, 1790].

111. Accounts for garments made for friendly Indians, BA March 16, 1789 [– February 21, 1790]. Julianna Barr describes the significance of gifting clothing as a means of "civilizing" Indians by dressing them in European clothing. Mission inventories reveal the extensive range of clothing available to indigenous residents. See Barr (2007), pp. 56–58; 149–50.

112. Index of document concerning expenditures incurred supporting Indian visitors, BA December 31, 1792; Amangual signed the document on the last day of 1792, but the amount indicated was from August 1790; this will explain the apparent discrepancy in the dates of this document and that contained in the next citation.

113. Revilla Gigedo to Muñoz, [discussion of] the Gratificación and Situado fund, BA December 8, 1790.

114. In Sonora, on March 23, 1785, Antonio Cordero ordered the merchant (and captain of the Dragones Provinciales de San Carlos militia) Joachim de Amezqueta to deliver to Leonardo María de Calo, as proxy for Alférez José Manuel de Ochoa of the Fourth Flying Company, one thousand pesos from the *fondo de gratificación* of

340 Notes to Pages 109–111

the Third *Compañía Volante*. Further, Amezqueta was to archive the order with its corresponding receipt into the company strongbox (*caxa*). See Cordero to Amezqueta, March 23, 1785, El Archivo de Hidalgo del Parral, 1631–1821 (frame 37/284), held in Special Collections at the University of Arizona Libraries, hereafter AHdP. A 1785 list of troops comprising the First Compañía Volante in Guajoquilla, provisioned by the merchant Joaquín de Ugarte and set to leave on an April 1 campaign, shows Teniente Rodallegas as captain, the position of sergeant filled by Nicolás Tarín, with two corporals, Juan Sauceda and Joaquín Soto; the carbineer Tiburcio de la O; and sixteen soldiers filling out the company. The list enumerates troop provisions of corn, flour, salt, *piloncillo*, cigarettes, meat, and lard for April 1785. See Rodallegas roster of troops of the First Compañía Volante, with provisioning by Ugarte, March 21, 1785, AHdP (frame 43/284). See the search for raiders by Alferez Josef Urías from the Primera Compañia Volante stationed in Chihuahua but on detachment to Presidio del Príncipe (Coyamé). Troops from the Third and Fourth flying squadrons from Presidio San Carlos had followed tracks earlier. Santiago (2018), pp. 12–15.

115. Certified detail of expenses incurred entertaining Indians, BA April 18, 1791.

116. [. . .] seventeen documents [regarding] distribution of gifts to Indians, BA August 14, 1790 ["No. 6, San Antonio de Béxar, January 13, 1792," signed Fran(cis)co Amangual].

117. Report of expenses incurred supporting Indian visitors, BA February 26, 1792.

118. These groups, unspecified by Amangual, entered in peace from February 26 until April 9, 1792. Accounting records of the company of Béxar, by Francisco de Amangual, paymaster, BA April 27, 1792; [. . .] Baca to Courbiére for boarding Indian visitors, BA August 14, 1792.

119. Merchants often dealt directly with commanders about subordinate debts as when José Rafael Sarracino discussed with Amezqueta a payment required from Eugenio Fernándes. On a related issue, due and owing were thirty-eight pesos used for sick soldiers in the district. See José Rafael Sarracino to Joaquín de Amezqueta, September 15, 1785, AHdP (frame 49/284). Moorhead mentions Joaquín de Ugarte in the context of a deposition by the Chihuahua merchant guild in a 1786 list of six vendors that received contracts in 1783. See Moorhead (1975), p. 216. For a study of administrative interactions with private merchants for troop provisioning, see Max Moorhead, "The Private Contract System of Presidio Supply in Northern New Spain," *Hispanic American Historical Review* 41, no. 1 (Feb. 1961): 31–54. A compressed version of this article appears in Moorhead (1975), pp. 216–19. For the travails of Francisco de Guizarnótegui and his contractual issues with supply in Nueva Vizcaya and Nuevo México, see also Frank (2000), pp. 95–101.

120. Pedro de Nava to Muñoz, and Muñoz to Espadas, [. . .] instructions to pay entertainment of Indians from mesteñas fund, BA December 14, 1790 [to January 28, 1791].

121. Amangual's acknowledgement of receipt of funds repaid to mesteñas fund, BA February 26, 1792. On this day, he noted that the *Mesteñas* Fund had been reimbursed for the sum of one hundred pesos, four *reales*, and nine *granos* from the governor and *alcaldes ordinarios* (municipal magistrates) of San Antonio. This amount is written in the margin as well, but it was not enough to fulfill Espadas' request. Espadas to Muñoz, concerning loan from mesteñas fund, BA February 24 [–March 2], 1792.

122. Francisco Amangual vs. Mariano Rodríguez, for slander, BA February 29, 1792, hereafter Slander suit (with progressing timeline). The following testimony originates

Notes to Pages 111–114

from the extant documentation of the proceeding. The deponents' statements were originally transcribed from the third-person point of view with only that of the presiding judge (Muñoz) presented in the grammatical first person. To sustain the narrative flow of events, I reconfigured the depositions of each individual soldier in the first person, both singular and plural. Minimal redaction of the testimony as recorded conveys the immediacy of the official recording. I intersperse in brackets the most salient Spanish terminology, and presumptive wording in gaps, exactly as it occurs in the documents.

123. Slander suit [Deposition of Alférez Manuel Urrutia, March 6]. In Spanish colonial bureaucratic terminology, *autos* constitute the testimony of judicial proceedings, or "records of procedure" as Priestley described them. (1916), p. 157.

124. Slander suit [Deposition of Alférez Manuel Urrutia, March 6]. After having it read back to him, Urrutia affirmed and ratified his deposition and gave his age as "more than fifty years old." This part of the proceeding will be repeated by each of the deponents followed by their respective signatures. In ratifications where a deponent could not write, a soldier would make the sign of the cross as a substitute for a signature.

125. Ibid. [Deposition of master tailor José Arreola, March 6]. Arreola affirmed his age as thirty-one years old, "more or less."

126. Slander suit [Deposition of Sgt. Andrés del Valle, March 6]. Even after all the mudslinging, Rodríguez and del Valle would have subsequent interactions related to commerce. It is likely that those occurrences were brief and purely mechanical, with little need for pleasantries. See Silva's detailed report [of horses and mules handed over by Rodríguez] to Andrés del Valle, BA August 10, 1795.

127. ["*le fue dolorosa por sindicarle su buen proceder y hombría de bien, de un defectto sumamente dinigrittibo*"/sic passim], Slander suit [Deposition of Corporal José Manuel Granados, March 6]. The use of the term *hombría de bien* is interesting in this context since its use here echoes that which was explored in an essay about "the opening of the world of politics" in México during the first half of the nineteenth century. In the post–Independence period, Costeloe argues that in place of the old ruling elite, there emerged a new circle of influencers [my terminology] known as the *hombres de bien*. He described them as "neither aristocrat nor proletariat, but from the middle class." While their number may have been divided politically, the group possessed "similar socioeconomic backgrounds" and "shared the same aspirations and values." The conservative Lucas Alemán described such a man as "un hombre religioso, de honor, de propiedad, de educación y de virtudes." On the other side of the aisle, the liberal José María Luis Mora similarly defined the *hombre de bien* as someone "que ocupe algún puesto a que deba su subsistencia, tenga alguna industria productiva, algún capital en giro o posesiones territoriales." Whether Alemán or Mora included military personnel as part of the equation, or not, is intriguing. The Amangual–Rodríguez conflict predated both Mexican thinkers' birth year, but the appellation may have emerged earlier and then, perhaps, coopted by status seekers and deponents like Granados and others in the army, even those stationed in the Comandancia. Michael P. Costeloe, "Hombres de Bien in the Age of Santa Anna," in *Mexico in the Age of Democratic Revolutions, 1750–1850*, ed. Jaime E. Rodríguez O. (Boulder: Lynne Rienner, 1994), pp. 16, 243–57.

128. Slander suit [Deposition of Corporal José Manuel Granados, March 6]. Granados gave his age as "thirty years, more or less."

342 Notes to Pages 114–117

129. Slander suit [Amangual to Muñoz, March 6]. [*se le castigue arreglado á la ordenanza del exercito*/sic]. Amangual may have referenced article 84, likely a carry-over from prior ordinances, regarding false testimony committed by soldiers. See *Recopilación 1806* (título X, tratado VIII, Ordenanza general), *Testigo falso*, pp. 35–36.

130. Slander suit [Summons and response of Sgt. Mariano Rodríguez, March 6]. As previously noted, *Título catorce* of the *Reglamento 1772* spelled out the election procedure for each presidio's choice of paymaster. Except for its final article, number thirteen, the entire content of Title 14 is devoted to the duties required by and selection of the soldier for *habilitado*.

131. Slander suit [Muñoz's summons to and response of Sgt. Mariano Rodríguez, March 6].

132. As we saw in the Zambrano corn case, Rodríguez's father-in-law was, from the year before, another accuser of Amangual.

133. Slander suit [Summons and response of Sgt. Mariano Rodríguez, March 6].

134. Slander suit [Muñoz's summons to Rodríguez, March 15]. The term *angaripola* is defined as "lienzo ordinario, estampado en listas de varios colores, que usaron las mujeres del siglo XVII para hacerse guardapiés [ordinary canvas/linen, printed with various colors on long strips, used by women in the seventeenth century to make coverings for the feet]." RAE, *Diccionario de la lengua española*, http://dle.rae.es/?id=2d6L3l7.

135. Slander suit [Deposition of Sgt. Mariano Rodríguez, March 15]. In this context, *pontiví* is a type of French cotton fabric. Elizabeth John suggests that it may have been a knitted, rather than woven, material. See John et al. (1994), p. 29 fn7.

136. Slander suit [Deposition of Sgt. Mariano Rodríguez, March 15]. Though never deposed, Gómez Moreno's participation in the slander suit would have come as no surprise to Amangual. A year earlier, Ygnacio de los Santos Coy, as sacristan of the villa of San Fernando and responsible for distribution of dispensations and receipt for those deliveries, alleged that he was physically abused by the priest during an incident on November 13, 1791. Where it involved Amangual, and according to testimony by Pedro Flores, (the *alcalde ordinario de segundo voto* dealing with civil cases in Béxar), the paymaster had delivered everything owed to Gómez Moreno as well as to his predecessor Pedro Fuentes, an acknowledgment overheard by Flores himself and the trigger for the priest's offense. See Proceedings in the case of Ignacio de los Santos Coy vs. Father Francisco Gómez Moreno for assault, BA November 14, 1791. Gómez Moreno maintained a high level of discontent in his daily life and was, apparently, rabid to see his indulgences serve his meddling ways at every opportunity. He took outrageous chances with those he targeted during his malicious follies, even going so far as to stir up the animosity of the Comanche against the military in murderous fashion. See Certified deposition of [Chávez giving evidence that Gómez Moreno is agitating] the Comanches, BA October 24, 1792.

137. Slander suit [Deposition of Sgt. Mariano Rodríguez, March 15].

138. Ibid. [Proceeding of confrontation, March 15]. In the margin of page 17 of the March 15 proceedings appear the abbreviated words "*Dilig*[enci] *a de Careo*," which can be translated as "face-to-face interrogatory." Mills writes of the significance of the oath as a juridical device of the Spanish legal tradition. Stemming from both Roman and Visigothic law, "it had evolved into two forms, the single oath, that of a lone individual, and compurgation, which required the swearor to support his oath with the oaths of a number of coswearors or compurgators [sic passim]." However, by

Notes to Pages 117–120   343

the sixteenth century Mills indicates that "there was apparently sufficient skepticism regarding the efficacy of the oath among legal circles" and, indeed "other kinds of proof that reinforced the evidence of the account book included witnesses to a transaction," among various accounting practices. See further Patti A. Mills, "The Probative Capacity of Accounts in Early-Modern Spain," *Accounting Historians Journal* 14, no. 1 (Spring 1987): 101–2.

139. Slander suit [Proceeding of confrontation, March 15].

140. Ibid. [*no es más de la verdad, y de negarlo el Sargento que está presente negará que no es luz la que está a la vista*].

141. Slander suit [Proceeding of confrontation, March 15].

142. Slander suit [Muñoz's order to Amangual for the examination of the storehouse of the paymaster's office, March 17, 1792]. With a date of March 16, the *ojo* (margin note) indicates this section of the document as an "auto relativo al merito de la ynformación y careo que se manda […] para que justifique y pruebe su exposicion [sic passim]."

143. Allan J. Kuethe and Juan Marchena Fernández, eds., *Soldados del rey, el ejército borbónico en América colonial en vísperas de la independencia* (Sevilla: Universitat Jaume, 2005), p. 26; for more on *comercio libre*, see Stanley J. Stein and Barbara H. Stein, *Apogee of Empire: Spain and New Spain in the Age of Charles III, 1759–1789* (Baltimore: Johns Hopkins University Press, 2003) and especially chapters 6, 8, and 9. As Barbier explains, *comercio libre* was extended to Nueva España in February 1789 through the elimination of tonnage restrictions. See Jacques A. Barbier, "The Culmination of the Bourbon Reforms, 1787–1792," *Hispanic American Historical Review* 57, no. 1 (Feb. 1977): 51–68.

144. Added to the list was hemp of 100 percent confirmable manufacture from the Peninsula, the islands of Mallorca (Amangual's birthplace) and Canarias, and silk weavings with a mixture of gold and silver thread manufactured in the "kingdom and the islands." See "*Punto veintidós*," in El Rey Yo, *Reglamento y aranceles reales para el comercio libre de España á Indias de 12 de octubre de 1778* (Madrid: Imprenta de Pedro Marín, 1778), pp. 28–29. The term *almojarifazgo* was defined by Priestley as an export and import duty dating from "Moorish times," which the "original pioneers of New Spain" were exempted from paying until 1543. Priestley (1916), p. 361–64. RAE similarly defines the word as an amount paid for products or merchandise that leave the kingdom's ports, for those introduced into its realm, or for those that trade from port to port within Spain.

145. Barbier (1977), pp. 61–62.

146. Kuethe, "Imperativos militares en la política comercial de Carlos III," in Kuethe and Marchena Fernández, *Soldados del rey* (2005), pp. 156–57.

147. One historian credited two influences on his study of verification procedures in inventories conducted in New Spain: the first was the groundwork laid in [publications] having shown the importance of, and increasing interest in, the study of Spanish accounting practices; and second, the scarcity of published work on accounting practices in the Spanish colonies. See David Baron, "Verification Procedures Used in Two Inventory Counts in New Spain, 1596–1597," *Accounting Historians Journal* 23, no. 1 (June 1996): 1–24. The research for my book took as one of its points of departure this same reasoning and especially so where inventories record the presence of historical artifacts, often of a purely functional, utilitarian nature, at the frontier presidio and among its resident consumers and itinerant visitors. Where it concerns material

344   **Notes to Pages 120–125**

culture and its relationship to social subjects, anthropologist Barbara Voss explains that "because of the durability and persistence of material culture, it can function to stabilize social identities that are otherwise quite volatile," with objects utilized for various purposes by different users. She argues that "meanings of place and things are never fixed," and studying "material practice allows us to investigate the ways that identities are often simultaneously ambiguous yet surprisingly enduring." Barbara L. Voss, *The Archaeology of Ethnogenesis: Race and Sexuality in Colonial San Francisco* (Berkeley: University of California Press, 2008), pp. 4–5.

148. Slander suit [Inventory of the paymaster's office, March 17].

149. Urrutia's presence at the March 17 inventory is questionable though his rubric exists on the document, and Muñoz confirms his presence on that date. General Castro had issued a note to Muñoz on this same day from Santa Rosa, ordering Urrutia to be set free from arrest. Castro added that Muñoz was to make certain that Urrutia knew "how displeasing to me is the report that obliged [Muñoz] to have him arrested, and that if [Urrutia did] not mend his ways, a serious measure" would occur. A note in the upper lefthand corner of Castro's directive indicates that Muñoz responded on March 24, 1792, potentially the same day he received it. Castro to Muñoz, ordering release of Alférez Manuel de Urrutia, BA March 18, 1792.

150. Slander suit [Inventory of the paymaster's office, March 17].

151. Ibid. [Inventory of the master tailor's goods, March 18, 1792].

152. *Reglamento 1772, Título catorce, artículos uno, dos, y tres.*

Chapter 4

1. Slander suit [Inventory of goods and supplies for the troops of Béxar presidio, April 19, 1792].

2. Ibid. [April 27, 1792]. *vara*: a unit of linear measure equal to about thirty-three inches (84 cm). One might wonder whether the appearance of both bretaña and pontiví cloth was an anomaly, given its foreign manufacture, or trafficked as contraband. According to Barbier, regularly forbidding textiles as allowable imports was part of the mercantile mechanism that was *comercio libre*. Apparently, New Spain's far northern provinces were exempt from certain restrictions of the *Reglamento*. See Barbier (1977), pp. 62–63; *Reglamento y aranceles* (1778), números 20–23. The "Cíbolo fund" likely referred to the two thousand pesos available for the construction of "an advance post" for the Béxar presidio, a fortification believed by Rubí to be an effective means of defending territory for settlement of uprooted Adaeseños and citizens of San Antonio. See Rubí's *dictamen* in Jackson and Foster (1995), pp. 187–88. The irony here is that under instructions from Governor Cabello, Amangual torched Fort Cíbolo ten years prior.

3. Slander suit [April 27, 1792]. The inspection committee, besides Muñoz, included Bernardo Fernández, Manuel de Urrutia, José Xavier Menchaca, Prudencio Rodríguez, Juan Antonio Urrutia, Alexandro de la Garza, with attesting witnesses Vicente de la Cuesta and José de Jesús Mansolo.

4. Ibid. Like some military personnel, a few missionaries in the colonial borderlands had lapses in judgement by acting upon personal motivations at the expense of ministering to their congregation's spiritual well–being. For other examples of ecclesiastical breaches of conduct, see, for example, Yetman (2012), chapter 5, passim; the biographical sketches in Rick Hendricks, *New Mexico in 1801: The Priests*

Notes to Pages 125–126   **345**

Report (Los Ranchos de Albuquerque: Rio Grande Books, 2008), pp. 143–64; and, for Franciscan interventions against Spanish imperial policies, see Ross Frank, "Demographic, Social, and Economic Change in New Mexico" in Jackson, ed. (1998), pp. 50–53. In other cases, the missionaries proved their valor and commitment to their duties by acting as competent if not voracious agents of the empire by taking control of potentially hazardous situations with Native populations and others. See Cabello to Croix, [...] Father Gonzáles' return from [Texas coast] to bring runaway Indians, BA June 13, 1780; for one missionary's desperate but determined plea in an overtly unofficial letter to persuade a Texas governor not to settle an Apache group in his mission, see Father Oliva to Martínez Pacheco, [...] settlement of Lipans in Texas mission, BA February 11, 1787; and the Governor's reply, BA February 14, 1787; Espadas to Martínez Pacheco, [request by] Copanes and Cuxanes Indians to have Father Reyes in charge of their mission, BA November 13, 1789; and for the angry response from another padre to the Indians' plea, see Fray José Francisco López to Martínez Pacheco, protesting Indian request concerning Father Reyes, BA November 14, 1789. For compliance when dealing with missionary requests for military assistance, see Espadas to Martínez Pacheco, [escort for cattle herd] as soon as Father Oliva requested it [...], BA June 3, 1789; Martínez Pacheco to Espadas, ordering an escort [...] for Father Cárdenas, BA November 7, 1789.

5. Defense presented by Mariano Rodríguez for release from jail, BA April 26, 1792.

6. Ibid. In fairness to Rodríguez, the paper had to be of a certain type for official documents and its scarcity was widespread across the borderlands. On May 7, 1792, in the town of Nuestra Señora del Pilar de Nacogdoches, the interim lieutenant governor Juan Cortés, who was also the captain of Presidio La Bahía del Espíritu Santo, brought charges against the accused Juan José Pena and produced the *sumaria* on "plain" paper, with the same explanation given for the Amangual-Rodríguez suit: absence of the proper kind in the province. Juan Cortés proceeding against Juan José Pena, BA May 27, 1792. By coincidence, the lack of proper paper caught the attention of the viceroy. Through his representative, Revillagigedo reminded the interim governor of Texas Escandón of the provisions of Article 156 of the Royal Ordinances of Intendants, prohibiting the use of plain paper for any pretext. He ordered official stamped paper necessary for administrative use be available so that the proper supplies would never be lacking. Díaz de Salcedo to Governor of Texas, [...] regulations for issuance of stamped legal paper, BA June 20, 1792. From a decade earlier, see the communication between the commander general and governor of Texas regarding the supply of stamped paper: Croix to Cabello, [stamped paper] for Béxar and La Bahía, BA June 2, 1780. A *bando* promulgated in 1783 found its way to Texas by way of a reminder from the commander general. Rengel to Cabello, [decree re: stamped paper], BA March 8, 1785. For the role of stamped paper as a new source of taxation for Spanish revenue to mitigate financial hardship, see María Luisa Martínez de Salinas, *La implantación del impuesto del papel sellado en Indias* (Caracas: Academia Nacional de la Historia, 1986). Gálvez nominally addressed the significance of stamped paper in his *Informe General del Marqués de Sonora al Virrey D. Antonio Bucarely con fecha de 31 de diciembre de 1774* (México, D.F.: Santiago White: 1867), pp. 120–21.

7. Defense presented by Mariano Rodríguez for release from jail, BA April 26, 1792.

8. Slander suit [April 27, 1792]. In truth, Muñoz's admonition merely echoed the prescribed duties of any presidio sergeant as conveyed in the Regulations of 1772. It required the sergeant to know from memory all the duties of the soldiers and the

346 Notes to Pages 126–129

corporals, and the penal laws, in order to instruct the company and to see to their compliance. Sergeants were not to overlook disorders, *prohibited conversations* [my emphasis], or incidents that might be contrary to obedience. The sergeant was to personally restrain and correct such things as quickly as possible, winning the respect of the soldiers by his good conduct and obedience and by the respect and deference he gave to the officers. *Reglamento 1772, Título trece, artículo diez.*

9. Defense presented by Mariano Rodríguez for release from jail, BA April 26, 1792.

10. Slander suit, [April 27, 1792]; Defense presented by Mariano Rodríguez for release from jail, BA April 26, 1792.

11. Some of that embarrassment can be attributed to a coterie of bad guys including army and navy deserters who banded together in numerous "herds of vagrants, smugglers, and highwaymen," and who "may have contributed" to disorder, damages, and excesses. Certified copy of royal decree concerning pardon for military deserters, BA October 10, 1783.

12. Muñoz to Ayuntamiento [...] complaint about conduct of priest [...], BA April 7, 1792. By August of the same year, even the viceroy was aware of the multitude of complaints about Gómez Moreno. In view of the "excesses" substantiated against the parish priest, Revilla Gigedo and the auditor of war forwarded an official letter to the bishop so that he might take proper action and then report what measures had been taken to correct Gómez Moreno's conduct. The *ayuntamiento* received an exact copy of the viceroy's letter to Muñoz. Revilla Gigedo to Muñoz, BA August 7, 1792; Revilla Gigedo to Ayuntamiento of San Antonio de Béxar, BA August 7, 1792.

13. Order issued by Muñoz for articles given to Indians, addressed to Amangual, Paymaster, BA March 16, 1792; Promissory note of Muñoz to Amangual, for four pesos worth of cigars for Comanche captains Soquina and Sojas BA March 27, 1792; Promissory note issued by Muñoz for two pesos worth of cigars for ten Comanche Indians, BA April 17, 1792.

14. Two weeks prior, Sojas and Soquina had received tobacco, biscuits, and other supplies from Muñoz; the soldiers were to take these provisions to Sgt. Valle and then charge to the account corresponding to expenditures for the Indians. Muñoz's order to send supplies to Comanche captains, [...], BA March 2, 1792; Castro to Muñoz, [...] deliver certain arms and ammunition to Comanche captains, BA March 24, 1792. By May 8, Viceroy Revillagigedo learned of the Castro order for provisions supplied to the two Comanche chiefs by Muñoz. Revilla Gigedo to Muñoz, [...] aid given by Muñoz to Comanche [...] as ordered by Castro, BA May 8, 1792. If certain weapons did not suit the soldiers of one company, they often did so for another. When in September 1785 the commander general described shotguns as not adaptable for troops at the Chihuahua presidio, he then determined their usefulness for the Cuerpo de Dragones Provinciales de San Carlos after contacting that company's commander. It is not known whether these weapons might eventually find their way to Native populations if frontier soldiers subsequently rejected the guns. Rengel to Commander of Provincial Dragoons Company of San Carlos, September 10, 1785, AHdP (frame 23/284). Of their number documented in the *Provincias Internas* in 1788, the *Dragones* consisted of seven companies with forty-three positions. See AGS, SGU, LEG 7022, images 16–10. Almost fifteen years later Lt. José Cortés lamented the trade of rifles and munitions between Anglo-American and English traders with the "nations on their borders." Cortés blamed the gifting of weapons as a misstep so pernicious it allowed an influx

Notes to Pages 129–131   **347**

of firearms sufficient to cross the frontier from one tribe to another, even reaching the "westernmost one," likely a reference to the Apache. Cortés (1789), pp. 69–71.

15. In this sense, a *manojo* may have equated to a bundle — that is, two pounds of raw tobacco. Castro to Muñoz, [...] forbidding hospitality to Apaches, BA March 10, 1792. Elizabeth John indicates that there is no weight equivalent for the term. John describes the human hand as a rough measure by volume, i.e., as the closest equivalent, the amount grasped in a handful. See John et al. (1994), p. 37, fn30.

16. Castro to Muñoz, [...] forbidding hospitality to Apaches, BA March 10, 1792. On March 22, 1792, the paymaster and later interim commander of the Bahía presidio Manuel de Espadas acknowledged the receipt of Muñoz' directive of March 16. In it, Castro made clear his superior order of absolutely no accommodation to "any Indian of the Apache race" until their suit for peace was carried out in good faith. Espadas to Muñoz, [...] orders regarding policies to follow with the Apache, BA March 22, 1792.

17. Castro to Muñoz, [...] forbidding hospitality to Apaches, BA March 10, 1792.

18. Moorhead (1975), pp. 96–98. And yet, if we are to believe the documentation generated by Spanish commanders from 1779 to 1791, they fluctuated back and forth between a desire to make peace with the Apache, to then recruiting Comanches to assist in making war against them. From an abundance of communication, see Cabello to Croix [Apache request for help to fight Tonkawa], BA March 18, 1779; Cabello to Croix, [preserving peace among Lipan, Apache, and Mescalero], BA August 19, 1779; Cabello to Croix [preservation of peace with Mescalero], BA September 14, 1779; Ibarvo to Muñoz, [preventing peace with Lipans or any other Apaches], BA October 24, 1791; Martínez Pacheco to Ugalde, [expenses for Friendly Apache], BA July 6, 1789; Martínez Pacheco to Ugalde [soldiers sent to drive out the Lipan from the Colorado River], BA October 15, 1789; Martínez Pacheco to Ugalde [securing peace with Lipan Apache], BA July 23, 1790; Gutiérrez de la Cueva to Muñoz [recruit as many Comanches for defense against Lipan Apaches], BA May 4, 1791; Espadas to Muñoz [plans for war against Apache by Tancahues, Vidaizes, Tejas, and Guachitas], BA May 5, 1791; Castro to Muñoz [Comanche plans to attack Apache], BA June 16, 1791; [Pedro de Nava's regulations treating the Apache, now at peace with Spain], BA October 14, 1791; Ibarvo to Muñoz [prevent peace arrangements with any Apaches], BA October 24, 1791.

19. Moorhead (1975), p. 99.

20. Reparaz has the date of April 24, 1779, as Gálvez's appointment as governor, while Worcester states that a September 1776 royal order conferred unto him the governorship. See Carmen de Reparaz, *I Alone: Bernardo de Gálvez and the Taking of Pensacola*, trans. Walter Rubin (Madrid: Ediciones de Cultura Hispánica, 1993), p. 20; Gálvez (1951), p. 22.

21. Moorhead (1975), pp. 98–103, 111. The latest plan was put into effect by the new viceroy Manuel Antonio Flores in 1788 (Worcester has the date as 1786) but signed on December 3, 1787. The Interior Provinces of the East included Coahuila y Téjas, Nuevo León, and Nuevo Santander ("las cuatro provincias del Oriente"), the latter under the governorship of the Conde de Escandón. The Interior Provinces of the West were composed of the Californias, Sonora, Nuevo México, and Nueva Vizcaya ("las cuatro provincias del Poniente"). Worcester and Velázquez concur on the territorial compositions. See "Decreto e instrucción dados por el Virrey Flores para la división de las comandancias" in Velázquez (1982), pp. 189–93; Gálvez, (1951), p. 23.

22. Cortés (1989), pp. 12–13.

348   Notes to Pages 132–134

23. The king resolved that Ugarte would have the same powers held by his predecessor Neve, but Ugarte was to follow the Gálvez Instructions "with exact subordination" and his compliance was to extend to "military as well as political and economic matters" under his command. Furthermore, he was "not to innovate in anything whatsoever" once ascended to the post. See Ugarte y Loyola to Governor of Texas, transmitting royal dispatch [of his appointment], BA April 20, 1786. But Gálvez extended more latitude in his final point (216), allowing "well-founded modifications" to dispel any "inconveniences or difficulties" as they arose. Gálvez, 1786, p. 85. And see Moorhead (1968), pp. 123–28; For the published *Instrucción*, see Velázquez (1982), pp. 151–93; Gálvez, 1786, pp. 27–146.

24. Gálvez, 1786, pp. 27–29. Arguably the best treatment of the Ugarte–Apache relationship and the newly minted commandant-general's impact on Spanish imperial policy before and after the Gálvez instructions is Moorhead (1968), passim.

25. Gálvez, 1786.

26. Moorhead indicates that Ugarte agreed with the content of the *Instrucción* "in all matters relating to war." He had a specific plan of offense that would assure a truce with the Lipan in Coahuila and force the Gileño and Mimbreño to sue for peace. Moorhead (1968), pp. 139–40.

27. In actuality, some parts of the Ordinance failed to be conclusively implemented, such as terminating the repartimiento. For a brief discussion of the intendancy system in France and its modifications for Spain, see the first chapter, "Modelos Europeos de la Intendencia," in Luis Navarro García, *Las reformas borbónicas en América. El plan de intendencias y su aplicación* (Sevilla: Universidad de Sevilla, 1995), pp. 13–37; and Fisher (1929), pp. 1, 8–9, 33. For the special relationship enjoyed but often abused by *subdelegados* in relation to enacting reforms among local communities, see Archer (1977), pp. 124–25. For the economic system of "forced distribution of manufactured goods in return for Native products," or *repartimiento de efectos* as a method for drawing indigenous communities into the New Mexico market, see Frank (2000), pp. 25–30. According to Smith, the sales tax rate doubled in 1632 when the Crown demanded additional funds for the support of its military and naval forces protecting its American possessions. For a discussion of the Spanish colonial experience with sales taxes, see Robert Sidney Smith, "Sales Taxes in New Spain, 1575–1770," *Hispanic American Historical Review* 28, no. 1 (Feb. 1948): 2–37.

28. Fisher (1929), p. 33. Rather than "departments," Fisher contends that "phases" would be a better word to describe the four entities. See also Horst Pietschmann, *Las reformas borbónicas y el sistema de intendencias en Nueva España. Un estudio político administrativo* (México, D.F.: Fondo de Cultura Económica, 1996), especially pp. 118–249.

29. *Gálvez*, 1786, artículos 91–92, 99–103.

30. Gálvez (1951), pp. 3–4. According to Britten, Western Apaches resided in the mountains and timbered uplands of New Mexico and Arizona, Eastern Apache lived on the plains of eastern New Mexico and West Texas, the Kiowa roamed the central plains and Oklahoma Panhandle. After pressure from the Wichita and Comanche, the Lipan made their way to Central Texas. Britten (2009), pp. 54–58. A concise summary of territory constituting the so-called *Gran Apachería* is found in Babcock (2016), pp. 4–6, and maps, pp. 4, 109; for the Gileño riverine presence, pp. 36–7, 42–3, 220–21. For the "Mimbreño" and "Gileño" presence, see Moorhead (1968), passim; and Griffen (1988), passim. For Cordero's campaign against the "Apachería Gileña," see Mark Santiago,

Notes to Pages 134–138   349

A Bad Peace and a Good War, Spain and the Mescalero Apache Uprising 1795–1799 (Norman: University of Oklahoma Press, 2018), p. 23.

31. Hadley (1997), pp. 175–226.

32. Moorhead (1968), pp. 44–49; from 1771–76 in Nueva Vizcaya alone, see Gálvez (1951), pp. 10–11.

33. Gálvez, 1786, artículos 20, 24, 33, 35. However, none of this meant that the Apache were pacified once and for all. Two years prior, Governor Cabello made clear to Commander General Neve that his men were too diminished in number and "preoccupied" with unnamed tasks to be sent to aid another presidio. This was part of the scheme to establish peace in the province of Nuevo Santander and news to this effect was requested by the viceroy. See Cabello to Neve, discussing proposed peace with the Apache, BA August 16, 1784. For the desperation of solitary captain Cabello, left to maintain security at a presidio lacking troops, see Monthly report of the cavalry division of Béxar, BA May 31, 1783.

34. Gálvez, 1786, artículo 52; Cabello to Ugarte y Loyola, reporting news of attack made upon Comanches by Mescalero Apache and Lipans, BA July 30, 1786.

35. According to Babcock, the term "establecimientos de paz" was never used by Spaniards. From 1786 to 1793, almost twelve thousand Ndé resettled in "establecimientos" near presidios. Babcock (2016), p. 2, 8.

36. But the Mescalero were holdouts in the 1790s, fighting on at a time most other Apache polities acquiesced to the Spaniards. Santiago (2018), pp. 3–4, passim.

37. DeLay (2008), p. 12. For the English translation of the Spanish Comanche Peace Treaty of 1786, see Thomas (1932), pp. 329–42.

38. DeLay (2008), pp. 12–14. In making these assertions, however, DeLay relies strictly on secondary sources. Documents housed at the Béxar Archives and from this same period reveal sporadic, but serious, even deadly attacks by Comanches and other Native groups upon travelers, missions, and the military. As late as 1798–99, correspondence between Cordero and other commanders proves Comanches caused great concern to frontier security such as it was.

39. Gálvez, 1786, a*rtículo* 79. His uncle José de Gálvez was more pessimistic, lamenting that even if the Spanish king had at his disposal all the "treasures, the armies and the storehouses of Europe," supplying the troops (especially those serving in the "imperial periphery"), their provisions, and fortifications would be an "impossible enterprise." Gabriel B. Paquette, *Enlightenment, Governance, and Reform in Spain and its Empire, 1759 — 1808* (Cambridge: Palgrave Macmillan, 2008), p. 106.

40. Referred to as Escandón within the documentation, his noble status as "Sierra Gorda" is predominantly used in the Béxar Archives document descriptions for the period covered in this study. For a detailed account of José de Escandón's emergence in New Spain's Far North as a colonizer and commander, see Jesús Canales Ruiz, *José de Escandón, La Sierra Gorda y el Nuevo Santander* (Santander: Institución Cultural de Cantabria, CEM, Diputación Regional de Cantabria, 1985); chapters 1 and 2 of Alonzo (1998); for summaries, see Chipman and Joseph (1992), pp. 169–72; and John A. Adams Jr., *Conflict and Commerce on the Rio Grande: Laredo, 1775–1955* (College Station: Texas A&M University Press, 2008), pp. 9–12.

41. Castro to Muñoz, transmitting Sierra Gorda's letter of March 17, […] campaign against Indians, BA March 24, 1792. Translation by John Wheat and myself. I retained the original punctuation.

42. Ibid. Exhorting the troops to greater glory was nothing new. Two years prior to the

350   Notes to Pages 138–140

events at Camargo and Revilla, His Majesty granted an *escudo de bentaja* (additional pay as reward) for soldiers distinguishing their performance in war. Symbolically, it served as a forceful stimulus to others by visibly displaying the honor with an insignia of a silver, starshaped galloon worn on the left sleeve. Espadas to Muñoz, […] rewards to soldiers distinguished in war actions, BA November 4, 1790.

43. Castro to Muñoz, transmitting Sierra Gorda's letter of March 17, […] campaign against Indians, BA March 24, 1792. By June 15, Manuel de Espadas informed Sierra Gorda that while Sgt. Río and the troops escorting the governor to Béxar were returning, they met along the way two Lipan Apache who alerted them to the death of Zapato Zas. This news, conveyed by either the two Indians or Corporal Granados from the Béxar Company, agitated the other Apaches to such a degree that they made threatening gestures of war and displayed unrestrained anguish. Luckily, the *presidiales* avoided death-by-association because of the intervention of a trio of Indians, "Bautista," "Jacinto," and "El Canoso," who managed to appease their distraught people. Espadas to Escandón, reporting hostile reaction of Indians to murder of Zapato Zas, BA June 15, 1792.

44. Gálvez, 1786, *artículos* 175–81. For a discussion of a "sustained surge in violence" between Spaniards and Mescalero Apaches, see Santiago (2018), passim; and for Castillo y Terán's 1767 description of other deserting apostate Indians, see Jackson (1995), pp. 167–69.

45. Naylor and Polzer (1988), pp. 270–72.

46. Castro to Muñoz, ordering troops to Laredo to escort Sierra Gorda [Escandón] to Béxar, BA February 13, 1792.

47. Menchaca had served the military for many years prior to his heading the convoy back to San Antonio. See Proceedings [Menchaca's appointment as Alférez], BA March 26, 1774.

48. Castro to Muñoz, ordering troops to Laredo to escort Sierra Gorda to Béxar, BA February 13, 1792; Revilla Gigedo to Muñoz, […] news of the Apaches who wounded […] Menchaca, BA April 17, 1792. For an insightful, condensed view of Juan Vicente de Güemes Pacheco de Padilla's (Segundo Conde de Revillagigedo) impact on the development of the colonial army, see Velázquez (1997), pp. 134–44. Whether written as a double-barreled surname or conjoined, spelling variations of Revillagigedo's patronymic exist. For footnoting, I chose the one used in Béxar Archives document descriptions.

49. I found no subsequent documentation related to the assault on Menchaca. Revilla Gigedo to Muñoz, […] arrival in Béxar of the Governor of Nuevo Santander, BA May 8, 1792; Espadas contacted Muñoz and acknowledged an "official letter dated [… May 27]" that Escandón had assumed command of the province, a notice that Espadas indicated he had already received from Castro. Sierra Gorda's provisional appointment as Governor of Texas, BA June 14, 1792; Roster of the company of Béxar, BA July 1, 1792; Roster of the company of Béxar, BA June 1, 1792. Muñoz had generated his last review of the same company on June 1, 1792.

50. Gálvez, 1786, artículos 21, 112.

51. Where it concerned the Yaquis, Mayos, and other Native people living in the mission pueblos of Sonora, credited by Gálvez as "the best workers in the mines and placers," these groups were to be attracted to work in those of La Cieneguilla, Bacoache, and Zaracache. Protection for laborers and the mineral wealth from that

Notes to Pages 140–145 351

labor came from "detachments of troopers" not needed in Apache country. Gálvez, 1786, artículos 113–14.

52. Out of desperation, perhaps, the two commanders found it convenient to "declare [the lands'] supply of water insufficient, to deny the existence of the Indians, and to exaggerate their fickleness." The commanders' protests were unsuccessful because of discrepancies within their argument. Thus, the missions were established with the protection of escorts from the garrisons of Los Adaes and La Bahía. Morfi (1935), pp. 300–1. For the difficulties and obstacles facing the personnel at Misión Concepción, see Habig (1968), pp. 126–28.

53. *Rivera's Proyecto, Tercer estado, artículo sesenta y siete.* The 1729 regulations contain fourteen articles addressing the use of escorts. The articles are regional specific, incorporate territory from Sinaloa to Texas, and dictate the number of soldiers assigned to protect missionaries, recruits, and civilians. *Reglamento de 1729, A quienes y en que tiempos se deberán dar escoltas de los presidios internos, artículos,* pp. 139–53.

54. [...] report on doubtful accounts of the company of Béxar [Cavo Franco], BA May 14 [– December 19], 1792.

55. Gálvez, 1786, artículos 38–52.

56. [...] report on doubtful accounts of the company of Béxar [...], BA May 14 [– December 19], 1792. Differences encountered in questionable balances gave the Accounting Office in Mexico City cause to generate a series of reports that ran with specified dates of service and a summary of the discrepancies existing in the fund's records. Report No. 1, which ran from January 8–30, 1787, concerns the salaries of four servants and the amount of the expenditures reported for the maintenance of the Indians; Report No. 2, from December 17, 1786, to February 23, 1787, lists the salaries of two servants and the amount of money lacking in the accounting; Reports No. 4 and 7, covering the dates January 31 to March 31, and, April 11 to June 5, 1787, respectively, covered a total of 116 days and indicated the same errors as did Reports numbered 8, 10, 15, 18 (which included similar errors in payments to servants but also showed discrepancies in the rent for two kettles, four ladles, and ten pots). Cavo Franco noted the same errors are evident in Reports No. 20 (February 19 to May 13, 1788), No. 22 (May 11 to June 12, 1788), No. 25 (July 5 to September 1, 1788), and No. 32 (November 19 to December 25, 1788). The grand total of days covered in these eight reports — not including the first four listed above — was 350 days.

57. [...] report on doubtful accounts of the company of Béxar [...], BA May 14 [–December 19], 1792. Account No. 9 covered the period March 24 to April 22, 1789, with discrepancies listed in the servant salaries and the rental of cooking utensils; Report No. 10 has the same information and includes the days of April 26 to August 17, 1789. Report No. 11, August 20 to September 17, 1789, concerns the same inaccuracies and for the same reasons as does Report No. 17, except for the utensils.

58. [...] report on doubtful accounts of the company of Béxar [...], BA May 14 [–December 19], 1792. The Béxar Archives' documents relating to Bustillo's expenditures for indigenous communities include his transactions with other notables found within this study. See Martínez Pacheco, Bustillos y Zeballos, and Courbiere, [expenses for] entertaining Comanche and Taovaya Indians, BA May 14, 1788; [Ibid], Orcoquizas, Cocos, and Mayeye Indians, BA July 5, 1788; Bustillos y Ceballos' statement of Indian expenses [...], BA June 17, 1791.

59. Correspondence between Castro and Sierra Gorda [...] concerning case against

352   Notes to Pages 145–146

Juan Cortés, BA July 14 [– September 9], 1792. Fact finders across the Comandancia
followed the usual procedures when conducting these types of investigations. In
January of 1780, Croix sent a certified copy of the assessor's opinion regarding a royal
cédula of 1776 ordering the prosecution of contraband in Texas. In turn, then-governor
Domingo Cabello, was able to dispatch the corresponding *títulos* (formal appointments) to individuals of his choice for remaining vigilant of illegal contraband trade
that might circulate in the province. Moreover, Cabello was responsible for drawing
up the instructions he considered most pertinent for exercising and discharging these
commissions. See further: Proceedings […] to prosecute contraband in Texas, BA
January 5, 1780; Croix to Cabello […] prosecution of contraband in Texas, BA January
10, 1780; Cabello to Croix […] prosecute contraband in Texas, BA March 18, 1780;
Croix to Cabello, [enforcement of Art.1 Title 6 of the Royal Regulations of Presidios]
to prevent paymasters from mishandling provisions assigned for the presidial troops,
BA January 6, 1780.
     60. Cabello to Croix, [contraband goods confiscated by] Amangual, BA March 18,
1780; Croix to Cabello, […] contraband goods confiscated by Amangual, BA June
9, 1780; Cabello to Croix, […] cases of Felix Menchaca and Juan Isurrieta charged
with contraband, BA June 15, 1780; Cabello to Croix [Menchaca and "Izurrieta"], BA
July 18, 1780; August 16, 1780; September 20, 1780; October 18, 1780; […] case against
Juan Cortés […] charged with smuggling, BA June 16, 1792. The translation of the
proceedings begins with a document dated June 16, 1792. These materials are hereafter
cited as "Cortés, smuggling, BA June 16, 1792" and may include a parenthetic timeline.
One month before Amangual began his inventory, then-governor of Texas Escandón
ordered Lt. Bernardo Fernández, himself recently held responsible for accounting inaccuracies, to go with ten privates in a secret maneuver to seize the loads and baggage
of Cortés without the slightest loss. Taking these steps was vital to Escandón's ordering
its proper inspection. Cortés, smuggling, BA June 16, 1792 (Escandón, June 17, 1792);
Cabello to Croix, […] seizure of contraband goods […] from Louisiana, BA May 9,
1780; Cortés to Muñoz, […] receipt of proclamation of amnesty to contrabandists,
BA November 4, 1791.
     61. Transcribed here exactly as it appears in the original. Nicholas Lamath (aka
Nicolás de Lamathé and Nicolas de la Matte, hereafter Lamath) was one of the
twenty-nine foreigners in Nacogdoches listed in the Muñoz census of May 1792. See
Correspondence between Castro and Sierra Gorda, concerning case against Juan
Cortés, BA July 14, 1792 [– September 9, 1792] (Amangual's inventory, June 18, 1792).
When Croix searched for a suitable "emissary of confidence" to appease clamoring by
the "Nations of the North," he found his man in Lamath. See Thomas (1941), pp. 79–81.
For Lamath's work at the pueblo of Bucareli, see Herbert Eugene Bolton, *Texas in the
Middle Eighteenth Century: Studies in Spanish Colonial History and Administration*
(Austin: University of Texas Press, 1915), pp. 118, 415, 427, 433.
     62. Correspondence between Castro and Sierra Gorda, concerning case against
Juan Cortés, BA July 14, 1792 [– September 9, 1792; Ybarvo, June 19, 1792; Amangual's
inventory, June 20, 1792]. Since Antonio Gil Ybarvo's surname across literature is
variously spelled "Ibarvo," "Ibarbo," and "Ibarvo," I cannot retain all cognates of the
name as they occur throughout this large document. Hereafter he is referred to as
Ibarvo, given its overwhelming frequency of use in the Béxar Archives. This officer
features in several studies for his presence in the conflictive domains of trade among
soldiers, settlers, and indigenous peoples. See David La Vere, "Between Kinship

Notes to Pages 146–150 353

and Capitalism: French and Spanish Rivalry in the Colonial Louisiana–Texas Indian Trade," *Journal of Southern History* 64, no. 2 (May 1998): 197–218; John et al. (1994): 26–56; Elizabeth A. H. John and John Wheat, "Governing Texas, 1779: The Karankawa Aspect," *Southwestern Historical Quarterly* 104, no. 4 (April 2001): 560–76; Bolton (1915), passim.

63. Given Spanish chroniclers' penchant for reinventing grammar for their reading audience, "Nachitos" is used in documents related to the Cortés case and others to refer to the French town and garrison of Natchitoches, located opposite from the presidio of Nuestra Señora de Pilar de Adaes (Los Adaes). The word is found nowhere in recent studies of Natchitoches or Los Adaes/Nacogdoches.

64. Cortés, smuggling, BA June 16, 1792 (Deposition of Treviño, June 20, 1792).

65. Ibid (Deposition of Maldonado, June 20, 1792). As in the Amangual–Rodríguez slander episode, for the remainder of the Cortés proceeding I retain the original Spanish language text as it occurs in the documents and to avoid overuse of the notations *sic* and *sic passim*.

66. Cortés, smuggling, BA June 16, 1792 (Deposition of Gómez, June 20, 1792). Studies of French trade in the borderlands are extensive but the most recent publications include: Francis Xavier Galán, "Presidio Los Adaes: Worship, Kinship, and Commerce with French Natchitoches on the Spanish-Franco-Caddo Borderlands, 1721–1773," *Louisiana History: The Journal of the Louisiana Historical Association* 49, no. 2 (Spring 2008): 191–208; H. Sophie Burton, "Vagabonds along the Spanish Louisiana–Texas Frontier, 1769–1803: Men Who Are Evil, Lazy, Gluttonous, Drunken, Libertinous, Dishonest, Mutinous, etc. etc. etc. — and Those Are Their Virtues," *Southwestern Historical Quarterly* 113, no. 4 (April 2010): 438–67. Archaeological evidence at Presidio Los Adaes suggests the "cooperative nature of the relationship between the Spanish, French, and Caddoan groups" with roughly equal amounts of artifacts representing these distinct polities. See H. F. Gregory, George Avery, Aubra L. Lee, and Jay C. Blaine, "Presidio Los Adaes: Spanish, French, and Caddoan Interaction on the Northern Frontier," in "Presidios of the North American Spanish Borderlands," edited by J. A. Bense, special issue, *Historical Archaeology* 38, no. 3 (2004): 69–71.

67. As with all given names and surnames in this study, I retain the spelling of Trexo's last name as it appears in the margin of the original document, the location of other individual identifiers in all the depositions. However, within the body of the deposition his name is spelled "Trejo." The same is true with Lamath's surname. In yet another instance of variations in spellings throughout a single folio related to one proceeding, the original document of Escandón's handwritten script — or that of his scribe — has Belanze's name written the same way and thus can be understood, and this will become evident, as either "Belame" or "Belanze" or "Blanz" or "Balanz." Cortés, smuggling, BA June 16, 1792 (Deposition of Trexo, June 20, 1792).

68. Cortés, smuggling, BA June 16, 1792 (Deposition of Rodríguez, June 20, 1792). Given its value as a commodity and its special significance to soldiers and civilians, the movement of tobacco from one point to another was bound to ride on legal and extralegal modes of transport. As Burton shows, the Bourbons successfully promoted tobacco and guaranteed markets in Spain and New Spain. For example, in Natchitoches alone, forty-nine residents raised 83,360 pounds of tobacco in 1766, while by 1791 eighty-three planters were harvesting 731,935 pounds. See H. Sophie Burton, "'To Establish a Stock Farm for the Raising of Mules, Horses, Horned Cattle, Sheep, and Hogs': The Role of the Spanish Bourbon Louisiana in the Establishment of Vacheries

354 Notes to Pages 150–154

along the Louisiana–Texas Borderland, 1766–1803," *Southwestern Historical Quarterly* 109, no. 1 (July 2005): 98–132.

69. Cortés to Sierra Gorda, reporting departure for Béxar of soldiers charged with contraband, BA August 19, 1792. By the following February, the still-injured Cortés appealed to Muñoz to contact *Comandante General* Castro so as to grant him leave for treatment of his arm at Valle de Santa Rosa. Because there was no physician available, Cortés told his superior that there was "no hope of healing." Cortés to Muñoz, [Castro seeks aid] for treatment of injured left arm, BA February 4, 1793.

70. Moorhead (1975), pp. 201–21. Abuses had reached such proportions that the commander general ordered Cabello to reiterate the requirements spelled out in Article 1, Title 6 of the regulations and that its content was to be observed to the letter. Indeed, the *Reglamento 1772* had as a key objective the curtailing of paymaster fraud and extortion. By 1780, Teodor de Croix had already noted the willingness of and freewill [*la voluntariedad y libre arvitrio*] by which some paymasters deviated from annotating with precision the annual stockpiles of goods and provisions for the *presidiales* and the *volantes* as called for in the 1772 mandate. Punishment leading even to the point of removal from their positions would descend upon those who refused to comply. Croix to Cabello, [enforcement of Title 6, Art.1 of the Royal Regulations of Presidios] to prevent paymasters from mishandling provisions assigned for the presidial troops, BA January 6, 1780.

71. Cortés, smuggling, BA June 16, 1792, (Deposition of Cortés, September 10, 1792). In the archival documentation, the Lamathé surname is variously spelled Lamath, Lamate, Lamat, de la Mate, and even Lamatte. Ethnohistorical considerations require that I mention all variations as they occur in the original documents, but practicality dictates that I use one consistent spelling.

72. Cortés, smuggling, BA June 16, 1792, (Deposition of Cortés, September 10, 1792).

73. Ibid.

74. Ibid. The Quiche or Kichai may be the Quicheis near the Trinity River, or the Quichas near the Sabine, and referred to by José Cortés (1989), p. 87. Self-identified as the K'itsäsh, a Caddoan tribe according to Hodge, their multiple identities for outsiders are generously noted in Hodge (1959, pp. 682–83.) The Tahuacanes or Tawakoni were considered part of the Wichita confederation of tribes. Smith (1995), passim; Barr (2007), passim. See a contemporaneous summary of the "Taucana" ("Tuacana") in Cortés (1989), p. 83.

75. Cortés, smuggling, BA June 16, 1792, (Deposition of Cortés, September 10, 1792).

76. Ibid. However, this had previously been ordered in the September 10 *auto* issued by Escandón. Though the original manuscript is torn, this section of the document attests to Cortés' presence specifically called for by the Lipan, an indication that Cortés had forged strong bonds in his efforts to maintain indigenous allies even among the more inconstant factions of the Apache.

77. Castro to Muñoz, [continue case against Cortés], BA October 27, 1792.

78. Ibid. (Ratification of Cortés, September 25, 1792). Cortés' willingness to part with buckskin for two essential components of soldier outfitting — the *cuera* and boots — prompts the question as to whether the items were for his personal use, or did he have particularly destitute soldiers in mind when he made the trade?

79. Ibid. (Ratification of Alférez Don Antonio Treviño, September 25, 1792). Patti Mills states that "the oath was a means by which a legal question or suit could be commended to God for resolution in the absence of other compelling evidence." But

Notes to Pages 154–158

doing so "depended on society's belief in the concept of immanent justice" which accepted both the possibility and probability of "divine intervention in human affairs on a regular basis." See Mills (1987), p.102. In the case of military justice, a soldier's insistence on multiple reiterations of the oath of ratification may have drawn on this form of mystical resolution, like making the sign of the cross, but, perhaps, not to the same extent as in civilian processes of adjudication.

80. Cortés, smuggling, BA June 16, 1792, (Ratification by Corporal Ylario Maldonado, September 26, 1792); for Arman's business of supplying horses and mules prior to, and even after, the Cortés case, see Ibarvo to Muñoz, [escape by José Gómez "Animas," who left with two horses of Arman], BA October 23, 1791; Correspondence between Cordoba and Muñoz [Navarro's mule sold in Natchitoches] by Arman, BA July 8, 1794.

81. Cortés, smuggling, BA June 16, 1792, (Ratification by Maldonado, September 26, 1792). According to the *Diccionario de la lengua española* (2006) of the RAE, a "candonga" (alternately spelled *condonga/o*) refers to a piece of canvas or silk, which, in this context, appears to constitute the bulk of the contraband items. *Malilla* refers to a card game played much like whist with much shuffling and trick playing.

82. Cortés, smuggling, BA June 16, 1792 (Ratification by Maldonado, September 26, 1792).

83. Ibid. (Deposition by Pvt. Joaquín Galán, September 26, 1792). I have not ascertained the identity of "Phelipe" but there is every reason to believe it was Philip Nolan, the young but hardened contrabandist discussed in Chapter 6. If so, Galán mistook an Irish accent for a British one. On a related note, Edward Murphy was a successful Irish merchant and landowner in Natchitoches, and formed a partnership with three other men, William Barr, who was Irish, and the other two, Americans. See La Vere (1998), pp. 382–83.

84. A *manojo* can describe a bundle of raw tobacco weighing approximately two pounds; it can also mean, simply, a bunch or handful. And see John et al. (1994), p. 37 fn30.

85. Cortés, smuggling, BA June 16, 1792 (Deposition by Galán, September 26, 1792).

86. Ibid.

87. For the Orcoquiza presence at trade distribution points in East Texas, see Galán (2020), pp. 134, 143, 152, 214. Described as neighbors of the Vidais and Texas, the "Orkoquisas" were settled along the Trinity River. Cortés (1989), p. 86.

88. Cortés, smuggling, BA June 16, 1792 (Deposition by Galán, September 26, 1792).

89. Cortés, smuggling, BA June 16, 1792 (Ratification of Private Antonio Gómez, September 26, 1792). After conducting excavations at the San Sabá presidio site, archaeologist Tamra Walter disclosed that clothing and associated items like buckles and buttons, as well as horse trappings, i.e., horseshoe nails and "jinglers" used to decorate bits, "attest to the elaborate nature of 18th-century Spanish colonial horse gear." Tamra L. Walter, "The Archaeology of Presidio San Sabá: A Preliminary Report," in "Presidios of the North American Spanish Borderlands," edited by J. A. Bense, special issue, *Historical Archaeology* 38, no. 3 (2004): pp. 94–105.

90. Cortés, smuggling, BA June 16, 1792 (Ratification of Gómez, September 26, 1792).

91. Ibid. There is no indication that the soldiers arrived on foot, walking next to their horses. These may have been horses long in service and accustomed to vocal commands from their riders without the need for head control gear.

92. Cortés, smuggling, BA June 16, 1792 (Ratification of Private Antonio Gómez, September 26, 1792).

356   Notes to Pages 158–161

93. Cortés, smuggling, BA June 16, 1792 (Ratification of Del Río, September 26, 1792). De la Zerda is likely the individual described in a 1799 census as "espanol," married, "natural de los Adais," fifty years old, and a carpenter/sic passim. Census report [Nacogdoches], BA December 31, 1799.

94. Ibid. More than likely, the variety was a dark aromatic tobacco called "perique" grown in Natchitoches and described in La Vere (1998), p. 376, fn15. Established in 1721 by the Marqués de Aguayo in northeast Texas, Los Adaes (Nuestra Señora del Pilar) sat opposite the French post of Natchitoches in Louisiana. It was the residence of the provincial governor until 1770 and lasted as a presidio for another three years. When the presidio was ordered abandoned, its inhabitants reluctantly moved to Béxar. However, many of them longed to return to East Texas. So, they did and eventually founded Nacogdoches very near to their old presidio location. See Moorhead (1975), pp. 30–31; Poyo and Hinojosa (1991), pp. 96–102. For an excellent discussion of material artifacts found at the site, see Gregory et al. (2004), pp. 65–77; for commercial and kinship links between French and Spanish groups at Los Adaes, see Galán (2008), pp. 191–208.

95. Cortés, smuggling, BA June 16, 1792 (Ratification of Del Río, September 26, 1792).

96. For example, see: [...] proceedings [...] investigation of French contraband trade and advance into the interior [...], BA February 10, 1750; [...] apprehension of certain contraband good coming from Natchitoches, BA November 16, 1766; and, for several cases in the 1780s see Cabello to Croix, [...] contraband cases in Texas, BA May 1, 1780; Cabello to Croix, [...] contraband goods introduced from Louisiana, BA May 9, 1780; Cabello to Croix, reporting on contraband cases, BA October 9, 1780; José Pereira de Castro to Martínez Pacheco [...] contraband trade in cattle, BA November 13, 1788. References to contraband and its function in the Spanish Atlantic system are abundant in recent scholarship. The common thread uniting discussion of its tenacity in the American dominions is the colonists' desire for overseas merchandise. As one historian explains, "the backwardness of Spanish industry meant that Spanish American consumers were largely dependent on non-Spanish manufacturers" for the items they craved. In the Spanish Atlantic ecosystem, "contraband [...] was the most effective form of protest against unpopular policies" emanating from its administrative centers and "the purchase of contraband goods had become second nature" to Spain's overseas subjects. See John Huxtable Elliot, *Empires of the Atlantic World: Britain and Spain in America, 1492–1830* (New Haven: Yale University Press, 2006), pp. 316–17. Paquette argues that Spanish policymakers were convinced that "prosperity, abundance, and low prices" and not "vigorous enforcement [of] punitive measures" could eradicate smuggling. See Paquette (2008), pp. 104; 146–51. For a discussion of the desirability of cloth among Spanish colonial consumers, see Caroline A. Williams, ed., *Bridging the Early Modern Atlantic World: People, Products, and Practices on the Move* (Farnham: Ashgate Publishing Ltd., 2009), pp. 14–15.

97. Rengel to Cabello, [...] royal order [...] vessels guarding against contraband trade, BA July 30, 1785.

98. [...] King's decree concerning seizure of contraband goods, BA May 23, 1791. It should be noted that neither term "considerable" nor "small" are precisely defined as numeric quantities in the original document when describing "amounts."

99. [...] King's decree concerning seizure of contraband goods, BA May 23, 1791. The *fiscal* during this time frame was Ramón de Posada y Soto, a bureaucrat who "carried out with efficiency" his position as Fiscal of the Royal Treasury of the Audiencia of

Notes to Pages 161–167 357

Mexico. For Posada's experience with twenty-nine bins of contraband tobacco in 1785, see Rodríguez García (1985), pp. 160–61, passim.

100. […] King's decree concerning seizure of contraband goods, BA May 23, 1791.

101. Ibid. Partial to his main character, one historian asserted that New Spain's tobacco monopoly made "genuine progress" through the efforts of Viceroy Bucareli, resulting in the imperial government's trajectory from mere competitors to dominators ultimately able to "force all nongovernment merchandizers out of the field." See Bobb (1962), pp. 253–57; for the period covered in this study, see Céspedes del Castillo and Anes y Álvarez de Castrillón (1992), pp. 89–169.

102. King's decree concerning seizure of contraband goods, BA May 23, 1791.

103. Revillagigedo to Muñoz, concerning contraband trade of Juan Cortés, BA September 26, 1792.

104. Ibid.

105. Ibid.

Chapter 5

1. As it pertained to colonial Mexico and its northern borderlands, the exact value of an *almud* varied by region. In the Spanish colonial frontier, it may have been approximately the equivalent of seven and a half liters. Haggard indicates the Chilean equivalent of one-half a *fanega*, and the US equivalent as 1.2885 bushels. Juan Haggard, *Handbook for Translators of Spanish Historical Documents* (Austin: Archives Collections, University of Texas, 1941), p. 17. Thomas gives its equivalency at "six bushels." (1932), p. 383. Guice calculates equivalency at 1.6 bushels. Norman Guice, "Texas in 1804," *Southwestern Historical Quarterly* 59, no. 1 (July 1955): 53.

2. Courbiére's account of expenses incurred for maintenance of visiting Indians, BA May 22, 1792. Esteban L. Portillo, *Apuntes para la historia antigua de Coahuila y Texas* (Saltillo: Edición Colegio San José, 2019/1886), pp. 13–21.

3. Courbiére's account of expenses incurred for maintenance of visiting Indians, BA May 22, 1792. Names and titles as written in the original document.

4. Morfi described "La Tortuga" as a pueblo of Tonkawa Indians located about fifteen leagues west of a Quitsey [Kichai] village. Morfi (1935), p. 56; Morfi (2010), p. 433.

5. Correspondence between Espadas and Muñoz, concerning Comanche depredations, BA May 25, 1792.

6. Ibid. (Muñoz to Espadas, May 26).

7. Correspondence between Espadas and Muñoz, concerning Comanche depredations, BA May 25, 1792. "[…] *debemos disimular sus ymperfecciones por ser nación que contiene a las demás*" [sic passim].

8. Correspondence between Espadas and Muñoz, concerning Comanche depredations, BA May 25, 1792.

9. Ibid. The relationship between cattle ranching, the *vaqueros* who worked in that enterprise, and mission personnel who oversaw and reaped the economic rewards of these endeavors has been substantively presented in frontier studies. For a few of the most comprehensive accounts, see Alonzo (1998); Jackson (1986); Terry G. Jordan, *North American Cattle-Ranching Frontiers: Origins, Diffusion, and Differentiation* (Albuquerque: University of New Mexico Press, 1993); and Odie B. Faulk, "Ranching in Spanish Texas," *Hispanic American Historical Review* 45, no. 2 (May 1965): 257–66.

10. Espadas to Muñoz, concerning policies toward the Comanche […], BA May 31,

358 Notes to Pages 167–168

1792. Perhaps it was an issue with guns. One year earlier, Ramón de Castro demanded to know from Governor Muñoz what number of weapons he thought was necessary to supply the Comanche so they would be content when it was necessary to accede to their repeated requests. See Castro to Muñoz, [...] treatment of Comanche captain "Ojos Azules" and his people, BA July 2, 1791.

11. Espadas to Sierra Gorda, reporting request of Canoso for a conference of peace, BA June 2, 1792. See the twelve-point plan presented by Comandancia officials to Canoso and other Lipan leaders in Britten (2009), pp. 160–65.

12. Espadas to Sierra Gorda, reporting request of Canoso for a conference of peace, BA June 2, 1792.

13. Castro to Sierra Gorda, transmitting Revilla Gigedo's letter of February 1, confirming shipment of guns for Béxar citizens, BA June 2, 1792. However, since the government in Texas had not responded to his repeated requests for information, by March 1793 Castro demanded reimbursement from Governor Muñoz in the amount of 886 pesos, one and a half *reales*, for the cost of the 117 muskets. There was an additional 101 pesos, six *reales* calculated as repayment to Leandro Pacheco and Pedro de Alva, the two *habilitados* who shipped the guns. Castro to Muñoz [...] to Amangual, [...] distribution of guns sent from San Luis Potosí for citizens of Béxar, BA March 15, 1793. It would be another six weeks before Muñoz contacted Amangual (indicating that Castro's order had just arrived in that day's mail) to send a report on the muskets that had been distributed to the citizens, then paid for, and deposited in the paymaster's office by then-governor Escandón. In order to decide the best way to proceed with Castro's request, Muñoz also asked Amangual for a list of the individuals who had received nothing. Castro to Muñoz [...] to Amangual, [...] distribution of guns sent from San Luis Potosí for citizens of Béxar, BA March 15, 1793. (Muñoz to Amangual, April 26, 1793).

14. Castro to Sierra Gorda, approving dispositions to Captain Canoso [...], BA June 16, 1792. By September, the reinstated Governor Muñoz received the same information from the commander general — the Lipan must be treated with great skill and cunning (*maña y astucia*). However, Castro alerted Muñoz to the potential return of the Lipan known as "Juan Bautista" who, like others from his nation, sought peace. In these instances, the governor was to immediately notify the general.

15. Castro sent his order on the same day as his instructions for the care of a Lipan escapee. If Castro seemed a hardhearted military man, an order to Muñoz only three months later would suggest differently. A Lipan woman sought refuge in San Antonio's Mission Valero since, according to the previous governor's account, she had escaped from her companions who wanted to kill her. Because of her plight, and given her Christian status, Castro ordered Muñoz to allow her to remain. Nonetheless, the governor was to maintain vigilance over her companions, to watch their movements so that they themselves would make it clear whether, or not, what the woman said was true. Castro to Muñoz, ordering him to let a Christian Lipan girl stay [...], BA September 29, 1792. Similarly, the spirited Capt. Juan Cortés of La Bahía informed Muñoz that another captive woman of thirty-four years had escaped from a *ranchería* of the upper Lipan, a group headed to the Bahía presidio to join the aforesaid El Canoso. According to Cortés' account, she had wandered lost for eleven days on foot and was so sick by the time she reached the presidio that she had already confessed. Once recovered, she described her story of escape and survival. Taken prisoner by the

Notes to Pages 168–171   359

militant Zapato Sax in 1791 at the Rancho de Palmitos, two of her children who came along were subsequently killed, as well as the one she bore on the road. She did not know if her husband had met the same fate. Cortés was attending to her, declaring she was well kept in his care. Cortés to Muñoz, [...] arrival of a woman, captive of the Indians [escaped] Lipan camp, BA October 3, 1792. One week later, the woman had recovered well enough to identify the *ranchería* as that of "Chief" Chiquito from which she had fled. There they had kept twelve women captives and three men, all of them taken at El Vallecillo, Revilla, and other *ranchos* in those jurisdictions. Encouraged by another Lipan, she took flight. However, she implied that Chiquito did not go out on raids or do any harm when he was with Zapato Sax. She confirmed the death of the latter and of others in his company, as well as a skirmish between the "Tahuayases" and the Lipanes of her *ranchería*. Cortés to Muñoz, with additional information on captive woman, BA October 10, 1792.

16. Espadas to Sierra Gorda, discussing policy toward Lipan Apaches, BA June 18, 1792. This "Jacinto" might be the same individual who helped to quell Lipan agitation over the death of Zapato Sax only three weeks prior.

17. Cortés to Sierra Gorda, [visit of two Lipan ... peace negotiations], BA July 5, 1792. The "Old Mission" is likely a reference to the relocated San Francisco Xavier [de Horcasitas] Mission, established in 1756. Donald E. Chipman, "San Francisco Xavier Mission On the Guadalupe River," *Handbook of Texas Online*, https://www.tshaonline.org/handbook/entries/san-francisco-xavier-mission-on-the-guadalupe-river.

18. Cortés to Muñoz, discussing exploration trip by Espadas, [...], BA Sept 9, 1791 (– September 11, 1791). Perhaps Espadas was just unlucky and therefore irresolute in most matters. Sent to reconnoiter the Guadalupe River, he withdrew on September 4 without having managed to get any farther than the Arroyo de las Animas due to the impassability of the terrain by heavy rains. Muñoz replied that he had in front of him a Lipan Indian prisoner, described as more than seventy years old, who gave a report of the headwaters of the Frio River and the area between the hill country and the San Sabá canyon. At that place were gathered the chiefs Zapatosas, Canoso, Chiquito, Josse [sic] Lombraña, and El Pinto. However, Muñoz doubted the report since Nava sent him word that Capt. José Tobar had killed both Canoso and Lombraña. As matters stood, even that turned out to be misinformation.

19. For the detailed account of this event and another suggesting the no-nonsense character of Cortés, see chapter 2.

20. Cortés to Sierra Gorda, [...] visit of Captain Canoso and a great number of braves, BA July 9, 1792. Julianna Barr has argued forcefully for the presence of women as negotiators for amity between Spaniards and indigenous nations. Barr (2007), for "women as noncombatant symbols of peace," see especially pp. 92–93, 246, 249, 252–53.

21. Cortés to Sierra Gorda, reporting on visiting Comanche [sic] captain, Jacinto, who is willing to visit the Governor, BA July 15, 1792. The Béxar Archives Online descriptor for this document is incorrect; Jacinto was a Lipan Apache.

22. Revilla Gigedo to Sierra Gorda, ordering Muñoz restored to office of Governor, BA August 8, 1792.

23. Cortés to Muñoz, discussing Indian activities, BA October 15, 1792.

24. Revilla Gigedo to Governor of Texas, [...] Lipan Indians at [Valero Mission] productive in agriculture, BA June 20, 1792.

360   **Notes to Pages 171–172**

25. Courbiére complied, describing large pots called *chancaqueros*, used when he arrived in September 1779. Courbiére included the rental price per day for these large pots and even the names of their owners: Flórez de Ábrego, Juan José de la Santa, and Antonio Sanches [sic]. However, medium-sized pots — the property of Juan Leal Boraz — found use when smaller groups of Natives appeared, and their cost was only two *reales* per day. Wooden basins (*artesones*) were available to serve food. Axes, hoes, and *beldúquez* (short swords) became handy for the slaughter of cattle and for the repair of the doors of the lodge (*jacalón*) housing the Indians. Courbiére retained copper pots brought from the storehouse of the presidio in order to have them ready for use by arrivals. Muñoz to Courbiére, […] pots used to cook for the Indian visitors, BA January 11, 1793.

26. *Belduque*: A type of short blade used to slaughter livestock.

27. Revilla Gigedo to Muñoz, […] Lipan policy and approving small gifts when necessary, BA January 16, 1793. See also Muñoz to Fernandez, [Viceroy's orders of January 16 emphasizing clause in peace treaty with Lipans], BA February 22, 1793; [Revilla Gigedo] to Castro, [Muñoz to collect information on Lipan], BA October 24, 1793.

28. Nava to Governor of Texas, […] proclamation forbidding trade with the Lipans, BA January 1, 1794.

29. Nava to Muñoz, instructing him not to urge the Lipans to move to Coahuila, BA February 13, 1794.

30. Barr (2007), pp. 270–71. Griffin (1988), pp. 75–81. Gálvez, 1786, artículos 52, 64, 65, among others.

31. Moorhead (1975), pp. 258–59. See also Babcock (2016), pp. 117–22. On April 12, 1790, "Capitan Cavezon [sic]" and eleven Lipan warriors made peace with a small squad of four privates and one corporal. Three Lipan including two working as interpreters accompanied the troops after several encounters with various "parties from [Béxar] and that of La Bahía." Though the Lipan party sued for peace, Governor Martínez Pacheco saw no other options for them but settlement in either missions or near towns. He was convinced that reduction of the Lipan to places of containment would prevent other nations from making war on the Spanish military and civilian populations. Barring that, their extermination constituted the only alternative in his eyes. See Martínez Pacheco to Ugalde, […] securing of peace with the Lipan Apache, BA July 23, 1790. Even before José de Gálvez's 1779 "royal" order, some commanders had of their own volition settled Native groups at presidios in apparent long-term status. Babcock (2016), pp. 75–80; for the Royal Order of 1779, see Babcock (2016), pp. 85–89; Britten (2009), pp. 140–41.

32. Nava to Governor of Texas, […] instructions […] governing treatment of friendly Apaches, BA April 18, 1794. See […] Nava's regulations to be observed [treatment of Apache], now at peace with Spain, BA October 14, 1791.

33. Revilla Gigedo to Sierra Gorda, ordering Muñoz restored to […] Governor, BA August 8 [– September 30], 1792. However, Commander General Castro generated a letter from Santa Rosa to Muñoz on August 25, conveying the August 7 pages received by Castro from Revillagigedo. In that document, the viceroy indicated that once the *autos* of investigation into the conduct of Muñoz had been finalized and if he was proven innocent of the charges brought against him, Muñoz's complete salary as governor would be credited to him as of August 26. Thus, Revillagigedo cleared him

Notes to Pages 172–174

361

of all charges, and he ordered Muñoz to immediately resume his duties as governor. Escandón received notification of the viceroy's decision. See Castro to Muñoz, [...] reappointment as governor, BA August 25, 1792. In this same cache of documents, Castro conveyed to Escandón two further resolutions from the viceroy. One concerned the complaint filed by Cipriano Sambrano against Muñoz; Sambrano claimed to have lost several days of profit from having to prove that a woman who had accompanied him on a trip was his lawful wife. See Castro to Sierra Gorda, [...] Revilla Gigedo's [...] acquitting Muñoz of charges from [...] Sambrano, BA August 25, 1792. In another, Ygnacio Flóres complained about Muñoz's manifold punishment of him by suspending his permit to round up *mesteño* cattle; his having to pay for mixing the *orejano* (unbranded) stock with the known (branded) livestock gave him reason to prepare a petition of grievance against this ruling. Again, the viceroy declared the Flóres suit unfounded. See Castro to Sierra Gorda, [...] Revilla Gigedo's [...] acquitting Muñoz of charges from Ignacio Flóres, BA August 25, 1792.

34. Roster of the company of San Antonio de Béxar, BA September 3, 1792.

35. Ibid.

36. Case against Toribio Durán for contraband trade, BA October 19, 1792. The document identifies Córdoba as the "commander and justice for the town of Nacogdoches due to the absence of Don Antonio Gil Ibarvo." (Muñoz to Revilla Gigedo, November 19, 1792). Later, Córdoba became the lieutenant governor of the town. Throughout 1793, he maintained frequent contact with Muñoz concerning Indian affairs and misbehavior on the part of a civilian of San Fernando named Francisco Travieso, an individual accused of robberies that incited ongoing retribution by Indians against other civilians. See Córdova to Muñoz, [Indian preparations for attack], BA April 27, 1793; [Travieso], April 27, 1793; [Apaches vs. other tribes], April 27, 1793; [Travieso stealing from Tawakoni, burning houses, causing retaliations], April 29, 1793. Clearly, Travieso was a dreadful man; see Proceedings against Francisco Travieso, charged with rape of María Martínez, BA August 16, 1794.

37. Case against Toribio Durán [...], BA October 19, 1792. The viceroy resolved that the proceedings be forwarded to the "senor intendant of that province" [sic] since he considered decision-making over the matter the purview of someone else. See Revilla Gigedo to Muñoz, ordering case of Toribio Durán sent to Commandant General, BA February 6, 1793. In fact, it was to be sent to the acting counsel of the intendancy Vicente Bernabeu (see below).

38. Case against Toribio Durán [...], BA October 19, 1792 (Muñoz to Revilla Gigedo, November 19, 1792). As in so many documents from the period, the spelling of names varies; in this case, the last name of the merchant is spelled, both, "Verasady" and "Verasadi."

39. Ibid. (Posada to Revilla Gigedo, December 31, 1792). For Posada's tenure in New Spain, see Rodríguez García, (1985), passim.

40. As described by Fisher (1969/1929, p. 111), "the intendant general of army and treasury, and each one of the intendants of province, must have a lieutenant-lawyer who shall exercise for them jurisdiction over civil and criminal litigation in the capital of their particular territory. At the same time, he shall be an ordinary assessor in all the business of the intendancy, exercising the authority of its superior official in [case of] his nonappearance, illness, and absences while visiting his province, or from any just cause." See also *Real Ordenanza* [*intendentes de exército y provincia en Nueva España*], *Año de 1786*, "Causa de justicia, artículo 15," which states "que al mismo

362 Notes to Pages 174–178

tiempo sea Asesor ordinario en todos los negocios de la Intendencia," Mantilla Troye et al. (2008), pp. 155–56.

41. From Revilla Gigedo's order of December 1, 1789, and approved by "His Majesty" on June 6, 1790. Case against Toribio Durán for contraband trade from Nacogdoches, BA Oct 19, 1792 (Posada to Revilla Gigedo, January 29, 1793).

42. Ibid. (Luna to Bernabeu, February 19, 1793). Within the same document, the word *guía* translates as, both, "bill of lading" and "passport." Bernabeu's appointment as the asesor ordinario met with accusations of corruption and gambling in a lively section of David A. Brading, "Power and Justice in Catorce 1799–1805," *Ibero-amerikanisches Archiv*, v.20, no. 3/4 (1994): 357–80.

43. Case against Toribo Durán for contraband trade from Nacogdoches, BA October 19, 1792. (Muñoz's *auto* . . . fine of 20 pesos . . . , February 6, 1794). See Military service record of José Gervacio de Silva, December 1796, CSWR, SAII.

44. Proceedings in the investigation of Ugalde's report on Indian expenditures, BA January 22, 1793; [. . .] report on doubtful accounts of the company of Béxar [Cavo Franco], BA May 14, 1792.

45. Proceedings in the investigation of Ugalde's report on Indian expenditures, BA January 22, 1793.

46. Ibid. Amangual shared many tasks with Fernández including becoming quite familiar with answering charges made against his job performance. Fourteen years earlier, as Presidio Béxar's paymaster, Fernández had been under suspicion of mismanagement of and profiting from company funds. In the summer of 1779, charges caught up with him and then-captain and governor Juan de Ripperdá, the latter investigated for abusing soldiers. See Certified copy of [proceedings against] Fernández, charged with mismanagement of affairs at Béxar, BA July 15, 1779. One year later, he was reelected to the same post, thus retaining the confidence of his colleagues. See Proceedings on the election of paymaster for Béxar, BA June 3, 1780.

47. Proceedings in the investigation of Ugalde's report on Indian expenditures, BA January 22, 1793. There is a difference in the dates of the viceroy's original directive from the previous year. On January 26, when Amangual received notice of Revillagigedo's December 19 inquiry (which initially prompted the proceedings) and subsequently obtained the documents for his own inspection, Muñoz wrote the date as *January* 19 of 1792.

48. Proceedings in the investigation of Ugalde's report on Indian expenditures, BA January 22, 1793.

49. Ibid. (Bernardo Fernández response, San Antonio de Béxar, January 16, 1795).

50. Proceedings in the investigation of Ugalde's report on Indian expenditures, BA January 22, 1793 [Bernardo Fernández response, San Antonio de Béxar, January 16, 1795]; my translation.

51. Ibid. According to Marchena Fernández, in some socio-geographic spaces across *Hispano-América* and on the peninsula, the designation of *distinguido* pointed to an individual that had requested their heraldry and the title of "hidalgo," which signaled their family's known quality but were still involved with arbitration to achieve a title of nobility, an often-protracted process. See further Marchena Fernández (1983), p. 126. In the contraband case that implicated Cortés, his brother-in-law José de Jesús Alderete bore the same honorific.

52. *All the soldiers are prohibited from bearing false witness in any circumstance. The officers will keep a watchful eye so that such a crime does not occur. If false witness*

Notes to Pages 178–181   **363**

is given in a civil case and is serious, the penalty incurred is ten years of service in the galleys. If it occurs in a criminal case, the penalty is the same as that which would have been imposed on the accused if he were legitimately proven guilty of the crime according to the law. Reglamento, 1729, artículo 121.

53. Fernández to Muñoz, with details of Indian visitors, BA February 2, 1793.

54. Bernardo Fernández' detail of Indian visitors, BA February 12, 1793.

55. Fernández to Muñoz, [...] dispatch of supplies and [...] events at Béxar, BA February 22, 1793.

56. Ibid. The original document lists the drummer's unit as "*3.a compañía volante*" but is translated as "Light." However, there are differences between presidial "light" and "flying/*volante*" companies, as I explain in chapter 1. One young drummer's experience over a two-day inspection of his unit in 1779 comes to light in Mark Santiago, "The Spanish Drummer Boy: A Glimpse of Soldier Life on the Apache Frontier," *Journal of Arizona History* 47, no. 4 (Winter 2006): 367–86. Described by de la Teja as both cadet and desk worker, Ramón de Murillo noted deficiencies across the military installations and so authored a well-intended proposal of ideas and suggestions to improve the administrative functions of the northern frontier. One of Murillo's firm beliefs was spelled out in point number 19 subtitled, "On the wastefulness of the drummer's position in these cavalry companies." His solution was to replace the "useless" drummers with buglers. See de la Teja/Wheat (2004), pp. 503, 523.

57. Fernández to Muñoz, [...] BA February 22, 1793. Less than two months later, Fernández's name would appear again in connection with an administrative blunder related to paperwork. Muñoz's census reports for the companies of San Antonio and Bahía del Espíritu Santo were not in compliance with Article 5 of the viceroy's circular of February 16, 1791. From San Luis Potosí, it fell to Bruno Díaz de Salcedo to inform Muñoz of the errors and to remind the governor that the February circular was sent to Texas in March 1792. Díaz de Salcedo to Muñoz [...] returning census of Texas to be corrected, BA April 10, 1793. Responding to the Díaz letter, Muñoz indicated that the first censuses were created by the *alcaldes ordinarios* of San Antonio de Béxar. Having recognized the errors but unable to make corrections since he was recovering from injuries suffered during a trip to the Texas coast, Muñoz assigned the task to Lieutenant Fernández. He apparently worked under the governor's supervision but without having crucial updated information from Nacogdoches. [Communication] between Díaz de Salcedo and Muñoz, [...] rosters of the companies of Béxar and La Bahía [...] according to Viceroy's instructions, BA April 10, 1793. Bruno Díaz de Salcedo was a former accountant at the Durango treasury, and once arrived in San Luis Potosí he became a controversial intendant in October 1787. See Brading (1994): 368–72.

58. Título tercero, *vestuario,* of the 1772 Reglamento called for a "red collar [collarín encarnado]," and is shown in the second frontispiece of Brinckerhoff and Faulk (1965), pp. vii, 19–21. For descriptions and images of the red collar as a ubiquitous, but not singular, coat accessory, see Chartrand (2011), passim.

59. [...] Cortés and Muñoz [...] military reports of the company of La Bahía, BA April 19 [– 26], 1793.

60. Cortés to Sierra Gorda, concerning Antonio Treviño, newly appointed lieutenant at Lampazos, BA August 10, 1792.

61. Fernández to Muñoz, reporting incidents [...] twenty-six Comanches [pursuing Lipan], BA February 16, 1793.

364   Notes to Pages 181–183

62. Fernández and Amangual to Governor of Texas, [four cannons are usable], BA July 14, 1793.

63. Revilla Gigedo to Muñoz, [...] cannon left at Bucarely [...], BA April 10, 1793. The following month, Nava contacted Muñoz regarding these same cannons but with a special interest in their vents (*"fogones"*) and calibers, or diameters, and their serviceability. Nava to Governor of Texas, [...] cannon brought to Béxar from Río de la Trinidad, BA May 14, 1793. A November 1792 royal directive forwarded by the Conde del Campo de Alange to Nava ordered the Commandancy General of the *Provincias Internas* to become one entity. Now independent of the viceroyalty, it was reestablished on the premise by which it was formed in a royal *cédula* of August 22, 1776. Added to Nava's command were the provinces of Coahuila and Texas, newly segregated to create what was now the extinguished Commandancy of the East. Nava became the superintendent general subdelegate of the royal treasury throughout its jurisdiction. Nava to [Muñoz], [...] independence of the Comandancia General and his appointment as Superintendent, BA March 5, 1793. See also Revilla Gigedo to Muñoz, [Comandancia General], BA February 12, 1793. For the decree, *Real cédula al Virrey Revillagigedo sobre la constitución de la Comandancia General, 24 de noviembre 1792*, see Velázquez (1982), pp. 197–99.

64. Castro to Muñoz, [...] send Manuel de Urrutia to Mexico, BA February 8, 1793.

65. Nava to Governor of Texas, concerning misbehavior of Alférez Manuel Urrutia, BA June 5, 1793.

66. Ibid.

67. Revilla Gigedo to Muñoz, concerning misbehavior of Alférez Manuel Urrutia, BA June 5, 1793.

68. Nava to Governor of Texas [report on officers and cadets] in Béxar and La Bahía, BA June 5, 1793.

69. Certified copy of royal orders to Alange [...] civil cases of military personnel under the jurisdiction of military courts, BA February 9, 1793. (Don) Manuel de Negrete y de la Torre, Conde del Campo d Alange, Marqués de Torremanzanal, was a member of the Great Cross of the Royal and Distinguished Order of Carlos III, Caballero de la [Orden] de Santiago, and Lieutenant General of His Majesty's royal armies, among his many titles. See the template documents with Alange's credentials in *Provincias Internas, Revistas de inspección*, AGS, SGU, Leg 7048 5-3 (recto), image 63/292. But, by 1793, Revillagigedo "provisionally conceded the fuero and preeminencias" of the provincial soldiers. McAlister (1957), p. 67. For extension of the fuero to some *pardo* and *moreno* militiamen who had survived downsizing of the free-colored units in major urban areas of New Spain, see Vinson (2001), pp. 173–98.

70. Certified copy of royal orders to Alange [military courts], BA February 9, 1793.

71. Ibid. Jacques Barbier describes the reign of Carlos IV (1788–1808) as a monarchy that "ruled over defeat and surrender" and the era of Carlos IV as "comprehensible only in terms of peninsular–colonial interaction." Further, because the "weight of colonialism" nurtured powerful interest groups, impacted developmental plans and "alone kept Spain a great power," Barbier argues that "it is difficult to see how true understanding can be sought outside an imperial perspective." Barbier and Kuethe (1984), p. 9. The *Real ordenanza ... de intendentes* of 1786 and its Department of Finance included articles 86–89 devoted to military jurisdiction. Fisher (1929), pp. 157–60.

72. Certified copy of royal orders to Alange [military courts], BA February 9, 1793.

Notes to Pages 183–188

365

73. Certified copy of Alange's letter [...] extension of legal rights of military personnel, BA February 9, 1793.

74. Antonio Cordero, Extracto de la revista de inspección [...], August 24, 1793, "Provincias Internas, Revistas de inspección [hereafter Revistas de inspección]," AGS, SGU, LEG, 7048, 5–7 (recto, verso), 8 (recto). Sgt. José Antonio Griego from the *Tercer Compañía Volante* received special recognition for twenty years of service; see Joseph Manuel de Ochoa, "Relacion de los Yndivid(uo)s de la expresada comp(ani) a [...] que tienen cumplidos plazas p(ar)a los premios señalados," August 8, 1793; Revistas de inspección, AGS, SGU, LEG, 7048, 5–13 (recto); and July 22, 1793. From the *Quarta* [sic] *Compañía Volante*, Maynez recommended José Ninfares, Ygnacio Rivas, Francisco Ramírez, and Pedro Rodríguez as deserving of the designation of *Ymbálido* based upon wounds received in the functions of war or from being just plain worn out [*cansado*]. *Revistas de inspección*, AGS, SGU, LEG, 7048, 5–3 (recto) 35/292.

75. Certified copy of Alange's letter [...], BA February 9, 1793.

76. As Julianna Barr explains, in the first year of permanent settlement for the Lipan, Gov. Martínez Pacheco sent Lt. José Antonio Curbelo and Alférez Urrutia to begin a "cyclical pattern of living among the Lipan settlements for at least half of each month." Apparently, the Lipan leaders and their families enthusiastically greeted Urrutia every two weeks, "expressing their joy in his company and their regret each time he had to leave." Barr (2007), pp. 274–75.

77. Bernardo Fernández vs. Manuel Urrutia charged with insubordination, BA January 25, 1792. This was not the alférez's first arrest. See Martínez Pacheco to Espadas, [...] arrest of Urrutia for insubordination and intoxication [...], BA April 26, 1790. See chapter 1 of this study for Urrutia's earlier drunken interactions with Francisco Amangual. Pedro de Nava eventually retired Urrutia. See Nava to [Munoz], announcing retirement of [Urrutia], BA June 26, 1793; Manuel de Urrutia to Muñoz [notified of his retirement], BA August 11, 1793.

78. Revilla Gigedo's orders to publish royal decree [...] granting amnesty for contraband trade, BA July 22, 1791.

79. Ibid. But by February 1794, a royal *cédula* specifically addressed those accused of homicide with a key caveat: the privilege of immunity did *not* extend to them. After making the rounds in Chihuahua, the document then targeted presidio soldiers in Texas when Nava sent a certified copy to the governor for publication and compliance throughout that province. Nava to Governor of Texas, [transmitting ... royal *cédula*] of February 28, concerning punishments for homicide, BA July 23, 1794.

80. Marchena Fernández stresses that "la palabra presidiario en realidad procede de cumplir pena en algún presidio militar, es decir, una plaza fuerte, Americana o del Norte de África" (1992), p. 254. Aside from its predominance as a descriptor of a garrison for soldiers, the RAE's varied definitions of *presidio* are closely aligned with notions of enclosure, deprivation of liberty, and custody. See https://dle.rae.es/presidio.

81. Revilla Gigedo's orders to publish royal decree [...] granting amnesty for contraband trade, BA July 22, 1791.

82. Ibid.

83. Ibid.

84. Ibid.

366   Notes to Pages 188-192

85. Title Eight of the *Reglamento 1772* and several articles within the 1786 *Instrucción* clarified — albeit using generalized language subject to nuanced interpretation — the attributes deemed necessary for the selection of officers. Commanders sought evidence of highly valued characteristics from men positioned for presidio captainship upon whose effectiveness manifested in large part the attainment of specific objectives for the garrison. Incorruptible dedication to task underscored at least two of the men's approach to the work at hand even as their professional reputations came under attack. In Cortés' case, it seems the allure of commodities proved too tempting to resist and his co-conspirators simply followed his lead. For the special status and privileges enjoyed by the officer class, see both Archer (1977), pp. 191-222, and Marchena Fernández (1983), especially pp. 69-80, 111-40, 141-63; and, for health designations of officers as found within military service records, see Marchena Fernández (1983), pp. 196-207.

86. Military service record of Francisco de Amangual, BA December 31, 1791.

87. Amangual to Muñoz, reporting that he is going to La Bahía to defend Juan José de la Garza, BA June 3, 1794. Two of the best studies of performative hierarchy within the military ranks are Marchena Fernández (1983), pp. 69-83, and *capítulo* ix (passim); and Archer (1977), chapters 8, 9, 10.

88. Cabello insisted that the voters convened for the election were to "exercise the utmost care" and thus "free themselves from painful circumstances that have occurred in other presidios," including the "scandalous losses" that brought out "well known breakdown[s], and loss for the individuals of the company." See Proceedings on the election of the paymaster for Béxar, BA June 3, 1780. Translation: author and John A. Orange Jr.

89. […] Cortés to Muñoz, […] Amangual's defense of [… Garza], charged with the murder of Vicente Serna, BA May 30, 1794. On June 1, Muñoz conveyed his approval to Amangual, urging him to conduct himself quickly to La Bahía.

90. Nava to [Munoz], transmitting copy of royal cedula of February 28, concerning punishments for homicide, BA July 23, 1794.

91. […] Cortés to Muñoz, concerning murderer Juan José de la Garza, BA November 6, 1794. For insight into work expected from those prosecuted as described by cédula, see Royal Decree concerning work of condemned criminals, BA April 3, 1794.

92. Nava to Governor of Texas, […] Cortés' cash payment of a public balance, BA January 2, 1794; Nava to Governor of Texas, acknowledging receipt of five accounting books of Juan Cortés, BA April 23, 1794.

93. Córdoba to Muñoz, concerning orders to forbid contraband, BA June 18, 1794. In his response, Muñoz provided the wrong date of Córdoba's letter indicating that it was dated June *13*, rather than the 18th.

94. Córdoba to Muñoz, concerning orders to forbid contraband, BA June 18, 1794. [– September 16, 1794].

95. Nava to Muñoz, giving instructions for training troops, BA July 17, 1794. In fact, four years earlier Gutiérrez reported on two flying squadrons he had inspected and the numbers he deemed necessary to achieve a "perfect state" of service. Gutiérrez noted the orderly instruction, discipline, and governance of the only flying squadron covering Nuevo León, established at Punta de Lampazos, and the Tercer [sic] Compañía Volante of Nuevo Santander. See Revilla Gigedo to Alange, AGS, SGU, leg.7299, 38 — Nueva España, extractos, November 26, 1790.

Notes to Pages 192–198   367

96. Fernández to Muñoz, acknowledging receipt of instructions for cavalry drill, BA September 9, 1794.

97. Cortés to Muñoz, requesting the return of his troops from military operations, BA November 7, 1794.

98. Nava to Governor of Texas, giving instructions for ascertaining ability of enlisted soldiers, BA February 4, 1795. For a summary of Muñoz's career and his enduring health difficulties, see Faulk (1964), pp. 24–27.

99. Nava to Muñoz, ordering careful examination of frontier [...], BA March 23, 1795.

100. Ibid. Gálvez, 1786, *artículo doscientos y dos*. See Additional instructions in tactical operations of patrols, BA June 19, 1793. This document is a four-page fragment of an apparently more complete text issued on this same date, but one I have failed to locate.

101. Nava to Muñoz [...], BA March 23, 1795.

102. Ibid.

103. Gálvez, 1786, *artículo veintitrés*.

104. Nava to Muñoz, ordering careful examination of frontier [...], BA March 23, 1795.

105. Ibid.

106. Gálvez, 1786, *artículo ciento treinta y ocho*. Rivera spent the night at an "uninhabited place called Anelo" during his expedition. Four decades later, Rubí described Anelo as a "farm," with horses and mules and spring water that was "more than a little warm." Jackson and Foster (1995), pp. 24, 102. On June 13, 1767, Lafora wrote that the expedition party slept at the "Anelo hacienda" at the border between Nueva Vizcaya and Coahuila. See Lafora and Kinnaird (1958), p. 161. For its foundation, see Alessio Robles (1938), pp. 235–36.

107. Gálvez, 1786, *artículo ciento cuarenta y dos*.

108. Ibid., *artículo ciento cuarenta y tres; artículo ciento cuarenta y cuatro*.

109. Ibid., *artículo ciento cuarenta y tres*.

110. Ibid., *artículo ciento cuarenta y cuatro*.

111. Ibid., *artículo ciento cuarenta y nueve*.

112. Ibid., *artículo ciento cuarenta y ocho*.

113. Ibid., artículo ciento cuarenta y cuatro.

114. The Provincias Internas del Oriente were comprised of Coahuila, Texas, Nuevo León, and Nuevo Santander. The districts of Parras and Saltillo came under Ugalde's jurisdiction. Worcester (1967), p. 23.

115. Gálvez, 1786, *artículo ciento cinquenta*. As Armando Alonzo reports, by 1798 Nuevo León relied on only one flying squadron with one hundred men, while Nuevo Santander had three such units, each consisting of seventy-five troops including officers. See Alonzo (1998), pp. 50–51.

116. Gálvez, 1786, *artículo ciento diecisiete*.

117. Ibid., *artículo ciento cinquenta y dos; artículo ciento cincuenta y tres*.

118. According to Secoy, leather employed as armor was imitated by Native warriors at the time of the Pueblo Revolt. Frank Raymond Secoy, *Changing Military Patterns of the Great Plains Indians* (Lincoln: University of Nebraska Press, 1953), pp. 18–20.

119. Ibid., *artículo ciento cinquenta y cuatro*. The leather-jacketed soldier, a ubiquitous figure in Spanish colonial historiography that has come to symbolize frontier

368 Notes to Pages 198–200

defense, is distinguished by the costume he wore as part of his body armor. Essentially, it was a vest composed of quilted buckskin that could also be a heavy, knee-length sleeveless coat or doublet. The *soldado de cuera* was the heavily armed presidial who received a salary of 290 pesos and described by Moorhead as a "veritable human fortress on horseback" and "a one-man arsenal." See Moorhead (1975), 88–89; 186–89; "The Soldado de Cuera: Stalwart of the Spanish Borderlands," *Journal of the West* 8, no. 1 (Jan. 1969): 38–55; for Lt. Pedro Fages' discrimination against the *cueras* while commanding the Free Company of Catalonian Volunteers, see Sánchez (1990), pp. 62–8; for images of the *cuera* and related military personnel costuming, see René Chartrand, *The Spanish Army in North America 1700–1793* (Oxford: Osprey, 2011), pp. 23–24, 26. For a contemporaneous report on the leather jacket's lifesaving impenetrability, see Domingo Cabello's monthly report of the cavalry division of Béxar, BA March 31, 1783 [March 13, 1783]. Croix criticized the *cuera* itself, likening it to a shroud rather than a protective garment. Thomas (1941), pp. 56–57.

120. Gálvez, 1786, *artículo ciento y cinco*. Documentary sources reveal enlistment efforts in the late seventeenth century acknowledging not only the participation of the *Ópata* at Babispe and Bacuachi as auxiliary forces (including a flying company) but also their known dexterity with horses and weapons. See for example AGS, SGU, LEG, 7022–16, images 9–11; Polzer and Sheridan (1997), p. 377. Missionaries and military commanders tried hard to protect Opata auxiliaries from abuse but, at times, it was elected Indian officials who toed the line for Spanish demands for boots on the ground. See Radding (1997), pp. 152–53. According to Moorhead, O'Conor failed to pay the Opata and the Seri for their help in a 1775 campaign against the Apache, and Sonora's Governor Anza reported mistreatment of the Opata by missionaries and military officers in 1777. Moorhead (1968), p. 55.

121. In his 1772 Regulations, the king himself acknowledged the well-known valor of the Ópata as well as their "constant fidelity." See Brinckerhoff and Faulk (1965), p. 5. Lt. José Cortés of the Royal Corp of Engineers hailed the Opata as "brave soldiers and loyal subjects" and advocated for their wages to be increased and for their communities to be conserved. Radding (1997), p. 262; Cortés (1989), pp. 26–27. Conversely, frontier functionary Ramón de Murillo blamed the "[im]possible to improve" Opatas "for all the advantages gained by our enemies" in Sonora. De la Teja and Wheat (2004), p. 532.

122. Nava to Governor of Texas, […] orders for sending muskets to Texas to give to friendly Indians, BA May 10, 1795.

123. Castañeda points out that the November 3, 1762, Treaty of Fontainebleau gave all of Louisiana to Spain, with Carlos III accepting the gift ten days later. However, it was not until April 21, 1764, that the king of France notified D'Abadie to turn the province over to Spanish officials. Things moved slowly, as usual, and only after O'Reilly came in 1769 did the Spanish establish dominion over Louisiana. Morfi (1935), p. 443, n.17. Chipman adds that French settlers in New Orleans opposed the transfer and delayed Spanish control of Louisiana until 1769. For a concise, albeit brief, discussion of the Seven Years' War's impact on Texas, see Chipman and Joseph (1992), pp. 174–77. For a brief summary of the Red River's appeal to the French, see Flores (1984), pp. 9–13.

124. Mattie Austin Hatcher, "The Louisiana Background of the Colonization of Texas, 1763–1803," *Southwestern Historical Quarterly* 24, no. 3 (Jan. 1921): 170–71.

125. See Translation of census and biographical data of foreigners, compiled by

Notes to Pages 200–202 369

Muñoz, BA May 21, 1792. However, in an earlier letter he failed to mention his deserter status. See Pedro José Lambremón to the Governor of Texas, stating reasons for residing in Texas, BA May 12, 1792.

126. Juan de Mouy to the Governor of Texas, stating reasons […], BA May 12, 1792. Colonial documents provide many examples of their authors, in this case presidio administrators, taking the usual liberties when spelling proper names. The varieties of (mis)spellings are numerous and may hint at gradations of literacy, knowledge of grammar, and familiarity with foreign names and places among the frontier soldiery. Juan de Mouy to the Governor of Texas, […] residing in Texas, BA May 12, 1792.

127. Apparently, de Mouy overstayed his welcome while in Texas. By September he had not returned to Natchitoches, and his commander Louis DeBlanc contacted Escandón to halt his journey and order his return. DeBlanc had only granted the second lieutenant leave so that he could bring his wife back with him, but that period had expired. Further, DeBlanc's commander wanted the militias in his district ready to march at a moment's notice for the benefit of the royal service. De Blanc to Sierra Gorda, requesting [return to Natchitoches of de Mouy], BA September 4, 1792.

128. Dupont was not an individual to be taken lightly by military personnel in Texas. In 1790, the viceroy issued a passport to Dupont, ordered Muñoz to prepare for his arrival, listen to his plans, attend to him, and then employ the Frenchman "as may best befit the royal service." Dupont's knowledge of maintaining amity with the Nations of the North and the Comanche guaranteed his importance to Revilla Gigedo and was therefore to be cultivated by Muñoz. See Revilla Gigedo to [Muñoz], instructing him to receive Dupont and listen to his suggestions, BA May 10, 1790; Revilla Gigedo to [Muñoz], Dupont would present order and instructions concerning Indian relations, BA May 10, 1790.

129. Pierre Chalis to the Governor of Texas, […] residing in Texas, BA May 14, 1792; the document spells "Chali" as "Sarly," further indicating that he is "Pedro" rather than "Pierre" — the name he signed at the bottom of the page—and the "legitimate son of Pedro de Sarly."

130. Angel [sic] Navarro to the Governor of Texas, […] residing in Texas, BA May 14, 1792. According to Hatcher, Italians were welcomed to settle in Louisiana since Carlos III ordered Gálvez to allow their admission to the borderlands along with Germans and the French. Hatcher (1921), p. 171. To enhance its pluralistic society, Gálvez may have included Corsicans, Ligurians, and the Genoese in that demographic.

131. Revilla Gigedo to Muñoz, requesting report of foreigners in Texas, BA April 17, 1792.

132. In this census, the name is spelled "Charli," whereas in the previous document of May 14, 1792, it is spelled two different ways.

133. Elguézabal's declaration of Leme's promotion, BA August 25, 1792.

134. Census and biographical data of foreigners compiled by Muñoz, BA May 21, 1792.

135. Possibly a presidial company stationed at the springs of San Marcos following the closure of Presidio San Xavier de Gigedo. Moorhead (1975), p.53.

136. Ibid. Like others who had provided Governor Muñoz with their "reasons for residing in Texas," Miñón had done so on May 14, and at that time he provided a bit more information than that provided by Muñoz in his biographical data. Having served as far as San Sabá, he lost an arm to cannon fire and injured both legs while

370   Notes to Pages 202–203

fighting the enemy and had since "remained crippled." His *ymbálido* status paid him eight pesos each month; Lambremon signed his testament since Miñón could not. Pedro Miñón to Muñoz, stating reasons for residing in Texas, BA May 14, 1792.

137. See chapter 4 for a discussion of Neve's direction to Governor Cabello to find a vacant post for the two sons of de Mézières.

138. Cabello to Croix, [proceedings in case of René] charged with contraband of tobacco, BA June 17, 1780; Rengel to Cabello, [payment of life pension to René], BA June 23, 1785.

139. Espadas to Muñoz, reporting on foreigners living at La Bahía, BA May 18, 1792. Muñoz's information is taken from documents sent to him by the captain of the Bahía presidio, Manuel de Espadas. There are two slight differences in the Muñoz redaction of the Espadas report: the captain included the king's name in his report, the deceased "Carlos III," and provided a statement about the "equally commendable conduct" of all three Frenchmen. However, Muñoz's seemingly odd insertion of Curbelo and the bison appears to be an afterthought, but one worth mentioning since its inclusion suggests the shoemaker René's reliability and value to the garrison despite his past indiscretions.

140. Sic passim. Census and biographical data of foreigners compiled by Muñoz, BA May 21, 1792. For much more specific information regarding foreigners in Nacogdoches, and Antonio Gil Ybarvo's response to the Texas Governor, see Muñoz to Ibarvo, [information] on foreigners residing in Nacogdoches [with report], BA May 12, 1792. See also Galán (2020), pp. 228–29. Juan Bosque's name emerged in the deposition provided by Private Galán during the Cortés smuggling proceedings.

141. Luis deBlanc to Muñoz, […] introduction of British–American subjects in […] Louisiana and Texas, BA April 26, 1793. Warnings about Anglo-American immigrants advancing with post–independence bravado is summarized in Chipman and Joseph (1992), pp. 202–5.

142. Census and biographical data of foreigners compiled by Muñoz, BA May 21, 1792. Armando Alonzo contends that Spanish officials hardly ever granted land to Anglos and Europeans in Nuevo Santander in light of the long history of ranchero occupation of the Lower Valley of Texas. The region achieved phenomenal growth during the late colonial period with the census of 1782 listing 21,991 persons; of 1788, 26,618; and the population of Nuevo Santander stood at about 31,000 Spanish and mestizo settlers and approximately 3,500 "Christian and Gentile Indians." See Alonzo (1998), pp. 40, 149.

143. Revilla Gigedo to Sierra Gorda, concerning census […] whereabouts of […] Dupont, BA May 23, 1792. *Cazador* is commonly used to mean hunter but here refers to shooters with expert aim. It can also mean soldiers of the light infantry. By September 23, the viceroy had heard nothing from Escandón (Sierra Gorda) regarding the enterprising Dupont. The ever conciliatory, but stringent, Revillagigedo reasoned that the former governor likely passed his inquiry on to the reinstated governor and so ordered Muñoz to locate Dupont. The viceroy was just as interested in the whereabouts of a Mr. Tolnei[y] whose physical characteristics, beverage preferences, and manner of speaking he described in detail to Muñoz. Though Revillagigedo asked for notification of these two Frenchmen as soon as the governor was able, it appears the information had for him become urgent. Revilla Gigedo to Muñoz, inquiring for the second time […] Dupont, BA September 22, 1792. It would be ten years before

Notes to Pages 203–208   **371**

Dupont was given permission to carry out his mining investigations. Nava [granting permission to Dupont], BA February 2, 1802.

144. Revilla Gigedo to Castro, […] Lipan situation around Laredo, BA January 15, 1793. On this same date, the viceroy contacted Muñoz directly, enclosing a copy of his letter to Castro and emphasizing the importance of the information concerning the Lipan in Laredo. Revilla Gigedo to Muñoz, [Lipans in Laredo], BA January 15, 1793. See also Gálvez, 1786, *artículo 186*; and Britten (2009), p. 161.

Chapter 6

1. […] report on doubtful accounts of the company of Béxar […], BA May 14 [– December 19], 1792.

2. Amangual to Muñoz, […] objections to accounting reports on expenditures for Indian[s], BA April 16, 1795. The auditor had sent the objections to him on January 26. Modifications to the translation by John Wheat are mine.

3. Congregate living arrangements may have been in so sad a state of disrepair as to be not only inconvenient but unsafe as well. In 1740, the Béxar presidio was described as consisting of forty "wretched huts." By 1767 its captain Luis Antonio Menchaca described the facility as vulnerable to attack and incapable of providing any advantage to its occupants. In 1790, Captain Muñoz made one final effort to "rebuild the presidio with plans and estimates made for the reconstruction of the enclosing wall." See Ivey (2004), pp. 110–11.

4. Amangual to Muñoz, […] objections to accounting reports on expenditures for Indian[s], BA April 16, 1795.

5. Ibid.

6. […] Muñoz' letter to Nava […] objections to financial report of Indian presents accounts have been satisfied, BA April 15, 1795.

7. Nava to Governor of Texas, […] mesteñas fund, and transmittal to Amangual, BA June 18, 1795 [–August 1, 1795].

8. Amangual to Muñoz, discussing collection of money for mesteñas fund, BA August 11, 1795. Some of this fiscal perplexity came to a conclusion by the end of the year. See […] Fernández and Muñoz, […] duties paid to mesteñas fund during 1795, BA December 24, 1795.

9. Amangual's detail of goods given to Indian visitors since May 1, 1795, BA August 16, 1795.

10. Nava to Governor of Texas, giving instructions as to settlement of Martínez Pacheco's accounts, BA March 3, 1796. Comanche and even Lipan people had indeed assisted Comandancia troops in the past and even now, but Nava may have meant to write *amigos* instead of "enemigos." It is possible he confused the two. See Nava to Governor of Texas, […] letting the Indians make war among themselves […], BA May 4, 1796. Based on one particularly harrowing, nonbattle experience, he may have had good reason to be muddled. See Britten (2009), p. 161.

11. Ternary reports on expenditures incurred for […] friendly Indian visitors during 1796, BA April 30, 1796.

12. […] Sierra Gorda to Muñoz, […] Viceroy's orders to increase alertness to avoid foreign infiltration, BA July 24, 1795. The urgency of the message was such that another warning of vigilance followed only two months later with communication

372   Notes to Pages 208–209

between the commander general and the lieutenant governor in Nacogdoches. See Fernández to Muñoz, discussing [Nava's] orders to arrest and question all suspicious foreigners, BA September 5, 1795.

13. Clarence J. Munford and Michael Zeuske, "Black Slavery, Class Struggle, Fear and Revolution in St. Domingue and Cuba, 1785–1795," *Journal of Negro History* 73, no. 1/4 (Winter–Autumn, 1988): 28.

14. [...] Sierra Gorda to Muñoz, [...] foreign infiltration, BA July 24, 1795.

15. Ibid.

16. Documentation of military units from Nuevo Santander show troop strength among veteran soldiers and *volantes*, and while they may not have been one and the same, the similarities were close enough to cause confusion. An 1801 monthly service report provided by Viceroy Marquina lists three Santander flying squadrons, with one established at San Juan Bautista with men from the Punta de Lampazos of Nuevo León but having notable vacancies. Individual identities, likely never before published until now, momentarily emerge from the ranks. For example, after ten years in the military, Joaquín Vidal de Lorca had attained the rank of lieutenant on November 25, 1796, while his Second Alférez José María de Barberena had served for seven years. Though Barberena was of "noble" status and had distinguished himself as an Indian fighter, Lorca described his conduct as "bad (*mala*)," his capacity as average (*mediana*), and, therefore, promised nothing more than what could be expected from one of his rank. José Antonio Tixerina, José Segundo Moreno, and José Maria Escandón defended New Spain's frontier with years of accumulated service among all three. At forty-three years of age, Tixerina had served over two decades as a soldier leading up to the rank of sergeant in the Compañía Veterana de San Agustín de Ahumada de Monterey, and in the First Flying Company of Nuevo Santander. Though Tixerina's effort (*aplicación*) is described as "little" and his capacity "limited," he is credited with fulfilling his obligations with the utmost care. See "Compañías Volantes de Nueva España" in AGS, SGU, LEG, 7277, images 10–1 recto, 10–5 recto; 10–6 recto.

17. [...] Sierra Gorda to Muñoz, [...] foreign infiltration, BA July 24, 1795. Herrera, a future captain of the *compañía volante* of Punta de Lampazos, is remembered as the proud father (and commander) of the fourteen-year-old enlistee José, who would join his father's squadron in 1797.

18. Nava to Governor of Texas, suggesting greater alertness in borders to stop foreign infiltration, BA July 30, 1795.

19. Ibid.

20. Naylor and Polzer (1988), p.159. "Abandoned" is not too strong a condemnation; Francois Lagarde uses it as well: *The French in Texas* (Austin: University of Texas Press, 2003), pp. 7–8. For more on the French plans aimed at "invading" Texas from 1693–1719, see José Ignacio Rubio Mañé, *El Virreinato III, Expansión y defensa, segunda parte* (México, D.F.: Instituto de Investigaciones Históricas, UNAM, 1983), pp. 60–104. Pursuant to the *Texas Almanac*, the Lavaca rises in extreme southeastern Fayette County and flows 117 miles into the Gulf of Mexico through Lavaca Bay. It is the principal stream running to the Gulf between the Guadalupe and Colorado rivers. The Spanish called it the Lavaca [*la vaca* = the cow] because of the numerous bison found near this water source. See http://texasalmanac.com/topics/environment/rivers.

21. See Chapter Three, p. 214. *Reglamento de 1729*, Tercer estado, artículo cuarenta y dos. For Aguayo's role as a "restorer of Spanish dominion in Texas," see Charles W. Hackett, "The Marquis of San Miguel de Aguayo and His Recovery of Texas from

the French, 1719–1723," *Southwestern Historical Quarterly* 49, no. 2 (Oct. 1945): 193–214. See Morfi's account (1935), pp. 192–228. For an account of the Aguayo expedition based on two English translations of Padre de la Peña's diary, see Foster (1995), pp. 145–61.

22. For an early perspective on the treaty's impact on the borderlands, see Arthur Preston Whitaker, "New Light on the Treaty of San Lorenzo: An Essay in Historical Criticism," *Mississippi Valley Historical Review* 15, no. 4 (March 1929): 435–54; and his "Godoy's Knowledge of the Terms of Jay's Treaty," *American Historical Review* 35, no. 4 (July 1930): 804–10. For more recent scholarship, see Charles A. Weeks, *Paths to a Middle Ground: The Diplomacy of Natchez, Boukfouka, Nogales, and San Fernando de las Barrancas, 1791–1795* (Tuscaloosa: University of Alabama Press, 2005).

23. Nava to Governor of Texas, [...] arrest of French in México, BA January 6, 1795. Only four weeks later it had become clear to Nava that Muñoz had not understood, and likely not even read, his instructions from the previous month. The exasperated commander general found himself having to repeat to an apparently incapacitated Muñoz not only the fundamental provisions of his January order but also its finer points. Nava rebuked Muñoz for proposing "annoying doubts [*dudas importunas*]" about his order. See Nava to Governor of Texas, [...] treatment of French found in Texas, BA February 4, 1795. Elizabeth John (1975, p. 764) mentions the "breakdown of responsibility" on the part of the Béxar commander and the "utter frustration" experienced by Nava in his communication with Muñoz.

24. Nava to Governor of Texas, [...] conditions in Louisiana due to threatened French war [...], BA January 15, 1795.

25. Nava to Governor of Texas, giving instructions [...] hostile plans of French and Americans, BA January 29, 1795.

26. Proceedings of investigation of French citizens [...], BA February 16, 1795; Nava to Governor of Texas, [treatment of French] under arrest, BA March 26, 1795; Nava to Governor of Texas [French and Louisiana-born residents], BA April 9, 1795; Nava to Governor of Texas [papers of Courbiere returned], BA April 14, 1795.

27. Nava to Governor of Texas, ordering release of [...] Courbiére and all French military, BA May 10, 1795.

28. Nava to Governor of Texas, [...] Courbiére's petition for payment of services, BA April 5, 1796.

29. Nava to Governor of Texas, ordering [...] Courbiére back into active service, BA August 5, 1796.

30. Cortés to Muñoz, [...] he has not arrested Louisiana residents in La Bahía [...] good conduct, BA May 9, 1795. Their good conduct may have been the result of intimidation in the form of eight working cannons being a visible deterrent to the population at Bahía. In a report to Muñoz in 1795, Cortés described the good condition of his presidio's cannon but admitted, "not a single soldier in the garrison" knew how to use them. See O'Connor (1966), pp. 52–54.

31. Nava to Governor of Texas, ordering to release all French prisoners, BA November 3, 1795.

32. Nava to Muñoz, announcing peace treaty between France and Spain [...], BA December 16, 1795. Probably the Peace of Basilea, signed June 22, 1795.

33. Amangual's reports on goods brought from Saltillo for Indian gifts, and evidence of payment, BA December 20, 1795; Amangual's statement of expenditures for Indian gifts, BA December 31, 1795; [...] Cortés and Muñoz, concerning La Bahía paymaster's answers to charges from paymaster of Béxar [Amangual], BA December 19, 1795.

374 Notes to Pages 212–213

34. Ternary reports [...] support of friendly Indian visitors [...] 1796, BA April 30, 1796. In an April 1795 response from Manuel Muñoz to Bernardo Fernández, Amangual is similarly described as "abilitado" when the paymaster sent bullets and a burlap-covered box to soldier Vicente Cabrera by way of Nacogdoches and with delivery to Lieutenant Bernardo Fernández. See Muñoz list of Indian presents [...], BA January 16, 1795.

35. Muñoz's certification concerning inventory of Tobacco Office at Béxar, BA January 4, 1796. Marchena Fernández describes urban commerce in terms of its flow and defines *libranzas* as a series of paper vouchers for *x* amount of money convertible by merchants in their stores and warehouses. With these vouchers, payments for salaries went to garrisons and toward certain arrears. They were exchangeable for coin in the accounting office upon arrival of allocated funds. This generated a strong price increase for products of first necessity since the vouchers, at times, specified in which store they could be exchanged and only in that store, and simultaneously [produced] ferocious inflation and high speculation [of that product/my translation]. Juan Marchena Fernández, "Capital, crédito e intereses comerciales a fines del periodo colonial: los costos del sistema defensivo americano, Cartagena de Indias y el sur del Caribe," in *Tiempos de America, Revista de Historia, Cultura, y Territorio*, No. 9 (Sevilla: Universitat Jaume, 2002), p. 28. For a contemporaneous account of the danger of free trade with foreigners, see Juan López Cancelada, *Ruina de la Nueva España si se declara el comercio libre con los extrangeros* (Cádiz: Manuel Santiago de Quintana, 1811). For the regulations and tariffs related to Spanish free trade, see El Rey Yo, *Reglamento y aranceles reales* (1778).

36. The names of these two men do not appear in the January 1, 1796, roster of the Béxar company, thereby precluding their status as soldiers of the company. See Roster of the company of Béxar, BA January 1, 1796. However, both names appear in a lengthy report of expenditures for multiple indigenous groups from January to April 1796. See Ternary reports on expenditures incurred for the support of friendly Indian visitors during 1796, BA April 30, 1796; and Arreola's statement of clothing [...], BA April 30, 1796.

37. Correspondence between Gutierrez de la Cueva and Muñoz, [election of paymaster], BA March 26, 1796.

38. Fernández to Muñoz, [...] Menchaca as Second Alférez at Béxar, [...] appointment as paymaster, BA February 25, 1796. Fernández had expedited the process and emphasized to Muñoz that Menchaca had already been duly elected to the position. Writing from Nacogdoches, Fernández voted for Menchaca, as did other officers, and he informed Muñoz that Cpl. Manuel Granados was to deliver the votes on behalf of the company. See Correspondence between Fernández and Muñoz, BA May 24, 1796.

39. Ternary reports [...] support of friendly Indian visitors [...] 1796, BA April 30, 1796. Orandain's [sic/gunsmith repair], BA April 30, 1796. The armorer here is named "Francisco" Orendain and is likely the same as a "Jose" Orendain mentioned in other documents. Years before, Amangual and Orendain cosigned a document related to weapon parts. See Price list for weapons in Béxar, signed by Amangual and Orendain, BA June 15, 1789. In all cases, the surname is consistently misspelled in the Béxar Archives holdings.

40. Fernández to Muñoz, [...] peace with France, BA February 25, 1796.

41. Nava to Governor of Texas, [...] letting the Indians make war among themselves [...], BA May 4, 1796. For the impact of budgeting restrictions towards the Apache

Notes to Pages 213–215   375

("de paz") and Spanish misunderstanding of their decentralized political structure, missteps that prompted Nava's three-prong policy change from five years prior, see Babcock (2016), pp. 177–83. By 1794, following the French declaration of war on Spain, Nava restricted food rations and even relocated "Mescaleros de paz" and other Apache bands thirty leagues distant from the presidios. Enacted to ease "the burden on the imperial treasury," these maneuvers proved onerous for the maintenance of peace. Santiago (2018), pp. 91–92.

42. Nava to Governor of Texas, […] letting the Indians make war among themselves […], BA May 4, 1796. Having described himself as a "vecino" of Villa San Fernando, Bueno eventually requested a license to round up cattle on the margins of the Medina River and accompanied by other citizens. See Juan José Bueno […] license to round up unbranded cattle, BA March 9, 1797. For Nava's abilities as a military strategist, see Santiago (2018), passim.

43. Nava to Muñoz, […] victory of soldiers over Indians near San Elisario, BA May 20, 1796. For sources on this venerable garrison, see Eugene Porter, *San Elizario, A History* (Austin: Pemberton Press, 1973); Jack S. Williams, "The Evolution of the Presidio in Northern New Spain," in "Presidios of the North American Spanish Borderlands," ed. J. A. Bense, special issue, *Historical Archaeology* 38, no. 3 (2004): 12, 19; for negotiations of peace at Elizario, see Griffen (1988), pp. 42–43, 46, passim; and for the physical layout and construction of the presidio, see Moorhead (1975), pp. 166–67.

44. Nava to Muñoz, […] victory of soldiers over Indians […], BA May 20, 1796. The "Indians" are not identified by tribe but simply described by Nava as "los enemigos" and "la Yndiada."

45. Ibid.

46. Cortés to Muñoz, […] action of Nicolás Madrid against the enemy Indians [announced per Nava's orders], BA July 1, 1796. Eleven years earlier, the same call to broadcast victory over enemies was urged by a commander general to a regional governor. See Rengel to Cabello, […] victory of troops over Apaches at San Agustín del Tucson, BA March 8, 1785. Returning to Namiquipa on June 23, 1789, Chihuahua's Second Compañía Volante similarly defended themselves with only eight men against an attack by "more than 130 enemies," earning a recommendation from General Ugarte for distinguished action. See AGS, SGU, LEG, 7019, 24, images recto/verso 3, Flores to Valdez, August 27, 1789.

47. Two orders of payment issued against the office of the paymaster were charged by the office of tariffs for the entry and exit of consumer goods collected. Both totaled 1,946 pesos and 7 *reales*. Inventory report of the Tobacco Office of Béxar, BA July 1, 1796.

48. Nava to Governor of Texas, forwarding copy of royal general pardon for publication in Texas, BA July 30, 1796.

49. Nava to Governor of Texas, reporting appointment of […] Fernández as captain of 3rd Flying Squadron of Chihuahua, BA May 20, 1796. Officers convened to find a solution. On August 23, 1796, Bernardo Fernández contacted Muñoz to discuss the impending change of administration with his departure east. Fernández cited a July 25 order concluding an adjustment to the Nacogdoches company accounts, a task undertaken by both Lieutenant Amangual and First Alférez Manuel Menchaca. The latter, elected in March as paymaster of the Béxar presidio, would soon assume his new position and, fittingly, longtime *habilitado* Amangual stood ready to assist his successor. Likely eager to accelerate his own career move, Fernández expressed

376 Notes to Pages 215–218

his compliance with ensuring a smooth transference of command by enumerating completed tasks. Motivated by self-determination, he took the opportunity to extol his success at maintaining harmony within the local constituency, an amalgamation of both transient and settled Native populations. Fernández to Muñoz, discussing future change of administration in Nacogdoches, August 23, 1796.

50. Certified copy of Croix's letter to Ibarvo, praising Gil Ibarvo's good work, BA January 13, 1779; Cabello to Croix [contraband] confiscated by Gil Ibarvo and Amangual, BA March 18, 1780; Croix to Cabello [auction contraband] confiscated by Amangual and Ibarvo, BA June 9, 1780. Morfi summarizes Ibarvo's reconnaissance of the Texas coast in 1777 and his investigation of the "mouths of several of the rivers [including] the Trinity and the Brazos." Ultimately, Morfi condemned as useless Ibarvo's efforts at producing a map of his explorations since it lacked relevant information. See Morfi pt. 2 (1935), pp. 427–28. For Ibarvo's map, see Hackett (1931), p. 388; and Ripperda to Croix [Ibarvo's map of Texas coast between Trinity and Colorado rivers], BA October 31, 1778.

51. Cabello to Neve, [relations] between La Mathe and Ibarvo, BA June 9, 1784; Cabello to Ugarte y Loyola, [Ibarvo's expulsion of] Frenchmen from Neches River, BA September 10, 1786; Certificate of award to Ibarvo for good work, BA October 31, 1786; Ibarvo to Martínez Pacheco, [trader Equis'] trouble with Tancagues, BA November 12, 1787; Martínez Pacheco to Ibarvo, discussing matters concerning Indian traders, BA February 6, 1788; Martínez Pacheco to Ugalde, [testimony in case of Hidalgo vs. Ibarvo], BA May 26, 1788; Gil Ibarvo to Martínez Pacheco, [capture and imprisonment of] the thief Juan Jose Pena, BA July 15, 1789.

52. Proceedings concerning Nava's decision in the Gil Ibarvo case [Nava to Muñoz], BA September 15, 1796.

53. Nava to Governor of Texas, retiring Antonio Gil Ibarvo from military service, BA September 15, 1796.

54. Nava to Governor of Texas, prohibiting Antonio Gil Ibarvo to establish residence in Nacogdoches, BA November 29, 1796.

55. Nava to Governor of Texas, […] order to Fernández, BA September 19, 1796.

56. Muñoz to Fernández, instructing him to give the command of Nacogdoches to Guadiana […] BA September 25, 1796.

57. Fernández to Muñoz, […] given the command of Nacogdoches to Guadiana […], BA October 24, 1796. The next day, Guadiana confirmed his October 16 ascendancy to commander of Nacogdoches. See Guadiana to Muñoz [installed as commander on October 16], BA October 25, 1796.

58. Guadiana to Muñoz, […] Gil Ibarvo will be returned his property, BA November 23, 1796.

59. Nava to Governor of Texas, copy of royal ordinance giving dishonorable discharges to personnel guilty of procuring, BA September 27, 1798.

60. Nava to Governor of Texas, forwarding Courbiére's discharge, BA September 30, 1796.

61. Muñoz to Elguézabal, forwarding monthly reports of the company, September 12, 1796.

62. Nava must have sensed the disheartening decision faced by Muñoz in handing over authority. But the commander general tried to reassure Muñoz of the perspicacity of his decision, telling him, "I do not doubt that the same zeal that has stimulated you not to let go of your knowledge will likewise move Elguézabal to carry out those

Notes to Pages 218–221   377

orders." Nava to Muñoz, approving measures taken by Muñoz to give [command] of Béxar to Elguézabal, BA October 16, 1796.

63. Nava to Governor of Texas, asking if his health forbids the prompt performance of his job, BA November 1, 1796.

64. Faulk (1964), p. 25.

65. Cortés to Muñoz, acknowledging receipt of royal ordinance […] penalties for mismanagement of official funds, BA November 18, 1796. Almost a quarter century had passed since the Regulation of 1772 explicitly warned against shortchanging soldiers and spelled out the consequences for culpable paymasters. *Reglamento 1772, Título catorce, Obligaciones y nombramiento del habilitado.* Not much had changed when, fourteen years later, Gálvez bemoaned the incompetence of the presidio paymasters in managing the "business affairs" of the troops. *Gálvez, 1786, artículo 90.*

66. Nava to Elguézabal, giving instructions […] sale of Juan Cortés' property, BA September 5, 1797.

67. Elguézabal to Muñoz, […] property of Cortés' wife to cover his debts, BA October 5, 1797.

68. Proceedings concerning announcement of sale of Cortés' house, BA October 13, 1797; Nava to Governor of Texas, […] Juan Cortés is to remain at Béxar, BA January 19, 1798.

69. Nava to Governor of Texas, reporting retirement of Juan Cortés, BA May 15, 1798.

70. Nava to Elguézabal, notifying of Fernández's appointment as Captain of La Bahía, BA October 17, 1797. I have found no evidence that Amangual assumed command of the Chihuahua *volantes.*

71. Elguézabal to Muñoz, reporting the return of Antonio Cadena with a recovered sum improperly paid by Espadas, BA September 18, 1797; Nava to Elguézabal, […] sums improperly paid out by Antonio Cadena, BA October 17, 1797. Someone must have had faith in Cadena. It strains credulity to envision how he became paymaster of La Bahía by the end of the year, especially during Cortés' unsavory exit. See Cordero to Commandant [approving nomination of Cadena for paymaster] of La Bahía, BA December 9, 1797.

72. Correspondence between Elguézabal and Muñoz, concerning trip of Espadas to Béxar to remain under arrest, BA September 22, 1797; Elguézabal to Muñoz, transmitting Nava's order concerning Espadas transfer to Béxar, BA September 30, 1797.

73. Nava to Governor of Texas, […] promissory notes from Espadas to be paid with funds from sale of Espadas' assets, BA December 15, 1798.

74. Nava to Elguézabal, agreeing to let [him] remain in La Bahía [if] he desires, BA October 17, 1797. And, yet, on this same day Nava told Elguézabal about Fernández's appointment to Presidio La Bahía. See fn70 above.

75. Nava to Elguézabal, […] instructions for payment of debts of Manuel de Espadas, BA January 19, 1798; Nava to Governor of Texas […] transfer the command of La Bahía to José Francisco Zozaya […], BA January 19, 1798. Espadas' fate might not have mattered to Nava even after he received news from Elguézabal on March 13 that the missions of Rosario and Refugio had failed to pay their debts to Espadas. Upon the paymaster's bankruptcy, the Father Minister of Mission Refugio made an agreement with creditors to repay 1,050 pesos. See Nava to Elguézabal [failure of both missions] to repay their debts to Espadas, BA April 17, 1798. On this same day, Nava reported to the governor that funds had emerged for collection and crediting of Espadas' debts. Nava to Elguézabal [receipt of liquid funds] to cover Espadas' debts, BA April 17, 1798.

378   Notes to Pages 221–224

76. Amangual's statement of expenses for Indians, BA April 30, 1798; Provisions included all types of cloth, buttons, gunpowder, bullets, cigarettes, and reimbursement for the freight charges on a box of rifles. The total charges amounted to 129 pesos, 8 *reales*, and 11 *granos*. The stupefying nomination of Cadena to the position of paymaster seems implausible and contrasts mightily with Amangual's rehiring in the same capacity at Béxar. Cordero to Commandant [approving nomination of Cadena, and election of Amangual, for paymaster] of La Bahía, BA December 9, 1797.

77. Francisco Amangual's […] articles supplied to visiting Indians, BA August 31, 1798. These groups received cigarettes, cloth from Queretaro and *serge*, tallow candles, payment for musicians, and paper for roses, all intended for the burial of an Indian woman. The list records a payment of thirty-six pesos to Vicente Michelá for three dozen knives, and an unspecified amount to the commander of the "pueblo of Nacogdoches" for the maintenance of Indians there from October to January 1798. Menchaca and Amangual are, again, listed as "los habilitados" at the beginning of the year. See Monthly report of company of Béxar, BA January 1, 1799.

78. Proceedings concerning payment for articles supplied to visiting Indians [page 8], BA December 31, 1798. The gifts totaled almost ninety-five pesos and the list was signed by Amangual in San Antonio on December 31, 1798. The items included cigarettes; an ox of "Matías Bargas" and cigarettes; in November, cigarettes, gunpowder and bullets, and payment to the blacksmith Manuel Flores for the nailing and ironwork (*clavazón y errage*) of the ten carriages (*cureñas*) constructed for the presidio artillery.

79. Amangual's affidavit certifying inventory of Tobacco Department (*casa de estanco*) managed by […] Barrera, BA January 4, 1799. A few days later, Nava ordered Muñoz to publish a proclamation in Texas concerning the prefixed term [of use] for the circulation of old stamped coinage. Nava to Muñoz, ordering […] proclamation concerning retirement of old coinage, BA January 15, 1799.

80. Díaz de la Vega to Muñoz, forwarding copy of Juan Barrera's letter requesting […] son's accounts from Tobacco Department be examined, BA January 26, 1799. Offerings from others failed to erase his debt. See [Elguézabal] to Arispe, [amount from Ibarvo to satisfy Barrera's debt], BA November 25, 1801.

81. Arispe to Muñoz, […] Juan Timoteo Barrera return to the paymaster the tobacco […], BA March 30, 1799; [Muñoz] to Arispe, [Barrera's Tobacco], BA April 17, 1799; Arispe's report [shipments charged to Barrera], BA October 24, 1799. A group of soldiers from Béxar and La Bahía and the "pueblo de Nacodoches[sic]," including volantes, must not have learned anything from Barrera's mistakes; they were accused of smuggling "48 libras de tobacco." Moral to Elguézabal, [list of soldiers] charged with contraband of tobacco, BA September 12, 1799.

82. [Elguézabal to Arispe] Galán's appointment as administrator of Tobacco […] approving Barrera's detention, BA January 8, 1800.

83. Arispe to Elguézabal, […] departure of Barrera […] to collect debts […], BA January 18, 1800. Barrera's aforementioned "detention" must have referred not to his being incarcerated but, rather, to his status as an enlisted soldier; that is, not yet forced out.

84. Arispe to Elguézabal, reporting exact amount of Barrera's debt, BA January 22, 1800.

85. […] Canalizo to Elguézabal, requesting action against […] Barrera, accused of embezzlement while […] collector of tithes of Béxar, BA January 30, 1800.

86. Arispe to Elguézabal, [allow] Barrera an additional three months' leave to

Notes to Pages 224–227 379

settle personal business, BA February 28, 1800. Money matters and irony perplexed the luckless Barrera. Ten years earlier, he filed an *expediente* for repayment of a debt owed to him by Simón de Arocha. See [Barrera vs. Arocha], demanding payment of debt, BA July 6, 1790.

87. McAlister (1957), p. 15.

88. By 1799, Lt. José Cortés of the Royal Corps of Engineers reported the virtues of, and the challenges faced by, the king's troops. He advocated for their faithfulness and "reverent obedience," their hardiness, tenacity, ability to survive on little sustenance, and devotion to service in the face of adversity. See Cortés (1989), pp. 25–26. One historian devotes an entire chapter to the army engineers, Manuel Mascaró and Gerónimo de la Rocha, called to assist with defense of the Comandancia General, in Janet H. Fireman, *The Spanish Royal Corps of Engineers in the Western Borderlands, Instrument of Bourbon Reform, 1764 to 1815* (Glendale: Arthur H. Clark, 1977), pp. 141–65.

89. Luís Navarro García, *Las provincias internas en el siglo xix* (Sevilla: Escuela de estudios hispano–americanos de Sevilla, 1965), pp. 1–4. These largescale occurrences signaled profound changes from a theoretical perspective for administrators in the metropole and in the context of international dynamics. However, for those working in the Commandancy some things remained constant, whether actual or imaginary. Navarro Garcia seems to forget that the Commandancy had undergone multiple divisions by 1800. As it is described in ongoing historiography, indigenous inhabitants representing many "nations" of long tenure predating Iberian incursion had established a presence that cannot be described as anything but international. That diversity of identities was recognized, sorted out, and recorded by European immigrants across time and space.

90. For a brief summary of international maneuverings in the Texas-Louisiana borderlands from 1800–1803, see Faulk (1964), pp. 119–22.

91. Navarro García (1965), pp. 26–28. The historiography on Philip Nolan is extensive and centers on his adventures not only as a horse trader but also as a key player on behalf of U. S. expansionist efforts. See Dan L. Flores, "Bringing Home All the Pretty Horses: The Horse Trade and the Early American West, 1775–1825," *Montana: The Magazine of Western History* 58, no. 2 (Summer 2008): 3–21, 94–96; and Flores, *Journal of an Indian Trader: Anthony Glass and the Texas Trading Frontier, 1790–1810* (College Station: Texas A&M University Press, 1985); Thomas Jefferson, Daniel Clark Jr., James Wilkenson, and William Dunbar, "Concerning Philip Nolan," *Quarterly of the Texas State Historical Association* 7, no. 4 (April 1904): 308–17; Maurine T. Wilson and Jack Jackson, *Philip Nolan and Texas: Expeditions to the Unknown Land, 1791–1801* (Waco: Texian Press, 1987); for Nolan's escapades and impact on Nava, Vidal, and Casa-Calvo, see Winston De Ville and Jack Jackson, "Wilderness Apollo: Louis Badins' Immortalization of the Ouachita Militia's Confrontation with the Philip Nolan Expedition of 1800," *Southwestern Historical Quarterly* 92, no. 3 (Jan. 1989): 449–61.

92. Nava to Governor of Texas, [...] arrival of Felipe Nolan with passport from the Governor of Louisiana, BA January 27, 1795; Monthly report of the Presidio of La Bahía, BA November 30, 1798; Nava to Governor of Texas, instructing him to aid Nolan [...], BA January 9, 1798; Nava to Governor of Texas, prohibiting all trade with foreigners and their introduction to Texas, with the exception of Nolan, BA March 20, 1798; Nava to Governor of Texas, refusing to permit Nolan to introduce goods into Texas, BA March 20, 1798.

93. Casa-Calvo to Elguézabal, promising to restrain Americans and French from

380 Notes to Pages 227–229

entering Texas, BA March 10, 1800. Nowhere is the patronymic hyphenated in the Béxar Archives, but indeed, the Marqués himself did so in his official signature as does his very recent biographer Gilbert Din.

94. Moral to Elguézabal, [...] Casa Calvo's [...] reporting attempts to prevent aggression by the English, Americans, and allied Indians [...], BA April 26, 1800. One historian suggests Casa-Calvo's "xenophobic" leanings may have stemmed from worry over which groups might be more patriotic to Spain. See Gilbert C. Din, *An Extraordinary Atlantic Life: Sebastián Nicolás Calvo de la Puerta y O'Farrill, Marqués de Casa-Calvo* (Lafayette: University of Louisiana at Lafayette Press, 2016).

95. Moral to Elguézabal, [...] Casa Calvo's [...] reporting attempts to prevent aggression by the English, Americans, and allied Indians [...], BA April 26, 1800. For a summary of the widening mistrust of Nolan, see Faulk (1964), pp. 117–19.

96. Nava to Governor of Texas, refusing to permit Nolan to [Elguézabal] to Governor [of Santander ...] ordering Nolan's arrest, BA November 8, 1800.

97. See Castañeda (1936–1958), p. 241. And for communication about Nolan in the fall of 1800, see [...] José Vidal to Commandant of Nacogdoches, reporting intentions of [Nolan's travels] to Texas and past the Rio Grande, BA October 6, 1800; [Elguézabal] to Governor [of Santander], reporting trip of [Nolan] to Mexico, and ordering Nolan's arrest, BA November 8, 1800; Músquiz to Elguézabal, [...] movements of Felipe Nolan, BA November 16, 1800; [Documents by] Layssard to Elguézabal, giving warning of suspicious actions of Felipe Nolan, BA November 25, 1800; [Elguézabal] to Cordero, [news from Nacogdoches] about Nolan and his robberies, BA November 30, 1800.

98. Nava to Elguézabal, [payments for] travel and maintenance expenses of Nolan's men, BA January 30, 1802.

99. Navarro García (1965), pp. 1–4.

100. Nemesio Salcedo to Elguézabal, [receipt of map of New Mexico] by [Fray Puelles], BA February 27, 1804. For a brief description of Salcedo's personal traits, see Faulk (1964), pp. 20–21.

101. Navarro García (1965), pp. 26–28.

102. Elguézabal's monthly report of the presidio of San Antonio de Béxar, BA January 1, 1800. In the absence of its now deceased Captain Muñoz, the interim governor of Texas was obliged to produce the monthly report for the *comandante inspector* Pedro de Nava. As Faulk explains, during the last months of Manuel Muñoz's illness Elguézabal achieved the rank of lieutenant colonel and was sent to the Béxar presidio to essentially carry out the duties of de facto captain. When Muñoz died in July 1799, Nava named Elguézabal as political and military governor of Texas. He did so partly to squash the Villa de San Fernando ayuntamiento's attempt to assume control of power in the province. See Faulk (1964), pp. 26–27.

103. Chiquito's appearances in three documents held at the Béxar Archives concern his alleged theft of cattle from the mission at "Bahía Santo," BA July 8, 1798; his request for gifts for his people from the Captain Bernardo Fernández, BA August 26, 1793; and his negotiations with the Governor of Texas for peace with the Lipan Apaches, BA September 12, 1793. He may be the same "Capitán Chiquito" described as Gileño by Griffen (1988), p. 55. He is intimately associated with Bacoachi in both Griffin and Moorhead (1968), pp. 183–85, 191–96. It is highly likely he is the same Chiquito mentioned as a kidnapper of civilians, including one woman who managed to escape from Rancho de Palmitos in October 1792. See Chapter 5.

Notes to Pages 229–231   **381**

104. Elguézabal's monthly report of the presidio of San Antonio de Béxar, BA January 1, 1800.

105. Ibid. Marchena Fernández (1992), pp. 193–219.

106. Elguézabal's monthly report of the presidio of San Antonio de Béxar, BA January 1, 1800. The Feast of Saint Thomas the Apostle had in times past been celebrated on December 21.

107. Elguézabal's monthly report of the presidio of San Antonio de Béxar, BA March 1, 1800.

108. Nava to Governor of Texas, [...] report on Comanche raid upon horses being smuggled into Louisiana, BA October 13, 1801. Castañeda, citing the same document, adds that "the herders had delayed reporting the outrage for obvious reasons and so made the venture futile." However, no such information is found in the original communication. See Castañeda (1936–1958), pp. 226–27.

109. *"El primer teniente Don Francisco Amangual es de conocido valor, de bastante aplicación, y honrrado* [sic] *proceder, con mediana capacidad, en su empleo sirve con utilidad."* Information concerning officers of [Béxar], BA January 1, 1802. Marchena Fernández (1983, p. 97) indicates that "the traditional military concept of the word 'medium' in ranking is different from the one commonly given and should be understood as insufficient but with possibilities of amendment, of correction, which still remains in force in today's Spanish army." Documents held at the Béxar Archives relative to Amangual's activity in 1802 are scarce.

110. See Military report of the *compañía volante* of San Carlos de Parras, BA January 15, 1803. Alférez Adam's name is alternately spelled *Adam* and *Adan* in original documentation. See "Revistas de inspección. Provincias Internas, AGS, SGU, LEG, 7047, 20–24, (97/110) 23 de Septiembre de 1801."

111. Nemesio Salcedo to Governor of Texas, ordering the return to Chihuahua of a detachment from the flying company of San Carlos de Parras, BA February 15, 1803. For "actual population" numbers totaling "362 souls," Elguézabal included the Parras company with Mission Valero's community for the year 1803. Juan Bautista Elguézabal, "Notes and Documents: A Description of Texas in 1803," ed. Odie Faulk, *Southwestern Historical Quarterly* 66, no. 4 (April 1963): 514. For more on military matters related to Parras, see Agustín Churruca Peláez, Al Kinsall, Glen P. Willeford, and Ellen A. Kelley, eds., *Before the Thundering Hordes: Historia Antigua de Parras*, Occasional Papers, No. 4 (Alpine: Sul Ross State University, Center for Big Bend Studies, 2000), pp. 31–32; and Agustín Churruca Peláez, Héctor Barraza A. *Historia Antigua de Parras* (Parras: "El Popular," 1989), pp. 188–89.

112. Nemesio Salcedo to Governor of Texas, ordering the return [...], BA February 15, 1803. These men constituted the pool from which appointments were to be drawn. And though a Cpl. Yldefonso Galavís (alternately spelled *Galaves*) stayed, Salcedo was to determine whether this soldier would rejoin his company, here unidentified. This reconciliation could only happen when he returned from detached service at the time the commander general wrote this letter.

113. Nemesio Salcedo to Governor of Texas, ordering the return [...], BA February 15, 1803.

114. Ibid. The military career of Col. Manuel Antonio Cordero y Bustamante is summarized in Faulk (1964), pp. 29–31; and amplified in Almaráz (1971), passim.

115. We learn the identity of the Indian tribes at the mission and of those that raided

382   Notes to Pages 232–234

and the first name of the Carancahua individual killed in this letter: Nemesio Salcedo to [Elguézabal taking steps] to reinforce Refugio [...], BA March 1, 1803.

116. Amangual to Elguézabal, reporting Indian raid on Refugio Mission, BA February 26, 1803. Some of the information missing in this letter is found in the March 1 letter above. As of the publication date of this book, I have not located the diary. Cadena, the formerly disreputable paymaster of an embarrassing 1797 episode of fiscal management had, by 1800, not only remained in service but also earned a glowing critique in a report from Elguézabal. He knew the "Apache idiom to perfection," and assisted with "practical knowledge of the field." See Elguézabal's [character of officers at Bahía], BA January 7, 1800.

117. Salcedo to [reinforce Refugio], BA March 1, 1803. Andrés Tijerina reports on the *volantes'* exploits in the 1820s involving pursuits into the "*despoblado*," going after "illegal" parties of travelers and "fugitives from civil jurisdiction." In one example, the commander of the Third Flying Squadron of Laredo, Nemesio Sánchez, sent one of his troops, José Antonio García, after an immigrant accused of murder named James Stuart. García eventually overtook the escapee and delivered him to the Laredo alcalde for trial. Tijerina (1994), pp. 81–82.

118. Amangual to Elguézabal, reporting departure of soldiers escorting [Sáenz], BA March 3, 1803.

119. Amangual to Elguézabal, [...] summary proceedings in case of Pedro Castañeda, deserter, BA March 12, 1803; Nemesio Salcedo to Governor of Texas [...] Manuel Flores, deserter, BA March 12, 1803; Nemesio Salcedo to Governor of Texas, discussing case of Juan José López, deserter from Parras, BA April 29, 1803.

120. Amangual to Elguézabal, reporting minor military details, BA April 13, 1803. For Elguézabal's low estimation of Béxar's inhabitants' work ethic and waste of corn, see Elguézabal (1803/1963), p. 513; and Faulk (1964), pp. 26–28.

121. Elguézabal to Cordero, transmitting Amangual's examination of presidial accounts, BA April 13, 1803. The designation of "*actual capitán*" is significant since this document is one of only two that I have encountered in the Béxar Archives that specifically addresses the rank and location of Amangual by correspondence from the Bahía presidio. See also Cadena to Arrambide [...] Pedro Castañeda, BA March 4, 1803.

122. Nemesio Salcedo to [Elguézabal], [proceed in the case of Denis], BA March 1, 1803.

123. Amangual to Elguézabal, transmitting records in case of mulatto Denis, BA April 23, 1803.

124. Amangual to Elguézabal, asking for a description of a fugitive priest, BA April 23, 1803. The following month, after conducting his own research, Amangual reported no luck in finding further information on the priest. See Amangual to Elguézabal, [...] lack of records [...], BA May 7, 1803. Clearly, the "truthful individual" implicated in the 1792 Amangual–Rodríguez slander suit, Fr. Gómez Moreno, was not the only troublemaker among borderlands clergy. For a fascinating, if somewhat troubling, account of not so virtuous members of religious society, see the biographical sketches found in Hendricks (2008), pp. 143–64.

125. Amangual to Elguézabal, transmitting census report of foreigners in La Bahía, BA April 23, 1803.

126. Elguézabal to Guadiana, ordering investigation of contraband trade at La Bahía reported by Amangual, BA June 4, 1803. Only two weeks later, Elguézabal described

Notes to Pages 234–238 383

the "capturing of wild horses" as an ongoing activity, second only to hunting buffalo, by the civilian population of Texas. Elguézabal (1963/1803), pp. 513–15.

127. Amangual to Elguézabal, [reputation of José López], soldier accused of theft, September 3, 1803. Nemesio Salcedo to [Elguézabal], reporting [Amangual's appointment] to collect military supplies at Saltillo, BA September 26, 1803.

128. [Ugarte's] Monthly report of detachment of Nacogdoches, February 4, 1804.

129. Chipman and Joseph (1992), pp. 237, 241. For the step-by-step process of putting the expedition together, see Flores pp. 39–68. Described as an agent working on behalf of the US government, Sibley's maneuverings were still evident in 1808. See Almaráz (1971), pp. 23–24. Sibley warrants further treatment in Thomas W. Kavanagh, *Comanche Political History: An Ethnohistorical Perspective, 1706–1875* (Lincoln: University of Nebraska Press, 1996), pp. 163–72, 175.

130. […] Ugarte's letter to Elguézabal, […] news of transfer of Louisiana to the United States […], BA February 4, 1804. See Chipman and Joseph (1992), p. 205.

131. […] Ugarte's letter to Elguézabal, […] news of transfer of Louisiana to the United States […], BA February 4, 1804. For a concise explanation of the suspicions by Spanish officials about boundary issues and American expansionist efforts, see Flores (1992), p. 27. Citing Acosta Rodríguez, in 1803 eighty-percent of Louisiana's free population was French. Ralph Lee Woodward, "Spanish Commercial Policy in Louisiana, 1763–1803," *Louisiana History: The Journal of the Louisiana Historical Association* 44, no. 2 (Spring 2003): 135.

132. Ugarte's list of soldiers at Nacogdoches requesting leave, BA February 4, 1804. In his 1719 *Reglamento*, Felipe V was unequivocal: he wanted the designation and post of "inpedido" abolished. But for those who met the criteria, salaries could continue for certain soldiers. Naylor and Polzer (1988), p. 36.

133. Velázquez (1982), p. 201; Navarro Garcia (1965), pp. 31–32; p. 31, fn 44; Moorhead (1968), pp. 277–8, fn 5 (May 30, 1804, royal decree).

134. Military report of the compañía volante of San Carlos de Parras, BA January 15, 1803

135. Nemesio Salcedo's instructions for removal of troops and families from Parras to Béxar, BA May 1, 1803.

136. [Elguézabal's] monthly report of military operations and events at Béxar, March 1, 1804; Correspondence between Amangual to Elguézabal, […] San Carlos de Parras, BA February 11, 1804.

137. [Elguézabal's] monthly report […], BA March 1, 1804.

138. [Elguézabal] to Amangual, transmitting military accounts of company of San Carlos, BA March 8, 1804. An early edition of a TSHA publication considers the origins of the name "Alamo" as applied to the Mission church of San Antonio de Valero and based on the "old records of the Mission and those of the Company of San Carlos there stationed." The authors argue that the mission's peregrinations were many from site to site until its eventual aggregation to the parish of San Fernando and the presidio of San Antonio de Béxar in 1793. From 1710 to 1718, its name varied in correspondence, but it was never called "Alamo" until much later in the registers of "Segunda Compania de Sn. Carlos de Parras." See Bethel Coopwood, Edmond J. P. Schmitt, and Lilia M. Casis, "Notes and Fragments," *Quarterly of the Texas State Historical Association* 3, no. 1 (July 1899): 66–70.

139. Pando's claim of years served, whether found in a military service record or other documentation, cannot be located at the time of research for this book. See

384 Notes to Pages 238–245

Amangual to Governor of Texas, [...] term of services of Miguel Pando, San Antonio de Valero, BA April 20, 1804.

140. Ibid.

141. Amangual to Elguézabal, [...] desertion of José Arellanes of the company of Béxar, San Antonio de Valero, BA April 23, 1804.

Chapter 7

1. Stationed now at the Béxar presidio, Álamo de Parras *volantes* performed escort duty as well. Monthly report of the military operations and events at Béxar, BA January 1, 1804.

2. Monthly report of the military operations and events at Béxar, BA January 1, 1804. Guadiana was a competent, reliable soldier. Once the French turned over Louisiana to the United States, Guadiana received orders to remain in Nacogdoches, a post he had commanded in 1796, in furtherance of assisting its current captain, Joseph Joaquín Ugarte. [Salcedo to Elguézabal] instructing him to station [Guadiana] at Nacogdoches [...] due to situation created by transfer of Louisiana, BA March 26, 1804.

3. Amangual to Elguézabal, [...] desertion of soldiers Bernardino Ocon and José Valencia, San Antonio de Valero, BA April 23, 1804. A few months before, Salcedo alerted the Texas governor about Ocon's dereliction and theft of clothing. Salcedo to [Elguézabal ... arrest of Ocon ... Álamo de Parras], BA December 19, 1803.

4. Consequently, Anze's place in the squadron would now be filled by Juan Pedro Walker. With this promotion, Anze straightaway reported to Antonio Cordero in Monterey. Drafts of [Elguézabal's] letters to [...] Amangual, Ugarte, [...] pertaining to civil and military matters, BA April 16, 1804. Juan Pedro Walker, a mapmaker and enlistee into the Spanish service, was a man of many talents according to Wilson and Jackson (1987), passim.

5. Nemesio Salcedo to Elguézabal, [...] Musquiz' diary on expedition to prevent entry of Anglo-Americans, BA May 21, 1804.

6. [...] Carpeta Número 2 [...] Salcedo's correspondence with José de Iturrigaray [et al.], BA June 12, 1804.

7. Ibid.

8. Ibid.

9. Casa-Calvo to Elguézabal, warning of exploration expeditions [from] the United States, BA June 27, 1804. Casa-Calvo may have conveniently conjured papal donation and the doctrine of discovery to justify his defensive maneuvers. One month later, José Ugarte followed up. Ugarte to Elguézabal, [USA exploration], BA July 25, 1804.

10. Casa-Calvo to Elguézabal, warning of exploration expeditions to be sent by the United States, BA June 27, 1804. By the following year, Casa-Calvo had reached the limits of his patience with outsider incursions and formed his own exploratory expedition. See Jack D. L. Holmes, "The Marqués de Casa-Calvo, Nicolás DeFiniels, and the 1805 Spanish Expedition through East Texas and Louisiana," *Southwestern Historical Quarterly* 69, no. 3 (Jan. 1966): 324–39.

11. Ugarte to Casa-Calvo, [...] Anglo-Americans' plans to reconnoiter the Mississippi River, BA August 1, 1804.

12. Nemesio Salcedo to Governor of Texas, [...] Anglo-American intrusion [...] Indian relations [...], BA August 11, 1804. See Ibid., [conduct of Ugarte], BA May 22, 1804; and Ibid., [report any attempt to move boundary], BA September 13, 1803.

Notes to Pages 245–246   **385**

"Tahuayases" and "Taboayazes" are misspellings or alternative spellings of Taovayas.

13. Navarro García (1965), pp. 26–9.

14. Amangual to Muñoz, regarding payment of expenses incurred in opening road to Santa Fé, BA February 7, 1791.

15. Ibid. Military rolls indicate that Louis Charles DeBlanc began as a cadet but eventually captained the Light Cavalry Company of the Militia of the Natchitoches post from 1757 to 1793. Elizabeth Shown Mills and Ellie Lennon. *Natchitoches Colonials: A Source Book: Censuses, Military Rolls & Tax Lists, 1722–1803*. Baltimore: Genealogical Publishing Co., 2017.

16. Cabello to Rengel, […] Juan Bousquet from trip to silver mine with Pedro Vial [and others], BA February 18, 1785; Cabello to Rengel, [progress made by Bousquet concerning metal in mine], BA May 19, 1785. See Cortés (1989), and his designating in 1799 the "Taobayaces" as the "most civilized" of the northern nations, pp. 84–86, 138 fn 89.

17. Ugarte y Loyola to Cabello, ordering payment to Vial […], discussing plan for exploring road to Santa Fé, BA August 17, 1786; Cabello to Anza [Vial's trip to Santa Fé], BA October 3, 1786; Ugarte y Loyola to Cabello, [Anza and Vial's plans for direct route between Béxar and Santa Fé], BA October 26, 1786.

18. Cabello to Ugarte y Loyola, […] Vial's journey to Santa Fé, BA September 24, 1786.

19. Loomis and Nasatir (1967), pp. 265–67. For the diary of Vial's trip from Béxar to Santa Fé, October 24, 1786, to May 26, 1787, see Loomis and Nasatir (1967), pp. 268–15. See, from among many, Gil Ibarvo to Martínez Pacheco, [arrival of Vial], BA October 20, 1788; Martínez Pacheco to Ugalde, [departure of Vial for New Mexico], BA July 4, 1789; Martínez Pacheco to Fernando de la Concha, [expedition of Vial to open new roads], BA December 8, 1788.

20. Loomis and Nasatir (1967), pp. 171–72. French by birth but in the service of the Spanish empire, Jarvay's name is variously spelled in the English and Spanish historiography of the period as Chalvert, Calbert, Jarvet (Jarvay), Tarbet, and so on.

21. Navarro Garcia (1965), pp. 28–29; this last date is likely incorrect and even the author's own footnote suggests the error. Navarro García may have intended to write "1804" since, by 1805, Vial was complying with orders from Governor Alencaster, who was answering to Salcedo. However, Loomis and Nasatir confirmed the 1804 trip, but stipulated that "the diary and report [Vial was required to have written had] not turned up." See Loomis and Nasatir (1967), pp. 423, fn4, 422–43, 428–37. These movements are summarized in Joseph P. Sánchez, Robert L. Spude, and Art Gómez, *New Mexico: A History* (Norman: University of Oklahoma Press, 2013), pp. 68–69. Governor Chacón figures most prominently in granting settlement land and reporting on the missionaries in Kessell (1979), pp. 415–28.

22. As it is well known, during the very short Gálvez administration the region had been split three ways: the western provinces consisted of Sonora and the two Californias; the central provinces consisted of Nueva Vizcaya and New Mexico; and Coahuila and Texas comprised the eastern section. Only two years later, Viceroy Flores divided the Provincias Internas into just two separate commands, only to have it reunited by Viceroy Revillagigedo in 1790 and then divided, again, in 1791. In an encore performance on November 23, 1792, a royal decree reunited the two divisions under Comandante General Pedro de Nava and made the provinces independent of the viceroy. Moorhead (1975), pp. 102–3, 111–12.

23. Certified copy of orders describing reorganization of the government of the Interior Provinces, BA May 18, 1804. The other reality made plain was the paucity

Notes to Pages 246–248

of human labor to verify the existence of seaports and "competent" people to work mineral resources. On August 20, 1804, Elguézabal provided an updated version of a relación estadística for the Real Tribunal del Consulado de Veracruz in which he listed information about the military force of the "Provincia de Texas," citing, for instance, "Infantry units, militia: None," "Cavalrymen: Ninety-five men," "Garrisons: four, including the Nacogdoches detachment with two presidial companies and one "Flying Squadron." Hinting at the lack of people skilled or competent enough to capably mine natural resources, Elguézabal revealed that Texas "settlers are skilled in hunting bison, deer, bears, wild pigs and capturing Wild Horses, preferring them to all others [occupations]." Guice (1955), pp. 46–56.

24. Certified copy of orders describing reorganization of the government of the Interior Provinces, BA May 18, 1804. Existing conditions in 1804 included the usual cheaters and hooligans. Ramón Murillo indicates in "número 2," of his reorganization plan that adjutant inspectors had been "ignorant of military matters" because their principles, which are unspecified, were incompatible with those of the profession they "lately adopted." Compounding the army's woes were the troops themselves having "sunk to such extreme incompetence," fearing the loss of their self-supplied horses in battle, which exposed "placing their own self-interest before the honor and glory of the armed service." Their cruelty to horses by spur wounding and crippling from "wild antics" while riding was matched only by their fear of being labeled as timid and not being men "of the outdoors," to them "the greatest dishonor." (De la Teja/ Wheat, 2004): 511- 512; 516.

25. Nemesio Salcedo to Governor of Texas, [. . .] Amangual [. . .] and Valle's new military commissions, BA August 13, 1804. Uranga served as an interim governor from May to November 1802. See Nava to Elguezabal [leave Uranga in charge of Texas], BA June 7, 1802.

26. Uranga to Elguézabal, [. . .] determination to start for Coahuila after delivering La Bahía company to Amangual, BA July 20, 1804.

27. Amangual to Elguézabal, reporting departure of detachment for Nacogdoches, BA July 24, 1804. Amangual to Elguézabal, [command turned over to him] by Uranga, BA July 29, 1804; Amangual to Elguézabal, discussing military supplies, BA August 12, 1804.

28. Cortes correlates a Muskogee group, the "Pacanas" from present Alabama, with the "Apalaches," both peoples who settled in between the Ouachita River and the "Misisipi" by the waters of the Río Colorado. Cortés (1989), pp. 90; 142, fn109. Ugarte to Elguézabal, promising to obey orders [. . .] immigration into Texas of Apalache Indians, BA August 1, 1804. Months before, settlement plans seemed to be on course. Certified copy [settlement of Apalache under] Tinza, BA April 3, 1804; Ugarte to Elguezabal, [inform Tinza of action on petition] for settlement, BA June 3, 1804.

29. List of Indian supplies from Barr and Davenport, BA September 27, 1803; for their favored status as traders, see J. Villasana Haggard, "The House of Barr and Davenport," *Southwestern Historical Quarterly* 49, no.1 (July 1945): 66–88; Census report of foreigners in Nacogdoches, BA January 1, 1804; Uranga to Elguézabal, [. . .] non–admission of Louisiana immigrants into territory under the Viceroy, BA February 11, 1804.

30. Nemesio Salcedo to Governor of Texas, [. . .] Viceroy has refused to permit immigrants from Louisiana to settle [. . .], BA January 9, 1804.

31. Ugarte's letter to Elguézabal, reporting no further news of Ashley and his band,

Notes to Pages 248–250 387

BA April 3, 1804. When Barr returned from Natchitoches, he informed Ugarte that an Englishman, "Capchan," confirmed Ashley's departure from Natchez with 143 men intending to secure "large supplies of meat" once they knew Louisiana was now in the possession of Americans. Once arrived in Tahuayas country, they intended to trade horses with them and to encourage depredations against the Spanish. See Ugarte [to Elguezabal, reporting Ashley's plans to trade …], BA February 9, 1804; Nemesio Salcedo to Governor of Texas, discussing precautions against Robert Ashley's band, BA March 13, 1804; Nemesio Salcedo to Elguézabal, […] receipt of Miguel Músquiz's diary on expedition to prevent entry of Anglo-Americans, BA May 21, 1804. Ashley's suspected meanderings among the Tahuayas spurred an investigation into such rumors during the previous year. See Nemesio Salcedo to [Elguézabal about plans to ascertain presence of Ashley among Tahuayas], BA September 27, 1803.

32. Upon the retirement of Col. Roque Medina, Nava announced the new appointment. Nava to [Elguézabal as Assistant Inspector of presidios], BA August 1, 1798.

33. Elguézabal to Commandant General, naming [Arciniega, Urrutia, Tarín] for promotion in the flying company of San Carlos de Parras, BA September 12, 1804. Since Elguezabal cites his "youth," the suggestion is strong of a boy who entered the army at a very young age.

34. Ibid. Urrutia had served thirty years, three months, and sixteen days with the presidial company of San Antonio de Béxar. He is not to be confused (except for one shared frailty) with the troublesome, abusive Manuel (de) Urrutia of previous chapters in this study; however, Elguézabal had a change of mind where it concerned Juan Antonio. In a short note presumably sent to General Salcedo ten days after his initial recommendations, Elguézabal rescinded his proposal of Urrutia for the post of second alférez, claiming that Urrutia was "ignorant of army tactics because he is fond of drinking to excess." Elguézabal added that, although "he does not indulge habitually in this vice — on account of the reprimands of his superior officers — he still falls into this bad habit." Elguézabal's opinion […] Urrutia's new military commission, BA September 22, 1804.

35. Elguézabal to Commandant General, naming [Arciniega, Urrutia, Tarín] for promotion in the flying company of San Carlos de Parras, BA September 12, 1804.

36. [Elguézabal's] monthly report of the military operations and events at Béxar, BA October 1, 1804.

37. Monthly report of military operations and events at Béxar, BA January 1, 1805. This same document records the December 16, 1804, death of Manuel Menchaca from natural causes. He was first alférez and former paymaster of the Béxar company and a frequent partner of Amangual in various assignments.

38. [Captain José Joaquín] Ugarte to Elguézabal, reporting news […] temporary settlement of boundary dispute with the Americans […] war declared by the English, BA January 4, 1805.

39. Antonio Cordero to Elguézabal, reporting that troops are being sent […], BA January 6, 1805. For a very recent summary of San Juan Bautista del Río Grande del Norte (or Presidio del Río Grande which, as Weddle indicates, the fort "was coming more and more to be known as"), see Duvall (2020), pp. 221–26. For the foundational monograph, see Weddle (1968) and for the quote, see p. 356.

40. Based on the three-page instructions of March 24, 1808, see also *Fuerza del destacamento que a las or*[de] *n*[e] *s del Capitan Don Francisco Amangual debe salir …*, Béxar Archives, e_bx_016887_001 — 003. Cordero had sent Amangual to visit Comanche

388   Notes to Pages 250–252

rancherias to "put a stop" to raids by making the leaders confront individuals in their midst "warring in [Spanish] territory." Kavanagh (1996), pp. 150–51.

41. Durán to Governor of Texas, [. . .] order for development of New Mexico, BA October 28, 1803; two months later Elguézabal reported his receipt of and compliance with the viceroy's proclamation. See Elguézabal [acknowledging proclamation regarding] New Mexico, BA December 7, 1803.

42. For a discussion of *gachupín* reaction to and nervousness about the Bourbon fracture on the peninsula, see among others the final chapter of Archer (1995); provincial response to the 1808 crisis and its impact in New Spain, see chapter 2 of Timothy Anna's *Forging Mexico: 1821–1835* (Lincoln: University of Nebraska Press, 2001); Feliciano Barrios and José Antonio Escudero, *España, 1808: el gobierno de la monarquía* (Madrid: Real Academia de la Historia, 2009), passim; and Eduardo Martiré, *1808 La clave de la emancipación hispanoamericana* (Buenos Aires: El Elefante Blanco, 2002), passim.

43. According to Flores, Salcedo was deeply suspicious of American intrusion coming under the guise of scientific explorations. He was convinced that such enterprises were intended "mainly to win over Indian allies." Dan L. Flores, *Southern Counterpart to Lewis and Clark: The Freeman & Custis Expedition of 1806* (Norman: University of Oklahoma Press, 2002), pp. 71–72. See Salcedo to [Elguézabal, presence of American flags among Indians], BA November 14, 1802; Salcedo to Cordero, [order not to attack American troops unless sure of victory], BA October 24, 1806; Salcedo to [Governor of Nuevo León to send troops to Texas], BA November 5, 1806; Salcedo to [Herrera, to transfer command and return to Béxar], BA November 25, 1806.

44. Herbert E. Bolton, "Papers of Zebulon M. Pike, 1806–1807," *American Historical Review* 13, no. 4 (July 1908): 798–827. One anthropologist argues that the Pacific crossing of Vitus Bering and Alexeii Chirikov in 1741–42 "brought back to Russia eyewitness accounts" of enough resources to precipitate a "fur rush" to the North Pacific and on the Alaskan mainland. In 1799, the Russian American Company, a consolidation of fur trade companies, gave rise to Russian colonization in the Américas, prompting Russian naval vessels to keep a "watchful eye on foreign intruders." See Kent G. Lightfoot, "Russian Colonization: The Implications of Mercantile Colonial Practices in the North Pacific," *Historical Archaeology* 37, no. 4 (2003): 14–28.

45. William C. Foster. *Spanish Expeditions into Texas, 1689–1768* (Austin: University of Texas Press, 1995), pp. 17, 33–49, 51–52. Summarized by Orellano Norris, the March 23, 1689, fourth expedition of De León was joined by approximately eighty-three troops from Nuevo León near the junction of the Nadadores and Sabinas Rivers. Orellano Norris (2017), pp. 20–24. Foster has the departure date as March 24, and the total number of soldiers at fifty from the five presidios of Nueva Vizcaya, and fifty from Nuevo León, the latter specifically formed by "two companies of loyal officers and soldiers accustomed to serving His Majesty." William C. Foster, *Texas and Northeastern Mexico, 1630–1690*, trans. Ned F. Brierly (Austin: University of Texas, 1997), pp. 122–23. Massanet (also Mazanet) reflected on Texas settlement in documents published in Hadley (1997), pp. 330–58.

46. Foster (1995), p. 95.

47. Ibid., pp. 109–23. Once the presidios and missions were established, the threat of French intrusion loomed as a potential menace to the mining regions of Nuevo León, Nueva Vizcaya, and even Coahuila and New Mexico. Jackson and Foster (1995), pp. 4–7.

Notes to Pages 252–253 389

48. Foster (1995), pp. 14, 30. As Barr contends, during the colonial period, the term "Tejas" was applied broadly to a collection of indigenous identities that formed the larger Hasinai Confederacy, consisting of the Hasinai, Kadohadacho, and Natchitoches peoples. Twenty-three bands of these confederacies and at least three other independent Caddo bands clustered in the river valleys of present-day northwestern Louisiana and northeastern Texas, along the Neches, Sabine, and the Red riverways. The Hasinai, later called "Cenis" by the French and "Tejas" by the Spaniards, were members of the Caddoan peoples. They had maintained a thriving culture in the region for over eight hundred years of agriculturally based communities encompassing hundreds of miles across present-day Louisiana, Texas, Arkansas, and Oklahoma. Barr (2007), pp. 19–20. Hadley and Naylor indicate that the Tejas, or Hasinai, were Caddoan speakers for whom the first mission of San Francisco was established in 1690. Hadley (1997), p. 377. For a focus on the Hasinai people and Kadohadacho confederacy leadership in the period covered in this study, see F. Todd Smith, *The Caddo Indians: Tribes at the Convergence of Empires, 1542–1854* (College Station: Texas A&M University Press, 1995), passim.

49. Foster (1995), p. 8.

50. Dennis Reinhartz, "Legado: The Information of the Entradas Portrayed through the Early Nineteenth Century," *The Mapping of the Entradas into the Greater Southwest*, ed. Dennis Reinhartz and Gerald D. Saxon (Norman: University of Oklahoma Press, 1995), pp. 141–43.

51. Hadley (1997), pp. 360–61. With final instructions released to him on March 11, 1718, requirements based on *dictámenes fiscales* of November 1716 and a final decision by a *junta general* one month later, Alarcón officially began his expedition. See Céliz (1935), pp. 21–23. By negotiating strategies from a regionally focused economic perspective, the Hasinai developed alliances via their settlements to access EuroAmerican commodities. See Martha McCollough, *Three Nations, One Place: A Comparative Ethnohistory of Social Change among the Comanches and Hasinais during Spain's Colonial Era, 1689–1821* (New York: Routledge, 2004), pp. 85–90.

52. Foster (1995), p.7

53. Ibid., p. 8. Inasmuch as daily movements and projections of distances traveled were estimations based on the use of the compass and the astrolabe, throughout history travelers depended on these devices. The astrolabe preceded the development of the sextant, an instrument necessary for recording longitude and latitude based on the angle of the sun at any given time.

54. *Reglamento 1772, Título décimo, trato con los indios enemigos ó indiferentes, artículo cinco*: "I especially charge [the] governors and captains of presidios to stipulate the release or exchange of prisoners as the first condition of the treaties or suspensions of fighting that they concede [and the] exchange will be man for man, etc., but if this is not possible and it is necessary to give more for my troops, it will be two or three Indians for each Spaniard. By no means will this extend to Indian auxiliaries or scouts."

55. Foster (1995), p. 11.

56. Though the Native polity is unspecified, the Marqués de Altamira describes the 110 soldiers who accompanied Governor de León on the expedition's missionizing foray, leaving the padres there with just "a few" troops so as not to upset the Indians. See *De el Parecer que el Señor Auditor de Guerra Marqués de Altamira expuso al Excelentisimo Señor Virrey Conde de Fonclara en 4 de Julio de 1744.*See Porrua Turanzas (1961), p. 155.

390   Notes to Pages 254–256

57. Foster (1995), pp. 7–11; Orellano Norris and Cavazos Garza (2017), pp. 130–32.

58. Loomis and Nasatir (1967, p. 462, fn5) write: "[There is] a copy of the Amangual Diary […] in the Mexican Archives […] under Tierra y Marina, 1836, legajo 7, number 2. A fuller but different copy is in the Béxar Archives and is found in the Indexed Translations. There are entries in the Guerra copy that are not in the Béxar copy, and there is considerable material in the Béxar copy that is not found in the Guerra copy. There are extensive omissions from each. Our copy is the Guerra copy, collated with the Béxar copy." Mattie Austin Hatcher, *Diary of Operations and Events Occurring in the Expedition Undertaken under Superior Orders from this Province of Texas to that of New Mexico by Captain Francisco Amangual, First Commandant, and Captain Don Jose Agabo de Ayala, Second Commandant, Beginning March 30, 1808* (sic passim/ hereafter Hatcher), Center for American History, the University of Texas at Austin (1934). The expedition is summarized in Kavanagh (1996), pp. 150–54.

59. Though there can never be consensus, across the decades maps from various sources refined the thinking of what span of territory most closely approximated the Comanchería of the eighteenth century. Several align with descriptive texts from scholars working in the field. See for example, W. A. Riney's 1933 image at https://texas history.unt.edu/ark:/67531/metapth493255/m1/1/; National Society of the Daughters of the American Revolution, Comanchería Chapter, image at https://www.texasdar. org/chapters/Comancheria/; Fort Phantom Hill image at https://fortphantom.org/ fort-heart-comancheria/. For what scholars consider the geospatial range of the Apachería during the years covered in this book, see Babcock (2016), pp. 4–6; and Britten (2009), pp. 54–58.

60. Salcedo, Chihuahua, re expedition of 200 soldiers between New Mexico and Texas, 5 mar 1808, SANM, 2014-\–2138, 1806–1808, #34.

61. Béxar Archives, e_bx_016887_003. Francisco Amangual, *Diario de las novedades y operaciones ocurridas en la expedicion que se hace desde esta Prov[inci] a de Texas, a la del Nuebo Mexico, de orden superior, siendo Primer Comand[ant] e el Capitán D[o] n Fran[cis] co Amangual, Segundo el Capitan D[o] n José Agabo de Ayala, en 30. de Marzo de 1808*, (sic passim/hereafter Amangual). See also J. R. Craddock's transcription of the Diary for the Cíbola Project (2019). UC Berkeley: Research Center for Romance Studies. https://escholarship.org/uc/item/22z409p1.

62. See Simon de Herrera, Copias del Oficio que Acompaña el Teniente Coronl. D. Simon de Herrera las de Ordenes que le Paso el Sor. Comande. Gral. para la Salida de una Expedicion Interna de 150 Milicianos de los Cuerpos de su Mando y Estado del en que Salieron, 25 de Marzo de 1808 (copia de 24 de Mayo de 1808) [sic passim]. Western Americana Collection, Beinecke Rare Book and Manuscript Library, Yale University. (hereafter BRBML).

63. Herrera to Calleja, BRBML 14905899, April 6, 1808; *Fuerza del destacamento* […] *de 12 de Enero y 19 de Febrero del presente año*, Béxar Archives, e_bx_016887_001; see the review table of all three companies in Simón de Herrera, *Cuerpos de caballería provincial del Nuevo R[ein] o de León y Colonia del Nuevo Santander*, BRBML 14905903, March 25, 1808. From June 19–20, 1808, Amador indicated his travel time from San Antonio. SANM, microfilm images 2119, 2123. There were dichotomies in the ethical standards of this mixed assemblage of soldiers and, as usual, adherence to duty or not could be dramatic. With the prospect of encountering non-Spanish-speaking sojourners, interpreters accompanied the troop: Juan Carlos Morarín provided his expertise with English and French, as did Luzgardo Montoya for speakers of Comanche, Tahuaya,

Wichita, and Tahuacana. In utter contrast and thus absent from the expedition was Nicolas Tomé, a soldier with the Compañía Volante of San Carlos de Parras, excluded since Nemesio Salcedo had very recently come to a decision about the robbery Tomé perpetrated against his fellow soldier Andrés Hernández. Acting on orders from the Auditor of War, Salcedo condemned Tomé to six years imprisonment. However, it is unclear where he was to complete his sentence. Nemesio Salcedo to Antonio Cordero, Béxar Archives, e_bx_016898_001. Volante, and alleged thief, Tomé was presumably set to travel, thus representing at least one member of the Parras squadron.

64. Fuerza del destacamento [...] de 12 de Enero y 19 de Febrero del presente año, [March 24, 1808] Béxar Archives, e_bx_016887_002.

65. Ibid. And in his own hand as he wrote in his diary, see "*deste Rio es el Colorado y por otro nombre el Rojo*" *Amangual*, June 1, 1808. Following Cordero's lead, Amangual may have simply been referring to the Caddo Nation (Kadohadachos, Natchitoches, and Hasinais) as the Indigenous group in the aggregate with whom the river is most closely associated. The "Rio Rojo," indeed has its source in the present-day Texas panhandle, as does the "Colorado" River also has its headwaters in northwest Texas. Further, both sources are close to each other. The East Texas-based Caddo people, and more specifically the Hasinais, never went further west than the vicinity of the Angelina and Neches Rivers. Smith (1995), pp. 5–8.

66. *Fuerza del destacamento* [...] *de 12 de Enero y 19 de Febrero del presente año* [1808], Béxar Archives, e_bx_016887_002. "Ymparica" is almost certainly a Spanish-language corruption of *Penateka*, identified as the southernmost band of the Comanche. Though the Hatcher translation uses the spelling "Ymparica," I retain the spelling "Yamparica" as found in both the 1808 instructions to Amangual and the Loomis and Nasatir text. This band ranged from the Edwards Plateau to the headwaters of the Central Texas rivers. Carol A. Lipscomb, "Comanche Indians," in *Handbook of Texas Online* (www.tshaonline.org/handbook/online/articles/bmc72). The Red River Valley proved compelling to explorers, spies, and adventurers representing competing empires. For a brief, but equally fascinating, summary of its appeal, see Flores (2002), pp. 9–24.

67. "Novillo" in Hatcher (1808/1934) and in Amangual's own text. "Novilla," in Loomis and Nasatir (1967): 462.

68. Hatcher, April 2–4 (1808/1934). I understand the term to mean longest serving and/or most experienced soldiers.

69. Hatcher, April 6–10 (1808/1934).

70. Possibly the same headman who attended a "formal peace council" sponsored by Governor Antonio Cordero and referred to in Britten (2009), p. 170.

71. Hatcher, April 11, 1808. This same description appears in the final chapter of Weddle (1999), pp. 196–98, and in Bennett R. Kimbell, "El Baluarte del Sur: Archeological and Historical Investigations of the Southeast Bastion at Presidio San Sabá (41MNI), Menard County, Texas," *Bulletin of the Texas Archeological Society* 81 (2010): 19. The stone wall may have originally been a log stockade, and later incorporated rooms used by the soldiers. The two-story structure may have been the captain's quarters or what remained of two towers on the northwest and southeast corners as suggested by archaeological investigations in 2000. See Walter (2004), pp. 96–97.

72. Hatcher, April 11 (1808/1934).

73. In the Hatcher translation and *Amangual*, pages for April 13–15 do not exist. As indicated above, Loomis and Nasatir (1967, pp. 467–68) used two "collated" sources.

392   Notes to Pages 258–262

In the Diary itself, the words "missing pages" are scrawled in the lower right of the page marked "dia 12 [de Abril/sic]."

74. In his assessment of the expedition, Kavanagh (1996, p. 151) cites Loomis and Nasatir's translation of Amangual's words as, "with much jubilation."

75. *Amangual*, April 17–20, 1808.

76. Ibid., April 20, 1808.

77. Sofais, alternately spelled "Chiojas," "Chofais," and "Sojas," interacted with Spanish travelers visiting Comanche *rancherías* between Béxar and Santa Fé, and apparently had significant political wherewithal to protect the interests of his people. Kavanagh (1996), pp. 137–39, 148–52. Pekka Hämäläinen indicates that Amangual's meeting with "Sofais [sic]" was intended to "resuscitate the alliance" between Spain and the Comanche since officials "sensed that their ties […] were in jeopardy." The author makes no mention of Cordero's 1808 order for finding a more expeditious route between Santa Fé and San Antonio de Béxar. Hämäläinen (2008), pp. 188–89. So went the official reasoning for the trip's primary objective, although other goals included strengthening alliances which would account for Amangual and his team being in the Colorado River area near the village of Chief Sofais.

78. *Amangual*, April 22–26, 1808.

79. Ibid., April 21–30, 1808. Hart and Butler assert that the Almagre is the same as the Arkansas River. See Stephen Harding Hart, and Archer Butler, eds., *The Southwestern Journals of Zebulon Pike, 1806–1807* (Albuquerque: University of New Mexico Press, 2007), p. 185. This is likely Verde Creek in *Bandera* County, southwest of present Kerrville.

80. *Amangual*, May 1–3, 1808. Or by expressing absolute faith in supernatural power, Amangual recorded "Dios nos guie." Loomis and Nasatir (1967, p. 479) translate his words as "May God take care of us."

81. *Amangual*, May 6, 1808.

82. Ibid. Unnamed by Amangual, Quegue was mercurial and usefully kept his adversaries attentive to him and his followers. Kavanagh (1996), pp. 144–45, 153–55.

83. Cabello to Rengel, [Indian relations and dealing with Indians], BA November 24, 1785. Peace negotiations were well under way by November 1785 which resulted in the high-profile "Comanche Peace" described in Thomas (1932), pp. 292–321; and Kavanagh (1996, pp. 110–21).

84. *Amangual*, May 7, 1808

85. The Loomis/Nasatir translation reads: "They displayed a deep understanding" (1967), p. 482.

86. *Amangual*, May 7, 1808.

87. Ibid. May 10, 1808; "[…] going uninvited into the tents and walking around among the troops." Loomis/Nasatir (1967), p. 483.

88. *Amangual*, May 12, 1808. Amangual within the same document alternately spells the name "Quegue" and "Quege."

89. Loomis and Nasatir translate the name as "Ysambanbi," but identified also as "Sabanbipit," a chief mentioned in the peace treaty with Anza in 1786, and almost certainly the same individual among several captains "who commanded detachments against the Apaches" in Thomas (1932), p. 327; as having "led eighty men" against Apaches in 1786, another "ninety-five warriors against the Faraone" in Kavanagh (1996, p. 140). Loomis and Nasatir (1967, p. 488) correctly indicate that in the Amangual diary the name appears as Ysambanbi, which is "probably closer to the correct

Notes to Pages 262–264 **393**

version." Reliably consistent in his grammar across the years, only a few pages later in the diary, however, Amangual writes the name as "Sambanbi." See *Amangual*, May 7, 1808. Loomis and Nasatir state that "in 1808 he [Ysambanbi] showed typical Comanche scorn for the Spaniards," p. 488. However, if this is the same "Capitan Grande" (alternately "Gran capitan" [sic]) of the Quegue retinue met by the Amangual party on May 6, such an attitude was nowhere in evidence based on Loomis and Nasatir's own narrative and annotations.

90. The visitor seems to fulfill the role of what Kavanagh calls an "intermediary" more accurately with "no political roles beyond the immediate interactions," rather than a "political leader" whose influence extended across time and space. (1996, p. 15).

91. *Amangual*, May 7, 1808. Again, the Hatcher translation differs, semantically, from that of Loomis/Nasatir. The latter translation reads like this: that the Indian was made to understand, "in a very kind way," that it would be better for him to sleep in the guardhouse. However, Hatcher translates this section, regarding the manner in which the visitor was advised, "as nearly as possible," suggesting to me that these translators working in different time periods emphasize the solicitous, perhaps patronizing, and definitely cautionary, overtures by the soldiers to the late-night visitor.

92. *Amangual*, May 17, 1808.

93. Ibid. Rather than ascribing the extension of friendship to "the Spanish government," the Hatcher translation reads "the love our sovereign felt for them," to suggest the king's virtual, if not visceral, role in cementing amicable relationships. Hatcher, May 17, 1808. The Loomis/Nasatir translation of the final section of this contentious episode included additional material from the Béxar copy of the Amangual diary. The "chief" further indicated that there "were several [men] ready to go at once [as guides], but that they were aware of the certain risk in going over the route." The Vial authors betray their biases favoring the Spaniards in a note about Quegue's response, describing it as "Typical Indian doubletalk" (1967, pp. 490–91, fn24).

94. Hatcher, May 19, 1808. Again, the translations from the same archive manifest in different ways. The Hatcher states that "the sick woman was left in the village of Chief Quegue because she became worse, but the Indian guide cheerfully continued with our company." Pursuant to Loomis and Nasatir (1967, p. 492), "we had left a sick Indian woman [a different one?] at the ranchería of Chief Quegue because she was extremely sick. But the Indian guide was quite satisfied to accompany us."

95. Loomis and Nasatir indicate "[Lipans or Llaneros?]" (1967), p. 493, Hatcher (May 21, 1808). Moorhead describes the "Lipiyanes" as allies in campaigns against the Mescaleros and other enemy Indian forces. See Moorhead (1968), pp. 252–54, and passim. In 1799, Cortés described the Lipiyanes as part of a "Llanero group" with "many warriors," occupying the plains and deserts between the Pecos River and the Rio Grande and divided into three categories of "Natajés, Lipiyanes, and Llaneros." Cortés (1989), p. 52.

96. Differences in the interpretation of language may provide a glimpse into translator bias about gender roles. Where Loomis and Nasatir credit the women, too, with being hunters, Hatcher has only the man carrying out that task. Hatcher may have assumed that women could not have been engaged in the presumptively male–only activity of "looking for meat." Foster (1995), pp. 191, 195 suggests that present-day Blanco Creek was once called Arroyo de Cunillo. In his *Itinerario* (diary), Rubí camped at "[El Arroyo de] Cunillo," in November 1767. Jackson (1995), p. 142–43.

394   Notes to Pages 264–265

97. For discussions of the hazards of eighteenth-century environmental challenges including drought and subsequent food scarcity, see Babcock (2016), pp. 29–30, 119–20; for its impact in Nueva Vizcaya, see Deeds (2003), pp. 129–30, 169–70.

98. "*terreno mui incomodo*" […] *muchisimas imposibilidades* […] *dando infinidad de bueltas*," *Amangual*, May 22–June 1, 1808 (Loomis and Nasatir, 1967, pp. 495–98). Loomis and Nasatir wondered why such strenuous work, with crowbars and pickaxes, should have been necessary for mounted men and a mule train (1967, p. 498, fn32). It seems to this writer that such labor might be a real possibility given the size of the expeditionary force (a fact that the authors will themselves point out as remarkable), the number of animals brought along, and the nature of the route being taken. Clearly, Amangual and his team were not retracing every trail of previous sojourners, whether those were Native people or outsiders. The expedition required water in exceptionally large quantity, and thus its participants were obliged to seek routes conducive to finding that resource. Consequently, this would have entailed travel over unchartered terrain and the use of implements designed for reshaping the environment to enable access and unfettered passage.

99. *Amangual*, June 1, 1808. By now the expedition had reached the present-day Texas Panhandle. Here is another discrepancy between the Hatcher translation and that of Loomis and Nasatir. Hatcher indicates that the Frenchman claimed the "Rio Colorado" did not flow past the Naypeste, but that both dumped into the Mississippi. Hatcher, June 1, 1808. Loomis and Nasatir state that after "a long distance" the Red River "joins the Napestle" but their translation concurs with the Hatcher in that both rivers joined the Mississippi (1967, p. 499). Giving multiple names to waterways was historic. Across several pages in his first volume, Pichardo attempts to settle the confusion. Pichardo (1931, Vol. I, pp. 485–515; for an entire chapter devoted to "the Red and its tributaries," see 1934, Vol. II, pp. 52–90). Pedro Vial's own expedition diary provided an explanation for the term Napestle, clearly a Spanish corruption of a word used by native people to describe the river. On June 22, 1792, Vial and his partners set out in search of the "Napeste" River, which, as he indicates "we call in French the Arkansas River." Five days later, they found it. See Louis Houck, *The Spanish Regime in Missouri: A Collection of Papers and Documents Relating to Upper Louisiana during the Dominion of Spain* (Chicago: R. R. Donnelley & Sons, 1909), p. 356. Gov. Tomás Vélez Cachupín of New Mexico described the river as a nexus for interactions between soldiers, settlers, and merchants. See Herbert Eugene Bolton, "French Intrusions into New Mexico, 1749-1752," in *The Pacific Ocean in History*, ed. Henry Morse Stephens and Herbert Eugene Bolton (New York: The Macmillan Company, 1917), pp. 396–98.

100. "Don Facundo" in the Hatcher translation, and more fully identified in Loomis and Nasatir as "Lieutenant Don Facundo [Melgares]," emerges forcefully in 1806 as an apparently astute expeditioner and skilled negotiator of peace. (1967, p. 500, 237–38, 455). Martínez could potentially be he that enlisted in the Béxar company in 1778. See […] Cabello [Manuel Martínez has enlisted], BA November 11, 1778.

101. *Amangual*, June 2–4, 1808. Amangual, Hatcher, and Loomis and Nasatir identify and spell the name: "Quitaray." Loomis and Nasatir (1967, p. 501) add the disclaimer, "We cannot identify the Quitaray Indians in [Frederick Webb] Hodge." *Handbook of American Indians North of Mexico*. 2 vols. (Washington, DC: Government Printing Office, 1912), p. 501. However, it may be that an entire group's identity was subsumed by its most prominent leader, one with the power to speak on behalf of his band about immediate concerns. Barr mentions a Taovaya chief named "Qui Te Sain" who had

Notes to Pages 265–269 **395**

dealings with Bernardo de Gálvez when he was Commandant General. Barr (2006), pp. 220, 224, 226. He is mentioned by Smith (2000), p. 74. It is possible that "Quitaray" was a Wichita chief, whose titular designation may have been corrupted into the suffix "-rey," but then spelled by translators and, even Amangual himself, as "ray." The result, then, would be *Qui Te Rey* or, resolving it cynically, *Quite* [el] *Rey* [Remove the King].

102. *Amangual*, June 5. I am inclined to agree with Loomis and Nasatir (1967, p. 501); the heretofore unidentified river must be the Canadian.

103. Ibid., June 6

104. Ibid., June 7–10

105. *Amangual*, June 11, 1808. Misread by the authors as *"desengeño claro"* but translated like Hatcher. Loomis and Nasatir (1967), p. 504. Hatcher, June 11, 1808.

106. *Amangual*, June 14, 1808.

107. *Francisco Amangual, San Miguel del Bado, reporting arrival of his expedition, June 16, 1808*; Twitchell #2117, Spanish Archives of New Mexico, 2014–2138, 1806–8, #34.

108. *Amangual*, June 17–19, 1808.

109. ["mande un sold[ado] a dar el parte al S[eñ]or Gov.or Ynterino de nuestra llegada"/sic passim] in *Amangual* June 19, 1808; The Hatcher translation reads: "I sent a soldier to give information to the acting governor of our arrival." Loomis and Nasatir identify the "squadron" as that of the Santa Fé company: "In this same place the squadron under the command of the interim governor was waiting" (1967, p. 508). Two days later, Amangual received orders from the governor, and by July, Nemesio Salcedo confirmed receipt of the diary. Amangual, Santa Fé, acknowledging receipt of orders from the governor, Twitchell #2127, Spanish Archives of New Mexico, 2014–2138, 1806–1808, #34. 2127; Nemesio Salcedo to [?], acknowledging receipt of diary and map of Amangual's trip, SANM, reel 16, frame 575, image 2139.

110. *Amangual*, September 20, 1808; the Vial translation states that: "another militia-man [singular] of said company broke his musket" (Loomis and Nasatir, 1967, p. 510). There is a noticeable gap in the Béxar Archives holdings of Amangual-related material between May 2, 1808, and September 11, 1808. However, his obligations to recording the daily activities and interactions while on expedition would have been curtailed during the extended stopover in Santa Fé. Once on the road for the trip back home, the diary is taken up again.

111. The abundance of documentary material related to desertion in the holdings of the Béxar Archives alone is considerable. *Sumarias* related to desertion and its perpe-trators fall under such headings as "cases and reports of"; "decrees on"; "punishment for"; "pursuit of"; "from Béxar"; "from La Bahía"; "from New Mexico"; and others too numerous to mention. See Adán Benavides, *The Béxar Archives (1717–1836): A Name Guide* (Austin: University of Texas Press, 1989), pp. 1141–42, 1166–67.

112. Nava to Governor of Texas, [royal order] deserters, BA July 27, 1801.

113. Copy of Caballero's communiqué of royal decree […] covering reinstatements after desertion, BA December 3, 1804. An assortment of conditions had to be met in order to receive His Majesty's pardon, and some of those included a loss of credit for time served.

114. See for example: Nemesio Salcedo to Governor of Texas, giving instructions on procedures in cases of second desertion, BA March 14, 1803; Cordero to Governor of Texas, […] case of Miguel Losaya, charged with second desertion, BA March 18, 1803; Nemesio Salcedo to Governor of Texas, […] punishment […] for desertion and […] trials dealing with repetition of desertion, BA June 4, 1803; […] Luzero and

396   **Notes to Pages 269–271**

Elguézabal, […] remittance to the Real Sala de México of all criminal cases in Texas dealing with desertion, BA June 22, 1803; Amangual to Elguézabal, […] desertion of Vicente Durán, Pedro García, Nepomuceno Ceballos and Blás Ramón, BA November 19, 1804. Not content to have merely defected, these same four men were, by the beginning of the following year, considered to be suspects in a robbery that took place at the Nacogdoches presidio where they landed after their desertion from La Bahía. See Nemesio Salcedo to Governor of Texas, [alleged theft], BA January 1, 1805.

115. *Amangual*, September 23, 1808.

116. Ibid., September 25–27, 1808.

117. Loomis and Nasatir (1967), p. 513 fn45.

118. *Amangual*, September 29 to October 1, 1808. The term "*mal pais*" can refer to arid, difficult terrain made so by volcanic rock, or, in geological terms, a lava field. In a note appended to the September 30 and October 1 entries, Amangual describes the land as impassable because of "las piedras calzinadas por el fuego, paresen el resumido de una mina de fierro [sic]." Throughout his Diary, Amangual uses the terms *rumbo* and *derrota* interchangeably.

119. *Amangual*, October 7, 1808. "His body was covered with lacerations," *Vial*, p. 516. Amangual wrote, "tiene el cuerpo abierto de las pruebas de la mas evidentes de la crueldad de estos Gentiles quienes sin piedad por su tierna edad le azotavan a cada ynstante [sic]."

120. *Amangual*, October 7, 1808. The Loomis and Nasatir text (1967), p. 516, identifies him as "Juan Cristobal" and even mentions his last name. They do not give his age but credit the "Béxar copy" with listing it as "about 10 or 12 years old." Amangual includes the first, middle, and last name "Padia" [Padilla/sic passim]. Amangual, October 7, 1808.

121. *Amangual*, October 7, 1808. Amangual identifies the Sierra on October 17.

122. Ibid., October 8–11, 1808.

123. Here, Amangual describes Agabo as the captain of a *militia*.

124. I can find no sources to confirm the presence of this mountain range, but a "Las Petacas" campground lies approximately four miles southeast of Taos, nowhere near to where the expedition party is at this point. Morfi, Chapa, Hackett, Alessio Robles make no mention of it, nor do Thonhoff, Moorhead, Frank, or Loomis and Nasatir. Perhaps Amangual meant to write *Pitalac* or *Pitala*, one (or two) of the Coahuiltecan-speaking Indian groups in the "region between Cíbolo Creek and the Río Grande" (too distant from Amangual's location) from which came the "bulk of neophytes for the San Antonio and Rio Grande missions." See Thonhoff (1992), pp. 12–13. Foster (1995, pp. 284, 313 fn22) indicates Rivera confirmed the "Pitalac (Pitala, Petalac)" resided in Texas in 1727. Hodge (1959, II p.264) describes the "Pitahay," as a tribe, evidently Coahuiltecan, met by Massanet in 1691, 11 leagues [east] of [the] middle Nueces [River], Texas." Lafora (1958, p. 185) spells the name "Petalac" and describes its members inhabiting "movable villages," and as one of several "savage" Indian nations. See Lafora and Kinnaird (1958), p. 185; Jackson (1995, p.43) adds the diacritical mark to "Pitalác.."

125. *Amangual*, October 14, 1808.

126. "Hurtaita" — *Vial*, p. 521. Amangual may have gotten the surname wrong. More than likely, it is "Sustaita."

127. *Amangual*, October 14, 1808. Benegas and Nañes are identified as militia soldiers.

Notes to Pages 271–282

128. "who declared that he was going to Santa Fé as a member of the detachment" — *Amangual*, October 16, 1808; "who said he was from the garrison of Santa Fé" — *Vial*, p. 521. I defer to earlier translations since this section of the original manuscript is torn, and therefore my reading of it cannot be conclusive.

129. (El) Brazito, New Mexico, southwest of Los Órganos Mountains. See Map 6 in Tigges (2013), p. 663. Lafora stopped to camp at "Los Bracitos" on August 7, 1766. Lafora and Kinnaird (1958), p. 85. Loomis and Nasatir (1967, p. 521) call it "El Bajio [sic]," — .

130. Quintero was captain of the Cavalry Corp of Nuevo Santander, as was Agabo of the Cavalry Corp of Nuevo León. Both units were, in fact, militias composed of volunteer soldiers.

131. *Amangual*, October 17, 1808.

132. "San Elzeario"; *Amangual*, October 19, 1808. "At 11 o'clock we encountered the *situado* [caballada?] of the Company of San Elzeario." Loomis and Nasatir (1967), p. 522.

133. *Amangual*, October 21, 1808.

134. *Amangual*, November 8–10, 1808.

135. Ibid., November 11–26, 1808.

136. Ibid., November 28, 1808. The Hatcher translation does not mention the fatigued horses, whereas the Loomis and Nasatir (1967, p. 528) text does, although they cite the "Béxar" copy.

137. *Amangual*, November 29–30, 1808.

138. Ibid., December 1–8, 1808.

139. Ibid., December 16, 1808; Loomis and Nasatir identify only Cpl. Francisco de León in this episode. (1967), p. 532.

140. *Amangual*, December 17–23, 1808.

Conclusion

1. Transfers management of Béxar military hospital to Mariano Varela, BA March 14, 1808. Amangual was the superintendent of the first hospital in Texas, housed at Mission Valero. According to Castañeda, a part of the abandoned mission was reconditioned at a cost of 352 pesos, and on January 1, 1806, the first patients were admitted. However, "Amangual found the position of superintendent incompatible with his military duties" and resigned shortly thereafter. See Castañeda (1936–1958, p.409).

2. [Amangual] Relieved as major of Viceregal Militia Corps, BA March 17, 1808. On this same day, Amangual appointed cashiers to supervise funds belonging to the militia corps of Nuevo León and Nuevo Santander. Nemesio Salcedo to Antonio Cordero, April 18, 1808. BRBML.

3. [Amangual] transfers command of Flying Company of San Carlos de Parras to José Antonio Aguilar, BA March 25, 1808; Francisco Viana to Antonio Cordero, BA March 29, 1808 (e_bx_016896_001.tif).

4. Kavanagh (1996), pp. 156–57. Gumption was theirs to claim given their steadily burgeoning commercial activities with Anglo-Americans in Red River country once the "Wichita blockade dissolved." Hämäläinen (2008, pp. 149–50).

Notes to Pages 283–284

Epilogue

1. Signed, rubric of Amangual, Béxar, February 9, 1808. In "Land Grants and Sales of the Béxar County Spanish Archives, no. 34," copy from the Robert Bruce Blake Collection, 976.4 R639r v. 3 (Francisco de Amangual), Daughters of the Republic of Texas Library. Amangual served as the manager of the Béxar military hospital, and though I have discovered no other documentation of that assignment, when he left on the Santa Fé expedition, the transfer of his job to Mariano Varela had occurred two weeks before. Transfers management of Béxar military hospital to Mariano Varela, BA March 14, 1808.

2. Without further information, we must assume that the girl is the daughter of his last wife, María Trinidad de los Reyes y García. Amangual's first wife was María Trinidad Castelo, and his second was María Fuentes. On February 13, Governor Cordero granted the property to Amangual for eighty-four pesos payable to the king and intended for "public works in Valero." There being no objections by any of the nearby property owners, Judge Vicente Amador placed Amangual in "quiet and peaceful possession" of the land by taking the captain by the hand, walking with him over the property, making him pull weeds and cast rocks to the four winds, all done as proof of actual ownership ("*hallarse pocesionado rlmente*"). BCSA, February 8–13, 1808, *Donacion de un solar y venta de una casa a Francisco Amangual, ano de 1808* [sic passim]. A solar was defined as a "plot of land with defined boundaries, located within the limits of a municipality." Félix D. Almaráz Jr., *The San Antonio Missions and Their System of Land Tenure* (Austin: University of Texas Press, 1989), pp. 13–14, 85.

3. "Last Will and Testament of Captain Francisco Amangual, Béxar, April 15, 1812." See http://www.sonsofdewittcolony.org//adp/history/bios/amangual/amangual.html. Printed in *Los Bexareños Genealogical Quarterly*, sourced from the Béxar County Archives.

4. As of July 2022, I have found no documentation for the cause of the younger Amangual's death. Maria Castelo died at the age of forty-four of pneumonia and was buried on January 5, 1805. Roman Catholic Archdiocese of San Antonio Sacramental Record, San Fernando y Presidio de San Antonio de Béxar (entierros), 1802–1817, Entry 190, 5 Jan 1805.

5. Roman Catholic Archdiocese of San Antonio Sacramental Record, San Fernando y Presidio de San Antonio de Béxar (entierros), 1802–1817, Entry 437, 21 May 1812. The sacramental record indicates that Francisco Amangual died of old age ("*murio de vejez*" [sic]). For a study of the history of land-use of a project area or *tierras realengas* (Lands of the King) that included the burial grounds and Old Catholic Cemetery, conducted from 1722 to the 1970s and reported by a team of researchers from UTSA, see C. M. M. McKenzie, C. Munoz, and R. Mauldin. Archival and Historical Review of the Children's Hospital of San Antonio Property, Downtown, San Antonio, Béxar County, Texas. Special Report No. 35. (San Antonio: Center for Archaeological Research, The University of Texas at San Antonio, 2020).

Bibliography

Archival Material

Archivo General de Indias. Expediente [...] presidios de las Provincias Internas y las Compañías Volantes. Guadalajara, 514, N.78 (Portal de Archivos Españoles).

Archivo General de Simancas. Compañías Presidiales y Volantes. Provincias Internas; Compañías Volantes de Nueva España; Companias Sueltas de Nueva España; Provincias Internas, Empleos; Provincias Internas, Contratas. (Portal de Archivos Españoles).

Béxar Archives. Briscoe Center for American History. The University of Texas at Austin.

Béxar County Spanish Archives. San Antonio, Texas.

Beinecke Rare Book and Manuscript Library. Western Americana Collection. Yale University.

Center for Southwest Research, University Libraries, University of New Mexico. Archivo de Simancas (Guerra Moderna); Spanish Archives of New Mexico II, Miscellaneous Documents, 1790.

Craddock, J. R. (2019). Diary of the Journey of Francisco Amangual from San Antonio, Texas, to Santa Fé, New Mexico, from there to San Elizario, New Mexico, and back to San Antonio March 30 to December 23, 1808. UC Berkeley: Research Center for Romance Studies. https://escholarship.org/uc/item/22z409p1.

Daughters of the Republic of Texas Library, Robert Bruce Blake Research Collection, Álamo de Parras company, Bustillo Family Papers, 1772–1936.

New Mexico State Records Center and Archives, Ted Otero Collection, Historical Documents, 1772–1867; Bernardo Vásquez-Franco Papers, 1791–1840; Spanish Archives of New Mexico I & II - New Mexico, U.S., Civil Records of New Spain, 1621–1821; New Mexico, U.S., Land Records of New Spain, 1692–1846.

Seleciónes del Archivo de Hidalgo del Parral, (MS 215). Special Collections, University of Arizona Libraries.

Unpublished Material

Amangual, Francisco. *Diario de las novedades y operaciones ocurridas en la expedición que se hace desde esta provincia de Texas, a la del Nuevo México, de orden superior siendo Primer Comandante el Capitan Don Francisco Amangual, Segundo el Capitán Don José Agabo de Ayala, en 30 de Marzo de 1808.*

Hatcher, Mattie Austin. *Diary of Operations and Events Occurring in the Expedition Undertaken under Superior Orders from this Province of Texas to that of New Mexico by Captain Francisco Amangual, First Commandant, and Captain Don*

José Agabo de Ayala, Second Commandant, Beginning March 30, 1808, Center for American History, the University of Texas at Austin (1934).

Lopez Cancelada, Juan. *Ruina de la Nueva España si se declara el comercio libre con los extrangeros.* Cádiz: Manuel Santiago de Quintana, 1811.

Published material (various authors, editors)

Recopilación de penas militares, segun ordenanza y reales ordines hasta noviembre de 1806 con las obligaciones del soldado, cabo y sargento de infantería, caballería, y dragones, y otros particulares para instrucción de los mismos. Madrid: Oficina de D. Francisco Martínez Dávila, impresor de cámara de S.M., 1825.

Various editors, *Documentos para la historia eclesiastica y civil de la provincia de Texas o Nuevas Philipinas, 1720-1779.* Madrid: Ediciones José Porrúa Turanzas, 1961.

Yo, El Rey. *Reglamento y aranceles reales para el comercio libre de España a Indias de 12 de octubre de 1778.* Madrid: Imprenta de Pedro Marín, 1778.

Published Material

Adams, John A., Jr. *Conflict and Commerce on the Río Grande: Laredo, 1775-1955.* College Station: Texas A&M University Press, 2008.

Aguilar, Joseph, and Robert W. Preucel, *The Continuous Path: Pueblo Movement and the Archaeology of Becoming.* Tucson: University of Arizona Press, 2019.

Albi, Julio. *La defensa de las Indias 1764-1799.* Madrid: Instituto de Cooperación Iberoamericana, 1987.

Alessio Robles, Vito. *Coahuila y Texas en la época colonial.* 2d ed. México, D.F.: Editorial Porrúa, 1978.

———. *Diario y derrotero de lo caminado, visto y observado en la visita que hizo a los presidios de la nueva españa septentrional el Brigadier Pedro de Rivera.* México, D.F.: Secretaría de la defensa nacional, Dirección de archivo militar, 1946.

———. *La Primera Imprenta en Las Provincias Internas de Oriente, Texas, Tamaulipas, Nuevo León y Coahuila.* México, D.F.: Antigua Librería Robredo de José Porrúa e Hijos, 1939.

Almaráz, Félix D., Jr. *The San Antonio Missions and Their System of Land Tenure.* Austin: University of Texas Press, 1989.

———. *Tragic Cavalier: Governor Manuel Salcedo of Texas, 1808-1813.* Austin: University of Texas Press, 1971.

Alonzo, Armando. *Tejano Legacy: Rancheros and Settlers in South Texas, 1734-1900.* Albuquerque: University of New Mexico Press, 1998.

Andújar Castillo, F. *Los militares en la Espana del siglo XVIII: Un estudio social.* Granada: Universidad de Granada, 1991.

Anna, Timothy. *Forging Mexico: 1821-1835.* Lincoln: University of Nebraska Press, 2001.

Appadurai, Arjun, ed. *The Social Life of Things: Commodities in Cultural Perspective.* Cambridge: Cambridge University Press, 1986.

Archer, Christon. *The Army in Bourbon Mexico, 1760-1810.* Albuquerque: University of New Mexico Press, 1995.

Babcock, Matthew. *Apache Adaptation to Hispanic Rule.* Cambridge: Cambridge University Press, 2016.

Bibliography

Bannon, John Francis. *The Spanish Borderlands Frontier, 1513-1821*. New York: Holt, Rinehart and Winston, 1970.

Barbier, Jacques A. "The Culmination of the Bourbon Reforms, 1787-1792." *Hispanic American Historical Review* 57, no. 1 (Feb. 1977): 51-68.

Baron, David. "Verification Procedures Used in Two Inventory Counts in New Spain, 1596-1597." *Accounting Historians Journal* 23, no. 1 (June 1996): 1-24.

Barr, Julianna. *Peace Came in the Form of a Woman: Indians and Spaniards in the Texas Borderlands*. Chapel Hill: University of North Carolina Press, 2007.

Barrios, Feliciano, and José Antonio Escudero. *España, 1808: el gobierno de la monarquía*. Madrid: Real Academia de la Historia, 2009.

Bauer, Arnold J. *Goods, Power, History: Latin America's Material Culture*. Cambridge: Cambridge University Press, 2001.

Belmonte Postigo, José Luis. "El color de los fusiles. Las milicias de pardos en Santiago de Cuba en los albores de la revolución haitiana." In *Las Armas de La Nación, Independencia y cuidadanía en Hispanoamérica (1750-1850)*, edited by Manuel Chust and Juan Marchena. Madrid: Iberoamericana, 2007.

Benavides, Adán, Jr. *The Bexar Archives (1717-1836): A Name Guide*. Austin: University of Texas Press, 1989.

———.W. Michael Mathes and Lawrence Clayton. "The Commandancy General Archive of the Eastern Interior Provinces." *The Américas* 43, no.2 (Oct. 1986): 203-225.

Blyth, Lance R. *Chiricahua and Janos. Communities of Violence in the Southwestern Borderlands, 1680-1880*. Lincoln: University of Nebraska Press, 2012.

Bobb, Bernard E. "Bucareli and the Interior Provinces." *Hispanic American Historical Revie* 34, no. 1 (Feb. 1954): 20-36.

———. *The Viceregency of Antonio Maria Bucareli in New Spain, 1771-1779*. Austin: University of Texas Press, 1962.

Bolton, Herbert Eugene. *Athanase De Mézières and the Louisiana-Texas Frontier, 1768-1780*. Cleveland: Arthur H. Clark, 1914.

———. "French Intrusions into New Mexico, 1749-1752." In *The Pacific Ocean in History*, edited by Henry Morse Stephens and Herbert Eugene Bolton, pp. 389-407. New York: The Macmillan Company, 1917.

———. "Papers of Zebulon M. Pike, 1806-1807." *American Historical Review* 13, no. 4 (July 1908): 798-827

———. *Texas in the Middle Eighteenth Century: Studies in Spanish Colonial History and Administration*. Austin: University of Texas Press, 1915

Borreguero Beltrán, Cristina. *El reclutamiento militar por quintas en la españa del siglo xviii, Orígines del servicio militar obligatorio*. Valladolid: Universidad de Valladolid, 1989.

Brading, David A. "Power and Justice in Catorce 1799 - 1805." *Ibero-Amerikanisches Archiv* 20, no. 3/4 (1994): 357-80.

Brinckerhoff, Sidney and Odie B. Faulk. *Lancers for the King. A Study of the Frontier Military System of Northern New Spain, With a Translation of the Royal Regulations of 1772*. Phoenix: Arizona Historical Foundation, 1965.

———. and Pierce Chamberlain. *Spanish Military Weapons in Colonial America*. Harrisburg: Stackpole, 1972.

Bringas, Father Diego Miguel Bringas de Manzaneda y Encinas, translated and edited by Daniel S. Matson, and Bernard L. Fontana. *Friar Bringas Reports to the King, Methods of Indoctrination on the Frontier of New Spain, 1796-1797*. Tucson: University of Arizona Press, 1977.

Britten, Thomas A. *The Lipan Apaches: People of Wind and Lightning*. Albuquerque: University of New Mexico Press, 2009.

Burns, Kathryn. *Into the Archive. Writing and Power in Colonial Peru*. Durham: Duke University Press, 2010.

Burton, H. Sophie. "'To Establish a Stock Farm for the Raising of Mules, Horses, Horned Cattle, Sheep, and Hogs': The Role of the Spanish Bourbon Louisiana in the Establishment of Vacheries along the Louisiana-Texas Borderland, 1766–1803." *Southwestern Historical Quarterly* 109, no. 1 (July 2005): 98–132.

———. "Vagabonds along the Spanish Louisiana-Texas Frontier, 1769–1803: Men Who Are Evil, Lazy, Gluttonous, Drunken, Libertinous, Dishonest, Mutinous, etc. etc. etc.—and Those Are Their Virtues." *Southwestern Historical Quarterly* 113, no. 4, (April 2010): 438–67.

Burton, H. Sophie and F. Todd Smith. *Colonial Natchitoches. A Creole Community on the Louisiana-Texas Frontier*. College Station: Texas A&M University Press, 2008.

Bushnell, Amy Turner. *Situado and Sabana. Spain's Support System for the Presidio and Mission Provinces of Florida*. Athens: Anthropological Papers of the American Museum of Natural History, 1994.

Calderón Quijano, José Antonio. *Historia de las Fortificaciones en Nueva España*. Veracruz: Gobierno del Estado de Veracruz, Consejo Superior de Investigaciones Científicas, Escuela de Estudios Hispanoamericanos, 1984.

Calloway, Colin G., ed. *Our Hearts Fell to the Ground: Plains Indian Views of How the West Was Lost*. Boston: Bedford/St. Martin's, 1996.

———. *One Vast Winter Count. The Native American West Before Lewis and Clark*. Lincoln: University of Nebraska Press, 2003.

Canales Ruiz, Jesús. *José de Escandón. La Sierra Gorda y El Nuevo Santander*. Cantabria: Institución Cultural de Cantabria, 1985.

Cañizares-Esguerra, Jorge. "Entangled Histories: Borderlands Historiographies in New Clothes?" *American Historical Review* 112, no. 3 (June 2007): 787–99.

Carlin, A. Roberta. *A Paleographic Guide to Spanish Abbreviations, 1500–1700*. N.p.: Universal Publishers, 1999.

Carrera Stampa, Manuel. "The Evolution of Weights and Measures in New Spain," translated by Robert Smith. *Hispanic American Historical Review* 29, no. 1 (Feb. 1949): 2–24.

Castañeda, Carlos E. *Our Catholic Heritage in Texas, 1519–1936*. Edited by Paul J. Foik, 7 vols., 4. Austin: Von Boeckmann-Jones, 1936–1958.

Castillo Crimm, Ana Carolina. *De León: A Tejano Family History*. Austin: University of Texas Press, 2003.

Céliz, Fray Francisco. *Diary of the Alarcón Expedition into Texas, 1718–1719*. Translated by Fritz Leo Hoffmann. Los Angeles: The Quivira Society, 1718/1935.

Céspedes del Castillo, Guillermo, and Gonzalo Anes y Álvarez de Castrillón, *El tabaco en Nueva España*. Madrid: Real Academia de la Historia, 1992.

Chabot, Frederick C. *Presidio de Texas at the Place Called San Antonio with a description of the Comandancia or the Governor's Palace*. San Antonio: Naylor Printing Co., 1929

Chapa, Juan Bautista. *Texas and Northeastern Mexico, 1630–1690* [Historia del Nuevo Reino de León de 1650 a 1690]. Edited by William C. Foster. Translated by Ned F. Brierley. Austin: University of Texas Press, 1997

Bibliography

Chapman, Charles Edward. *Catalogue of Materials in the Archivo General de Indias for the History of the Pacific Coast and the American Southwest*. Berkeley: University of California Press, 1919.

Chartrand, René. *The Spanish Army in North America 1700-1793*. Oxford: Osprey, 2011.

Chipman, Donald E., and Luis López Elizondo. "New Light on Felipe de Rábago y Terán." *Southwestern Historical Quarterly* 111, no. 2 (Oct. 2007): 160–81.

Chipman, Donald E., and Harriet Denise Joseph. *Spanish Texas 1519-1821*. Rev. ed. Austin: University of Texas Press, 1992.

Churruca Peláez, Agustín, Al Kinsall, Glen P. Willeford, and Ellen A. Kelley, eds. *Before the Thundering Hordes: Historia Antigua de Parras*. Occasional Papers, no. 4. Alpine: Sul Ross State University, Center for Big Bend Studies, 2000.

Churruca Peláez, Agustín, Héctor Barraza A., et al. *Historia Antigua de Parras*. Parras: "El Popular", 1989.

Chust, Manuel, and Juan Marchena, eds. *Las Armas de La Nación, Independencia y cuidadanía en Hispanoamérica (1750-1850)*. Madrid: Iberoamericana, 2007.

Coopwood, Bethel, Edmond J. P. Schmitt, and Lilia M. Casis. "Notes and Fragments." *Quarterly of the Texas State Historical Association* 3, no. 1 (July 1899): 66–70.

Cortés, José. *Views from the Apache Frontier: Report on the Northern Provinces of New Spain*. Edited by Elizabeth A. H. John. Translated by John Wheat. Norman: University of Oklahoma Press, 1989.

Costeloe, Michael P. "Hombres de Bien in the Age of Santa Anna." In *Mexico in the Age of Democratic Revolutions, 1750-1850*, edited by Jaime E. Rodríguez O., pp. 243–57. Boulder: Lynne Rienner, 1994.

Cruz, Gilbert R. *Let There Be Towns. Spanish Municipal Origins in the American Southwest, 1610-1810*. College Station: Texas A&M University Press, 1988.

Cunningham, Debbie. *The Natives of the Seno Mexicano as Documented in the Escandon Hierro Manuscripts from 1747-1749* in *Southern Quarterly* 4, v. 51. Hattiesburg, 2014: 54–71.

Cummins, Light Townsend. *To the Vast and Beautiful Land. Anglo Migration into Spanish Louisiana and Texas, 1760s-1820s*. College Station: Texas A&M University Press, 2019.

Curbelo Fuentes, Armando. *The Canary Islanders in Texas: The Story of the Founding of San Antonio*. San Antonio: Trinity University Press, 2019.

Cutter, Charles R. *The Legal Culture of Northern New Spain, 1700-1810*. Albuquerque: University of New Mexico Press, 1995.

Cutter, Donald C., ed. and trans. *The Defenses of Northern New Spain: Hugo O'Conor's Report to Teodoro de Croix, July 22, 1777*. Dallas: Southern Methodist University Press, 1994.

Cutter, Donald C., and Iris Engstrand. *Quest for Empire: Spanish Settlement in the Southwest*. Ann Arbor: Fulcrum, 1996.

Daniel, James M., and Pedro José de la Fuente, "Diary of Pedro José de la Fuente, Captain of the Presidio of El Paso del Norte, August–December 1765." *Southwestern Historical Quarterly* 83, no. 3 (Jan. 1980): 261–78.

Deeds, Susan M. *Defiance and Deference in Mexico's Colonial North, Indians under Spanish Rule in Nueva Vizcaya*. Austin: University of Texas Press, 2003.

de la Plaza Bores, Angel. *Archivo General de Simancas. Guia del investigador*. Madrid: Ministerio de Cultura, 1992.

Bibliography

de la Teja, Jesús. "Forgotten Founders: The Military Settlers in Eighteenth-Century San Antonio de Béxar." In *Tejano Origins in Eighteenth-Century San Antonio*, edited by Gerald E. Poyo and Gilberto M. Hinojosa, pp. 27–40. Austin: University of Texas Press, 1991.

———. *San Antonio de Bexar: A Community on New Spain's Northern Frontier* Albuquerque: University of New Mexico Press, 1996.

———. "Spanish Colonial Texas." In *New Views of Borderlands History*, edited by Robert H. Jackson, pp. 107–130. Albuquerque: University of New Mexico Press, 1998.

de la Teja, Jesús, and Ross Frank, eds. *Choice, Persuasion, and Coercion: Social Control on Spain's North American Frontiers*. Albuquerque: University of New Mexico Press, 2005.

de la Teja, Jesús, and John Wheat. "Béxar: Profile of a Tejano Community, 1820–1832." In *Tejano Origins in Eighteenth-Century San Antonio*, edited by Gerald E. Poyo and Gilberto M. Hinojosa, pp. 1–27. Austin: University of Texas Press, 1991.

———. "Ramón de Murillo's Plan for the Reform of New Spain's Frontier Defenses." *Southwestern Historical Quarterly* 107, no. 4 (April 2004): 501–33.

DeLay, Brian. *War of a Thousand Deserts: Indian Raids and the US Mexican War*. New Haven: Yale University Press, 2008.

Del Rio, Ignacio. *La aplicación regional de las reformas borbónicas en Nueva España, Sonora y Sinaloa, 1768–1787*. México, D.F.: Universidad Nacional Autónoma de México, 1995.

De Ville, Winston, and Jack Jackson, "Wilderness Apollo: Louis Badins's Immortalization of the Ouachita Militia's Confrontation with the Philip Nolan Expedition of 1800." *Southwestern Historical Quarterly* 92, no. 3 (Jan. 1989): 449–61.

Din, Gilbert C. *An Extraordinary Atlantic Life: Sebastián Nicolás Calvo de La Puerta y O'Farrill, Marqués de Casa-Calvo*. Lafayette: University of Louisiana at Lafayette Press, 2016.

Douglass, Carrie B. *Bulls, Bullfighting, and Spanish Identities*. Tucson: University of Arizona Press, 1997.

Dunn, William E. "Spanish Reaction against the French Advance toward New Mexico, 1717–1727." *Mississippi Valley Historical Review* 2, no. 3 (December 1915): 348–62.

Duvall, Tracy. *Drawing the Line. The Marqués de Rubí's Inspection of the Presidios, 1766–1772*. Self-published, 2020.

Eissa-Barroso, Francisco A. "Of Experience, Zeal, and Selflessness": Military Officers as Viceroys in Early Eighteen-Century Spanish America." *The Americas* 68, no. 3 (Jan. 2021): 317–45

Elguézabal, Juan Bautista. "Notes and Documents: A Description of Texas in 1803." Edited by Odie Faulk. *Southwestern Historical Quarterly* 66, no. 4 (April 1963): 513–15.

Elliot, John Huxtable. *Empires of the Atlantic World: Britain and Spain in America, 1492–1830*. New Haven: Yale University Press, 2006.

Faulk, Odie B. *The Last Years of Spanish Texas, 1778–1821*. The Hague: Mouton, 1964.

———. "Ranching in Spanish Texas." *Hispanic American Historical Review* 45, no. 2 (May 1965): 257–66.

———. *The Leather Jacket Soldier: Spanish Military Equipment and Institutions of the Late 18th Century*. Pasadena: Socio-Technical Publications, 1971.

Faulk, Odie B. and Laura E. Faulk, *Defenders of the Interior Provinces: Presidial Soldiers on the Northern Frontier of New Spain*. Albuquerque: The Albuquerque Museum, 1988.

Bibliography 405

Fireman, Janet R. *The Spanish Royal Corps of Engineers in the Western Borderlands: Instrument of Bourbon Reform 1764 to 1815*. Glendale: The Arthur H. Clark Company, 1977.

Fisher, Lillian Estelle. *The Intendant System in Spanish America*. New York: Gordian Press, 1969/1929.

———. *Viceregal Administration in the Spanish American Colonies*. New York: Russell & Russell, 1967/1926.

Fisher, Nora. "Colcha Embroidery." In *Rio Grande Textiles, Spanish Textile Traditions of New Mexico and Colorado*, compiled and edited by Nora Fisher. Santa Fé: Museum of New Mexico Press, 1994.

Flores, Dan L. "Bringing Home All the Pretty Horses: The Horse Trade and the Early American West, 1775–1825." *Montana: The Magazine of Western History* 58, no. 2 (Summer 2008): 3–21.

———. *Journal of an Indian Trader: Anthony Glass and the Texas Trading Frontier, 1790–1810*. College Station: Texas A&M University Press, 1985.

———, ed. *Southern Counterpart to Lewis & Clark: The Freeman & Custis Expedition of 1806*. Norman: University of Oklahoma Press, 1986.

Foster, William C. *Spanish Expeditions into Texas, 1689–1768*. Austin: University of Texas Press, 1995.

———. *The La Salle Expedition on the Mississippi River. A Lost Manuscript of Nicolas de La Salle, 1682*. Austin: Texas State Historical Association, 2003.

Fox, Anne A., Feris A. Bass Jr., and Thomas R. Hester. *The Archaeology and History of Alamo Plaza*. San Antonio: Center for Archaeological Research, The University of Texas at San Antonio, Archaeology Survey Report, No. 16, 1977.

Franco López, Pedro. *Breve relación del Nuevo Reino de Galicia y provincia de la Nueva Vizcaya de don Alonso de la Mota y Escobar*. Jalisco: El Colegio de Jalisco, 1996.

Frank, Larry and Skip Keith Miller. *A Land So Remote. Wooden Artifacts of Frontier New Mexico, 1700s–1900s*, vol. 3. Santa Fé: Red Crane Books, 2001.

Frank, Ross. "Demographic, Social, and Economic Change in New Mexico." In *New Views of Borderlands History*, edited by Robert Jackson, pp. 50–53. Albuquerque: University of New Mexico Press, 1998.

———. *From Settler to Citizen: New Mexican Economic Development and the Creation of Vecino Society, 1750–1820*. Berkeley: University of California Press, 2000.

Friedrichs, Irene Hohmann. *History of Goliad*. Victoria: Regal Printers, 1961.

Galán, Francis X. *Los Adaes, the First Capital of Spanish Texas*. College Station: Texas A&M University Press, 2020.

———. "Presidio Los Adaes: Worship, Kinship, and Commerce with French Natchitoches on the Spanish-Franco-Caddo Borderlands, 1721–1773." *Louisiana History: The Journal of the Louisiana Historical Association* 49, no. 2 (Spring 2008): 191–208.

Gálvez, Bernardo. *Instructions for Governing the Interior Provinces of New Spain, 1786*. Translated by Donald E. Worcester. Berkeley: The Quivira Society, 1951.

Gálvez, José de. *Informe General que en virtud de Real Orden Instruyó y Entregó el Excmo. Sr. Marqués de Sonora al Excmo. Sr. Virrey Frey D. Antonio Bucarely y Ursúa: Con fecha de 31 de Diciembre de 1771*. México, D.F.: Imprenta de Santiago White, 1867.

García Pérez, Rafael D. "Revisiting the America's Colonial Status under the Spanish Monarchy." In *New Horizons in Spanish Colonial Law*, edited by Thomas Duve and Heikki Pihlajamäki, pp. 29-74. Frankfurt: Max Planck Institute for Legal History and Legal Theory, 2015.

García Ruiz, Jorge Luis and Antonio Gragera. *San Antonio de Valero. Libro de Casamientos de la Misión, 1709-1788, vol. 3.* Self-published, 2022.

Gatschet, Albert Samuel. *The Karankawa Indians, the Coast People of Texas.* Cambridge, MA: Peabody Museum, 1891.

George, W. Eugene. *Lost Architecture of the Rio Grande Borderlands.* College Station: Texas A&M University Press, 2008.

Gómez Pérez, Carmen. "La recluta en el ejército de América." In *Aportaciones militares a la cultura, arte y ciencia en el siglo xviii hispanoamericano*, pp. 79-84. Sevilla: Capitanía General de la Región Militar Sur, 1993.

González, Anibal. "The Legend of Joseph de Urrutia." *Sayersville Historical Association Bulletin* 6 (Summer 1985): 14-19.

Gould, Eliga H. "Entangled Histories, Entangled Worlds." *American Historical Review* 112, no. 3 (June 2007): 64-86.

Gregory, H. F., George Avery, Aubra L. Lee, and Jay C. Blaine. "Presidio Los Adaes: Spanish, French, and Caddoan Interaction on the Northern Frontier." In "Presidios of the North American Spanish Borderlands," edited by J. A. Bense. Special issue, *Historical Archaeology* 38, no. 3 (2004): 65-77.

Griffen, William B. *Apaches at War and Peace: The Janos Presidio, 1750-1858.* Norman: University of Oklahoma Press, 1988.

Guice, Norman. "Texas in 1804." *Southwestern Historical Quarterly* 59, no. 1 (July 1955): 46-56.

Guy, Donna J. and Thomas E. Sheridan, eds. *Contested Ground: Comparative Frontiers on the Northern and Southern Edges of the Spanish Empire.* Tucson: University of Arizona, 1998.

Habig, Marion. *The Alamo Chain of Missions: A History of San Antonio's Five Old Missions.* Chicago: Franciscan Herald Press, 1968.

———. *San Antonio's Mission San José.* Chicago: Franciscan Herald Press, 1968.

Hackett, Charles W., ed. *Historical Documents relating to Mexico, Nueva Vizcaya, and Approaches Thereto, to 1773.* Vols. 1, 2, and 3. Washington, DC: Carnegie Institution of Washington, 1923-37.

———. "The Marquis of San Miguel de Aguayo and His Recovery of Texas from the French, 1719-1723." *Southwestern Historical Quarterly* 49, no. 2 (Oct. 1945): 193-214.

Hackett, Charles W. and José Antonio Pichardo. *Pichardo's Treatise on the Limits of Louisiana and Texas.* Vols. 1 and 2. Austin: University of Texas Press, 1931, 1934.

Hadley, Diana, Thomas H. Naylor, and Mardith K. Schuetz-Miller. *The Presidio and the Militia on the Northern Frontier of New Spain: A Documentary History.* Vol. 2, part 2, *The Central Corridor and the Texas Corridor, 1700-1765.* Tucson: University of Arizona Press, 1997.

Hämäläinen, Pekka. *The Comanche Empire.* New Haven: Yale University Press, 2008.

Hart, Stephen Harding, and Archer Butler, eds., *The Southwestern Journals of Zebulon Pike, 1806-1807.* Albuquerque: University of New Mexico Press, 2007.

Hatcher, Mattie Austin. "The Louisiana Background of the Colonization of Texas, 1763-1803." *Southwestern Historical Quarterly* 24, no. 3 (January 1921): 170-71.

Hendricks, Rick. *New Mexico in 1801: The Priests Report.* Los Ranchos de Albuquerque: Rio Grande Books, 2008.

Bibliography

Heredia Herrera, Antonio. *Fuentes para la historia militar en los archivos espanoles.* Sevilla: Capitanía General de la Región Militar Sur, 1996

Hinojosa, Gilberto Miguel. *A Borderlands Town in Transition. Laredo, 1755–1870.* College Station: Texas A&M University Press, 1983.

Hodge, Frederick W. *Handbook of American Indians North of Mexico, I & II.* New York: Pageant, 1959.

Holmes, Jack D. L. "The Marqués de Casa-Calvo, Nicolás DeFiniels, and the 1805 Spanish Expedition through East Texas and Louisiana." *Southwestern Historical Quarterly* 69, no. 3 (Jan. 1966): 329–39.

Holmes, Sarah A., Sandra T. Welch and Laura R. Knudson. "The Role of Accounting Practices in the Disempowerment of the Coahuiltecan Indians," in *Accounting Historians Journal*, 32, Issue 2 (December 2005).

Houck, Louis. *The Spanish Regime in Missouri: A Collection of Papers and Documents Relating to Upper Louisiana during the Dominion of Spain.* Chicago: R.R. Donnelley & Sons, 1909.

Islas Escarcega, Leovigildo, and Rodolfo Garcia Bravo y Olivera. *Diccionario y refranero charro, el caballo de raza Azteca en la charrería.* México, D.F.: Editores Asociados Mexicanos, S.A. de C.V., 1992.

Ivey, James E. "The Presidio of San Antonio de Béxar: Historical and Archaeological Research." In "Presidios of the North American Spanish Borderlands," edited by J. A. Bense. Special issue, *Historical Archaeology* 38, no. 3 (2004): 106–20.

Jackson, Jack. "The 1780 Cabello Map: New Evidence That There Were Two Mission Rosarios, and a Possible Correction on the Site of El Fuerte del Cíbolo." *Southwestern Historical Quarterly* 107, no. 2 (Oct. 2003): 202–16.

———. *Almonte's Texas.* Translated by John Wheat. Austin: Texas State Historical Association, 2003.

———. *Los Mesteños: Spanish Ranching in Texas, 1721–1821.* College Station: Texas A&M University Press, 1986.

Jackson, Jack, and William C. Foster. *Imaginary Kingdom: Texas as Seen by the Rivera and Rubí Military Expeditions, 1727 and 1767.* Austin: Texas State Historical Association, 1995.

Jackson, Robert, ed. *New Views of Borderlands History.* Albuquerque: University of New Mexico Press, 1998.

Janin, Hunt, and Ursula Carlson. *Trails of Historic New Mexico: Routes Used by Indian, Spanish, and American Travelers through 1886.* Jefferson: McFarland & Co., 2010.

Jefferson, Thomas, Daniel Clark Jr., James Wilkenson, and William Dunbar. "Concerning Philip Nolan." *Quarterly of the Texas State Historical Association* 7, no. 4 (April 1904): 308–17.

John, Elizabeth A. H. *Storms Brewed in Other Men's Worlds: The Confrontation of Indians, Spanish, and French in the Southwest, 1540–1795.* College Station: Texas A&M University Press, 1975.

———. Adán Benavides Jr., Pedro Vial, and Francisco Xavier Chaves. "Inside the Comanchería, 1785: The Diary of Pedro Vial and Francisco Xavier Chaves." *Southwestern Historical Quarterly* 98, no. 1 (July 1994): 26–56.

———. and John Wheat. "Governing Texas, 1779: The Karankawa Aspect," *Southwestern Historical Quarterly* 104, no. 4 (April 2001): 560–76.

Jones, Oakah L. *Nueva Vizcaya: Heartland of the Spanish Frontier.* Albuquerque: University of New Mexico Press, 1988.

Jordan, Terry G. *North American Cattle-Ranching Frontiers: Origins, Diffusion, and Differentiation*. Albuquerque: University of New Mexico Press, 1993.

Juarez, Paola, and Reidezel Mendoza. *Ni presidio ni misión. Historia de la capilla de San José de Paso del Norte*. Chihuahua: Self-published, 2021.

Kavanagh, Thomas W. *Comanche Political History: An Ethnohistorical Perspective, 1706–1875*. Lincoln: University of Nebraska Press, 1996.

———. *The Comanches: A History, 1706–1875*. Lincoln: University of Nebraska Press, 1999.

Kessell, John L. *Kiva, Cross, and Crown. The Pecos Indians and New Mexico, 1540–1840*. Washington, DC: National Park Service, 1979.

———. *Remote Beyond Compare. Letters of don Diego de Vargas to his Family from New Spain and New Mexico, 1675–1706*. Albuquerque: University of New Mexico Press, 1989.

———. "The Puzzling Presidio: San Phelipe de Guevavi, alias Terrenate" in *New Mexico Historical Review* 41, (Jan., 1966): 21–46.

Kicza, John E. *Resilient Cultures: America's Native Peoples Confront European Colonization, 1500–1800*. Upper Saddle River: Prentice-Hall, 2003.

Kimbell, Bennett R. "El Baluarte del Sur: Archeological and Historical Investigations of the Southeast Bastion at Presidio San Sabá (41MNI), Menard County, Texas." *Bulletin of the Texas Archeological Society* 81 (2010): 1–102.

Knowles, Thomas W. *They Rode for the Lone Star: The Saga of the Texas Rangers*. Dallas: Taylor, 1999.

Kuethe, Alan J., and Kenneth J. Andrien, *The Spanish Atlantic World in the Eighteenth Century, War, and the Bourbon Reforms, 1713–1796*. New York: Cambridge University Press, 2014.

Kuethe, Alan J., and Juan Marchena Fernández, eds. *Soldados del rey, el ejército borbónico en América colonial en vísperas de la independencia*. Seville: Universitat Jaume, 2005.

Lafora, Nicolás, and Vito Alessio Robles, *Relación del viaje que hizo a los presidios internos situados en la frontera de la América septentrional*. México, D. F.: Editorial Pedro Robredo, 1939.

———. Lawrence Kinnaird, *The Frontiers of New Spain, Nicolás de Lafora's Description 1766–1768*. Berkeley: The Quivira Society, 1958.

Lagarde, Francois, ed. *The French in Texas*. Austin: University of Texas Press, 2003.

Langelier, John Phillip. *El Presidio de San Francisco: A History under Spain and Mexico, 1776–1846*. Denver: US Department of the Interior, National Park Service, 1992.

La Vere, David. "Between Kinship and Capitalism: French and Spanish Rivalry in the Colonial Louisiana–Texas Indian Trade." *Journal of Southern History* 64, no. 2 (May 1998): 197–218.

Lepe, José I. *Diccionario enciclopédico sobre asuntos ecuestres e hípicos*. Mexico, D.F.: Editorial Porrua, S.A., 1972/1951.

Liebmann, Matthew. *Revolt: An Archaeological History of Pueblo Resistance and Revitalization in 17th Century New Mexico*. Tucson: University of Arizona Press, 2012.

———. T. J. Ferguson, and Robert W. Preucel. "Pueblo Settlement, Architecture, and Social Change in the Pueblo Revolt Era, A.D. 1680–1696." *Journal of Field Archaeology* 30, no. 1 (Spring 2005): 45–60.

Lightfoot, Kent G. "Russian Colonization: The Implications of Mercantile Colonial Practices in the North Pacific." *Historical Archaeology* 37, no. 4 (2003): 14–28.

Bibliography

Loomis, Noel M., and Abraham P. Nasatir. *Pedro Vial and the Roads to Santa Fé*. Norman: University of Oklahoma Press, 1967.

Looscan, Adele B., Julia Lee Sinks, and Lester G. Bugbee. "Notes and Fragments." *Quarterly of the Texas State Historical Association* 2, no. 3 (Jan. 1899): 243–47.

López Cancelada, Juan. *Ruina de la Nueva España si se declara el comercio libre con los extrangeros*. Cádiz: Manuel Santiago de Quintana, 1811.

Machado Carilla, José Luis. *Familias canarias en el poblamiento de La Luisiana de Bernardo de Gálvez*. Self-published, 2023.

MacMillan, Esther. *San Antonio in the Eighteenth Century*. San Antonio: San Antonio Bicentennial Heritage Committee, 1976.

Mantilla Trolle, Marina, and Rafael Diego-Fernández Sotelo and Agustín Moreno Torres. *Real Ordenanza para el establecimiento é instrucción de intendentes de exército y provincia en el reino de la Nueva España*, 1786. Guadalajara: Universidad de Guadalajara, 2008.

Marchena Fernández, Juan. "Capital, crédito e intereses comerciales a fines del periodo colonial: los costos del sistema defensivo americano, Cartagena de Indias y el sur del Caribe." In *Tiempos de America, Revista de Historia, Cultura, y Territorio*. No. 9. Sevilla: Universitat Jaume, 2002.

———. *Oficiales y soldados en el ejército de América*. Sevilla: Escuela de Estudios Hispano-Americanos de Sevilla, 1983.

———. *La vida de guarnición en las ciudades americanas de la ilustración*. Sevilla: Ministerio de Defensa, 1992.

Marchena Fernández, Juan, and Manuel Chust, eds. *Por la fuerza de las armas, ejército e independencias en Iberoamérica*. Castelló de la Plana: Publicaciones de la Universitat Jaume I, 2007.

Martínez, Leroy. *From Across the Spanish Empire: Spanish Soldiers Who Helped Win the American Revolutionary War, 1776–1783. Arizona, California, Louisiana, New Mexico, and Texas Military Rosters*. Baltimore: Genealogical Publishing Company, 2015.

Martínez de Salinas, María Luisa. *La implantación del impuesto del papel sellado en Indias*. Caracas: Academia Nacional de la Historia, 1986.

Martiré, Eduardo. *1808 La clave de la emancipación hispanoamericana*. Buenos Aires: El Elefante Blanco, 2002.

———. *Las Audiencias y la Administración de Justicia en Las Indias, Del judex perfectus al judex solutus*. Madrid: Universidad Autónoma de Madrid, 2005.

Marshall, Joseph M. *The Day the World Ended at Little Big Horn*. New York: Viking Penguin, 2007.

McAlister, Kyle N. *The "Fuero Militar" in New Spain, 1764–1800*. Westport: Greenwood Press, 1957.

McCarty, Kieran, and Mark Santiago. "The Founder of Spanish Tucson Petitions the King: Don Hugo O'Conor's 1770 'Relacion.'" *Journal of Arizona History* 39, no. 1 (Spring 1998): 85–98.

McCollough, Martha. *Three Nations, One Place: A Comparative Ethnohistory of Social Change among the Comanches and Hasinais during Spain's Colonial Era, 1689–1821*. New York: Routledge, 2004.

———. "Reasons for the Marginal Incorporation of the Comanches by the Spanish," in *Great Plains Research* 12, no. 2 (Fall 2002): 369–383.

Bibliography

McDermott, John Francis, ed. *The Spanish in the Mississippi Valley, 1762-1804.* Urbana: University of Illinois Press, 1974.

McKenzie, C.M.M., C. Munoz, and R. Mauldin. (2020). *Archival and Historical Review of the Children's Hospital of San Antonio Property, Downtown, San Antonio, Bexar County, Texas.* Special Report No. 35. Center for Archaeological Research, The University of Texas at San Antonio.

Mecham, J. Lloyd. *Francisco de Ibarra and New Vizcaya.* Durham: Duke University Press, 1927.

Meyer, Michael C. *Water in the Hispanic Southwest: A Social and Legal History, 1550-1850.* Tucson: University of Arizona Press, 1984.

Mills, Elizabeth Shown, and Ellie Lennon. *Natchitoches Colonials: A Source Book: Censuses, Military Rolls & Tax Lists, 1722-1803.* Baltimore: Genealogical Publishing Co., 2017.

Mills, Patti A. "Financial Reporting and Stewardship Accounting in Sixteenth-Century Spain." *Accounting Historians Journal* 13, no. 2 (Fall 1986): 65-76.

———. "The Probative Capacity of Accounts in Early-Modern Spain." *Accounting Historians Journal* 14, no. 1 (Spring 1987): 95-108.

Moorhead, Max. *The Apache Frontier, Jacobo Ugarte and Spanish-Indian Relations in Northern New Spain, 1769-1791.* Norman: University of Oklahoma Press, 1968.

———. *The Presidio: Bastion of the Spanish Borderlands.* Norman: University of Oklahoma Press, 1975.

———. "The Private Contract System of Presidio Supply in Northern New Spain." *Hispanic American Historical Review* 41, no. 1 (Feb. 1961): 31-54.

———. "The Soldado de Cuera: Stalwart of the Spanish Borderlands." *Journal of the West* 8, no. 1 (Jan. 1969): 38-55.

Morales, Francisco, O.F.M. *Ethnic and Social Background of the Franciscan Friars in Seventeenth Century Mexico.* Washington, D.C.: Academy of American Franciscan History, 1973.

Moreno, Frank Jay. "A Spanish Colonial System: A Functional Approach." *Western Historical Quarterly* 20, no. 2, part 1 (June 1967): 308-20.

Morfi, Fray Juan Agustín. *History of Texas 1673-1779.* Translated by Carlos Eduardo Castañeda. Albuquerque: The Quivira Society, 1935.

———. *Relacion geográfica e histórica de la provincia de Texas o Nuevas Filipinas, 1673-1779.* Edited by Guadalupe Curiel Defossé. México, D.F: Dirección de Publicaciones del Consejo Nacional para la Cultura y las Artes, 2010.

Munford, Clarence J., and Michael Zeuske. "Black Slavery, Class Struggle, Fear and Revolution in St. Domingue and Cuba, 1785-1795." *Journal of Negro History* 73, no. 1/4 (Winter-Autumn, 1988): 12-32.

Navarro García, Luis. "*La expansión de las fronteras indianas en el siglo XVIII.*" In *Aportaciones militares a la cultura, arte y ciencia en el siglo xviii hispanoamericano*, pp. 227-28. Sevilla: Capitanía General de la Región Militar Sur, 1993.

———. *Don José de Gálvez y la comandancia general de las provincias internas del norte de Nueva España.* Sevilla: Escuela de Estudios Hispano-Americanos, 1964.

———. *Las provincias internas en el siglo xix.* Sevilla: Escuela de estudios hispano-americanos de Sevilla, 1965.

———. *Las reformas borbónicas en América. El plan de intendencias y su aplicación.* Sevilla: Universidad de Sevilla, 1995.

Bibliography

Naylor, Thomas H., and Charles W. Polzer. *Pedro Rivera and the Military Regulations for Northern New Spain, 1724–1729*. Tucson: University of Arizona Press, 1988.

Nieto-Phillips, John. *The Language of Blood: The Making of Spanish-American Identity in New Mexico, 1880s–1930s*. Albuquerque: University of New Mexico Press, 2008.

O'Connor, Kathryn Stoner. *The Presidio La Bahía del Espíritu Santo de Zuñiga, 1721–1846*. Austin: Von Boeckmann–Jones, 1966.

Ortelli, Sara. *Trama de una guerra conveniente: Nueva Vizcaya y la sombra de los apaches (1748–1791)*. México, D.F.: Centro de Estudios Históricos, El Colegio de México, 2007.

Ozanam, Didier. *Los capitanes y comandantes generales de provincias en la España del siglo XVIII*. Córdoba: Servicio de publicaciones, Universidad de Córdoba, 2008.

Norris, Lola Orellano, and Israel Cavazos Garza. *General Alonso de Leon's Expeditions into Texas, 1686–1690*. College Station: Texas A&M University Press, 2017.

Paquette, Gabriel B. *Enlightenment, Governance, and Reform in Spain and Its Empire, 1759–1808*. Cambridge: Palgrave Macmillan, 2008.

Pérez, Alexander Joseph. *Karankawa Kadla - mixed tongue - : Medicine for the Land & our Peoples*. Charleston: Palmetto Publishing, 2021.

Pezzi, Rafael. *Los presidios menores de África y la influencia española en El Rif*. Madrid: La Real Academia de La Historia, 1893.

Phelan, John Leddy. "Authority and Flexibility in the Spanish Imperial Bureaucracy." *Administrative Science Quarterly* 5, no. 1 (June 1960): 47–65.

Pietschmann, Horst. *Las reformas borbónicas y el sistema de intendencias en Nueva España*. Rolf Roland Meyer Misteli, trans. México, D.F.: Fondo de Cultura Económica, 1996.

Polzer, Charles W., and Thomas E. Sheridan, *The Presidio and the Militia on the Northern Frontier of New Spain: A Documentary History*. Vol. 2, part 1, *The Californias and Sinaloa-Sonora, 1700–1765*. Tucson: University of Arizona Press, 1997.

Porrua Turanzas, José, José Manuel, and Enrique Porrua Venero, eds. *Documentos para la historia eclesiástica y civil de la provincia de Texas o Nuevas Philipinas, 1720–1779*. Madrid: Ediciones José Porrúa Turanzas, 1961.

Porter, Eugene. *San Elizario, A History*. Austin: The Pemberton Press, 1973.

Portugués, Joseph Antonio. *Colección general de las ordenanzas militares, sus innovaciones, y aditamientos dispuesta en diez tomos, con separación de clases*. Vol. 2. Madrid: Antonio Marín, 1764.

Poyo, Gerald E., and Gilberto M. Hinojosa, eds. *Tejano Origins in Eighteenth-Century San Antonio*. Austin: University of Texas Press, 1991.

Priestley, Herbert Ingram. *José de Gálvez, Visitor-General of New Spain (1765–1771)*. Vol. 5. Berkeley: University of California Press, 1916.

Quesada, Alejandro de. *Spanish Colonial Fortificaciones in North America, 1565–1822*. Oxford: Osprey Publishing, 2010.

Radding, Cynthia. *Landscapes of Power and Identity. Comparative Histories in the Sonoran Desert and the Forests of Amazonia from Colony to Republic*. Durham: Duke University Press, 2005.

———. *Wandering Peoples. Colonialism, Ethnic Spaces, and Ecological Frontiers in Northwestern Mexico, 1700–1850*. Durham: Duke University Press, 1997.

Rama, Ángel. *The Lettered City*. Edited and translated by John Charles Chasteen. Durham: Duke University Press, 1996.

Bibliography

Ramón, Regino F. *Historia General del Estado de Coahuila*. Saltillo: Leonor Ramón de Garza, 1990.

Ramos de Arizpe, Jose Miguel, Nettie Lee Benson, tran. R*eport on the Natural, Political and Civil Condition of the provinces of Coahuila, Nuevo León, Nuevo Santander and Texas of the Four Eastern Provinces of the Kingdom of Mexico, with an Exposition of the Defects of the System in General, Especially the Government, and of the Reforms and Improvements Necessary to their Prosperity*. Austin: The University of Texas Press, 1950/1812.

Rangel Silva, José Alfredo. "Milicias en el oriente de San Luis Potosí, 1793-1813." In *Las armas de la nación. Independencia y ciudadanía en hispanoamérica (1750-1850)*, edited by Manuel Chust and Juan Marchena, Madrid: Iberoamericana, 2007.

Reinhartz, Dennis and Gerald D. Saxon, eds.. *The Mapping of the Entradas into the Greater Southwest*. Norman: University of Oklahoma Press, 1995.

Reparaz, Carmen de. *I Alone: Bernardo de Gálvez and the Taking of Pensacola*. Translated by Walter Rubin. Madrid: Ediciones de Cultura Hispánica, 1993.

Reséndez, Andrés. *Changing National Identities at the Frontier: Texas and New Mexico, 1800-1850*. New York: Cambridge University Press, 2004.

Ricklis, Robert A. *The Karankawa Indians of Texas: An Ecological Study of Cultural Tradition and Change*. Austin: University of Texas Press, 1996.

Robertson, James Alexander. *Louisiana under the Rule of Spain, France, and the United States, 1785-1807*. Vol. 1 and 2. Cleveland: The Arthur H. Clark Company, 1911.

Rodríguez de la Flor, Fernando, German Labrador Méndez, and Patricia A. Marshall. "Baroque Toxicology: Discourses on Smoke and the Polemics of Tobacco in 17th Century Spain." In "Cultural Studies in the Spanish Golden Age," edited by Elena del Río Parro. Special issue, *South Atlantic Review* 72, no. 1 (Winter 2007): 112-42.

Rodríguez García, Vicente. *El Fiscal de Real Hacienda en Nueva España (Don Ramón de Posada y Soto, 1781-1793)*. Oviedo: Secretariado de publicaciones de la Universidad de Oviedo, 1985.

Rodríguez O., Jaime E. *Mexico in the Age of Democratic Revolutions, 1750-1850*. Boulder: Lynne Rienner, 1994.

Rubio Mañé, José Ignacio. "Nota Introductoria" in "El Teniente Coronel Don Hugo O'Conor y la situación en Chihuahua, 1771" and "Itinerario del Teniente Coronel Don Hugo O'Conor, de la Ciudad de México a la villa de Chihuahua, 1771." *Boletín del Archivo General de la Nación* 30 (1959): 355-91, 395-471, 647-55.

———. *El virreinato III. Expansión y defensa. Segunda parte*. México, D.F.: Fondo de Cultura Económica, Universidad Nacional Autónoma de Mexico, 1983a.

———. *El virreinato IV. Obras públicas y educación universitaria*. México, D.F.: Fondo de Cultura Económica, Universidad Nacional Autónoma de México, 1983b.

Saavedra Fajardo, Diego de. *Idea de un príncipe político cristiano representada en cien empresas*, vol. 2., Vicente García de Diego, ed. Madrid: Espasa-Calpe, S.A., 1955.

Sánchez, Joseph P. *Spanish Bluecoats. The Catalonian Volunteers in Northwestern New Spain, 1767-1810*. Albuquerque: University of New Press, 1990.

———. Robert L. Spude, and Art Gomez. *New Mexico: A History*. Norman: University of Oklahoma Press, 2013.

Sánchez Rodríguez, David. *Soldados del Rey (1508-1524)*. Self-published, 2006.

Santiago, Mark. *A Bad Peace and a Good War: Spain and the Mescalero Apache Uprising of 1795-1799*. Norman: University of Oklahoma Press, 2018.

Bibliography

———. *The Red Captain: The Life of Hugo O'Conor.* Tucson: Arizona Historical Society, 1994

———. "The Spanish Drummer Boy: A Glimpse of Soldier Life on the Apache Frontier." *Journal of Arizona History* 47, no. 4 (Winter 2006): 367–86.

Sanz, Raimundo de, Francisco Gago Jover, and F. Tejedo Herrero, eds. *Diccionario Militar.* Zaragoza: Institución Fernando el Católico, 2007/1749.

Schilz, Thomas Frank, and Donald E. Worcester. "The Spread of Firearms among the Indian Tribes on the Northern Frontier of New Spain." *American Indian Quarterly* 11, no. 1 (Winter 1987): 1–10.

Secoy, Frank Raymond. *Changing Military Patterns of the Great Plains Indians.* Lincoln: University of Nebraska Press, 1953.

Segovia, Rodolfo. *Las Fortificaciones de Cartagena de Indias.* Bogotá: El Áncora Editores, 2009.

Sellers-García, Sylvia. *Distance and Documents at the Spanish Empire's Periphery.* Stanford: Stanford University Press, 2014.

Seymour, Deni J. and Oscar Rodriguez. *To the Corner of the Province: The 1780 Ugarte-Rocha Sonoran Reconnaissance and Implications for Environmental & Cultural Change.* Salt Lake City: The University of Utah Press, 2020.

Simmons, Marc. *Spanish Pathways. Readings in the History of Hispanic New Mexico.* Albuquerque: University of New Mexico Press, 2001.

Simpson, Leslie Byrd, ed., and Paul Nathan, trans. *The San Sabá Papers: A Documentary Account of the Founding and Destruction of San Sabá Mission.* Dallas: Southern Methodist University Press, 2000 (1959).

Sims, Harold Dana. *The Expulsion of Mexico's Spaniards, 1821–1836.* Pittsburgh: University of Pittsburgh, 1990.

Smith, F. Todd. "Athanase de Mézières and the French in Texas, 1750–1803." In *The French in Texas*, edited by Francois Lagarde. Austin: University of Texas Press, 2003.

———. *The Caddo Indians: Tribes at the Convergence of Empires, 1542–1854.* College Station: Texas A&M University Press, 1995.

———. *The Wichita Indians. Traders of Texas and the Southern Plains, 1540–1845.* College Station: Texas A&M University Press, 2000.

Smith, Fay Jackson. *Captain of the Phantom Presidio: A History of the Presidio of Fronteras, Sonora, New Spain 1686–1735.* Spokane: The Arthur H. Clark Company, 1993.

Smith, Robert Sidney. "Sales Taxes in New Spain, 1575–1770." *Hispanic American Historical Review* 28, no. 1 (Feb. 1948): 2–37.

Stein, Stanley J. and Barbara H. Stein, *Apogee of Empire: Spain and New Spain in the Age of Charles III, 1759–1789.* Baltimore: Johns Hopkins University Press, 2003.

Stern, Peter. "Marginals and Acculturation in Frontier Society." In *New Views of Borderlands History*, edited by Robert Jackson, pp. 157–88. Albuquerque: University of New Mexico Press, 1998.

Stevens, Donald Fithian. *Origins of Instability in Early Republican Mexico.* Durham: Duke University Press, 1991.

Temkin, Samuel. *Luis de Carvajal. The Origins of Nuevo Reino de León.* Santa Fé: Sunstone Press, 2011.

Bibliography

Thomas, Alfred Barnaby. *Forgotten Frontiers: A Study of the Spanish Indian Policy of Don Juan Bautista de Anza Governor of New Mexico, 1777-1787*. Norman: University of New Mexico Press, 1932.

————. *Teodor de Croix and the Northern Frontier of New Spain, 1776-1783*. Norman: University of Oklahoma Press, 1941.

Thompson, Jerry D., and Lawrence T. Jones III. *Civil War and Revolution on the Rio Grande Frontier: A Narrative and Photographic History*. Austin: Texas State Historical Association, 2004.

Thonhoff, Robert H. *El Fuerte del Cíbolo, Sentinel of the Béxar-La Bahía Ranches*. Austin: Eakin Press, 1992.

Tigges, Linda, ed., and J. Richard Salazar, trans. *Spanish Colonial Lives, Documents from the Spanish Colonial Archives of New Mexico, 1705-1774*. Santa Fé: Sunstone Press, 2013.

Tijerina, Andrés. *Tejanos and Texans under the Mexican Flag, 1821-1836*. College Station: Texas A&M University Press, 1994.

Topik, Steven C., Carlos Marichal, and Zephyr Frank. *From Silver to Cocaine: Latin American Commodity Chains and the Building of the World Economy, 1500-2000*. Durham: Duke University Press, 2006.

Turpin, Solveig A. and Herbert H. Eling, Jr. "Aguaverde: A Forgotten Presidio of the Line, 1773-1781." *Journal of Big Bend Studies*, Volume 16: 83-128. Alpine: Center for Big Bend Studies, Sul Ross State University, 2004.

Twitchell, Ralph Emerson. *The Spanish Archives of New Mexico*, vol. 2. Cedar Rapids: Torch Press, 1914.

Velázquez, María del Carmen. *Establecimiento y pérdida del Septentrión de Nueva España*. México, D.F.: El Colegio de México, 1997.

————. *El estado de guerra en nueva españa, 1760-1808*. México, D.F.: El Colegio de México, 1950.

————. *La frontera norte y la experiencia colonial*. México, D.F.: Secretaría de Relaciones Exteriores, 1982.

Victoria Ojeda, Jorge. *Las tropas auxiliares de Carlos IV. De Saint-Domingue al Mundo Hispano*. Castelló de la Plana: Publicaciones de la Universitat Jaume, 2011.

Villasana Haggard, Juan. "The House of Barr and Davenport." *Southwestern Historical Quarterly* 49, no. 1 (July 1945): 66-88.

————. *Handbook for Translators of Spanish Historical Documents*. Austin: Archives Collections, University of Texas, 1941.

Vinson, Ben. *Bearing Arms for His Majesty: The Free-Colored Militia in Colonial Mexico*. Stanford: Stanford University Press, 2001.

Vizcarra, Catalina. "Bourbon Intervention in the Peruvian Tobacco Industry, 1752-1813." *Journal of Latin American Studies* 39, no.3 (Aug. 2007): 567-93.

Voss, Barbara L. *The Archaeology of Ethnogenesis: Race and Sexuality in Colonial San Francisco*. Berkeley: University of California Press, 2008.

Walter, Tamra L. "The Archaeology of Presidio San Sabá: A Preliminary Report." In "Presidios of the North American Spanish Borderlands," edited by J. A. Bense. Special issue, *Historical Archaeology* 38, no. 3 (2004): 94-105.

Warner, Ted J., ed., and Fray Angélico Chávez, trans. *The Domínguez-Escalante Journal: Their Expedition through Colorado, Utah, Arizona, and New Mexico in 1776*. Salt Lake City: University of Utah Press, 1995.

Bibliography

Weber, David J. *The Spanish Frontier in North America*. New Haven: Yale University Press, 1992.

Weddle, Robert S., and Carol Lipscomb, trans. *After the Massacre. The Violent Legacy of the San Sabá Mission*. Lubbock: Texas Tech University Press, 2007.

———. *San Juan Bautista: Gateway to Spanish Texas*. Austin: University of Texas Press, 1999.

———. *The San Sabá Mission: Spanish Pivot in Texas*. Austin: University of Texas Press, 1964.

———., and Mary Christine Morkovsky, and Patricia Galloway, eds. *La Salle, the Mississippi, and the Gulf: Three Primary Documents*. College Station: Texas A&M University Press, 1987.

Weeks, Charles A. *Paths to a Middle Ground: The Diplomacy of Natchez, Boukfouka, Nogales, and San Fernando de las Barrancas, 1791-1795*. Tuscaloosa: University of Alabama Press, 2005.

West, Elizabeth Howard, and Marqués de Altamira, "Bonilla's Brief Compendium of the History of Texas, 1772 (an Annotated Translation)." *Quarterly of the Texas State Historical Association* 8, no. 1 (July 1904): 3–78.

Whitaker, Arthur Preston. "Godoy's Knowledge of the Terms of Jay's Treaty." *American Historical Review* 35, no. 4 (July 1930): 804-10.

———. "New Light on the Treaty of San Lorenzo: An Essay in Historical Criticism." *Mississippi Valley Historical Review* 15, no. 4 (March 1929): 435-54.

Williams, Caroline A., ed. *Bridging the Early Modern Atlantic World: People, Products, and Practices on the Move*. Farnham: Ashgate, 2009.

Williams, Jack S. "The Evolution of the Presidio in Northern New Spain." In "Presidios of the North American Spanish Borderlands," edited by J. A. Bense. Special issue, *Historical Archaeology* 38, no. 3 (2004): 6–23.

Wilson, Maurine T., and Jack Jackson. *Philip Nolan and Texas: Expeditions to the Unknown Land, 1791-1801*. Waco: Texian Press, 1987.

Wolff, Thomas. "The Karankawa Indians: Their Conflict with the White Man in Texas." *Ethnohistory* 16, no. 1 (Winter 1969): 1–32.

Woodward, Ralph Lee. "Spanish Commercial Policy in Louisiana, 1763-1803." *Louisiana History: The Journal of the Louisiana Historical Association* 44, no. 2 (Spring 2003): 133–64.

Wunder, John R. "'That No Thorn Will Pierce Our Friendship': The Ute-Comanche Treaty of 1786." *Western Historical Quarterly* 42, no. 1 (Spring 2011): 4–27.

Yetman, David. *Conflict in Colonial Sonora. Indians, Priests, and Settlers*. Albuquerque: University of New Mexico Press, 2012.

Index

Álamo de Parras *compañía volante*, 27, 234
Alange, Conde del Campo de: and royal
order related to military courts, 182;
military reports to, 184
alférez (second lieutenant), 45
Álvarez Tuñón y Quirós, Gregorio, 2; captain
at the Fronteras (Sonora) presidio, 2;
misconduct of, 2
Amangual, Francisco (lieutenant; paymaster): accused by Zambrano, José Macario
(merchant), for breach of contract, 56–57,
68–70; and *Fondo de Gratificación*, 109;
and incident related to drunken Urrutia,
Manuel de (first *alférez*), 65–68; and
Mesteñas fund, 64, 72; appointed to head
Presidio La Bahía by Governor Salcedo,
247; as borderlands operative (1770-1808),
2; as fiduciary, 12; assigned to the San
Antonio de Béxar presidio, 45; believed
Comanches killed Rondein, Juan, 29;
born in Mallorca, 45; commander of
the Segunda *Compañía Volante de* San
Carlos de Parras, 1, 23; complaint filed by
Menchaca, Joaquín, against, 60; debts of,
45–46; discovery of contraband tobacco,
28; died (1812), 284; expected integrity
and honor of *habilitado*, 54; expedition
across Indigenous and European territories, 1, 251; expenditures from *Mesteñas*
fund for Indigenous groups, 109–10; gift
of cigars to Captains Sojas and Soquina
(Comanche), 71; given the position of
paymaster (1788), 45; Governor Cabello
depended on, 83; *habilitado* (elected
paymaster, 1788), 1, 2, 54; high deference
to superiors, 11; killed twenty-six Comanches, 45; led sorties against Comanches,
31; married Los Reyes y García, María
Trinidad de, 283; member of the Batavian Regimen of Dragoons (*Dragones
de España*), 45; on actions taken against
Rodríguez, Mariano (sergeant), 74–76; on
habilitados privilege of extracting a commission on goods, 57; on reimbursement
of *Fondo de Mesteña*, 72–73; ordered to
stop paying drafts without prior authorization by Governor Muñoz, Manuel, 72;
over a decade of participating in the army
in the Iberian peninsula, 63; participated
in the Sonora Expedition (1767–71), 45;
paymaster role and significance to borderlands commerce, 53; *presidial* (presidio
soldier), 1; promoted to second lieutenant,
61; promoted to sergeant (1774), 45; raids
against Comanches, 30, 31; report on
itemized payments, 73–74; responsibilities
as paymaster, 2; responsibilities of the
habilitado, 54; returned to Béxar with the
heads of Comanches killed, 30; role of
paymaster under suspicion, 180; stationed
at Fort Cíbolo (Big Spring), 28; succeeded
Valdés, Marcelo (*alférez*/paymaster),
31–32; valued his Indigenous scouts, 44
Amangual-Cavo Franco, José del (Superior
Accounting Office of the Royal Tribunal
of Accounts) case: accounting notes
compiled by Amangual, 142–43; Amangual responded three years later to Cavo
Franco, 144; Cavo Franco issued a report
suggesting "questionable balances" on
the part of Amangual (1792), 141; central
concern was the expenditures of gifting
to Indigenous groups, 142–43; concluded
that Courbiére, Andrés Benito (French
merchant) as source of accounting problems, 177–78; period covered included
that of Fernández, Bernardo (previous
paymaster) and Amangual, 142

417

418 Index

Amangual-Cortés contraband case: alleged contraband related to a trip from Natchitoches, Louisiana to Nacogdoches, Texas, 144–45; Amangual held a public auction of confiscated goods, 162; Amangual took inventory of items, 145, 146, *147–148*; Castro, Ramón de (*Comandante General*), ordered Escandón, José (interim governor) to investigate contraband allegation against Cortés, Juan (captain) and his soldiers, 144; Cortés argued that the activity in question complied with Castro's intentions, 152; Cortés indicated to Escandón that he was unaware of the prohibition on trade with the French, 152; depositions and ratifications, 148–50, 154–60; Escandón considered the case unworthy of consideration, 154; Escandón deposed Cortés, 152; Escandón reminded Cortés that trade with the French was prohibited, 152; Governor Muñoz ordered Cortés's house to be auctioned to pay for he owed, 220; items included four enslaved persons of African descent, 146; items not present included goods and horses taken by hostile Indians, 146. *See also* Cortés, Juan

Amangual-Expedition to Santa Fé, New Mexico (1808): accompanied by three-hundred soldiers, 228; accompanied by two-hundred soldiers, 1, 250; Amangual kept an expedition diary, 23; Amangual remained in Santa Fé for three months, 268; Amangual traveled from Santa Fé to El Paso and San Elizario, 268–69; Amangual was directed to inspire fidelity and love for the Spanish king among Indigenous groups encountered, 257; arrived on 16 June in Santa Fé, 266; encountered a Spaniard boy who had been kidnapped, 270; *compañia volante* of Álamo de Parras participated in, 27; departed on 30 March, 250; desertions by soldiers, 269; encountered "Don Pedro" (a Frenchman), 264; encountered limited water sources, 260–61; encountered "Yndio Cordero" (Comanche), 258; expedition started in San Antonio de Béxar, 1, 23; named by Governor Cordero y Bustamante to undertake expedition, 44; nine-month expedition, 1, 23, 250;

return to San Antonio, 272–74; theft of iron chain from a Comanche guide by a Spanish soldier, 259; undertaken to assert Spanish presence, 251; Vial, Pedro ("Pierre;" Frenchman), previously undertook a similar expedition, 246

Amangual-Muñoz-Ugalde reimbursement dispute: actual expenditures were not specified, 109; Amangual requested reimbursement from the *Fondo de Mesteñas,* though denied by Governor Muñoz, 64; Governor Muñoz allocated funds before receipt of Viceroy Revillagigedo's order, 109; Revillagigedo prohibition on use of funds from the royal treasury, 109

Amangual-Rodríguez slander dispute, 144; Amangual accused Rodríguez, Mariano (sergeant), of defaming his character, 111; Amangual exonerated, 184; Amangual provided testimony, 113; Amangual viewed punishment of Rodríguez as too lenient, 127; final accounting of funds and goods, 124; Governor Muñoz ordered an accounting of financial and supply records, 119, 124; Muñoz asked Amangual to forgive Rodríguez, 125; Muñoz heard witness testimony, 111–18; resident petition denouncing Gómez Moreno, Francisco (priest), 128; review of funds and supplies accepted as correct, 124; Rodríguez accused Amangual of theft of property, 114; Rodríguez apologized for making the accusation, 126; Rodríguez asked for a pardon, 124; Rodríguez implicated the priest Gómez Moreno as the source of the account, 115–17, 124; time spent in confinement by Rodríguez, 125; witnesses deposed, 111. *See also* Rodríguez, Mariano; Zambrano, José Macario

Amangual, José María (son of Amangual, Francisco), 242; a cadet in the military, 241; after his death, father assumed debts of, 284; stationed at the Béxar presidio, 241; death of, 284

Amangual, María Antonia (daughter of Amangual, Francisco), 284

Amangual, María Gertrudis (daughter of Amangual, Francisco), 284

Anglo-Americans: and Louisiana Purchase, 242; as interlopers, 9; entrance into Nacogdoches area, 203; given sanctuary by

Index

Indigenous communities, 203; Spaniard officials concern with the dangerous presence of, 235; theft of horses and other illegal activities, 203; unauthorized entry into French territory, 202; unauthorized entry into Spanish territory, 23, 203, 227, 247–48. *See also* Ashley, Robert; Nolan, Philip; Sibley, John

Apaches (Ndé), 6, 9, 79, 84, 86, 95; Agar (Lipan leader), 31; Amangual's use of guides identified as, 172; Amangual's view of members as "savages," 270; and assistance to friendly members in Nueva Vizcaya and Sonora, 172; as key nemesis to Spaniards, 22; "Bautista" (Lipan intermediary), 179; Captain Chiquito (Lipan leader), 229; cooperated with Spanish related to Comanches, 31; Gileño, 94, 95, 135, 199; housed at the San Antonio mission, 171; Jicarilla, 134, 135; Lipan, 22, 30, 109, 136; list of Apache subgroups, 94; Mescalero, 94, 134, 172; Mescalero as "declared enemies," 138; Mescalero pacification in Nueva Vizcaya, 135; on sheltering of Lipan members at the San Antonio de Valero mission, 171; rancherias, 43; refused Spanish plan to relocate to Coahuila, 171–72; surveillance of horses at the Béxar presidio, 139; Spanish declaration of war against, 95, 134; Spanish estimate of the number of men among, 94; Spanish hope that Apaches leave the region in peace, 104; taken prisoners by Spaniards, 168; waged war against Spaniards over forty years, 94; Zapato Sax/Zas (Lipan leader), 31, 137, 168; Zapato Sax/Zas conducted raid in Nuevo Santander, 168; Zapato Sax/Zas considered "cruel and warlike," 138

Ashley, Robert: Anglo-American friend of Nolan, Philip, 228; led a band of Anglo-American interlopers in Spanish territory, 247–248; pursued by Spanish military, 228

Barragán, José Florencio: created and provisioned a *compañía volante* for a villa, 13; part of landed elite, 13

Barrios y Jáuregi, Jacinto de (governor), 56, 201; succeeded by Martos y Navarette, Ángel de, 56

Bourbon Reforms, 19, 26, 119; an effort to assert presence of authority in New Spain's frontiers, 77; fostered a transition from a religious-based to a military oriented frontier, 77; shift centralized authority within the empire, 77

Branciforte, Miguel de la Grúa Talamanca (viceroy; Marqués), 205; on news of American colonists ("*colonas*") plan to send emissaries to Spain, 208

Bucareli y Ursa, Antonio María de (viceroy): admonished Ripperdá to practice vigilance, 104; received negative report from Croix, Teodoro de (Commander General) on adherence to regulations by troops, 92; recommended deployment of missionaries to control local Indigenous communities, 105; scolded Ripperdá, (governor), 92; succeeded Croix, Carlos Francisco de (viceroy), 104; suggested that soldiers serve as escorts to civilians, 104–5; trust in Ripperdá, Juan María, 105

Bustamante, Ramón de (captain), 137, 141; battle victory at Paloblanco, 138–139, 214; mutilation of Indigenous corpses, 139; possible glorification of, 138; promotion of battle victory as stimulus for other soldiers, 138; Zapato Sax/Zas (Lipan Apache leader) killed at Paloblanco, 138

Cabello, Domingo (governor): aided by *Comandante General* Rengel in locating needed horses, 49; and contraband tobacco discovery, 28–29; argues that shortage of soldiers weakened presidios against Comanches, 49, 51; considered the complete extermination of Indigenous groups as a solution, 48; constraints in conducting sweeps, 82; explanation for shortages of horses and mules at the Béxar presidio, 30, 49–50; initiated investigation of Cazorla, Luis (captain), 59; key figure in colonial Spanish borderlands, 21; lowered duty on horses caught, 63; on application of same livestock rules to missionaries, 63; on soldiers' debts, 46; on perennial troop deficit, 31, 82–83; reminded by *Comandante General* Rengel of previous field operations directives issued, 81; response to Croix, Teodor de (*Comandante General*), 46, 48–49, 51; selected Vial, Pedro (itinerant traveler) to carry exploration of new routes, 245; shortage of firearms, 49; succeeded Governor Ripperdá, 63; superior to Amangual, 28, 31; supported and promoted Amangual to paymaster, 31–32; viewed month-long field campaigns as impractical due to safety for the presidios, 80, 82

Canary Islanders: arrival at San Antonio de Béxar area, 41

Canoso, El (Lipan Apache leader), 23, 168, 170; communicated that Lipan peoples meant no harm to Spaniards as a peace offer, 167; requested to meet alone with Vásquez, Francisco, 167

Carlos III (Spanish king), 45, 53; aims of reorganization of presidios, 78–79; appointed Croix, Teodoro de (his nephew) as *Comandante General*, 78; authorized the *Reglamento de Comercio Libre* in the Americas, 119; gained the Louisiana territory, 200; issued decree (1781) to incentivize soldiers to remain in the military, 52; issued 1772 *Reglamento*, 78; mandated adoption of *Instrucciones*, 132; tensions between stimulation of free trade and strength of the military, 120

Carlos IV (Spanish king): abdicated the crown, and was followed by Fernando VII (his son), 250; abolished the *fuero*, 182; allowed soldiers violating military rules to retain bonuses, 268; created military courts, 162, 183; enacted criteria for the investigation of seized contraband (1791), 161; granted amnesty to *contrabandistas* (1791), 186; on legal rights of soldiers, 183–4

Castro, Ramón de (*Comandante General*): considered Indigenous friendship as essential to Spanish success, 168; not generous with Apaches, 129; on the king's desire to exterminate Indigenous groups deemed as enemies, 129; recommended good treatment of Comanches and other friendly nations, 129; thought that too many missions existed, 130; upset that missionaries did not follow his commands regarding Lipan Apache members, 129; viewed Canoso's request for a meeting to discuss peace as deceitful, 168

Catholic missionaries, 4: abuse of soldiers by, 40–41; and Franciscan order, 252; Canary Islanders complaint to viceroy regarding, 41; complaint by ranchers against, 41; contentious relationship between the military and, 41; demands on soldiers by, 40; Governor Cabello sought the mustang restriction to also apply to, 63; implicated in the Amangual-Cortés contraband case, 150; restrictions influenced the location of *volantes* units, 34, 37; part of military explorations along with troops, 34; prevented settlers from accessing Indigenous labor, 41; *Reglamento* of 1729 addressed abuses against *volantes* by, 42; resident petition denouncing Gómez Moreno, Francisco (priest), 128; role in intra presidio politics such as the Amangual-Rodríguez slander case, 116; soldiers as assistants to, 38; soldiers denied land and water by some missionaries, 37; tensions with military units, 37. *See also* presidios

Cavo Franco, José del (Superior Accounting Office of the Royal Tribunal of Accounts): reiterated accounting issues in Texas to Viceroy Revillagigedo, 175. *See also* Amangual-Cavo Franco, José del, case

Cazorla, Luís/Luis (captain; military inspector): appealed to de Neve, Felipe (Commandant Inspector of the *Provincias Internas*), to continue his military assignment in the northern frontier, 81; Cabello, Domingo (governor) brought charges against, 59; captain of the La Bahía presidio, 58; granted royal assignment to the dragoon unit in Mexico City, 81; reported to superiors that Karankawa had become aggressive, 106; requested amnesty for a despondent soldier, Méndez, Manuel (private), 96; requested a pardon for Méndez, 97; submitted opinion to Croix, Teodoro de (Commander General), 59; took personal care of Méndez, 97

children: Amangual fathered three, 242, 284; Amangual's expedition encountered a child of ten to eleven years of age who had been kidnapped by Apaches, 270; Apache captivity of, 94; arrival at presidios, 54–55; benefits to children of

Index

retired soldiers, 53; boys as servants, 145; cadet, 26; death of Amangual's son, 284; death of servant boy of Urrutia, Manuel de, 31; Governor Muñoz reported that in Nacogdoches a total residence of thirty-one non-Spanish, 202; Karankawa departure from Misión El Rosario left behind Karankawa, 105; Spanish care of children in their Spanish father's custody, 102; Spanish order to kill and capture Apache (Ndé), 86; Spanish speculation on danger of Spanish children taken captive by Indigenous groups, 94

Comanches (Numunuu): 22, 33, 109, 164, 179; aiding Spaniards against Apaches, 136, 275; as opponents to Apaches, 95; by 1810 resumed raids in Texas, 275; Captain Manco, 212; Captain Sojas, 71, 128, 129, 179, 212, 261; Captain Soquinas (intermediary), 71, 128, 129; Captain Sordo, 165; Cojo, 164–65; Courbiére, Andrés Benito (French merchant), role in provisioning, 164; Cuerno Verde (leader) insisted on continuous war against Spanish, 136; death of Cayetano Travieso, 106; domination of territory, 9; factions within, 257; Governor Muñoz's distribution of cigars to, 128; items given to, 129; "Sanbanbi" (Yamparica) 261; Spanish decision not to pursue relatives of Captain Sojas, 179; strategy to contain and punish, 106; "Yamparica/Ymparica," 257, 261–63, 265

Comandancia General, 3, 32; and separate governance of presidios, 12; and removal of viceroy's control of the *Provincias Internas,* 78; as a reimagined militarized *Provincias Internas,* 3; enacted by Viceroy Croix and Inspector Gálvez, Bernardo, de (viceroy), 12; estimated force of soldiers in the, 197; *Fondo de Mesteñas* as a major revenue source for the, 62, 63, 110; formally authorized in 1776, 78; involved violence and asymmetric warfare, 15–16; local commanders at odds with imperial strategies, 23, 79; militarization of, 3, 47, 236; ongoing reorganization of the, 276; separate governance of presidios under the, 12; 1768 plan for a, 77–78; smuggling within the, 160; soldier waywardness within the, 225; strategy to increase the

population of Texas as a buffer against the United States and France, 246

compañía de campaña, 36; composed of "field" soldiers, 36

Compañía del Álamo (de Parras/El Álamo), 27

compañías milicianas (militia companies), 32

compañías veteranas (longest serving military companies), 32

compañías volantes (flying squadrons): also referred to as *cuerpos volantes, escuadra volante,* or *tropas volantes,* 4; and mobility and permanence, 5; and transformation into a presidial company, 6, 33; charged with military control and defense of *Provincias Internas,* 1, 4, 26; commonalities with presidial units, 9; contrast to *tropa ligera,* 47; development of, 4; important actors in Spanish colonial history, 10; local council members employed soldiers for their own interests, 37; multiple responsibilities of, 15; some focused on escorting officials and travelers, 38; Spanish at-the-ready mounted military units, 1, 15; *tropa ligera* at Béxar presidio, 29; units housing themselves, 38; units without a commander, 37-38; were more formal organizations by 1772, 12–13

contrabandistas (smugglers), 160–63; and French trade, 160; Carlos VI granting of amnesty to (1791), 186; commonly smuggled goods included cattle, tobacco, and cloth, 160; decree related to, 187; Menchaca, Felix, as suspected, 145; resisted governmental regulations, 7; 1796 pardon of, 217; soldiers collaborated with, 151; within military units, 7; Ysurieta, Juan de, as suspected, 145. *See also* Amangual-Cortés contraband case

Cortés, Juan (captain): and desire for non-Apache communities to declare themselves enemies of Lipan Apaches, 170; assigned to the Presidio La Bahía, 21; considered a leader of great military acumen, 169; forced to retire, 220; Governor Muñoz cancelled his order related to transferring of soldiers, 85; investigated for a contraband charge, 144–45; opposed transfer of soldiers by Muñoz, 84–85; received a viceregal order pardoning smugglers of prohibited beverages,

145; reported tensions between Vidaes, Orcoquizacs and Karankawa, against Lipan Apaches, 170; and the limits of state power, 160. *See also* Amangual-Cortés contraband case

Croix, Carlos Francisco de (viceroy of New Spain; Marqués)): formation of *Comandancia General* governing structure, 12; succeeded by de Bucareli y Ursa, Antonio María, 104

Croix, Teodoro de (*Comandante General*): developed plan for management of horses, 48; first Commander General of a *Comandancia General*, 3; ordered renewal of operations against Apaches, 130; rule regarding unbranded animals, 62; set process for electing *habilitados*, 58–59; stipulated requirement of a livestock license, 62; succeeded by de Neve, Felipe, 130; formulated plan for the *Fondo de Mesteñas*, 62; ordered the undoing of alliance between Karankawas and Orcoquiza, 106

Courbiére, Andrés Benito (French merchant), 128, 164, 206, 210; Amangual concluded that he was the source of accounting mistakes, 206; Amangual's interpreter for Friendly Nations of the North, 65; as *soldado distinguido*, 22, 177; *Comandante General* Nava ordered Governor Muñoz to send him on various assignments, 210–11, 217–18; contracted to provide lodging and supplies to Indigenous groups at the Béxar and La Bahia presidios, 164, 177; dominated commerce in the borderlands, 210; forced retiree, 220; Governor Muñoz's desire to banish, 218; jailed but allowed to retain his assets and salary, 210; named by Fernández, Bernardo, (paymaster) as source of accounting problems, 177–78; purchased materials from Béxar presidio for use by Indigenous groups, 108, 164–65, 171; released from jail, 210

DeBlanc, Louis (commander): discovered Indians in the Natchitoches (Louisiana) area were providing sanctuary to Anglo-American interlopers, 203; informed Muñoz, Manuel (governor of Texas), of Anglo-American unauthorized entry into French Territory, 202; suggested he would encourage Indians to plunder the Anglo-Americans, 202

De la Garza, José Alexandro (private): participated in verifying supplies in the Amangual-Rodríguez slander dispute, 119, 121; conveyed Rodríguez's, Mariano (sergeant), retraction of accusation against Amangual, 124; communicated his wish to leave military unit, 235

dereliction of duty by soldiers, 98, 185, 261, 269; alcoholic soldiers, 185; and desertion by, 7–8, 10, 96, 236; by desperate troops, 120; chronic, 191; contraband, 28–29, 160, 202, 216; criminality, 8; desertion by Castañeda, Pedro, and Flores, Manuel, 233; desertion by two drummers, 269; disobedience, 8; harboring bootleg liquor, 191; illicit activities, 3, 7–8, 160; insubordination, 191; soldier accusations of other soldiers, 281; theft of livestock, 269; Urrutia, Manuel de (first *alférez*) refusal to follow orders, 68; Urrutia, Manuel de, violence and intoxication events, 65, 181; vandalism, 215–16; within the *Comandancia General*, 185. *See also contrabandistas* (smugglers); Amangual-Cortés contraband case; Durán, Toribio; soldiers

documentation: Amangual's roles as *habilitado* and soldier, 2; central role of *habilitados* (paymasters) in borderlands military history, 1, 54, 57, 59, 61, 65, 68, 79, 101, 113, 123, 141, 150, 174; disreputable habilitados, 151, 223; importance of examining link between military actions and administrative tasks, 2; importance of military accounting practices, 142; importance of examining *Reglamentos* of 1729 and 1772, 131; mishandling of financial affairs, 151; multiple layers of tax collection, 197; need to examine Spanish colonial military history, 1, 2, 8, 45, 78; relevance of Spanish governmental *ordenanzas, reglamentos, and dictámenes*, 2; Spanish obsession with corroboration (documentary and testimonial), 59. *See also* Amangual; Amangual-Expedition to Santa Fé, New Mexico (1808); *hojas de servicio;* inventory

Dunbar and Hunter Expedition, 235

Durán, Toribio (soldier/civilian), 174–75, 186, 216; Amangual took inventory of confiscated good, 174; appeared before

Index

423

Governor Muñoz, 173; Governor Muñoz ordered he pay for all goods seized, 175; received a fine for transporting unclaimed goods, 174; transferred contraband from Nacogdoches to San Antonio, 22, 173

Elguézabal, Juan Bautista de (governor), 224; and bookkeeping discrepancies, 220; Governor Muñoz assigned the Béxar presidio to, 218; Nava, Pedro de, (*Comandante General*) transferred command of La Bahía presidio to Zozaya, Joseph Francisco (lieutenant) 221; Nava provided instructions on the payment of Espadas' debts, 221; ordered an investigation of Guadiana, José María (alférez) for possible role in contraband trade, 234; ordered detention of Nolan, Philip (American), 227; ordered the search for Nolan, 227–28; ordered to take strong measures to prevent unauthorized entry of American and French interlopers into Spanish territory, 227; presented his assessment of Amangual's performance, 230; recorded arrivals and departures of Indigenous persons, 229; upon quitting, Governor Muñoz handed his authority to, 218

Escandón, José de/Sierra Gorda (*Conde de* Sierra Gorda; governor): account of Indigenous resistance, 137–38; and organization of investors, 13; colonizer, 13; delays in escort from Laredo to San Antonio, 139–40; governor of Nuevo Santander, 22; interim governor of Texas (1792), 140; investigated contraband charge against Captain Juan Cortés, 144–45; reorganized the militia corps in Nuevo Santander, 13; viewed the Lipan Apaches as never acting in good faith, 168

Espadas, Manuel (paymaster) 23, 165; Governor Muñoz denied the request from, 110–11; requested funds from the *Mesteñas* fund from Governor Muñoz, 110

Esparza, Antonio Casimiro de (captain): and battle loss considered in the 1778 *junta de guerra*, 93; lack of troop cohesion and leadership blamed for lost battle, 93; Spaniard troops killed in a battle by Comanches, 92–93

Esparza tragedy (1775): discussed at the *junta de guerra* (1778), 93; unit led by Esparza,

Antonio Casimiro (captain) suffered major loss to Comanches, 92–93. *See also* Ripperdá, Juan María (governor); Rubio, José (*Comandante Inspector*)

Felipe V (Spanish king): ordered inspection of presidios in Northern provinces, 78

Fernández, Bernardo (first lieutenant; paymaster), 60, 68, 124, 144, 179; assigned to review accounts and supplies in Amangual's slander case, 119, 121; directed by Nava, Pedro de, (*Comandante General*) to arrest foreigners, 209; escorted witnesses to be deposed by Governor Escandón, 158; Governor Muñoz concluded investigation involving, 178; implicated by Cavo Franco, José del (Superior Accounting Office of the Royal Tribunal of Accounts) on questionable accounts, 175–76; named Courbiére, Andrés Benito (French merchant) as source of accounting problems, 177–78; ordered to take possession of goods transported by Durán, Toribio, 173; preceded Amangual, 57, 142, 144, 204; presented a peace proposal to Canoso (Lipan Apache leader), 168; reported the actions of Pobedano, José Francisco (blacksmith) to Governor Muñoz, 181; responded to Cavo Franco's allegations, 144; role of paymaster under suspicion, 180; testimony by, 176–77

Fondo de Mesteñas, 73, 74; an important revenue source for presidios, 62, 63, 110; explained, 62, 63; funds requested for Cortéz, Juan, (second lieutenant), 61–62; to be used for payment of goods for maintenance of Indigenous groups, 62, 64; used for needs of soldiers, 72, 110–11

Fondo de Gratificación, 121, 124, 191; activities charged against, 103; as common fund of the presidios, 103; movement of funds between the *Fondo de Mesteñas* and, 109

France: Spain granted special privileges to wealthy merchants of, 210; Spanish prohibition on trade with, 152; spread of firearms among Indigenous groups in Louisiana and Texas, 33

Gálvez, Bernardo de (viceroy): and fund to encourage migration to territory, 200; and militaristic orientation, 133;

as military commander for Nueva Vizcaya and Sonora, 130; considered recruiting Indian auxiliaries to supplant Spanish troops, 199; considered using "unneeded" military funds for gifting to Indigenous "peaceful" groups, 136; enacted the *Instrucción* (1786), 7, 22, 131, 134, 196; expressed a divine destiny for Spanish colonies, 132; formation of *Comandancia General* governing structure and, 12; formulated the *Instrucciones* as ordered by Carlos III, 132; general view of Apaches, 135; highlighted the importance of surveillance of the frontier to counter resistance from Indigenous groups, 193–94; inspection of presidios, 12; ordered continuous war against unfriendly Indigenous groups, 136; ordered that soldiers be excluded from escort duty, 140; promoted the strategy of making Indigenous communities dependent on the Spanish, 142, 256; proviso in *Instrucción* on Apaches, 135; recognized the horseback skills of Apaches, 135; recommended the elimination of unfit Spaniard soldiers from presidial and *compañías volantes*, 134, 278; served as governor of Louisiana, 130; wish to reduce the number of soldiers in the *Comandancia*, 197

Gálvez, José de (visitor-general), 199

gandules (Indigenous warriors), 89, 165, 169; accompanied El Canoso, 170; killing of nine, 214

gente der razon ("civilized people"), 166

Gómez Moreno, Francisco (priest), 150, 174; colony residents signed a petition against, 128; implicated by Sergeant Rodríguez as the source of the account against Amangual, 115–17, 124; labeled as "truthful" by Sergeant Rodríguez, 127. *See also* Amangual-Rodríguez slander dispute

Grand Pragmatic of Free Commerce (1778), 133

Herbante del Camino, Agustín (fiscal): on mobility of *compañías volantes*, 5, 35; on *volantes* remaining at presidios, 36

Herrera Britdale, José de, 83; fourteen-year old military volunteer, 25; member of *compañía volante* of Punto de Lampazos, 25; related to Captain de Herrera, Simón, 25

Herrera, Simón de (governor), 256; stationed in Monterrey, 208; related to Herrera Britdale, José de, 25

hojas de servicio (military service records), 10, 21, 86–90, 281; as indicators of social status ("calidad"), 86; contents of, 86; racial and class hierarchy within military, 89–90; relevant to individual identification, 22, 86, 89

Ibarvo, Antonio Gil (captain), 19, 148; attempted to conceal contraband, 216; captain of the militia and justiciar mayor of Nuestra Señora del Pilar de Bucareli, 216; confiscated pirated cloth and tobacco, 216; discharged from military unit, 216; forced retirement, 216–17; named in Amangual-Cortés contraband case, 146; Nava, Pedro de, (*Comandante General*) ordered his banishment from Nacogdoches, 216; positive recognition by superiors, 216

Ibero-Franco-Anglo-Indian borderlands, 19; Spanish-French-Indian borderlands, 55

Indigenous resistance, 26; and political strategies, 131; as invading barbarians, 34, 35; by Mescalero Apaches, 136; by Ndé (Apaches), 9, 22; by Pueblos, 26; Comanche attack on Béxar presidio, 29, 92; Comanche strategies to avoid capture by Spanish troops, 83; Karankawa strategies to assert spatial control. 16; periodic attacks against mission-presidios, 43; Quegue (Yamparica) leader refusal to order guides for Amangual's expedition, 263; strategies to avoid capture while pursued by Spanish troops, 83. *See also* Apaches; Comanches

Indigenous individuals and communities: Acaxee, 26; "Araname," 107; Arkansas, 227; as allies, 36; as "Friendly Nations," 16; as treacherous, 129; Bidais/Vidais/Vidaes, 106, 108; Caddo (Kadohadacho), 33, 264; "Cancaraquases," 107; Captain Cabezón (Tancague), 207; Captain Hoyoso, 229; Cherokee (*Aniyvwiya/Anigaduwagi/ Kituwah*), 227; Chickasaw (*Chikasha*), 227; Chiojas (Sofais/Sojas), 259–60, 261; Chiso, 26; "Coapites," 107; Cocos, 106, 107; Concho, 26; considered "weak and cowardly" by Spaniards, 105; "Copanes,"

107; "Cujanes," 107; El Mudo (Taguacano), 164-165; Faraon, 94; geographic distribution of, 134; Guichita/Guchitas (*Wichita/Kitikiti'sh/Kirikirish*), 22, 136, 164, 207, 229; Guichita acquisition of firearms from the French, 33; Guichita control of region, 9; Jasinto/Jacinto, 164-65, 169, 170; Janos, 26; Julime, 26; Karankawa, 31, 105-6, 164; Karankawa alliance with Orcoquiza, 106; Karankawa use of canoes to escape from Spaniards, 83; leaders deployed multiple strategies against Spanish forces, 131; Lipillanes, 94; Manso, 26; "Mayaye," 107; "Menchaca" (Taguacano), 164-65; Mimbreños, 134; Natagé, 94, 134; Navajo (Diné), 94, 95, 135, 136; on access to the labor of, 41; on good relations with Indigenous communities, 136; on view that captured Spaniard children were the most harmful to Spaniards, 94; Opata auxiliaries, 80; Orcoquizas/ Orcoquizacs/Orcoquisac, 55, 108, 157; Orcoquiza alliance with Karankawa, 106; "Pamposa," 107; "Pastia," 107; Pawnees/ Panana (*Chahiksichahiks/Chatiks se chatiks*), 33, 245, 246; Pima/Upper Pima, 6, 199; political control of region by, 9, 16; Quegue/Quege, 261, 262, 263; Quiches, 153; soldiers as overseers of, 42; Spaniard cohabitation with Indigenous women, 65–66, 67; Spanish desire for complete extermination of, 48, 129; Spanish effort to prevent alliance between Apaches, Tejas and Bidais, 106; Spanish order to kill male Apache warriors and capture women and children, 86; Spanish political gifting to, 106, 107–8, 110, 128, 136; Spanish traders use of "peace by deceit" with Indigenous groups, 142; Suma, 26; "Tacame,: 107; Taguacanos/Tahuacanes (Tawakoni), 108, 110, 153, 155, 157, 164, 179; Taguayas, 60, 65, 153, 164; Tahuacanes provide restitution to Lipan Apaches, 213; Tahuaias, 108; Tancagues (Tonkawa), 71, 73, 109, 164–65; Taovayas/Taboayazes/ Tavoayaze, 33, 95, 245; Tarahumara, 26; "Tecocodames," 34; Tejas, 106, 251, 252, 252; tensions between Karankawa, Lipan, Orcoquizacs, and Vidaes, 170; Tepehuan, 26; Tinza, Luis ("Apalache" general), 247; "Tlascalan" families from the interior of

New Spain, 56; Toboso, 26; Ute, 65, 135; Ute peaceful relations with Diné (Navajo) and Gileño Apaches, 95; view of all Indians as "inconstant," 166; warfare role of Apache women, 94; Xaranames, 170; Xixime, 26; Yaqui, 35; Yuma, 140. *See also* Apaches; Comanches

Instrucción (1786). *See* Gálvez, Bernardo de (viceroy)

inventory, 2, 277, 280; Amangual's experience with, 204; and confiscated goods from Durán, Toribio, 173-75; and gifting to Indigenous groups, 211–12; brought to Béxar presidio by Amangual, 57; importance to Amangual-Rodríguez slander dispute, 75, 115, 119–22, 123–24, 126, 145; of contraband, 22; of tobacco, 11, 72, 215, 223; salient to Amangual-Cortés contraband case, 144–48, 150-51, 153, 155, 157, 162, 223

Junta de Guerra, 34; attendees at the 1778, 93; conclusion that Apaches were "declared enemies," 94; council speculated that Spaniards kidnapped as children were the most dangerous to Spanish presidios, 94; noted presidios were few and were at great distances from one another, 94

Ladrón de Guevara, Antonio: created a compañía volante, 27; founded villa of Nuevo Santander (1749), 27; part of Escandón, José de/Sierra Gorda (*Conde de* Sierra Gorda; governor), forces, 27

Laws of the Indies: viewed as outdated, 11, 278

Lewis and Clark Expedition, 235, 245, 246: Governor Chacón, Fernando, dispatched a unit to observe Anglo-American exploration, 228; report on Lewis, Meriwether, reaching the Missouri River, 228; secret expedition by Lewis, Meriwether and Clark, William, 242

limited scholarship: on analysis of the *Reglamentos* of 1729 and 1772, 131; on link between military duties and administrative tasks, 2;

Marín, José Francisco (field marshal): charged with evaluating conditions in the *Provincias Internas*, 35; on reduction of presidial forces and enlistment of

Index

"Indian friends," as a cost-savings action, 35; recommendations on presidios and flying squadrons (1693), 6, 12–13, 35; recommended a military headquarters and supply base at "Teuricache," 35

Marmolejo, Francisco (auditor-general of the *Junta de Guerra*), 34

Martínez Pacheco, Rafael (governor), 177, 205–6; as a captain, disregarded an order from Governor Muñoz, 64; implicated by Fernández, Bernardo (first lieutenant; paymaster) of mismanagement of accounts, 177; received complaint by Menchaca, Joaquín against Amangual, 60

Martos y Navarette, Ángel de (governor), 55; and political offices and presidios as principal buyers of local civilian products, 55–56; on absence of a market, 55–56; succeeded Barrios y Jáuregi, Jacinto de, 56;

Menchaca, Felix: named in contraband case, 145; goods confiscated, 159

Menchaca, Joaquín: filed complaint against Amangual (1788), 60, 74, 279; Martínez Pacheco, Rafael (governor) admonished, 60; possessed a livestock license, 62–62

Menchaca, José (lieutenant): appointed to commander of the Aguaverde presidio by Neve, Felipe de (Commandant Inspector of the *Provincias Internas*), 80; ordered Méndez, Manuel (private) to surrender, 96

Menchaca, Manuel (second lieutenant): a member of the *Compañía Volante* de Santiago del Saltillo, 87; elected to paymaster, 87–88; entered the Béxar company as its second alférez, 212; promoted to first *alférez*, 87–88; served for twenty-five years, 87

Méndez, Manuel (private): alleged to have suffered a sword attack by another soldier, 96; despondent soldier, 96-98; granted amnesty for desertion and insubordination, 98; imprisoned for insubordination, 97; royal *yndulto* of 1776 applied to, 98; superior requested amnesty for, 96; took refuge in the church at *Presidio La Bahía*, 96. *See also* Cazorla, Luís/Luis (captain; military inspector)

Mesteñas, Fondo de (Fund): 61–62, 63, 64, 207; explained, 62; reimbursement to, 73, 110

Mestizos, 65, 260, 261

Mézières, Antonio/Athanasio de (*alférez*; lieutenant governor), 19, 93, 106, 205; and Anglo-American unauthorized entry into French territory, 202; attack on Karankawa, 31; governor of Fort Natchitoches (Louisiana), 93; native of Louisiana, 202

microhistory: importance of mundane actions, 20; of borderlands, 11, 16

missions and missionaries: and presidio complex, 36; competition with Indigenous and military units, 39; abuse of authority by, 40–41; tensions with military units, 41. *See also* presidios

Muñoz, Manuel (Governor of Texas), 23, 61; decided to overlook some Comanche anti-Spanish actions, 166; dispatched a unit of soldiers to La Tortuga in response to confrontation with Comanches, 165–167; multiple roles in the Spanish empire, 111; prohibition on the slaughter of *mesteña* cows, 171; quit his post, 218; relationship with French merchants Lamath, Nicholas, and Courbiére, Andrés Benito, 164; restored to governor of Texas and captain of the Béxar presidio, 170; Amangual notified Nava, Pedro de, (*Comandante General*), that Muñoz's had suffered an accident, 218–19; communicated that he was well and able to carry out his duties, despite Amangual's letter, 218–19. *See also* Amangual-Muñoz-Ugalde dispute

"Nachitos" (Natchitoches), 148–49, 152–160, 205

Nava, Pedro de (*Comandante General*), 27; and reimbursement to the *Mesteñas* Fund, 61–62; *compañías volantes* created in 1781, 27–28; description of *soldado distinguido* and their privileges, 147; did not hesitate to reprimand subordinates, 213; directed Governor Muñoz to limit Urrutia, Manuel de (first *alférez*), activities and distance from the presidio, 181–82; forwarded the decision to pardon prisoners for specified offenses, 215; imposed penalties on those who improperly traded with the Lipan Apaches, 171; issued instructions on interactions with Lipan Apaches, 172; issued instructions to Governor Muñoz on training of soldiers

Index

427

and warfare, 192–94; issued orders for the guarding of Nacogdoches against American and French intruders, 210; on regulation regarding use of the *Mesteñas* Fund, 64, 110; ordered that Nolan's, Philip, goods be prohibited in Texas, 227; ordered the capturing of foreigners in Spanish territory, 209; praised the military actions of Fernández, Bernardo de (lieutenant), 215; requested reports on Urrutia, 181

Navarro, Ángel (merchant): came from the island of "Córzega," 201; left home at the age of thirteen or fourteen, 201; migrated to the San Antonio presidio as a merchant, 201; named in Amangual-Rodríguez slander dispute, 111–18

need for comparison of the *Reglamentos* of 1729 and 1772, and the Gálvez *Instrucción* of 1786, 131

Neve, Felipe de (*Comandante Inspector de las Provincias Internas*), 79, 84; adhered to the 1782 royal order to engage Indigenous enemies, 80; allowed Cazorla, Luis (captain) to retain his captaincy at the La Bahía presidio, 81; conflicting assignment given to Cazorla, 81; death of (1784), 130; directed Cabello, Domingo (captain) to continue role of *comandante inspector*, 80; favorable view of the management of troops by Croix, Teodoro de, 79; granted Cabello discretion on military field actions, 82; reorganized troop units, 80, 130; reported attack on the Karankawa, 31; succeeded Croix, Teodoro de, 79

Nolan, Philip (American), 227; activities among presidios by, 227; executed in 1801, 228; Irish immigrant, 226; part of Anglo-American interlopers in Spanish territory, 226; Spanish toleration of, 226, 227

Nueva Vizcaya, 6, 26, 46; abolishment of presidios at Cametla and San Hipólito, 5; addition of presidios at El Pasaje, El Gallo, Conchos, and Casas Grandes, 5; Spanish decision to retain presidios in, 36

Nuevo Santander, 22, 27, 72, 77, 196–97, 208, 246; Amangual Expedition to Santa Fé and cavalry Corp of, 256; Escandón, José de/Sierra Gorda (*Conde de* Sierra Gorda; governor), report on Paloblanco incident in, 137–38; Lipan Apache raids in, 171;

newcomers not to be mistreated in, 203; Nolan, Philip, in, 226, 228; *Reglamento* of 1772 and *volantes* in, 47; settlement of, 13; *volante* drummer boy from, 180; Zapato Sax in, 168. See also Escandón, José de/Sierra Gorda (*Conde de* Sierra Gorda; governor)

Ojos Azules (Comanche leader), 65: angrily departed from La Bahía presidio, 167; confrontation with Urrutia, Joseph (captain), 65-66; felt offended by Urrutia's disrespect, 67; on behalf of Comanches received rifles sent by Castro, Ramón de (Commander General), 129

Orcoquisac mission/presidio, 55

Ordenanzas de Intendencias (Ordinance of Intendants, 1786), 7, 12, 278; aim to protect and support merchants, 133; and creation of militias, 133; intendants functioned as assistant to the viceroy, 133; governor of Coahuila and Texas lacked intendants, 174; replaced four departments of government, 133; sought to replace *alcaldes mayores* with intendants and *subdelegados*, 133

peace by purchase, 4, 22, 70, 95, 107; actions involving irony and amnesty, 179; as a gamble, 109; as an enigmatic and tenuous interaction, 213; as an indispensable action between Spaniards and friendly Indigenous groups, 136, 275; as a strategy involving deceit, 171; Gálvez, Bernardo de (viceroy), referred to it as "peace by malice," 70; Spanish provision of European goods and weapons to Comanches as a form of, 129

Prada, Policarpo: accompanied Amangual from Coahuila to San Antonio, 45, 61; former sergeant in the "*Dragones de España*," 45; second *alférez* at La Bahía del Espíritu Santo presidio, 45

presidial military units: converted into *compañías volantes*, 33; and transformation of *compañías* volantes into, 6, 33

presidios (military outposts): and deficiency of troops at, 51, 82, 83, 127; and mission complex, 36; as ecosystem, 7, 21, 70; as two-pronged apparatus, 78; at Monclova (Coahuila), 1; at San Antonio de Béxar, 1; at Santa Fé (New Mexico), 1; at Tucsón

428   Index

(Arizona), 1; companies at, 32; complex of misión-rancheria and, 7; corrupt captains/commanders at, 46, 58; crises within, 12; defrauding of soldiers' salaries, 57; dissonance between, 182; erosion of morale by indebtedness, 54; family members provided goods intended for soldiers, 58; Felipe V (Spanish king) ordered an inspection of, 78; hunger at, 58; land and water distribution privileges for soldiers, 55; length of military work imposed, 52; mass desertions uncommon, 96; military hierarchy, 51–52; misconduct and desertion of soldiers at, 33; ongoing debts of soldiers, 46; on profiteering and price gouging by presidial captains, 58; on reserve funds for soldiers, 102; payroll at, 72; relations within, 18; Presidio La Bahía del Espíritu Santo, 81; retirement pay, 52; reward for bravery and service, 53; shortage of horses, 49; siphoning of goods for family members intended for troops, 58; soldiers' disability, 52–53; stampedes and theft of horses and mules at, 30; stipends for widows of dead soldiers, 53; tensions with missionaries, 41, 129; *tropas ligeras* lacking armaments, 49; unscrupulous paymasters or administrators, 46; *yndulto* promulgated to benefit deserters who returned to their posts and completed their military contract, 96, 127. *See also* soldiers

Provincias Internas (Far North territories of *Nueva España*): and *compañías volantes*, 4; and creation of two general commandancies (1804), 236, 246; *compañías volantes* mission to defend the, 26; Croix, Teodoro, named *Comandante General* of the, 78; defined, 1; divide into two military districts, 130; enactment of *Comandancia General* excluded the viceroy's jurisdiction, 78; established by the Seven Years' War, 47; explained, 77; Felipe V (Spanish king) ordered an inspection of presidios in the, 78; included twenty-three presidios by 1760, 55; militarization of, 3, 47, 236; Neve, Felipe de, appointed as *Comandante Inspector* for the, 79; public works implemented in the, 246–47; reported as deplorable, 93; Rivera, Pedro de (general) inspected the presidios in the (1724-1728), 36; split into two distinct military dis-

tricts, 130. See also *Septentrión*; Ugalde, Juan de; Ugarte y Loyola, Jacobo

Pueblo Revolt (1680), 5, 26

Ramón, Diego (captain): assigned to assist the mission of San Juan Bautista del Río Grande del Norte (Coahuila) presidio, 34; ordered to form and lead a new *compañía volante* at San Juan Bautista del Rio Grande del Norte, 34; placed in charge of the presidio at San Juan Bautista del Rio Grande del Norte, 34

Ramón, Domingo (captain): accompanied by Tejas Indians, 253; Espinosa, Isidro de, authored a "trail diary," 253; expedition aided by French traders, 252; led expedition with Espinosa, Isidro de (fray), 252

rancherías, 85, 107, 197, 261; numerous, 43, 131; places to flee from Spanish, 136, 194; mobile locations of, 172; Spanish effort to integrate, 200; Spanish spying on, 270

rastreros (Indian scouts), 31

Real declaración (1767), 11

Reglamento de Habana (1719), 42

Reglamento de 1729, 78, 131; addressed soldier discipline and training, 90; and the political relations between presidials and Indigenous cohabitants, 106; annual gunpowder and bullet distribution per soldier, 90; authored by Rivera, Pedro de (general), 44, 57; enacted by Viceroy Casafuerte, 199; on unnecessary services by soldiers, 141; prohibition on war against friendly non-baptized Indians, 105; sought to address cash payments to soldiers, 57

Reglamento de 1772, 87, 131; addressed conduct, compensation and composition of *volante* units, 47; addressed soldier discipline and training, 87, 90, 99; annual gunpowder and bullet distribution per soldier, 90; called for blind obedience of soldiers, 96; duties of paymaster enumerated in, 53–54, 101–2; enacted by Carlos III, 78, 199; integrated provisions in the *Reglamento de* 1729, 78; mandated incessant war against hostile Indigenous groups, 81; Naylor, Thomas, and Polzer, Charles W., discuss the significance of, 78; on governing of mounts, 48; on soldiers' governing of civilians, 56; provided for

Index

429

recruitment of Indigenous scouts, 47; provision related to civilians, 55; required captains to ensure proper uniforms for soldiers, 46; required officers to know regulations by memory, 96; required prompt receipt of soldier pay and rations, 101; set prices for goods, 59; specified composition and hierarchy of presidio military units, 47

Rengel, José Antonio (*Comandante General*): Governor Cabello questioned the practicality of month long operations, 82; intervened to address shortage of horses in the presidios, 49; Neve (*Comandante Inspector de las Provincias Internas*) granted discretion to governors in managing field operations, 82; plan to reorganize *volantes* units, 196, 198; reinforced directive that troop units should pursue field operations for at least a month, 81; succeeded Neve, Felipe de, 82, 130; suggested that detachments choose the most practical routes, 82

Revillagigedo I/II, Francisco (viceroy; conde), 64; approved Muñoz's decision on killing of *mesteña* and gifting of small items to Lipan Apaches, 171; approved the taking of Indigenous families as prisoners, 171; declared war on Apaches (1748), 134; on proper allocation of royal funds, 109; ordered Governor Muñoz to banish Lamath, Nicolas de, from Nacogdoches, 163; ordered military escort for Escandón, 139; ordered that Urrutia, Manuel de (*alférez*), present himself in Mexico City, 181

Ripperdá, Juan María (governor), 21, 52, 53; and questionable competency of, 90–92; low balance in the *Fondo de Mesteñas* at the end of his tenure, 63; numerous correspondence from superiors to, 104, 160; received instructions on how to proceed with smuggling cases, 160; scolded by Viceroy Bucareli, 92, 104; ultimately trusted by Viceroy Bucareli, 105

Rivera, Pedro de (general): abuse of *volantes* by religious orders, 42; authored the *Reglamento* of 1729, 44, 57; considered some soldiers as lazy and indulgent in vices, 38; found disarray at San Bartolomé presidio, 38; inspection of presidios (1724–28), 6, 12, 57; noted problems in each presidio, 36; on contrast between *volantes* and presidial

companies, 6; on importance of land use for control and cohesion in frontier settlements, 40, 41; on nomenclature for *compañías volantes*, 40, 41; on possible pay cuts for apathetic soldiers, 57–58; on the creation of *compañías volantes*, 39; on the function of *volantes*, 40; recommendation on the naming of captains of *volantes*, 39; recommendations by, 6; recommended disbanding *volante* unit at San Bartolomé, 38; reminded borderlands residents that the land belonged to the king and no one else, 41; troubled by flying squadrons, 6, 40

Rodríguez, Mariano (*cuera*; first sergeant): accused by Amangual for defamation, 111; known for fighting with other soldiers and associated with disorder, 87; Muñoz, Manuel (Governor of Texas) admonished, 126; participated in campaign against Comanches, 87; placed under arrest, 123–124; plea presented to Muñoz, 125–26; served in the cavalry unit of the presidio of San Antonio de Béxar for thirty-three years, 87; son-in-law of Zambrano, José Macario (merchant), 70, 279; was a witness to an accounting report by Amangual, 73. *See also* Amangual-Rodríguez slander dispute; Zambrano, José Macario

Royal Regulations of Presidios (1772), 12–13, 21, 46; mandated obedience to superiors, 93; on distribution of lands and town lots, 55; provision related to "Political Government," 55; required monthly review of military forces, 99

Rubí Corbera, Cayetano María Pignatelli (Marqués de; field marshal): inspection of presidios, 12, 21, 199; ordered the use of the prices for goods in the 1729 regulations, 58

Rubio, José (*Comandante Inspector*): and comparison to soldiers in Europe and the pursuit of glory, 99; castigated Ripperdá, Juan María (governor) for the battle lost to Comanches, and led by Esparza, Antonio Casimiro de (captain), 92; conflictive interactions with Ripperdá, 21; critical of Ripperdá's management of troops, 92–93; directed Ripperdá to discourage soldiers from discrediting the militia, 99; informed Ripperdá that Carlos III (Spanish king) would not support soldiers incapable of military duties, 52; issued instructions to improve the management of presidios, including fiscal issues, 100–103; mandated policies to reward soldiers, 98; reminded Ripperdá of the utility of target practice exercises for soldiers, 90, 91; sought to regulate charges against the *fondo de gratificación*, 103; Viceroy Bucareli y Ursa scolded Ripperdá, 92. *See also* Esparza tragedy (1775)

salidas (military raids/campaigns), 82; against Comanches, 30
San Juan Bautista de Río Grande presidio, 53, 80; a point of departure for expeditions, 252; dual charge of troops to protect the mission and forestall French intrusions, 33; established in 1701, 33; located adjacent to mission, 37; original *compañía volante* converted into a presidial unit, 33, 34; Sarmiento y Valladares (viceroy) ordered the creation of a *compañía volante* at, 34; *volantes* unit consisted of thirty soldiers, 34
Sarmiento y Valladares, José (viceroy; Conde de Moctezuma), 43; created a flying squadron in 1698, 36; directive regarding the San Juan Bautista del Río Grande military organization (1701), 34; on protection of missionaries, 34
Segunda Compañía Volante de San Carlos de Parras, 1, 23, 27, 230, 236–237, 240; law enforcement and subsequent weakening of cohesion of, 248–249; full command transferred to Aguilar, José Antonio, 275; included one-hundred soldiers, 27–28; led by Captain Fernández Carmona, Juan, 27–28; temporary command by Valle, Dionisio (lieutenant), 247, 266–267
Septentrión, 9, 18; area encompassed by, 1; defined, 1; long history of contraband goods in the, 163; military and political problems in the, 130; unwelcomed incursion into the, 23
Seven Years' War (1756–63), 11, 45; established the northern provinces of New Spain, 47; impacted the European political boundaries in North America, 47, 200; reinforced Spanish colonial administration and governance of territories, 133
Sibley, John (American), 235
Silva, José Gervacio de (first *alférez*): served

for twenty-six years, 88; served as sergeant in the *Compañía Volante* of San Juan Bautista de Lampazos; promoted to *alférez*, 88; served as paymaster, 88
situational strategizing: described, 84, 169, 216, 247, 279
soldiers: accumulation of debt, 100; adherence and resistance to regulations, 7–8; amnesty granted to deserters willing to resume their duties (1783), 127; and unacknowledged documents produced by, 131; challenges to survival, 8; concern with the spread of firearms among Indigenous communities in Louisiana and Texas, 33; confronted hardships, low pay, and difficult working conditions, 182; difficulty in fighting Indigenous communities, 99; expressed occasional resistance to authority, 132; Ferrero, Felipe (second corporal) arrived at San Antonio presidio with debts, 45–46; mundanity of tasks and chores of, 20, 179, 181, 214, 233, 237, 249, 266, 277; on military hierarchy and promotion within, 51; preference for tobacco harvested by the French, 159; some actions seen as parallel to that of the enemy, 132; vandalism by civilians and, 215–16; variable quality of, 140–41. *See also* presidios
Spanish empire: and decisions by local commanders, 108, 132; and limits of state power, 160, 225; close scrutiny of commanders in the Provinces by superiors, 103–4; contrast in resources in the frontiers with those in urban places in, 8; deployed enmity and amity in conducting war against Indigenous groups, 139; founded on the action of soldiers facing multiple obstacles, 25, 196; gifting to Indigenous leaders and communities as a central policy within the, 70, 106, 275; grounded on the concepts of dominance and assent, 258; habitual transgressions within the, 225; incomplete project to create Indigenous dependence on Spanish, 108; interpersonal tensions between military commanders, 21, 85; link between Spanish hegemony in the "Greater Southwest" and political challenges in Europe, 252; military strategy of accommodation and tolerance, 9; on goal to establish

Index   **431**

provinces with law-abiding royal subjects, 56; ongoing resistance by Indigenous groups, 131; ordinance system replaced four departments of government, 133; organization of commerce to support the, 119–20, 133; settlement and military encroachment, 16; shuffling available soldiers from post to post, 217; structural tensions within, 225, 275; the handling of finances an ongoing concern, 100; waning of dominion and habitual transgression in the frontier, 225, 239

tobacco, 187; a commodity confiscated under the Amangual-Rodríguez slander suit, 145, 148–50; Amangual's careful accounting of, 72, 223; as contraband, 28–29, 160, 202, 216; commodity noted in the Amangual-Cortés contraband case, 152–59; and *"estanco"* (Tobacco Office), 212, 215; finding of unclaimed eleven *manojos* of (Ft. Cibolo and El Cleto), 28–29, 216; formation of a colonial monopoly of, 133; Galán, Luis, appointed the administrator of the Tobacco Department, 224; gifted to Comanche and Lipan Apache leaders, 129; Governor Escandón ordered the selling of confiscated, 162; held high value among frontier communities (Indigenous and Spanish), 50, 71, 72, 276; prudent bureaucratic accounting of unclaimed cache of, 28–29; revenues from distribution of, 11; scrutiny of department funds of, 72; royal decree on the proper management of revenues from, 162; special provision in royal order on, 186

Truxillo, Juan (second lieutenant): member of *volantes* in Nueva Vizcaya, 89; served for twenty-three years, 89

Ugalde, Juan de (general; *Comandante de las Armas*), 60, 109, 177; approved promotion of Amangual, 61; assigned the eastern district of the *Provincias Internas*, 130; held Amangual responsible for miscalculation by Bustillo, José (cashier), 179. *See also* Amangual-Muñoz-Ugalde reimbursement dispute

Ugarte, José Joaquin (captain): observed attrition of soldier, including desertion, 236; on presence of Sibley, John (American) in the Nacogdoches area, 235; report on mobility of soldiers at Nacogdoches presidio, 234; reported news of transfer of New Orleans to the Unites States (1803), 235; suspected territorial acquisition aims of Anglo-Americans, 235; warned by Governor Casa-Calvo to be aware of questionable territorial intentions of persons from the United States, 244

Ugarte y Loyola, Jacobo (general; military commander), 133, 138, 194; and *Instrucciones*, 132, 134; and postponement of peace agreement with Mescalero Apaches, 172; assigned the western district of the *Provincias Internas*, 130; attended the 1778 *junta de guerra*, 93; directed by Viceroy Gálvez to remain neutral with the Yumas. 140; governor elect of Sonora, 93; on responsibility to protect local ranchers, 195–96

Ureña, Mariano (first sergeant), 46; appointed as first sergeant by Amangual, 45; debts of, 45–46; former sergeant in the "Dragones de España," 45; joined Amangual in trip from Coahuila to San Antonio (1779), 45, 61; lacked full a uniform and sword, 46

Urrutia, Joseph (captain): lived for seven years among the Ndé (Apaches), 43–44

Urrutia, Juan de (second lieutenant; first sergeant of a *tropa ligera*): considered for position of second *alférez*, 248; reported to have killed eighteen Indigenous males and females, 88; served as a cadet and later a soldier in various units, 88

Urrutia, Manuel de (first *alférez*): an embarrassment for Amangual, 67; arrested for insubordination related to alcohol related incident, 185; assignments by Amangual, 66; close friendship with two young Comanche warriors, 65; cohabitated with a Ute woman, 65–68; dead servant boy of, 31; embarrassed Amangual's, Francisco, leadership and management of troops, 29, 65–68; esteemed by the Tawakoni and Lipan Apaches, 185; first sergeant of the *tropa ligera* at the Béxar presidio, 29; filled Amangual's vacancy at Fort Cíbolo, 29; Governor Muñoz arrange for his reporting to Mexico City, 182; his intoxication episodes of, 65–68, 181; jailed for violence and intoxication, 65, 181; Nava, Pedro de, (*Comandante General*) ordered Governor Muñoz to restrain the actions of, 181–82; overheard comments by Rodríguez, Mariano (sergeant) critical of Amangual and deposed by Governor Muñoz, 111–18, 181; part of inspection staff, 121; refused to follow an order, 68; report to Amangual by nephew of, 66

Valdés, Marcelo (first *alférez*), 29; Governor Cabello depended on, 83; led sorties against Comanches, 31; was succeeded by Amangual as paymaster, 31–32
vaqueros, 42, 63, 165, 167; worked for Padre Camarena, 167

woman/women: accompanied Canoso (Lipan Apache) in his trip seeking peace, 170; and Apache visit to La Bahía presidio, 170; and goods intended for, 146; and ownership of livestock by, 181; "Bautista" reported capture of a, 179; Captain Chiquito reported Comanche killing of four, 229; Captain Domingo Ramón's travel diary notes the presence of eight married, 253; Captain Sojas (Comanche) accompanied by two, 179; Comanche, 66; illness of Quege guide's wife, 263–64; Indigenous males escape from Misión El Rosario left behind children and, 105; Karankawa males reuniting with Karankawa children and, 106; Karankawa

male warriors' efforts to rescue detained Karankawa, 31; listed in the accounts related to Amangual-Cortés contraband case, 146; on expected arrival of Spanish, 54–55; reporting of a female Indigenous warrior, 264; reporting of an Indigenous female participating in a hunt, 264; sister of Ojos Azules (Comanche leader), 66; Spanish concern with the supportive war efforts by Apache, 94; Spanish order to kill and capture Apache (Ndé), 86; Urrutia's, Manuel de (alférez), cohabitation with Ute, 65–68; Truxillo, Juan (second lieutenant), with his bare hands killed a, 89

Ysurieta, Juan de: named in contraband case, 145

Zambrano, José Macario (merchant): a soldier stationed at the Béxar presidio, 68; accused Amangual of breach of contract, 56–57, 74, 279; disagreement related to a payment demanded by Amangual, 68; father-in-law to Rodríguez, Mariano (sergeant), 70, 279; mistrusted Governor Muñoz and his impartiality, 69; presented his case to Castro, Ramón de (*Comandante General*), 69; resident of the villa of San Fernando, 68
Zozaya, José/Joseph Francisco (lieutenant): assumed command of La Bahia presidio, 221